Theatre Histories: An Introduction

"A work that more than any other currently available suggests the range and richness of theatre and performance history study today." – Marvin Carlson, *City University of New York*

"This book will significantly change theatre education." – Janelle Reinelt, *University of California, Irvine*

"Globally ambitious in its scope, innovative in design, and open-ended in its challenge to the received histories, this new grand narrative will engage scholars and students at every level, whatever their particular interests in past performance." – Jacky Bratton, *Royal Holloway, University of London*

"Finally we have a book that conceives theatre history in world terms and breaks down the Euro-American boundaries that have marginalised the theatres of other cultures for so long." – Brian Singleton, *The University of Dublin, Trinity College*

Theatre Histories: An Introduction is a bold and innovative way of looking at the ways we understand performance and the ways in which history is written. Its chapters offer clearly written overviews of theatre and drama in many world cultures and periods. These and its unique, in-depth case studies demonstrate the methods used by today's theatre historians.

Using a new narrative strategy that challenges the standard format of one-volume theatre history texts, the authors help the reader think critically about performance in all its global diversity. *Theatre Histories* explores aesthetic and interpretive approaches from many cultures, continents and time periods. The authors explore contemporary Japanese theatre, kabuki, and kathakali with as much range and depth as Shakespeare, vaudeville, and realism.

Theatre Histories: An Introduction is organized to provide:

- an understanding of how key shifts in human communication shaped developments in the history of theatre and performance throughout the world
- an introduction to the methodologies employed by today's theatre historians
- in-depth case studies demonstrating "history at work"
- a truly global perspective on drama, theatre, and performance

Keeping performance, drama, and culture at center stage, *Theatre Histories: An Introduction* is compatible with standard play anthologies and offers many pedagogical resources including a website with additional references, discussion questions, and links to related sites at www.routledge.com/textbooks/0415227283.

What the reviewers say:

"Perhaps most significantly, this book integrates the studies of western and non-western traditions of performance practice and it uses carefully detailed case studies to exemplify and to probe an issue in more depth. Thus, *Theatre Histories: An Introduction* is notable not only for how it records the past but for how it critiques our study of that past."

Harry J. Elam, Jr, Olive H. Palmer Professor in the Humanities,
Department of Drama, *Stanford University*

"Provides a fresh and most welcome look at this field, offering not a single totalizing view but multiple narratives from multiple perspectives. By looking at theatre and performance from a global perspective and utilizing a range of critical methodologies, the authors have provided a work that more than any other currently available suggests the range and richness of theatre and performance history study today."

Marvin Carlson, *City University of New York*

"*Theatre Histories* has finally achieved a new synthesis of performance studies and traditional theatre history, inflected with methodological insights from cultural studies and critical theory, that provides an appropriate pedagogy for the twenty-first century. . . . Williams, best known for his scholarship on Shakespeare; Zarrilli, a specialist in Indian theatre and actor training; Sorgenfrei, an established scholar of Japanese theatre; and McConachie, whose American performance research has been blended with community-based research and performance, constitute a strong team of historians whose collective expertise is richly appropriate to the scope of this project."

Janelle Reinelt, *University of California*

"As a sophisticated introduction to 'history at work' in theatre, this book should provide a refreshing alternative to traditional undergraduate texts."

Judith Milhous, *City University of New York*

"Perhaps the first theatre history text to treat non-Western theatre with such intelligence and seriousness . . . This text will revolutionize theatre history pedagogy."

E.J. Westlake, *University of Michigan*

Theatre Histories:
An Introduction

Phillip B. Zarrilli, Bruce McConachie,

Gary Jay Williams, Carol Fisher Sorgenfrei

General Editor: Gary Jay Williams

Routledge
Taylor & Francis Group

NEW YORK AND LONDON

First published in the USA and Canada 2006
By Routledge
270 Madison Ave, New York, NY10016

Simultaneously published
By Routledge
2 Park Square, Milton Park, Abingdon, Oxon OX14 4RN

Routledge is an imprint of the Taylor & Francis Group, an informa business

Typeset in Bembo by
Florence Production Ltd, Stoodleigh, Devon

Printed and bound in Great Britain by
Bell and Bain Ltd, Glasgow

Library of Congress Cataloging in Publication Data
Theatre histories: an introduction/by Phillip B. Zarrilli . . . [et al.]
    p. cm.
    Includes bibliographical references and index.
    1. Theatre–History.   2. Performing arts – History.   I. Zarrilli, Phillip.
    PN2101.T44 2006
    792.09–dc22   2005027639

British Library Cataloguing in Publication Data
A catalogue record for this book is available from the British Library

ISBN10: 0–415–22727–5 (hbk)
ISBN10: 0–415–22728–3 (pbk)

ISBN13: 978–0–415–22727–8 (hbk)
ISBN13: 978–0–415–22728–5 (pbk)

Contents

CONTENTS

CONTENTS

Contributors

Phillip B. Zarrilli is Professor of Performance Practice in the Department of Drama at the University of Exeter. From 1976–1998 he was Professor of Theatre, Folklore, and South Asian Studies at the University of Wisconsin–Madison. He has also taught at U.C.L.A., Northwestern, N.Y.U., and the University of Surrey. His books include *Kathakali Dance-Drama: Where Gods and Demons Come to Play* (London: Routledge, 2000); "*When the Body Becomes All Eyes*": *Paradigms, Practices, and Discourses of Power in Kalarippayattu*, 2nd ed. (Oxford University Press, 2000); *Acting (Re)Considered: Theories and Practices*, 2nd ed. (ed., London: Routledge, 2002); *Asian Martial Arts in Actor Training* (ed., Madison, 1993); *Indian Theatre: Traditions of Performance* (co-author; University of Hawaii Press, 1990); *Wilhelm Tell in America's Little Switzerland* (co-author; Onalaska: Crescent Printing Company, 1987); and *The Kathakali Complex: Actor, Performance, Structure* (New Delhi: Abhinav, 1984). He is internationally known for training actors using a psychophysical process combining yoga and Asian martial arts, and as a director. His recent productions of Samuel Beckett's plays in Los Angeles, Austria, and Ireland have won considerable critical acclaim.

Bruce McConachie is Director of Graduate Studies in Theatre and Performance Studies at the University of Pittsburgh. He has published widely in American theatre history, theatre historiography, and in the emerging field of performance and cognitive studies. Some of his major books and websites include: *Theatre for Working-class Audiences in the U.S., 1830–1980* (with Dan Freidman, 1985); *Interpreting the Theatrical Past* (with Thomas Postlewait, University of Iowa Press, 1989); *Melodramatic Formations: American Theatre and Society, 1820–1870* (University of Iowa Press, 1992, awarded the Barnard Hewitt Prize in Theatre History); *American*

Theater in the Culture of the Cold War: Producing and Contesting Containment, 1947–1962 (University of Iowa Press, 2003); and *Virtual Vaudeville* (with David Saltz and others, 2004). Professor McConachie is also a former President of the American Society for Theatre Research.

Gary Jay Williams is Professor Emeritus, Department of Drama, The Catholic University of America in Washington D.C., where he directed productions and taught theatre history, theory, and Shakespeare in performance for 29 years. He is the author of *Our Moonlight Revels: A Midsummer Night's Dream in the Theatre* (University of Iowa Press, 1997), winner of Theatre Library Association's George Freedley Award. He was Editor of *Theatre Survey*, journal of the American Society for Theatre Research from 1995 to 2001, and is the author of over fifty articles in journals, encyclopedias, and anthologies. He was a professional New York critic and a professional actor.

Carol Fisher Sorgenfrei is Professor of Theater at U.C.L.A., where she formerly headed both the playwriting and critical studies programs. She is a scholar, translator, playwright, and director focusing on Japanese, intercultural, and fusion theatre. She is the author of *Unspeakable Acts: The Avant-Garde Theatre of Terayama Shûji and Postwar Japan* (University of Hawaii Press, 2005), as well as many articles in journals such as *TDR*, *Theatre Journal*, and *Asian Theatre Journal*, essays in books, play translations, and encyclopedia entries. Her fifteen original plays include the award-winning *Medea: A Nô Cycle Based on the Greek Myth* and the kabuki-flamenco *Blood Wine, Blood Wedding*. With Israeli director Zvika Serper, she created the internationally acclaimed Japanese–Israeli fusion play *The Dybbuk: Between Two Worlds*. She is Associate Editor of *Asian Theatre Journal*, editor of the *Newsletter of the Association for Asian Performance*, and a former member of the Executive Committee of the American Society for Theater Research.

Acknowledgments

We want to express our gratitude to Routledge's Talia Rodgers, Commissioning Editor, and to Moira Taylor, Senior Development Editor, Textbooks, for their belief in, and long support for this project, from conception to realization. Moira Taylor has guided, inspired, and sustained us throughout, coordinating each stage of the evolution of the book, taking a keen, knowledgeable interest in every essay and every photograph, keeping us grounded in our mission, and providing wisdom and patience at every turn.

A history of this scope is possible in great part, of course, because of the specialized works of many dedicated scholars. We have drawn on them often and happily here; their works are cited in this text and in the extended bibliographies on our website: www.Routledge.com/textbooks/0415227283. But we wish to add this expression of our gratitude for their scholarship and their vitality, and with it our hope that this book will serve them.

Tobin Nellhaus's insights into the importance of major new communication technologies for theatre history helped us shape the periodization of our book. Many of our colleagues have been supportive. We especially wish to thank for their advice and encouragement Dave Escoffery, Faye C. Fei, Richard Hornby, David Jortner, David Mayer, Paul Murphy, Stuart Sillars, Gary Taylor, Andrew Weintraub, E.J. Westlake, S.E. Wilmer, and W.B. Worthen. Simon Williams was initially involved in this project and provided valuable contributions at an early stage. We have listened to, and benefited from the external reviewers of our work, including our severest critics; they have helped us serve our readers better. We look forward to future conversations with our readers.

We are grateful to our students, who have been there at every stage of the journey that resulted in this text, helping to shape what we think is a necessary new step for thinking about theatre and performance history. We have each benefited from the long-term research support of our universities: the University of Exeter; the University of Wisconsin–Madison; the University of Pittsburgh; the Catholic University of America, Washington, D.C.; and the University of California, Los Angeles.

We have each had the strong, enduring support of our families and partners whose sacrifices made it possible for the work to get done, and we express our heartfelt thanks to all of them, including Caitlin O'Reilly, Stephanie McConachie, Josephine S. Williams, and Richard Hornby.

It has been our privilege to write these histories of performances, theatres, and cultures, and we look back on the variety and the depth of imagination that we have encountered with wonder, profound respect, and gratitude.

Phillip B. Zarrilli
Bruce McConachie
Gary Jay Williams
Carol Fisher Sorgenfrei

Preface: Interpreting performances and cultures

A first mapping: About this book

Theatre Histories attempts to take a fresh approach to the historical study of world performance, theatre, and drama. It is designed to provide a global perspective that allows the performances of many cultures to be considered, not in the margins of western theatre but in and of themselves, and as they illuminate each other and our understanding of human expressiveness at large. To do this, our narrative is organized unlike that of any other theatre history text. We relate the histories of performance and theatre throughout the world to the key developments in modes of human communication that have reshaped human perception. Performances and cultures are center stage throughout.

We have also designed this book to challenge our readers to reflect on the very methods by which history is written. In recent years, there has been much healthy new critical thinking about the writing of history, for reasons we shall explain. We illustrate a variety of interpretive approaches to the history of performance, theatre, and drama. We have sought to make these accessible to the reader new to them.

We do not attempt, then, to provide the reader with *a* history of *the* theatre. Rather, we consider many cultures and multiple methods of interpreting performances, theatre, and drama from around the world. We do not privilege chronologies or lists or attempt the impossible task of covering the entire history of theatre and drama in the world. We have aimed for inclusiveness of both cultural and historiographical kinds as pedagogical strategies, intended to stimulate the appreciation and interpretation of many kinds of performance and theatre, and many kinds of critical thinking about them.

Our book is divided into four parts, each with an introduction and three chapters, and with supporting case studies following each chapter. At each level – part introductions, chapters, and case studies – we take specific approaches to interpreting historical phenomena, with respect for primary source materials and often with an eye to opening up fresh perspectives. *Theatre Histories* aims to stimulate interest in the process and practice of the interpretation of performance, theatre, and drama, past and present. Reading and writing history responsibly requires being aware of the historical methods being used and being able to critique them. There are no value-free histories; it is always a matter of what values and whose inform a particular historical work. Among other things, our purposes reflect our understanding of the material cultural forces that shape the work of both the theatre historian and the theatre artist, both of whom engage, in their different ways of knowing and representing human experience, in processes of interpretation. *Theatre Histories* is about making the study of history part of an ongoing inquiry into our relationship with our various pasts and part of an inquiry into the various theatres in which we are engaged, inquiries that we hope will open to theatres yet to be imagined.

To summarize, *Theatre Histories*

- Offers a global perspective on the theatre and performance of many cultures, allowing cultural performances that are relatively neglected in the West to be considered, and not in the margins of western theatre or according to its criteria but in and of themselves and as a means for illuminating our understanding of human expressiveness at large.
- Shows how key developments in the history of performance and theatre throughout the world are related to the key developments in modes of human communication that have reshaped human perception.
- Challenges readers to read the history of theatre and performance actively and critically by introducing them to a variety of interpretive approaches in ways accessible to the reader new to these approaches.

A second mapping: Cultural performances, theatre, and drama

> What is important is to go out, open up a way, get drunk on noise, people, colors.
>
> (Octavio Paz 1959)

This is how the highly celebrated Mexican author, Octavio Paz, described what he regarded as Mexico's primary mode of cultural performance – the "fiesta." In contrast to "theatre and vacations, Anglo-Saxon 'weekends' and cocktail parties, bourgeois receptions and the Mediterranean café," Paz proclaimed that "Mexico is in fiesta." While some might argue that Paz's characterization of Mexico as "in fiesta" encourages a stereotype, his assertion that "fiesta" rather than theatre is central to Mexican identity, culture, and history points to a significant problem in how histories of theatre are written. What happens when a specific culture's history or view of its cultural and artistic identity is shaped not by drama and theatre as defined by European standards,

Figure 0.1 Two male Xantolo dancers dressed as women, during celebrations in Zapotila, Hidalgo, for the Day of the Dead celebration, the Mexican version of the Christian feasts of All Saints' and All Souls' days.

[Source: © Chloe Sayer. Color Plate No. 29, after p.128 in *The Skeleton at the Feast: The Day of the Dead in Mexico*, by Elizabeth Carmichael and Chloe Sayer. British Museum Press, 1991.]

but rather by other indigenous modes of performance? Is a history of "world theatre" to leave out cultural performances like fiesta?

Jane Plastow, a specialist in the history of African theatre, explains the issue:

> The definition of theatre commonly advocated is simply that which pertained to Europe at the time of . . . colonization. . . . This definition became outmoded almost from the time of its inception, for Europe rapidly moved on to experiment with forms such as surrealism, absurdism, 'total' theatre, whilst leaving Africa in the grip of ideas of naturalistic production imported from the world of British amateur dramatics.
>
> (Plastow 1996:12–13)

Plastow makes the important point that in twentieth-century western "theatre," the boundaries between theatre and performance are not what they were in the eighteenth or nineteenth centuries. Throughout the twentieth and into the twenty-first century, avant-garde performance artists revolted against bourgeois theatre, and were often inspired in their experiments by examining non-theatrical performances of the past or from other cultures. Yet, the discourse of most histories of theatre is shaped by their concentration on western and pre-twentieth-century forms of drama and theatre. Moreover, the discourse of these histories is shaped by western humanistic expectations at large, in great part because of the western emphasis on the text of a play (see Chapter 1, Part 2 – Introduction, and Chapter 11). This is quite limiting even for an understanding of western theatre/performance practices, past and present. Western humanism is much more limiting for our understanding of theatre and performance in non-western cultures.

To avoid some of the limitations of western humanism, we focus on the more inclusive category of cultural performances. Cultural performances are expressive events performed by at least one person for at least one other. They range from small scale practices such as story-telling and puppetry to large scale events such as sports contests, religious rituals, and Mexican fiestas. All theatrical events are also cultural performances. When we experience a specific performance, whether as performers, participants, or spectators, the experience flows from and partly shapes our individual and collective identities. Cultural performances are usually set off from everyday life by their:

- **Spatio-temporal frames**. Because cultural performances typically take place at special times in special places, spectators usually know they are watching a performance. Broadway plays are framed as special events which occur at certain times in specific locations. Worshipers gather at a specific place and time for a religious service. The fire-eating street juggler frames his performance for his audience at the beginning of his act, usually with a grand gesture that attracts attention.
- **Structures**. Each form of cultural performance possesses a clear set of characteristics, identifiable by its rules, conventions, and/or techniques, such as actors singing lyrics (western opera), actors crossing a bridgeway on each entry/exit that joins the green-room to a specially constructed, resonant wooden stage (Japanese noh theatre), or performers in Kerala, India, sanctifying the stage with extensive rituals prior to each kūṭiyāṭṭam performance (given without diacritical markings hereafter).
- **Content**. Cultural performances may have content based on traditional tales or myths, contemporary events, or any human experience. The contents allow members of the community to reflect upon the ideas, meanings, images, and/or experience of the performance.

Within and across cultures or sub-cultures, the boundaries and markers that identify a particular mode of performance are more or less flexible. Some modern theatre directors, for instance, have merged the conventions and techniques of dance, puppetry, and theatre. Cultural performances may be creative blends of a variety of popular sources and entertainments (see Chapter 7). For example, British pantomime is a nineteenth-century invention that uniquely combines elements of English drama, music hall, and fairy tales to create what is still a popular form of theatre in England today (see the Chapter 7 case study). Some cultural performances, such as 1960s "happenings" or overtly political street theatre, intentionally transgress normal expectations regarding space, time, style, and content (see Chapter 11). Performances, like societies and cultures, are not static but always in the process of being reinvented. Shakespeare in perform-ance is always a dialectical interaction between volatile texts and cultural dynamics (see Chapter 11 case study).

Cultural performances range from simple to complex in terms of their means and manner of production. The solo orator who tells, recites, or sings a repertory of oral narratives may employ simple means of staging but bring to bear virtuosic skills on an art rich in complexity. More complexly staged cultural performances, such as those of the Japanese kabuki theatre, engage multiple specialists in interactive skills, including author-composers, actor-dancers, designers (the first revolving stage was devised for kabuki), technicians (for flying), managers, and producers.

All cultures and subcultures have distinctive modes of behavior, thinking, or acting. Such practices include habitual daily activities, special extra-daily practices such as sports events, theatre performances, religious observances, and other cultural performances. Extra-daily practices often require the practitioner to undergo specialized bodily and/or mental training in order to become accomplished in attaining a certain specialized state of consciousness or physicality in order to gain access to a certain type of power or

Figure 0.2
A Balinese shadow-theatre dalang (puppeteer) with four-gender instruments and a stage. [Source: Angela Hobart. Photo: P. Homer.]

agency. An Olympic games weight lifter trains through repetition over time to attain a strong, muscular body. The solo Balinese shadow-puppet performer (*dalang*) trains to attain the spiritual and physical abilities necessary to sustain an all-night performance of a lengthy play in which he enacts all the characters of the drama (Figure 0.2). Extraordinary energy, time, and cultural resources are often invested by a society to enable such specialists to become virtuosic in their practices.

The historical perspectives we utilize in this book allow us to trace the way modes of performance practice emerge, are valued through patronage or other means of support, go out of fashion, change, or even die over time. These perspectives help us show that what was lost or out of fashion is sometimes rediscovered, remade, or reinvented in a later historical period. For example, in the renaissance, Italian opera was born from a reimagining of ancient Greek performance. Anthropologist Edward Schieffelen argues that "performativity, whether in ritual performance, theatrical entertainment or the social articulation of ordinary human situations, is the imaginative creation of a human world" (1998:205). The myriad forms of cultural performance examined here all engage the human imagination in configuring a "world," as performances that are structured, written, staged, elaborated, and/or enacted according to culturally and historically specific conventions and aesthetics.

The English word aesthetic is derived from the Greek *aisthetikos* meaning sense perception. Aesthetics became a special branch of western philosophy concerned at first with beauty in art. Our use of the term aesthetic emphasizes the operation of perception and experience in producing particular pleasures in particular contexts. Different aesthetics produce quite different pleasures intended for particular contexts. It is useful to consider the aesthetics of a performance in order to consider how it operates in delivering various kinds of pleasure for its audience through a specific set of conventions. Some forms of cultural performance intentionally work against commonly accepted conventions in order to challenge the usual pleasures such performances can deliver.

Theatre and drama

Like other types of cultural performance, theatrical performances are usually set apart from everyday life by spatio-temporal frames, formal structures, and expressive content. Theatre emerged in some cultures with the invention of writing, as we will see in Part I. The English word "theatre" derives from the ancient Greek *theatron*, which meant "seeing place" and referred to the hillside area on which Greek citizens gathered to experience the plays competitively produced in the context of an annual religious festival (see Chapter 2). The term can refer both to permanent, purpose-built theatres or temporary structures where spectators experience performances from stand-up comedy to operas and plays.

In many cultures since the invention of writing, the enactment of drama has been a major mode of theatrical performance. The English word "drama" derives from the Greek *dran*, meaning to do or to act. In the active sense of the original Greek term, a dramatist is an individual who undertakes, singly or with others, the act of writing a play intended for performance. In the western humanistic tradition that privileges texts, the word "drama" has come to refer to a kind of literature intended to be read as well as performed. Performers in many cultures, however, used and continue to rely on scripts, the written record of a performance, to ensure the repeatability of their efforts. In this book, we often use drama as a synonym for script; both primarily serve as blueprints for performance. (Scripts are not the only basis for the repeatability of a performance. India's kathakali actors keep manuals which record performative additions to the "original" text.) Drama primarily relies on narrative for its structure; its enactment tells a story. The types of stories told and the way they are enacted differ widely from culture to culture and in different periods within a culture. Many dramas use invented stories involving fictitious actions, while others are based on historical or quasi-historical epic and mythological events. Some dramas are enacted within a religious context with the intent of achieving a "real" effect in the world or cosmos, as we will see in Chapter 2.

In the past, the western study of theatre and drama focused on the dramatic text, almost to the exclusion of acting, directing, and design. The bias against some forms of cultural performance, such as indigenous, non-western rituals and dramas, developed during the fifteenth century when Europe began to explore and colonize the Americas, Africa, and Asia. In addition to economic gain, a primary justification for colonization was to bring western ideas of civilization to cultures considered barbarous, primitive, and pagan. As we shall see in Parts I, II, and IV, Europeans disdained and suppressed forms of performance that did not fit western prototypes of drama or theatre and in many areas actively eradicated them. When Europeans encountered dramas and/or theatre that better fit their prototypes, they were surprised to discover these among peoples and cultures otherwise thought inferior.

For example, when Sir William Jones's English translation of Kālidāsa's Indian Sanskrit drama, Sakuntala (probably written in the fifth century C.E.) appeared in 1789, there was an enthusiastic response to the play throughout Germany, Italy, and France. It was widely translated, and numerous adaptations were produced as ballets, dramas, or operas. The famous German playwright and spokesman for high art in the western tradition, Johann Wolfgang von Goethe (1749–1832), viewed Sakuntala as "a rich source of archetypal values." Even as he appreciated Sakuntala as poetry, he made an effort to dissociate "this poetic work from Indian art, religion, and philosophy" (Figueira 1991:13). Goethe's view of Sakuntala tells us more about the nineteenth-century German idealism than it does about Kalidasa's play or Indian culture (for a discussion of Goethe's theatre at Weimar, see Chapter 6).

What historical methods might be more fruitful for examining and interpreting cultural performances, theatre, and drama?

A third mapping: About history, historiography, and historical methods

History – an everyday thing, saturating every moment of our cultural existence. Making sense of what has happened is how we live. We do it in all sorts of ways.

We sing it, dance it, carve it, paint it, tell it, write it . . . The ways we make sense of the past are almost innumerable, but we are culturally astute in knowing how these different ways are to be interpreted. . . .

(Dening 1996:xiv)

The historian's task

For most of the twentieth century, history as a discipline shared with most other academic fields a single set of assumptions about the world and the role of the historian in examining it. This view, termed "positivism," assumed that the historian was a kind of scientist who, by dispassionately observing discrete "facts" could arrive at essential, objective truths about significant events in the past. Positivists were confident that the "facts" would speak for themselves when it came to understanding and explaining historical events. The positivist historian believed that she or he was able to distill the "facts" from documentary records filled with the biases and misperceptions of past observers. Important historiographical texts like G.R. Elton's *The Practice of History* (1969) defended the notion that a proper analysis of the documentary record was sufficient to establish objective truths about the past. Further, Elton, like many positivists, believed that historians could correct past errors and could learn to tell ever more objective stories; present historians could build on the positive knowledge of past histories.

More recently, however, many historians have questioned the possibility of positivistic historical knowledge. The publication of Thomas Kuhn's *The Structure of Scientific Revolutions* in 1962 challenged the view that the discipline of science (and hence the field of positivist history) was a process entailing ever more objective means of determining truth. Instead, Kuhn demonstrated, scientists worked within historical "paradigms," each with different notions of objectivity. This, in effect, rendered untenable the claim that "the scientific method" established universal truth. What had seemed universally true with Newtonian physics, for example, became a relative, local truth in Einsteinian physics. Kuhn's insights have had an impact on how historians view their work. Most historians today have a much more guarded notion of objectivity, recognizing that the writing of history has been, and can be deeply affected by the historical, cultural formations within which historians work. Critiquing past historical interpretations is possible in part because of a heightened awareness of diverse cultural perspectives, especially the perspectives of those who, having neither power nor wealth, have had little voice in how history is written.

None of this is to say that historical explanations from the past are not helpful in shaping historical knowledge now. Today, historians who consider themselves philosophical realists view the attempt at objectivity as a process, not a result – a process of negotiation between the curiosity and scholarly rigor of the historian and a documentary record that admits of several possible interpretations. Most historians now understand their hypotheses about how and why a series of related events occurred as "partial and provisional" interpretations, are likely to be challenged by later historians (Evans 1997:249). What were the causes of the French Revolution? Why did realism

Figure 0.3 *Mr. Garrick in "Richard III,"* engraving by William Hogarth and Charles Grignion, 1746, based on Hogarth's painting. The image served several narratives of English national identity (see Chapter 5), and was being printed and sold throughout most of David Garrick's career. [Source: © Gary Jay and Josephine S. Williams.]

dominate the stages of the twentieth century? Why has Shakespeare become a global phenomenon? Tentative answers can be offered, and some answers, some interpretations, will prove more persuasive than will others.

The historian's sources

If the truth does not simply emerge from an unbiased or "neutral" reading of the primary sources, how is the historian to approach the documentary record? Certainly the historian must still carefully attend to primary sources – the material remains of a culture, be those architectural ruins, writings, or paintings, that were produced by a people for their own purposes. These must be distinguished from secondary sources, that is, interpretations of the culture produced by historians later.

Primary sources or documents available to theatre and performance historians include many kinds of materials, such as the ruins of theatres, inscriptions that document a building's date or patron, original dramatic texts, visual records of performances (whether on a wall, vase, or in a painting), period costumes, a theatre's financial records and attendance figures, and original playbills or programs. All require care in interpretation. Sources available to the historian can never be taken as direct reflections of some past reality. An actor's autobiography may not represent the unfavorable reviews that critics wrote about him. As Mark Monmonier illustrates in his book, *How to Lie with Maps* (1991), something as seemingly factual as a map of the geography and topography of an area can be used to deceive (or can be given a skewed interpretation). The validity of all sources and the interpretations of them should be tested.

Although primary sources may differ, some evidence is incontrovertible. For example, a few revisionist historians have attempted to argue that the evidence for the Holocaust is unreliable. However, there is a consensus among respected, reliable historians that there is massive evidence, verifiable and incontrovertible, of how and when the German Nazis exterminated millions of Jews, gypsies, homosexuals, and political opponents during World War II. All historical explanations involve some judgments but not all are equally valid. One must always test a particular interpretation against the available evidence and source material. As historian Richard Evans explains, "Documents are always written from somebody's point of view, with a specific purpose and audience in mind, and unless we can find all that out, we may be misled" (Evans 1997:80). The historian's tasks include attempting to understand documents from the point of view governing them when written and articulating what distinguishes them from other documents.

New theories and approaches to historical interpretation

New historical knowledge may be generated by the discovery of new evidence and by the imaginative reinterpretation of existing sources, sometimes under new cultural imperatives. As an example of the first, when T. Ganapati Sastri made the chance discovery in 1909 of a cache of thirteen previously unknown manuscripts of plays by the playwright Bhasa, who lived around C.E. 400, the entire history of India's Sanskrit theatre and its dramatic literature had to be re-examined (see Chapter 3). New technologies sometimes lead to the imaginative reinterpretation of "old" sources. The invention of carbon dating has allowed much greater precision in determining the dates of certain types of material evidence of early human life, leading to reassessments of human evolution. To take an example of reinterpretations that occur because cultural perspectives change, historians today have a special concern for critiquing histories that are inscribed with habits of viewing the world from the position of the powerful and the privileged. Such histories have, and continue to reinforce social and political structures and habits of thinking in which there is little place for the history of subjugated peoples and minorities.

The historian's tasks often involve bridging gaps between cultures, time periods, experiences, and key concepts or ideas "through the use of a disciplined historical imagination" (Evans 1997:214). "Theories" might be thought of as the explanatory bridges we construct in order to be able to better link the past and present. Theories grow out of the concerns we have in a particular "present" moment. The "theories" that guided positivist historiography grew out of assumptions and concerns prevailing from the late nineteenth through the mid-twentieth century, as we have seen. Following the "scientific" method, historians often attempted to look for "first causes" in history. This point of view naively assumed that if one could find a first cause or pattern of causality for an event, similar phenomena could be understood and thereby controlled or managed. Finding the origin of an historical event or a situation would substantially explain its outcome. In this way of thinking, the processes of history bore some resemblance to Darwin's idea of the processes of biological evolution. While it is still useful to inquire into the origins of a phenomenon, such as a performance or theatre, historians are today less likely than nineteenth-century historians to assume that an initial cause determines all subsequent development or that what happened in one culture is the pattern for all.

Throughout this book we engage a variety of contemporary critical theories that have arisen from re-examining the assumptions about what it means to know and examine a subject. Some of these theories have emerged from our concerns with neglected cultures, with western dominance, colonialism, race and gender discrimination, and other discursive formations that protect privilege. These concerns have helped shape some of the kinds of questions we ask about the past and the ways we examine and interpret the sources available to us.

Let us take an issue arising out of attitudes about gender, a subject we take up on a number of occasions in this book. In some ways, theatre has always been "about" gender and its cultural performance. In the performance of Greek tragedies and comedies during the fifth century B.C.E. in Athens, males performed female as well as male roles. In the comic satyr plays, male actors donned erect phalluses as part of their costumes for the half-human, half-animal satyr. Even though historians knew that Athenian males performed the female roles on the ancient Greek stage, it was only very recently that this aroused significant interest. There was no discussion of what men playing women might reveal to us about fifth-century Athenian notions of gender and sexuality.

As this and numerous other examples illustrate, theatre at its most vital tends to be a "'queer' institution" – to borrow a term from gay studies. That is, theatre seems to be "most itself when challenging the norms of its ambient culture. One of the most powerful means of doing so is shape-changing, particularly with regard to sex and gender" (Senelick 2000:10). However, with few exceptions, until the 1980s studies of theatre or drama seldom focused specifically on the issues or implications of gender or sexuality in theatre. As social, political, and economic concerns with issues of gender and race became paramount in the West during the 1960s and 1970s, prompting public debate of issues of equality and access to fundamental human rights, these concerns became manifest in "new" theories, such as feminist and then queer studies. By the 1980s, these theories had begun to assist historians in re-examining gender and sexuality in theatre and performance throughout the world, often allowing them to read "against the grain," that is, to reinterpret or re-examine sources to understand how gender or racial bias may be silently embedded in the practices of a culture or in the histories written about it. Gender theories may not provide new primary sources but they do prompt the historian to make sure that she or he is taking into account the "facts" of the practices of a culture in matters of gender or race or sexuality, practices that might have previously been overlooked, ignored, or misinterpreted.

Problems of representation and interpretation

One of the major problems in writing a history of performance is how to represent forms of performance from other cultures. Let us take the example of Japanese noh theatre, developed by the actor-playwright-theorist Zeami Motokiyo (1363–1443) (see Chapter 3). Textbooks usually represent noh as a courtly, masked, medieval dance-music-drama, created and performed solely by males, with beautiful costumes, ancient and delicate masks, and a simple stage setting. It has been described as being performed to "strangely dissonant" music, with "excruciatingly slow" dances, and a structure "more like lyric poetry than drama" because noh plays are said to "lack conflict." Such accounts may quote French playwright Paul Claudel's famous dictum that "in drama something happens; in noh, someone appears." They may also note that performing or viewing noh can be a form of Zen Buddhist meditation, suggestive of the mystical nature of "the Japanese mind," which cannot be grasped by the intellect. While such descriptions are not totally wrong, they are superficial and deeply misleading. Such accounts may, in part, be described as formalistic in their concerns, that is, they focus on matters of form – costumes, masks, the physical stage, or the structure of a play. In this formalist operation, there is also the suggestion that noh is a kind of frozen image of a picturesque ancient Japanese culture, unchanged and unchanging; there is, therefore, no pursuing the cultural question of how the Japanese regard this art today. Western accounts of noh drama as lacking in conflict imply that it is inferior because it doesn't measure up to any criteria for dramatic form. Such accounts are often also Orientalist, that is, they reiterate the idea of a mystical, exotic, "incomprehensible East." (For more on Orientalism, see the Chapter 9 case study, "Global Shakespeare.") In this text, when we describe non-western genres of performance, we attempt to do so in culturally appropriate terms. When applying a particular interpretive approach to any historical period or culture, we have tried to be sensitive to the linguistic, aesthetic, religious, and/or socio-cultural dimensions that distinguish a particular historical period and culture.

A fourth mapping: periodization through modes of human communication

One of the identifying characteristics of human awareness and consciousness is the development of the ability to reflect upon and communicate who we are. Theatre and performance are complex, culturally embedded, historically specific kinds of communal reflection and communication. Because major new developments in modes of human communication led to profound changes in the ways people thought about, related to, and organized their worlds, each of the four parts of this book are organized to mark such transformations and relate them to theatre and performance. Part I, Performance and Theatre in Oral and Written Cultures before 1600, traces developments in human communication from the emergence of language 50,000 years ago, through oral, ritual and shamanic modes of performance born out of human languages, down to the development of systems of writing and the invention of a variety of types of theatre and drama in some literate cultures. Part II, entitled Theatre and Print Cultures, 1500–1900, begins with the period when print technologies developed in China and Europe and began to have a major effect on communication worldwide. Part III, Theatre in Modern Media Cultures, 1850–1970, explores the development of photography and traces the impact on theatre and performance of innovations in such audiophonic modes of communication as telephone and radio. Finally, Part IV, Theatre and Performance in the Age of Global Communications, 1950-present, takes us into the era of "virtual" communication that began with the proliferation of television and led to the microchip technologies of the twenty-first century. Our periodization strategy derives in part from arguments developed by Tobin Nellhaus (2000), and Walter Ong (1982).

As we will see throughout this book, new forms of communication never completely replace old media. When writing was invented (around 3,000 B.C.E.) it changed, but never completely displaced significant modes of oral transmission and performance. Even today, despite the ubiquitous presence of computers, the print media continues to be an important mode of communication, albeit one that has reshaped itself. Film and television have not replaced live theatre, although theatre today certainly bears the influence of film (see Parts III and IV). Our continuing use of metaphors taken from older modes of communication or technologies testifies to the durability of previously dominant media. To say that an event makes an "impression" on us is to use a metaphor based on printing, comparing our minds to a blank piece of paper and the event to the imprint of a printing press. Thinking of mental images from the past as "snapshots" or offering one's "take" on a recent occurrence engages metaphors from photography and film. When an event is inscribed on your memory, it is as if a sharp instrument were used to form letters or hieroglyphs in clay, as in the early days of writing. To "rewind" or "replay" a moment from a conversation is to compare the reiteration of a human performance to a tape or video recording.

As the above examples suggest, communication technologies derive from, and shape the ways we think about ourselves and the world. A new mode of communication produces "reality effects" that, in effect, set the stage for alterations in human behavior and social organization, as well as in performance and theatre. The kinds of media a culture uses in effect structure the way it perceives reality, enabling some practices and constraining, even preventing others. Before writing, history could not be completely separated from myth. Photography altered the nineteenth century's perceptions of "reality." Of course, any new medium must be deployed by people and institutions with power in a culture before it begins to alter general perception. Although printing texts on wood blocks developed first in China, the "reality effects" of printing were not felt worldwide until the invention of the new form of printing with moveable type in

Europe in 1455, a development that allowed mass production and wide distribution of books. Until corporations and national defense strategists began to explore the possible uses of computing, the computer had little influence on world cultures. By the late twentieth century, as we shall see in Part IV, new communications media were having a profound impact on many of the traditional practices and institutions of world cultures, including the production and reception of live performance.

Of course, significant innovations in modes of communication are not the only reasons that theatre and performance have changed over time. Accordingly, while we use new modes of communication as markers of the beginnings of major periods of theatre history, we are keenly aware of and examine many other causes. When tracing examples of theatre censorship in Chapter 4, for example, we rely primarily on political explanations. Sometimes, multiple causal factors must be introduced to account for theatrical change. One cannot understand theatre and performance in what is known today as Southeast Asia without some knowledge of the many waves of different cultural influence that have crossed the peninsula that spreads southward from the Asian mainland for 2,000 miles, from Myanmar (Burma) to the far-flung eastern islands of Indonesia. These include religious infusions from Buddhism, Hinduism, and Islam, plus military conquests by Mongol armies and several European powers. As theatre scholar James R. Brandon writes:

> Kingdoms have risen, have conquered their neighbors, and have imposed their culture – and theatre forms – on the conquered; they in turn have been conquered by *their* neighbors who have imposed on them *their* culture – and theatre forms. Some parts of Southeast Asia have changed hands eight or ten times during the period of recorded history.
>
> (1967:3)

While writing and print technologies helped to make these influences and impositions more or less successful, it is clear that changes in media alone cannot account for the many forms of theatre that have arisen in Southeast Asia over the centuries.

Case studies and interpretive approaches: the historian at work

In our case studies following each chapter, we use selective interpretive approaches to examine specific subjects in theatre history within their historical and cultural contexts. These demonstrate how historians do the work of interpretation. Each case study provides an introductory explanation of the theory and method being used, as well as applying that interpretive approach to the material at hand. The approaches we have selected include theories of play and improvisation (Chapter 1), semiotics (Chapter 9), cognitive studies (Chapters 2 and 6), and deconstruction (Chapter 11). The case studies introduce the reader to a wide-ranging, but by no means exhaustive set of examples of possible interpretive approaches used by theatre historians today. Following each study is a selective list of related sources. On our website readers will find additional lists of readings, and for the case studies, discussion questions that offer further guidance for using the interpretive approaches: www.Routledge.com/textbooks/0145227283.

A note on diacritics, spellings, and names

In the matter of diacritical markings and romanized spellings of the terms from the many languages used in this text, we have followed common usage, seeking to strike a balance between being accessible to many different readers and sensitive to many cultures. In the matter of Japanese and Chinese names, we place the family name first (e.g., Suzuki Tadashi), unless the person has adopted western usage.

The Authors

Key references

Brandon, J.R. (1967) *Theatre in Southeast Asia*, Cambridge, Mass.: Harvard University Press.

Dening, G. (1996) *Performances*, Chicago: University of Chicago Press.

Elton, G.R. (1969) *The Practice of History*, London: Fontana.

Evans, R.J. (1997) *In Defence of History*, London: Granta Books.

Figueira, D.M. (1991) *Translating the Orient: The Reception of* Sakuntala *in Nineteenth Century Europe*, Albany: SUNY Press.

Kuhn, T. (1962) *The Structure of Scientific Revolutions*, Chicago: University of Chicago Press.

Monmonier, M. (1991) *How to Lie with Maps*, Chicago: University of Chicago Press.

Nellhaus, T. (2000) "Social ontology and (meta)theatricality: reflexions on performance and communication in history," *Journal of Dramatic Theory and Criticism*, 14, 2:3–40.

Ong, W.J. (1982) *Orality and Literacy: The Technologizing of the World*, London and New York: Methuen.

Plastow, J. (1996) *African Theatre and Politics*, Amsterdam: Rodopi.

Postlewait, T. (1991) "Historiography and the theatrical event: a primer with twelve cruxes," *Theatre Journal*, 43:157–78.

Postlewait, T. (1998) "The criteria for periodization in theatre history," *Theatre Journal*, 40:299–318.

Postlewait, T. (2000) "Writing history today," *Theatre Survey*, 41, 1:83–106.

Postlewait, T. and McConachie, B. (1989) (eds) *Interpreting the Theatrical Past*, Iowa City: University of Iowa Press.

Senelick, L. (2000) *The Changing Room: Sex, Drag and Theatre*, London and New York: Routledge.

Schieffelen, E.L. (1998) "Problematizing Performance," in F. Hughes-Freeland (ed.) *Ritual, Performance, Media*, London and New York: Routledge.

PART I

Performance and theatre in oral and written cultures before 1600

Edited by **Phillip B. Zarrilli**

Performance and theatre in oral and written cultures before 1600

INTRODUCTION

The evolution of human speech and language, and the invention of writing both had a revolutionary impact on human consciousness. Each changed fundamentally the way humans interacted with each other and their environment, and how they imagined themselves and their place in the world. Part I examines cultural performance and theatre as they emerged throughout the world before A.D. 1600. It looks at performance and theatre from the evolution of human speech, through the birth of language and the development of systems of writing, to the invention of printing, first in China (seventh century) and later in Europe (fifteenth century).

Human history stretches back across five million years, yet the majority of historical accounts of our collective endeavors focus on life since the invention of writing, around 3,000 B.C.E. Given this historical focus on literate rather than non-literate cultures and peoples, 99.9 percent of human history receives little serious study. Historians of theatre and performance usually focus where evidence exists in the form of written texts or in archeological ruins of purpose-built performance structures. Chapter 1 discusses the historiographical problems of interpreting and understanding performance in pre-literate cultures. It also provides an overview of the wide range of oral, ritual, and shamanic performances that developed during pre-literate human history but which still inform and interact with literate performance practices in many cultures today. In Chapters 2 and 3, we examine how drama and theatre developed as distinctive forms of performance practice alongside extant oral and ritual performance in some literate state societies.

In this Introduction, we consider what human consciousness might have been like before language as we know it, examining how perception, action, and imitation were central to early human existence. We trace one theory of the evolution of speech and language that explains how humans developed the unique ability for symbolic communication – an ability essential for story-telling and for writing and performing drama. We examine the ways in which the human imagination and the ability to communicate through performance are engaged in different types of social organization.

We then consider the impact of the invention of complete systems of writing, by the Sumerians in Mesopotamia (approximately 3,000 B.C.E.), and by Native American societies in Mesoamerica (probably in southern Mexico around 600 B.C.E). The invention of writing and the concomitant act of reading produced a revolution in both human consciousness and social organization as profound as the invention of speech and language. In some cultures, this revolution produced highly reflexive modes of writing/reading/performance, such as poetry, drama, and criticism.

The evolution of human language and consciousness

Episodic and mimetic modes of communication

For our earliest human ancestors, direct perception via the senses played an essential role in survival for hundreds of thousands of years. Our five senses allow us directly and immediately to perceive and respond to the environment in the here-and-now. While our senses and perception continue to be important to us today, we do not depend on them for survival to the extent we once did, except in natural disasters or violent conflict.

Early in human history, engaging in participatory, communal, bodily-based activities such as early forms of hunting, music, dance, and archaic ritual served both to heighten one's sensory perceptions and awareness, and to further orient and attune each person to others in the immediate group and to the environment. In these early practices, the human operated primarily as a perceiver/doer/actor-in-the-world. One engaged the world directly and immediately, without the mediation of "thinking" about an activity. Archaic forms of music, dance, and ritual engaged people in voicing or moving together – a means of attuning one's sensory awareness to others and for developing social bonds (McNeill 1995:*passim*). Success in hunting with archaic weapons depended on the ability of individual and group to move silently, quickly, and with stealth while sustaining synchronous coordination through non-verbal communication with others. Survival was no doubt enhanced for those best attuned to their senses and those who could form strong bonds with others in small communal groups fighting for life in harsh environments.

In his outline of four phases of human evolution – the episodic, the mimetic, the mythic, and the theoretic – Merlin Donald describes this earliest stage of human evolution as being part of an "episodic" culture, wherein one lives completely within the here-and-now (1991). There is no past or future, only the present.

Ethnologists' studies of animal behavior show that many animals, and especially our primate ancestors, also engaged in simple mimesis (imitation). The ability to learn by imitating behavior is essential to survival. Mimesis can also be autotelic; that is, it has its own rewards that are experienced as enjoyable and even playful. Mimetic behavior can thereby generate a sense of well-being. Merlin Donald uses the term "mimetic" to describe this second phase of human development beyond the episodic. In the mimetic phase, gesture, posture, and facial expression begin to be used as early forms of non-verbal communication.

Both the episodic mode of staying in the moment and the mimetic mode have been central to the activities of the performer and actor throughout history and across cultures. The episodic and mimetic modes are prerequisite aspects of performance, although various kinds of training have been invented to meet the needs of specific genres of performance.

The evolution of human speech

Language is a term that is now applied to the myriad forms of communication that evolved over millions of years to allow all living beings to communicate with other animates, especially those of the same species. Ethnologists study everything from the dance language of honey bees, to the chemical "language" used by ants, to various bio-acoustic modes of communication such as those of birds, frogs, blue whales, and elephants. The pitches of accoustic "languages" are often above or below the range of the human ear. Scientists studying Bermudan humpback whales have discovered that they vocalize lengthy "love songs" varying in pitch and lasting from six to 30 minutes. Such songs change over time, with a constant process of development in which new elements are composed, repeated, and elaborated. Dolphins and especially miniature chimps, the bonobos – with whom humans share 99 percent of the same genetic makeup – can be trained to communicate spontaneously and creatively.

But humankind and our closest ancestors developed more sophisticated modes of both natural and unnatural communication. How did this happen? Although the great apes that preceded hominid development possessed the neural pathways necessary for complex modes of communicative expression to convey information, what humans in particular eventually possessed were the lips, tongue, and modes of controlled exhalation that would anatomically allow us to speak (see Figure I.1).

Some forms of human development, such as tool-making, do not necessarily require language. More complex social activities, for example crossing a sea mass such as the Strait of Gibraltar (between southern Spain and North Africa) in a planned migration, certainly do. Similarly, cooperative hunting requires the use of speech.

As the anatomical ability to breathe properly to support speech evolved, the brain continued to enlarge, and as more complex modes of thought processes and language use evolved, the necessary neural pathways developed. What resulted was not a single "primeval" language, but rather, the distinctive capacity to use language self-referentially, that is, the ability to use words that point to other words via syntax. This development was only complete anatomically when modern humans, *Homo sapiens*, became dominant, approximately 150,000 years ago.

Mythic and theoretic modes of communication

By 120,000 years ago a *Homo sapiens* recognizable as our identical ancestor had emerged. One particular group of "modern" *H.sapiens*, living in a cave at the mouth of the Klasies River in South Africa between 120,000 to 60,000, were settled permanently, engaged in complex domestic life, felled giant buffaloes with spears, possessed a complex knowledge of their environment, practiced music and art (using red ochre "crayons"), engaged in ritual burial of the dead, and used language much as we do today. *H.sapiens* either absorbed or replaced *H.neanderthalensis* and *H.erectus*.

The period brought a "cultural explosion." The species could depict humans, animals, symbols, and perhaps even note the passage of time (lunar calendars) in bone and ivory, on stone and wood. They fashioned flutes, drums, and stringed instruments, and painted or etched the walls of caves (see

Australopithecus (4.1 million years ago)

Gestures and vocations (grunts, shrieks, sighs, etc.)

Homo habilis (2.4 million years ago)

Approximately 2.4 million yeas ago in Africa, an early form of human voca language probably first developed with the genus *Homo habilis*. *Habilis* also developed the ability to make stone tools, and to control fire. Possessing a larger brain, and eventually achieving food supluses, *habilis* developed larger and more complex social groupings, necessitating a synergistic process of more complex development of a part of the brain (Broca s area) fundamental to the production of sign language and speech. But for both *habilis* and his successor, *Homo ergaster*, the complete set of physical attributes in the larynx (voice box) and control of exhalation were still not sufficiently developed for human articulate speech to appear; therefore, communication remained primarily gestures, grunts, shrieks, etc.

Homo erectus (2 million years ago)

It is only with the wholly new species, *Homo erectus*, that a major shift in hominid evolution occurred. With *erectus*, some form of speech evolved as early as 900,000 years ago. This may have been short utterances, with conditional propositions.

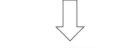

From erectus *came apparently two main divergences*

1. Homo neanderthalensis (300,000 to 30,000 years ago)

During the Middle Pleistocene era between 300,000 and 230,00 years ago, the manufacture of tools and high level of social complexity that marked *Homo neanderthalensis* point to the use of a rudimentary mode of vocalization somewhat close to *Homo sapiens*. The *neanderthalensis* anatomy suggests that pitch and melody played a key role in the ability to communicate complex ideas and the development of a speech/sound/song-based society. Voices would have been high-pitched and melodic, but [i], [a], and [u] could not have been pronounced by this species.

Homo sapiens (300,000 years ago)

The development of complex thought processes and complex sentences allowed speech-based societies to develop. While archaic forms of *sapiens* probably developed as early as half a million years ago, it took over 100,000 years for *Homo sapiens* to replace *Homo neanderthalensis* in Europe and the Middle East, and *erectus* in the Far East.

Modern humans (150,000 years ago)

Posessed all the physical features necessary for speech as we know it today.

Figure I.1 One charting of the evolution of human language. Adapted from Steven Roger Fischer, *History of Language* (1999). [Source: Steven Roger Fischer, *History of Language*, Reaktion Books, 1999.]

Figure I.2). As Fischer notes, "By now articulate speech – and the symbolic reasoning it allowed – was certainly being used in all the ways we are familiar with today, and hominids were no longer merely the 'talking ape', but the 'symbolic ape'" (Fischer 1999:56).

Early forms of speech allowed communication and planning sufficient for humans to cross seas, settle villages, and further develop technology, hunting, music, dance, rituals, and narratives. According to Merlin Donald, the evolution of human speech and language transformed our mimetic capabilities into the "mythic" phase of our development. Telling stories about ourselves, our communities, and our place in the world allowed an entirely new way of understanding and representing reality. It is these earliest pre-literate oral, ritual, and shamanic performances that are examined in Chapter 1 as they developed in relatively intimate, small-scale communal settings.

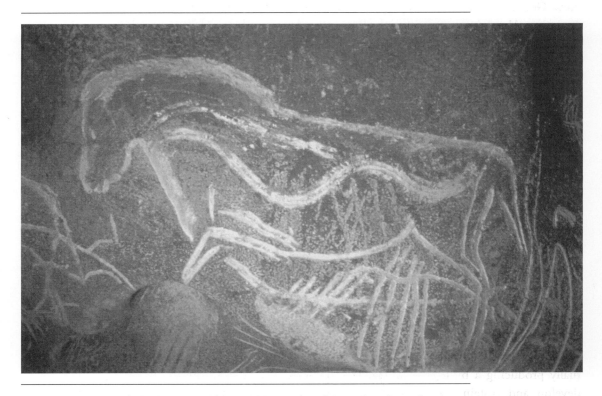

Figure I.2 Artwork in Lascaux, Chauvet Cave, showing a drawing of a horse with possible spring moulting on its coat. [Source: French Ministry of Culture and Communication, Regional Director for Cultural Affairs, Rhone-Alpes Region, Regional Department Archaeology.]

Human language, writing, and society

Band, tribe, chiefdom, state

The need for survival and for a sense of belonging or connectedness to others leads human beings to organize themselves into communities. Each type and scale of social organization engages in different ways our communicative abilities, our imagining of ourselves, and our relationships to others. Jared Diamond has identified four types of societies ranging from intimate, relatively simple, nomadic bands through settlements organized as tribes and chiefdoms, to the highly complex, centralized model of the state (1997:267ff).

By the time fully articulate speech developed (35,000 years ago), all humans lived in bands. Most continued to do so until as recently as 11,000 years ago. Today only a few bands live autonomously in remote regions of New Guinea and the Amazon (other bands such as the South African San, Australian Aborigines, and North American Inuit have come under the control of states, been threatened with extinction, and/or been assimilated). Bands range in size from five to 80 people and are the smallest, most intimate forms of human society, with all or most of those in the band closely related by birth or marriage. Bands are nomadic; base their relationships on kinship; share a common language; exchange stories, words, dances, music, rituals, and goods; and make decisions in relatively egalitarian, informal ways. Within bands there is no social stratification by class, nor are there hereditary or formal modes of leadership or monopolization of decision-making. Leaders emerge informally through strength of character, intelligence, and/or the ability to fight. For people living within bands, experience is shaped primarily through ever-evolving relationships with the immediate environment and through face-to-face contact with those with whom one has daily involvement, often shaped by collective performances and rituals.

By 14,000 years ago, *Homo sapiens* was the only hominid species surviving, differentiated by hundreds of language families and thousands of languages, and organized into small bands. By 12,000 years ago, a warming climate pushed the Ice Age to the two poles. Rising ocean levels divided peoples. The warming climate allowed the growth and domestication of wild grains, eventually producing a biological revolution. Major population settlements could develop and sustain themselves in resource-rich regions of the world by growing wheat and barley, and keeping goats and sheep.

In the Fertile Crescent of the Near East (today's Iraq between the Tigris and Euphrates Rivers; see Figure I.3) and perhaps a few other places in the world, a new form of settled social organization began to emerge – tribes. Improved technology allowed the extraction and preservation of food. Permanent dwellings were built in which hundreds rather than dozens of people lived in settlements, sharing a common language and culture, including performance and rituals. Tribal organization is characterized by its pattern of settled residence, and its larger groupings consisting of more than one kinship group (clans). Particular clans possess rights to plots of land. Tribes are still small enough that all individuals are known by relationships and names. Like bands, tribes may be governed by a somewhat informal "egalitarian" system with information and decision-making being communally shared. In some

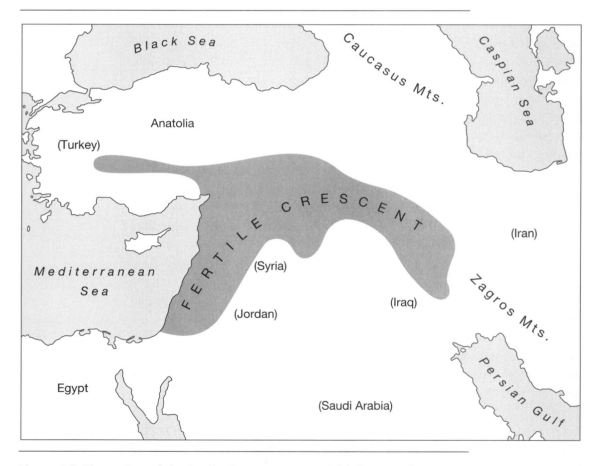

Figure I.3 The region of the Fertile Crescent – an area rich in natural resources and capable of sustaining a large, settled, centrally-controlled society.
[Source: Jared Diamond 1997:135.]

tribes, a "big-man" may emerge who achieves high status through the strength of his individual character. Reciprocal exchange and a participatory mode of socio-economic organization continue to characterize interaction in both tribes as well as bands. As peoples settle, particular languages become associated with specific geographical regions. Language becomes associated with land.

Chiefdoms emerged by approximately 5,500 B.C.E in the region of the Fertile Crescent and by around 1,000 B.C.E in Mesoamerica and the Andes. Chiefdoms are considerably larger than tribes, numbering from several thousand to as many as tens of thousands of people. Chiefdoms were the first societies organized around a central hereditary authority figure, who often held a monopoly over the exercise of power, centralizing information and decision-making. A chief's decisions were usually implemented by one or two levels of bureaucrats who often played multiple roles, such as in Polynesian Hawaii where *konohiki* oversaw labor, irrigation, and collection of tribute. Some chiefs, such as those in Hawaii, were assumed to be divine, or of divine descent, and either combined in their own role the authority of being chief priest, or supported a separate group of priests who provided justification for their authority. While bands and tribes possessed supernatural beliefs and ritual practices, these beliefs and practices were not used to

> justify central authority, justify transfer of wealth, or maintain peace between unrelated individuals. When supernatural beliefs gained those functions and became institutionalized, they were thereby transformed into what we term religion.
>
> (Diamond 1997:278)

Some chiefdoms were large enough to exist as multiple villages (with the chief's village as primary), to have specialized craftspeople producing specialized luxury goods, and to delegate some menial jobs to slaves – those captured in raids. Chiefdoms for the first time shifted from reliance on reciprocal exchange characteristic of bands and tribes, to a form of tribute in which a portion of one's harvest was given to the chief – most of which was retained centrally while a small amount might be redistributed as part of a feast or other public occasion. Chiefs could also require commoners to undertake labor, for example the erection of public architecture such as temples, burial tombs, henges (large circular structures with a surrounding back, see Chapter 1), or irrigation systems. Luxury goods were usually reserved for chiefs, as archaeological excavations of their burial sites reveal.

The development of larger and more complex modes of social organization such as chiefdoms (and states) creates a social setting where, for the first time, individuals understand that they are connected to other people they have never seen. For example, Javanese and Indian villagers traditionally know that they are connected to people they have never met through particular nets of kinship and/or clientship. Therefore, there was no word in Javanese for the abstract concept of "society" until very recently. The identification of individuals' places within society was identified by such markers as "lord of X" or "mother of Y" or "client of Z." One's ties to others are not necessarily forged only within the immediate group and environment, but rather are "imagined." Within larger communities like chiefdoms (and states), the imagining of the larger community to which one belongs is shaped and styled differently at different times in different cultures.

As late as 1492 C.E., chiefdoms were common in productive areas of South and Central America and some parts of sub-Saharan Africa, the Eastern United States, and Polynesia. But by the twentieth century they had disappeared as chiefdoms were conquered by centralized states. Today, states are the most familiar form of social, political, and economic organization; indeed, the entire land mass of the world, with the exception of Antarctica, is now ruled by modern nation-states (see Chapter 6 for a discussion of modern nation-states). Early and modern states share some characteristics. Both have a high degree of centralized control and economic specialization, which often includes mass production and the execution of public works. In both we find economic redistribution (taxes rather than tribute) and a proliferation of specialized and professional administrators, selected at least partly on the basis of training and ability. In both, internal conflicts are settled by recourse to laws. Both have a judiciary and police, and in both, modes of organization are based not on kinship but on political allegiance and territorial lines. Unlike bands, tribes, and chiefdoms, which consist of a single ethnic and linguistic group, states and especially empires (formed by the conquest of several states) are multilingual and multi-ethnic.

The earliest forms of state organization arose around 3,700 B.C.E. in Mesopotamia and 3,000 B.C.E. in Mesoamerica, some 2,000 years ago in China, Southeast Asia, and the Andes region of South America, and over 1,000 years ago in West Africa. Features of these early states were: leadership by a titled, hereditary leader – either a king considered divine or an equivalent leader; the adoption of slavery on a larger scale than chiefdoms; and the development of state religions, often with standardized temples. No chiefdom developed writing, except those in the process of becoming states. Indeed, the first "complete" systems of writing developed about the same time as the formation of early states in Mesopotamia and Mesoamerica. Where such complete systems of writing developed, literate elites emerged in early states, creating some of the socio-cultural conditions within which drama and theatre developed, as we shall see in Chapters 2 and 3.

The invention of systems of writing

For approximately 40,000–50,000 years as modern languages continued to evolve, not only were new technologies invented, but modes of oral and expressive culture developed which allowed particular societies and groups to remember, reflect upon, celebrate, and perform their evolving stories and identities through oral/verbal, bodily, and artistic modes of expression. Precursors of complete systems of writing appeared as early as 100,000 years ago when humans began to invent a wide variety of graphic symbols and mnemonics (memory tools) to store information. Graphic symbols were usually reproductions of commonplace phenomena of the physical world such as the sun, stars, fauna, flora, human-like figures, and so on. Aids to memory such as knot records, notches made on bone or a staff, or pictographs served a linguistic function. Knot records date back to the early Neolithic period and reached their peak with the South American Incas' *quipus* – an elaborate system of counting. While knots and notches record numbers, prompt memory, and suggest categories, pictures are able to record much more information and suggest characteristics and qualities as well. Tens of thousands of years ago, pictorial communication appeared in early cave art (see Figure I.4), and, among some Native Americans, pictography was long used to convey complex

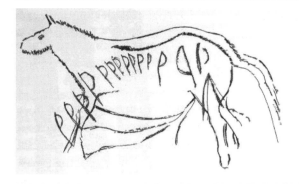

Figure I.4 Some cave art such as this horse at Les Trois in southern France is considered a form of pictorial communication. The significance of the series of " P "s engraved over the horse is unknown.
[Source: Steven Roger Fischer, *A History of Writing*, London: Reaktion Books, 2001, p.18.]

messages with no recourse to articulate speech. Knots, notches and pictographs remain "incomplete" or "pre"-writing in that they do not use their marks or pictures to communicate articulate speech.

Complete systems of writing did not evolve like language, but were invented to communicate articulate speech via the use of conventional, artificial marks on a durable surface. The spoken word is transformed into a representative sign. It was in Mesopotamia that clay tokens were used as early as 8,000 B.C.E. to count grain and animals in the region's early farming settlements. Somewhat before 3,000 B.C.E. the Sumerians in Mesopotamia managed to develop from a repertoire of pictograms and symbols the first complete system of writing – cuneiform. Cuneiform is a form of writing scratched or inscribed on clay tablets with a pointed tool (stylus). With the invention of Sumerian, individuals began to read a sign inscribed on clay as a sound with its own independent value.

By 2,500 B.C.E the Sumerians' simple cuneiform script was capable of "conveying 'any and all thought' . . . adequately fulfil[ling] the needs of its society" (Fischer 2001:52). The earliest inscriptions are lists accounting for payments, goods, people, etc. Of all the cuneiform inscriptions discovered, 75 percent are administrative and book-keeping records. Among the remaining 25 percent are legal, religious, astronomical, and medical writings, and dictionaries and recipes. Also in this 25 percent – and most significant for our purposes – are the first and oldest of many literatures of the world. These include hymns, laments, descriptions of activities of the gods, and quasi-epic stories. The extant poetic works include two poems of Enmerker, two poems of Lugulbanda, and a cycle of five poems known as *Gilgamesh*. The *Gilgamesh* cycle dates approximately from 2,700 B.C.E Like the later Greek epics, the *Iliad* and the *Odyssey*, the epic of *Gilgamesh* was most likely a collection of disparate but related stories gathered and elaborated by tale-tellers and eventually written down after hundreds of years of oral transmission and performance. It enjoyed wide popularity throughout the Near East, and also exists in Sumerian, Hittite, and Hurrian versions.

The transition from oral communication to writing was not universal, and its development took place at different times and with different systems in different cultures and historical periods. The second documentable case of an independent development of writing is among Native American societies in Mesoamerica, most likely southern Mexico from approximately 600 B.C.E. It is possible that Chinese, Egyptian, and Easter Island modes of writing *may* have also developed independently. Whether this is the case or not, linguists agree that all other systems of writing were inspired by if not direct descendents of either the Sumerian or Mesoamerican systems.

Most pre-literate peoples who developed writing did so by borrowing and then adapting systems of writing they encountered. For example, on Syria's northern coast, Semitic scribes of Ugarit borrowed the outer physical form of Sumerian cuneiform script to write the Hurrian language (Figure I.5). In East Asia, some scholars believe that it was in the Shang state in north central China (c.1,500–1,545 B.C.E.) that an early version of the Chinese system of character writing developed (arguably originating in Mesopotamia), later to be influential in the development of the writing systems used in Korea, Japan, and Vietnam. On the Indian subcontinent where well over 200 scripts eventually developed, they all derived from one source script – Brahmi – which itself derived from a Semitic (probably Aramaic) source by c.253–250 B.C.E. The success of a particular system of writing does not entail superiority but adaptability. It is not "the efficiency of a writing system or script that determines its longevity and influence, but rather the economic power and prestige

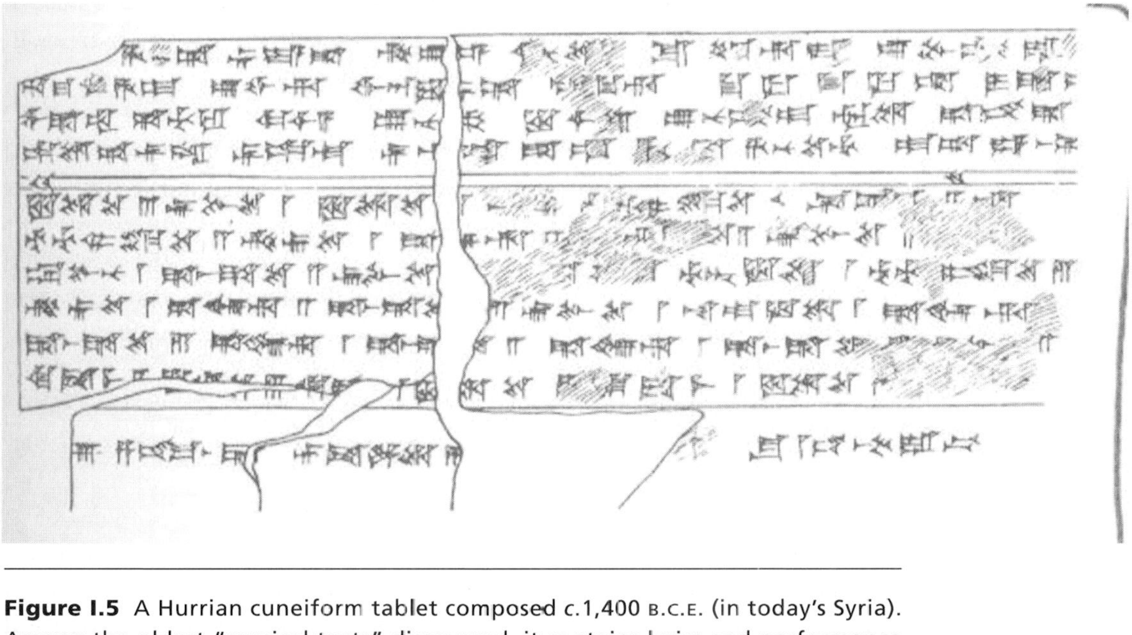

Figure I.5 A Hurrian cuneiform tablet composed c.1,400 B.C.E. (in today's Syria). Among the oldest "musical texts" discovered, it contains lyrics and performance information. It is one of many examples of how the outer form of Sumerian cuneiform script was borrowed to write different languages. [Source: Steven Roger Fischer, *A History of Writing*, London: Reaktion Books, 2001, p.55.]

of those using it. . . . A powerful society's writing system – the consonantal alphabet – will mark history, while a weak society's will perish" (Fischer 2001:119).

Historians of early writing systems have argued that writing emerged only when and where there was a need for a system of writing within a context that provided the social, economic, and human resources necessary to support specialists in written language, such as copyists, librarians, teachers, religious specialists, poets, and eventually in a few cases, dramatists and the companies of actors/dancers who could perform a play. All of the societies that invented writing (Sumer, Mesoamerica, China, Egypt) or were early in creating their own systems (Crete, Iran, Turkey, the Indus Valley, and Mayan cultures) "involved socially stratified societies with complex and centralized political institutions." They stored food surpluses grown by peasants sufficient to support these institutions and the specialists (Diamond 1999:236).

Writing never developed among hunter-gatherer societies organized into bands or tribes or even among more settled chiefdoms, because they did not possess the need, institutions, or agricultural resources necessary to support it. For example, among many of the Pacific islands, writing remained unnecessary for centuries. In many Pacific societies elaborate states never developed, so there was no need for a complex system of bookkeeping.

Performance, communication, and remembrance

All societies, whether organized as an intimate band or a large-scale state, have a need for communication and remembrance. In Chapter 1, we examine how oral cultures do this through recitations of lengthy genealogies, elaborating epics and myths, or reciting religious/ritual texts, performances that often required remarkable feats of memorization. Rich storehouses of oral lore, epics, myths, and tales were adapted to a variety of modes of oral performance by storytellers and bards. Sometimes they informed rituals, dance, and music which served to knit people together into a community with a particular world-view. In Chapters 2 and 3 we interrogate selected forms of drama and theatre as they emerged in larger-scale literate state societies. Chapter 2 discusses the ways in which the religious/civic festivals within some early state societies produced two very different models of drama and theatre: (1) commemorative ritual/religious dramas re-enacting a mythological/historical event of the past and (2) independently authored, original "literary" dramas. We examine how each type of drama and its performance is shaped by the particular religious/ritual context of its invention; how each choreographs in its structure and performance a particular form of state authority; and how each negotiates a particular relationship with writing and textuality. Finally, Chapter 3 examines specific models of pleasure and/or aesthetics generated by, and shaped within the context of, court or imperial-state patronage.

PZ

Key references

Anderson, B. (1983) *Imagined Communities*, London: Verso.

Diamond, J. (1997) *Guns, Germs, and Steel: The Fates of Human Societies*, New York: W.W. Norton & Co.

Donald, M. (1991) *The Origins of the Modern Mind: Three Stages in the Evolution of Culture and Cognition*, Cambridge, Mass.: Harvard University Press.

Donald, M. (2001) *A Mind so Rare: The Evolution of Human Consciousness*, New York: W.W. Norton.

Fischer, S.R. (1999) *A History of Language*, London: Reaktion Books.

Fischer, S.R. (2001) *A History of Writing*, London: Reaktion Books.

Fischer, S.R. (2003) *A History of Reading*, London: Reaktion Books.

McNeill, W.H. (1995) *Keeping Together in Time: Dance and Drill in Human History*, Cambridge, Mass.: Harvard University Press.

Mithen, S. (2005) *The Singing Neanderthal: The Origin of Language, Music, Body and Mind*, Forthcoming.

CHAPTER 1

Oral, ritual, and shamanic performance

In this chapter we focus on oral, ritual, and shamanic performance practices, the earliest to emerge in primary oral cultures before theatre – part of that pre-literate past that is 99.9 percent of human history. Our main purpose is to discover as much as we can about archaic forms of performance from historiographic methods used to interpret pre-literate, especially smaller-scale societies. A secondary purpose is to understand that oral, ritual, and shamanic performance are not part of a "primitive" past, but dynamic and often adaptable forms of performance that continue to shape many peoples' personal, social, and/or cosmological identities today.

All we can know of performances in the pre-literate past before 3,000 B.C.E. is what can be gleaned from scant archeological evidence, interpretation of the verbal arts of oral performance, oral compositions fixed when systems of writing developed, and analysis of early written texts that provide some fragmentary (and usually biased) information about pre-literate beliefs and cultural practices. We can also make careful use of contemporary ethnographic studies of extant oral, ritual, and shamanic performances by scholars of anthropology, folklore,

and performance (on ethnography and history, see the Chapter 5 case study on kathakali dance-drama). This combination of historiographic methods necessarily involves a high degree of inference in the act of interpretation. Any written evidence is secondary, and therefore inherently problematic.

We begin by examining the fundamental historiographic problem of how to understand primary orality and oral performance in pre-literate societies. We then provide an account of key features of early oral performance, and of oral performance under the "sign" of writing.

We next consider a central question of orality and ritual. How did early peoples orient themselves to the world as they knew and understood it? We can try to answer that by analyzing dynamic and often unstable notions of power – a central force in most archaic performance. Turning to ritual and shamanic performance practices, we describe how they are understood to act upon the world, or "do" something fundamental. However, these practices serve a variety of worldviews and accomplish their "doing" in a variety of ways. Because no single definition of ritual can contain all its possibilities, the remainder of the chapter analyzes ritual and shamanic performance practices across a wide range of historical periods and cultures. The examples of oral, ritual, and shamanic performance selected for discussion are organized according to the different types of evidence available to us:

- What can we learn about archaic performance from archeology alone? We answer this question with a brief account of one ritual landscape in Neolithic England (*c*.3,500–2,500 B.C.E.).
- What can we learn about performance in a culture for which there is both archeological evidence and early written accounts? Here we (re)construct pre-literate Celtic oral and ritual/festival performance circa the sixth century C.E.
- What can we learn about ritual and shamanic performance by examining contemporary ethnographic accounts? Here and in the case studies following this chapter, we examine Hopi, Balinese, Yoruba, and Korean performances – all with historical roots in antiquity.

Each example illustrates the way in which performance orients its participants to the "world" as they imagine and understand it. As bodily-based practices, these performances helped "make" these worlds in the past, and continue to do so for peoples still practicing them in the present.

Primary orality

Just as a distinctive human consciousness and society developed with the evolution of language, the invention of complete writing systems necessarily altered human consciousness. This immediately poses fundamental problems for the historian. If the invention of writing fundamentally transformed human consciousness, to what degree is it possible in today's literate world to re-imagine what life was like before writing? If the earliest proto-written scripts date only from 5,000–6,000 years ago, how can we know what the world was like during the thousands of years in which there was no writing or literacy? Walter J.

Ong takes as his subject "thought and its verbal expression in oral culture," and secondarily "literate thought and expression" as they emerged from, and in relation to orality (1988:1).

Ong asserts the obvious – we are so literate today that "it is very difficult for us to conceive of an oral universe of communication or thought except as a variant of a literate universe" (ibid.:2). Most cultures today have some knowledge of a form of writing in their history. For anyone reading this book, it is impossible to "fully recover a sense of what the word is to purely oral people" (ibid.:12). To help us understand the difference between our literate modes of communication, and those before writing, Ong identifies two forms of orality – primary and secondary. Primary orality refers to those peoples who have never encountered writing and whose entire worldview and modes of communication are untouched by any form of writing. In contrast are present-day high-technology cultures and societies, in which "secondary orality," an orality "sustained by telephone, radio, television, and other electronic devices that depend for their existence and functioning on writing and print" (ibid.:11). Modern media are discussed in Part IV of this book.

When words are committed to writing, oral communication is translated into a manual/spatial mode of communication that necessarily restructures thought. The residue left in writing – the marks inscribed on clay or on the surface of parchment or paper – are not present in primary oral cultures. Simple oral dialects usually consist of only a few thousand words, and users have no knowledge of the history of their vocabulary.

For people within primary oral cultures, there is no differentiation between a thought and the words which express it. Saying something is intending something. One's word is the final authority – no signature in writing is required. One's actions require no authority outside themselves. While primary oral communication is to some degree analytic in that it breaks things down into component units, in contrast, written records "fix" words. They can be studied. The very materiality of written words historically encouraged the development of a distinction between what is written and the ideas the words represent. From the root word for the act of speaking, "oration," is derived the word "ratio" for rational thought. It has been argued that literacy creates two separate worlds – the world which we hear and see, or the world of talk and action. The second world is the imperceptible mental world of thoughts, desires, and intentions. As we shall see in Chapter 2, the literate Greeks by the time of Plato and Aristotle created for the West this second space which houses thoughts, intentions, and desires. This western metaphorical space was called psyche, and is usually known today as "the mind."

Oral performance

Voicing and listening in the mythic mode

Tete ka asom ene Kakyere
Ancient things remain in the ear

(an Akan [Ghanaian] proverb,
Vansina 1985:xi)

In primary oral cultures, the perception, action, and doing fundamental to early human survival remains central to what one does and how things are known. What is known is learned through direct participation and/or apprenticeship rather than abstract study. In primary oral cultures, human beings are the only potential repository for traditional oral narratives, myths, tales, proverbs, classificatory names, information on how to perform a ritual, tell/sing a monumental epic story, etc.

Here speaks the storyteller, telling by voice what was learned by ear. Here speaks a poet who did not learn language structure from one teacher and language meaning from another,

nor plot structure from one and characterization from another, nor even an art of storytelling from one and an art of hermeneutics from another, but always heard all these things working together in the stories of other storytellers. And this poet, or mythopoet, not only narrates what characters do, but speaks when they speak, chants when they chant, and sings when they sing.

(Tedlock 1983:3)

Apprenticeship in verbal arts of performance, drumming, hunting, dancing, or ritual requires some form of discipleship. Initial learning through listening, doing, direct imitation of a teacher/elder, and repetition, allows a neophyte to reach a sufficient level of mastery to enable improvisation within the limits of accepted conventions.

Rich and complex early oral texts were eventually transcribed, such as the Sumerian epic known as *Gilgamesh*, India's *Mahabharata*, and the well-known Greek epics, the *Iliad* and the *Odyssey*. But a fundamental shift occurred when such texts were no longer simply *heard*, but *read* for their meaning. As Walter Ong explains:

the scholarly focus on texts had ideological consequences. With their attention directed to texts, scholars often went on to assume, often without reflection, that oral verbalization was essentially the same as the written verbalization they normally dealt with, and that oral art forms were to all intents and purposes simply texts, except for the fact that they were not written down. The impression grew that, apart from the oration (governed by written rhetorical rules), oral art forms were essentially unskillful and not worth serious study

(1988:10)

Recent research by folklorists studying oral performance reveals the creativity and complexity of oral modes of composition. Archaic forms of skilled oral performance and discourse might best be thought of as "weaving or stitching – '*rhapsodein*,' to 'rhapsodize' . . . to stitch songs together" (ibid.:13). For some forms of oral performance such as epic/heroic tales there is no fixed text. Each performance is composed as it happens. The mechanisms of remembering involve cueing and scanning – highly creative processes that take place as a particular story is "stitched" together in performance.

Primary oral cultures are "episodic" locations of listening, hearing, and voicing where "mythic" worlds are created. The hearer does not attempt to analyze, understand, or interpret what is heard, but experiences and absorbs the musicality of the voice – its timbre, tone, amplitude, pitch, resonance, vibration, and shape as the voice moves between sounding and silence(s) – the pauses of varying lengths that help mark, set off, and/or accentuate what is voiced. Reception is perception, not "meaning."

By examining an extant tradition in which the experience of "hearing" is central, we can gain insights into performance in primary oral cultures, with the understanding that the extant practices of indigenous peoples today cannot be taken to be exactly the same as practices in archaic periods. The Sami are an indigenous people whose homeland stretched across northern Finland, Sweden and Norway, and into the Kola Peninsula. Like most indigenous peoples, the Sami have suffered years of cultural and political oppression, in this case at the hands of Norway. Like all indigenous peoples, they have been in a constant process of negotiating their traditions and ways of understanding their relationship to their world and their immediate environment. The Sami have been thrust into both national (Norwegian) and transnational global worlds. They are also one of the most modernized indigenous peoples in the world. They used to be called Lapps – the peoples who herd reindeers. But the "Lapps" are actually a very diverse group of peoples with at least a dozen distinct language and culture groups.

One of these groups is the northern "reindeer Sami" whose homeland is the northernmost part of the country called Norway today.

The relationship of the Sami to nature was based traditionally on an acceptance of the provisional nature of human existence – a view necessitated by living in close relationship within a particular ecosystem. The necessities of survival produced a worldview in which all creatures and their environments are seen as fundamentally interdependent. One Sami practice illustrates this understanding of a relational world – "serious listening," that is, hearing and obeying the heartbeats of the Earth itself. Among the many stories still part of the extant Sami tradition is the myth of the creator god who plucked a beating heart from a two-year-old reindeer and placed it at the center of the earth so that its living pulse beat in the ground of all being(s). When life becomes difficult, people press their ears to the ground and listen. If they hear the reindeer's beating heart, all will be well. If not, they are doomed.

"Seeing" words in the mythic mode

Just as "listening" is an episodic mode of communication that helps create a "mythic" world, so does "seeing." Among the Yoruba of Nigeria and Benin, West Africa, the oral elaboration of a story by an excellent teller makes the story a "spectacle" (*ìran*) in that "it is visible through the storyteller's dramatization, and the spectator visualizes it further in his mind's eye" (Drewal and Drewal 1983:1). As seen in early cave paintings, some of the earliest forms of oral performance no doubt literally made use of images as a memory aid for the teller and to enhance the pleasure of the audience. Imagery is a way for humans to access the "invisible" where their language is not written. But images also played a key role in the development of some writing systems such as Sumerian cuneiform, Egyptian hieroglyphs, and Chinese characters. For literate westerners raised in alphabetic cultures, the central role of images in early communication may be difficult to comprehend.

Figure 1.1 Iranian *parda-dar*, outside Masjid-I Juma' in Savara. Photo © Samuel R. Peterson. [Source: Victor H. Mair, *Painting and Performance*, Honolulu: University of Hawaii Press, 1988.]

"Picture-recitation" – the telling of lengthy stories with pictures – exemplifies the central importance of images in some archaic performances. One scholar hypothesizes that picture-recitation originated in India (*sáubhika, citrakathī,* and *paṛ*) and spread through Indonesia (*wayang bèbèr*), Japan (*etoki*), China (*chuan-pien*), Iran (*parda-dar*) (Figure 1.1), Turkey, Italy, and Germany (Mair 1988, passim). When this genre first developed, it is likely that the pictures were primary and the "texts" (eventually written down) were oral elaborations of the stories told by the pictures.

Chinese "transformation texts" (*pien-wen*) date from the T'ang period (C.E. 618–906), and are part of the central history of Chinese fiction and drama since they represent the first extended vernacular narratives in China. The *pien* story-tellers were lay entertainers – mostly men, but occasionally women as well – inhabiting a niche in society between the sacred and the secular. The contents of this once flourishing popular performance tradition were both secular and religious, and in China mainly Buddhist. *Pien-wen* became a well-known literary genre, but

derived from a much earlier form of oral story-telling with pictures, first called *chuan-pien*, literally "turning transformation [picture scrolls]" (ibid.:1). The term "transformation" refers to miraculous powers of transformation and manifestation of early Buddhist figures. Artists represented these manifestations in wall-paintings, on silk or paper, known as *pien-hsiang* – "transformation scenes or tableaux" which a story-teller used during performance. Like most such "folk art" traditions, in China these modes of performance were neglected in historical records which exclusively documented the products of elite, high society.

In the Javanese version of picture-recitation, *wayang beber* ("unfolding/unrolled shadows"), a narrator (*dalang*) unrolls a long, horizontal scroll on which are painted a series of scenes as he chants and speaks the story the scroll reveals (Figure 1.2). Six to eight scrolls are required to perform an entire story. It is likely that *wayang beber* was at first "closely connected with animistic rites of ancestor worship" (Brandon 1970:5). Some scholars have argued that Java's most popular and well-known form of traditional theatre today, *wayang kulit* (literally, "shadows

Figure 1.2 A Javanese *wayang beber* scroll, with painted scenes, used by the narrator (*dalang*) as he speaks and chants a story. © Archives Internationales d'Ethnographie. [Source: *Archives Internationales d'Ethnographie*, 16 (1903), taf.18.2. In Victor H. Mair, *Painting and Performance*, Honolulu: University of Hawaii Press, 1988.]

made of leather"), developed as specific figures on a scroll, were detached from the scroll to become individual puppets. With a host of puppet-characters to manipulate independently, the shadow puppeteer was able to literally bring the shadows to life on his screen. This allowed shadow-puppetry to supersede in popularity the older, more static picture-recitation form. As explained in the Balinese example below, it also became a powerful efficacious ritual practice through which to exorcise witches (Mair 1988:60)

"Serious listening" and/or "seeing" characterize many archaic modes of performance which engage the spectator's senses directly, and help create one's relationship to the world understood through myth, not history. Myths, epics, and even tales are traditionally context-specific; that is, like rituals they are told or enacted within a context that specifies precisely when or where each story is to be communicated. Among the Zuni of New Mexico a story such as "The Girl and the Protector" is only to be

> told late at night; if you tell it during the day you will hasten the coming of the darkness. If you tell it after the snakes have come out in the spring and before they go underground in the fall, take care to omit the first and last lines and to hold a flower in one hand while you speak. Otherwise the story may attract the attention of the snakes.
>
> (Tedlock 1983:68)

In primary oral cultures, everything has its place and time, usually within a recurring cycle. One's experience of the day, the waxing and waning of the moon, the passing and return of seasons, the placement of the stars in the sky, and the marking of larger units of 'annual' time help create an experience of time as cyclical – not linear or historical.

But what happened to early oral performances when they encountered writing for the first time?

Oral texts and their transmission under the written sign: Vedic chanting in India

Where complex writing systems *did* develop, they did not displace many modes of oral, verbal, expressive communication. We examine the history of how a once completely oral mode of performing and transmitting sacred texts – the Vedas of India – has continued to exist to the present day "under" the written word.

Most well-known oral compositions – Homer's the *Iliad* and the *Odyssey* or the Sumerian Epic of *Gilgamesh* – died out as oral performances. All we possess of these traditions, especially in the West, is a suggestion of these traditions in the form of texts set down in writing. But in other parts of the world, among native peoples in Asia and Africa for example, oral performances still abound.

The oldest sustained form of continuous oral performance in the world is chanting of the Vedas in India. Four different Vedas exist, the oldest of which is the *Ṛg Veda*, dating from as early as 1,200 B.C.E. The four Vedas are collections of poems, hymns, and invocations derived from ritual and religious practices which originated in the Central Asiatic region. Since their composition, they have continued to be transmitted orally from generation to generation down to the present by socially high-ranking, male priestly communities, for whom recitation of the Vedas is their life's work and purpose – an unbroken line of transmission for over 3,000 years.

With the development of written Sanskrit (eighth century B.C.E.) these priestly families became literate; however, their texts were not committed to writing until very recently. Vedic education is not an intellectual undertaking, but a rigorous training in ritual chanting. It is traditionally undertaken by all Brahmin boys who must learn to recite in its entirety the specific Veda inherited by their families (for an early twentieth-century account, see Wood 1985:58–89). This prodigious task of memorization is necessary so that each boy can chant the Vedic verses appropriate for each of the specific rituals required to sustain Brahmin life, function as a priest in the temples, and collectively perform the lengthy sacrificial rituals understood to be necessary to sustain the universe.

Until the late twentieth century, full-time training for young Brahmin boys started soon after the ceremony of the investiture of the sacred thread (*upanayanam*) at approximately the age of seven and continued for eight to 12 years. With the exception of a few individuals who specialize in the study of Sanskrit, for the majority of teachers as well as students, both undertake instruction in recitation of the Vedas with little if any intellectual understanding of the meaning of the texts they are learning. The process of transmission is an entirely oral, embodied process. In the Sama Veda tradition of Kerala, in southwest India, the most musical of the four Vedic traditions, the teacher literally places his hands on the student as he chants the text, manipulating the student's head and body to the particular rhythm of the text so that the student learns not in his head by memorizing, but through his body's engagement with the text (Figure 1.3).

When writing was introduced, Brahmins saw writing as inferior to speech. Indeed, writing down the sacred chants was at first forbidden, because a Veda is intended *only to be heard* as it is chanted. The Vedas are distinguished from written texts which are "remembered." Since the written word is not directly heard, it is a recollection of something heard or spoken in the past. The religious prohibition against writing the Vedas is probably one reason among many that writing did not develop on the Indian subcontinent until about the eighth century B.C.E.

But when writing did develop, oral transmission continued to play a central and even dominant role in many modes of traditional knowledge and learning, from religious ritual to hands-on therapies within traditional medicine and performance down to the present day – as we will see in the case studies of *kutiyattam* in Chapter 3 and kathakali in Chapter 5. Simultaneously, a great body of literature emerged. India produced the world's first linguists who categorized letters according to the specific place of articulation – a very "modern" practice. From the

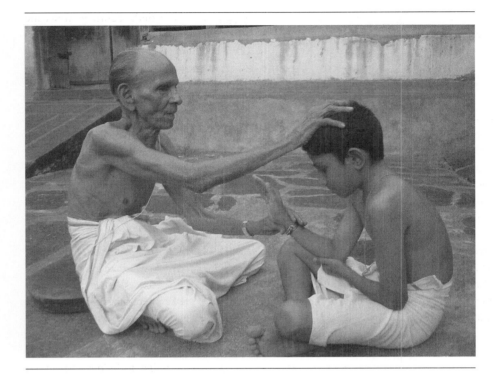

Figure 1.3 Sama Veda chanting in Kerala, India. Photo © by Kunju Vasudevan Namboodiripad.

time that Sanskrit texts began to be written down and eventually composed, the way of writing Sanskrit has always born the marks of the centrality of the aural/oral dimension of the language. Scribes traditionally did not distinguish one word from another, but rather used *sandhi* to mark and distinguish "breath groups," so that the text would be chanted correctly (these are not markings for understanding in silent reading).

Among the oral traditions briefly discussed thus far, Vedic chanting and *wayang berber* in its earliest form served sacred, ritual purposes. Although the term "ritual" is very familiar to us today, our understanding of ritual is usually secondary, that is, we have not been initiated into our understanding of the world by a set of sacred, ritual practices. Just as orality can be primary or secondary, so can ritual practices.

In early archaic cultures, primary ritual practices shaped one's consciousness and awareness as much as primary orality. Early complex states in Egypt and Greece (with its city-states) organized their societies around ritual much more than we do in modern Euro-American societies, as we shall see in Chapter 2. Unlike Christianity, especially the Protestant tradition with its emphasis on personal faith and a written word considered divine, early societies often "had no holy books and no interest in what individuals privately believed. Piety was a matter of performing ritual acts in honor of the gods, and these acts were the glue that held society together" (Wiles 2000:27). While rituals continue to be practiced by many peoples today, like orality they are secondary in shaping most people's consciousness and relationship to their world.

In the remainder of this chapter, we interrogate and reflect upon ritual practices, beginning with an examination of the dynamic notion of "power."

Ritual specialists: Accessing sacred power

In twenty-first century cosmopolitan cultures, commonplace understandings of "power" and "energy" are based on biomedical, scientific assumptions. It is typical to presume that power and energy are stable, rationally measurable, and quantifiable. But this has not always been so.

Traditional systems of medicine throughout the world are based on rational observation of illness, diagnosis, and treatment via a wide variety of indigenous medicinal herbs, plants, or hands-on therapies. For many conditions, highly successful systems of treatment have been developed through trial and error such as Chinese acupuncture. However, side-by-side with the scientific aspect of traditional medicines exists the assumption that disease or systemic imbalance can be caused not only by natural causes, but also by divine and/or magical sources. For example, according to one of the two most important early Indian medical texts by Susruta, texts central to *Ayurveda* (the science of life), one of the seven classes of disease was described as "the providential type," thought to be brought about through charms and spells.

In many historical periods and cultures, agency and power are viewed as a complex set of interactions between humanly-acquired techniques of virtuosity and power within the microcosm, and the exercise of divine powers in relation to both microcosm and macrocosm. Many traditional concepts of power and agency consider neither to be absolute, but rather contingent, unstable, capricious, dangerous, and locally immanent. Within a contingent "world," it is necessary to have cultural specialists who gain specific forms of agency that enable them to engage, interact with, and/or control unstable powers.

Many archaic prayers, incantations, rituals, and the like were developed and performed in order to actualize, stabilize, or rectify human relationships to the immanent powers of the cosmos within the immediate environment. Sacred words or ritual landscapes do not "represent" or "mean" something, nor is it necessary for them to be interpreted; rather they are understood to have "power" in and of themselves. By its very design, a particular ritual landscape is assumed to actualize a relationship to the sacred.

Saying certain words also can actualize a particular power. In the oral transmission of the Vedas in India, discussed above, the Brahmins chanted *mantras* – a series of sacred words and/or syllables, often not translatable. They are instruments of power, that is, tools designed for a specific task. Their transmission is usually circumscribed by secrecy. Once a *mantra* is given by a master who possesses its power to a student, it must be brought to accomplishment, usually by undergoing austerities and through thousands or hundreds of thousands of cycles of repetition. *Mantra* today are ubiquitous throughout South, Southeast and East Asia, and are used for either good ("light") or evil ("dark") purposes.

Different types of cultural specialists are understood to possess as a divine gift the ability to access and develop special powers to diagnose and/or heal an illness, to read signs of the future, to conquer an opponent or an enemy army, or to uphold the universe itself. In small-scale bands, tribes, or even in somewhat larger chiefdoms, multiple powers are often assumed to be present in single individuals – ritual specialists and/or shamans. The term *shaman* derives from the original Siberian Tungus word, *saman*, meaning "one who is excited, moved, raised" (Laderman 1991:7). Shaman refers to a traditional branch of religious specialists believed to be able to heal a variety of illnesses, counteract misfortune, or to solve personal or social dilemmas after entering a state of trance to communicate with the powers in the unseen world.

As societies grew larger and more complex, some individuals became specialized in applying their powers within a single sphere. Where states developed, individuals with special powers continued to function, but their powers were sometimes circumscribed by the centralization of authority in official religious practices. Specialist groups of priests acted on behalf of the state (Chapter 2).

In the sections that follow, we examine a range of ritual landscapes, practices, and performances within which small-scale communities experienced and/or special agents accessed powers within their world for a variety of purposes. We examine how some specialists utilize techniques of masking, rhythm, music, impersonation, and/or costumes to help access power or contact the sacred through invocation, transformation, and the like. Based on archeological evidence, we begin with a discussion of one type of ritual landscape in England that oriented a pre-literate people to their "world."

Late Neolithic ritual landscapes and pilgrimage in England

Among the 100 monuments of the Late Neolithic period in Britain, the complex at Thornborough, North Yorkshire, was possibly the most important sacred site of the day. In use from approximately 3,500 B.C.E. to at least 2,500 B.C.E., the henge monuments here were the site of major calendrical rituals that attracted masses of short-term pilgrims from across the entire northern region. A henge is a circular structure with a surrounding bank. On a flat gravel plateau near the River Ure, the ancient peoples of the period constructed the only linked cluster of three massive henge monuments ever built (see <http://thornborough.ncl.ac.uk/>). Each of the three primary henges measures a staggering 250m in diameter and 15m in height, capped at the time with local white pumice. Each has a double entrance, with an external ditch. The three henge monuments are equally spaced, and extend over 1.7km (more than a mile) on an orientation running

northwest to southeast. As seen in Figure 1.4 in an aerial view, the three henges are linked by passageways. The central henge was constructed on top of an earlier cursus monument measuring at least 1.1km, indicating that the site had already long been used for ritual purposes. Additional Neolithic-early Bronze Age monuments, including three other henges in areas close-by, at least ten burial mounds, and traces of contemporary settlements are scattered near the site. The massive scale of the linked henges indicate that it accommodated significantly large gatherings of pilgrims. It is as if the three major cathedrals in England (Westminster, York and Canterbury) had all been placed in one location.

Henges are specially constructed to interact with the landscape and thereby create what is known as a "ritual landscape." Once inside a circular henge, one enters a 360-degree universe, environmentally and architecturally self-contained, bounded by the henge whose white-pumace face joins the sky. One hypothesis is that the henges were built to align with, for example, the three middle stars within the constellation Orion known as "Orion's Belt" on specific dates. When pilgrims gathered inside the site facing one of the openings, they witnessed a spectacular moment – the appearance on the horizon of the constellation, Orion. Since the three linked henges reproduce the precise configuration of Orion's Belt, those gathered would have experienced a moment of union between earth and sky – a womb-like encirclement of self/community within their cosmos. It must have been an awe-inspiring annual moment for those making the pilgrimage.

These sacred, ritual spaces were kept apart from everyday activities. Camps were set up at a distance of approximately 600m from the henges. Beyond the camps, at least some individuals performed a "ritual deposition" of highly valuable Cumbrian stone axes and perhaps other objects of high value. The monuments themselves are part a wider landscape that contains burial monuments and settlement areas.

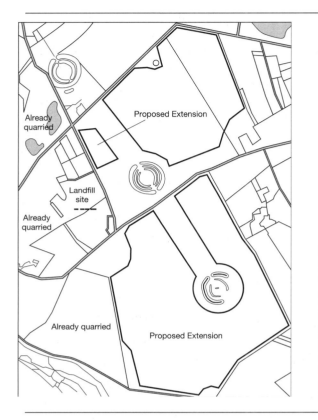

Figure 1.4 Aerial view of the three linked Thornborough Henges. From <http://thornborough.ncl.ac.uk/>

[Source: Reproduced by permission of Ordnance Survey on behalf of HMSO. © Crown Copyright 2005. All rights reserved. Ordnance Survey Licence number 100038806.]

While much remains speculative, what can be concluded from the existence of these Neolithic sites is that there was a richly elaborated system of ritual performance taking place within them that literally served to orient the peoples of the period within personally, socially, and cosmologically specific spatial and temporal frames that must have given shape and "meaning" to their lives. The shape and meaning derived from their involvement in and experience of the act of pilgrimage and participation in the rites that no doubt occurred within this extraordinary ritual landscape.

The Thornborough Neolithic site provides us with a tantalizing view of early ritual performance in a sacred, ritual landscape. Sketchy as the picture is, it is soundly based on the archeological evidence

of this and comparable sites of the period. In the next section we provide an overview of oral and ritual/festival performance practices in early Celtic cultures in Ireland and Wales – an era for which there is archeological evidence, as well as some problematic textual evidence.

Early Celtic oral and ritual festival performance

We focus here on the Celts who possessed rich traditions of oral (bardic) performance as well as ritual/festival performance. At its peak in the later first millennium B.C.E., the Celtic world stretched from Ireland, Wales, and Spain in the West, and Scotland in the north to the Czech Republic in the east and northern Italy in the south and even beyond

Europe to Asia Minor (Figure 1.5). During most of the first millennium B.C.E., the entire region of northern Europe inhabited by the Celts was virtually non-literate. So, of the three traditional primary sources of evidence for interpreting ancient history – archaeological, linguistic, and literary – our only ample evidence for the early Celts is archeological. The earliest linguistic evidence is sparse before the Roman period. The first allusion to the Celts by name (*Keltoi*) is in the writing of the Greek historians, Hecataeus of Miletus, in about 500 B.C.E., and Herodotus in the fifth century B.C.E. To what extent the Celts possessed some consciousness of their identity as a peoples is not clear.

By the end of the first century B.C.E., Celtic culture per se seems to have ended as Europe came under the control of the Roman Empire. A new hybrid culture emerged from the interaction between Roman and Celtic traditions and practices. The new "Romano-Celtic" culture is nowhere better witnessed than in the bardic traditions.

After the collapse of the Roman Empire in the West during the fifth century C.E., Europe was overrun by a new Germanic culture. The Celts virtually disappeared, except in the furthest western extremes of Ireland, Wales, Scotland, and Brittany, together with Cornwall and the Isle of Man. There the Celtic languages survived, and a vernacular Celtic

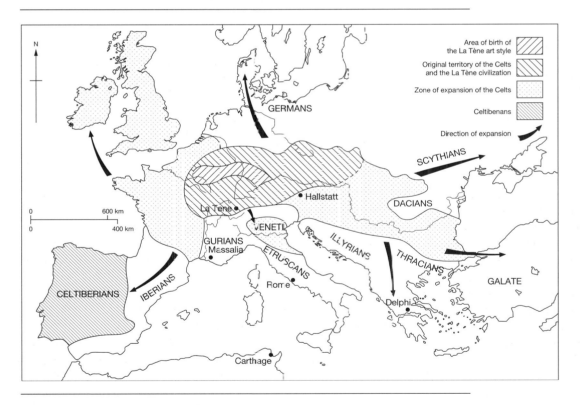

Figure 1.5 Territories occupied by Celts from the fifth century B.C.E. until the Roman conquest.
[Source: After R. and V. Megaw, *Celtic Art*, London: Thames & Hudson, 1989. In *The Celtic World* edited by Miranda J. Green (London: Routledge), 1986.]

mythic tradition developed during the first and second millennium C.E.

Written Irish dates from the sixth century from within a monastic milieu and remained so for 600 years. Can these texts reveal much about the earlier, oral Celtic traditions? Scholars do not agree. From the sixth century on, Irish and Welsh thought and learning were an amalgam and interweaving of indigenous and monastic elements. All that remains of course is what the monks chose to record and transmit. "Of the learned oral tradition which preceded the written and which continued along-side it, obviously we know nothing except by written reference or by extrapolation from the written texts," writes Celtic scholar, Proinsias Mac Cana (1995:782). The extant ecclesiastic literature is a vast collection of prose and verse texts covering historical and genealogical, mythico-historic, lyrical, tribal and family lore, social and legal procedures, medicine, and dramatic materials. In Wales the corpus of lore was known as *cyfarwyddyd*, meaning "guidance, direction, instruction, knowledge."

With regard to stories of Ireland's greatest epic hero, Cu Chulainn, Mac Cana explains that Cu Chulainn's birth tale is

> a coherent mythico-heroic text and is evidently a tersely phrased version of an oral narrative. The primary reason why there was such a carry-over from the oral to the written phase was that oral literature and learning enjoyed high status long before the coming of writing, and that mainly because, in their more formal mode, they were cultivated and controlled by an elitist and privileged class of semi-sacred savants and poets: the druids and, subsequently, the *filidh*, who were closely associated with religion and ideology and had their close counterparts in Wales, and, earlier still, among the Celts of Britain and the Continent.
>
> (1995:783)

Oral performance in the telling of such tales no doubt played a central role in pre-literate Celtic culture. Although very late, the following eleventh-century tale from Wales tells what happened when Gwydion and his companions visited the court of Pryderi as poets:

> They made them welcome. Gwydion was placed at Pryderi's one hand that night. 'Why,' said Pryderi, 'gladly would we have a tale [*cfar-wyddyd*] from some of the young men yonder.' 'Lord,' said Gwydion, 'it is a custom with us that the first night after one come to a great man, the chief bard [*pencerdd*] shall have the say. I will tell a tale gladly.' Gwydion was the best teller of tales [*cyfarwdd*] in the world. And that night he entertained the court with pleasant tales and story-telling [*cyfarwyddyd*] till he was praised by everyone in the court.
>
> (Davies 1995:786)

In another story, Gwydion is welcomed at a North Wales court where he narrates stories after a feast. Clearly, such tales were the product of a verbal culture, told to entertain, with rules for oral art playing a key role in their composition. Only eleven native Welsh tales have survived. The earliest texts that have emerged, though, are clearly a result of the interweaving of two cultures – one oral, and the other literate. The chief texts are preserved in two very late Welsh collections – the White Book of Rhydderch (*c*.1350), and the Red Book of Hergest (*c*.1400). Today, these tales are known as the *Mabinogion* – a title first given to the tales by Lady Charlotte Guest who did the first English translation (1849) (she derived the title from a term of questionable correctness in the final line of each of the four branches, "Here ends this branch of the Mabinogi"). Like all such collections, they are not from a single hand, do not form a unified whole, and vary widely in background, date, and content.

The picture of the early bards that emerges from Irish and Welsh sources is that the early, pre-Christian Celtic bards sang praises to the gods. They composed praise poetry bringing benefits to their patrons and the people in general. Their words also had power in them. When praising the qualities of a ruler, the singing bard was in effect calling these qualities into existence in the ruler (Ross 1995:431). Bards also might sing satirical songs, which were understood to bring physical blemish, bad luck, or even death to the person against whom they were sung. Training as a bard traditionally involved seven years of apprenticeship.

The early monastic literature also provides glimpses into the early ritual and religious life of the Celts. To judge from the lives of the Irish saints written in Latin and early medieval Gaelic, their authors attributed many miracles and powers to them to make them competitive with the Celtic druids. In pre-Christian Celtic cultures, the druids were the religious and ritual specialists who possessed special powers, knowledge, and the ability to communicate directly with the gods (the druids correspond to the Brahmins of India and flamines of early Rome – all three descended from the ancient Indo-European priestly tradition). The druids were therefore in charge of all ritual, assisted by other specialists including the bards. Druids deployed magical powers through incantations and had the ability to foresee the future and predict events, serving therefore as prophets. Rulers relied in decision-making on druids' ability to tell the future. They may have received their divinatory powers through trance states, prompted at times by chewing acorns. They possessed knowledge of astrology and did calendrical computations. They reputedly possessed powers as shape-shifters and could either change their own shape, or that of others, into animals or birds. They were masters of illusion, and skilled healers through the use of therapeutic and other treatments. Even natural phenomena supposedly obeyed the dictates of the druids – they commanded winds, fires, and

mists. Finally, they were teachers of songs for noblemen, and guardians of hereditary learning and oral traditions. Oaths sworn before druids were considered sacred and binding. Druidic teaching was completely oral. Irish druids "sang over" (for-cain, a word which can also mean "prophesy, predict") their pupils; the pupils repeated the lesson in chorus.

Under the aegis of the druidic orders, great national assemblies and festivals took place annually in ritual landscapes. The druids possessed a clear concept of time and created a liturgical calendar of sacred times and festivals. Great sacrificial rituals were held every five years. The most widespread and enduring of the seasonal festivals in Ireland is Lughnasa, the pan-Celtic "Games or Assembly." Held at Lugh annually in August, Lughnasa was a religious/ritual occasion and a feast celebrating the first fruits. Like most traditional festivals, it also included competitive games, horse-racing (still an Irish passion), feasting, and drinking. Traditionally, sacrifice and fire magic were central parts of Lughnasa and all Celtic rituals – fire and water being the most revered of elements. Druids held all souls immortal. Young animals were sacrificed, and kings and druids hosted feasts as a sign of wealth and authority.

In the cycle of Celtic festivals in Ireland, Samain was the celebration of the new year every 1 November. It was the most dangerous and portentous of all festivals since it was a time when gods moved freely in the world of man and could play cruel tricks.

As late as the seventh- and eighth-century compilation of Irish law books, druids still had a place in legal codices, but under the influence of Christianity they were negatively regarded as "witch-doctors" or "sorcerers." As Celtic culture was Christianized, only vestiges of early Celtic oral and ritual traditions remained.

We now briefly consider how to interpret and understand the complex phenomenon of early ritual. We will then consider how accounts of extant ritual and shamanic practice might further help us understand archaic performance practices.

Interpreting and understanding ritual

If in primary oral cultures saying something is intending something, performing a traditional ritual is similar in that it is understood to "do" or "accomplish" something. Rituals are not done "for nothing." When performed fully and correctly, a traditional ritual is sufficient to itself and therefore requires no authority outside itself. Early in the development of ritual activity, what was accomplished may have been nothing more than fully engaging in ritual activity as part of a small community – the structuring of movement, gesture, voice into patterns that pleased or bound people together, thereby creating its own intrinsic value. Today the practice of ritual and religion has become a matter of individual choice rather than social or cosmological necessity. Indeed, the term ritual is used often to refer not only to traditional sacred or religious rites, but also to "rituals of everyday life" or "secular" rituals, constituted by the performance, for example, of the ceremonies of a monarchy or state government. Given our focus here on the early history of performance, we examine traditional rituals.

Traditional rituals are special occasions, made distinct from everyday time, that form and re-form self and social identity, and in which self and one's relationships are "constituted and ordered" (Kapferer 1984:179). Many rituals are performed to achieve a purpose or result, that is, they are efficacious. Specific rituals may be intended to heal, to protect, to harm, to propitiate an ancestor spirit or a god, or to mark a major transition or transformation in one's status, such as birth, puberty (initiation), a new relationship, or death. Whatever the purpose of a ritual, as Richard Schechner reminds us, there are usually elements within a ritual process which provide some form of pleasure or entertainment (2002:70–71).

Masking, costuming, impersonation, dance, music, narrative, and humor are strategically utilized in some rituals, not only to achieve their efficacious end but to please the gods, ancestors, and/or humans gathered to participate or witness. Consequently, efficacy and entertainment are not binary opposites, but rather form a continuum.

Of the many types of rituals which exist, ethnographer/folklorist Arnold van Gennep has examined "rites of passage" as they mark major transitions in one's life within both simple and complex societies (1960). Van Gennep identified a three-fold structure of ritual action through which an individual passes – separation from society, existing in a marginal or liminal state, and reintegration based on achieving a new condition or status. The investiture of the sacred thread for Brahmin boys described above is one example – a rite of passage into one's life-work of chanting the Vedas. Among the Gisu of Uganda, an extensive ritual of initiation marks a young boy's transition from boyhood to manhood whereby he becomes able to serve as male provider and sexual partner. Here young boys are sequestered from their family and undergo a series of rites that culminate in circumcision. For the ritual initiation to achieve its efficacious end of transforming boy to man, the neophyte must not flinch or in any way register a response to the tremendous pain and blood-letting as his foreskin is cut off. Male powers and courage are thereby tested (La Fontaine 1985:117ff).

Anthropologist Victor Turner describes how at the time of undergoing such rites, the individual is "neither here nor there" but rather is "betwixt and between the positions assigned and arrayed by law, custom, convention, and ceremonial" (Turner 1969:95). In the post-liminal phase at the conclusion of the rites, the individual exists within a "new" reality – one's fundamental state, condition, and/or status has changed. The transformations that take place within ritual processes can be generative, profoundly changing an individual. As discussed in Chapter 2, other rites of passage, such as ceremonies of death, mark the crossing of different thresholds – in this case from life to another dimension or world.

Some rituals are highly prescribed processes, requiring specialist knowledge. Others allow for improvisation within the context of performance (see the Yoruba case study below). What does one experience when performing a very strictly prescribed ritual? Frits Staal argues that ritual structures follow rules that may have no single, explicit meaning (1996). More like the pleasure, purpose and function inherent in music, some rituals have a satisfaction and pleasure all their own that are part of the practice and structure of the ritual per se, that is, rituals do not *have* to be *about* something other than themselves.

> The structural properties of ritual ... require not only consummate skill and expertise but also a lot of the priests' attention – not less than is required, say, from the member of an orchestra, a ballet company or a team of engineers set upon the execution of a common task. ... It is characteristic of a ritual performance, however, that it is self-contained and self-absorbed. The performers are totally immersed in the proper execution of their complex tasks. Isolated in their sacred enclosure, they concentrate on correctness of act, recitation, and chant. Their primary concern, if not obsession, is with rules. There are no symbolic meanings going through their minds when they are engaged in performing ritual. ... [W]hat counts in ritual is what the ritualist *does*.
>
> (ibid.:115; 453)

Staal's focus on the experience of the ritual participant is a useful antidote to the over-emphasis that some western scholars have given to the "symbolic" dimension of ritual – to what ritual represents. Symbolic interpretations of ritual were developed by westerners whose early speculation about the nature of ritual was informed by the Christian assumption that all ceremonies symbolize religious truths and

eternal values. But historically, Christian preoccupation with symbolic interpretation of Christian rites developed very late, at the time of the Carolingian Renaissance during the eighth century C.E. in Europe (ibid.:124–125).

Some forms of ritual or shamanic performance require either the ritual specialist or a member of the community to undergo possession or to enter an ecstatic state of trance. What happens when an individual experiences possession? Anthropologist Edward Schieffelin provides the following analysis based on ethnographic research among the Kaluli people of Papua New Guinea.

> Kaluli spirit séances in Papua New Guinea were highly entertaining, even thrilling events, but they could only ethnocentrically be called performances in a western sense. ... This is because, in séance, the issue is not performative illusion but the exact opposite: it is the presence of spirits. If anything, it is the spirits themselves who perform.
>
> Kaluli spectators know very well that spirit séances can be faked and keep a sharp eye for signs of 'performing' or, as they see it, deception. Spirits in séance cured illness and revealed the identity of witches, both of which were activities of considerable (even life-and-death) social and politic consequence, and people did not fool around with them. ... A 'performance' in the western sense was precisely what speaking with the spirits through a medium was not and could not be. It had more of the character of a telephone conversation. The Kaluli themselves likened it to speaking with someone over two-way radio. To describe Kaluli séance as a performance in the popular western sense would be to violate its ethnographic nature.
>
> (1998:203)

When discussing traditional rituals, we must also be careful not to assume that the participant/spectator relationship is like that at most theatre performances. Schieffelin describes what the relationship is like between dancers and spectators in the Gisalo ceremony of the Kaluli of Papua New Guinea:

> In Gisalo, the dancers sing nostalgic songs about the lands and rivers of their audience's community. Members of the audience are moved so deeply they burst into tears, and then, becoming enraged, they leap up and burn the dancers on the shoulder blades with the resin torches used to light the performance. Indeed, this remarkable response could be interpreted as virtually necessary to the performance, since if the audience is not moved and the tension between performers and audiences does not rise to the pitch of violence, the ceremony falls apart and is abandoned in the middle of the night. . . . [A]fter a successful performance, the dancers pay compensation to those whom they made weep. . . . It is real grief and rage that are evoked. . . . The performers are held accountable for the painful emotions they evoke – and the retaliation upon them (and the compensation they must pay) return that account – as well as those emotions being an indication of the beauty and effectiveness of the performance. The dancers and song composers . . . are extremely pleased if they have managed to provoke numbers of the spectators to tears, despite the consequences to themselves.
>
> (ibid.:203; 1976:21–25)

Clearly, traditional rituals are understood to have real consequences, attain fundamental change, and/or access specific powers in particular contexts.

Between ritual and theatre

Just as oral performance and verbal arts continue to be practiced and interact with complete systems of writing, oral, ritual and shamanic performance practices interacted with the new forms of dramatic performance (or theatre) wherever they began to develop, such as in Greece, India, China, and Japan. Ritual and shamanic performance helped shape dramatic conventions, aesthetics, and/or performance context. Oral and ritual performance remain an integral part of many cultures and sub-cultures today; therefore, it is wrong to assume that cultures where ritual or shamanic performance persist are somehow "primitive."

Until fairly recently, theatre historians accepted the argument that theatre was born out of ritual. This theory was put forward by a group of Cambridge University classics scholars known as "the Cambridge Anthropologists" – Gilbert Murray (1866–1957), Francis Cornford (1874–1943), and Jane Ellen Harrison (1850–1928). These arguments have been revealed as spurious, since they are based on a mistaken notion of social Darwinism. Underlying social Darwinism is the assumption that cultures have evolved, so they are viewed hierarchically, from the "primitive" culture at the bottom, to the "great civilizations" at the top – with such western genres as "tragedy" considered the pinnacle of theatrical culture. This theory of the "origins of theatre" is now thoroughly discredited. The assumption that it is possible to find a single origin of "theatre" is in itself a problematic proposition, since theatre is not one "thing," but rather a complex set of human communicative activities involving, as does the practice of ritual, fundamental human desires to imitate, play, imagine, and structure our experience. In Chapter 2 we examine the history of several forms of drama/theatre within particular contexts, but we will make no attempt there to create a general theory of origins of (all) theatre.

Many scholars have fruitfully used theories of ritual as a tool for the interpretation of "ritual action" of later forms of drama and theatre. Naomi Conn Liebler has argued recently for a reading of Shakespeare's tragedies as "festive," a term which marks "the celebration of a community's survival" (1995:8). Liebler builds on theories of ritual and the "festive," especially the early work of C.L. Barber in *Shakespeare's Festive Comedy* (1959). She argues for an analogous understanding of tragedy's relationship to the "festive," i.e. the social, communal. Lieblein concludes that "tragedy is not ritual; ritualistic elements in tragedy are not themselves actual rituals. In theatre, we are always in the realm of 'as if,' of semblance or resemblance. Ritual and theatre do not share similar efficacies, but they do share similar intents" (1995:25–26).

In the remainder of this chapter and the case studies that follow, we examine ethnographic accounts of four types of ritual and shamanic practice which help form (or reform) historical "selves" and/or "social identities." We offer two examples of ritual/ceremonial practice which emphasize the social and collective domains of social (re)formation – an annual cycle of traditional ceremonies that constitutes an elaborate ritual drama for the Hopi people of Arizona, explained below, and a study of ritual as "play" among the Yoruba people of Nigeria in a case study to follow. We conclude this chapter with an exorcistic shadow-puppet performance in Bali, Indonesia. This and a case study of *kut* – a Korean shamanic performance – which follow this chapter offer two examples of the wielding of special powers to "heal" by individual ritual/shamanic specialists. The Hopi, Balinese, Yoruba, and Korean practitioners constantly (re)negotiate their traditional ways of understanding, organizing, and performing their rituals with today's new and often conflicting social, political, and economic realities.

Ritual, ceremony, and collective social life

Hopi ritual performance cycles

Perhaps 30,000 years ago, the first ancestors of today's Native Americans arrived in North America. Ice still covered much of the northern parts of the Eurasian and North American continents, with some corridors of tundra grass where humans and animals roamed. At least occasionally, the Bering Sea bottom was exposed as a land bridge between northeastern Asia and Alaska. In pursuit of mammoths, bear, and reindeer, proto-Mongoloid groups living in northern China and northeast Asia crossed the Bering Strait. These immigrants, now called Native Americans, were at first exclusively groups of hunters who eventually diversified as they moved south and as the climate they encountered changed. Some key traditions, practices, and beliefs have survived the centuries, such as dwellings (earth lodges, conical tents, birchbark lodges), use of feathered ornaments, and a relatively democratic political organization featuring tribal/group councils. A strong ceremonialism attached to hunting survived, as did elaborate ceremonies and rituals practiced in order to contact and make present the spirits. Three classes of traditional healers and ceremonialists developed among the early Native Americans, consistent with their proto-Mongoloid origins. There were herbalists who cared for everyday wounds and aches, the medicine man who sought to access the supernatural to make ill persons well, and the shaman – a medicine man who, like the shamans in Siberia, underwent a trance state to discover disease or cure the sick.

Until about 5,000 B.C.E., Native Americans continued to live as hunters, while some descendents lived as fishermen and collectors. A new era dawned in Mexico at this time when humans in the region developed the ability to produce food. Squash, beans and maize became staple foods allowing the development, as in early Sumeria, of fixed, agriculturally-based settlements. For some Native Americans, annual hunting rituals were displaced by rituals and ceremonies centered on the growth of vegetation and marking harvest seasons. Those living settled lives developed an integrated interpretation of spiritual harmony with the cosmos and environment. In the American southwest, one settled form of Native American culture that developed is known as Pueblo. Among the Pueblo peoples are the Hopi and Zuni, whose ritual/ceremonial life was elaborated as a means of securing rain and fertility. Each society developed its own ceremonial organizations to keep their world in harmony.

We focus here on the ritual practices of the Hopi whose traditional homeland is on three mesas in northeastern Arizona (Figure 1.6). In prehistoric times, Hopis cultivated a variety of crops including kidney and tepary beans, cotton, pumpkins, and maize. The most ancient Hopi village, Oraibi, dates from around 1,125 C.E., suggesting it is either the

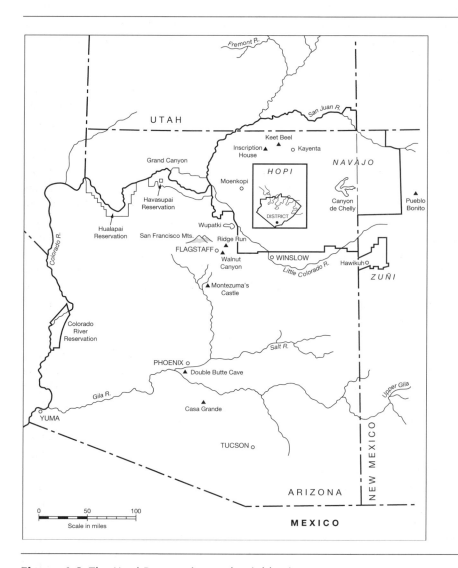

Figure 1.6 The Hopi Reservation and neighboring areas. [Source: In *The Kachina and the White Man* by Frederick J. Dockstader. Albuquerque: University of New Mexico Press, 1985, p.3. Copyright uncertain.]

oldest, or one of the oldest, continually inhabited locales in an area now known as the United States of America.

When the Spanish first encountered the Hopi people (whom they called "Moqui") in 1540, they imagined (or desired) that the high cities on rocky mesas, gleaming like gold in the desert sun, were the legendary Seven Cities of Cibola. Although not made of gold, Hopi villages were thriving urban centers.

In 1629 Franciscan friars were sent to evangelize the Hopi and their neighbors – the Zuni and Acoma. Although the Hopis converted peacefully to Catholicism, their native religion centering around ritual dances of the Kachinas never died out. Spanish descriptions of the period, while failing to understand the purpose of what they were seeing, demonstrate that the ritual Kachina dances were similar to those still performed, though certainly they originate in a much earlier period.

Traditional Hopi religion and beliefs are organized around an annual ritual calendar intended to maintain equilibrium with their environment For a period of approximately seven months each year Hopis interact with the Kachinas (from *kachi*, life or spirit and *na*, father) – unseen supernatural beings and spirits of the dead. Kachinas have the power to "bring rain, exercise control over the weather, help in many of the activities of the villages, punish offenders of ceremonial or social laws, and in general act as a link between gods and mortals" (Dockstader 1985:9). The Kachinas visit during the months beginning with the Winter Solstice (*Soyala*) (21 December) until just after the Summer Solstice (21 June) when the Home Dance (*Nimán*) takes place. As beneficent supernatural beings, the Kachinas are thought to have always been with the Hopi, having come with the original Hopi ancestors when they emerged from the Underworld at the beginning of time. They wandered together until they settled where they are located today in Arizona.

Hopi interact with these beings via male masked dancers – also known as Kachinas. As in other Native American ritual societies, such as the Yaqui peoples, it is a great honor and responsibility to become a Kachina. To become a particular Kachina by enveloping oneself in a complete costume and "helmet-mask" covering the entire head, is to lose "one's personal identity and . . . [become] imbued with the spirit of that being" (ibid.:10). At the time of the ceremonies, one must follow specific prescriptions for behavior and deportment, remaining pure and celibate in order to serve as a suitable messenger. The performers embody and impersonate these beings through a series of dances from their initial emergence at Winter Solstice until they return "home" in July. From August through November, non-Kachina rites occupy the ritual calendar, with the Snake or Flute Dance (*Chuchubti*) in August. Women's Society rituals in September/October (*Marû* and *Oáqöle*), and the Tribal Initiation (*Wuwuchim*) in November.

Hopi religious ceremonies are conducted between underground chambers (*kiva*) reached by ladders, and public areas of villages, especially the plaza. The *kiva* are both sacred spaces for secret ceremonies as well as communal lodges.

The nine day *Powamú* (Bean Dance) ceremony celebrates fertility each January. It is the major ritual of the Kachina cult. Sixteen days before Powamu, beans are planted inside warm, humid kivas, in order to force new growth. There are eight days of secret rituals and preparations. Some performances are dramatic enactments of Hopi mythology, with clan ancestor Kachinas, such as Eótoto – the father of the Kachinas – putting in an appearance. On the night of the fifth day of the ceremony, Kachina Mother Hahai-I Wuhti demands to see the sleeping children. The following afternoon, she and her monster children, the Nataşka Kachinas, are joined by Ogre Woman, Soyok' Wuhti Kachina, who carries a bloodstained knife and long crook to capture young children to eat. Parents threaten their disobedient children with the monsters' wrath, and bribe the monsters with food.

Eótoto Kachina is the chief of all Kachinas. Aided by the loyal Aholi Kachina (who once cut his own throat to permit Eótoto to escape), Eótoto draws cloud symbols in corn flour on the earth, pointing towards the village. Aholi calls out loudly while striking the picture with his staff. Carrying green shoots of corn, Eótoto performs a water ritual in six directions to guide the rain-clouds to the village. Simultaneously, other Kachinas bring gifts to the children.

During Kachina dances, a number of *Táchkutí* appear – the clowns (Figure 1.7). Commonly known as "Mudheads" since their heads are covered with sack-like masks, they dash around the village making crude jokes, eating like gluttons, and tripping over themselves. They mime falling down dead, and are only revived by the performance of explicit sexual acts. They then distribute seeds to young women, who plant them to ensure fertility. Long-Billed

Wapamu Kachina is a guard who uses his yucca whip to keep the clowns moving, and to prevent onlookers from disrupting the Kachina processions. During Powamu, people with rheumatism can be cured if Wapamu whips the affected body part.

On the ninth day, the public ceremonies occur. As many as a hundred masked Kachinas may dance in the plaza. Warrior Maid He'e'e Kachina waves her arms from the rooftops, signaling other Kachinas to chase people into their houses and whip those who refuse. The young bean plants in the kivas are cut and taken to a shrine. Finally, the Kachinas distribute the beans to the households. Various clownish Kachinas mimic the serious rituals. Sometimes, they even impersonate obnoxious tourists, pushing, taking photos, and shouting in crude English.

Every four years when children between the ages of six and ten are to be initiated, they are brought to the kivas. After rituals and songs, the

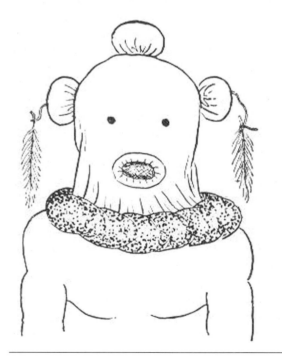

Figure 1.7 *Tachukti Kachina.* One of several types of "Mudhead" clown masks. [Source: In *Kachina and the White Man* by Frederick J. Dockstader. Albuquerque: University of New Mexico Press, 1985, p.20. (Line drawing) Copyright uncertain.]

elders depart. It is dark. The sound of pounding feet on the roof signals the entrance of the Kachinas who climb down the ladder. The children suddenly recognize their fathers, uncles and brothers. Hú'Kachinas whip the children with yucca whips, then whip themselves, fiercely warning the children to keep their new knowledge secret.

This annual cycle of traditional ceremonies constitutes an elaborate ritual drama through which "men, animals, plants and spirits are inter-transposable in a seemingly unbroken chain of being" (Ortiz 1969:143). Historically, this type of ceremonial cycle is typical of peoples who created settled, agricultural communities. For Hopi and others still practicing complete ritual cycles today, the ceremonies point to a common past, usually articulated in an origin myth, and also serve as the primary touchstone of individual and social identity in a changing world. In the case study of Yoruba Egungun which follows this chapter, we examine how creative ritual can be in negotiating past and present.

The healing powers of ritual/ shamanic specialists

An exorcistic shadow puppet performance in Bali

The performance of the Balinese shadow-puppet play, *wayang Calon Arang*, is, in effect, a ritual exorcism. The play demonstrates the early historical roots of shadow puppet theatre in animistic ritual/religious practice. It also demonstrates how the serious business of ritual may quite logically involve humor, including ribald comedy, scatological word-play, or sexual innuendo, such we have seen in the comic "Mudmen" in Hopi Kachina ceremonies.

Calon Arang is the supreme or "Queen Sorceress" in Balinese ritual drama . . . the semi-historical manifestation of the widow (Rangda)" (Hobart 2003:103). Performances of *Calon Arang* are arranged with a specialist puppeteer when villagers wish to expose and exorcise witches in their area. Involving

learned/scholarly healers, spirit mediums, and masked ritual dramas, the performance of *Calon Arang* engages one or more of the diverse, sometimes demonic, dark, or evil powers in order to "heal" an individual or community. In Bali, illness, death, and a considerable number of human troubles in everyday life are attributed to *leak* (in high Balinese *desti*) – usually translated as witches. Healers refer to them as "agents of power" or "poison wind" – people whose practices access the destructive and the malign, rather than the positive aspects of power (ibid.:104). They are able to transform at night into monkeys, tigers, pigs, chickens or flickering lights. In such transformed states, *leak* can enter households to bring a variety of troubles, illness, or even death. If someone wishes to victimize or curse another, one goes to a sorcerer to acquire a drawing inscribed with magical syllables (Figure 1.8).

The performance of *Calong Arang's* story in the form of a traditional shadow puppet play takes place outside the local village death temple at night. It is dangerous for the puppeteer to undertake, since it temporarily exposes the dangerous, invisible realm of dark powers. The puppeteer, therefore, is usually also a healer who regularly encounters both demonic and protective powers. He must be an individual with strong spiritual powers since narrating the story "tests [his] capacity to combat and contain malevolent forces and energies" (ibid.:112). During the performance, at a certain point in the story, the puppeteer "'summons the witches' . . . of the area to attend. Only a few witches may come, but many may be drawn to the show, like heavy gusts of wind, in order to 'test' the power of the puppeteer" (ibid:114). The local witches who come are called out by the shadows on the screen. In such performances, past and present, the invisible is made visible, at least temporarily, so that the invisible, in its malevolent form, can be engaged and controlled, at least temporarily, by the healing powers of the puppeteer.

Humor, like ritual, often plays at the transition points or boundaries where darkness, horror, and

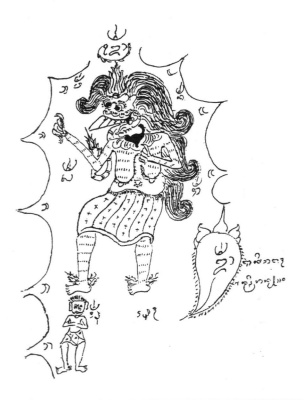

Figure 1.8 In the Balinese shadow-puppet play, *wayan Calon Arang*, a witch charged with power puts her foot on a man's head. Alongside are magical syllables.

[Source: Angela Hobart, *Healing Performances in Bali*. N.Y. and Oxford: Berghahn Books, 2003, line drawing 4.1 on p.109. © Museum der Kulturen, Basel.]

human fear lurk. The opening scene of *Calon Arang* is set in the court of the great Balinese prince, Erlangga. Erlangga has ordered his two servants, the proto-typical comic duo, Wayan Geligir and Nang Kinyan, to deliver a message to the widow from Dirah. The comic duo hold the "screen" as they discuss their fears about their forthcoming journey. The naive and simple Nang Kinyan whispers to his companion:

> Agents of power will approach us at night . . . .
> [D]o you know any mantras so that it will become light?

WAYAN GELIGIR: Why should I learn mantras? These days we have electricity! Lights can now be switched on and off with ease in the villages.

Matches can also be bought for a few Rupiah. It takes at least one year of study to become sufficiently *sakti* [powerful], just to transmit mystic fire from the hands.

NANG KINYAN: Wadah!

WAYAN GELIGIR: [M]oreover witches who take on the forms of monkeys, chicken, pigs, or fierce ogres may these days be electrocuted!

Attending the 1993 performance of the play in Tegallalang, Gianyar, Bali, anthropologist Angela Hobart relates how the audience, in response to the servant's comic repartee, "bursts out in laughter" while simultaneously "tension mounts as [they are] alerted to the presence of *leak* . . . who may be lurking nearby" (ibid.:116). Here comedy, so far from being separate from ritual, serves the serious business of exorcistic ritual. Also, while the Hopi Kachina ceremony and Korean *kut* performance (explained in a case study following this chapter) include comic "acts" or "mini-dramas," only the Balinese shadow-puppet performance of *Calong Arang* performs a fully developed dramatic narrative

Summary of Chapter 1

This chapter has considered oral, ritual, and shamanic performance practices in pre-literate cultures, and their encounter with writing when it developed. We considered the nature of primary orality and discussed key features of oral performance. We discussed how traditional ritual is organized to "do" something, and surveyed a variety of ways in which this is accomplished. We examined a Neolithic ritual landscape in northern England using archeological evidence, oral and ritual performance among the Celts in Ireland and Wales using archeology and problematic early monastic texts. We considered four examples of ritual or shamanic performance in the ethnographic present.

We have seen how many of the elements utilized in theatre are present in oral, ritual, and shamanic performance including masking, impersonation, and costuming. The Hopi Kachina ceremonies and (as we shall see) the Korean *kut* include comic "acts" or "mini-dramas," and the Balinese shadow-puppet performance of *Calong Arang* performs a fully-developed dramatic narrative. Although Balinese shadow theatre probably had its origins in Javanese/Balinese ancestor and/or animistic worship, it exemplifies how a genre of theatrical performance in certain contexts functions as a ritual intended to have a real effect – identifying and exorcising witches in a particular village. We will want to keep this particular example in mind as we turn, in Chapter 2, to the specific history of the development of specific forms of drama and theatre with the emergence of early states.

PZ

Key references

Anderson, B. (1983) *Imagined Communities*, London: Verso.

Barber, C.L. (1959) *Shakespeare's Festive Comedy*, Princeton, N.J.: Princeton University Press.

Brandon, J.R. (ed.) (1970) *On Thrones of Gold: Three Javanese Shadow Plays*, Cambridge, Mass.: Harvard University Press.

Davies, S. (1995) "Mythology and the Oral Tradition: Wales," in M. Green (ed.) *The Celtic World*, London: Routledge.

Dockstader, F.J. (1985) *The Kachina and the White Man*, Albuquerque: University of New Mexico Press.

Drewal, M.J. and Drewal, M.T. (1983) *Gelede: Art and Female Power Among the Yoruba*, Bloomington: Indiana University Press.

Gennep, A. van (1960 [1st edn 1909]) *The Rites of Passage*, Chicago: University of Chicago Press.

Green, M. (ed.) (1995) *The Celtic World*, London: Routledge.

Hobart, A. (2003) *Healing Performances of Bali*, New York: Berghahn Books.

Kapferer, B. (1983) *A Celebration of Demons*, Bloomington: Indiana University Press.

Kapferer, B. (1984) "The Ritual Process and the Problem of Reflexivity in Sinhalese Demon Exorcisms," in B. Kapferer (ed.) *Rite, Drama, Festival, Spectacle*, Philadelphia: Institute for Human Studies Issues.

Kirby, E.T. (1975) *Ur-Drama: The Origins of Theatre*, New York: NYU Press.

Laderman, C. (1991) *Taming the Wind of Desire: Psychology, Medicine, and Aesthetics in Malay Shamanistic Performance*, Berkeley: University of California Press.

La Fontaine, J.S. (1985) *Initiation: Ritual Drama and Secret Knowledge Across the World*, London: Penguin.

Liebler, N.C. (1995) *Shakespeare's Festive Tragedy: the Ritual Foundations of Genre*, London: Routledge.

MacAloon, J.J. (1984) *Rite, Drama, Festival, Spectacle*, Philadelphia: University of Pennsylvania Press.

Mac Cana, P. (1995) "Mythology and the Oral Tradition: Ireland," in M. Green (ed.) *The Celtic World*, London: Routledge.

Mair, V.H. (1988) *Painting and Performance: Chinese Picture Recitation and Its Indian Genesis*, Honolulu: University of Hawaii Press.

Ong, W.J. (1988 [1st edn 1982]) *Orality and Literacy*, London: Routledge.

Ortiz, A. (1969) *The Tewa World: Space, Time, Being, and Becoming in a Pueblo Society*, Chicago: University of Chicago Press.

Ross, A. (1995) "Ritual and the Druids," in M. Green (ed.) *The Celtic World*, London: Routledge.

Schechner, R. (2002) *Performance Studies: An Introduction*, London: Routledge.

Schieffelin, E.L. (1976) *The Sorrow of the Lonely and the Burning of the Dancers*, New York: St. Martin's Press.

Schieffelin, E.L. (1998) "Problematizing performance," in F. Hughes-Freeland (ed.) *Ritual, Performance, Media*, London: Routledge.

Staal, F. (1996 [1990]) *Rituals and Mantras: Rules Without Meaning*, Delhi: Motilal.

Tedlock, D. (1983) *The Spoken Word and the Work of Interpretation*, Philadelphia: University of Pennsylvania Press.

Turner, V. (1969) *The Ritual Process*, Chicago: Aldine Publishing Company.

Turner, V. (1982) *From Ritual to Theatre: The Human Seriousness of Play*, New York: PAJ Publications.

Vansina, J. (1985) *Oral Tradition as History*, Madison: University of Wisconsin Press.

Wiles, D. (2000) *Greek Theatre Performance: An Introduction*, Cambridge: Cambridge University Press.

Wood, A. (1985) *Knowledge Before Printing and After: The Indian Tradition in Changing Kerala*, Delhi: Oxford University Press.

CASE STUDY: Yoruba ritual as "play," and "contingency" in the ritual process

Aiyé l'ojà, òrun n'ilé
"The world is a market, the otherworld is home."

Drewal and Drewal 1983:2

If this world is a market, and one's permanent residence is the otherworld, then life in this world is contingent and transitory. For the Yoruba, life in this world is a constant process of balancing or "playing" with and between opposing forces. As a cultural designator, the term "Yoruba" has been used only since the nineteenth century to identify this large, socially and culturally diverse set of subgroups speaking many different, but related dialects of Yoruba. The Yoruba peoples are spread across the coastal region of West Africa (Togo, Benin, and Western Nigeria) (Figure 1.9). They are also in diasporic communities in Brazil, Cuba, or the United

States. One prominent, early subgroup among the Yoruba is Ketu, whose antiquity has been established from at least the fourteenth century. It was via the Ketu that Islam began to have an impact on the area by the late seventeenth century.

Balance and symmetry are central to Yoruba religion and are embedded in all aspects of Yoruba life – dance, speech, and ritual. Traditional Yoruba deities who have boundless energy and provoke action are classified as "hot," and must be counterbalanced by those who are "cool" – "whose strength is in the patience and gentleness they radiate" (Ajayi 1998:38). Èṣù, the capricious trickster god of the crossroads and Òrúnmìlà, the god of fate are two opposites who complement one another, as reflected in the Yoruba's primordial creation myth. Dances of all types are informed by an aesthetic of balance and symmetry – in practice, a constant process of shifting

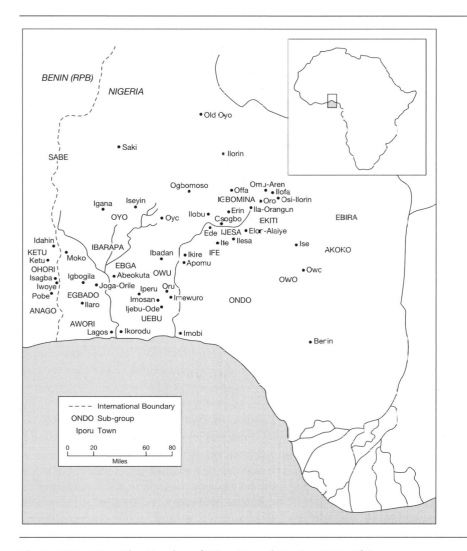

Figure 1.9 Map: The Yoruba of Nigeria and Benin, West Africa.

between right and left (*ìwọ̀ntúnwọnsì*). Indeed, Yoruba society does not expect rigid conformity, but "appreciates occasional lapses and personal idiosyncrasies" (ibid.:29). This is also evidenced in the delight people take when engaging in both *ẹ̀dà-ọ̀rọ̀* (inverted discourse) and in the indirect handling of the "truths" of riddles and proverbs – a trait some westerners ethnocentrically deride as "never straight-forward" (ibid.:31).

We have seen that some rituals are highly prescriptive in form, inviting absorption of ritual specialists in the intricacies of the repetition of highly codified scores. While all rituals have a structure, not all ritual structures possess a rigid score. Indeed,

Yoruba ritual practices are founded on the transformative possibilities of ritual becoming a "journey" for its participants through which deep-learning takes place by "playing" in the moment.

The concept of Yoruba ritual (*ètùtu*) encompasses "annual festivals (*ọdún*), weekly rites (*ọ̀sẹ̀*), funerals (*ìsìnkú*), divinations (*idafa*), and initiations and installations of all kinds" (Drewal 1992:19). As Margaret Drewal explains, Yoruba say they go to "play" ritual, that is to say they spontaneously "improvise" dance steps or rhythmic patterns, and improvise through parody, elaboration, or invention. Some forms of improvisation are obvious, such as when the Yoruba incorporate in their Egúngún masquerade festival (described below) parodies of western behavior or dress (using tuxedos or World War II gas masks, for example).

Journey as a metaphor for this contingent life is embedded in all Yoruba ritual, as reflected in the final two lines of these verses by diviner, Kolawole Ositola:

> We are going in search of knowledge, truth, and justice . . .
> We are searching for knowledge continuously.
> (ibid.:33)

This is not a journey from predetermined point A to point Z, but rather a life-long processual journey of exploration and discovery through which consciousness is to be transformed.

INTERPRETIVE APPROACH: Theories of play and improvisation

In her study of Yoruba ritual, Margaret Thompson Drewal asserts that "playing is the power Yoruba actors exercise in transforming ritual itself, and indeed it may be more precise to say that ritual structures, or strategies, have no existence apart from the tactics, or play, of actors. It is in play that ritual's very efficacy resides" (1992:28). Here Drewal is counteracting many earlier anthropological accounts of ritual that overemphasize structure, convention, rigidity, and the role that "rules" play in the efficacy of ritual.

Drewal adopts an "actor-centered approach" focused on "the relationship between actors and the forms they operate on" (1983:xvi). This locates the "power" of ritual not in the structure, but in the active engagement of the individual "actor" within the experience of the structure as it is performed/practiced. Drewal's emphasis on the centrality of play and improvisation within Yoruba ritual is specific to the ethnographic present – to the way in which the Yoruba people situate the contingency of "playing" as central to both their worldview and to their engagement of ritual structures. It relates to the general theories of play as developed by sociologists Huizinga (1970), Callois (1979), and Sutton-Smith (1997). Theories of play emphasize the autotelic enjoyment of engaging, stretching, and breaking rule-governed activities. Given its ephemeral mode of engagement "in the moment," "play" is usually lost in the writing of theatre histories. But the joy of "playing" or "attending to play" is central to the moment of both ritual and theatrical performance. An "actor-centered" approach to the study of performance histories necessarily will mean attempting to understand and interpret what cultural actors experience and how they engage in the moment of performance/practice.

▷

▷ Questions to ask when considering any type of performance in light of this theory.

KEY QUESTIONS

1   How might an "actor-centered" approach be applied to performances in another culture or era?

2   How much attention do specific historical studies give to understanding and interpreting what particular actors within specific cultures were experiencing and how they were engaging in the moment of performance/practice?

Egúngún masquerade spectacle

From the many forms of Yoruba ritual, we have selected for brief description here the masquerade spectacle, Egúngún, which honors the spirits of ancestors. On dates set by diviners and publicly announced, Egúngún festivals are organized by Egúngún societies and held in the open air in villages or towns annually, biannually, or on the occasion of a funeral. Each occasion is unique, with great variation in the numbers and types of masked and unmasked performers that appear, in the order of performance, and in the type, range, and quality of audience engagement. During performances, the spectators' attention is never directed to one place at one time. Their attention is drawn to what is happening in particular (often improvised) moments rather than to "repetition of a stock formal segment" (Drewal 1992:93).

Egúngún begins at night in the center of the town when a spirit (Agan) "brings the festival into the world" (Drewal and Drewal 1983:2). Egúngún society members invoke the elusive Agan into the world by using idiophonic language that simulates the "actual dynamic qualities" Agan possesses. He is likened to the "[small, quick, light, drizzling] . . . early night rain" (ibid.:2–4). It is forbidden that anyone see Agan's entry into the world; therefore, all non-members must lock themselves in their houses as Agan is beckoned. The first rhythms played on the bata drum summoning ancestors or deities for this and other festivals are called aliwási, literally "drums come into the world."

Egúngún is an opportunity for the unseen ancestral spirits to visit. Performers are understood to possess àṣẹ, the "activating force or energy" (ibid.:5), with "the power to bring things into existence" (Drewal 1992:90). Egúngún performances temporally weave together a series of equal, but quite different stylistic and thematic segments, each of which has its own independent origin myth.

These myths are available to particular segments of performance as source traditions, but each occasion of performance is a completely unique negotiation of that past with the present. Drewal witnessed the appearance of four maskers in a performance in the town of Imasai, in the Egbado area, one of whom appeared as the Gorilla (Inoki), with "naturalistically carved wooden testicles and a penis painted red on the tip" (ibid.:93) (Figure 1.10). He represented a character that features significantly in the Egúngún origin myth in which a gorilla rapes Iya Mose, who thereby gives birth to a half-human, half-monkey child. The child eventually grows up to be "'One-Who-Brings-Sweetness' to the community" (ibid.:92). At this performance, Gorilla "sneaks up behind unsuspecting women in the performing space, raising his penis as if he is going to rape them" to the ideophonic sound (sabala-sabala-sa-o) of the drums aurally simulating the sounds of Gorilla's sexual movements. Because the attention of spectators was not centrally focused, the Gorilla masker was able to catch-out women in the audience, much to the amusement of the other spectators.

Figure 1.10 The masks worn in Egúngún are called *idan*, literally meaning "miracle." The "miracle" depicted here represents Gorilla, a character that figures significantly in Egúngún origin myths. Ẹgbado area, town of Imạsai, 23 December 1977. From Margaret Drewal, *Yoruba Ritual*, p.161, by kind permission of Indiana University Press.

Numerous other examples of improvisational intervention exemplify the underlying creativity and sense of play informing Yoruba ritual, most obvious when a segment of Egúngún is a competitive performance where individual skills and techniques are tested. So fluid is an Egúngún masquerade that master performers "continue to refine their skills," while "neophytes learn in plain sight of everyone" (ibid.:89). At the conclusion of the festival, a different spirit (from Agan), known as Aránta or Olọdúngbọ́dún ("The-Owner-of-the-Festival-Takes-the-Festival") "carries the spectacle back to the otherworld" (Drewal and Drewal 1983:4). The playful improvisation at the heart of Yoruba practice points to an important dimension of many historical forms of ritual. It has allowed the

Yoruba to creatively interact with, and respond to neighboring peoples such as the mask of the Hausa (Meat Seller), or to changing historical circumstances, from the introduction of Islam to European colonialism.

PZ

Key references

Ajayi, O.S. (1998) *Yoruba Dance*, Trenton, N.J.: Africa World Press.

Callois, R. (1979) *Man, Play, and Games*, New York: Schocken Books.

Drewal, M.T. (1992) *Yoruba Ritual: Performers, Play, Agency*, Bloomington: Indiana University Press. A video-tape companion to this book includes sequences from Agemo, Egúngún, and Jigbo masking and dancing; divination rituals; an Osugbo elder's dance; and a Muslim Yoruba celebration. Contact Indiana University Press, 601 North Morton Street, Bloomington, Indiana 47404–3797

Drewal, H.J. and Drewal, M.T. (1983) *Gelede: Art and Female Power Among the Yoruba*, Bloomington: Indiana University Press.

Huizinga, J. (1970) *Homo Ludens*, New York: Harper.

Sutton-Smith, B. (1997) *The Ambiguity of Play*, Cambridge, Mass.: Harvard University Press.

CASE STUDY: Korean shamanism and the power of speech

Korean shamanistic performance can be analyzed from various perspectives that emphasize its aesthetics, its cultural functions, or its linguistic place in Korean society. For many people today, the term "shaman" may suggest a masked dancer from a long-vanished tribe, or a grass-skirted "witch-doctor," offering dubious cures to those deprived of modern medicine. However, in industrialized, twenty-first century South Korea, "[t]he rituals of the shamans are very much in demand because many people consider them an effective way to cope with the material and spiritual needs of modern society" (Bruno 2002:1).

We begin by looking at Korean shamanistic performance in light of the contested theory of ritual origins. Next we consider the formal structure of *kut* and offer an interpretive approach to its performance, that of speech act theory.

Shamanism, ritual, and theories of the origins of theatre

The term "shaman" originally derived from Siberian (Tungus), referring to religious specialists able to mediate between the human world and the spirit world by means of an altered state of consciousness described as trance, spirit possession, or ecstasy. The shaman's goal is to control the spirits in order to heal the sick and protect society from evil. Shamans are, or have been active in every continent inhabited by humans.

Mircea Eliade's *Shamanism: Archaic Techniques of Ecstasy* (1964) is considered the classic work on shamanism from the perspective of comparative religious study. Eliade noted that all shamans share a number of traits, including the experience of a complex, sometimes psychologically painful initiation. All shamans embark on spirit journeys to the realms of gods or demons; they are trained in song, dance, and the skills of impersonation; they serve as priests and personal advisors; they cure the sick and exorcise malignant spirits; and they aid the dead to find peace. In some societies, the shaman's journey or initiation involves imbibing hallucinogenic plants.

Despite his insights, Eliade has been criticized for failing to make sociological distinctions between cultures and for overgeneralization in terminology. Nevertheless, performance scholars such as Richard Schechner and Eugenio Barba, inspired by anthropologist Victor Turner, embrace shamanism as the root of theatre. They note that both shamans and actors are "liminal" beings who mediate between the everyday world of the audience (or believer) and another realm that only these beings can enter. Both willfully "become" or "call down" another persona (a spiritual being or a character); both use "ritually repeated" special words, movements, gestures, costumes, objects, and spaces, differently than in everyday life. In both cases, audiences are aware of the performer's or ritual practitioner's "doubleness"; that is, audiences know who the enactor is in real life and who she is impersonating or becoming in the ritual or play. This theory suggests that the shaman or religious practitioner performs rituals to change reality (for example, to purify a sinner, answer prayers, cure the sick, talk to the dead, or bring rain), while the goal of the actor is primarily to entertain and/or enlighten.

Recently, such comparisons have been challenged. Eli Rozik (2002) cites the lack of empirical historical evidence of connections between shamanism and theatre, and questions why the idea of ritual origin should be reserved exclusively for theatre, when other arts share elements with ritual (music, song, dance, art, or architecture). He suggests instead that "theatre is a specific imagistic medium (i.e. a method of representation or, rather, an instrument of thinking and communication), and as such its roots lie in the spontaneous image-making faculty of the human psyche" (ibid.:xi). He maintains that theatre and ritual are different types of human activity:

> Theatre is a medium that can serve different intentions and purposes; and ritual is a particular mode of action, with definite intentions and purposes, which can use any medium. Ritual and theatre do not constitute a binary opposition: they operate on different ontological levels.
>
> (ibid.:337)

Rozik proposes that theatre exists at the borderline between the conscious and the unconscious, "an arena where culture confronts and subdues nature" (ibid.:347). Theatre comes into being when "the human psyche spontaneously formulates thoughts in the shape of fictional worlds (i.e. worlds populated by characters and their actions). . . . Theatre . . . affords an imagistic medium for imagistic thinking" (ibid.:343–344). In this view, spectators at theatrical performances confront their own consciousness and subconsciousness, rather than observing a staged world with which they may or may not identify. Korean *kut* poses an interesting problem, employing as it does both ritual and theatre, sometimes making a clear distinction between the two and sometimes blurring the boundaries.

Performing Korean *kut*

Kut is a type of Korean ritual performed by shamans (mostly female), called *mudang*. The "*mu*" (shaman) in *mudang* is written with the Chinese character formed by two horizontal lines (at the top and bottom, symbolizing heaven and earth), with a central vertical line uniting them; on either side is a human being dancing in the air (Hogarth 1999:2). The very character describes a *mudang* as one whose dance links the material and spiritual realms. In anthropologist Victor Turner's term, she is a "liminal being" (Figures 1.11 and 1.12).

Kut may be performed to let the dead vent anger, regrets, or desires in order to rest in peace; to heal the sick and control epidemics; or to obtain good luck. A *kut* can last for several days. It may include choosing a colored flag to determine the mood of a spirit, consuming ritual wine and food, playing music, singing, reciting long tales, chanting Buddhist sutras, performing spirit-possession dances (both by the *mudang* who is inhabited by the spirit, and by non-possessed audience/participants who impersonate the *mudang*), and performing dances purely for fun. Separate (non-ritual) theatrical pieces are usually performed at the end of the *kut*.

The most famous of such independent plays is the masked dance drama of Hahoe village. It contains not only an invocation to the spirits but crude and obscene elements, which in former days served as a social "safety valve," allowing the oppressed to poke

Figure 1.11 The Chinese character *mu*, part of *mudang*, the term for the shaman in the Korean ritual, *kut*.
[Source: Carol Fisher Sorgenfrei.]

Figure 1.12 A group of Korean shamans performs a grand ritual in which they entertain a general of the divine, petitioning him to comfort troubled spirits and bring happiness to the village. Seated in the foreground are musicians. From Traditional Performing Arts of Korea. © Korean National Commission for UNESCO, 1975.

fun at their masters. For example, a servant boy sits on the head of a nobleman, a girl urinating in public excites a monk sexually, and a butcher tries to convince a pair of hypocritical aristocrats to buy bull's testicles and heart to increase sexual potency. Such comic reversals, obscenity, and the incongruous are parts of life often suppressed in "official" or "classical" art, as well as in many religions. Nevertheless, such elements appear in traditional belief systems throughout the world. They are found in spring festivals marking fertility and rebirth, and sometimes serve as a means of releasing aggression against the ruling class in stratified or unjust societies (see the Molière and Bahktin case study, Chapter 4.)

In addition, the entire *kut* has a dramatic structure. It includes an opening invitation to the spirits, a central portion in which the shaman and her clients entertain and supplicate the visiting spirits, and a conclusion in which the spirits are sent back to their own realm. During the *kut*, the possessed *mudang* enacts various spirit-characters, while the audience/participants take on roles as they speak with, coax, plead with, or even try to bribe the spirit-characters with food, wine, entertainment, and money. If the *kut* is successful, the audience/participants experience deep emotional satisfaction or a sense of release.

Some *mudang* have been invited to international festivals to perform *kut*. While some members of the audience may be seeking a genuine spiritual experience, others want exotic secular entertainment. Similarly, the financial backers may be believers, promoters of cross-cultural understanding, or people out to make money. Generally, shamanistic performances at non-religious venues require significant changes in the rituals. Holledge and Tompkins note, in analyzing the 1994 Australian tour by the Korean *mudang*, Kim Kum hwa, that "The packaging of spirituality as a commodity – and particularly the spirituality of an indigenous culture defined by the West as primitive, mythic, and irrational – presents peculiar problems for the marketplace" (Holledge and Tompkins 2000:60). They suggest that "the future of intercultural work is more likely to be tied to patterns of consumption than to idealistic notions of cultural exchange" (ibid.:182). Not all scholars and artists agree with this assessment, and Chapter 12 will consider some of the controversies and ethics of cross-cultural, intercultural, and fusion performance.

Anthropologist Choi Chungmoo has employed performance analysis (including the methods used by Schechner) in her study of *kut*. The shaman's language communicates her liminal status, which must be real for the ritual to be effective (unlike theatre, where liminality is symbolic or suggested). For example, when invoking and impersonating the spirit of her client's dead son, the shaman shifts between the third person and first person. Using "he" to refer to the spirit of the son emphasizes the distance between this world and the realm of the dead; using "I" in impersonating the son's spirit emphasizes the presence of the spirit in the material world. The shaman is simultaneously "I" and "Not I." In Richard Schechner's terms, she is a "between persona" (Schechner 1981:88). In Rozik's terms, however, the shaman's impersonation and doubleness stimulate the brain's imagistic capabilities.

By skillful impersonation and transformation, the shaman creates an emotionally and aesthetically satisfying dialog between herself and her characters, and between each of these and the audience. The solo performer/shaman consciously shifts roles between narrator (herself) and character (the dead spirit) in a manner similar to that of contemporary "one-person shows," traditional Korean *p'ansori* (solo story-telling to music), or Brechtian acting (see Chapter 9). In addition, the shaman must sense the desires and tastes of her audience. She must be able to vary the length of a song, dance, dialog, and all other elements to give the audience/participants the greatest emotional satisfaction. Although performing ritual actions, she must be willing to improvise and "break the rules." Choi concludes that the shaman balances "ritual efficacy and aesthetic felicity to come up with a convincing dramatic performance" (Choi 1989:236). Her conclusion also accords with Rozik's analysis of theatre as the creation of an "imagistic" world of the mind, peopled by fictional characters and situations.

Using speech act theory to interpret Korean *kut*

Antonetta Lucia Bruno agrees that the shaman's language choices are crucial, while emphasizing the importance of non-written communication. Her methodology is inspired by "speech act theory," originally defined by philosopher John L. Austin.

INTERPRETIVE APPROACH: Speech act theory

Speech act theory may be stated simply as "to say something is to do something." Austin's 1962 *How to Do Things with Words*, like Eliade's monumental book, has proven useful for various academic disciplines. However, like Eliade, Austin has been criticized for his failure to emphasize differences between languages and cultures. In addition, some scholars fault him for failing to consider adequately non-linguistic factors, particularly the speaker's "intention" and the listener's active role. But the basic theory is so useful it has often been re-interpreted and modified.

Speech communicates not merely by words, but also by gestures, tone of voice, style of language, level of discourse, word choice, speed of delivery, and so on. Such communication (taking words, grammar, and mode of delivery together) is called a "locutionary act." If the words spoken are meant to do something (that is, if the words are "performative"), such as making a promise, an assurance or a threat, they are called "illocutionary acts." Illocutionary acts are especially important for actors and directors, since they must learn to think in terms of active verbs and intentions. A third type of speech is called a

▷

> "perlocutionary act." Here, circumstances determine how the speech act affects the listener's feelings, thoughts, or actions – for example, persuading someone to do something. The meaning of the communication (from the perspective of both speaker and listener) varies depending on how the speaker delivers the words and gestures. For example, does the shaman or actor sing, whisper, dance, mime, use an unknown language, stutter, or suddenly speak in the voice of a dead person? Like theatre, speech acts take place in both time and space. Dance, mime, and music are also communication. Depending on rhythm and movement qualities, a dance may be a dance of joy or a dance of lamentation; drum beats might encourage a feeling of dread or of elation. Similarly, people mingling in a theatre lobby (or those awaiting the arrival of the spirit of a dead relative) perform gestures and words that are appropriate to the situation. Even without intending to, they are clearly communicating by performing "speech acts," although an outside observer might "misread" the communication, especially if she comes from a different culture. Thus, both the intention of the speaker and the effect of the speech on the listener are crucial in determining the meaning of a speech act.
>
> These are examples of the kinds of questions one would ask using speech act theory, which is interested in the "performative" nature of language, language that makes something happen.

KEY QUESTIONS

1 **When is the language spoken by one person simply informative and when is it performative – designed to affect another, provoke a response, force a reaction, change an opinion or change the circumstances? What especially powerful words are used to do these things? (One might ask these questions about a scene in a play.)**

2 **Does the oral delivery of this language support the speaker's design (or not)? Consider such factors as tone, volume, rate, particular inflections, or emotional coloring. What effect does the delivery have on the listeners? (One might ask these questions of the delivery of an exchange of lines in a scene.)**

In her insightful *The Gate of Words: Language in the Rituals of Korean Shamans*, Bruno employs variations of Austin's theory that emphasize performance. She defines speech as dialog rather than as monologue. That is, the speaker (shaman, character, invoked spirit, or actor) does not merely speak to a passive listener. She has a social and physical relationship with the world; communication goes both ways – that is, the audience (and/or the spirit who is being addressed) can also affect her performance. Bruno writes that during a *kut*, the speaker, whether human (shaman) or supernatural (ancestor or divinity), possesses a special authority or power to perform speech acts. These acts consist of utterances (including chanting or singing) of a particular nature and are accompanied by particular actions (ritual action, including dance and music) performed at specific moments of the *kut*. The meanings of speech acts are created and recreated during the entire *kut* by all the participants.

(2002:13)

Since words and gestures mean different things depending on the context, "speech act theory [must be] reinterpreted, focusing on a continuous transformation of meaning according to the speech event, which is constituted by both linguistic forms and social norms" (ibid.:11).

To analyze a specific ritual using speech act theory, one must focus on the effective combination of ritual speech (magic spells and incantations) with ritual actions (the manipulation of objects). For example, when performing a divination, the *mudang* takes bits and pieces of her clients's casual conversations and re-contextualizes them, so that she is able to use them in a new text when she speaks in the voice of the spirit. This re-contextualization of remembered dialog does not mean that the *mudang* is "faking"; rather, she is in control, making the ritual emotionally effective for the audience. Similarly, her choice of words and style of performance will help the audience "see" and "hear" a god or ancestor rather than the *mudang* herself, who is a person her audience knows in daily life. The differences between daily and "extra-daily" activities and words, performed by a special person in a special setting with special ritual objects, mark the *kut* as a powerful event.

Speech act theory, here modified for ritual analysis, is a valuable tool that can help us understand all types of theatrical as well as social performance.

CFS

Key references

Austin, J.L. (1962) *How to Do Things with Words*, London: Oxford University Press.

Barba, E. (1982) "Theatre anthropology," *The Drama Review*, 26:5–32.

Bruno, A.L. (2002) *The Gate of Words: Language in the Rituals of Korean Shamans*, Leiden, The Netherlands: Research School CNWS, Leiden University.

Choi, C. (1989) "The artistry and ritual aesthetics of urban Korean shamans," *Journal of Ritual Studies*, 3:235–250.

Eliade, M. (1964, [1st edn 1951]) *Shamanism: Archaic Techniques of Ecstasy*, Princeton: Princeton University Press.

Hogarth, H.K. (1999) *Korean Shamanism and Cultural Nationalism*, Seoul, Korea: Jimoondang Publishing Co.

Holledge, J. and Tompkins, J. (2000) *Women's Intercultural Performance*, London and New York: Routledge.

Rozik, E. (2002) *The Roots of Theatre: Rethinking Ritual and Other Theories of Origin*, Iowa City: University of Iowa Press.

Schechner, R. (1981) "Performers and spectators transported and transformed," *American Ethnologist*, 12:707–727.

Schechner, R. (1985) *Between Theatre and Anthropology*, Philadelphia: University of Pennsylvania Press.

Turner, V. (1986) *The Anthropology of Performance*, New York: Performing Arts Journal Publications.

Turner, V. (1982) *From Ritual to Theatre: The Human Seriousness of Play*, New York: Performing Arts Journal Publications.

CHAPTER 2

Religious and civic festivals: Early drama and theatre in context

In large-scale states where centralized authority developed, public life was organized around elaborate annual religious festivals featuring commemorative celebrations, rituals, and performances held on specific dates in the sacred calendar. Early religions are best understood not as matters of personal faith but as apparatuses for enacting highly choreographed performances believed necessary for maintaining social, civic, and cosmic cohesion.

Festivals lasting days or weeks create a "time out of time" (Falassi 1987:*passim*). At festival time, people leave behind everyday concerns to be subsumed within a larger whole. They participate in the large-scale celebratory practices that constitute a festival – processions, pilgrimages, rituals, singing, dancing, performances, and competitions/games. Social codes are played out and social memories invoked and reinforced as people process, dance, sing, prostrate themselves, or engage in self-flagellation.

In large-scale societies where writing developed, it stimulated economic and cultural growth. A writing system is a technology which, similar to the clock or the map, transforms what is recorded, measured, or encoded. The precise nature of that transformation differs according to context. In some societies, writing shaped new forms of cultural performance like drama and theatre, providing distinctive ways of encountering myths, epics, or narratives. This chapter examines a variety of different types of early drama and theatre that emerged in the context of religious festivals in large-scale literate societies – in Egypt, Greece, Mesoamerica, Persia (Iran), and medieval Europe.

Many early forms of drama or quasi-dramatic activities were part of commemorative ritual/ religious ceremonies that celebrated, re-enacted, or elaborated a fundamental mythological, cosmic, or historical event or source of power. Commemorative ceremonies sometimes provided dramatic means of encountering a power or a past event in the present, reminding a community of "its identity as represented by and told in a master narrative . . . making sense of [its] past as a kind of collective autobiography" (Connerton 1989:70). Commemorative "dramas" are often anonymously created by one or more individuals. Although great artistry and imagination may be involved in their creation, they are usually not judged on artistic merit. Rather, these works are assembled, "authored," and performed to enhance the relationship of the community or the individual to the divine or to achieve a ritual purpose; the boundaries between spectating and participation may be blurred. The commemorative performances in Egypt, Mesoamerica, Persia, and Europe that are discussed in this chapter range from "dramatic" elaborations of a ritual or liturgy to dramas that enact a narrative. Commemorative dramas may be enacted to liturgically honor appropriate deities; to ritually pacify cosmic or natural forces (winter/summer solstices, etc.); to enhance communication with the divine; or to commemorate mythic, quasi-historical or historical moments in human history.

Individually-authored dramas, by contrast, are (usually) authored by one person, bear both the name and imprimatur of an individual's poetic voice, engage narrative in some way, and are judged by a set of specific aesthetic criteria. Writing is clearly a necessary but not sufficient cause for the invention of literary drama. While the spectator is ideally engaged in an aesthetic experience, some degree of reflection or critical response to the drama, to its ideological content, or to the performance is expected. This chapter discusses the earliest forms of literary drama authored for the annual dramatic competitions in the fifth century B.C.E. during the festivals in Athens, Greece, honoring Dionysus (god of fertility and wine). This discussion continues in Chapter 3, focusing on aesthetics in the context of royal/imperial patronage.

Some early forms of drama and theatre discussed in Chapters 2 and 3, whether commemorative or literary, might be described as exemplifying "total theatre." They combine acting, music/song, and dance/movement. They employ non-realistic modes of representation in costuming/masking/make-up and acting in order to depict larger-than-life figures, such as epic heroes, gods, and ghosts. Staging conventions obviously differ from those of contemporary western realist theatre. Consider, for example, the relationship between actor and character. In

ancient Greek tragedy, three actors played all the speaking roles in a play, with each playing at least two different roles in a play, rather than a single actor playing one character. In Japanese noh (Chapter 3), the main actor (*shite*) takes one role in the first part of the performance and returns in the second part in a transformed state, while the onstage chorus occasionally chants in first person some of the character's lines, expressing her innermost thoughts, thereby helping make present that figure. In many cultures, "impersonation" is not theatre's ultimate goal.

Among the questions we address as we examine early forms of drama and theatre are these:

- What were the religious and social contexts within which specific early forms of drama and theatre developed?
- How did the structure, context, and content of performance "choreograph" civic and religious authority?
- What was recorded in early dramatic texts, and who composed/authored them? As these dramatic versions of myths, tales, or epics were transcribed for the first time, were they "fixed" or did they vary in performance?

We begin our examination in Egypt where the myth of Osiris was re-enacted annually at a festival in the god's honor.

Commemorative ritual "drama" in Abydos, Egypt

The earliest settled agricultural activity in Egypt was in the region of el-Badari, Upper Egypt, around 4,400–4,000 B.C.E. The Upper and Lower Kingdoms were unified between 3,200 and 3,000, by which time a distinctive Egyptian civilization had evolved that had a highly complex set of polytheistic religious practices and beliefs. For well over 3,000 years, Egyptian religious and cultural life exhibited a tolerant openness to the worship of old and new deities – local and foreign gods and goddesses. The Egyptian pantheon included a spectacular array of deities to be propitiated and worshipped. Their myths and legends were often contradictory. Three different, but interconnected accounts of creation existed, each focusing on a different group of deities and each considered equally valid.

A series of dualities was fundamental to the Egyptian world-view, within which chaos was balanced by order. In the fragile physical environment of Egypt, the "Black Land" of the rich, fertile banks of the river Nile and its annual life-giving waters balanced the "Red Land" of the surrounding barren deserts. Day balanced night. Their regular alternation demonstrated how the gods controlled the cosmos. The god Ra was both lord of time and the sun-god who ruled the day. His counterpart was Osiris – ruler of death and the underworld. Death and life were not two different states, but two aspects of one state; therefore, life balanced death. The after-life – an idealized version of Egyptian daily life – was assumed to be an "underworld," located in the heavens where the dead lived as *akhs* – eternally blessed spirits, transfigured both by their difficult journey through a dark underworld and their final judgment by the great god, Osiris.

Life was associated with day and death with night. The sun god, Ra, was born in the morning, aged during each day, and then sank into Osiris's underworld at night, to be reborn at dawn. The daily rebirth of the sun mirrored the constant rebirth of the dead in afterlife. Elaborate mortuary rituals were developed to ensure that this rite of passage was successfully accomplished by the souls of the dead. In the underworld, Ra and Osiris became one. According to the Egyptian *Book of the Dead*, "Osiris is yesterday and Ra is tomorrow."

Cosmic equilibrium could be maintained only through the cooperation of the gods and goddesses. Chaos was kept at bay by the earthly representative of the gods – the pharaoh. As the intermediary between divine and mortal worlds, the pharaoh (male or female) possessed the inherent dualities of the cosmos. Only the pharaoh was empowered to

intercede on behalf of humankind; therefore, s/he was considered the main priest of every Egyptian temple. Temple rituals, offerings, public ceremonies, and secret esoteric rites replenished the power of the gods who kept the universe in order. As high priest, the pharaoh delegated most daily temple obligations to a hierarchy of male and female priests. These "servants of the gods" ranged from a few at small temples to 81,000 serving the great Karnak temple during the rule of Rameses III (1,184–1,153 B.C.E.).

The pharaoh was at first regarded as a servant of the gods, but later was considered divinely conceived, therefore equal to the gods. Each pharaoh was considered an incarnation of Horus, son of Osiris. When a pharaoh died, he was immediately identified with Osiris.

Ritual/ceremonial practices and the commemorative ritual-drama of Osiris at Abydos

The elaborate ritual life of Egyptian temples was based on making offerings that nourished the gods – food, libations, song, dance, incense, and annual festivals. Before conducting daily worship or public ceremonies, priests and priestesses purified themselves by bathing, chewing natron salts, and removing body hair. Song and dance were especially central to worship of the goddess, Hathor, at her temple at Dendera. One hymn describes how even the king danced and sang before the goddess while wielding a sacred, golden rattle:

> He comes to dance,
> comes to sing,
> Hathor, see his dancing,
> see his skipping!
>
> . . . O Golden One,
> how fine is the song
> like the song of Horus himself,
> which Ra's son sings as the finest singer.
> He is Horus, a musician!
>
> (Fletcher 2002:83)

The sacred Egyptian calendar featured numerous annual festivals, astrologically determined, during which statues of gods and goddesses housed in sacred barques (boat-shaped shrines, Figure 2.1). These barques usually were hidden from sight and were the subject of secret rituals inside temples. When they were taken in procession by land and water to visit other temples or burial tombs, the barques were carried out of the temple on the shoulders of priests and accompanied by dancers and musicians (Figure 2.2), making that deity's power present for the people.

The festival season began each year with the celebration of New Year's Day (19 July) during the first Egyptian month of Akhet (Inundation) – the season when the Nile floods. Four other major festivals were celebrated in this month alone. The festival of Osiris at Abydos took place in the fourth Egyptian month, among other festivals honoring Hathor and Sokar (god of cemeteries).

Arguably the most important Egyptian myth is that of Osiris and his sister and consort, Isis. Before human-time, when Osiris and Isis ruled the world, prosperity and peace reigned. But Osiris's brother, Seth, became jealous. Therefore, Seth killed Osiris by sealing him in a coffin and drowning him in the Nile at a location near Abydos, thereby bringing conflict to the world. When Isis recovered Osiris's

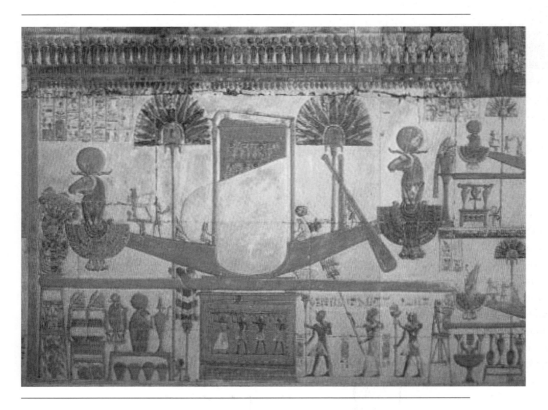

Figure 2.1 The sacred barque of Amun-Ra in a relief from a temple of Seti I.

[Source: p.103 of *The Egyptian Book of Living and Dying* by Joann Fletcher. London: Duncan Baird Publishers, 2002.]

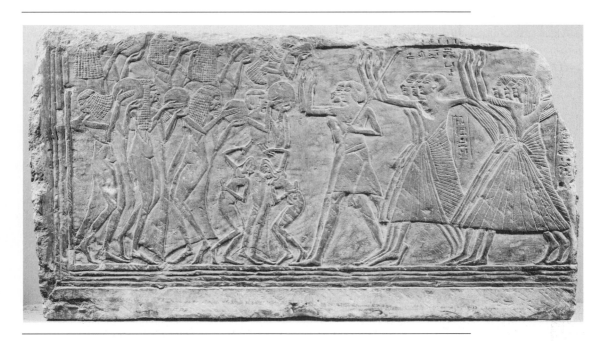

Figure 2.2 Fragment from a relief from a tomb at Sakkara (c.1250 B.C.E.) shows women and young girls playing tambourines and clapsticks and dancing at a festival procession (right), led by a baton-carrying official and other male officials, their arms raised in rejoicing. © Cairo/Jurgen Liepe, Berlin.

body, Seth took the body from her, and dismembering it, scattered it over the far expanses of Egypt Isis and her sister Nephthys (protectors and restorers of the dead) scoured the kingdom, locating every piece of his body. After reassembling the body, Isis used her great powers to revive Osiris. From their union was born their son, Horus – raised to avenge his father's death. Osiris left to become ruler of Duat – the underworld.

This legend was central to Egyptian belief in the rebirth of the dead into an afterlife. In the Egyptian view, Seth represented chaos and Horus the divine nature of kingship, always to be reborn. Osiris was the god who restored life, and therefore was regarded as the fecund god of fertility, agriculture, and the Nile.

The deity most honored with great public ceremonies was Osiris, especially at the main center of his worship in Abydos by the period of the Middle Kingdom (after 2,055 B.C.E.). Middle Kingdom rulers lavished patronage on the cult. Osiris's statue was re-housed in a new "everlasting great barque," lavishly constructed of "gold, silver, lapis lazuli, bronze, and cedar." Annually, the barque containing Osiris processed from the temple to the desert site of his tomb and back again. At the center of this liturgy lasting a few days (if not several weeks) was a commemorative re-enactment of dramatic moments of Osiris's story.

The little that is known to us of this quasi-dramatic commemorative ritual is the information inscribed on a single stele (a flat stone), dating from the rule of Senusret III (1,870–1,831 B.C.E.). It provides a description of the dual roles of the chief priest/organizer of the festival, Ikhernofert, who was both overseer of the ceremonies and a participant/ actor playing the role of the "beloved son of Osiris."

> I arranged the expedition of Wepwawet when he went to the aid of his father. I beat back those who attacked the Barque of Neshmet. I overthrew the foes of Osiris. I arranged the Great Procession and escorted the god [Osiris] on his journey. I launched the god's ship . . . I decked the ship with gorgeous trappings so that it might sail to the region of Peker [near Abydos]. I conducted the god to his grave in Peker. I championed [avenged] Wenn-nefru [Osiris as the re-risen god] on the day of the Great Combat and overthrew all his adversaries beside the waters of Nedit. I caused him to sail in his ship. It was laden with his beauty. I caused the hearts of the Easterners to swell with joy, and I brought the gladness to the Westerners at the sight of the Barque of Neshment. . . .
>
> (Gaster 1950:41–42)

Other major roles were taken by priests and priest-esses, supported by a large group of "extras" who constituted the warring factions of Seth and Horus/Osiris. The "Great Combat" was a spectac-ular occasion, with thousands of participants on the two sides. The Greek historian, Herodotus recorded in his *Histories* how the massed armies engaged in "a hard fight with staves . . . they break one another's heads, and I am of the opinion that many even die of the wounds they receive; the Egyptians however told me that no one died."

Hieroglyphic texts as mnemonic manuscript records

Egyptians borrowed the idea of writing from Sumer – a mixed form of writing using hieroglyphs ("sacred carvings"). Egyptian writing dates from 3,400 B.C.E.,

before the establishment of the first dynasty of the pharaohs. Since writing was considered a gift of the god, Thoth, the healer, lord of wisdom, and scribe of the gods, it recorded *mdw-ntr*, "god's words." Egyptian hieroglyphs were first used for accountancy and then as a bureaucratic tool. With less than 1 percent of the populous literate, scribes were a learned, specialist community. Colorful hieroglyphic inscriptions decorated tombs and temples and were decorated with special symbols and images of animals, birds, and humans to "activate" the scenes. Learning was highly respected, and papyrus texts devoted to astrology, law, history, mathematics, medicine, geography, and sacred liturgy were stored in great libraries attached to temples.

The reign of Senusret III during the Middle Kingdom "was a time when art, architecture, and religion reached new heights, but, above all, it was an age of confidence in writing" (Shah 2000:183). Many literary forms flourished. Narratives such as *The Story of Sinuhe* and *The Shipwrecked Sailor* were composed. "Wisdom texts" recorded maxims on how to gain well-being in life, while "dream books" guided priests in their interpretation of dreams. Manuscripts such as *All Rituals Concerning the God Leaving His Temple in Procession on Festival Days* recorded sacred words and the correct performance of rites.

No specific manuscript has been located for the rites of Osiris at Abydos. If any manuscript had been used, it would have recorded the sacred words used to animate and honor Osiris; there would have been no "dialog" specially authored for the figures central to the re-enactment. The focus of the performance would have been on the processional spectacle and re-enactment manifesting the presence and power of Osiris in his annual going-forth, his conquering of death, and rebirth. Perhaps the contemporary focus on narrative in literary works of the Middle Kingdom helped create a climate within which dramatizing parts of the Osiris story was an obvious means of enhancing the efficacy of the annual commemoration.

The way in which Egyptians "imagined" their place within the world and cosmos was informed by two paradigms of great antiquity – the assumption that society was organized around "high centers," headed by divinely-ordained monarchs, and the assumption that cosmology and history were indistinguishable. Both assumptions are evident in the commemorative ritual drama of Osiris at Abydos.

In the early centuries of the Christian era, when the Romans began to rule over Egypt, traditional religious beliefs and rituals began to lose their hold on cultural life throughout Egypt. When Christianity was declared the official religion of the Roman Empire in the fourth century C.E., non-Christian places of worship were closed and ancient Egyptian religion and culture died.

Dialogic drama in the city-state of Athens

The divine god-kings of Egypt located authority in a single person and produced hieratic festivals honoring gods like Osiris. A very different way of negotiating the relationship between divine and civic authority, and between the cosmos and history developed in Athens, Greece during the fifth century, B.C.E., where distinctive forms of literary drama and theatre flourished. The spectacular quasi-dramatic re-enactment of Osiris's story was monologic in its reification of Osiris within a ritual/liturgical context that invited no reflexive engagement. The forms of drama that developed in the context of the annual festival of Dionysus in Athens were dialogic and agonistic in that they invited social political, critical, and aesthetic debate.

As in Egypt, ancient Greek religion was polytheistic. Within the Greek pantheon, a complex host of anthropomorphic gods and goddesses vied for power, prestige and influence, and (mis)behaved much as did the great epic heroes. The most powerful of the gods were assumed to reside on mount Olympus – the highest peak in Greece. Zeus was considered both king of the gods and ruler of the sky. Zeus's siblings and children each had their own spheres of influence, and each god or goddess embodied a complex set of ways in which the Greeks understood their world. For example, Artemis, the goddess of the hunt, twin to Apollo, was a keen hunter of wild animals and their protector, a virgin goddess who was associated with both chastity and fertility, and a protector of maidens and of women in childbirth.

The gods associated with oral epic poetry (Apollo) and later forms of choral dance and drama (Dionysus), reflect contrasting dimensions of human experience. As David Wiles writes:

> Apollo is associated with light, thus intellectual enlightenment, and far-sighted prophecy. Dionysus the wine-god is associated with darkness, with nocturnal drinking bouts, and the loss of mental clarity in moments of collective emotion, with the loss of boundaries around the self experienced in a crowd, and the hiding of self behind a theatrical mask. Apollo makes music with the measured chords of his lyre, whilst the instrument of Dionysus is the haunting double oboe which can whip up wild dances. The worshippers of Apollo tend to be male, those of Dionysus more often female.
>
> (2000:7–8)

Living inside the earth were the furies or demons. Important forces active in the world, such as justice and destruction, were imagined as powerful in their own right as semi-personal deities. Ancestors could exert influence over the living; therefore, death rituals and burial rites were important. All the gods and forces active in the world were often in conflict. This in itself reflected the fact that Greeks did not share one set of core values or beliefs, contrary to some romanticizing views of Greek civilization. None of the gods was inherently good or evil, but each needed to be appropriately honored, propitiated, and worshipped to access their potential beneficence or prevent their wrath.

In the eighth and ninth centuries, B.C.E., epic bards like Homer "recited or sang" their own monologic versions of lengthy stories of the gods and epic heroes of bygone eras, such as *The Iliad* and *The Odyssey*. Their performances gave life to the deeds of a heroic aristocracy, populating a murky, distant, quasi-mythic/quasi-historical past.

Alphabetic writing, debate, and "democracy"

Around 850 B.C.E., a system of alphabetic writing adapted from the Phoenicians was introduced into Greece (Fischer 2001:123). In a remarkably short time – by the end of the fifth century B.C.E. – there was a literacy revolution in Athens. "Everyday life was so overrun with books . . . that cheap editions of philosophy could be picked up from the bookstalls for a drachma" (Wise 1998:21). Most poet/performers refocused their creative work, and, rather than composing solo oral epics, they began to write tragedies or comedies in which multiple actors spoke dialog and choruses played a central role, with choreographed dancing/singing. The high place once accorded to bardic performance was soon replaced by the celebration of dramatists who were awarded prizes for plays. How and why did this revolution occur? The nature of Greek alphabetic writing, the competitive spirit in Greek culture, and the Greek creation of an early form of democracy all played roles.

In the Greek alphabet syllabic notation was broken down into phonemes, consonants, and vowels for the first time. Alphabetic writing separates meaning from sounds, the effect of which is to open up the possibility and space of difference within the operation of written language. Alphabetic writing thereby invites debate, and debate became central to Greek, and especially Athenian, culture and society.

A unique set of socio-political circumstances had developed in Greece by 508 B.C.E. An amorphous, polytheistic tradition of myths had combined with an emergent political system of autonomous and independent city-states and alphabetic writing

to produce a totally new form of governance – an early form of democracy – all of which perhaps spurred the drama's development. The governing arrangement was unlike that of Egypt, in which the Upper and Lower Kingdoms combined to form a single, vast empire ruled centrally by their god-kings for over 3,000 years. The Greek city-states, which included Athens, Sparta, and Corinth, were discreet socio-political entities that alternatively vied with one another for ascendancy and occasionally joined forces in alliances to face a common outside threat – such as that of the Persians (defeated in 479 B.C.E.).

The focus of our attention here is the city-state of fifth-century Athens, comprised of the entire region known as Attica, within which were 139 smaller townships (*demes*). Citizenship was restricted to male Athenians (perhaps 30,000), who were expected to fulfill civic obligations as soldiers/sailors, athletes, debaters, or judges, and as participants/ spectators at annual public religious festivals. Citizens whose wealth exceeded a certain sum were expected to take on such civic obligations as maintaining a warship, equipping a religious procession, or financing a "chorus," which meant underwriting the production of a set of plays in one of the annual theatre festivals. The civic obligations of male citizens were shaped also by their location within a township and by their lineage within one of Attica's ten tribes.

The give-and-take of competition (*agon*) was central to the spirit of the age. This is exemplified not only in the struggles among the gods and heroes in Greek myths and epics, but also in public debate and oratory, newly developing modes of education emphasizing the art of rhetoric. It is evident in new ways of thinking, such as stoicism and skepticism, in the many forms of public contests (athletics, choral dancing, and later drama), and in the constant state of bellicosity requiring the training and readiness of extensive sea and ground forces to protect the city-state or expand its territorial power.

The centrality of the art of rhetoric, originally known as *techne rhetorike*, translated as "speech art," or oratory and exemplified in Aristotle's (384–322 B.C.E.) *Art of Rhetoric*, demonstrates how the invention of writing led to an organized, abstract analysis of speech itself. In this sense, writing in fifth-century Athens enhanced some forms of oral communication since speeches were given extempore – no orator would ever speak from a prepared text. For the Greeks (and later the Romans – see Chapter 3), oratory and reading were social activities. They always read aloud, even when there was no audience. Literature existed for hearing, not for a silent, private activity. Manuscripts were intended for declamation. Composition continued to take place in the very art and act of telling, even as the principles of the act of telling were becoming the object of a separate art and science.

Clearly, increasing attention was being paid in Athens to the give-and-take of dialogic forms of thought, reflection, and civic engagement. These were exemplified in the teaching of Socrates and the later writings of Plato (*c.*428–348 B.C.E.), especially in Plato's *Republic*. One significant philosophical result was that by the end of the fifth century B.C.E. a mental world of thoughts, desires, and intentions the Greeks called "psyche" was postulated – today usually known as "the mind" – and was conceived as separate from the body. Thus was one pervasive form of philosophical dualism created in the West.

Dialogic drama in the context of the Great Dionysia (festival) in Athens

The theatrical performance of tragedy and comedy in ancient Athens needs to be understood also in the context of all the civic/religious rituals and ceremonies of which it was a part. Fifth-century Greek theatre was woven into the fabric of civic/religious discourse, a matter obscured by the purely literary considerations of Greek tragedy that began with Aristotle's *Poetics*, written almost a century after the height of the great tragic playwrights, and which long dominated western approaches to drama. To read the idealized accounts of ancient Greece of the nineteenth and much of the twentieth century, one would hardly believe that the Greek theatre gave voice to a volatile, competitive culture, one often involved in war and often debating difficult internal social issues.

By the fifth century B.C.E., Greek religious festivals typically included processions, sacrifices, celebrations, and (in some cases) competitions. The worship of dead heroes was among the most important rites of ancient Greece from at least Homeric time forward. Their propitiation enacted and reflected the belief that the dead enjoyed some of the same activities in death as in life. Their spirits could be recalled by the re-enactment of their past deeds. They could be propitiated through athletic feasts, contests of horsemanship, offerings of cakes, and the performance of choral laments – group singing and dancing. Since communication between the living and the dead was thought to be essential to the well-being of the nation itself, each township held a festival at its local burial site where local heroes were appeased. Eventually these local rites were expanded to include deities from the larger pantheon, including Zeus, Apollo, Poseidon, and Dionysus.

These religious rites often included competitions in honor of the gods, best exemplified in the well-known pan-Greek Olympic games (from 776 B.C.E.), held in honor of Zeus every four years following the summer solstice. Young male competitors trained for thirty days in foot and chariot racing, boxing, wrestling, *pankration* (martial arts), discus, and javelin – all of which contributed to military preparedness. Competitions were often violent and brutal, and could end in death. A religious ceremony and two day procession preceded the games. Spectators were exclusively male, with the exception of the priestess of Demeter, the goddess of agriculture. At the concluding ceremony on the fifth day, there was feasting, giving thanks to the gods, and the awarding to the victors of olive branches cut from Zeus's sacred grove. The rites and ceremonies constituted an important framework that, while honoring

Zeus, in effect allowed athletic competitions to become increasingly professionalized and secular.

Every mid-summer the Panathenaia honored Athena, the patron deity of Athens. Following a great procession, a new dress was presented to clothe the image of the goddess. To further popularize this festival and achieve civic cohesion, athletic contests were held every four years, starting in 566–65 B.C.E. Among the team events was the *pyrrhic* – a martial dance in which the dancers wore the full armor of the ancient Greek foot soldier and executed military movements. Additional competitions eventually included solo recitations of works by Homer, and musical contests.

There were four major festivals annually in honor of Dionysus, the god of fertility and wine-making. The Lenaea festival (from 440 B.C.E.), named after the Lenai or maenads who danced ecstatically under the influence of Dionysus, took place in January–February. It was first devoted to comedies and later included tragedies. The Rural Dionysia was a series of smaller township festivals in December–January. It featured phallic chants, sacrifices, and wine-drinking, and ultimately incorporated performances of tragedies and comedies that had been performed at the City Dionysia. The Anthesteria festival was an early spring festival in February–March which celebrated the opening of new wine, and began to include comedies quite late,

perhaps around 326 B.C.E. The most notable of the Dionysian festivals was the Great, or City Dionysia, which was also the second most important of all the city's annual festivals. It was as part of this festival that dramas were first performed. They were staged ultimately in a large outdoor amphitheatre, seating 10,000–15,000, located near the temple of Dionysus. The temple and the theatre were just below the Acropolis, the promontory at the center of Athens that served as both a stronghold and center of public life. Scholars have long believed the tragedy competitions were instituted at this festival in 534 B.C.E., and that Thespis was the first winner. Some scholars have suggested recently that the tragedy competitions came only later, with the advent of Athenian democracy in the last decade of the sixth century.

Each March or April, the Great Dionysia began with a raucous procession, celebrating the coming of the god Dionysus to Athens. This was followed by sacrificial rituals, civic ceremonies, and competitions in dithyrambs – choral songs and dances – and competitions of tragedies and comedies. The procession, which began just outside the geographical boundary of the city-state, incorporated the citizens of Athens as well as visitors. It opened a complex series of events, civic and religious, and the theatrical performances are best understood within the fullness of this civic and religious context. The probable order of events is described below.

The Great Dionysia in fifth century Athens: Probable order of events

Day 1: Procession of the statue of Dionysus and the Proagon

The coming of Dionysus to Athens from Eleutherai was re-enacted. After a ritual sacrifice, Dionysus's statue was brought from a temple near Eleutherai in a procession to his temple in

Athens, at the base of the Acropolis. The procession was probably conducted by a group of young men (ephebes) in the midst of their military training (Winkler 1990:37). They offered another sacrifice at the base of the Acropolis, within the sacred precinct of Dionysus's temple. In the *proagon* that followed, the playwrights and their choruses who were competing in the tragic competition were introduced to the public and the subject of their plays announced.

▷

▷ ### Day 2: Dithyramb competitions

Dithyrambs were performed – choral songs and dances in honor of Dionysus, first regularized by Arion at Corinth around 600 B.C.E. Each of the ten tribes of Athens sent representative performers with a poet who composed/choreographed the year's entry. These works were danced/sung by two choruses of fifty – one of younger boys, and a second of mature men. Although the verses were originally dedicated to Dionysus, the contest was eventually opened up to other myths, leading some to scoff that the dithyrambs had "nothing to do with Dionysus."

Day 3: Comedy competition (beginning in 486 B.C.E.)

Five different playwrights competed with comedies that offered keen satirical commentary on current socio-political matters, such as war, education, politics, the legal system, or even tragic poetry. The comedies of Aristophanes (c.448–380 B.C.E.) freely caricatured well-known individuals, including Socrates the philosopher, Cleon the politician, and Aeschylus and Euripides – who, together with Sophocles were the greatest of the fifth-century writers of tragedy. The only comedies of this type to survive, in fact, are the eleven by Aristophanes. The genre came to be referred to as "old comedy" to distinguish it from the later genre of domestic situation comedies, known as "new comedy."

Days 4, 5, and 6: Tragedy competition

Important civic-religious ceremonies were held before the assembled public on the day of the opening of the tragedy competition (Goldhill 1990:104–109). These included the display of tributes by outlying cities under Athenian rule and the appearance of young men in full military address, whose training was provided by Athens after their fathers had died in battle in service to the state. The names of those citizens who had benefited the city-state that year were read out, and these citizens were presented a crown or garland.

The playwrights then presented their sets of four plays, probably one set by each playwright per day. Each set – three tragedies and a final satyr play – were original variations on a Greek myth. The satyr plays were farcical renditions of incidents from the same myth as the tragedies. These ribald pieces were named after the satyrs – the half-horse, half-human wine-drinking companions of Dionysus who constituted the chorus of these plays. Their costumes (Figure 2.3) included a horse's tail, an erect phallus, and a head-mask with pointed/equine ears, snub-nose, and wild hair and beard. Only one satyr play survives: *Cyclops* by Euripides (c.480–407/6 B.C.E.). The satyr plays were characterized by broad physical sight-gags and scatological humor.

Probably on the last day, the judges of each category of the competition announced the winners of the tragedy and comedy competitions and awarded prizes. At the end of the festival, officials held an open public assembly to receive any criticism of the proceedings, including complaints about the plays selected or the judging.

The tragedy competitions would have fostered keen debates. The dramatists reworked the myths over and again – usually the stories of conflicts within ruling families, such as the house of Atreus, conflicts that have consequences for the *polis* – the civic body of the whole. The myth of the house of Atreus was the basis for the tragic trilogy of *The Orestia*, by Aeschylus (c.525–456 B.C.E.), the only complete set

Figure 2.3 Actors and chorus for a satyr play. At the center top are Dionysus, Ariadne (his wife), and a muse. Below, the playwright (with scroll), choral trainer (with lyre), and piper. To either side of Dionysus are three mature actors (with beards, holding their masks) – one costumed as a king, one as Kerakles (with club), and the third as Silenus (leader of satyrs). The young beardless men (*ephebes*) are costumed as satyrs with erect phalluses. Drawing by E.R. Malyon from the Pronomos Vase, a pot for mixing wine, late fifth or early fourth century B.C.E. © Museo Nazionale, Naples.

of three related tragedies to survive. Each playwright re-imagined these stories from the distant bronze age; they were imbued with contemporary relevance. The characters they created inhabited "the mental universe of the audience," and their values were, David Wiles believes, "substantially those in the democratic period" (2000:10–11). There are, it should be noted, considerable differences between the vision, structure, and poetic style of the plays of Aeschylus, written in the first half of the fifth century, and those of Euripides, written in the latter half. Euripides was influenced by the development of Sophism, the philosophical movement that brought disciplined processes of reason and critical thinking to Athens. Athenians associated Euripides with Socrates, and he was a controversial figure. His tragedies critiqued traditional values and religion, no longer showing reverence for the heroes and gods of the myths.

The theatre audience consisted primarily of male citizens of Athens who constituted the *polis*. Seated in tribal order, each tribe occupied one wedge in the amphitheatre, mirroring the seating of the Athenian Assembly, with the tribe's Council seated in a special section or at the front. As we have seen, the third day of the festivities of the City Dionysia, the day on which the performances of the tragedies took place, was preceded by the performance of important civic/religious ceremonies. The sons of fathers who died in battle and whose training and education had been undertaken by the state processed annually in military dress in the theatre where Sophocles's *Antigone* was played, with its central conflict between the rules of a state at war and the interests of the individual. Generals from each of the ten tribes offered ritual libations to Dionysus in the theatre where Euripides's *The Trojan*

Women was played. In that tragedy, Euripides used one of the most famous war stories in Greek history – Greece's conquest of Troy – to focus on the brutality of war and the suffering it brings to the innocent. In one year, the playwright, Phrynicus (writing between 511 and 475 B.C.E.), was heavily fined for dealing with the painful subject of the destruction of Miletus by the Persians, a city Athens had pledged to defend but did not. Its fall precipitated the invasion of the Persians. Throughout the fifth century, there was almost no year without an Athenian military engagement, and the festival ceremonies would have prompted the citizens of Athens to reflect upon state decision-making (Winkler 1990:21).

The degree of direct civic engagement in the festival is staggering – at least 2,500–3,000 male citizens were directly involved as participants in the processions, ceremonies, rites, or dramatic competitions constituting the festival. For the choral dithyrambs alone each of ten tribes organized 50 boys under 18 and 50 men (aged 20–30) – a total of 2,000. The three days of tragedies utilized somewhere between 36 and 45 young men (at first 12 and later 15 in each chorus) and nine mature men (three speaking roles). While the boys dancing their first dithyramb were under 18, the young men dancing in the tragic choruses were in the prime of their youth, aged 18 to 20, and in the process of undergoing two years of military training. At any one time (by the fifth century), there were two cohorts of 450–500 young men, known as *ephebes*, drawn from the ten tribes, who were undergoing training. The second year cadets put on a public demonstration in the theatre of their "hoplite military manoeuvres [combat exercises in battle dress] and close-order drill", while at least 36 of those in their first year were selected to perform as the chorus members in each of the three sets of tragedies (ibid.:22–23). The philosopher Chameleon (fifth century B.C.E.) described choral dancing as "practically a manoeuvre in arms and a display not only of precision marching in general but more particularly of physical preparedness." It is these young "citizen soldiers in training" who are depicted on the famous Pronomos Vase (Figure 2.3) as members of the chorus in a satyr play.

The City Dionysia offers a festival model within which ritual practices frame competitive performances in a civic/religious event, an event that flows from and constitutes life within the *polis*. It was a rite of transition for young men as they moved from boyhood to manhood, taking their place as citizen-soldiers in civic society. Within the festival, the performances of tragedies, satyr plays, and comedies were not simple acts of affirmation of some ideally homogeneous community (a notion dear to classicists in the nineteenth and twentieth centuries). Rather, these performances staged the current tensions of the *polis* in negotiation with stories of the past. As such, they often provoked a critical examination of the *polis* of the present. To take an example in addition to those cited, there are many strong women characters in the surviving tragedies, from Clytemnestra in Aeschylus's *The Orestia* through Sophocles's *Antigone* and Euripides's *Medea*. The women in Aristophanes's comedy, *Lysistrata*, protest against war by refusing to sleep with their husbands. These strong women on stage are, as Helene Foley has observed, quite surprising in a patriarchal society in which women were largely restricted to the domestic sphere (Foley 1981:*passim*). Some scholars are suspicious because these women were authored by men and played by male actors in a phallocentric culture (Case 1985:*passim*), but it seems likely that Athenians expected their theatre to stage contemporary cultural issues in its dialogic process, stirring debate.

To judge from the scant evidence of the judging procedures, the playwriting competitions must have produced some controversies. Great care was taken to select judges of plays who would be beyond reproach. The methods of selecting the winner was elaborate. In one year, the judges cast their ballots, and then a blind drawing from those ballots was conducted to produce a winner. The introduction of randomness in the selection was apparently intended to stave off any accusations of corruption. All of this was undertaken under the sign of the delirious Dionysus – the irrepressible god of wine and fertility who was able to condone at least temporary transgression and ecstatic excess.

After the fifth century B.C.E.

At the City Dionysia in 449 (or Lenaia in 442) a competition among the actors of tragedy was introduced, marking public recognition of the actor's art. An actor could win although he might appear in a losing tetralogy. Actors were celebrated or critiqued on the basis of their day-long performances. By the fourth century B.C.E. when, instead of new plays, previously authored plays were re-presented and/or toured other cities, the emphasis shifted further toward celebrating actors such as Polos, rather than playwriting. The Roman Aulus Gellius recorded a story of a performance by the famous fourth-century Greek actor, Polos, in the title role of Sophocles's *Electra*, who takes the ashes of her brother, Orestes, from his tomb. Polos used the ashes of his own recently deceased son, and, according to Gellius's version of the story, Polos "filled the whole place, not with the appearance and imitation of sorrow, but with genuine grief and unfeigned lamentation" (Gellius 1927: II,35–37).

It was nearly a century following the peak achievements of Athenian theatre that Aristotle gave his lectures that have come down to us as his *Poetics* (*c.*330 B.C.E.). He focused on the formal attributes and proper aesthetic effects of tragedy. Drawing on plays that had won the City Dionysia competitions, he discussed the kinds of plots, characters, and language appropriate to achieve the effects of a genre he considered a "natural" form. Sophocles's *Oedipus the King* is a frequent reference point. He thought that *mimesis* – direct imitation of reality – was theatre's goal. One of tragedy's chief effects, he

believed, was catharsis, a term that for the Greeks had associations with both religious purification and medical purging. Aristotle suggested that an audience experiencing tragedy would achieve a sense of proportion once purged or purified of emotional and/or intellectual error. When rediscovered in the fifteenth century, Aristotle's *Poetics* was used pervasively as a model for European dramatic writing and analysis. While he was the first to offer such insights into the drama, Aristotle's discussion was also a rationalized processing of the complex Greek art of theatre. He dismissed performance as unnecessary for tragedy's effects, making the play text the chief object of the study of theatre. From his formalistic analysis, the reader would have little idea of the civic context in which the dialogic drama of Athens took place in the fifth century B.C.E. (The legacy of the Aristotelian tradition is discussed in Chapter 11.)

Beyond Athens, an independent comic tradition developed in Syracuse in the fifth century. Syracuse became a second major center of performance. In the fourth century B.C.E., the legacy of Greek theatre was spread by the conquests of Alexander the Great – once a student of Aristotle – in his campaign to "Hellenize" non-Greek peoples. As we will see in Chapter 3, this Hellenic era of theatre (317–86 B.C.E.) developed through the period of the Roman Republic and eventually gave way to a theatre transformed by the Roman Empire (86 B.C.E.–692 C.E.). Greco-Roman drama then gave way to spectacular popular entertainments during the period of imperial rule. After Rome's fall, classical drama was sustained in the medieval scholastic imagination, and, from the renaissance's investigation of the classical past, it emerged within the rational, logocentric discourse of humanism.

Mesoamerican performance

'If only they'd come make a show for us we'd wonder at them and marvel,' the Xibalba said, referring to the two sacred 'boys' – Hunahpu and Xbalanque. 'Please entertain us . . . ' So they began their songs

and dances . . . the spectators crowded the floor, and they danced . . . the Weasel . . . the Poorwill . . . the Armadillo.

(Tedlock 1985:151–152)

This passage from the centuries-old sacred book of the Maya Quiché peoples – *Popul Vuh* – provides clear evidence of a rich Mesoamerican performance culture, one stretching back to as early as 3,000 B.C.E. The Mexica (Aztecs), Maya, and Inca kingdoms ruled Central and South America until the late fifteenth and sixteenth centuries, when the Spanish conquered the indigenous peoples of the Americas.

Throughout Mesoamerica, public celebrations before the conquest always involved a religious element while also serving as a means of social integration. Performances could involve thousands of highly skilled performers who "used elaborate and highly colorful costumes, masks, body makeup and, at times puppets and stilts. The sets were lavishly adorned with arches, flowers, animals, and all sorts of natural and artfully designed elements" (Taylor 2004:357). Most performances were outdoors in public spaces (courtyards and temples), while some were in private patios. Rigorous training in specific genres of music and dance was normal for boys and girls from ages twelve to fifteen and took place in "houses of song." Rulers performed "a 'princely dance' on special occasions," and priests "embodied god-figures" (ibid.:358). Such performances were staged in the context of religious festivals and set against the great architectural spaces of Mesoamerican cities, which included massive pyramids. Temples were regarded as the "navel of the world" and "the human-made equivalent of nature's mountains [. . .] forming a living link that conjoined the heavens above, the earth, and the underworlds below" (ibid.:364). They were situated to cast shadows or catch the rays of the sun at the equinox. Public ceremonies were synchronized with the movement of heavenly bodies, making cosmic time palpable and elaborate calendar-keeping essential.

Within this ceremonial context, there were practices for paying debts and offering important sacrifices. Among the Aztecs, these ceremonies included human sacrifice.

> At the apex of the pyramid, contact point between the heavens and earth, the high priests reenacted the ur-scene of the giving and taking of human life. Victims – often illustrious war captives but also women and children – were bathed and prepared. The six priests who performed the sacrifice appeared on the pyramid dressed in large, colorful vestments, their bodies and faces painted. They adorned themselves like the god, 'whom they represented on that day.'
>
> (ibid.:361)

Naked, the sacrificial victims were led up the stairs of the temple. One special priest displayed for the victims an image of the god (*ixiptlatl*). Following a set formula, each victim was ritually slain as the high priest cut out the heart, held it up to the sun, and threw it to the image of Huitzilopochtli. The body of each victim was then thrown down the temple steps. Diane Taylor explains the concept behind a practice regarded as inhumane today:

> While the practice sounds cruel, it reflected the belief that there was no firm division between life and death. Being was not considered ontologically stable but in flux, a transitive condition between here and there. The sacrificial victims would be joining the gods, at times taking messages from those on earth, while the victims' energy and force would be transferred to others on earth through the donning of the skin. Notions of continuity and constantly recycling life forces, rather than cruelty or revenge, sustained these practices. The Mayas, for example, referred to certain forms of sacrifice as *ahil* (acts of creation).
>
> (ibid.:361–362)

Religious rites create a synergy between the divine and human realms. If the gods sacrificed themselves for humans as the world was formed, then the gods require similar sacrifices in return.

Sacrificial rites performed by divinely-ordained priests or kings maintained the social and cosmological orders mandated by the gods at the time of creation. Constant human sacrifice was therefore considered a necessity, manifesting the economic and military power of the state.

Sung dance-drama: The Mayan Rabinal Achi

There were two general types of overtly dramatic and theatrical performance among Mesoamericans. Comedic figures performed caricatures, ridiculing those who were ethnically different, and sung dance-drama (*mitote* in Nahuatl; *taqui* in Quechua) recounted and commemorated group and individual histories and past glories. We examine here a specific Mayan song-dance-drama, *Rabinal Achi*. We also will see in this an example of the Spanish suppression of indigenous systems of belief and cultural performances with Spain's conquest of the New World.

Rabinal Achi is a Quiché language song-dance still performed today in the highlands of Guatemala. It is known both as *Rabinal Achi*, meaning "Man of Rabinal," and *Xajoj Tun*, "Dance of the Trumpets" – a reference to the fact that during parts of the performance characters dance to the playing of trumpets. It is one of few extant plays with Mayan (rather than Spanish) dialog. *Rabinal Achi* relates and dances the story of conflict between the noble warriors and leaders of two indigenous Mayan city-states (Quiché and Rabinal) that reached a climax in the early fifteenth century, well before the arrival of the Spanish.

The first form of the Spanish invasion of the Guatemala highlands is known among Mayans as "the great death of the flesh" or "the sickness" because the coming of Europeans to these isolated peoples was accompanied by a smallpox epidemic

that struck in 1520. The Quiché were finally conquered by the Spanish in 1524, the Cakchiquel nation in 1530, and Rabinal in 1537.

The primary historical incident around which the performance score for *Rabinal Achi* evolved is the story of a famous Quiché king, Quicab – a member of the lineage of the house of Cawek of the Forest People. In the fourteenth and fifteenth centuries, Quicab ruled a confederation of the Rabinal, Cakchiquel, and Tzutuhil nations. While Quicab was away on a military campaign expanding his kingdom, there was a revolt at home. One of those involved was his fifth son, who may have been the historical figure on whom the character Cawek in the play is based.

In the play, the main characters are Lord Five Thunder – ruler of the mountaintop fortress of Rabinal, the Man of Rabinal (serving at his behest), who together uphold a traditional order, and the renegade who disrupts that order, Cawek, the son of the Lord of Quiché. All three wear distinctive helmet-masks and carry axes and shields, symbols of royal power (Figure 2.4). Cawek's father was a noble who fought alongside the neighboring city-state of Rabinal. Rabinal's boundaries are guarded by Eagle and Jaguar, priests in the service of Lord Five Thunder, whose names are taken from the source of their spiritual power to protect. At Lord Five Thunder's court resides his wife and his unmarried daughter, "Mother of Quetzal Feathers." Cawek becomes a renegade warrior when he betrays the people of Rabinal, causing much suffering. As the drama opens, Cawek has already betrayed his father's former allies and been captured by Man of Rabinal. The drama presents the confrontation between Man of Rabinal and Cawek in the context of Cawek's trial. Cawek remains defiant toward his captors throughout, but accepts death by beheading at the end of the drama. Before dying, he is allowed to view aspects of the world he will leave. He is shown the lovely daughter of Lord Five Thunder and dances depicting the beauty of nature.

Figure 2.4 Man of Rabinal similar to the eighth-century lord from the temple of the Inscriptions at Palenque (not depicted). He wears a feathered headdress, mask, short cape, and kilt, and carries an upraised axe and a small round shield. Drawing by Jamie Borowicz. © Dennis Tedlock.

As a representation of Mayan royalty and culture, *Rabinal Achi* does reflect some early history. But it is not an historical drama per se, but rather a commemorative ritual drama. It is a montage of fragments of royal stories from across six different generations, gathered into the confrontation between Man of Rabinal and Cawek. Generic character names allow the story and its examination of the power negotiations between rulers and city-states to remain open.

Episodes from the history of royal lineages were the subject of many other early pre-Spanish dramas. In all such plays, the actors represented the main characters through costuming and dancing, while dialog was sung or chanted by separate choruses to musical accompaniment.

After the Conquest, Spanish missionaries recognized that the participation of the people in annual cycles of ceremonial performances at which dramas like *Rabinal Achi* were performed had great meaning for the Maya. The Spanish attempted to suppress and/or alter the performances by a variety of means. They insisted that Christian hymns be substituted for Mayan songs, and eventually, as early as 1593 and as late as 1770, they issued bans against indigenous plays, "warning that representations of human sacrifices would lead to real ones" (Tedlock 2003:5). The Spaniards also introduced Christian biblical theatre from medieval Europe.

The first European play performed in the Americas, *The Final Judgment*, attributed to Andres de Olmos, was staged in Tlatelolco (*c.*1531–1533). It threatened natives with damnation in hell if they did not marry. Most significantly, Time appeared as a character. This Western European figure represented a "linear, universalizing force, antithetical to native understandings of cyclical motion." Also, death was "depicted as an individual fate" (Taylor 2004:369). As we have seen, the Mayan worldviews governing *Rabinal Achi* and other Mesoamerican indigenous performances were very different.

In order to save their performance of *Rabinal Achi* from censorship, Mayans separated the words of their play from its music, and removed "all but the main outlines of the original religious content from public view" (Tedlock 2003:2). Religious aspects of the performance today are the primary responsibility of the play's "Road Guide" (*K'amol B'e*) – the native ritual specialist, or priest-shaman whose prayers and offerings circumscribe and punctuate the performance.

Today's performance of *Rabinal Achi* offers some hints of what Mayan drama might have been like before the Spanish conquest. In the plays the Spanish had created since the middle ages, dramatizing battles between Moors and Christians (see the case study following this chapter), the characters danced in parallel files, confronting one another. In *Rabinal Achi* "when the actors dance, they move around the perimeter of a square, and when they promenade they move in a circle. These pathways locate them all in one world . . ." (ibid.:14). The Mayans' counter-clockwise movements within a square, together with their temporal marking of the 260 days of the divinatory calendar during which Cawek says farewell to his homeland by moving "on all four edges/in all four corners," suggests the distinctive rhythms of the Mayan calendar. In the Spanish plays, when Moors confront Christians or Indians confront Spaniards, their costumes are from two different worlds – one "evil" and the other "good." In *Rabinal Achi*, both Cawek and his captors dress alike, and their arguments are shaped by a shared, rather than

opposite, set of values. In *Rabinal Achi*, one of the opponents may be misguided or wrong but he is not, as in the dramas of the Moors and Indians, "evil" or living in "falsehood."

The aesthetic conventions governing performances of *Rabinal Achi* are presentational – not representational or realistic. The audience is located on four sides of the playing space. The drama unfolds. The actors deliver lengthy speeches as solos, similar to the renderings of ancient Mayan court songs. There is no fast-paced realistic dialog, and actors never attempt a conversational tone. The main characters narrate more events from the past than they re-enact in the dramatic present (reminiscent of the style of the Japanese noh theatre – see Chapter 3). When Rabinal captures Cawek by "roping" him with the rope he wears around his waist, he does not realistically lasso him, but rather, as the two remain still, a stage assistant appears and ties the end of the rope carried by Rabinal around Cawek. Toward the conclusion of the play, when Cawek is to die by beheading, he simply kneels, and other characters dance around him. In a simple and unhurried manner, those with axes simply bring them toward but not to Cawek's neck. Immediately following his "beheading," Cawek stands, and joins the other dancers in a final collective dance. It is as if he and all the other characters were ghosts again, returning to the parallel world, where they lead lives visible only to dreamers. Shoulder to shoulder, they dance westward until they reach the foot of the steps leading to the door of the cemetery chapel. There the actors all kneel, and the Road Guide leads them in a prayer to their ancestors (ibid.:19). According to Tedlock, today's Mayan actors are speaking to and for their ancestors as much as anyone else, including all those who ever acted in the play. Acting in this play is not so much a matter of impersonating historical individuals – as if their lives could be relived in realistic detail – as it is a matter of impersonating their ghosts. All the ghosts except Cawek are thought to have their home in a cave beneath the ruins on

Red Mountain, where they remember what they did when their bones wore flesh (ibid.:14–15).

The figure of Road Guide maintains links between the present and past. He visits the ruins each day, making burnt offerings to the original spirits and "praying for permission to make their memories visible and audible in the waking world" (ibid.:15). During the play, it is revealed that Cawek secretly laid a curse on Rabinal land, a curse understood to be still in effect today. So each time Cawek mentions a place at which he stopped, Road Guide says prayers and burns offerings to counteract the curse as the performance continues.

Mayan texts

A system of writing was independently invented among native peoples in Mesoamerica, most likely in southern Mexico, around 600 B.C.E. but the Mayans never used their own system of writing to record what performers spoke in their performances. It was only in the sixteenth century, under the influence of Christian missionaries that Mayans wrote down "texts" like *Rabinal Achi* in their own language, using the Roman alphabet. The missionaries had created handwritten scripts for the European Bible and saints plays that they introduced, translating some speeches into local Mayan languages. Under the guidance of the missionaries, Mayas wrote out some plays such as *Rabinal Achi*. This was new. These alphabetic texts contained details and content never included in the older Mayan hieroglyphic texts. Tedlock attributes these differences not to alphabetic writing per se, but to the fact that indigenous authors were responding to the missionary suppression of their performances and "the destruction of hieroglyphic texts". Therefore, "they sought to conserve the audible words of endangered performances for which those books provided prompts" (ibid.:158). Their "texts" of the sixteenth century were, then, written as records of oral performances and, according to Tedlock, are more like "a set of program notes than

a libretto" (ibid.:158). They are not single-author works but collectively created, mnemonic records of performance. The earliest of these "texts" followed an oral model that participants would have elaborated on in the moment of performance.

For Mesoamericans, such annual performances were necessary to sustain the universe and their place within it. Performances such as *Rabinal Achi* were commemorative, not representational in the western sense, in which a performance was long thought to have only a secondary authenticity, deriving from a text. In many extant fiestas and celebrations throughout the Americas (such as those on the Day of the Dead), such performances continue this tradition in which commemorative performances are understood to do something fundamental in the world.

Texts in other traditions

In other religious traditions, such as Confucianism, Buddhism, Hinduism, Islam, and Christianity, people saw themselves as communities bound less by ethnicity and geography than by language and sacred, written script (Anderson 1983:20). Texts held the truths fundamental to communities (Chinese, Pali, Sanskrit, Arabic, Latin). We conclude our discussion of commemorative religious drama in this chapter by examining the liturgies and "dramas" produced within two monotheistic traditions originating in the Middle East – Christianity and Islam. Each was founded on the notion that God acted in human history through a specific individual – Jesus Christ and Muhammad, respectively. In the case of Christianity, Jesus (4? B.C.E.–C.E. 29?) was one of the sons of Mary and her carpenter-husband, Joseph, Aramaic-speaking Jewish residents who lived in the semi-pagan village of Nazareth, within the area known as Galilee (Palestine). Jesus was proclaimed by his followers to be the "anointed one" or the new "messiah." In the case of Islam, Muhammad (*c.*C.E. 570–632) was a merchant living in the city of Mecca (in today's Saudi Arabia), to whom, his followers believe, God chose to reveal his eternal message.

Medieval Christian liturgy and drama

When the Jewish people returned from exile in Babylon (586–538 B.C.E.) to their homeland in the volatile basin of the eastern Mediterranean, their trials and tribulations continued under a series of mostly foreign rulers. From 63 B.C.E., when the Roman general Pompey conquered Jerusalem, the area remained under either direct or indirect Roman rule until the end of the Roman Empire. When Jesus began to carry out his public ministry in Galilee, like John the Baptist before him, he was one of a number of contemporary Jewish prophets declaring the imminent arrival of a "new" kingdom of god. When he arrived in Jerusalem for a celebration of the Jewish Feast of the Passover with his followers, he extended his teaching and healing into an aggressive public protest by driving traders and moneychangers out of the main Jewish temple. He was arrested by the Roman authorities, put on trial, condemned to death, and crucified – a common mode of execution. Thrown into turmoil by Jesus's death, his small group of disciples gathered to share a memorial meal that recreated their last supper with Jesus and that commemorated his crucifixion and resurrection.

To the authorities of the period, whether Roman or Jewish, Jesus was a minor figure. According to Tacitus in his *Annals* (15.4, second century C.E.), "Christus" had been "sentenced to death by the procurator, Pontius Pilate, during the Reign of Tiberius." He was the leader of the "Christians," Tacitus writes, those who shared a

> detestable superstition . . . suppressed for awhile, spread anew not only in Judea where the evil had started, but also in Rome, where everything that is horrid and wicked in the world gathers and finds numerous followers.

Many such "enemies of mankind" were sentenced to death in the Roman public spectacles on the command of the Emperor Nero (*c.*C.E. 64; see Chapter 3).

For his followers, the period immediately after Jesus's death was fraught with uncertainty. Was the new "Kingdom of God" imminent? As decades, and years passed, and Jesus's death and resurrection receded further into the background, common worship among his followers evolved to mark the key events in his life and ministry. Christian liturgy came to focus on recreating the memorial meal (the Eucharist or "thanksgiving"), and Christ's suffering at the hands of the Roman authorities, his death, and his resurrection (the "Passion").

In spite of the dismissive attitude of authorities, followers of Christ grew in numbers. St. Paul (d. approximately C.E. 67) ministered to the new groups of non-Jewish believers throughout Greece, including the cities of Corinth and Ephesus. By the time of Paul's ministry, a very simple and informal Christian ceremony was being conducted in Greek – then the language of the eastern Mediterranean. It included readings from the "old law" of Moses as well as the "new law" of the Christian prophets, communal singing, perhaps a commentary by an elder in the community; and the blessing and distribution of bread and wine, as Christ had at his last supper with his disciples.

The conversion of the Roman Emperor Constantine to Christianity in C.E. 312 ended the persecution of the Christians and made Christianity the official religion of the Roman Empire. Although a service in Latin existed from the second century, with separate forms for the Syrian and Greek Orthodox Churches in the East, the Latin Mass, with its specific structure, did not become universal until the fifth century – the moment at which the vast Roman Empire was beginning to crumble in the face of invasions from the Goths and Lombards. Perhaps it was in the face of the collapse of world order as they knew it that Christian leaders fixed the order of the Mass and their symbolic vestments. By the sixth century, St. Gregory established a common form for the Mass throughout Western Europe, realized when his book of rules, *Sacramentary*, became the pattern for the Catholic Mass under the Frankish King Pepin in 754.

Just as European vernacular languages were developing (Spanish, French, Italian, etc.), the standard liturgy was being written and delivered in Latin. Since priests were coming largely from well-to-do families, they were educated in Latin and well versed in ancient literature. Knowledge of ancient rhetoric, poetry, drama (especially Roman drama, being accessible in Latin) was central to medieval thought. Drama was not equated with the excesses of theatrical spectacle during the days of the Roman Empire (Dox 2004:*passim*). This is exemplified in the adaptations from Terence's plays by Hrotsvitha (c.935–973), a noble lay member of the all-female Abbey of Gandersheim, in Saxony. Her writings in Latin included six plays, based on the comedies of the Roman playwright, Terence (see Chapter 3). Her adaptations put them to use for the personal discipline of young Christian women, especially for the suppression of female sexuality in favor of virginity. The plays may well have been intended for reading, reflection, and semi-dramatic recitation, rather than performance.

Dramatic and performative elements related to the Latin liturgy

For lay Christians of the ninth through the twelfth centuries, the "Word of God" came to them not via printed texts but through other media, including homilies (sermons in the Mass), visual symbolism (the sacrificial Christ as the lamb of God), and the visual narratives of stained-glass windows and church wall paintings. Embodied modes of worship were developed, such as prayerful processions to the "stations of the cross," depictions in the churches of episodes in the sequence of Christ's suffering including Christ carrying the Cross, Christ being nailed to the Cross, his death, and the removal of his body for burial. The liturgy manifested and commemorated the saving "acts" of Christ, prefigured in the Old Testament and played out in the

New. Early in the tenth century, inventive clergy in monasteries that were centers of learning and the arts, such as the Benedictine Abbey of Fleury in France, began elaborating on key moments of the liturgy to heighten devotion among both cloistered communities and lay congregations.

Interpolations were added to the Mass for special occasions and to the cycle of community prayers known as the Divine Office that marked the stages of the day from sunrise to midnight. Amalarius, Bishop of Metz, used a service for the consecration of a new church as an occasion for "remembering" one important moment in the sacred history of Christ known as the Harrowing of Hell. Christ is believed to have descended into hell after his "death" on the cross to release righteous souls from the devil. When the Bishop, representing Christ, knocked on the doors of the new church, this was understood as symbolizing Christ's knocking on the gates of Hell. The devil (played by a clergyman) appeared to defy the Bishop, but when the doors were opened, the devil fled, and the edifice was purged of any evil.

By the tenth century, melodies taken from Greek and Jewish originals were standardized within Pope Gregory the Great's *Antiphonarium*. Known as psalmody, these melodies were attached to liturgical texts as plain chant and responsorial – a question and answer form in which the text was divided between a single singer (*cantor*) and the remainder of the community (*decani responsores*). Such musical elaboration eventually allowed for harmony and ornamentation – melismatic chant – in which the final syllable of a text was elaborated with forty or more notes. Eventually, further small pieces of text were added to expand a melody through responsorial singing – *tropes*.

[T]ropes encouraged rhythmical and emotional variations which reflected the mood of a text – where the material was sad the syllables could be prolonged, where it was joyful they could be sharp and lively. . . . So it became possible to reflect the emotional and physical action of the text in the music, and the musical characterization of any biblical personage whose words were being sung became almost inevitable.

(Harris 1992:27)

Early tropes in the tenth century set to music a biblical passage of key importance to Christians. It begins, "*Quem Queritis in sepulchre, Christicolae,*" meaning "Whom do you seek in the tomb, followers of Christ?" The words, sung in plainchant, are those of an angel greeting the three Marys, including Jesus's mother, who came to the tomb to which Christ had been taken after his crucifixion in order to properly anoint his body. The women reply, "Jesus of Nazareth who was crucified, heavenly ones." The angel's reply is of supreme importance for the young Christian community: "He is not here. He is risen." This is the first confirmation of Christ's resurrection from the dead, which for Christians carries with it the possibility of redemption for all humankind (the episode is related in Matthew 28:1–7 and Mark 16:1–7). Many versions of the sung text exist. Sometimes they were performed as part of verses in the introductory portion of the Easter morning Mass and sometimes in an earlier prayer service at midnight, heightening the drama of the discovery of the empty tomb and Christ's defeat of death.

> At the second hour after midnight on Easter morning, the bells of the abbey were set joyfully ringing. The great Paschal Candle was lifted onto the altar, and six smaller lighted candles were added to it, three on each side. . . . The bells still continued to ring, whilst a procession formed at the altar and travelled round the building, eventually returning to the 'sepulchre' . . . [where] two acolytes concealed inside the structure, representing the angels at the tomb, sang in Latin . . . 'Whom do you seek in the

sepulchre, Christian women?' The two singing deacons replied . . . 'Jesus of Nazareth who was crucified, heavenly ones' . . . [To which the angels replied] 'He is not here. He has risen as predicted. Go! Proclaim the news that he has risen from the tomb!' A priest dressed in a white alb then emerged from the sepulchre carrying the special Easter chalice containing the *Corpus Christi*, or 'body of Christ'.

(ibid.:29–30)

In the tenth century, the Bishop of Winchester wrote out detailed instructions for the performing of this scene in Benedictine monasteries. Other tropes were soon used for other holy seasons, including the celebration of Christ's birth. While moving and dramatic, tropes were not dramas per se, but allowed a heightened experience of personal/collective worship and devotion commemorating Christ.

Biblical dramas, Latin and vernacular

As early as the tenth century, a few stories associated with Christ's birth were being dramatized in Latin within churches, but perhaps not as part of the liturgy proper. Early biblical plays in Latin dramatized the visit of the shepherds to the manger to see the newly-born Christ, performed on Christmas morning, and the visit of the Magi – the wise men or Three Kings who bring gifts to the Christ child, performed on the 6 January. By the end of the eleventh century, the *Procession of the Prophets* was being performed, based on a popular sermon from the fifth or sixth century. After the initial spectacle of a musical procession, costumed priests playing Old Testament prophets, including Isaiah, Jeremiah, Daniel, and Moses, stepped forward to deliver their prophecies of the coming of Christ. The monastery of Benedictbeuren in Bavaria combined the prophets play with its Christmas plays.

One of the most sophisticated examples of Bible music-drama in Latin is *The Play of Daniel*, derived from the Old Testament story of Daniel in the lion's den. It was performed in the cathedral of Beauvais sometime during the Christmas season in the twelfth and thirteenth centuries. Here the prophet Daniel from the Old Testament prefigures the Messiah. In this play, there are at least nine opportunities for processions through the cathedral, making use of harps, zithers, and drums to accompany chant singing. Daniel sings a musically-compelling passage in which he deciphers the mysterious handwriting on the wall that predicts the fall of King Belshazzar. (*The Play of Daniel* and *The Play of Herod*, another Latin music-drama based in scripture, were staged and recorded by the New York Pro Musica in the mid-twentieth century. See the list of references following this chapter.) The scenes in *The Play of Daniel* and other early music-dramas were staged on elevated platforms set up in the open spaces of the cathedrals (there were no fixed pews), such as the nave or in the choir or chancel – spaces near the altar for the choir and clergy. These platforms, sometimes designated in Latin as *mansions*, were not self-contained, illusionistic stages. Actors moved freely from one mansion to another, using the common floor area, referred to in some stage directions as the *platea*. This was, in effect, a neutral, unlocalized playing area, with mansions bordering it, that could be whatever the text required at a given moment; the actor's lines identified locale and atmosphere for the audience. It carried over into the later vernacular Bible plays staged outside the church. The fluid, open stage that Shakespeare later wrote for was somewhat indebted to this staging tradition.

During the later twelfth century, the biblical plays began to be written in vernacular languages and performed outside churches. These were still based on incidents in the Old or New Testaments but were more dramatic in structure and inventive in characterization. An important early example is *The Play of Adam* (c.1150) from Norman France. It dramatizes the fall of Adam and Eve in the garden of Eden and the story of their sons, Cain and Abel. The detailed

stage directions make clear that it was performed adjacent to a church or cathedral, and the stage directions provide many details about scenic décor, costuming, and acting.

During the fourteenth century, there was a flowering of vernacular Bible drama. One reason was the institution of the new Feast of Corpus Christi in 1311 by Pope Clement V, widely observed by 1350. It was created to celebrate the importance and meaning of the priest's consecration at Mass of the bread and wine, understood to become, by virtue of that consecration, the actual body and blood of Christ, as established by Christ at the last supper. The feast of Corpus Christi was created to celebrate the redemptive power of this sacrament and the presence of Christ in the world in general. It was observed near Trinity Sunday, between late May and late June. In a common Corpus Christi ritual, priests processed through the city displaying the "Host," a consecrated wafer encased in a vessel known as monstrance, signifying the real presence of Christ. The procession of the Host was often accompanied by tableaux of biblical scenes representing Christian sacred history and testifying to the humanity of Christ. In this way, the "cycle plays" may have developed. In Paris in 1313, actors began to recite the story of the Passion – the events leading up to and including Christ's crucifixion and resurrection – as part of the living tableaux. Short speeches were introduced in Innsbruck, Austria, in 1391 with the appearance of Adam, Eve, and the twelve disciples of Christ. By 1394, sets of plays based on key biblical episodes providing a whole history of salvation – "cycle plays" – were being performed in York, England, using pageant wagons (see Figure 2.5).

The flowering was also possible because of the growth of towns as entities independent of feudal lords, and the development of the medieval trade guilds – the bakers, tailors, and goldsmiths who trained apprentices and regulated wages and working conditions. Many guilds undertook charitable projects, including the sponsorship of plays. A Noah's

Figure 2.5 Pageant wagon of Christ's nativity, with tableaux, in a procession in Brussels in 1615 for Queen Isabella. Painting by Dennis Van Alsoot. © the Board of Trustees of the Victoria and Albert Museum, London.

ark play would be produced by shipwrights or fishermen's guilds and the play of the three kings by the goldsmiths guild. At this point, religious, civic, and commercial motives were involved in the production of the religious plays. In communities like York and Chester, the annual cycles attracted numerous visitors and provided a major economic boost for the community. Some towns organized Bible plays to give thanks for their deliverance from the plague or other disasters. (A quarter of Europe's population died of the "Black Death" between 1347 and 1350.) The Catholic community of Oberammergau in the Bavarian Alps began to perform its Passion Play in 1634 in fulfillment of a pledge to God that if the plague would cease, they would perform a play on Christ's sufferings every ten years. This the village has done, with few exceptions,

until the present, with various script changes since the 1960s to remove anti-Semitic passages.

Among the stories the vernacular Bible plays dramatized were those of the creation of the world; the building of Noah's Ark; Abraham's sacrifice of his son; the Nativity, with the visits of the shepherds and the Magi; Herod's attempt to slay the new child-king by dispatching his army to slay all newborn children; Christ's raising of his friend, Lazarus, from the dead; and Christ's crucifixion and resurrection. Forty-eight plays survive in manuscript from York, the longest of which is 546 lines and the shortest 86. Thirty-two plays survive from Wakefield, and 25 from Chester. Not being attached to the liturgy as such, vernacular Bible dramas of all types combined instruction with dramatic freedom, creating local characters and providing comic humor. God talks like one's neighbor, shepherds suffer from oppressive landlords, and Noah's wife seriously doubts her husband's big ark project. The plays are episodic and certainly not Aristotelian, mixing comedy and tragedy and held together by the frame of God's plan of salvation, more heavenly in their logic than historical or chronological. They abound in anachronisms. At Christ's birth, King Herod can swear by the Trinity. Some plays reflect the then-common anti-Semitism: Jews were blamed for Christ's death.

Where pageant wagons were used, they provided stages for the tableaux in the processions and/or for performances at certain stations along the way in the processions ("processional staging"). In some cases, some of the wagons might have been moved into some contiguous staging arrangement, perhaps adjacent to a large platform, a city square, or a green, which would have provided a neutral playing area – a *platea*. More than a single 12ft wide pageant wagon certainly would have been necessary for the final play of the Chester cycle on the Last Judgment, in which Christ appears to determine the fate of the souls of all humankind. The action requires four contiguous mansions, including Heaven, Hell, and Earth, and 20 characters. It is not clear that all the plays in these surviving manuscripts were played in these cities in every year; the manuscripts were written by different hands at different times. One disputed source for the city of Chester says its 25 plays were played over three days.

Some vernacular religious plays were performed on fixed stages and over several days. The illuminations and stage directions of the text for the 1547 performance of the Mystère de la Passion in Valencienne, France, indicates elaborate fixed stage arrangements that allowed complex scenic spectacles, including the descent of an angel, flying devils, and the ascension of Christ into the clouds with angels. The late sixteenth-century Passion Play at Lucerne, Switzerland, was performed in the city's Weinmarkt over two days. The three-part Cornish play known as the Cornish *Ordinalia* used mansions in a circular arrangement, perhaps within a circular earthen embankment, and it played over three days.

Other Christian religious plays

Vernacular religious dramas of other kinds included saint's plays, devoted to the lives of the saints, especially their miracles, and the morality plays, probably derived from sermons given by the clergy to elaborate important points from the day's scriptural readings. One of the earliest morality plays was authored by Hildegard of Bingen (1098–1179), a learned and gifted Benedictine mystic, abbess, healer, and author. She experienced a set of profound religious visions about which she wrote at length. Her creative musical output included the composition of 77 songs and a musical morality play, *Ordo Virtutum* (*c*.1155). Like her songs, the *Ordo* was probably composed and written for performance by nuns within her convent, and therefore not performed for a general public. Drawing upon the fourth-century Latin work by Prudentius, *Psychomachia*, this sung-drama features the battle for a human soul between the forces of evil and 16 personified virtues. A late example of the saint's play genre is the play *Mary Magdalene* (late fifteenth century), which dramatizes incidents, scriptural and apocryphal, in the life of the fallen woman saved by Christ, who came to be Jesus's follower. Its staging required a large cast, several mansions, including heaven and hell, and a wheeled ship on which Mary Magdalene sails around the *platea* to several destinations. The play includes Jesus and Peter alongside several allegorical characters like those in the morality plays, including Pride, Lechery, Flesh, and Curiosity.

Morality plays developed widely during the fourteenth century. Allegorical in nature, the publicly-performed plays were locally produced by groups of citizens, sometimes elaborately. They usually focused on an "everyman" figure who faced a choice between good and bad behavior. This idea of the Christian "in conflict" is taken from St. Paul:

Put on the whole armour of God, that ye may be able to stand against the wiles of the devil. For we wrestle not against flesh and blood, but against principalities, against powers, against the rules of the darkness of this world, against spiritual wickedness in high places.

(Ephesians 6:11–12)

Since God had given humankind "free will" to choose good or evil, the individual who chose badly would suffer the consequences – damnation and the fires of Hell. In *The Castle of Perseverance* (*c.*1475, Figure 2.6) the main character, Mankind, is seduced by the Bad Angel who tells him there will be time in old age to be virtuous. Mankind then encounters a wide range of allegorical characters who attempt to influence him. They include the Seven Deadly Sins, the figures of Conscience, Confession, and Penance, and the Virtues, including Meekness,

Patience, Charity, and Chastity. At his trial before God, Mercy and Peace plead for him against Righteousness and Truth. God judges mercifully in the end.

Dramas of Christian conquest: "In this sign"

A sense of "struggle" has been part of Christian history since its inception as a millenarian religion. In the first centuries the struggle was for survival of communities of believers in an overtly hostile climate. Once established as the religion of the Roman Empire, the struggle turned within, where factions fought over interpretations of doctrine, for control of decision-making power at formative church councils, or, externally, for control of civil power. As medieval western Christian power was eventually concentrated in Rome and in the figure of a pope, the Church constructed the idea of the

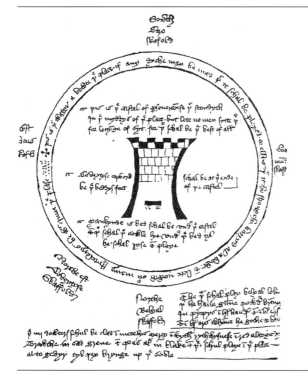

Figure 2.6 Plan of the mansions and playing area for the morality play, *The Castle of Perseverance*, c.1450, possibly for a performance in an ancient earthen round. Mankind's castle is at center, the location of the five mansions is indicated outside the circle, and the direction within the double circles reads: "This is the water about the place [*platea*], if any ditch be made where it shall be played, or else let it be strongly barred all about." © The Folger Shakespeare Library.

"Holy Land," that set of sites where sacred history had unfolded – and it became a site of Christian pilgrimage.

From the eleventh century, it also became a site of bitter, bloody struggle for power and ascendancy in a series of engagements eventually described as the "Crusades." (The term first appeared in Spain in the thirteenth century.) In these wars, Christian Europe sought to "liberate" Jerusalem from the Muslim "infidels."

> 'Crusade' has from the beginning been a floating, highly mobile and adaptive term, precisely denoting very little but replete with connotations. It has always been a versatile theory. Popes championed a useful concept that allowed them to declare a holy war on any individual or group, proscribing them as enemies of Christ. There were holy wars against Muslim infidels; against heretics like the Albigensians of Provence; against recalcitrant Christian monarchs; even against humble towns that failed to toe the papal line. But the first category, war against the Muslim infidel, was always popularly regarded as the true war 'for and by the Cross.' Sanctified war was an innovation within the Christian Church, which had for centuries struggled to impose the peace of God upon adversaries.
>
> (Wheatcroft 2004:187)

The sense of holy empowerment and the accompanying evangelistic zeal to conquer under the "sign of the cross" exemplified the spirit of the Crusades. It ignited the re-conquest of the Iberian peninsula in which Arab Islamicists who had occupied it for centuries were defeated. It also fired the first Spanish and Portuguese quests to conquer and colonize – Spain to the West (the Americas) and Portugal to the East (India and beyond). This expansionism was fed in part by a complex set of social/civic performances of privilege and power embedded in the growth and

expansion of medieval chivalry – a set of practices that performed heroic and romantic gestures in song, jousting, and court pageantry.

When Christian kingdoms began to re-conquer the Iberian peninsula and/or colonize the world, a variety of dramas of conquest resulted. In some, western Christian modes of performance were imposed on indigenous populations, as happened in Mesoamerica. The second case study in this chapter analyzes one from a genre of dramas of conquest that involved battles between the Christians and the Moors.

Even as the newly emergent kingdoms of Europe colonized much of the world, secular drama and performances, long suppressed or controlled by church or civic authorities, gradually gained ascendancy under newfound royal patronage. Moralities, for example, were taken up by small professional companies of five or six who performed them in court banqueting halls. Eventually called interludes, these performances became common at banquets. Biblical dramas were being suppressed by the latter half of the sixteenth century, due in part because of the struggle between Catholics and emergent militant Protestantism. King Henry VIII's split with the Roman Catholic Church effectively ended the Bible play tradition in England, although Shakespeare seems to be remembering a performance of a *Play of Herod* in Hamlet's speech of advice to the players. The morality plays, less explicitly tied to Catholic doctrine and traditions, died a slower death. They provided some reference point for the development of secular plays, written by individual authors for public stages. Theatre, religion, and the state, once closely bound together in western history, were evolving toward new and often conflicting relationships.

Islamic commemorative mourning "dramas": The Ta'zieh of Iran

"Islam" is an Arabic word meaning submission to God. In the Islamic tradition, God revealed his message to Muhammad in a series of visions from

612 B.C.E. For Muslims the Qur'an is nothing less than the transmission in simple, clear Arabic language, of a divine archetype that is kept in Heaven for eternity, and is graven on the "guarded Tablet." It was that archetype that was directly revealed to Muhammad. Muhammad said he did nothing except transmit the message of Allah, adding and removing nothing. Muhammad probably did not read and would have transmitted what he received orally. The word "Qur'an" is from a verb originally meaning "vocal recitation." It was only after 622 that some of Muhammad's disciples began to inscribe fragments of what they heard onto bits of leather. After the Prophet's death, the Qur'anic revelations were gathered into a number of corpora, collected by the first Caliph, Abu Bakr. For several centuries, written versions provided little more than a guide to memory for repeating aloud a text already memorized.

Muslims consider the Qur'an a record of the precise words God spoke to Muhammad. Copying the Qur'an is therefore writing down the divine words of God. As the writing of the Qur'an grew in significance, possessing a copy of this holy book meant possessing God's very words. The Qur'an has great poetic power, is essentially abstract, and unlike the stories of Jesus or Rama (see Chapter 3), only rarely refers to specific places.

Given the importance of the sanctifying act of writing down divine words, the most esteemed art in Islam is calligraphy, an art that evolved historically as different styles of script evolved (Figure 2.7). Since Islam generally prohibits representation of living or dead people in order to maintain a clear distinction between the Creator and the created, the Qur'an is never illustrated, but it can be illuminated. Each of its 114 chapters can be marked by a decorative heading, and marginal roundels guide one's reading, indicating places for required ritual prostration. The main decorative elements of Islamic illumination are geometric vegetal patterns and interlacements.

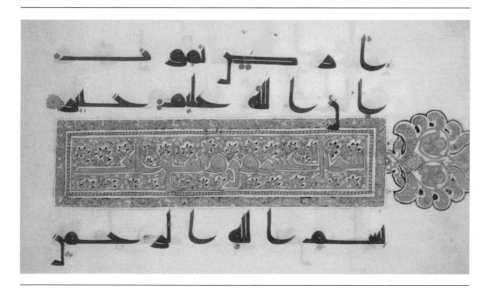

Figure 2.7 Qur'an fragment, showing the heading for Chapter 32, "The Prostration" (al-Sajda). Arabic text in kufic script on vellum. Ninth century C.E. Near East, possibly Iraq. © the Trustees of the Chester Beatty Library, Dublin.

Secular Islamic books often do contain illustrations or illuminations. Sultans, shahs, princes, and members of the aristocracy or wealthy merchants throughout the Islamic world valued manuscripts highly. From at least the ninth century onwards, two attributes of royalty in Iran were maintaining a library and patronage of fine manuscripts, and Persian princes themselves were often artists or calligraphers. Other non-representational arts such as poetry, music, and dance also flourished under the patronage of Islamic rulers.

Commemorative mourning rituals and the development of Ta'zieh

When Muhammad died in 632, the Muslim community faced a crisis over his successor as caliph or iman (spiritual and temporal ruler). Those who believe that the Prophet had passed special, divine knowledge to his son-in-law and cousin Ali, supported Ali and his descendents. They were called Shi'a (members of the Shi'i sect). However, others (members of the Sunni sect) held that the succession should fall to the best person, not necessarily a direct relative of Muhammad. After the murders of Ali's father and older brother, Ali's son, Husayn, led a rebellion to regain control. But Husayn, his family, and followers were surrounded by the opposing army on the plain of Karbala (in present day Iraq). On the tenth day of Muharram in the Islamic year 61 (10 October 680), after ten battle-filled days without water in which all the males – except a single small boy – were massacred, Husayn himself was killed and the women taken captive.

The two main branches of Islam – Sunni and Shi'i – reflect the historical and theological struggle over succession of the Prophet. Most followers of Shi'i Islam live in present-day Iran, Iraq, Yemen, and Bahrain, with smaller communities in India, Pakistan, Bangladesh, and Afghanistan. The Sunnis constitute about 85–90 percent of the world's Muslim population and live in the Middle East, North Africa, Central Asia, and Indonesia.

For Shi'i Muslims, the first month of the Muslim lunar calendar, Muharram, soon became a period for performing mourning rituals to commemorate the moment when Husayn, his family, and followers were martyred. Since at least the tenth century, ritual processions in Baghdad featured mourners with black-painted faces and disheveled hair, singing songs of lamentation and beating their chests in mourning. Acts of self-flagellation have remained a central part of participants' identification with the martyred Husayn to the present day. In the area that is today known as Iran, the term Ta'zieh (Persian meaning "condolence" or "expression of grief") began to be used as early as the Safavid dynasty (1200–1786) to refer to commemorative rituals marking Husayn's death. When Persia became a separate nation in the sixteenth century and adopted Shi'i Islam as the state religion, these rituals received royal patronage.

Around the middle of the eighteenth century, Ta'zieh began to take the shape of dramatic, commemorative festivals born from older mourning rituals. The events surrounding Husayn's martyrdom form the narrative core recounted in these commemorative dramas. During the first ten days of Muharram, a cycle of ten Ta'zieh plays is performed, one each day. Each chronicles a single episode of the brutal events, or focuses on the heroic deaths of specific members of Husayn's family and followers. The only prescribed play is the death of Husayn – always performed on the tenth day. Observances often continue through the remainder of the month of Muharram and into the month of Safar, specifically to mourn the torment of Husayn's female relatives taken as captives to Damascus. Some communities perform less ornate Ta'ziehs not necessarily about the events of Karbala throughout the year.

Non-representational "reading" and representation in Ta'zieh

Ta'zieh was originally performed at a cross-roads or in other outdoor areas. By the early nineteenth century, special performance spaces (Takiyeh) were built for Ta'zieh. Some staging elements may be remnants of pre-Islamic entertainments and rituals, including a mourning ritual for the legendary prince Siyavosh, a sinless hero unjustly killed, like Husayn.

Ta'zieh is performed in the round, with a raised central platform surrounded by a huge circular, sand-covered space used for spectacular effects, such as equestrian events and foot battles. Additional raised stages erected around the edges of the circular space are used for subplots, enemy camps, or special scenes. These often extend into the audience area. Corridors stretch from the central stage through the audience so that messengers and processions of horses, camels, and vehicles can pass. Battle scenes can surround the entire audience. Audience and performers alike are immersed in a whirling, centrifugal experience of tumultuous action, songs, music, recitations, and battles (Figure 2.8).

Properties and costumes are simple and sometimes symbolic. A basin of water represents the Euphrates River. Protagonists wear green or white and sing in lyrical Persian chants, while the antagonists wear red and declaim in a fierce, uncouth manner. Women's roles are played by veiled males dressed in black. Some characters, such as demons, are masked.

Ta'zieh participant-performers are not "actors" who represent characters. They do not memorize lines. Rather, they are "readers" who sing or recite in a non-realistic manner from segments of the script held in hand. Like many forms of commemorative

Figure 2.8 A nineteenth-century performance of Ta'zieh. In the 1870s, the Takiyeh Dowlat was erected in Tehran in the Royal Compound. Its walls, canvas ceiling, and circular stage were copied in takiyehs and husseinyehs all over the country. Tehran 1976 (after Kemalal-Mulk's paintings. Photo © Peter Chelkowski.)

ritual-drama, Ta'zieh has all the trappings of "theatre," as westerners would understand the term, but it is not theatre. Rather, it is a participatory, epic re-enactment of an historical event that makes the past present for Shi'ite participants and spectators. To participate in Ta'zieh is to participate in a deeply religious event filled with intense grief, mourning, and lamentation. Husayn's martyrdom at Karbala exemplified supreme self-sacrifice, human suffering, and a profound act of divine redemption. The pain participants inflict on themselves is the pain of Husayn.

Ta'zieh ties contemporary Iranians to their complex past, reminding them of their intimate connection with Husayn and the Shi'a battle of resistance against a powerful, alien invader. For those who participate, Ta'zieh brings the past into the present, and the site of performance becomes the physical locus of martyrdom.

Summary discussion

In this chapter we examined two early forms of drama and theatre – commemorative religious/ritual "drama" in Egypt, Mesoamerica, medieval Christian Europe, Persia (Iran), and literary drama in Athens. Several striking commonalities exist among these diverse forms of early drama and theatre. Most involve the physical act of processing in the context of a religious festival. Processions incorporate a specific local topography, and usually inscribe onto that locale a cosmic, sacred geography. Processions are a means of including huge numbers of people in an activity with a common purpose – the annual celebration of a deity or a specific act of devotion. Processions are also a means of reminding all that the act of celebration or devotion is set aside in a special frame, a "time out of time." They are also spectacles, offering a means of elaborating key symbols associated with a god or cosmic power. They bring private symbols into the public domain, offering the community at large an opportunity for individual or group celebration and/or devotion.

As we have seen, commemorative religious/ritual dramas are a means to an end – providing spectator-participants or devotees with immediate and synesthetic encounters with the cosmic/divine in a ritual/religious context. Other examples of commemorative drama include Ramlila and Raslila in India (see Chapter 3), Tibetan Buddhist Cham, and the closely related Mani-Rimdu, performed by the Sherpas of Nepal (Jerstad 1969). While there are often elements of humor, satire, or comic caricature within religious/ritual dramas or a festival, as a whole, these moments enhance or reinforce divine and/or civic authority. "Drama" or "theatre" then are not wholly adequate terms to describe such a diverse set of commemorative religious/ritual practices. While many forms of commemorative religious/ritual drama continue to exist today, others were lost with the collapse of such great early civilizations as Egypt, or when western colonial powers suppressed the commemorative rites of indigenous peoples, as in Meso- and Native America.

In the context of fifth-century Athens, the earliest forms of dialogic literary dramas were invented for performance as part of religious festivals honoring Dionysus. Greek comedy and tragedy, as well as the physical theatres within which they were performed, were transformed in both Rome (see Chapter 3) and the renaissance. In the renaissance, the dialogic dramas of Athens, Aristotle's *Poetics*, the Roman poet Horace's *Ars Poetica* (*c.*19 B.C.E.), and Vitruvius's studies of the architecture of Greco-Roman theatres (*c.*15 B.C.E.) were "re-discovered" and deployed in the academy in the service of humanism's project of demonstrating the reasoned ordering of knowledge of a well-ordered world. Nothing to do with Dionysus.

PZ

Key references

Anderson, B. (1983) *Imagined Communities*, London: Verso.

Beeman, W.O. (1982) *Culture, Performance and Communication in Iran*, Tokyo: Institute for the Study of Languages and Cultures of Asia and Africa.

Bevington, D. (1975) *Medieval Drama*, Boston: Houghton Mifflin Company.

Case, S.E. (1985) "Classic drag: the Greek creation of female parts," *Theatre Journal*, 37:317–327.

Chelkowski, P.J. (1979) *Ta'ziyeh Ritual and Drama in Iran*, N.Y.: New York University Press.

Connerton, P. (1989) *How Societies Remember*, Cambridge: Cambridge University Press.

Dox, D. (2004) *The Idea of the Theater in Latin Christian Thought*, Ann Arbor: University of Michigan Press.

Falassi, A. (ed.) (1987) *Time Out of Time: Essays on the Festival*, Albuquerque: University of New Mexico Press.

Fischer, S.R. (2001) *A History of Writing*, London: Reaktion Books.

Fletcher, J. (2002) *The Egyptian Book of Living and Dying*, London: Duncan Baird Publishers.

Foley, H.P. (1981) "The Concept of Women in Athenian Drama," in H.P. Foley (comp.) *Reflections on Women in Antiquity*, London: Gordon and Breach.

Frankfort, H. (1948) *Ancient Egyptian Religion*, N.Y.: Harper & Row.

Gaster, T. (1950) *Thespis, Ritual, Myth and Drama in the Ancient Near East*, New York: Henry Schuman.

Gellius, A. (1927) *The Attic Nights of Aulus Gellius*, trans. J.C. Rolfe, Cambridge, Mass.: Harvard University Press.

Goldhill, S. (1990) "The Great Dionysia and Civic Ideology," in J.J. Winkler and F.I. Zeitlin (eds) *Nothing to Do with Dionysus? Athenian Drama in Its Social Context*, Princeton: Princeton University Press.

Harris, J.W. (1992) *Medieval Theatre in Context*, London: Routledge.

Izeki, M. (1998) "The Aztec ritual sacrifices," *Performance Research*, 3:25–32.

Jerstad, L.G. (1969) *Mani-Rimdu: Sherpa Dance-Drama*, Seattle: University of Washington Press.

Shah, I. (2000) *The Oxford History of Ancient Egypt*, Oxford: Oxford University Press.

Taylor, D. (2004) "Scenes of cognition: performance and conquest," *Theatre Journal*, 56:353–372.

Tedlock, D. (1985 [2nd edn 1996]) *Popul Vuh: The Mayan Book of the Dawn of Life*, N.Y.: Simon and Shuster

Tedlock, D. (2003) *Rabinal Achi: A Mayan Drama of War and Sacrifice*, Oxford: Oxford University Press.

Tydeman, W. (1978) *The Theatre in the Middle Ages*, Cambridge: Cambridge University Press.

Wheatcroft, A. (2004) *Infidels: A History of the Conflict Between Christendom and Islam*, New York: Random House.

Wiles, D. (2000) *Greek Theatre Performance: An Introduction*, Cambridge: Cambridge University Press.

Winkler, J.J. (1990) "The Ephebes' Song: *Tragoidia* and *Polis*," in J.J. Winkler and F.I. Zeitlin (eds) *Nothing to Do with Dionysus? Athenian Drama in Its Social Context*, Princeton: Princeton University Press.

Wise, J. (1998) *Dionysus Writes: The Invention of Theatre in Ancient Greece*, Ithaca: Cornell University Press.

Audio-visual resources

Anon. (1958) *The Play of Daniel*, New York Pro Musica, Noah Greenberg, musical director. Music transcribed by Bishop Rembert Weakland. Charles Bressler as Daniel and Russell Oberlin as the angels. Decca Records, DL 79402.

Anon. (1964) *The Play of Herod*, New York Pro Musica, Noah Greenberg, musical director. Scored by Noah Greenberg and staged by Nicholas Psacarpoulos. Brayton Lewis as Herod. Decca Records, DL 710,095–6.

CASE STUDY: Classical Greek theatre: Looking at *Oedipus*

Oedipus the King in classical Athens

Although the initial presentation of *Oedipus the King* cannot be dated with certainty, most historians assume that the play was staged in Athens in 427 B.C.E. Sophocles's (496–404) tragedy centers on a plague that is afflicting the ancient city of Thebes, where the play is set (Sophocles 1993:45). The citizens of Athens were just recovering from a plague that had ravaged their city in that year. The playwrights, performers, and producers in fifth-century Athens often presented plays that commented on current social and political problems. *Oedipus* would have fulfilled an expectation of the Athenian community. In the drama, King Oedipus must discover who killed Laius, the former king, in order to prevent the plague from killing more Thebians. Through keen detective work and his own memory, Oedipus learns that he himself was the killer and

that Laius was his father. Also in 427 B.C.E., the Athenians were fighting a war with Sparta, another Greek city-state, and they needed strong leaders who were not afraid to face the consequences of their past actions. *Oedipus* is partly a play about the need for leadership in the midst of a political crisis.

The tragedy is also about roots. In pursuit of the truth, Oedipus interviews characters from the many places of his past. He discovers the place that gave him birth and the womb that nurtured him. Believing at first that he was born in Corinth, Oedipus learns he was born in Thebes and that his wife Jocasta, the former Queen of King Laius, is also his mother (Figure 2.9). Recognizing his lack of true vision and knowledge, Oedipus blinds himself, prophesizes the barrenness of his two daughters, and seeks exile from Thebes. In *Oedipus the King*, as in many other Greek tragedies, people are tragically linked to place; Oedipus gains self-knowledge by

Figure 2.9 The scene on this fragmentary bowl (Sicily, c.330s) is evocative of the moment from the scene in *Oedipus the King* in which Jocasta (half covering her face) first realizes the truth. Oedipus's face (masked) is turned to the audience. In this positioning, he would not see his wife/mother's face and begin to recognize the implications of what he is telling her. © Syracuse Archeological Museum.

learning his true place in his family, his city, and in the Greek cosmos.

Ironically, classicists have much to say about Sophocles's use of place in the text of his tragedy, but they know little for certain about place and space in the initial staging of *Oedipus*. In the theatre today, architects, designers, and directors work to make sure that the spatial dynamics of a production – the interior of the theatre, the setting on stage, the blocking of the actors, their use of stage properties, and other spatial considerations – complement and amplify the emotions and meanings they wish to communicate to the audience. While the architecture, statuary, vases, and other remains of classical Greek civilization leave no doubt that the Athenians used space with great sophistication, there is little that can be said with certainty about the spatial dynamics of their theatrical productions. None of the surviving plays from this era – 44 in total, written by Aeschylus (*c*.543–456), Euripides (480–406), and Aristophanes (*c*.448–*c*.380) as well as Sophocles – include stage directions. The more than 1,500 plays from fifth century Greece that have vanished probably would have given us more clues about staging. Playwrights staged their own works during much of this period and so had no need to write out instructions for the performers. Also, a "play" was an outgrowth of an oral tradition and conceived for performance, not as a stand-alone literary text headed for print.

Nonetheless, we can draw some conclusions about staging from the remaining plays and from other ancient texts. Later writers noted that the Greeks were only allowed to use three actors, who might play several roles, for their dramatic contests. The text of *Oedipus the King* can be played by this number. Many plays also demand an interior, offstage space where the performers could change costumes and masks and prepare for entrances through double doors. Tableau representations of interior scenes could also be wheeled out through these doors on a wagon, called an *ekkyklema*. But what did the acting area look like, where was the nearby interior space, and how many doors did it contain? In *Oedipus*, as in several other plays, much of the action occurs around a significant set piece – an altar in the case of Sophocles's tragedy. This property may have been placed center stage, but the evidence for this is not conclusive. Like other Greek tragedies, *Oedipus* demands a performing chorus, probably fifteen dancers and singers led by the player of an *aulos*, a double pipe instrument that may have sounded like an oboe. Again, however, the surviving evidence does not permit the historian to reconstruct the sight and sound of the chorus in the initial production of *Oedipus* with accuracy. The best the historian can do in considering the possible staging of *Oedipus* in the fifth century is to put forward a hypothesis based on a careful reading of the play in the context of the culture and the physical evidence.

The physical evidence

The primary physical remains of the classical, fifth-century B.C.E. Greek theatre include the rough stone outlines of two small *theatrons* ("seeing places") in small communities near Athens, and a few stones from a retaining wall on the hillside at the base of the Athenian acropolis (most of the remains of theatres are from the late fourth century B.C.E. and after). When *Oedipus* was produced in 427 B.C.E., the Athenians relied on the downward slope of a hill, augmented with low wooden grandstands that probably hugged the contours of the hillside, for seating the 15,000 or so spectators and in a way that allowed a clear view of the playing area. The playing area was at the base of this curving hillside and was leveled to form the *orchestra*, or "dancing place." (This space may have been defined originally for the dancing and singing in the dithyramb contests, which predated the earliest plays.) As classicist Rush Rehm notes, the theatre of ancient Athens was then "less a building than what we would call landscape architecture" (2002:37). Fragmentary records suggest that the spectators looking downhill at the performers in the *orchestra* sometimes responded with stomping, whistling, and prolonged noise-making, as well as hearty applause.

The precise shape of the fifth-century *orchestra*, however, has been a source of much controversy. Although some later *orchestras* were designed as full, or nearly full circles, the evidence for the classical era suggests that the *orchestra* at the theatre in Athens was more rectangular or even trapezoidal in shape. Before moving their festival performances theatre to the hillside, the Athenians had mounted productions in the marketplace. The wooden bleachers built there would most likely have produced a rectangular playing space. One of the surviving theatres from the classical era, at Thorikos, has a rectangular *orchestra*, curved at the edges facing the audience when stone seating was added later. Several of the later Greek theatres with circular *orchestras* show evidence of an

earlier orchestral shape on the site that was roughly rectangular or trapezoidal. The construction of wooden bleachers fronting a playing area in a hollow created by three sides of a hill — the configuration of the *theatron* in Athens — would likely have created a trapezoidal *orchestra* (see Figure 2.10). The symmetrical image of a circular *orchestra*, such as we find in the remains of many Hellenistic stone theatres built in the later fourth century and after, such as the theatre at Epidauros (340–330 B.C.E.) has long fascinated scholars (Figure 2.11). But for the fifth century theatre in Athens, with its wooden bleachers, the evidence for a trapezoidal *orchestra* is strong.

For the interior house behind the *orchestra*, the offstage area for changes and entrances, some of the best evidence comes from paintings on vases and vase fragments dating from the classical era and later. This

Top view:

Partial side views:

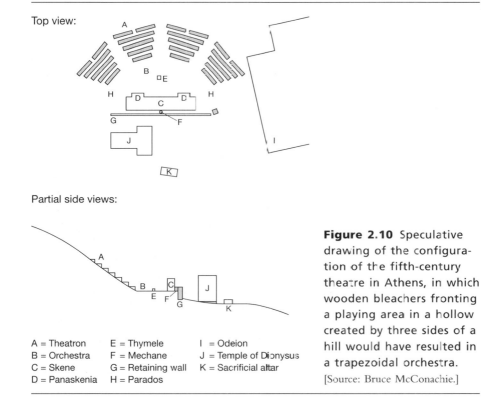

A = Theatron   E = Thymele   I = Odeion
B = Orchestra   F = Mechane   J = Temple of Dionysus
C = Skene   G = Retaining wall K = Sacrificial altar
D = Panaskenia   H = Parados

Figure 2.10 Speculative drawing of the configuration of the fifth-century theatre in Athens, in which wooden bleachers fronting a playing area in a hollow created by three sides of a hill would have resulted in a trapezoidal orchestra.
[Source: Bruce McConachie.]

Figure 2.11 The theatre at Epidaurus (330–340 B.C., showing the theatron, orchestra, parodoi (see double gates), and fragments of the skene. While such extant Greek stone theatres might have derived some features from the fifth-century theatres, they were built long after the richest period of Greek drama, in the Hellenistic period. Photo © Gary Jay Williams.

evidence must be approached with care, however, because the vase painters stylized their figures and structures, rather than rendering them realistically. Several show actors and others framed by pole-like columns and horizontal beams, a type of structure that could only have been made of wood. Other evidence points to the use of such wooden structures in dithyrambs, the choral dance and chants performed by members of the ten tribes of Athens on the day before the play contests began. The sources suggest that a fifty-member dithyramb chorus might have entered into the *orchestra* through double doors, one pair on each side of this house.

The Greeks called this wooden building a *skene*. Vase paintings suggest that colonnaded wings called *paraskenia* extended out toward the *orchestra* from double doors on either side of the *skene* (see Figure 2.10). Some plays called for the roof of the *skene* to be used as an acting space; the watchmen in the opening scene of the *Agamemnon* in Aeschylus's trilogy, *The Orestia* (458 B.C.E.) seems to be perched on the *skene* roof. Some plays require that gods be lowered into the *orchestra*, perhaps from a crane (*mechane*) that rested on or behind the *skene* house. (The later Latin phrase, "*deus ex machina*," or "God from the machine," derives from this practice and came to be used to indicate any dramatic device that miraculously resolves matters in the last act.) The *skene*, then, was probably an enclosed and roofed wooden building at the rear of the *orchestra*, with colonnaded wings extending from double doors on either side. Many classical scholars suppose that the *skene* house also had a large central door between the *paraskenia*. Much later Greek stone theatres had several large openings, but all the extant Greek plays could have been performed with two.

While the *dithyramb* dancer-singers may have used the *skene* for their entrances, the play choruses (which were smaller) may have entered into the *orchestra* through two passages called the *paradoi*, passages between the *skene* and the *theatron*. In ancient Athens, the *parados* passage was initially part of a road leading out of one part of the city into the surrounding countryside. When the Athenians moved their *theatron* to the hillside, they likely incorporated this road into their open-air theatre. By the time *Oedipus* was produced, the road wound around a large building called the *Odeion* on the eastern side of the *orchestra* (audience left), opened into the *orchestra*, and then continued on the other side of the *orchestra* and *skene* building into the countryside. On their first entrance, then, the 15-member chorus for *Oedipus* may have entered through the *parados* near the *Odeion*, at the eastern side of the *orchestra*, and, after remaining in the *orchestra* for the duration of the play, exited through *parados* on the western side (Figure 2.10). Evidence from the plays suggests that actors playing characters also occasionally entered and exited through the *paradoi*; a character arriving from or exiting to the countryside might have conventionally used the *parados* on the western side of the *orchestra*.

The first scene of *Oedipus* features an actor playing an old priest with some children gathered around him as they offer sacrifices at an altar. Evidently, this scene occurred in the *orchestra*, but where in the *orchestra* was the altar located? To propose an answer to this question, we need to move from the immediate context of the space of performance into the wider arena of fifth-century Athenian culture.

Cultural evidence

The Athenians produced theatre to honor Dionysus, the god of fertility associated with wine, drunkenness, and male sexuality. In several rituals during the winter months, the residents of Athens paraded through the streets carrying emblematic phalluses and a statue of Dionysus. The largest of these festivals was the City Dionysia, which lasted for five days in March. Following the procession on the first day of the ritual, priests of Dionysus slaughtered bulls, a symbol of the god, and distributed their meat to the revelers. *Dithyramb* contests followed on the next day, with the last three days of the civic-religious festival devoted to dramatic contests – two days of tragedies and satyr plays followed by a final day of comedies. The production of *Oedipus* in 427 B.C.E., then, was preceded by a ritual sacrifice and this certainly involved altars for slaughtering and roasting the bulls.

The altars for the Dionysiac rituals, however, were not the same as the altar used by the Priest in *Oedipus*. At the base of the hillside *theatron*, downhill from the *orchestra* and *skene*, was a small grove of trees with a temple and altars for the worship of Dionysus (Figure 2.10). It is likely that the procession on the first day of the City Dionysia ended in this grove and that the bulls were slaughtered and roasted on the large altars near that temple. In contrast, the altar on the *orchestra* stage was probably a much smaller, portable, stage property altar. While *Oedipus* requires an altar, other plays need tombs or statues for their performance and all of these properties would have been removed after the production of each play.

Where was the prop altar for *Oedipus* located? Perhaps at the center of the *orchestra*, placed over a flat stone called the *thymele*. Archaeologists have discovered such a stone embedded in the ground of the *orchesta* in several ancient theatres, usually at or near the geometric centers of their circles or trapezoids. For the audience looking down at the *orchestra* from the three sides of the *theatron* hill, the *thymele*, or a prop covering it, would have provided a significant focal point for their view. It may be that the *thymele* also organized some of the on-stage movement of the actors and chorus. Some vase paintings show the *aulos* player, who led the chorus into the *orchestra* and accompanied their chanting and movement, standing on this center stone. Historians have conjectured that the *thymele* or a prop in the same location provided the central axis around which much of the choral movement probably swirled.

Such speculations, however, depend upon general cultural orientations to spatiality, that is to say, the social use of space. How did the classical Greeks think about and use space? The evidence thus far for theatrical space suggests two general orientations: inside/outside and center/periphery. Quite simply, the plays and the space of performance allowed actors to locate themselves either inside or outside of the *skene* building. Also, actors and chorus could place themselves near the center of the action, at the *thymele*, or on its periphery, at the edges of the *orchestra* or even in the *paradoi*. This spatiality is very different from the ways in which actors in contemporary theatres generally use the space of the stage and theatre. For a perspective on the spatial orientations of different cultures, it is helpful to look at spatiality through the lens of cognitive studies.

INTERPRETIVE APPROACH: Cognitive studies

Theatre scholars have been using insights from cognitive studies for several years to explore the construction of narrative in drama, to understand acting and audience response, and to analyze the spatiality of a performance. In brief, cognitive linguists, psychologists, and philosophers are exploring how humans perceive the world, engage emotionally with it, and make meaning from their experiences. Most have concluded that the mind/brain sorts experience into categories that are largely the result of human evolution and early childhood learning. Further, this process of categorization takes place at mostly unconscious levels. Cognitive linguist George Lakoff and philosopher Mark Johnson speak of "basic level," "spatial relation," and "bodily action" metaphors that derive from these categories in the mind/brain and shape all notions of human action, culture, and history. For example, the "source-path-goal" concept, learned in infancy by crawling toward an object, is one of many bodily action metaphors. This pattern charts goal-oriented movement from one place, the "source," across a "path," to an end location, or "goal." This category in the mind/brain allows us to conceive of future purposeful action and to enjoy reading a narrative or following a piece of music with a beginning, a middle, and an end (Lakoff and Johnson 1999:30–36).

In *Philosophy in the Flesh* (1999), Lakoff and Johnson devote significant discussion to the several ways humans experience space. Categories in the mind/brain relating to spatiality include inside/outside, part-whole, center/periphery, balance, up/down, near/far, and link. In early childhood, we learn differences between what is inside of us and what is on the outside, what is nearby and what is far away, and how to keep our bodies in balance. Like

▷

▷

the source-path-goal schema, humans learn these concepts of spatiality through their bodies; later applications of balance, for instance, to notions of symmetry in architecture and ideals of justice in legal systems derive from this embodied knowledge. When we consider making a telephone call, counting the peas in a pod, or inviting another person to join a group circle, we are using categories in the mind/brain based on the spatial relations concepts of link, part-whole, and inside/outside. Further, these orientations to space shape human behavior in all cultures. Drawing on cross-cultural linguistic experiments, Lakoff and Johnson point out that human beings everywhere use language that organizes their relations to space through these same general categories.

However, because of significant cultural differences, specific historical societies have different spatial relations concepts, different orientations to space. These cultural differences are evident in the organization of space in a typical dwelling, in a town or city, and in the theatre. Since the renaissance, Western Europeans (and, later, settlers in the Americas) have been putting frames around the space of the stage to separate the fiction of the on-stage action from the audience and from the natural world. This frame, called a proscenium arch, was not a part of Greek theatre practice, which provided no architectural separation between the audience and the performers and sited the theatrical experience in the midst of the natural world. Consequently, the general orientations we use to build and comprehend proscenium productions today – the importance of the downstage center positon for an actor, the significance of strong verticality in scene design, the ways directors treat the transition from the offstage "wings" to the on-stage playing area, and the logic of scene changes to indicate a change in locale – probably would have not worked for classical Athenians producing and enjoying plays in their *theatron*, *orchestra*, and *skene*. From the perspective of cognitive studies, modern proscenium production generally emphasizes the spatial relations concepts of inside/outside, up/down, balance, and link. It is not difficult to see that these spatial relations concepts massively shape western orientations to space generally today.

These are some key questions to ask in thinking about cognitive studies, spatiality, and staging:

KEY QUESTIONS

1   What mental concepts have humans unconsciously used in their historical cultures to shape their spatial relations?

2   Among these spatial relations concepts, which were the primary ones used by people in a specific culture to locate themselves and others in space?

3   How did these dominant concepts shape theatre architecture and staging practices in that culture?

Spatiality in Athenian culture

If the concepts of inside/outside and center/periphery oriented the classical Greeks to the spatiality of their theatrical productions, the historian would expect to find these orientations in many other areas of fifth-century Athenian culture. Certainly the concept of inside/outside exerted significant pressure in Athenian life. It shaped gender roles, for instance, because women were generally expected to stay inside their father's or husband's dwellings, while Athenian society looked to males for most of its exterior, public life. City walls surrounding Athens and extending down to its seaport clearly separated an inside "us" from an outside "them." This separation was made more acute by the political practice of ostracism, which occurred when the male citizens of Athens voted to permanently exclude a resident from the city.

Ostracized Athenians were effectively banished from the center of society to the periphery. This practice, in other words, points not only to the category of inside/outside, but also to the prominence of center-periphery in generating and maintaining much of Athenian spatial practice. The spatial organization of Greek temples, which drew worshippers from surrounding areas to the center of each temple, also underscores the importance of this category. Ancient Greek biologists considered the heart to be at the center of the body and wrote about blood circulation as a flow from the periphery to the center and back again. When the classical Greeks drew maps of the world, they placed Greece at the center and arranged other lands and continents on the periphery around it.

Consequently, when fifth-century Athenians went to their *theatron* on the hill to watch *Oedipus the King* in 427 B.C.E., they came with minds/brains already accustomed to organizing space in the world through the categories of inside/outside and center/periphery. Further, it is clear that the tragedy itself took advantage of these spatial orientations in the minds of its audience. Sophocles used the *skene* house to represent the palace in which Oedipus was born – even, symbolically, the womb from which he sprang. In the course of the tragedy, the palace became firmly associated with Jocasta: she tries to keep the family feud between Oedipus and Creon inside of its doors, and she ultimately kills herself within the *skene*. Regarding center/periphery, Rush Rehm notes that in many Greek tragedies characters are "pulled in from far away [to a center] as if drawn by a magnet" (Rehm 2002:44). This was certainly true for the production of *Oedipus*. Characters came from the periphery – from the nearby town of Thebes and from Delphi, Corinth, and Mount Cithaeron – to the religious and political center of the city, the altar in the *orchestra* in front of the palace. And in the end, the blind Oedipus sought ostracism from Thebes, a type of banishment that drew on both inside/outside and center/periphery orientations.

Historians cannot know for sure how Greek audiences understood the spatial organization of their theatre and, specifically, the spatiality of the initial performance of *Oedipus the King*. But they can assemble the evidence of spatial practice from the physical and textual remains and examine it through the lens of cognitive studies to arrive at a probable hypothesis.

BMc

Key references

Ashby, C. (1999) *Classical Greek Theatre: New Views of an Old Subject*, Iowa City, IA.: University of Iowa Press.

Lakoff, G. and Johnson, M. (1999) *Philosophy in the Flesh: The Embodied Mind and Its Challenge to Western Thought*, New York: Basic Books.

Rehm, R. (2002) *The Play of Space: Spatial Transformation in Greek Tragedy*, Princeton: Princeton University Press.

Sophocles (1993) *Oedipus Rex*, trans. D. Fitts and R. Fitzgerald, in W.B. Worthen (ed.) *The HBJ Anthology of Drama*, Fort Worth: Harcourt Brace Janovich.

Taplin, O. (1977) *The Stagecraft of Aeschylus: The Dramatic Use of Entrances and Exits in Greek Tragedy*, Oxford: Oxford University Press.

Wiles, D. (1997) *Tragedy in Athens: Performance Space and Theatrical Meaning*, Cambridge: Cambridge University Press.

CASE STUDY: Christians and Moors: Medieval performance in Spain and the New World

A play of conquest

To celebrate their conquest of New Mexico (the present-day Southwest of the United States) in 1598, Spanish *conquistadores* threw themselves a week-long party, which included a variety of performances. According to one participant, there were: "Tilts with cane-spears, bullfights, tilts at the ring, / A jolly drama, well composed, / Playing at Moors and Christians, / With much artillery, whose roar / Did cause notable fear and marveling, /To many bold barbarians. . . . " (Harris 1994:145).

How might we understand this important historical document? Many Spanish-speaking cultures continue to enjoy "bullfights," of course, and "tilts with cane-spears" is easily explained as jousting matches on horseback with breakable lances (so as to avoid injuring the riders). Similarly, "tilts at the ring," another game dating from medieval tournaments, challenges the rider to thrust his lance through a small ring. But what was the "jolly drama" with "Moors and Christians" that involved noisy "artillery?" And why might a drama about Moors, the Spanish term for Muslims living in northern Africa, be performed to celebrate the conquest of land in North America?

Plays focused on a symbolic fight between Moors and Christians derived from the tournament tradition of medieval aristocratic culture in Spain. By the time Spaniards in the New World crossed the Rio Grande to claim New Mexico, Christian kings, princes, and counts in Spain had been staging *moros y cristianos* spectacles for popular and aristocratic

audiences for over three hundred years. These choreographed battles typically pitted two groups of knights against each other – blackfaced Moors with exotic silk gowns and Christian crusaders in shining armor. Following exchanges of verbal abuse from both sides, the Moors usually won the initial battles, but the Christian knights always triumphed in the end, sometimes returning with facsimiles of Moorish heads on their lances. In other performances, the Moors would recognize the error of their ways, convert to Christianity, and bow down before a symbol of Catholic power. By 1598 in New Mexico, these symbolic gang wars between rival religious fanatics had been modernized to include swords rather than lances and noisy harqubuses, the forerunner of the shotgun.

Why were the *moros y cristianos* performances popular in medieval Spain, how did these performance events compare to other kinds of medieval theatre, and why do they retain their popularity today?

The medieval context

Medieval Spaniards' desire to stage and enjoy *moros y cristianos* performances had to do with the ongoing struggle between Christian and Islamic powers for control of the Iberian peninsula for most of the middle ages (Figure 2.12). Following victories in the eighth century over Christian kingdoms on the peninsula, the Moors established a culture and society in what is now present-day Portugal and most of Spain that was more advanced and tolerant than the rest of medieval Christian Europe. The Christian kingdoms of Castile and Aragon, from their mountain strongholds in the north and east, waged intermittent wars against the Moors that finally culminated in the expulsion of Islamic forces from the peninsula in 1492. This seven-hundred year crusade left an indelible impression on Spanish history and culture. Hardened by constant warfare, the Christian aristocrats of Castile and Aragon forged a culture of religious fanaticism and military valor that shaped the Catholic Inquisition at home and Spanish conquest abroad. After 1492, the rulers of Spain expelled all infidels from the peninsula, tortured thousands of *Moriscos* (Christians of Moorish background) and *Marranos* (Christians of Jewish background) suspected of un-Christian belief, and extended their crusade of conversion or extinction to the natives of the New World. When the *conquistadores* of New Mexico performed the "jolly drama" of *moros y cristianos*, they were honoring a tradition of militant Christianity that had brought them victory for hundreds of years. There can be little doubt that the Spaniards rejoiced in the "fear and marveling" that the spectacle produced among the Native Americans who were watching the show.

As in the New Mexico production of 1598, performances of *moros y cristianos* in medieval Spain normally occurred in the midst of a festival. In January and February of 1461, for example, Count Miguel Lucas de Iranzo, the Castilian ruler of Jaen, threw a party for the populace of the town that lasted for 21 days. In addition to celebrating his wedding, Lucas's festival was also designed to shore up his power and prestige in the wake of a recent plague and frequent attacks by the Moors. For his wedding celebration, the Count and his retinue claimed the blessing of God by dressing themselves in images of Christian power. Lucas transformed the entire town into a stage using an array of torches, symbolic tapestries, and musicians to heighten the effects of the processions, games, dances, and plays. Mock battles

between Christians and Moors occurred in the midst of other dramatic spectacles, such as the freeing of Christian captives from a Moorish dragon and the conversion of the King of Morocco to Christianity. Like many of his subjects, Lucas appeared both as himself, a magnanimous ruler, and as a performer, enacting one of the kings who visits the Christ child in Bethlehem in a Nativity play, for instance.

Count Lucas's wedding festival of 1461 illustrates several aspects of late medieval performance in Spain. Just as many of the people of Jaen participated both as actors and spectators, most public spaces in the town could be used for either acting or spectating, depending on the occasion. Fixed stages and fixed distinctions between performer and spectator were unnecessary. The genres of such carnival entertainment were also fluid; aristocratic games of combat flowed into popular dances, and church rituals could inform pageant processions. For instance, for his winter wedding celebration, the Count likely re-used some of the same pageant wagons that paraded through the streets to celebrate the spring feast of Corpus Christi, a celebration of Christ's redeeming presence in the world in which plays depicted episodes in Christian salvation history. Festival celebrants made few distinctions between religious observance and secular practice. Finally, politics was never far from the center of these pageants, tournaments, and plays. Lucas, like other kings and counts in Castile and in all medieval Christian kingdoms, notes one historian, staged his festivals as "deliberately complex symbolic ceremonies, frequently laden with polemical or propagandistic intent" (Holme 1987:5). (The Count's lavish spending on celebrations seems to have made little difference in his political fortunes, however; rivals in Jaen murdered him in 1473.) Overall, the performances sponsored by Count Lucas in late medieval Spain were like a stained-glass window of religious and political symbols brought to life and set to music.

INTERPRETIVE APPROACH: Cultural hierarchy

Many cultures use verticality to signal ethical differences. Thus, whatever is "high" – the human head, a mountain top, heaven – becomes "good," while the "bad" is associated with the "low" – sexual organs, the sewer, Hell. In *The Politics and Poetics of Transgression*, Peter Stallybrass and Allon White use this human proclivity to align ethics with verticality in order to analyze how cultures create images of what they term "the low other." When mainstream cultures classify minority groups as immoral, dirty, noisy, and/or unworthy, they are defining these people as "low others." By separating themselves from "low others," people in the dominant culture create an image of themselves as "high" and "moral." As Stallybrass and White comment, "the human body, psychic forms, geographical space, and the social formation are all constructed within interrelating and dependent hierarchies of high and low" (1986:2).

Although usually excluded from normal participation in society and politics, "low others" remain objects of fascination and attraction to people in dominant groups. Stallybrass and White note the "psychological dependence" of the dominant culture upon images of "low others." They conclude that "this is the reason that what is *socially* peripheral is so frequently *symbolically* central" (ibid.:5). The insights of Stallybrass and White have obvious relevance to the interactions between many dominant and subordinate groups throughout history, including "white" and "black" Americans, Eastern Europeans and Jews, and Castilians and Moors in medieval Spain.

Students of theatre history can begin to read for the "low other" in past performances by asking these questions:

KEY QUESTIONS

1   How did make-up, costuming, characterization, and other modes of theatrical communication denigrate specific kinds of roles, social groups, and/or forms of belief?

2   What types of characters and beliefs were made to appear "high" through the contrast with these "low others?"

3   What were the historical reasons for and the consequences of depicting this ethical contrast between the "high" and the "low"?

The "low other" in medieval performance

Performances in medieval festivals and religious holidays, especially of plays like *moros y cristianos*, often defined proper Christian behavior by denigrating and defeating its un–Christian opposite. Because vertical relations of authority and belief were so important in medieval Christian culture, stereotypes of "low others" proliferated in European performances from the twelfth through the sixteenth centuries. Characters associated with vice in morality plays designed for ethical instruction – the female temptress, Sloth, Gluttony, Pride, the rest of the Seven Deadly Sins, and Lucifer himself – were typically costumed and played in ways that aligned them with dirt, feces, and rampant sexuality (Figure 2.12). In the day-long religious plays depicting important incidents of Christian history, Jews, Romans, and infidels were often characterized as buffoons, villains, or other "low" types. Mummers plays, Christianized versions of pagan rituals designed to ensure the return of spring after the winter solstice, often featured a blackened Turk as the antagonist of a white Christian knight. Another winter solstice performance, the Sword Dance, symbolically sacrificed a hairy wild man or a "greenman" from the forest to incite the resurrection of the springtime sun (and the Christian Son of God).

In medieval Spain, Moors and Jews became the primary symbols of the "low other" in festival performances. Medieval writers often characterized Moors as treacherous and cowardly in *moros y cristianos* plays. The Jews who served as advisors to King Herod were usually foolish buffoons. Before 1492, when all Moors and Jews who refused to convert to Christianity were driven out of Spain, however, the Castilians often sought to include these minorities living within their cities in their religious festivities. Records from earlier in the fifteenth century indicate that actual Jews were sometimes asked to

Figure 2.12 Stonework depicting a sexualized Lucifer tempting Christ. Carved on a capital of Autun Cathedral in France in the twelfth century by Gisilbertus. © Abbé Denis Grivot, Autun, France.

perform the roles of Jewish rabbis in the Cycle plays and that Moors were invited to perform their own dances during Christian religious processions Nonetheless, anti-Semitic and anti-Islamic prejudices, coupled with the desire to purify Catholic Spain, eradicated the previous Spanish toleration of minority religious groups after 1492.

Moros y cristianos in New Mexico today

The legacy of Spanish medieval theatre continues to shape popular and religious celebrations in Spanish-speaking countries today. It is especially evident in nativity plays at Christmas, scenes deriving from the cycle plays performed during the Easter season, and *moros y cristianos* mock battles presented at festivals in the countries of Latin America and the southwestern

United States. A grant from the United States National Endowment for the Arts in 1976 enabled Latinos in Chimayo, New Mexico, to upgrade their performances of *moros y cristianos* with new costumes and properties. During a June fiesta, about two dozen men and women dress in thirteenth-century costumes, mount horses, wield swords and scimitars, and engage in symbolic battle. To create the illusion of darker skin, the Latinos playing Moors also wear black veils, thus continuing the tradition of the Moor as "low other." As during the days of Spanish imperialism, the ideology of militant Christianity continues to shape the ending of the play. Convinced by the outcome of the battle that their own religion is false, the Moors convert to Christianity, and all performers join together in a hymn of praise to the Holy Cross.

Figure 2.13 Map showing extent of Christian and Moorish territories in 1490.
[Source: Bruce McConachie.]

Some native Americans living in the Southwest also perform versions of *moros y cristianos*, partly to honor their conversion to Christianity under Spanish rule but also to gain a wry revenge against their historical persecutors (Figure 2.14). These performances typically involve Indians on hobby-horses playing both groups of antagonists, with historic native Americans on one side and Spaniards and "white" Americans on the other. Instead of dramatizing conquest and conversion, however, the performance points up the foolishness of the "whites," who, in this revised version of *moros y cristianos*, flee a symbolic bull, portrayed by an Indian.

In 1598 when the Spanish conquerors first performed the dance drama, they understood the Native Americans as symbolic Moors, to be converted or exterminated. Today, in situations in which American Indians control and perform the dance, they have turned white soldiers, saints, and traders into the "low others" that Indians once had been.

BMc

Key references

Glick, T.F. (1979) *Islamic and Christian Spain in the Early Middle Ages: Comparative Perspectives on Social and Cultural Formation*, Princeton: Princeton University Press.

Harris, M. (1994) "The Arrival of the Europeans: Folk Dramatizations of Conquest and Conversion in New Mexico," in C. Davidson and John Stroupe (eds) *Early and Traditional Drama: Africa, Asia, and the New World*, Kalamazoo, M.I.: Medieval Institute Publications.

Holme, B. (1987) *Medieval Pageantry*, London: Thames and Hudson.

Shergold, N.D. (1967) *A History of the Spanish Stage from Medieval Times Until the End of the Seventeenth Century*, Oxford: Clarendon Press.

Stallybrass, P. and A. White, (1986) *The Politics and Poetics of Transgression*, Ithaca, N.Y.: Cornell University Press.

Stern, C. (1996) *The Medieval Theater in Castile*, Medieval and Renaissance Texts and Studies, Vol 156. Binghamton, N.Y.: Center for Medieval and Renaissance Studies.

Wickham, G. (1987) *The Medieval Theatre*, 3rd edn, Cambridge: Cambridge University Press.

Figure 2.14 1942 drawing of a Native American as a Spanish Christian saint on a horse in a *moros y cristianos* production. From Papers of the Michigan Academy of Arts and Sciences. © The Michigan Academy.

Imperial theatre: Pleasure, power, and aesthetics

Chapter 2 focused primarily on the religious and socio-cultural contexts within which early forms of drama and theatre originated and were performed. In Chapter 3, we give more attention to aesthetic considerations, that is, to the ways in which dramatic performances deliver particular kinds of pleasure(s) for particular audiences through specific sets of dramatic and/or theatrical conventions. One example of a theatrical convention is the aside – a moment where an actor playing a specific role talks directly to the audience without other characters on stage being aware of the exchange

Because any discussion of aesthetics necessarily involves analysis of context, we also consider how and why particular state formations have historically generated particular aesthetics and therefore different pleasures. What pleasures are produced for an "elite" audience at court, for "the masses" in a Roman public arena, or for devotees participating in a commemorative drama?

The concentration of economic resources in hierarchically ordered, centralized states allowed the development of specialists – copyists, teachers, priests (keepers/interpreters of sacred texts), poets/

dramatists, actors, dancers, musicians, and grammarians, or critics. What position within social or artistic hierarchy does each of these specialists hold? Are poets/dramatists/critics more highly valued than actors, or vice-versa?

Where elite "interpretive communities" develop, both critical theory and the artist's work are shaped by reflection upon the form and structure of a genre. Such literate self-consciousness takes two forms – the production of specialist works of critical reflection on the structure, form, artistic techniques, and/or conventions of performance such as Aristotle's *Poetics* (*c*.330 B.C.E.), Horace's *Art of Poetry* (Rome, *c*.19 B.C.E.), Bharata's *Nāṭyaśastra* (India, between the second century B.C.E. and the second century C.E.), the secret treatises on noh drama by Zeami (Japan, C.E. 1363–1443), or the theory of theatre of Li Yu (China, 1611–80?) in *Casual Notes in a Leisurely Mode* (*Xianqing ouji*, also known as *A Temporary Lodge for My Leisure Thoughts*, 1671). A second manifestation of literary self-consciousness is when art forms demonstrate an awareness of their artistry and conventions. Drama/theatre takes itself as an object by calling attention to its performance conventions. When theatre becomes conscious of its own conventions, it openly points to itself through asides, monologues, role-playing, eavesdropping, or the play-within-a-play, and it is non-illusionistic. As Niall Slater explains, "As the theatre games become ever cleverer and cleverer, the object of the audience's admiration becomes the dramatic skill, not the illusion" (1985:15). As we shall see in this chapter, both the plays of the Roman playwright, Plautus, and the Sanskrit dramas might be described as "meta-theatrical" in so far as the theatrical performance is, at times, about theatre. Such reflexivity is exploited for its own (often comic) sake, and sometimes invites reflection on the culture.

In some historical periods and cultures, sustained royal patronage provided a (momentarily stable) context within which artists were able to concentrate and reflect on the nuances of their artistry. Because court life often isolated powerful rulers from "the people," this allowed the development of idiosyncratic behavior, the indulgence of particular likes and dislikes, and the creation of intricate networks of socio-political intrigue vying for influence and power within a court.

The concentration of power and patronage in a single individual or an elite hierarchy means that some arts or artists find favor and are promoted, while others fall out of favor and are censored or even banished. How do artists find favour, win influence, or simply gain permission to ply their trade? What role do advisors, courtiers, or poets and jesters play in these power games – especially given the reflexive role of the poet or "jester" who writes for, or entertains a ruler? How far can comedy or satire go in testing the limits of social or political power? What if a ruler is a poet or actor?

We cannot answer all of these questions here, but we begin to address a few of them by examining developments in Greco-Roman drama, theatre, and performance during the periods of the Roman Republic and Roman Empire, and the emergence of early literary and commemorative drama and theatre in India, China, and Japan.

Drama, theatre, and performance in the Roman Republic and Empire

Greek drama and theatre were disseminated under Alexander the Great throughout the greater Mediterranean region during the fourth century B.C.E. By 300 B.C.E., theatres were to be found throughout all of Greece. Actors became powerful public figures enlisted for political negotiations or as ambassadors, and some became wealthy. With the reorganizing of dramatic performances at the end of the fourth century that put the choruses under the command and budget of a state official, the *agonothetes* – "arranger of contests," the move toward professionalizing and institutionalizing theatre was almost complete. In the bristling fifth century, the theatre had given expression to all the contestations of a dynamic, evolving civic and religious sphere. As the theatre began to be professionalized and the support of the choruses was institutionalized, the role of the community in engendering and producing Athenian dialogic drama seems to have effectively diminished.

The decline and defeat of Athens at the end of the long and agonizing Peloponnesian wars in 404 B.C.E., to which Athenian expansionism had contributed, virtually ended the era of Athenian Old Comedy, with its broad socio-political satire. Aristophanes and his successors could no longer lampoon generals and politicians. Old Comedy was replaced by domestic comedies (New Comedy) – exemplified in the work of the highly popular playwright, Menander (*c*.341–291 B.C.E.). What little we know of Menander's output is from two complete or nearly complete plays, *The Bad-Tempered Man* and *The Woman of Samos*, and fragments of others (Figure 3.1). Their domestic plots focus on love affairs and family relationships, with somewhat generic characters, defined by gender, age, or class. Menander's

Figure 3.1 An image probably of the popular Menander, with three masks of Greek New Comedy: the mask of a young man (in his hand), and masks of a young woman and an older man or a comic slave. Marble relief sculpture of the first or second century, after a third-century B.C.E. work. © 2004 The Trustees of Princeton Museum. Photo: Bruce M. White.

plays were considered at the time to reflect and speak to everyday social concerns. Aristophanes of Byzantium once commented, "O Menander and Life! Which of you imitated the other?" Clearly, the expectations of audiences in Athens and throughout Greece had changed from those informing fifth-century reception of Old Comedy.

Comedies in the Republic

When the Greek playwright, Philemon, died (*c.*263 B.C.E.), New Comedy did not receive a fillip until it was reinvented in Rome as *fabula palliata* – "plays

in Greek dress" and Greek locations. Two Roman playwrights of note adapted Greek New Comedies from the previous 200 years for their Roman audiences: Titus Maccius Plautus (254–184 B.C.E.) and Terence (195/185–157 B.C.E.). In the context of the Roman Republic (fourth century to mid-first century B.C.E.), drama was no longer dialogic as it had been in fifth-century Athens. Drama became one of many professional entertainments for consumption as part of the festivities of public holidays known as *ludi* – "games" – the counterpart of the Greek festivals.

The Elder Tarquin (616–578 B.C.E.) is credited with the founding of the largest of these, the *Ludi Romani* – held early in September to honor Jupiter. Many additional *ludi* were later added, including festivals in other months in honor of Flora, Jupiter, and Apollo. While the Greek festivals had celebrated specific deities with specific kinds of events, such as the tragedies celebrating Dionysus at the City Dionysia or the athletic games performed in honor of Zeus at Olympus, the Roman *ludi* were eclectic, including numerous types of games and entertainments. Chariot and horse racing were among the earliest events, followed by boxing, gladiatorial contests (264 B.C.E.), and dramatic performances (240 B.C.E.).

Ludi were also held to celebrate great funerals, birthdays, or state occasions, such as military victories. Romans worshiped a conglomeration of indigenous deities such as the great Jupiter and deities borrowed from Greek and oriental cultures. To find favor with these deities, worship was undertaken by a special priesthood using rituals that were legalistic and magical. A college of priests developed a complex system to foretell the future, read omens, and practice augury – reading signs revealed in the viscera of freshly sacrificed animals.

It was at the *Ludi Romani* in the mid-fourth century that *ludi scaenici* (scenic/stage shows) were first presented as part of the festival. The first play was produced as part of the *Ludi Romani* in 240 B.C.E., authored by the former Greek slave, Livius Andronicus. Like all his later comedies and tragedies, his first was a translation of a Greek play. Andronicus produced and acted in all his plays.

Along with adaptations of Greek comedies and tragedies, mimes (*mimos*) were also popular. Mime originated in Syracuse and was performed as early as the fourth century B.C.E. in Athens. Featuring both men and women as performers, mime used monologue, dialog, dance, song, and variety skills such as acrobatics to elaborate either everyday scenes or those from mythology. In contrast to dramas in which action developed through plot devices and characterization of masked actors, interest in mime was maintained by the range and plasticity of a performer's expressive abilities.

Plautus transformed Greek New Comedy beginning with his first production in 205 B.C.E. by bringing to his adaptations some of the conventions of indigenous Italian performance, especially those of the southern Italian tradition of Atellan farce (*fabulae atellanae*). Improvised from simple core narratives, easily recognizable stock characters wove together jokes and physically-based comic stage-business. An audience would expect an old man to oppose his son's amorous adventures and the slave to cleverly thwart his old master. Both early Atellan farces and Plautus's dramas were performed on temporarily constructed wooden stages set up for each *ludi*. This simple playing space was not bound by a realistic depiction of locale or space; it could represent a harbor-front or a street. A scene building backed the playing space, and its three openings serviced many different plots. Actors wore masks for all performances, and music played an important role, in Plautus's plays in particular (Figure 3.10).

Because dramatic performances took place in the context of public games, Roman playwrights had to write plays that captured the attention of an audience. This is exemplified in the Prologue to Plautus's *Poenulus*. An actor steps onstage and directly addresses the raucous audience:

Hush and be silent and pay attention; that you listen is the order of the general-manager, that both those who have come hungry and those who have come well-filled may cheerfully be seated on the benches. Those of you who have eaten have done much more wisely, but you who haven't eaten can have your fill of the play. . . . Arise, Herald, order the people to be silent. . . . Let no worn out harlot sit in front of the stage, or the lector or his rods make a sound, nor the usher roam about in front of people or show anyone to a seat while the actor is on the stage. Those who have had a long leisurely nap at home should now cheerfully stand, or at least refrain from sleeping. Keep slaves from occupying the seats, that there be room for free men, or let them pay money for their freedom. If they can't do that, let them go home and avoid a double misfortune – being raked with rods here, and with whips at home if their masters return and find they haven't done their work.

(Duckworth 1941: I,727–728)

The era of the mid-Republic during which Plautus wrote has been described as conservative in the extreme. Spartan, puritanical, and moralistic "blue law" legislation, as well as official and semi-official educational propaganda, all attempted to constrain behavior and encourage a return to virtues of the past. The ancient virtues embedded in restrictive laws were founded on "the way of the fathers" (*mos maiorum*) and clearly shaped the expectations of Roman audiences. Looking to legends of the past which embodied virtues such as honor, dignity, and uprightness, Romans were expected to subordinate their individual personalities to the larger social good. In legal terms, the male head of each family (*pater familias*) held absolute power over members of his household. In 340 B.C.E., Manlius Torquatus had his son executed for disobeying orders during the Great Latin War, even though his son's unauthorized attack resulted in military victory. Every Roman institution operated as a sacred patriarchy, and each family was a state in miniature.

Two types of behavior shaped and constrained Roman males during the Republican period – *pietas* and *gravitas*. *Pietas* is usually translated as "respect for elders," but also implies respect for authority, loyalty of wife to the husband, and devotion to the gods. Usually translated as "dignity," *gravitas* is a weighty quality, ideally manifest in behavior that is sober and enduring.

Plautus's comedies, known primarily for the fast traffic of their comic plots and low antic business, are also interesting because they turn patriarchal order and gravitas on their heads, as we will see in the case study following this chapter. Those with the least power in the Roman hierarchy – slaves, wives, and sons – are often those who win out (albeit the stakes are not large). The reference to the rod and whippings for slaves in the Prologue to *Poenulus* cited above reflects the reality that Roman slaves were the lowest among the low in Roman society – objects with no rights who could be tortured or killed. In Plautus's plays, the clever slave often outsmarts his master.

The later comedies authored by Terence – who had been a slave brought to Rome from northern Africa – were more constrained than those of Plautus. From his first production in 166 B.C.E., Terence followed the model of Menander's Greek social commentaries and may have appealed to a more cosmopolitan strain of the Roman audience. His characters were less in the vein of stock types and drawn with somewhat more dimension than those of Plautus. Terence's language is often elegant and witty. In his six extant plays, he often combines plots and characters from several Greek comedies into one play with nuanced action.

In spite, or perhaps because of this, Terence at times had trouble holding the attention of his Roman audience. At the first performance of *Hecya*, written for the *Ludi Megalenses* in 165 B.C.E., the audience left to go and see the rope dancers. At a second staging, they left to see the gladiators fight. Other of his plays were more successful. Terence's plays became important in Latin education in the medieval period and informed the development of drama and performance during the early renaissance.

The well-known politician, philosopher, and teacher, Lucius Annaeus Seneca (5/4 B.C.E.–C.E. 65) authored nine tragedies loosely based on Greek originals, including his *Medea*, *Phaedra*, *Oedipus*, *Agamemnon*, and *Thyestes*. Informed by the late

Roman version of stoicism, which taught self-sufficiency and the avoidance of high emotion, his plays are characterized by instances of sensational violence and horror. Although the issue is open to debate, it is likely that Seneca's plays were not staged, but written for recitation at small gatherings. As important as Terence to the renaissance, Seneca's philosophical essays and plays influenced Montaigne and Shakespeare respectively.

Imperial spectacles

The powerful patriarchy operating throughout the Roman Republic eventually gave way to a centralized authoritarian state with the establishment of the Roman Empire in 27 B.C.E., when Caesar Octavian received the honorific title of Augustus. Absolute power was surrendered by noble/landed families to a now all-powerful emperor, later called the father of the country (*pater patriae*). The service once extended to one's family was now to be extended to the state.

Immediately before the advent of Empire, in the period of the late Republic, dramatic performances increasingly depended on spectacle to create their impact, sponsored by wealthy men who sought reputation in public (self-) presentations. By the end of the first century B.C.E., both comedy and tragedy ceased to be viable dramatic forms that could be used by new writers to reflect new sensibilities. They were replaced by spectacular re-staging of extant dramas, or alternative forms of popular entertainments, often including bloody contests.

The first permanent theatre was built in Rome by Pompey the Great in 55 B.C.E. (Figure 3.2). This grand building sat 20,000 spectators and featured a stage 300 ft in width, backed by a three-story façade (*scaenae frons*) with decorative statues. It was constructed less to serve the art of drama than to be a highly visible platform where Pompey (and subsequent rulers) could preside over the gathered populace, displaying his authority and the grandeur of Empire. With the decline of new dramatic writing,

it was an artistic anachronism. A large temple was incorporated into the outer wall of the auditorium (*cavea*) for Venus Victrix, perhaps so the goddess could oversee each spectacle or perhaps because this allowed Pompey to build a permanent theatre at a time when, for legalistic religious reasons, theatres were usually erected temporarily for special occasions and then dismantled. In any case, the religious purpose of the *ludi* to honor Venus Victrix seems by this point to have been purely vestigial.

In addition to the revival of tragedies and comedies, both mime and a relatively new art called pantomime were popular in the early Empire. In pantomime, a chorus and/or musicians accompanied a solo, non-speaking actor (in a mask with a closed mouth), who played all the roles in a lavishly staged myth or the re-staging of a drama. A young boy, Paris, who was the Emperor Nero's favorite pantomime dancer, was reportedly put to death by him because he was so much better a dancer than the Emperor. In the second century C.E., Lucian wrote of pantomime:

> You will find that his is no easy profession, nor lightly to be undertaken; requiring as it does the highest standard of culture in all its branches, and involving a knowledge not of music only, but of rhythm and meter, and above all of your beloved philosophy, both natural and moral, the subtleties of dialectic alone being rejected as serving no useful purpose. . . . The pantomime is above all things an actor; that is his first aim, in the pursuit of which he resembles the orator, and especially the composer of declamations, whose success . . . depends like him upon verisimilitude, upon the adaptation of language to character: prince or tyrannicide, pauper or farmer, each must be shown with the peculiarities that belong to him.
>
> (Nagler 1952:28–29)

Pantomime and mime artists were often controversial figures denied citizenship (as were all actors),

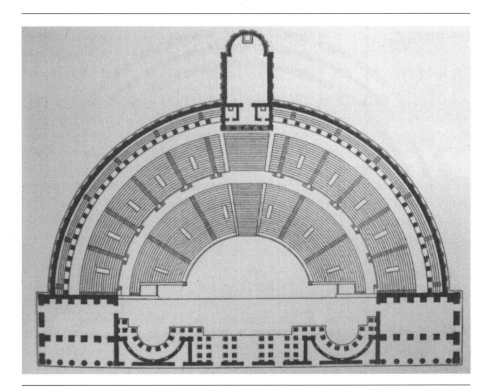

Figure 3.2 Ground plan of the Theatre of Pompey (55 B.C.E.), Rome, as reconstructed in the renaissance. Connected to the rear of this theatre was an enormous public plaza with open colonnaded structures, what the Greeks had called a *stoa*.

but nevertheless gained a large public following and were treated as stars. When Julius Caesar served as dictator of Rome (48–45 B.C.E.), the noted producer and actor of mime, Laberius, was called out of retirement by Caesar himself to celebrate Caesar's victories. When Laberius appeared as a beaten slave in one mime performance, he was bold enough to pronounce on stage that "Henceforth, O citizens, we have lost our liberty!" A further public challenge to Caesar's authority was suggested when Laberius reportedly said, "He must fear many, whom many fear" – whereupon it is reported that the entire audience of 20,000 turned to see Caesar's reaction to Laberius's words. While Caesar awarded the palm

of victory for acting to Laberius's rival, Pubilius Syrus, he nevertheless treated Laberius genially and tolerantly.

Such was not often the case in the increasingly popular blood spectacles taking place in specially built circuses – huge new buildings in which chariot racing and other events were staged. These included animal fights, gladiatorial contests, and *naumachiae* – the staging of sea fights based upon episodes from Greek history. In 46 B.C.E., Julius Caesar commissioned the staging of a battle between Tyre and Egypt on an artificial lake in Rome, and in C.E. 52 Claudius staged a fight between Rhodes and Sicily using 19,000 prisoners. *Naumachiae* were another means of staging an emperor's power to rewrite and control history. Later, the Emperors Caligula and Nero further encouraged and patronized the expansion of this wide range of public games and entertainments to please a mass public.

The Emperor Constantine converted to Christianity in 312, and by the early fifth century, there was some decline in the more excessive blood spectacles. The games and the theatre had long been opposed by the growing Christian community. By the end of the second century, the Christian writer Tertullian had urged Christians to look instead to the spectacle of the church. In 398, the church decreed excommunication for anyone going to the theatre rather than church on holy days. Actors were forbidden the sacraments unless they renounced their profession, a decree that remained in force down through Molière's lifetime and into the eighteenth century. Nevertheless, Roman *ludi* continued, with festivals in the fourth century lasting as much as 100 days. With the economic and political decay of the Empire and its division into independent parts, ruled by Rome and Constantinople, a weakened Rome fell in 476. The last record of a Roman theatre performance is dated C.E. 549.

Indian literary and commemorative drama and theatre

If fifth-century Athens produced the earliest examples of literary drama, the Indian sub-continent was a second location where multiple types of both literary and commemorative drama flourished. The early history of drama in India is difficult to reconstruct, but one source of early quasi-dramatic and then dramatic activity no doubt originated in the variety of early forms of story-telling, such as picture-recitation (see Chapter 1), which developed from antiquity. *Kathā* is the Sanskrit word for "story," most often understood as something "which is true," that is, a story that involves consequences that reverberate throughout cosmic history. The Sanskrit

root, *kath*, means to "converse with, tell, relate, narrate, speak about, explain." *Kathā* then might be better translated as "telling or narration" (Lutgendorf 1991:115). Listening to interesting and inspiring stories told, narrated, sung, and/or enacted was a common practice from the early Vedic period. Learned teller-scholars have long offered discourses on the meaning of a story as part of each telling/singing. The legacy of story-performance is still very much alive today in numerous genres that exist across the sub-continent such as Tamil Nadu's *Kathākālaksepa* – literally "spending time listening to stories."

These "stories that matter" might be classified today as "myths," "epics," or "tales," but any *kathā* that matters carries its own important "truth," and therefore is understood as needing to be heard. Some of India's greatest "stories" that became important sources for playwrights composing literary or commemorative dramas are the two great pan-Indian epics known as the *Mahabharata* and *Ramayana*, and the *pūraṇas* – specific collections of traditional stories, lore, wisdom, genealogy, and techniques, gathered into books at a certain time in history impossible to pinpoint precisely. For neither the *Mahabharata* or the *Ramayana* is there a single authoritative version. Rather, each region of India possesses its own version in the regional language. Valmiki's Sanskrit version of the *Ramayana*, dating from between 200 B.C.E. and C.E. 200, is held in the highest regard, but it is only one of many Sanskrit versions. When regional languages developed, Valmiki's Sanskrit version was replaced with easily accessible vernacular versions. The *Mahabharata* is eight times the length of Homer's *Iliad* and *Odyssey* combined, and it dates back to at least the mid-first millennium B.C.E. Many other compendiums of stories exist, such as the *Kathāsaritsāgara*, or "An Ocean of Streams of Stories," a Sanskrit compilation by Soma of 22,000 stanzas (*c.*C.E. 1063–1081). This storehouse of myths, epics, and tales is the primary resource authors began to mine when literary and commemorative dramas were invented.

The story of the origins of drama and early Sanskrit theatre

The fact that stories have always mattered in India is nowhere better seen than in the story of the origins of drama and theatre contained in the *Nātyaśastra* – an encyclopedic work on all aspects of drama (*nātya*) attributed to the sage, Bharata, authored or collected between 200 B.C.E. and C.E. 200. The story relates how Indra organized a group of the gods to approach the creator, Lord Brahma, to request that he create a pastime that would provide all manner of people with visual as well as auditory pleasures. Brahma accepted their argument, and, using his yogic powers, resolved to add to the four existing Vedas – books of hymns sacred to the Hindus – a fifth. This Veda was on

> the *Natya* [drama] with the Semi-historical Tales (*ithāsa*), which will conduce to duty (*dharma*), wealth (*artha*) as well as fame, will give guidance to people of the future as well, in all their actions, will be enriched by the teaching of all authoritative works (*śastras*), and will give a review of all arts and crafts (1:15).
>
> (Ghosh 1967:1)

It is thought that when Brahma created the Veda of drama, he gave this gift to the sage, Bharata, and gave his hundred sons the task of putting this form into practice. Drama was to represent people from all walks of life and be accessible to all. Its aim was to educate and teach by dramatizing stories that could hold people's attention through their depiction of the experiences of life in all its diversity, from war to sexual sensuality. It was to offer "good counsel" and "guidance to people" (Ghosh 1967:2–3; 14–15). A performance was to result in an ideal aesthetic experience in which an audience would "taste" (*rasa*) the states of being/doing (*bhāva*) conveyed by the characters. The term *nātya*, usually translated as "drama," does not mean, then, simply the written dramatic text. Rather, *nātya* embraces all aspects of dramatic

production through which artists skillfully embody the work and provide an audience with an aesthetic experience.

The *Nātyaśastra* is the single most important source we have on the early history of Indian drama and theatre. As a *śastra* it is still considered an authoritative guide to both the theory and practice of theatre, just as *śastras* are authoritative in other fields of practice such as medicine or architecture. Its 36 chapters classify and describe in minute detail every aspect of production necessary for an acting company to achieve success. It traces the origins of drama and explains how to construct an appropriate theatre building (Figure 3.3). It explains how to worship the gods prior to performance, discusses types of plays, and provides a guide to playwriting, including rules governing metrical patterns and prosody. It provides instruction in costuming and make-up and in the types of characters and the behavior appropriate to each. It categorizes and describes movement and gesture and the internal methods of acting the moods and states of being of characters. Although the *Nātyaśastra* is considered authoritative by some, the text is unknown to practitioners of many traditional genres of Indian theatre. As we shall see in the case study on South Asian Sanskrit theatre following this chapter, even where the text is known, practitioners have not necessarily followed what is described or prescribed in the text. Like other *śastras*, the *Nātyaśastra* is honored as a divine gift, like a respected elder, but not slavishly imitated.

The earliest indication of the art of acting is recorded in Panini's *Aṣṭādhyāyi, c.*500 B.C.E. Given the highly developed nature of dramaturgy and performance practice recorded in the *Nātyaśastra*, it is safe to assume that early literary drama and the conventions and aesthetics governing its performance developed between 500–200 B.C.E. Highly professional companies included male and female performers specializing in specific role-types, led by a male manager/actor (*sutradhara*). In some later genres of regional theatre such as Ramlila and

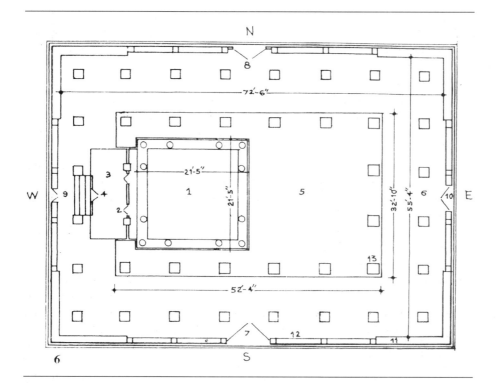

Figure 3.3 Floor plan of a playhouse for Sanskrit Theatre in India, as described by Bharata in the *Nātyaśastra*, to be constructed on a consecrated piece of land on an East–West axis, and divided into equal halves for dressing room and acting areas. The audience is to be seated on the floor or a raked bank of seats in the east half. [Source: Line drawing. After Sketch No. 3, p.47 in Tarla Mehta, *Sanskrit Play Production in Ancient India* (1995) New Delhi: Motilal Banarsidass, 41 U.A. Bungalow Rd, Jawarhar Nagar, Delhi 100 007.]

kathakali (Chapter 5), all the actors are traditionally male.

Over five hundred Sanskrit dramas exist today – all composed in Sanskrit and Prakrits – dialects evolved from Sanskrit. *Rūpaka* is the Sanskrit term for a literary drama intended for performance on stage. *Rupa* literally means "form," and *rūpaka* specifically refers to a form of poetry meant for representation on stage as opposed to poetic forms intended only for hearing or reading. As discussed

in a case study that follows this chapter, while Sanskrit dramas have characters and plots, the focus is on how the *performance* produces a satisfying aesthetic experience.

Like their Greek counterparts, when Indian playwrights dealt with traditional stories drawn from epic and puranic sources, they used their imaginations to reinvent and reinterpret each story. Authored some time in the fourth century C.E., Bhasa's one act drama, *The Breaking of Thighs* (*Urubhangam*), is based on a story in the *Mahabharata*. In the epic itself, the leader of the Kauravas, Duryodhana, is the primary force for unleashing tremendous conflict and therefore "evil" in the struggle for supremacy between two sets of warring cousins. However, in Bhasa's play, he creates a Duryodhana who is the central sympathetic character of the play and serves as a vehicle for the audience's aesthetic experience of *rasa*.

Commemorative devotional drama

In addition to Sanskrit literary drama and theatre in which aesthetic experience is the *raison d'etre* of performances first patronized at courts, a second of many important theatrical traditions in early India were commemorative devotional dramas intended for mass audiences. Devotional dramas allow devotees immediate access to an encounter with one of many specific manifestations of the divine – an experience sometimes described as *bhakti rasa* – an aesthetic experience of deep devotion that is a creative interpretation of the *rasa* aesthetic.

We examine here one of many commemorative devotional dramas, North India's *Rāmlīlā* – an enormously popular, pluralistic form of open-air performance that re-enacts episodes from the life of Ram. Its present form is attributed to a disciple of the poet Tulsidas about 1625. *Līlā* literally means an act of cosmic or divine "play," that is, a moment when the divine interacts with the human world. In the case of *Rāmlīlā* and its earlier quasi-dramatic precursors, the divine's vehicle for this interaction is Ram (or Rama) – one of the ten incarnations of Lord Vishnu (the preserver of the universe). The story of Ram is recorded in the various versions of the epic mentioned above – the *Ramayana*, and since its first telling, the *Ramayana* has been a source for performance. The earliest evidence for worship of Vishnu (as Ram or Krishna, etc.) in the region of Uttar Pradesh, North India, is established in legend. The first direct citation of this fact is from Greek geographers drawing on documents of the fourth

and third centuries B.C.E. Norvein Hein (1972) postulates that the earliest forerunner of today's immensely popular *Rāmlīlā* were dramatizations of parts of the *Ramayana* under royal patronage during the early centuries C.E. One early text, the *Harivaṁśa* (no later than C.E. 400), relates how part of the *Ramayana* was sung by a background chorus while actor-dancers in the foreground danced/enacted the story. Hein hypothesizes that this early form of dance-drama eventually died out in North India under Muslim rule (1200–1500), but elements of the early performance were still reflected in the rebirth of devotional drama during the fifteenth and sixteenth centuries, when the popular Bhakti devotional movement swept across north India (ibid.:124).

We focus here on the extant *Rāmlīlā* tradition as it emerged after 1625. Since Vaishnavite concern is with creating a devotional experience in which a devotee enters into "the fabric of mythic narrative" (Lutgendorf 1991:251), *Rāmlīlā* has become a highly participatory form of drama. It draws millions of pilgrim-devotees from across India – especially the north and central regions. In the very geographical location where it is assumed that Lord Rama was born (Ayodhya) and lived in the distant past, *Rāmlīlā* re-enacts the trials and tribulations of Ram. Some performances last three to five days and others for over a month. Audiences can exceed one hundred thousand – including not only Hindus, but also minority Muslims and Christians. Performances culminate with the festival of Dussehra in which an effigy of the evil ten-headed demon-king, Ravana, is burned – a spectacular celebration of the victory of good over evil (Figure 3.4). The vast majority of these are based upon the lengthy poem, *Rāmcharitamānas*, authored by the poet Tulsidas (1532–1623), in a special local dialect of the regional vernacular – Hindi. The performances are done by amateur castes under the sponsorship of wealthy patrons.

In contrast to the highly decorative mode of composition of Sanskrit poetry still in use at the

Figure 3.4 Ravana, the ten-headed demon-king as an effigy as part of the Ramnagar *Rāmlīlā*. Photo © Richard Schechner.

time he wrote, Tulsidas authored his version of the *Ramayana* in accessible language. He records the moment he began composing his version of the story:

> Now reverently bowing my head to Shiva
> I narrate the spotless saga of Ram's deeds.
> In this year 1631 I tell the tale,
> laying my head at the Lord's feet.
> On Tuesday, the ninth of the gentle month,
> in the city of Avadh, these acts are revealed.
> 1.34.3–5 (Lutgendorf 1991:8)

In performance, Tulsidas's version of Ram's story is mapped onto the specific geographical locations understood to be dear to Lord Ram, so in effect, "the pageant came to express notions of cosmography and pilgrimage that aim at reclaiming and transforming the mundane world" (ibid.:255). The entire year becomes "for sadhus and other mobile devotees, a series of pilgrimages that re-enact the Lord's own movements and bring worshipers to the sites at which they re-experience his salvific deeds" (ibid.:250). Therefore, for Vivah Pancham – the celebration of Ram and Sita's wedding anniversary – the ideal site is pilgrimage to Mithila (Janakpur) in Nepal. The pilgrims able to travel there "identify themselves as members of Ram's . . . wedding party, and they trade humorous insults with the people of the bride's hometown" (ibid.:250). All *Rāmlīlās* involve the re-enactment of specific events from Ram's life and role playing. Some are brief, while others are elaborated at length.

> On the marriage day in Ayodhya . . . wedding processions mounted by major temples wind through the city for hours. They consist of lampbearers, drummers and shehnai players, "English-style" marching bands (all requisites of

a modern North Indian wedding), and of course the bridegrooms – Ram and his three brothers – astride horses or riding in ornate carriages. The grooms are usually *svarups* – young Brahman boys impersonating deities [Figure 3.5]. But a few processions feature temple images borne on palanquins. After receiving the homage of devotees before whose homes and shops they briefly halt, the processions return to their sponsoring establishments, where a marriage ceremony is performed. The crowds of devotees attending these rites are not merely spectators; they are encouraged to take the roles of members of the wedding party.

(ibid.:251)

At the most famous re-enactment at Ramnagar near Banaras, after a special set of offerings is given (*pūjā*), Tulsidas's version of Ram's sacred story is chanted/sung in its entirety by a group of 12 men

known as Ramayanis. They are accompanied by a *mṛdangam* drum. A prescribed number of couplets are sung daily. Only on the tenth day of recitation do the Ramayanis arrive at couplet 175 when the *Rāmlīlā* re-enactment of scenes per se begins. Their singing is then incorporated into the larger context of the *līlā*, and continues until they reach the last book of the *Rāmacharitamānasa*, when the *līlā* ends. But the recitation of the full text is not complete, so the Ramayanis continue their quiet reading until each word of the text has been read so that the final ritual passing of a flame (*aarti*) is held in Ayodhya, closing the full performance of 30–32 days.

Since the text is chanted, the actors do not simply recite the text of the drama, but rather like the dancers of old they "bring to life and . . . interpret the words of the recitation" (Hein 1972:124). All actors are males, with the roles of Sita, Ram, and his brother taken by prepubescent boys. They are worshiped as divine embodiments of those

Figure 3.5 A *Rāmlīlā* svarup on Hanuman's shoulders. Such young pre-pubescent boys play the holiest roles of Ram and Sita in performances where they are worshiped as the gods. Photo © Sam Schechner.

they impersonate (Figure 3.5). Other characters such as Hanuman the monkey king who helps Ram and the ten-headed demon-king Ravana, wear masks, and all the performers are amateurs. Some actors of a specific *Rāmlīlā* claim that their roles are inherited within their families, such as one actor playing the role of Ravana in 1990 who claimed the role had been in his family since the time of Ishvari Prasad Narayan Singh (1835–1889). The performance style is a combination of wordless tableaux and processional drama, in which actors move from place to place with occasional dialog that most of the devotees will not hear. Some locations are specially constructed for a *līlā* while others are actual landmarks in the town.

A deep, personal piety and devotion is at the heart of the *Rāmlīlā*, and motivates devotees to participate annually. The heartland of *Rāmlīlā* enactments is in the Banaras region where it is presumed the tradition was born, and the most famous dates from the nineteenth century under the sponsorship of the royal house of Banaras, where the Maharaja and Rama become "mirror images of each other, the twin heroes of the Ramnagar Ramlila" (Schechner and Hess 1977:74). The performance at Banaras reflects the traditional Hindu elision of the king as upholder of the cosmos.

In 1987–1988, the hugely popular Indian television serialization of the "Ramayan" was based primarily on Tulsidas's version. Hindu nationalists have recently recast Ram's kingship as a narrowly militant ideology which excludes minority Muslims and Christians who used to attend the *Rāmlīlās* in large numbers.

Early Chinese and Japanese drama, theatre, and performance

Song, dance, and impersonation central to Siberian-type shamanism in Korea constituted some of the earliest archaic forms of ritual and performance in pre-literate China and Japan (see Chapter 1). In China, male and female shamans date from before the Zhou dynasty (1027–256 B.C.E.). Early Chinese performance also featured court entertainers, dancers, jesters, and a form of story-telling in which the performer took on some roles during the telling.

In the state of Northern Qi during the sixth century, some performances integrated song, dance, and acrobatics with enactments based on actual events, such as "The Big Face," which tells of a beautiful prince who donned a terrifying battle mask in order to scare his enemies. This is said to be the origin of one type of elaborate face-painting used in what is known today as Beijing Opera, or *jingxi* "drama of the capital," also commonly known as *jingju*. Similarly, the swinging arms of an abused wife in "The Stomping-Swaying Wife" is thought to prefigure the graceful movements of the long, flowing "water sleeves" that some characters wear. The Chinese word *xi* (seen at the end of *jingxi* and similar terms) means both "game" and "play," and refers "to virtually any entertainment, acrobatics, sport, jest, or children's amusement" (Dolby 1976:4). The lay Chinese storytellers discussed in Chapter 1 gave picture-recitation performances of both sacred and secular stories from as early as the Tang period (C.E. 618–906) and represent the first extended vernacular narratives in China.

The first significant dramatic musical performance (Figure 3.6) enacting an extended narrative appeared during the Yuan Dynasty (1279–1368). Yuan dramas (*zaju*) are popular variety plays consisting of song, dance, monologues and even farce, most often written in four acts with a shorter "wedge." Each act featured a single singing role and musical mode, though these modes might change for each of the four acts. Only the wedge might contain variations. Male and female actors performed roles of either gender. Performances took place as part of temple or court ritual occasions, as well as in large urban theatres or teahouses as commercial enterprises. Many of these plays were written by classically educated Confucian scholars who had been

Figure 3.6 Thirteenth-century (Song dynasty) music drama (*zaju*). The period is just before the Mongol invasion that ushered in the Yuan dynasty. From a thirteenth-century tomb sculpture.
[Source: In William Dolby, *A History of Chinese Drama*. N.Y.: Barnes and Noble, 1976, Figure No. 1 facing p.100. Original source: Shao Jingshen, *Xiqu bitan*, Peking, Zong-hua Shuju Publishers, 1962, p.234.]

deprived of their court positions by Mongol invaders. Yuan dramas therefore contain both highly literate and highly entertaining elements, including crusading bandits fighting corrupt officials, romantic adventures, and supernatural rescues. In composing their dramas, Yuan playwrights drew on literary tales, dynastic histories, and popular oral narratives in which Confucian values were embedded. Many deal with lawsuits and justice (including murder cases), suggesting that the ousted scholars harbored and tapped into an undercurrent of dissatisfaction with the Mongol rulers. One of the best is *Injustice Done to Dou E* (*Dou E yuan*, also known as *Snow in Midsummer*) by Guan Hanqing (active late thirteenth century). It concerns a chaste young widow who is framed for murder by a man she refused to have sex with. At her execution, she calls on heaven to exonerate her, and indeed, the three miracles she prays for occur. After several years, her ghost appears to her long-lost father, now a righteous judge who is investigating corruption. The actual murderer is punished, and the girl's name is posthumously cleared.

This type of music drama continued to be popular even after the Yuan dynasty was replaced by the Ming dynasty (1368–1644). Among the most

well-known of all classical Chinese plays is the Ming drama, *The Peony Pavilion* (*Mudan ting*, 1598). Written in the same decade as *Romeo and Juliet*, this work by Tang Xianzu (1550–1617) also tells of a young couple's star-crossed love. However, *The Peony Pavilion* ends happily. Here a young girl dreams repeatedly of a lover she has never met, finally dying of longing. The young man sees the dead girl's portrait, falls in love, and braves the underworld to bring her back to life. Her father refuses to believe in her resurrection and accuses the young man of fraud. Political intrigues create further complications, but supernatural intervention leads to a happy ending. The music dramas that developed during the Yuan and Ming dynasties set the stage for the later development of numerous forms of regional sung dramas.

Chinese writing became the vehicle for the spread of Chinese models of culture, civilization, and values throughout East Asia. From its inception as a character-based system of early writing (*c.*1500–1545 B.C.E.), Chinese calligraphy evolved a distinctive aesthetic. Each individual character can be seen as an individual work of art; therefore, like Arabic, Chinese calligraphy developed into an art as important as any other — music, painting, or poetry.

In Japan, there had been no system of writing prior to the fourth century. This fact helps to explain the continuing power of the oral tradition in Japan (for example, story-telling and the presence of a chorus or narrator in many plays). After Japan invaded Korea in C.E. 370, Chinese writing and literature were introduced to the Japanese court by the Korean scholars who were brought there to educate the Crown Prince. However, since Japanese and Chinese are not related linguistically, Japanese scholars were forced to learn Chinese. The influence of Chinese writing and culture on Japan increased when Chinese Buddhism became the official religion of Japan during the mid-sixth century. By 645, Japan established a Confucian-based central administration, and Chinese writing was adapted to communicate old Japanese. Eventually, a complex system of writing developed that combined Chinese characters and Japanese phonetic writing.

The earliest pre-Buddhist/pre-Chinese forms of Japanese performance are Shinto-inspired forms of shamanistic propitiatory ceremonies and dances. Shinto is a set of utilitarian ritual practices intended to harness the natural forces of the environment in which it is assumed that everything – trees, birds, seas, animals, mountains, wind and thunder, etc. – has its own soul or spirit (*kami*). *Kami* are the natural energies and agents understood to animate matter and influence human behavior, and are sometimes identified as gods or goddesses.

When Buddhism came to Japan, it did not displace Shinto; rather, Buddhas and *kami* were and are often worshiped side by side. Interaction with China also brought the religious and philosophical influences of Confucianism and Taoism. Confucianism emphasizes maintenance of social harmony through hierarchical relationships in which the subordinate person (such as a child or wife) remains obedient and loyal to the higher-ranked person (such as a father, older brother, or husband) who behaves beneficently to the individual below. The

influence of Taoism in Japan is seen in the official incorporation of Taoistic practices into the state structure where, for example, a Bureau of Divination determined the auspicious timing of state occasions and officially interpreted good and bad omens.

One of the most significant Buddhist practices for the majority of Japanese became rituals honoring one's family ancestors. As we shall see, Japanese noh drama eventually became suffused with issues of the resolution of the pain or agony of restless, wandering spirits, both living and dead.

Along with Buddhism, Confucianism, and Taoism, contact with Chinese culture in the sixth century also brought the introduction of proto-theatrical court performances, including several types of masked dance dramas such as *bugaku* and *gigaku*. Some *gigaku* and *bugaku* masks depicting warriors, gods, and semi-mythical beasts dating from the Nara Period (710–84) are preserved in temple collections. These early masks may have influenced the design of some masks later used in noh theatre.

It was under the leadership of Kan'ami (1333–84) and his son Zeami (1363–1443) that noh evolved into a unique form of Japanese theatre and drama. Kan'ami was head of a troupe of *sarugaku* ("monkey music") actors that included Zeami. Originally, *sarugaku* was one of several types of traveling entertainments popular throughout the country. It was filled with visual variety and lively acts. In 1374, the troupe was offered patronage by the shogun, Ashikaga Yoshimitsu (1305–1358). Kan'ami's troupe began to live at court, and *sarugaku* became more refined as it transformed into a courtly genre. At court, the teenage Zeami not only performed, but he was trained in traditional aristocratic arts, including classical poetry. The new rulers of the Ashikaga clan were brash samurai warriors rather than elegant aristocrats. It was important for them to demonstrate their legitimate right to rule. With this in mind, they moved the seat of government back to the old imperial capital of Kyoto and began to adopt the tastes and practices of the aristocrats they replaced. Thus their rule gradually reunified the cultural and political centers.

Kan'ami's greatest innovation was the combination of popular mimetic drama with an elegant, aristocratic style. After his father's death, Zeami continued to refine artistic practice and transformed the social perception of formerly outcast actors. Noh came to be considered an elegant, refined, and philosophically self-reflexive set of artistic practices. As he matured, Zeami wrote many noh plays and a series of highly sophisticated treatises on the arts of acting and playwriting. These were meant only for his descendants, and they did not come to public attention until the early twentieth century. Today, Zeami is acknowledged as one of the world's most important dramatic theorists.

Today, noh is appreciated as a distinctive theatrical art drawing on many sources including indigenous shamanic and Shinto ritual practices, early performance traditions, and Buddhist spirituality and philosophy. It draws on literary masterpieces such as *The Tale of Genji* (*Genji monogatari*), written by the court lady Murasaki Shikibu around C.E. 1000, often considered to be the world's first novel. It also is indebted to historical accounts of clan warfare, such as are chronicled in *The Tale of the Heike*. All these elements were creatively adapted and crafted into plays by Kan'ami, Zeami, and their descendants. For example, when masks were adopted as part of the early development of noh, it was "a practical move by performers, intended to increase the credibility of, and give poignancy to, their performances in the roles of supernatural beings and ghosts" (Ortolani 1984:179). As the noh stage evolved, it began to be modeled on the architecture of Shinto shrines (Figure 3.7).

Figure 3.7 A Japanese noh stage. It achieved the shape shown here by the sixteenth century. At first a separate structure, located in a courtyard, as seen here at the Buddhist temple of Nishi Honganji in Kyoto, it was housed within a larger building by the late nineteenth century. The stage proper remained covered by its own roof and linked to the green room by a raised passageway (*hashigakari*). © Monica Bethe and Karen Brazell. [Source: Figure 1.9, p.14 in *Dance in the Nô Theatre: Volume One. Dance Analysis* by Monica Bethe and Karen Brazell. Cornell University: China-Japan Program. Ithaca, 1982. The Cornell East Asia Papers series Published with permission.]

Although the period of Ashikaga rule (1336–1573, also known as the Muromachi period) was created by samurai warriors, the noh plays they preferred to watch were seldom about military victory. Rather, in keeping with the tastes of the aristocrats they had displaced, they preferred plays dealing with tragic love affairs, unrequited passions, the agony of defeated warriors, the elegance of old age, or supernatural events. The majority of the approximately 240 noh plays still performed today were written during the Muromachi period.

The centrality of supernatural beings and ghosts and the traces of shamanic practices in the early development of noh can be seen in the Japanese noh play, *Aoi no ue* (*Lady Aoi*, c.fifteenth century as revised by Zeami). The play was inspired by a chapter in *The Tale of Genji*. At the opening of the play, the audience sees an elaborate folded robe in the middle of a highly polished wooden floor of the stage (Figures 3.7, 3.8). The empty robe represents the prostrate figure of the mortally ill Princess Aoi, the pregnant wife of Prince Genji. She has been

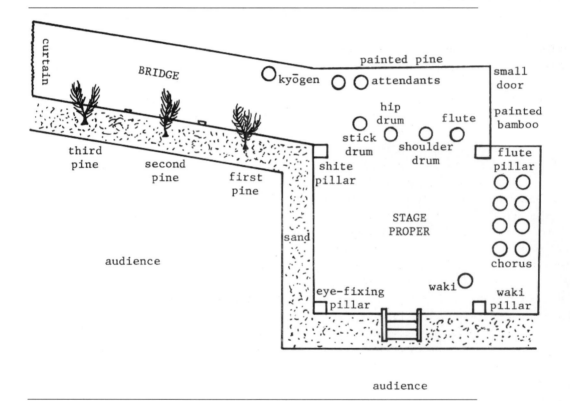

Figure 3.8 Noh stage plan, indicating locations of musicians, chorus, and attendants. The painted pine and bamboo on the upstage wall and the three pine trees arranged along the passageway reflect the outdoor origins of the theatre. Stage and passageway are separated from the audience by a strip of sand or gravel. © Monica Bethe and Karen Brazell. [Source: Bethe and Brazell, as in Figure 3.7: Figure 1.11, p.151.]

possessed by the angry, restless spirit of Lady Rokujô, Genji's former mistress, whose living spirit leaves her body when she sleeps. A Shinto shamaness performs a ritual to call forth this spirit that is possessing Lady Aoi. At the far end of the bridgeway (hashigakari), the curtain is lifted by stage attendants, and from the green room emerges the spirit of Lady Rokujô, performed by a male actor in an exquisitely carved female mask. Lady Rokujô eventually reveals her identity:

> In this mortal world ephemeral as lightning,
> I should hate nobody,
> nor should my life be one of sorrow.
> When ever did my spirit begin to wander?
> Who do you think this person is
> who appears before you now
> drawn by the sound of the catalpa bow!
> I am the vengeful spirit of Lady Rokujô.
> (Goff 1991:135)

Since the shamaness only has sufficient power to call forth but not exorcise this invading spirit, a male Buddhist mountain priest (a "warrior priest" or *yamabushi*) is summoned to perform the exorcism. For feminist critics today, his successful exorcism, together with other factors, marks an interesting difference between the male-authored play and its female-authored source. In the original tale, Lady Aoi dies. In the male-authored play, the male Buddhist priest succeeds where, in the female-authored tale, the female Shinto shamaness does not. In the case study following this chapter, the feminist critical approach is seen to be fruitful in the analysis of another famous noh play, *Dôjôji*.

Although noh plays are characterized by and appreciated for their finely crafted, suggestive poetry, Zeami was most concerned with the performer's superior artistry as shaped by Zen Buddhist thought and practice. This concern with the development of artistic skill is revealed in the remarkable set of treatises that Zeami wrote, in which he considers both the practical and philosophical "secrets" of his evolving artistry. His texts cover key principles such as finding ways to please an audience, the rhythmic development of plays and performance (jo, ha, kyû, "introduction, intensification, and rapid close"). He offers an analysis of mask/character types and advice on how to play each, metaphysical reflections on the path of the actor, treatises on writing plays, and complex discussions of aesthetic principles.

The concern with artistic elaboration that constitutes noh performance is also reflected in the acting versions of noh plays in their recording of the scores chanted by the actors of each of the five schools. Figure 3.9 provides a modern example of a syllable-by-syllable translation of the text as it is vocally elaborated in specific chant styles cued by the score. Because Japanese syllables end in vowels – "kyo . . . o . . . o . . . mo . . . I . . . ta . . . tsu" – chant styles developed that allowed the actor to elaborate and elongate the vowel that ends each syllable.

The vagaries and uncertainties of court patronage that first produced noh are revealed in the fact that Zeami, in his seventies, was banished to the island of Sado in 1434, to be granted an amnesty in 1441. The case study on noh below provides a further description and analysis of this earliest form of Japanese drama and theatre in performance and in cultural context.

Summary discussion

Throughout Part I, we have explored the earliest forms of performance and then drama and theatre as they emerged in several different regions of the world. In this chapter, we often have focused, especially in the three case studies, on formal, aesthetic issues, trying also to consider the socio-cultural and religious context that produced each mode of appreciation and pleasure. One striking similarity among Greek, Roman, Indian, and Japanese playwrights is their utilization of archaic, epic stories as the basis for their creative work. What was familiar became "new," transformed and elaborated by each particular

次第立わ
（小ノ川）強衆き

WAKI &
WAKIZURE

I	SET		KYO	TO-
TSU	EYES		O	DAY
TO	ON		O	WE
SA	MI-		MO	BOLD-
DA	YA-		I	LY
ME	KO		TA	PUT
N	AGAIN		TSU	ON
			TA	OUR
			BI	TRA-
			GO	VE-
			RO	LING
			MO	CLOTHES

KYO	TO-
O	DAY
O	WE
MO	BOLD-
I	LY
TA	PUT
TSU	ON
TA	OUR
BI	TRA-
GO	VE-
RO	LING
MO	CLOTHES
KI	AND
RA	WHEN
KU	SHALL
O	WE

Figure 3.9 A modern noh acting score for *Funa Benkei*, showing the first part of the chanted text in Royal Tyler's performance translation of the Kita School acting score of the play, directed by Akira Matsui in Madison, Wisconsin (1982). Reading down the right column, one can see that the English acting version has been scored syllable-by-syllable to match the original Japanese, allowing English-speaking actors to chant the text as closely as possible to the original.
[Unpublished performance translation.]

artistic genius, refracted through the prism of his or her cultural sensibility.

PZ

Key references

Bhasa (1985 [1930]) *Thirteen Plays*, trans. A.C. Woolner and L. Sarup, Delhi: Molilal Banarsidass.

Bieber, M. (1961) *The History of the Greek and Roman Theater*, Princeton: Princeton University Press.

Blacker, C. (1975) *The Catalpa Bow: A Study of Shamanistic Practices in Japan*, London: George Allen & Unwin Ltd.

Dolby, W. (1976) *A History of Chinese Drama*, New York: Harper and Row.

Duckworth, G.E. (trans.) (1941) *The Complete Roman Drama*, New York: Random House.

Fei, F.C. (ed.) (1999) *Chinese Theories of Theater and Performance from Confucius to the Present*, Ann Arbor: University of Michigan Press.

George, D.E.R. (1999) *Buddhism as/in Performance: Analysis of Meditation and Theatrical Practice*, New Delhi: D.K. Printworld(P), Ltd.

Ghosh, M. (ed. and trans.) (1967, 1961) *The Nātyśastra*, vol. I, Calcutta: Manisha Granthalaya, 1967; vol. II, Calcutta: Asiatic Society, 1961.

Goff, J. (1991) *Noh Drama and The Tale of Genji*, Princeton: Princeton University Press.

Hawley, J.S. (1981) *At Play with Krishna: Pilgrimage Dramas from Brindavan*, Princeton: Princeton University Press.

Hein, N. (1972) *The Miracle Plays of Mathura*, New Haven: Yale University Press.

Inoura, Y. and Kawatake, T. (1981) *The Traditional Theatre of Japan*, New York: Weatherhill.

Kapur, A. (1990) *Actors, Pilgrims, Kings and Gods: The Ramlila at Ramnagar*, Calcutta: Seagull Press.

Keene, D. (1966) *Nô: The Classical Theatre of Japan*, New York: Kodansha International.

Keene, D. (1970) *Twenty Plays of the Nô Theatre*, New York: Columbia.

Lidova, N. (1994) *Drama and Ritual of Early Hinduism*, Delhi: Motilal Banarsidass.

Lutgendorf, P. (1991) *The Life of a Text: Performing the Ramcaritmanas of Tulsidas*, Berkeley: University of California Press.

Mahabharata (1970) translated and summarized by C. Rajogopalachari, 10th edn, Chowpatty, Bombay: Bharatya Vidya Bhavan.

Mahabharata (1998) English version based on selected verses, by Chakravarthi V. Narasimhan, rev. edn, New York: Columbia University Press.

Marasinghe, E.W. (1989) *The Sanskrit Theatre and Stagecraft*, Delhi: Sri Satguru Publications.

Mehta, T. (1995) *Sanskrit Play Production in Ancient India*, Delhi: Motilal Banarsidass.

Murasaki, S. (1935) *The Tale of Genji*, trans. A. Waley, Boston, New York: Houghton Mifflin Co.

Nagler, A.M. (1952) *A Source Book in Theatrical History*, New York: Dover Publications, Inc., citing *The Works of Lucian of Samosata*, trans. H.W. Fowler and F.G. Fowler, Oxford: The Clarendon Press, III, 249–263.

Ortolani, B. (1984) "Shamanism in the Origins of the Nô Theatre," *Asian Theatre Journal*, 1, 2:166–190.

Ortolani, B. (1995) *The Japanese Theatre: From Shamanistic Ritual to Contemporary Pluralism*, Princeton: Princeton University Press.

Schechner, R. (1983) "Ramlila of Ramnagar: An Introduction," in *Performative Circumstances from the Avant Garde to Ramlila*, Calcutta: Seagull Press, 238–288.

Schechner, R. and Hess, L. (1977) "The Ramlila of Ramnagar," *TDR*, 21, 3:51–82.

Shih, C.-W. (1976) *The Golden Age of Chinese Drama: Yuan Tsa-Chu*, Princeton: Princeton University Press.

Slater, N.W. (1985) *Plautus in Performance*, Princeton: Princeton University Press.

Tang, X. (2002) *The Peony Pavilion*, trans. Cyril Birch, 2nd edn, Bloomington: University of Indiana Press.

Walton, J.M. and Arnott, P.D. (1996) *Menander and the Making of Comedy*, Westport, Conn.: Greenwood Press.

Wiles, D. (1991) *The Masks of Menander: Sign and Meaning in Greek and Roman Performance*, Cambridge: Cambridge University Press.

CASE STUDY: Plautus's plays: What's so funny?

Comedy has been more important to the human race than the history of western dramatic criticism would suggest. Tragedy dominated that history for over two thousand years. Aristotle (384–322 B.C.E.) devoted his famous *Poetics* (*c.*330 B.C.E.) to Greek tragedy, only glancing at comedy. If his promised book on comedy was ever written, it has never been recovered (Janko 1984: Parts I, IV). In western theory since, comedy has played second fiddle to tragedy because of tragedy's high-born characters, its elevated language, the moral weight of its issues of human suffering, and its ultimate idealism about human potential under duress. Yet the early Greek philosophers did recognize that the theatre's rendering of human experience would be incomplete without a comic vision; Socrates, while drinking with friends, once made the fruitful suggestion that the genius of comedy is the same as that for tragedy (Plato 1942:215–216). The Greeks and Romans kept the two separate, however, unlike Shakespeare, who mingled kings and clowns in his tragedies such as *Hamlet* and *Macbeth* – a sore point for the neoclassical critics who came after him. This case study looks at selected plays of the Roman

comic playwright, Titus Maccius Plautus (254–184 B.C.E.) in the light of the comic theory of French philosopher, Henri Bergson (1859–1941), whose book on laughter in 1900 took comedy seriously.

First, it will be useful to consider some of the major western notions about the formal characteristics of comedy as a genre, including Aristotle's brief comments. Aristotle's critical method was inductive, reasoning from a number of specific Athenian examples toward what he believed to be universal laws for the drama. Distinguishing between tragedy and comedy, he reasoned that comedy "tends naturally to imitate men worse, [tragedy] to imitate men better, than the average." Comedy will be populated by "characters of a lower type," he observed, while tragedy's chief characters will be from great and "illustrious" families (nobility or ruling families). (Aristotle 1957:376; Aristotle 1984:2319, 2325). Comedy's home, it follows, is not the court but the domestic household or neighborhood street. Comedy's affairs being on a domestic scale, it may be added, comedy's plots almost invariably involve food, money, sex, or social status. Also, as the principal character in a tragedy will have, according to

Figure 3.10 This Roman marble relief show a performance of masked characters typical of Roman comedy, including the two older men at left and the young man at right with a scheming servant at his side. Between them, a musician plays the double-reed aulos, suggestive of the important place of music in some of the comedies. Behind the actors is a door of the façade backing the stage and a small curtain (*siparia*), perhaps concealing a painted panel not relevant to this particular scene. © Museo Nazionale, Naples.

Figure 3.11 Statue of a masked slave character from Roman comedy, leaning casually on a pillar. Archaeological Museum, Istanbul. Photo © Gary Jay Williams.

Aristotle, a flaw leading to his/her fall, so too, it may be inferred from Aristotle, will the chief character in comedy. The chief humor of comedy, Aristotle says, will derive from a defect that is neither painful nor destructive (Aristotle 1957:183).

Following Aristotle's mode of formal analysis, later theorists made distinctions between high and low comedy. In high comedy, much of the humor derives from ideas and witty language. (The more socially oriented critic would point out that these are the prerogatives of an economically privileged class.) In low comedy, the humor derives less from refined reflection than from fast-developing events and physical action, with the body being a major player. The phallus is a standing joke in the oldest of western comic forms – built into the costumes of the characters in the Greek satyr plays. To these major ideas about western comedy may be added Northrop

Frye's fruitful observation in his archetypal theory of comedy that comedies usually end with some festive ritual, such as dinner or a wedding, signaling the formation of a new society (Frye 1957:163–168).

Plautus wrote some 130 plays according to contemporary reports, sometime between 205 and 184 B.C.E. The 21 extant plays show the work of an experienced theatrical craftsman. They are characterized by inventive fast-moving plots in domestic Roman settings, with efficiently-defined characters, clever language, and broad physical business (Figure 3.10). In their overflow of comic energies, they stand in contrast to the comedies of Terence (c.195–159 B.C.E.), which are built around relatively more complex characters and ideas and are somewhat more rational and constrained. In Plautus's comedies, there are many examples of the operation of Henri Bergson's principles of the comic.

INTERPRETIVE APPROACH, PART I: Henry Bergson's theory of laughter

Bergson was a philosopher and known specifically for his philosophy of vitalism, a spiritualized concept of evolutionary life processes and personal development being informed by a vital impulse, an *élan vital* that materialism and science cannot explain, working toward perfection. (George Bernard Shaw's Fabian "life force" was a variation on the idea; see Chapter 9). Bergson's philosophy was in some part a resistant response to the scientific rationalism of his time and to the increasingly clockwork mechanization of humanity in the workplace and in middle-class life generally.

His theory of comedy suggests that we find it funny when "something mechanical is encrusted on something living." He writes, "The attitudes, gestures, and movements of the human body are laughable in exact proportion as that body reminds us of a mere machine" (Bergson 1956:84, 97, 79). We laugh when we watch a human being so single-minded that he or she "resembles a piece of clockwork wound up once for all and capable of working automatically" (ibid.:156). We laugh at the character who behaves less like a fully-engaged human being and more like an automaton, driven by some fixed idea (ibid.:180). The ingredients of comic character, Bergson suggests, are "rigidity, automatism, absentmindedness, and unsociability" (ibid.:156). Laughter is society's corrective for such asocial creatures (ibid.:187–189).

These are some key questions that can be asked of any comedy when using Bergson's theory.

KEY QUESTIONS

1   In which dramatic character(s) do we see human behavior that makes us laugh because it is comically machine-like, rigid, inflexible, unsociable?

2   Where does the action of the play seem to take on a mechanized life of its own?

3   Where does the language of the play seem to take on a mechanical life of its own?

Vanity, in Bergson's opinion, is one of the best fuels for the mechanized comic character, who is generally comic in proportion to his ignorance of himself (ibid.:171–173, 71). The central character of Plautus's *The Braggart Soldier* (*Miles Gloriosus*, 205 B.C.E.) is wholly infatuated with himself, bragging about his victories, his strength (he says he killed an elephant with his fist), and his sexual prowess. His slave, who struggles to carry his master's oversized shield, feeds his ridiculous appetite for flattery, once describing his master as "Destiny's dashing dauntless debonair darling" (Plautus 1963:9). Late in the play, sure that every woman wants him, the vain soldier flatters himself preposterously, confiding that he was born only one day after Jove and is the grandson of Venus (ibid.:80). His servant's scheme, and the play's whole purpose, is to wind him up to strut like this. When a collaborating servant girl greets him with "Hail, you gorgeous creature! / Oh, man of every hour, beyond all other men / Beloved of two gods – " he interrupts her to ask, "Which two?" (ibid.:90). In Plautus's *The Pot of Gold*, the miserly old Euclio is Bergson's automaton. Euclio is obsessed with money and so fears that someone will steal the pot of gold he has hidden that he suspects everyone, including the rooster he finds scratching near it, which he instantly kills. The foxy slave of his daughter's suitor does steal Euclio's gold, and when Euclio ultimately gives the suitor permission to marry his daughter, he does so only because that will get him his pot of gold back.

Bergson's idea of the mechanization of the human as a source of humor extends to plot situations and sequences. We laugh when "the history of a person or of a group . . . sometimes appears like a game worked by strings, or gearings, or springs" (ibid.:116). So it is in Plautus's *The Menaechmi*, which features identical twin brothers (a happily practical idea for a theatre in which all characters wore masks). Long lost to each other by misfortune, the twins are reunited by fate in the city of Epidamnum, but only after a chain of events in which each brother is repeatedly mistaken for the other. In twins, there is the momentary suggestion that life's reproducing machine was inadvertently left turned on. Twins pose the disconcerting possibility that people are but an arithmetic of interchangeable features, destabilizing our assumptions about individual identity. In *The Menaechmi*, the plot is a calculus of complications set off by the presence of the twins. Menaechmus II, from Syracuse, searching the world for his brother, arrives in Epidamnum where his brother, Menaechmus I, lives. The mistress of Menaechmus I, Erotium, mistakenly invites Menaechmus II into her house, supposing him to be her lover. So, too, the angry wife of Menaechmus I and all the household servants of MI mistake MII for MI. Each twin concludes that the world around him has gone mad.

Everyone else believes the twins to be mad, including the doctor who is called in by Erotium's father. In exasperation at one point, Menaechmus II feigns madness to be rid of them all. Plautus multiplies the confusions by repeatedly having one twin exit by one door just as the other enters by another. All the characters revolve in and out of the doors of the houses of Erotium and Menaechmus I like figures on a mechanical clock gone haywire. (The Roman stage consisted of a platform backed by a façade with two or more doorways representing the houses.) The audience is always in on the joke because Plautus is always careful to have the entering twin identify himself clearly. At the play's climax, the twins finally meet at center stage, mirroring one another, and to the relief of everyone, they sort out the confusion.

Bergson's mechanization principle can also be seen operating in portions of Plautus's dialog. Near the end of *The Rope*, Daemones and the slave, Trachalio, who serves the suitor of Daemones's daughter, have a rapid-fire exchange of lines in which the response "All right" is repeated seventeen times. After Trachalio exits, Plautus caps the sequence:

DAEMONES: All Right, all right, nothing but "all right". He'll find all right's all wrong one of these days, I hope.
[Enter Gripus, another slave]
GRIPUS: Will it be all right [Daemones jumps] if I have a word with you, sir?
                                        (Plautus 1964:145–146)

A moment later, Trachalio has a series of exchanges with his young master, Plesidippus, who is love with Daemones's daughter:

PLESIDIPPUS: Do you think we shall be betrothed today?
TRACHALIO: I do.
PLESIDIPPUS: Do you think I should congratulate the old man on finding her?
TRACHALIO: I do.

PLESIDIPPUS: And the mother?

TRACHALIO: I do.

PLESIDIPPUS: And what do you think?

TRACHALIO: I do.

PLESIDIPPUS: You do what?

TRACHALIO: I think.

PLESIDIPPUS: You do think what?

TRACHALIO: I do think what you think.

PLESIDIPPUS: Don't you think you could think for yourself?

TRACHALIO: I do.

(Plautus 1964:147–148)

In both cases, the robotic responses of the slave, Trachalio, produce a comic momentum that threatens to unravel language itself (Figure 3:10). (Compare Abbot and Costello's famous skit, "Who's on First?")

Bergson offers other ideas about what is funny, such as inversion (the robber robbed or the parent being lectured by the child) and the snowball effect (something sets off a chain reaction of events that accelerates toward total collapse) (Bergson 1956: 121–122; 112). To Bergson's ideas we may add a final source of humor: theatre mocking its own conventions. Consider the following lines in Plautus's prologue to *Amphitryo*, which is delivered by the god Mercury in disguise as a lowly servant.

But I still haven't told you

About this favor I came to ask of you –

Not to mention explaining the plot of this tragedy.

I must get on . . .

What's that? Are you disappointed

To find it's a *tragedy*? Well, I can easily change it.

I'm a god after all. I can easily make it a comedy. . . .

(Plautus 1964:230)

The passage is amusing not only because Mercury is treated with irreverent familiarity, but also because Plautus is mocking theatrical conventions here, including prologs. Overall, this prolog suggests a familiarity with comic performance that would support the speculation that Plautus was a comic actor. The middle name that he took, Maccius, may be derivative of Maccus, the name of a clown figure in the ancient Atellan farces (see Chapter 3) who was greedy and gluttonous, the type of character that Plautus might have played (ibid.:8–9).

Bergson's theories will not make Plautus's plays any deeper. Plautus was apparently happy entertaining a relatively broad-based audience. In *The Rope*, he mocks comedies that pretend to aspire higher. After the character Daemones gives a pretentious speech about how wonderful it is to be as moral as he is, his slave comments: "Huh! I've heard actors in comedies spouting that sort of stuff, telling people how to behave, and getting applause for it. But I never heard of any of the audience behaving any the better for it, after they got home" (ibid.:147).

Plautus's plays have had staying power. One century after his death the critic M. Terentius Varro put together a collection of 20 of the 21 plays of his that survived. They may well have been performed – or variations on them – down through the early years of the Roman Empire. Plautus brought over some of his stock characters and plots from the prolific Greek comic playwright, Menander (342–291 B.C.E.) (Figure 3.1), but only one of Menander's plays survives – *Dyskolos*, translated as *The Grouch*. So, it is through Plautus that many classical prototypes – characters and plots – survived down through the early modern period and beyond. Among the many descendants of Plautus's *miles gloriosus* – the braggart soldier – are the Capitano and Scaramouche of the *commedia dell'arte* and Shakespeare's Falstaff in *Henry IV, Part 1* (1598). Plautus's *The Menaechmi* is the source of Shakespeare's *Comedy of Errors* (1598), to which Shakespeare added a second set of identical twin slaves from Plautus's *Amphitryon*. The *Comedy of Errors* was the source for Rodgers and Hart's musical comedy, *The Boys from Syracuse*, adapted by

George Abbot (1938). *Amphitryon* was the source for no fewer than 38 versions down to Jean Giradoux's *Amphitryon 38* (1929), and Plautus's *The Pot of Gold* was the source of Molière's *The Miser* (1668). The 1962 American musical comedy, *A Funny Thing Happened on the Way to the Forum* (book by Burt Shevelove, Larry Gelbart, and music by Steven Sondheim) was a long-running concoction derived from Plautus (a 1966 film version is a tiresome catalog of unfunny mugging).

INTERPRETIVE APPROACH, PART II: Bergson's theory in historical perspective

To some degree, all theories reflect the cultural discourse of their time. As Bergson set out at the end of the nineteenth century to theorize universal laws of comedy, he was operating, unquestioningly, from his experience as a French white male of privilege, in a nation that had long been a major colonizing power, especially in Africa. His examples are preponderantly French, from the seventeenth-century plays of Molière to the nineteenth-century plays of Eugene Labiche. He does not test his theory with plays outside western culture.

Some parts of his analysis are painful to sensibilities today. In a discussion of comic disguise, Bergson asks "Why does one laugh at the negro?" His answer is that a black face, "in our imagination, is one daubed over with ink or soot . . . though the black . . . color is indeed inherent in the skin, we look upon it as artificially laid on, because it surprises us" (Bergson 1956:86–87). The third person plural refers to Bergson and his assumed white readers. In our globalized world a century later, variations in skin color are neither a source of surprise nor amusement; the concept of fundamental human rights has made possible some progress toward making it repugnant to use race or color as bases for oppressive judgments. Nor would Bergson's method lead us to ask about the status of Plautus's comic slaves.

Bergson's Victorian ideas of gender inform his analysis, as is in evidence in his discussion of comic effects generally in language. He observes that the phrase "*Tous les arts sont frères*" (all the arts are brothers) is commonly accepted because, he believes, the masculine *frères* always will be understood as symbolizing humankind. It would be comic, he says, to say, "*Tous les arts sont soeurs*" (all the arts are sisters), because, "sisters" could never be understood symbolically (ibid.:135–136). Here, Bergson represents as a matter of universal law what was in fact the result of a culturally limiting notion of women in his time. Not surprisingly, in his essay, male characters form the basis of his "universal" proofs.

To dismiss Bergson's work entirely for such embedded values would be to overlook the insights that remain viable. But the case is instructive. The study of theatre brings with it ethical responsibilities to identify the values, implicit or explicit, in any historical coverage and any critical approach one chooses. Reading a variety of interpretive approaches in theatre and performance helps one to form one's own critical sensibilities and to make ethically-informed decisions.

GJW

Key references

Aristotle (1957) *Aristotle's Poetics: The Argument*, trans. G.F. Else, Cambridge, Mass.: Harvard University Press.

Aristotle (1984) *Poetics*, trans. I. Bywater in *The Complete Works of Aristotle*, rev. edn, J. Barnes (ed.), vol. 2, Princeton: Princeton University Press.

Bergson, H. (1956) "Laughter," in *Comedy*, Garden City, N.Y.: Doubleday Anchor Books.

Duckworth, G.E. (1942) *The Complete Roman Drama*, vol. 1, New York: Random House.

Frye, N. (1957) *Anatomy of Criticism*, Princeton: Princeton University Press.

Janko, R. (1984) *Aristotle on Comedy, Toward a Reconstruction of Poetics II*, Berkeley: University of California Press.

Plato (1942) *Symposium*, in *Plato, Five Great Dialogues,* trans. B. Jowett, Roslyn, N.Y.: Walter J. Black.

Plautus, T.M. (1974) *The Twin Menaechmi*, trans. Edward C. Wiest and Richard W. Hyde in O.G. Brockett and L. Brockett (eds), *Plays for the Theatre*, 2nd edn, New York: Holt, Rinehart and Winston.

Plautus, T.M. (1958) *The Pot of Gold*, trans. Peter Arnott, New York: Appleton-Century-Crofts.

Plautus, T.M. (1963) *The Braggart Soldier*, trans. Erich Segal, New York: Samuel French.

Plautus, T.M. (1964) "Amphityro," in *The Rope and Other Plays*, trans. E.F. Watling, Baltimore: Penguin Books.

Slater, N.W. (1985) *Plautus in Performance*, Princeton: Princeton University Press.

CASE STUDY: Kutiyattam Sanskrit theatre of India: *Rasa-bhāva* aesthetic theory and the question of taste

Sometime in the fifteenth century, an unknown, highly educated connoisseur/scholar, writing in Sanskrit, attacked the "unfounded foul practices" of a specialized community of male and female actors (*cākyārs* and *naṅgyārs*) in Kerala, India. In his "Goad on the Actors," he wrote:

> Our only point is this – the sacred drama (*nāṭya*), by the force of ill-fate, now stands defiled. The ambrosial moon and the sacred drama – both are sweet and great. A black spot mars the beauty of the former; unrestrained movements that of the latter. 'What should we do then' [to correct these defilements]?
>
> Listen. The performance should strictly adhere to the precepts of Bharata [author of the *Nāṭyaśastra*]. Keep out the interruption of the story. Remove things unconnected. Stop your elaboration. . . . Reject the regional tongue. Discard the reluctance to present the characters.

> . . . Always keep the self of the assumed character. This is the essence of acting. One follows the principles of drama if things are presented in this way.
>
> (Paulose 1993:158–159)

Today the Kerala actors still perform Sanskrit dramas in their distinct regional style, known as kutiyattam. The fifteenth-century author was attacking the kutiyattam actors for their "blasphemous" and "ill-logical" deviations from precepts for staging Sanskrit dramas found in the *Nāṭyaśastra*, written at least 1,200 years earlier, which he considered definitive. The "defects" were obstacles in the path by which he expected to come to a proper aesthetic experience of Sanskrit drama.

The *Nāṭyaśastra*, summarized in Chapter 3, is attributed to the sage Bharata (*c*.200 B.C.E.–C.E. 200). As with many "authoritative" texts dating from antiquity, no manuscripts exist from the period of its composition. The earliest extant version dates from 1,000 years or more later. Today scholars construct editions from 52 different copies.

It is unclear if the author, "Bharata," was a single historical person, an assumed name, a name representing a school of thought/practice, or an acronym in which the first syllable, *Bhā* stood for *bhāva*, the states of being/doing embodied by the actors (Vatsyayan 1996:6). Whoever he was, the author/compiler was an accomplished, modest practitioner/theorist following a lineage of practice: "I am not able by any means to exhaust all the topics about drama; for knowledge, and arts and crafts connected with it are respectively manifold and endless in number." Although focused primarily on theatre, the *Nātyaśastra* became the authoritative sourcebook for subsequent practice and aesthetic theory in all India's arts, including literature, music, architecture, painting, and sculpture.

Early Sanskrit drama in performance

Sanskrit drama was written in the melodic language within the Indo-Aryan language subgroup closely related to Latin, Greek and most European languages. The earliest Sanskrit texts date back some 3,000 years to the oldest book of Hindu hymns, the *Rg Veda*. The earliest Hindu sacred texts, including drama and the *Nātyaśastra*, were composed in Sanskrit. Probably reflecting social status, these dramas use Sanskrit for high-status male characters, while all women, children, men of inferior status, and the stock comic character (Vidusaka) speak in varieties of Prakrits – dialects evolved from Sanskrit. As these dialects fell into disuse over the years, they became less and less comprehensible to audiences.

Early troupes and/or performances, patronized by the courts, were often part of religious festivals. Ideally, performances took place in specially constructed theatres or in halls at court, intimate enough for the nuances of an actor-dancer's performance to be appreciated. As described in the *Nātyaśastra*, actors followed a rigorous training regime that included a special diet, full body massages, yoga, and extensive

training in "dance postures, physical exercise . . . [and] rhythm" (Kale 1974:57–58). Actors trained rigorously in order to embody each role mentally and physically and thereby "carry forward" (*abhinaya*) the appropriate experience for an audience to "taste." Their regimen included training in body movement, the language of hand-gestures, voice, emotional expression, and costumes and make-up. Actors learned physical vocabularies for representing both the ordinary things in nature – for the miming of a deer – and for abstract concepts. The Indian actor's body was to become a vehicle through which the performance of each role allowed the audience to "taste" the experience. Emphasis was on developing fourfold expression in bodily movement, including hand gestures, vocal expression, inner expressivity of emotions, and external aspects, especially important being costumes and makeup since scenery was minimal.

Of the many types of Sanskrit dramas, the best known are heroic dramas, such as *Sākuntala* by Kalidasa (*c.*100 B.C.E.–C.E. 400), a seven-act play based on well known epic sources, and invented dramas such as *The Little Clay Cart* by Sudraka (active sometime between the third and sixth century C.E.). Minor forms included one-act farces, two of which were written by the seventh-century South Indian king, Mahendravarman, *A Farce of Drunken Sport* and *The Hermit/Harlot*.

Regardless of type, Sanskrit dramas follow a set of conventions. All begin with an invocation (*nandī*), followed by a prolog, and all conclude with a benedictory prayer. The prolog is in effect a metatheatrical playlet in which the Sutradhara – the leader of the company of actors who often played the leading male role – engages with another actor in a brief conversation that foreshadows the plot and reflects upon the characters and the theatrical conventions of the performance to come.

The language of the texts alternates between simple prose and ornate verse in a variety of meters. Both are chanted and/or sung to musical accompaniment, though perhaps some small prose sections may be spoken. The purpose of the verse passages is not to carry forward the narrative, but to allow reflection, commentary, and a deepening of the state of mind of the main character(s). The opening passage of the play proper in King Mahendravarman's seventh century one-act farce, *The Hermit/Harlot*, illustrates the difference between prose and verse. The ill-tempered Bhagavan enters looking for his wayward student, and calls out:

> Shandilya! Shandilya! He's not to be seen. Quite fitting for one who is surrounded by the darkness of ignorance. For:
>
> > *The body, a mine of diseases, subject to old age,*
> > *Poised on the brink of hidden Death,*
> > *Is like a tree on a river bank,*
> > *About to be uprooted by the ever-battering wave.*
> >
> > *And though such human embodiment is earned*
> > *Through numerous good deeds, yet,*
> > *Deluded by materialism intoxicated with his strength,*

> > *Good looks, and youth, man is blind to those defects grave.*
>
> Therefore, really, this poor fellow can't be blamed. I'll call him once again. Shandilya! Shandilya!
>
> (Lockwood and Bhat 1994 (Part II:20)

The Sanskrit verse (*italics*) provides the actor with numerous images rich for physical elaboration.

The stage was conventionally assumed by audience and actors to be divided into zones. Actors moving from one part of the stage to another indicated a shift in locale. This convention also allowed the action to shift back and forth between two groups of actors on stage. In *The Hermit/Harlot* the comedic exchange of souls between the Bhagavan and the courtesan takes place in two locales – the part of the garden where the Bhagavan is undergoing his meditation and the part where the courtesan awaits her lover.

The Hermit/Harlot

The prolog establishes both the structure and comedic tone of the farce to follow. The Sutradhara, leader of the troupe and main actor (later playing the role of the Bhagavan) announces to the Vidusaka (played by the actor who later plays Shandilya) that their acting company will soon be invited to perform a play "at the royal palace," and that they must be pleasing to the King.

VIDUSAKA: What type of play, sir, are you going to put on?

SUTRADHARA: [After consulting various] critical treatises on drama . . . [and considering] the various *rasas* discussed . . . the primary, the most important *rasa* is the one that provokes laughter. Therefore, I'm going to put on a farce.

VIDUSAKA: Sir, though I'm a comedian, I know nothing about farce!

SUTRADHARA: Then learn!

The Sutradhara's conclusion that he should put on a farce because it is the "most important *rasa*" is amusing because farce is a "minor" dramatic form, and comedy always takes secondary place to the heroic and erotic sentiments. A metatheatrical layer of humor is created by the fact that the company of actors is, at the moment, performing a farce written by the King himself.

In the play proper, a young man, Shandilya, has become a wandering mendicant who also "must learn" at the feet of a supposedly learned teacher/practitioner, Bhagavan, who belongs to a severe Hindu Saivite sect that practices yoga and austerities.

▷

SUTRADHARA: I was born in a family which flourished on the remains of the food of crows . . . [with] tongues untouched by learning. . . . [With] no food in our house, I became a convert to Buddhism. But because those bastards eat only once a day . . . I gave up that religion too [to follow the Bhagavan].

As mendicants, they have just begun their daily round to beg alms from households with their skull-bowls. When the Bhagavan and Shandilya stop for repose and meditation in a garden, the Bhagavan begins his meditation, but Shandilya spots a young courtesan awaiting her lover, falls in love with her, and therefore meditates on "wine, women, and song." The play title derives from the subsequent exchange of souls between the courtesan, whose soul has been mistakenly taken by the servant of the god of death (Yama), disguised as a serpent, and the Bhagavan himself, who uses his powers to inject his soul into the body of the courtesan in order to teach his recalcitrant student, Shandilya, a lesson. The plot turns on farcical mistaken identities with a distinctly yogic twist.

King Mahendravarman's farce is an entertaining as well as trenchant send-up of the religious orders of seventh-century South India. The Bhagavan is a "teacher" who becomes caught in the (il)logic of his own philosophical speculations. The "student" is one who, like the Vidushaka, ought to be learning but cannot.

INTERPRETIVE APPROACH: Reception theory

Reader-response and reception theory first developed in German literary studies during the 1960s and 1970s in order to shift focus from the meanings assumed to be *in* texts to a more interactive model. Reception theorists explore how a reader makes sense of a book or how an audience understands its experience of a production. This more interactive view sees audiences as being active agents in the process of meaning-making at a theatrical event. Analyses of audience reception have used a variety of tools, from quantitative use of data derived from questionnaires to qualitative studies making use of interviews of audience members.

Focusing on reception in a given historical period and culture involves exploring: (1) the nature of the culture's theories/expectations of aesthetic experience; (2) the conventions through which its art forms attempt to create this experience, and (3) the ways in which the theories have been interpreted and changed over time. Literary scholar Stanley Fish has argued that there is no meaning inherent in any work of art except that which is constructed by an "interpretive community" within a particular historical moment (Fish 1980). One way that the historian can identify a particular interpretive community is to focus on the *negative* reactions of critics or audiences (even a riot). Such responses are often reactions to changes in one or more modes of theatre production. These may be responses to changes in artistic practices – acting, playwriting, scene design, or theatre architecture, or to changes

▷

▷

in business practices – ticket prices. The expectations of members of a particular interpretive community can reflect a fierce sense of ownership of the standards for an art form, as in the trenchant critique of the Kerala actors above.

Welcome as the move of western criticism toward examining audience reception is, it belies the fact that many non-western aesthetic theories have, from their beginnings, been much less concerned with (ostensibly) self-enclosed meanings in texts than with the ways in which *performances* of plays can provide heightened experiences for the audience, including considerations of adaptive strategies. Western theory and philosophy often have been driven by a *logocentric* focus on the text (logo = word) and interpretation. Even western theories of reception have somewhat limited themselves to trying to determine what a performance means by "reading" its codes, which is to say parsing other kinds of (ostensibly) fixed "texts." It remains to be seen whether this process can account fully for the multi-sensory experience of a complex and particularized performance, such as those of Sanskrit theatre are, and in which music, song, dance, spectacle, and acting seek to create a "total" experience.

Unlike Aristotle's *Poetics*, which was largely devoted to analyzing the attributes and effects appropriate to a particular genre of scripted drama – tragedy, Bharata's *Nāṭyaśastra* articulated theories of how performance could produce the experience of *rasa*. In Japan, Zeami specified the means for achieving the proper aesthetic effects of performance in noh theatre. These eastern practitioner-philosophers were offering performance-oriented systems of production and reception. This case study examines India's *rasa* aesthetic theory and its development within a special interpretive community in Kerala.

Reception theory can be useful to the performance historian, of course, in many periods and cultures. Below are two examples of questions one might ask using reception theory.

KEY QUESTIONS

1 **How has reception of a play like Samuel Beckett's *Waiting for Godot* changed since the extremely negative reaction to its first performances? What historical and/or critical shifts are reflected in this change in reception and perception?**

2 **How have audiences in another historical period shown agency on the occasion of a performance they have seen?**

Rasa-bhāva *aesthetic theory*

The *Nāṭyaśastra* clearly establishes the *rasa-bhāva* aesthetic as the central theoretical and practical organizational concept for theatre when it states, "nothing has meaning in drama except through *rasa*." *Rasa* is so called "because it is capable of being

tasted" (Bharata 1967:105). The analogy of *rasa* as the tasting or savoring of a meal is offered to explain the process by which a theatrical performance of a play attains its own coherence. "The 'taste' of the various ingredients of a meal is both their common ground and organizes them as its end" (Gerow

bhāva (states of being/doing the actor embodies)		rasa ("tasted" by the audience)
pleasure or delight (*rati*)	*corresponds to*	the erotic (*srngāra*)
laughter or humor (*hāsa*)		the comic (*hāsya*)
sorrow or pain (*śōka*)		pathos/compassion (*karuṇa*)
anger (*krōdha*)		the furious (*raudra*)
heroism or courage (*utsāha*)		the heroic/valorous (*vīra*)
fear (*bhaya*)		the terrible (*bhayānaka*)
disgust (*jugupsa*)		the odious (*bībhatsa*)
wonder (*vismaya*)		the marvelous (*adbhuta*)

1981:230). What the actors offer as the "meal" to be tasted is each character's state of being/doing (*bhāva*), which is specific to the ever-shifting context of the performance. The accompanying *rasas* are made available for "tasting" as each *bhāva* is embodied and elaborated in performance.

The *Nātyaśastra* identified eight permanent states of being/doing (*sthayibhāva*), each with its accompanying *rasa* (see diagram above).

These basic states are enhanced by many other transitory and involuntary states.

Rasa theory operates simultaneously on two levels: (1) the audience's experience of the various states or moods arising from the actor's embodiment of the character, and (2) the process of aesthetic perception of the whole. Playwrights and composers structure their work around those modes most useful for elaboration. In this sense, the "seed" of the *rasa* experience is implicit in a drama and made explicit by the actors as they perform. In the rather simple one-act farce, *The Hermit/Harlot*, the prolog as well as the play proper elaborates the comic (*hāsya rasa*), although the forms that this takes can vary with the performance circumstances. Here is what the *Nātyaśastra* has to say about the physical expression of the comic (*hāsya*):

This is created by . . . showing unseemly dress or ornament, impudence, greediness, quarrel, defective limb, use of irrelevant words, men-

tioning different faults, [etc., the result is represented] . . . by consequents [*sic*] like the throbbing of lips, the nose and the cheek, opening the eyes wide or contracting them, perspiration, color of the face, and taking hold of the sides.
(Bharata 1967:172)

In *The Hermit/Harlot*, the gamut of comedic situations ranging from obvious physical humor and byplay to the subtler play of philosophical ideas would have given rise to an equally wide range of audience responses.

Although the basis of the permanent states of being/doing embodied by actors are the emotions we experience in everyday situations (becoming angry or guffawing with laughter), these everyday emotions are not the same as the ultimate aesthetic experience of *rasa*. To understand this dimension of *rasa* aesthetic theory, we must go beyond Bharata's *Nātyaśastra*, which focuses pragmatically on the means for evoking *rasa*. It is the later commentators who explicate this aesthetic dimension of rasa, each reflecting on the nature of aesthetic experience from their own particular historical and philosophical perspectives, creating a dynamic history of Indian aesthetics.

The most influential among them is the philosopher, Abhinavagupta (tenth to eleventh centuries), from Kashmir. His *Abhinavabhāratī* sought to define the nature of the *rasa* experience. The *Nātyaśastra* clearly expected an audience to be educated into the sensibilities needed to appreciate the subtleties of an actor's performance, of course, but Abhinavagupta refined this, defining the ideal spectator and audience member as a *sahṛdaya* – one whose heart/mind is "attuned" to appreciate the performance.

> The artistic creation is the direct or unconventionalized expression of a feeling of passion "generalized," that is, freed from distinctions in time or space and therefore from individual relationships and practical interests, through an inner force of the artistic or creative intuition within the artist. This state of consciousness (*rasa*) embodied in the poem is transferred to the actor, the dancer, the reciter and to the spectator. Born in the heart of the poet, it flowers as it were in the actor and bears fruit in the spectator.
>
> If the artist or poet has the inner force of the creative intuition, the spectator is the man of cultivated emotion, in whom lies dormant the different states of being, and when he sees them manifested, revealed on the stage through movement, sound and decor, he is lifted to that ultimate state of bliss, known as *ānanda*.
>
> (Vatsyayan 1968:155)

The decline of Sanskrit theatre and the birth of kutiyattam

During the ninth and tenth centuries C.E., just as Sanskrit theatre was reaching its zenith in most of India and becoming the subject more of commentators such as Abhinavagupta than of actual practice, a distinctive style of staging Sanskrit dramas known as kutiyattam ("combined acting") emerged in Kerala on the far southwest coast. It was developed with the patronage and direct involvement of King Kulasekhara Varman, around C.E. 900. The king himself authored two dramas still staged today in this style – *Subhadrādhananjaya* and *Tapatīsamvarana*. Assisted by a well known high-caste brahmin scholar, Tolan, King Kulasekhara is credited with the introduction of a number of innovations. These

became the controversial hall-marks of this distinctive style of performance: (1) the use of the local language, Malayalam, by the Vidusaka to explain key passages of the Sanskrit and Prakrit dramas; (2) the introduction of each character of a play with a brief narration of his past; (3) allowance for deviation from a script in performance to provide elaboration on the meaning and/or the state of mind/being of a character; and (4) the development of stage manuals for staging dramas in this emergent style and acting manuals on how actors should elaborate passages in a play. One practical reason for the introduction of Malayalam into performances was that Sanskrit was ceasing to be an everyday spoken language. After the tenth century, it was used only by certain educated communities.

Perhaps the most crucial feature of the development of kutiyattam during this period was its exclusive performance within particular high-caste temples of Kerala as a "visual sacrifice" to the deities of these temples. Theatres of the kind prescribed by Bharata for Sanskrit drama were built within compounds of few wealthy, high-caste temples in Kerala (Figures 3.12, 3.13). Other changes ensued, still to be seen today. In kutiyattam, Sanskrit dramas are not performed in full. Rather, sections of the drama become dramas in and of themselves, with lengthy preliminaries and elaborations of the story featuring one of the main characters on each night. On the final one to three nights, there is the "combined acting," *kūṭiyāṭṭam*, the term from which the style takes its name, that brings all the actors to the stage to perform the act or scene being staged. Still today, enacting a single scene of a drama in the kutiyattam style can take from five nights to as many as 41.

One of the oldest plays in the kutiyattam repertory is the one-act farce, *The Hermit/Harlot* (Figures 3.14, 3.15). One traditional stage-manual for the *Hermit/Harlot* gives instructions on how to stage the play over 35 nights, including the nights of "combined acting." For seven of these nights, the Vidusaka explains and comments in the local language on the philosophical issues raised by the play (Raja 1964:17). Only certain sections are

Figure 3.12 A temple theatre, known as a *kuttampalam*, built for Kutiyattam in the Lord Vadakkunnathan (Siva) temple in Trissur, central Kerala. The temple compound containing this one is set apart from the outside world by high walls and massive gates. The main shrine housing Vadakkunnathan is to the right. © Phillip Zarrilli.

enacted on specific nights. Indeed, when a portion of the scene between the Bhagavan and Shandilya is enacted in this tradition, the evening becomes less about the farcical humor than about a serious allegory on the "interaction between God and the human soul" (Lockwood and Bhat 1995(Part II):9) The scene with the courtesan and her attendant in the garden before the exchange of souls becomes an opportunity for the two women performers (*nangyārs*) to elaborate the erotic pleasures associated with the poetic images of the garden, emphasized through dance and facial expression.

For the fifteenth-century anonymous author of *The Goad on Actors*, it was the very different experience and meaning of kutiyattam's way of staging King Mahendravarman's farce that he thought necessary to attack as "blasphemous" and "illogical." As an audience member, he decried the fact that the actors of the kutiyattam tradition were depriving him of an experience of *The Hermit/Harlot* as the farce he expected. Looking back at least 1,200 years to Bharata, he demanded a return to a staging of the drama in its entirety, uninterrupted by the actors' lengthy elaborations. His displeasure notwithstanding, the kutiyattam tradition of staging Sanskrit dramas, with all its "faults" and "defilements," persisted down to the present. For centuries, kutiyattam has been appreciated within its high-caste interpretative community of educated connoisseurs for its unique delights, including the Vidusaka's

Figure 3.13 Cross-section of the interior of the theatre in a temple in Trissur. Inside the high-ceilinged *kuttampalam*, the audience sits on the polished floor, facing the roofed stage. A drummer sits upstage, behind the actor. The dressing room is through two entry/exits doors behind the drummer. [Source: Line drawing No. 14 located on p.79, from *Kuttampalam and Kutiyattam* by Goverdhan Panchal. New Delhi: Sangeet Natak Akademi, 1984. The author indicates that "most of the drawings in this book are based on my own drawings and sketches" and then rendered by Shri Ajit Parikh and Shri Ajit Joshi of the School of Architecture, Ahmedabad.]

lengthy seven nights of humorous, philosophical elaborations. Today, the audience base for kutiyattam is considerably smaller than it once was.

Reception theory, with its emphasis on the agency of the audience/reader in the process of making meaning from the experience of a work, opens opportunities for understanding Sanskrit theatre. This theatre's practitioners were not logo-centric but concentrated on the means by which performance itself should evoke the proper aesthetic pleasures. The distinctive style of staging Sanskrit drama in the kutiyattam tradition still was guided by the *rasa-bhāva* aesthetic – ubiquitous in India even where the *Nāṭyaśāstra* itself is unknown. But kutiy-

attam was developed within Kerala's culturally distinctive, regional interpretive community and reflected a major language change – the decline of Sanskrit itself. Audience and theatre artists were cultural partners in this development. The connoisseur's trenchant negative criticism of the kutiyattam actors in Kerala with which we began this case study is evidence of an aesthetic shift; the record of his negative response helps the historian to further understand the modified aesthetic of kutiyattam. This development was not unique. As we saw in Chapter 3, in the commemorative devotional dramas dating from the fifteenth and sixteenth centuries, *rasa* theory and practice were reinvented to accommodate

Figures 3.14 and 3.15 The Bhagavan or Herm t (Figure 3.14), and his wayward student, Shandilya (Figure 3.15), played, respectively by Raman Cakyar and Kalamandalam Shivan, in a kutiyattam production of *The Hermit/Harlot* in Thiruvananthapuram, Kerala, in 1977. From a reconstructed staging based on traditional acting and staging manuals, under the supervision of Ram Cakyar of the Kerala Kalamdalam. The costume of Shandilya (Figure 3.15) is the traditional one worn in kutiyattam by the stock comic character, Vidusaka, who plays Shandilya here. Photo © Phillip B. Zarrilli.

an aesthetic experience of deep devotion known as *bhakti*, which became a new *rasa*. This is especially evident in several genres of North Indian devotional drama including *Rāmlīlā* which, as discussed earlier, celebrates the life of Ram, and the genre known as *raslīlā* which celebrates the life of Lord Krishna.

PZ

Key references

Baumer, R. Van M., and Brandon, J.R. (eds) (1981) *Sanskrit Drama in Performance*, Honolulu: University of Hawaii Press.

Bennett, S. (1990) *Theatre Audiences: A Theory of Production and Reception*, London: Routledge.

Bharata (1961, 1967) *Natyasastra*, 2nd edn, trans. and ed. M. Ghosh, vol. I, Calcutta: Manisha Granthalaya, 1967; vol. II, Calcutta: Asiatic Society, 1961.

Byrski, M.C. (1974) *Concept of Ancient Indian Theatre*, New Delhi: Munshiram Manoharlal.

Coulson, M. (1981) *Three Sanskrit Plays*, New York: Penguin.

Eagleton, T. (1983) *Literary Theory: An Introduction*, Minneapolis: University of Minnesota Press.

Fish, S. (1980) *Is There a Text in This Class? The Authority of Interpretive Communities*, Cambridge, Mass.: Harvard University Press.

Fortier, M. (1997) *Theory/Theatre: An Introduction*, London: Routledge.

Gerow, E. (1977) "Indian Poetics," in J. Gonda (ed.) *A History of Indian Literature*, vol. V, Wiesbaden: Otto Harrassowitz, 217–301.

Gerow, E. (1981) "*Rasa* as a Category of Literary Criticism," in R. van M. Baumer and J.R. Brandon (eds), *Sanskrit Drama in Performance*, Honolulu: University of Hawaii.

Haksar, A.N.D. (1993) *The Shattered Thigh and the Other Mahabharata Plays*, New Delhi: Penguin.

Holub, R.C. (1984) *Reception Theory: A Critical Introduction*, London: Methuen.

Jones, C.R. (1984) *The Wondrous Crest-Jewel in Performance*, New Delhi: Oxford University Press.

Kale, P. (1974) *The Theatric Universe*, Bombay: Popular Prakashan.

Lockwood, M. and Bhat, A.V. (1994) *Metatheatre and Sanskrit Drama*, New Delhi: Munshiram Manoharlal Publishers.

Miller, B.S. (ed.) (1984) *Theater of Memory: The Plays of Kalidasa*, New York: Columbia University Press.

Panchal, G. (1984) *Kuttampalam and Kutiyattam*, New Delhi: Sangeet Natak Akademi.

Paulose, K.G. (ed.) (1993) *Natankusa: A Critique on Dramaturgy*, Tripunithura: Government Sanskrit College Committee [Ravivarma Samskrta Grathavali–26].

Raghavan, V. (1993) *Sanskrit Drama: Its Aesthetics and Production*, Madras: Paprinpack.

Raja, K.K. (1964) *Kutiyattam: An Introduction*, New Delhi: Sangeet Natak Akademi.

Richmond, F. (1999) *Kutiyattam: Sanskrit Theater of Kerala*, Ann Arbor: University of Michigan Press (CD-Rom).

Richmond, F., Swann, D. and Zarrilli, P. (1990) *Indian Theatre: Traditions of Performance*, Honolulu: University of Hawaii Press.

Vatsyayan, K. (1996) *Bharata: The Natyasastra*, New Delhi: Sahitya Akademi.

Vatsyayan, K. (1968) *Classical Indian Dance in Literature and the Arts*, New Delhi: Sangeet Natak Akademi.

CASE STUDY: The Silent Bell: The Japanese noh play, *Dôjôji*

Does attending an outdoor performance of a fifteenth century noh play at a Buddhist temple sound like a hot date? In contemporary Japan, growing numbers of trendy young urbanites flock to summertime performances of noh plays such as *Dôjôji*, performed as *takigi nô* (noh by firelight). What might be the fascination of a genre that many Japanese consider outdated, slow, and incomprehensible?

One answer may be the allure of the main character in the noh plays (*shite*, the one who does). Many, including *Dôjôji*, feature main characters who are agonized females or their ghosts, often formerly great beauties, women who have been betrayed, who are possessed by demonic forces, or who are crazed. Their angry spirits make battle against the prayers that the Buddhist priests (male characters) say to try to calm them. Powerful dance, hypnotic music, and stunning costumes and masks combine with the atmospheric firelight to create an ideal occasion for a stylish date. But beyond this, might there be deeper, cultural reasons in Japan's past and present? To explore this, we need to know something of the cultural context in which noh developed. Considering the interest in plays like *Dôjôji*, with their special kind of female characters and their mythic femaleness, we also should inquire into the place of such portraits of women that the all-male noh theatre developed. In doing so, this case study will employ contemporary feminist and gender theories, adapted to the subject. (Some Japanese terms are used here without the diacriticals and italics sometimes used in English transliteration; for example, we use noh for *nô* and kyogen for *kyôgen*.)

INTERPRETIVE APPROACH: Feminist and gender theory, modified for medieval Japan

"Feminism begins with a keen awareness of exclusion from male cultural, social, sexual, political, and intellectual discourse. It is a critique of prevailing social conditions that formulate women's position as outside of dominant male discourse" (Dolan 1988:3). Feminist theory first appeared in Europe and America around the end of the nineteenth century and has since entered the thinking of many cultures. Nevertheless, some women in developing countries have rejected western feminism as not relevant to their situations. As Chandra Mohanty explains: "Western feminist discourse, by assuming women as a coherent, already constituted group which is placed in kinship, legal, and other structures, defines third world women as subjects *outside* social relations, instead of looking at the way women are constituted *through* these very structures" (1991b:72). Mohanty also notes that "third world women have always engaged with feminism, even if the label has been rejected in a number of instances" (1991a:7). By this she means that such women have actively attempted to improve their material situations. Thus, while acknowledging that cultural differences must be considered, and that solutions or explanations posed for one culture or time may not be appropriate in another context, Mohanty suggests that in male-defined societies, all women struggle to negotiate a place for themselves.

The social and economic roles of women and men as depicted in theatre can indicate the stresses and ruptures that define an actual time and place. Until recently, Japanese theatre studies focused almost exclusively on theatre written and performed by males, and on the male spectator's perspective. The role of women as creators and spectators was seldom considered. Extensive feminist theatre research is now being done to more fully understand women's roles in Japanese theatre history.

In Europe and America, feminist theory was first systematically applied to theatre in the early 1980s, building on concepts developed during the women's liberation movement of the previous decade. Early feminist theatre historians worked to recover or retrieve neglected works by female playwrights and to document the activities of female actors, managers, directors, critics, and designers. One goal of this case study is to emphasize the often overlooked early female performers whose innovations made the all-male noh possible.

▷

Multiple feminisms and the idea of gender

Feminist theory is not a unified whole, but includes various approaches such as materialist, liberal, radical, lesbian, black, and Lacanian (psychoanalytic). Paralleling Mohanty's concern regarding women in "non-western" or "third-world" countries, Judith Butler argues that "the premature insistence on a stable subject of feminism, understood as a seamless category of women, inevitably generates multiple refusals to accept that category" (1990:4). We must look at the many ways that gender and sexuality (male and female, heterosexual and homosexual, normative and alternative) are performed and perceived in various societies.

Butler (ibid.) insists that the body's external gestures (not some "inner essence") define gender (as opposed to biological sex). She notes that the body publicly performs repeated, planned, stylized actions that are understood by the society in which they occur. Gender is therefore not stable; only physical gestures make gender readable to the outside observer. Even when done unconsciously or by habit, these gestures result in a performance that is as stylized and as choreographed as a ballet.

Materialist feminism

"Cultural materialism" seeks to understand how literature is both a product of, and a participant in, a wide range of oppressive social formations and practices, from a society's language to its constructions of class, race, ethnicity, gender, or nationhood. (For further explanation of materialist criticism, see the Chapter 9 case study on Ibsen's *A Doll House*.) Materialist feminists deny the existence of a natural female (or male) essence. They argue that gender is constructed by the repetition of accepted social practices, an argument that seeks to counter traditional western concepts of "natural" gender identities.

Sue-Ellen Case (1988) asks how the audience in a society that denies women economic and social opportunities "reads" the staged image or sign of "woman," when that sign is created by a male playwright and performed by a male actor. Materialist feminists suggest that the female performing body in societies in which women are allowed to perform might actively create an alternative (even subversive) version to that created in male-written or male-directed plays. She might do this by her choice of costume, gesture, intonation, rhythm, movement, expression, or her personal lifestyle. In so doing, she might, necessarily, challenge conventional ideas about women characters in classical plays, including ancient Greek tragedy or the plays of Shakespeare.

Gender and the spectator

The Platonic-Aristotelian idea of mimesis seems to assume that theatre's purpose is to mirror reality, and reality as males see it. The spectator is assumed to be male and traditional male values frame the play. But suppose that a female (or male) spectator were to resist

▷

identification with the male hero and values. Materialist feminist Elin Diamond advocates that women on stage might use Bertolt Brecht's distancing or "alienating" acting techniques to disrupt the narrative conventions of realism – which Case terms "the prison-house of art" (ibid.:124). Diamond believes that feminist performance must focus on Brechtian "gestus." The influential twentieth century German playwright, Bertolt Brecht (1898–1956) sought to break from realism in his plays and in his innovative methods for performance and production. Influenced by Karl Marx, Brecht sought to make his audiences critically aware of the social and economic conditions of characters so that audiences would challenge such conditions (Brecht's work is further discussed in a Chapter 9 case study). The term "gestus" refers to the expressive means an actor can employ – such as a way of standing or moving or a pattern of behavior – that indicates to the audience the social position or condition of the character the actor is playing. (Various devices can be used to this end including unexpected costuming choices, cross-gender casting, or puppetry.) Applying Brecht to feminist performance, Diamond suggests that in contrast to realistic theatre, in which the actor "laminates body to character," actors (especially women) perform in ways in which the body "stands visibly and palpably separate from the 'role' of the actor as well as the role of the character" (Diamond 1988:89). The goal of gestic acting would be to make the female (or male) body an active agent who chooses the way she or he is looked at, rather than being a passive object.

This case study uses materialist feminism and gender theory, modified for Japanese medieval culture, to better understand the female origins of noh. It considers the social position of women in medieval Japan, various "distancing" techniques of noh performance, and the "mythic dimensions of femaleness" as perceived by many Japanese.

What is noh?

Noh plays are performed on a raised wooden stage, over which is a roof held up by four pillars, even when the stage is indoors (Figures 3.7, 3.8). The main acting area is about fifteen square feet. Beneath the floorboards, ceramic jars enhance the sound of the actors' stamping feet. Noh stages have a painted pine tree on the back wall, representative of the "epiphany pine" where a god-possessed priest once danced. There are no special settings or lighting, and only minimal stage properties. A bridgeway (*hashigakari*) connects the stage with the curtained "mirror room" where the actors prepare (Figure 3.18); the *hashigakari* is seen as a passage from this world (the realm of the audience) to the world of spirits (embodied by the actor who crosses this bridge). The audience, usually about 400 people, sits on two sides of the stage. Steps lead from the stage into the auditorium (Figure 3.17), a vestige of the Tokugawa era (1603–1868) when actors would descend them to receive valuable gifts from the shogun and his entourage.

Professional noh actors today are almost all male, training from childhood with older relatives. To prepare to peform properly, the actor stares at his masked (or sometimes unmasked) reflection in the "mirror room." He will embody the character, but will not go into trance. The main character, the *shite*

Figure 3.16 In a performance of the noh play *Dôjôji* at the Kanze Theatre, Tokyo, 1962, the ghost of the maiden, dressed as a beautiful *shirabyôshi* dancer, approaches the bell at Dôjô Temple. Here, the actor moves from the *hashigakari* (bridgeway) onto the main stage, symbolizing the passage from the spirit world to this world. Photo © Gary Jay Williams.

and the secondary character, the *waki* meaning the listener or sideman, may have companions called *tsure*. Usually the *waki* arrives first and establishes the situation; then the *shite* enters. The *shite* dances while retelling and reliving past woes; the *waki* is often a traveling Buddhist priest asked to pray for the release of the *shite*'s suffering soul. While the *shite* dances, the chorus chants his words.

Eight to fifteen chorus members kneel onstage at the audience's right (opposite the *hashigakari*). Unlike the Greek chorus, they do not dance and have no identity particular to a given play. Musicians (flute and drums) sit upstage, in front of the painted tree. They vocalize rhythmical sounds (*kakegoe*) as part of the musical score. Stage assistants (*kôken*) handle props, straighten costumes, or prompt actors.

They are unobtrusive but clearly visible to the audience.

When masks are used, they are worn only by the *shite* (and sometimes the *shite*'s companion). Smaller than the adult male face, they allow the audience to see simultaneously the role portrayed by the mask and the actor's living flesh. Costumes are elegant, costly, and conventional. The scripts are in an archaic language, using a "brocade style" that weaves together well-known stories, poetry, and Buddhist references.

Alternation of serious and comic plays

In the past, a full day's performance consisted of five noh plays, with short, comic plays (kyogen) in

Figure 3.17 After the maiden has danced around the bell and seemed to fly into it, the bell decends over her and rises, as here, to reveal the differently masked actor (who has done a quick change) as a horned, demon serpent that is the ghost-maiden's true form. The abbot and the priests attempt an exorcism. Photo © Gary Jay Williams.

between them. Today, most programs have one or two noh plays and one kyogen. Kyogen plays (the literal meaning of kyogen is "crazy words") emphasize comic inversions of social roles and stereotypical behavior. Unlike noh, kyogen uses everyday speech, few masks, no chorus, and reserves song and dance for comic effect. Powerless characters, such as women, thieves, servants, or sons-in-law, outwit masters, husbands, priests, or gods. They play practical jokes and are carried away by song, dance, and uncontrollable urges (for wine, food, prestige, mischief, or even cruelty). For example, in *Tied to a Pole* (*Boshibari*), the master ties up his two servants to prevent them from drinking his wine. In a complex, physically comic sequence, they cleverly help each other get drunk anyway. Kyogen actors also perform minor roles during the interlude between two-part noh plays.

Actor-playwright-theorist Zeami Motokiyo (1363–1443), who refined the art that became noh, maintained that actors should gauge the style of performance to please the audience, changing it as needed. However, during the Edo (or Tokugawa) period (1603–1863), noh became a state ritual rather than entertainment, and no variations were permitted. Although noh seems slow today, it is performed about three times faster than it was during the eighteenth century.

What happens in Dôjôji?

As noted in our Preface, western scholars did not always consider noh to be "drama," because it focuses on sustained lyrical moments rather than on logical plot development. French poet-playwright Paul Claudel (1868–1955) once said, "In drama something happens; in noh someone appears." What did he mean?

Dôjôji (author unknown; formerly attributed to Kanze Kojirô Nobumitsu, 1435–1516), one of the most popular and theatrically flamboyant noh plays, begins when the *waki*, the male Buddhist Abbot of Dôjôji (Dôjô Temple), announces that for many years, no bell has hung in the temple. Today, a new bell will be raised and dedicated. He leaves, forbidding the priests to admit women. The *shite* – an elegant woman – appears, maintaining that she, as a *shirabyôshi* dancer, should be allowed to perform at the dedication (Figure 3.16). The foolish priest agrees to let her enter.

She dons a special hat (*eboshi*) normally worn by male courtiers. Her dance gradually becomes chaotic and animalistic, entrancing the priests. The music, used only in *Dôjôji*, is the exotic, hypnotic *rambyôshi*, a secular version of the music of a Shinto demon-quelling ritual. Her feet move in triangular patterns, mimicking the fish-scale triangles on the actor's inner robe. Finally, the dancer knocks the hat from her head, stamps her feet, and looks at the bell. She swings her fan back and forth like the ringing hammer of a bell, as the Chorus sings: "This loathsome bell, now I remember it! / Placing her hand on the dragon-head boss, / she seems to fly upward into the bell" (Brazell 1998:199). She leaps up, and the giant bell falls crashing to the ground around her.

In the *ai-kyôgen* (interlude), the priests discover that the bell is red hot. When the Abbot returns, he angrily explains why women were forbidden. Long ago, a girl's father told her that a visiting priest would one day marry her. When she asked to be his bride, he fled in horror. She chased him, but he crossed the river by boat. In her fury, she transformed into a serpent, dove into the river, and swam across. On the other shore, she followed him to the temple of Dôjôji, where he had hidden beneath an unraised

bell. Again becoming a snake, she entwined her body around the bell. The heat of her passion was so intense that the bell metal became fiery hot, burning alive the priest inside. The dancer in the play is this woman's furious ghost.

During this interlude, the *shite* remains inside the giant bell, where the actor changes mask and costume. When the bell rises, we see a female snake-demon, the dancer's true form (Figure 3.17). The Abbot and priests battle her, attempting an exorcism, but they cannot overpower her; they can only chase her off. As the play ends, the Chorus chants:

> Again she springs to her feet,
> the breath she vomits at the bell
> has turned to raging flames.
> Her body burns in her own fire.
> She leaps into the river pool,
> into the wavers of the river Hitaka,
> and there she vanishes.
> The priests, their prayers granted,
> return to the temple,
> return to the temple.
>
> (Brazell 1998: 206)

In order to interpret this play, we must consider its cultural and historical context. Zeami did much to develop noh theatre, but he did not create it from thin air.

Zeami and the female origins of noh

Japanese performance is said to originate in the shocking dance of Uzume, a female Shinto deity. According to the myth, because the sun-goddess, Amaterasu – the direct ancestor of the Emperor and thus of the Japanese people – was angry with her trickster brother, she hid herself in a cave. Deprived of the sun's light and fertility, the universe would have died. In desperation, the goddess Uzume leaped onto an overturned rain barrel, stamping her feet in dance and lifting her skirts to reveal her genitals. The other deities roared with laughter. The curious Amaterasu peeked out. But she did not witness Uzume's dance; instead, she saw her own reflection in a mirror. Entranced, she emerged from the cave. The laughter caused by Uzume's sexy dance had saved the universe from eternal death. In his secret treatises, Zeami wrote that this myth proved noh's divine origin and relationship to the royal household. But is that all the myth tells us today?

Amaterasu is a female identified with the life-giving sun. Her emotional, irrational response to the bad behavior of an unruly male dangerously disrupts the balance of nature. She cloaks her body in darkness. In contrast, Uzume intentionally displays her body in a kind of divine striptease. She uses explicit nakedness not to create a sexual spectacle for the pleasure of male viewers of the dance, but to make the gods laugh and thereby to control events. Feminist theory suggests that she was performing not as a sexual object, but rather as an active agent. Also, these two female deities are reverse images that complement each other: light and dark, anger and laughter, life and death. Females have the power to give and to withdraw life.

In the sixth century, Korean emissaries introduced the patriarchal religion of Buddhism to Japan, challenging the dominance of female-oriented Shinto. Powerful leaders allied themselves with these opposing religions, vying for political control. Many sects combined aspects of both religions. Eventually, Shinto rituals became associated with the female realm and with life-affirming acts (fertility, marriage, sex, and birth), while Buddhist rites were tied primarily to the male realm, death, and the afterlife.

Noh theatre reflects this gendered religious syncretism, which remains today. The texts are primarily Buddhist, emphasizing karma (the results of sin that determine reincarnation status) and salvation in the afterlife. In contrast, most performance elements derive from Shinto (or Shinto-Buddhist) rituals, including demon-quelling dances, stamping feet, ritual purifications, trance-possession by gods, and

the invasion of the present by spirits and ghosts. The noh stage is based on Shinto shrine architecture.

Noh incorporated elements of female dances. Shinto shrine maidens (miko) performed sacred kagura dances as well as nembutsu-odori, Buddhist-Shinto ritual dances meant to pacify angry ghosts. Female prostitute-entertainers performed Buddhist funeral rituals for the imperial family and entertained aristocratic, male clients on river boats. Their outcast status diminished as their religious importance grew. Zeami's family may have belonged to their clan (Kwon, 1998).

Kusemai and shirabyôshi were popular, secular entertainments mainly performed by women dressed in male clothing. Critics feared that their unconventional, disturbing musical rhythms and dance styles were contributing to "an age of turmoil" and were a sign of "a nation in ruins" (O'Neill 1958: 43–44). Like Uzume, these female ritualists and performers disrupted notions of social and religious stability.

Since Zeami's time, only males have performed noh; nevertheless, Zeami praised and valued his female predecessors. He wrote that his father Kan'ami had trained with Otozuru, a female kusemai dancer. The shite's main dance is still termed kusemai, and many plays, including Dôjôji, feature female shirabyôshi or kusemai dancers as characters.

The aesthetics of noh

Zeami's treatises were written in his maturity. Intended as training manuals for his family of actors and playwrights, they also include profound meditations on aesthetics. This case study considers two of Zeami's many aesthetic concepts – monomane and yûgen.

Monomane, often inaccurately translated as "mimesis," is the imitation of character, not action. Unlike western mimesis, which is representational and idealistic, monomane is non-representational and physical. By imitating "the three roles" (male, female, or old person), the actor reveals the fictional character's invisible body. For Zeami, a mask allows the actor to become another character; his body becomes a vessel inhabited by another's "essence," which resides in the mask (the Buddhist concept of "essence" is clearly at odds with materialist philosophy). According to Steven T. Brown, "Underneath the actor's costume and mask is the body of the actor transformed into the virtual body of the other" (2001:26).

Noh uses many elements of non-realistic, "gestic" performance as identified by Elin Diamond. These include stylized movement and gesture, music, conventionalized vocal patterns and wordless sounds, choral and narrative speech, a single character performed by several actors (as when the chorus takes up the *shite*'s speech), dialog that cites other literary works, masks that do not fully hide the actor's face, and costumes that do not emphasize the actor's gender, class or physical body. These might be described as "gestic" performance elements. They are further supported by aesthetic concepts such as *yûgen*, one of many ideas infused with the mystical, non-dualistic philosophy of Zen Buddhism, the sect that was especially popular among the aristocrats and samurai who were Zeami's patrons.

Yûgen is a deep, quiet, mysterious beauty tinged with sadness. Zeami expands its meaning to refer to both text and performance, emphasizing the fleeting, melancholy nature of human existence. The greatest *yûgen* appears in plays about aged, dispossessed, or formerly beautiful women, who are reduced to poverty, madness, or regret. Steven T. Brown's analysis of *yûgen* is indebted to materialist feminism and other contemporary interpretive approaches. He has revised the definition of *yûgen* to include the idea of "symbolic capital" (Pierre Bourdieu's term), which stresses that actors could enhance their political position by representing characters in a way that appealed to powerful patrons. By displaying aristocratic female bodies in exquisite emotional agony, Zeami and his troupe could please all members of the shôgun's court (ibid.:30–33). By combining

yûgen with *monomane* in plays about often Shinto-identified females in need of male Buddhist healing or exorcism, Zeami consolidated the position of formerly outcast actors in a changing court, and paved the way for noh's transition from popular entertainment to elite art (Sorgenfrei 1998).

A materialist perspective on the shôgun's court

Although written after Zeami's death, *Dôjôji* represents the maturity of the form that Zeami solidified. Zeami lived during a time of peace, enforced by samurai warriors after centuries of civil war. The elegant culture of the older imperial court clashed with the rather uncouth style of the warrior-rulers, the samurai. These new rulers had fostered legal changes to centralize military power and weaken noble branch families. These changes encouraged a porous social structure that increased the individual's opportunity for changing class, rather than reinforcing the strict class divisions typical of most feudal societies. Such a pattern does not fully accord with materialist interpretations of history; however, since the new laws forced the material position of aristocratic females downward, a materialist feminist interpretation proves valuable in understanding the representation of such characters in noh.

Among the new laws were those that shifted inheritance rights away from female aristocrats and toward first-born sons. Suddenly, a divorced or abandoned woman found herself dispossessed both financially and emotionally. Her fury at an unfaithful spouse would be intensified by the loss of property she would previously have retained. Many people believed that the angry spirits of such dispossessed females and those of the dispossessed male rivals of the ruling Ashikaga clan, were responsible for a century of natural disasters that devastated Kyoto. Beginning around the time that the Ashikaga clan took power in 1336, there were at least fourteen earthquakes and numerous plagues, typhoons, droughts, famines, fires, and floods (Brown 2001:49).

Various Buddhist and Shinto rituals and festivals were established to calm these enraged spirits. As noted earlier, most noh plays, including *Dôjôji*, center on the anger or madness of dispossessed spirits (dead or alive). The great majority of *shite* are agonized females. Although Zeami's main patrons were male samurai, they preferred plays about women. Only 16 of 240 currently performed noh plays focus on warriors.

Aristocrats also feared dispossession. Court poet Nijô Yoshimoto tried to retain power by transforming the military court into a bastion of cultural refinement. In 1374, he encouraged the seventeen-year-old *shôgun* (military ruler) Ashikaga Yoshimitsu – famous for his wild excesses and vulgar taste – to attend a performance of popular *sarugaku* (monkey music) acted by the talented, eleven year old Zeami. Nijô hoped to wean his master from *dengaku* (field music), the more shocking type of performance he usually patronized. The plan succeeded too well. Overwhelmed by Zeami's beauty and skill, Yoshimitsu invited the entire troupe of rough and tumble, wandering, outcast performers, headed by Zeami's father Kan'ami, to live in his court. Since sexual relations between male samurai warriors and their young male pages or protégés were not uncommon, Zeami became the *shogun's* lover.

Powerful aristocrats and samurai now feared they would lose influence to these upstart favorites. To protect his own position, Nijô tutored Zeami in the aristocratic arts. Under his guidance, Zeami gradually altered the popular street entertainment, *sarugaku*, into the stately, poetic, all-male, Buddhist-oriented genre later known as noh.

Nijô's strategy involved differentiating *sarugaku* from its rival *dengaku*, the form that Yoshimitsu had originally preferred. By Zeami's time, masked *dengaku* (originally connected to Shinto fertility rites) was performed by both males and females. It had become associated with political turmoil and recurring bouts of mass hysteria called "*dengaku* madness" People of all classes would commit acts of larceny or lewdness, dance semi-naked in the streets for weeks on end, and dress in clothing forbidden to their class or gender. *Dengaku* actors were accused of being animal spirits disguised as humans (O'Neill 1958; Fujiwara-Skrobak 1996). An eyewitness to a 1349 *dengaku* performance described golden curtains, exotic animal skins, and actors dressed in embroidered, silver brocade. The huge audience caused the wooden stands to collapse. The eyewitness wrote:

> The number of those who died among the great piles of fallen timber is past all knowing. In the confusion thieves began stealing swords. . . . Cries and shouts rose up from people who had had limbs broken or slashed; from others, stained with blood, who had been run through with swords or halberds . . . and from others still who had scalded themselves with the boiling water used for making tea. . . . The *dengaku* players, still wearing devil masks and brandishing red canes, gave chase to thieves escaping with stolen costumes. . . . Young servants unsheathed their weapons and went after men who had carried off their masters' ladies. . . . It was as if Hell's unending battles and the tortures of its demons were being carried out before one's eyes.
>
> (O'Neill 1958:75–77)

Because *dengaku* had originated in native Shinto fertility dances, it was tied to supernatural female powers and unbridled female sexuality. In contrast, *sarugaku's* origin is connected to Buddhist burial rites. *Sarugaku* (and eventually noh) would need to suggest victory over wild, emotional female forces by calm, "rational" Buddhism and stoic male warriors. Male fear of female sexuality and the idea that the female body is the source of evil are evident in *Dôjôji*.

Gestic performance and Dôjôji

Both the content and performance style of most noh plays suggest doublenesss rather than a seamless fusion of opposites. In terms of gender, the audience sees masked, obviously male actors playing primarily female characters, who perform dances derived mainly from female or Shinto genres. In terms of class, formerly outcast actors are dressed in gorgeous robes tossed on stage historically by grateful aristocratic patrons. Even noh's commoner characters possess aristocratic traits.

The acting is "gestic" because gender and class are defined not by realistic imitation, but by conventionalized gesture, movement, and costume. The complex non-duality of these acting bodies mirrored the ideal new Japanese ruler, who combined a crass male warrior's martial fortitude with nostalgia for the faded delicacy, elegance, gentleness, and poetic skills of aristocrats – often female, dead, and dispossessed. In *Dôjôji*, the body of the male actor portraying a female dancer "enacts a complex double masquerade of both masculine and feminine" (Klein 1995:118). The male noh actor's body stands in for the absent female body of the *shirabyôshi* dancer, which stands in for the absent male monk as well as the invisible demonic snake. By leaping into the bell, the *shirabyôshi* dancer imitates what happened to the male. Instead of being burned to death, she is revealed in her true form. In fact, her physical body has vanished, since it was only an illusion, a disguise.

The audience sees a male actor masked as a female *shirabyôshi* dancer, who is really the snake-demon in disguise. But all of these represent another absent female, the woman of the past who is now a tormented ghost. Seeing the ghost of a woman whose lust-filled pursuit of the monk marked her as a demon-snake should inspire horror and disgust. The climax of the play becomes a cosmic battle between demonic, female forces and holy, male forces, but it is not conclusive – the demon will continue to lurk in the river, able to resurface at any time. Female sexual power can be contained but not destroyed.

The fear of women displayed in *Dôjôji* reflects not only a misogynistic undercurrent in some types of Buddhist thought, but the historical fact that "the position of women at the elite levels of Japanese society was taking a distinct downward turn" (ibid.:117). The ambiguous ending suggests that chaos could erupt if the rulers failed to guard against all those (male as well as female) they had dispossessed.

Dôjôji *today*

The continuing popularity of *Dôjôji* (and its numerous adaptations for modern theatre, film and even *anime*) suggests that the play holds a deep fascination for the public. Like the Muromachi period (1336–1573) in which it was created, late twentieth- and early twenty-first-century Japan is a time of dissonance. Though outwardly serene, smooth-running, and seemingly homogeneous, Japanese society is filled with contradictions and turmoil. Men can no longer count on life-time employment; young, unmarried women live with parents while working at mind-numbing jobs; the elderly are no longer cared for by their adult children. Asian neighbors demand official Japanese apologies and reparations for atrocities committed in World War II. The victims (and their descendants) of the atomic bombings at Hiroshima and Nagasaki suffer physical and psychological disease. Industries have collapsed, inflation is out of control, pollution mars the environment, and even basic food such as sushi is considered dangerous to eat.

For some, the age is defined by incomprehensible acts of antisocial rage such as the sarin poison gas attacks by religious extremists. For others, it is defined by nature out of control, represented by the devastating Kobe earthquake of 1995. Still others point to governmental scandals, the apparent nervous breakdown of the Crown Princess, or the government's violation of Japan's "Peace Constitution" by sending troops to aid American military ventures, as proof that the cracks in Japanese society are irreparable. Material dispossession and spiritual betrayal are not confined to the past.

The silent bell of *Dôjôji* may speak to the spiritually and materially dispossessed: the huge, bronze temple bell no longer is able to intone warnings, announce religious services, celebrate victories, or mark the time of day. The silent bell harbors unseen forces of evil that might break forth at any moment. *Dôjôji*, with its silent bell, performed by the light of bonfires on a summer night, is theatrically stunning but it also may suggest the difficult transformation Japan is undergoing today, from a troubling past to an uncertain future.

CFS

Key references

Brazell, K. (ed.) (1998) *Traditional Japanese Theater*, New York: Columbia University Press. [Includes a revised translation of *Dôjôji*.]

Brown, S.T. (2001) *Theatricalities of Power The Cultural Politics of Noh*, Stanford, C.A.: Stanford University Press.

Butler, J. (1990) *Gender Trouble: Feminism and the Subversion of Identity*, London and New York: Routledge.

Case, S.E. (1988) *Feminism and Theatre*, New York: Methuen.

Case, S.E. (ed.) (1990) *Performing Feminisms: Feminist Critical Theory and Theatre*, Baltimore and London: Johns Hopkins University Press.

Diamond, E. (1988) "Brechtian theory/feminist theory toward a gestic feminist criticism," *The Drama Review* 32:82–94.

Diamond, E. (1997) *Mimesis Unmasked*, London and New York: Routledge.

Dolan, J. (1988) *The Feminist Spectator as Critic*, Ann Arbor, Michigan: UMI Research Press.

Fujiwara-Skrobak, M. (1996) "Social consciousness and madness in Zeami's life and works, or, the ritualistic shamanistic-divine aspects of Sarugaku for an ideal society," Unpublished Ph.D. dissertation, U.C.L.A.

Keene, D. (1998) "Dôjôji", rev. version, in K. Brazell (ed.) *Traditional Japanese Theater*, New York: Columbia.

Keene, D. (1970) *Twenty Plays of the Nô Theatre*, New York: Columbia. [Includes an early translation of *Dôjôji*].

Klein, S.B. (1995) "Woman as Serpent: The Demonic Feminine in the Noh Play *Dôjôji*," in J.M. Law (ed.) *Religious Reflections on the Human Body*, Bloomington, I.N.: Indiana University Press.

Komparu, K. (1983) *The Noh Theater: Principals and Perspectives*, New York and Tokyo: Weatherhill/Tankosha.

Kwon, Y.-H.K. (1988) "The female entertainment tradition in medieval Japan: the case of *Asobi*," *Theatre Journal*, 40:205–216.

O'Neill, P.G. (1958) *Early Noh Drama*, London: Lund Humphries.

Ortolanti, B. and Leiter, S.L. (eds) (1998) *Zeami and the Nô Theatre in the World*, New York: CASTA.

Mohanty, C. (1991a) "Cartographies of Struggle: Third World Women and the Politics of Feminism," in C.T. Mohanty, A. Russo and L. Torres (eds) *Third World Women and the Politics of Feminism*, Bloomington, I.N.: Indiana University Press.

Mohanty, C. (1991b) "Under western eyes: feminist scholarship and colonial discourses," in C.T. Mohanty, A. Russo and L. Torres (eds) *Third World Women and the Politics of Feminism*, Bloomington, I.N.: Indiana University Press.

Sorgenfrei, C.F. (1998) "Zeami and the Aesthetics of Contemporary Japanese Performance," in B. Ortolanti and S.L. Leiter (eds), *Zeami and the Nô Theater in the World*, New York: CASTA.

Zeami, M. (1984) *On The Art of the Nô Drama: The Major Treatises of Zeami*, trans. J. Thomas Rimer and Y. Masakazu, Princeton: Princeton University Press.

PART II

Theatre and print cultures, 1500–1900

Edited by **Bruce McConachie**

Theatre and print cultures, 1500–1900

INTRODUCTION: CHINA AND WESTERN EUROPE

If asked in 1500 to choose the world's most advanced culture, an observer on the moon looking through a high-powered telescope would probably have chosen China. By the middle of the Ming Dynasty (1368–1644), the Chinese enjoyed the highest standard of living, the most advanced technology and medical care, the most reliable government, and arguably the most sophisticated culture in the world. In the previous century, Chinese explorers, using their invention of the compass, had established hegemony over key ports in the Indian Ocean and landed on the east coast of Africa. New discoveries in rice cultivation had multiplied China's food-producing capacity. Landed interests and officials controlled the government, which ruled an enormous population through an imperial bureaucracy noted for its educational accomplishments. Stabilizing this authority was gunpowder, another Chinese invention, and the ideology of Confucianism, which honored learning, tolerance, decorum, and governance. Confucianism also denigrated the merchant class as unworthy of that of gentlemen, with the consequence that money made in trade and manufacturing was usually invested in education and culture rather than enhancing commercial profits. Many sons of merchants aspired to join the Confucian elite, where they could attain a high rank in the university system or imperial bureaucracy.

Chinese spectators enjoyed many kinds of theatre during the Ming Dynasty. These included *zaju*, a kind of variety performance dating from earlier times, and *kunqua*, a type of musical drama accompanied by dancing and singing that gained popularity with Confucian elite audiences. Musician Wei Liangfu (*c.*1500–*c.*1573) synthesized several modes of southern Chinese music to initiate *kunqua*, which typically centered on mellifluous, plaintive singing to flute accompaniment. Performances of *kunqua* plays, usually about the complications of young love, also featured string and percussion instruments, slow but fluid dance movements, and lyrical, melancholy monologues. Early performances of *kunqua*, often staged at court or in elite houses, might last three days and nights. The Ming Dynasty also spawned many regional forms of opera, which later innovators would synthesize into Beijing Opera, or *jingxi*.

The foundations of Chinese society and culture changed little in the four hundred years after 1500 in comparison to Western Europe. In the West, the Protestant Reformation and the religious wars that followed in its wake (1520–1648), ensured that no single ideology such as Confucianism would unify western belief. Whereas the Ming Dynasty in China turned its back on the rest of the world – the emperor even forbade the construction of seagoing vessels – the smaller, weaker kingdoms of Spain, Portugal, England, and France sent out explorers and colonizers after 1492 to spread their religious views and enrich their kingdoms. Confucian belief and bureaucratic control regulated new discoveries in China, but the science of Galileo, Newton, and others challenged the authority of Church and state in the West during the seventeenth century and later. In the eighteenth century, the idea of a public emerged in Europe – a literate group of merchants, scientists, philosophers, artists, and others with their own political agenda, a sphere of influence unthinkable in imperial China. China had experienced conquest from abroad when the Mongols invaded, but never revolution from below. In contrast, some workers and peasants helped to lead the French Revolution (1789–1799), which challenged the kind of absolutist rule in Europe that Chinese emperors took for granted. After 1500, a new class arose in Western Europe that eventually supplanted landed aristocrats and royal sovereigns as national rulers. The bourgeoisie, merely a necessary evil in Confucian morality, began an industrial revolution in the late eighteenth century that transformed European society and led to the political power of their class in the twentieth.

By 1500, both China and Western Europe had the printing press. In China, where moveable type had been in use since the eleventh century, the Confucian elite used print primarily to standardize its bureaucratic procedures and to spread traditional learning, including extensive criticism of *kunqua* music. Print culture began in Europe in the mid-fifteenth century; Gutenberg printed his famous Bible in 1456. In sharp contrast to China, early printing was mostly unregulated in the West and soon it had entered into all of the debates that divided literate Europeans. Protestants printed Bibles for lay readers, explorers published new maps, and scientists relied on the press to communicate their findings. Print helped sovereigns maintain their rule and, eventually, revolutionaries to overthrow them, and the early capitalists relied on the press for land titles, legal notices, and binding contracts. From 1500 to 1700 in Europe, most printers were kept busy with Bibles and religious tracts, scholarly books, and legal documents. After 1700, print culture went into high gear with the addition of newspapers and journals, novels and histories, and many more pamphlets, manuals, and plays. New inventions, coupled with more widespread literacy, led to an explosion of cheap texts in the nineteenth century. In China, socially and ideologically conservative institutions maintained a near monopoly on print culture. In Western Europe, the most dynamic, even the most radical institutions and movements turned to print to advance their goals. By 1900, print and its reality effects pervaded all social and cultural practices in Western Europe, including the theatre.

This introduction focuses on the many ways that print impressed itself on Western European theatre between 1500 and 1900. Subsequent chapters in Part II will show in some detail that print also played a role in Japanese theatre, while in India the continuation of a culture based in orality and writing rather than print shaped theatrical performances during these years. In western theatre, however, many developments could not have occurred without the theatre's immersion in print culture. The legitimation of dramatic, text-based theatre as an independent institution, the development of perspective scenery within a proscenium frame, the authority accorded to dramatic authors, and the legibility of the gestures and characters presented by Western European actors were all dependent on the reality effects of print culture. For all of these developments in the period between 1500 and 1900, print was a necessary, but by no means sufficient cause.

The rise of European professional theatres

Although print would prove vitally important to western theatre, the struggling professional troupes of the mid-sixteenth century relied very little on printed plays. In Spain and England, traveling companies of actors benefited from the gradual decline of medieval forms of theatre by enacting traditional

farces, moralities, banquet performances, and occasional new scripts – typically cobbled together by the actor-manager – for popular and aristocratic
audiences. Much as troupes of minstrels had done in medieval times, the acting
companies of the early 1500s attached themselves to a noble family, entertained in their households when they could, and traveled with the permission
and under the protection of a nobleman's name for much of the season. Despite
this apparent extension of feudal relationships in the theatre, however, Western
European actor-managers and their companies both drew on noble patronage
and supported themselves economically by charging admission.

In a parallel development, renaissance humanist scholars in the major
universities of Italy, England, Spain, and France had been rediscovering and
printing ancient Greek and Roman texts related to the theatre. By 1520,
editions of Aristotle's *Poetics*, the major plays of Plautus, Terence, Sophocles,
and Seneca, and the illustrated discussions of theatre buildings and scenery by
Vitruvius were available in print. Fired by an interest in these ancient texts,
renaissance scholars and their aristocratic patrons began writing their own
plays in imitation of the classics and soon they were seeking to produce them.
In Italy, Gian Giorgio Trissino (1478–1550) wrote and published the first
classical-style tragedy, *Sofonisba* (1515). Italian political theorist Niccolo
Machiavelli (1469–1527) borrowed the form of classical comedy to write
The Mandrake (*c*.1518). Like Machiavelli, university-trained Nicholas Udall
(1505–1566) in England leaned heavily on Plautus to shape his *Ralph Roister
Doister* sometime in the 1530s. Earlier in the century, Juan del Encina
(1469–1529) and Gil Vicente (*c*.1453–*c*.1537) were writing classically-based
entertainments for royal courts on the Iberian peninsula. Because of the religious disturbances that wracked France during these years, classically-inspired
plays and performances developed somewhat later in Paris, with the first of
them coming to the French court in the 1550s.

While most academics and aristocrats produced their plays on temporary
stages for student or court audiences, one group of scholars built the first
permanent theatre in Italy since antiquity, the Teatro Olimpico. Its architect,
Andrea Palladio (1518–1580), based much of his design on the architectural
drawings of the Roman writer, Vitruvius. From Vitruvius, Palladio borrowed
the look of the *scenae frons* from the Roman theatre (see Chapter 3) for the
scenic façade of the Teatro Olimpico. In the completed theatre, perspective
scenery was placed behind the five openings in the façade and the side
entrances, in effect a merging of the renaissance rediscovery of the ancient
past and renaissance's own new technological development. The Teatro

Olimpico opened in 1585 with a production of *Oedipus Rex* to an audience of academics and nobility. Such productions, however, were mostly occasional, amateur undertakings intended for pedagogical, honorific, celebratory, and scholarly purposes. Renaissance academic theatre might occasionally employ professional actors, especially in Italy, but it never challenged the professionals' popularity with the public. Nonetheless, the literary resources of the academic theatre offered substantial opportunities to the early professional troupes. Two major theatrical traditions, *commedia dell'arte* and dramatic, text-based theatre, flowed from the intersection of amateur and professional theatre in the mid-sixteenth century.

Commedia dell'arte

Although its origins are uncertain, troupes in northern Italy apparently began performing *commedia dell'arte* in the 1540s. In a typical *commedia* scenario, lustful or miserly old fathers block the romantic hopes of a young couple, who turn to their servants for help. Through successful trickery and often lucky discoveries (such as lost family relationships), the foolish old men are foiled and the lovers happily united. Nearly all of the characters and plot devices of *commedia* derive directly from the plays of Plautus and Terence, which the Italian troupes probably learned while reading and performing *commedia erudita* (academic comedy) for aristocratic patrons. Even though they were indebted to academic comedy, the acting troupes styled themselves *dell'arte*, that is, professional, to distinguish their work from the amateur efforts of academic theatre.

Most *commedia dell'arte* improvisation was carefully planned. Somewhat like stand-up comedians, the actors relied on memorized lines from *commedia erudita* and pre-arranged comic business and then plugged these speeches and gags into pre-set scenarios. This ready store of comic material freed *commedia dell'arte* performers to charm and entertain the public with their considerable skills, charisma, and virtuosity. Indeed, once a few troupes had mastered the fundamentals of their craft, *commedia dell'arte* spread rapidly. Professional companies were performing in Venice and Milan in the 1550s and by the 1570s troupes were appearing in southern France, Spain, and even London. During the next century, it was a mark of status for royal and ducal courts to patronize and house a *commedia* troupe; *commedia dell'arte* traveled as far as Stockholm and Moscow.

By 1600, the typical company employed eight to twelve performers, each with his or her own specialized character (Figure II.1). The actors playing the

Figure II.1 Late sixteenth-century engraving showing three stock characters from the *commedia dell'arte* – from left, Arlecchino, Zanni the cuckold, and Pantalone – serenading an unseen lady in in her house on the right. © Bibliothèque Nationale de France. [Source: Le Recueil Fossard – Paris: Librairie théâtrale, 1981 (lote 4–V–43809). Conserved in the National Museum, Stockholm.]

old men (*vecchi*) wore grotesque half-masks and used specific dialects: Pantalone always spoke Venetian and the Doctor railed in Latin or Bolognese, for instance. The lovers (*innamorati*) appeared without masks and often quoted poems and romantic dialog from *commedia erudita*. The servants (*servi*) were the most diverse, with names such as Arlecchino and Brighella for the males and Franceschina and Colombina for the women. With their sequences of comic business called *lazzi*, the servants carried much of the comedy of the show. For example, Arlecchino, always hungry, catches and eats a fly with relish. Most were masked, though some of the younger female servants may have occasionally appeared without the conventional half-mask. Women had acted in a few medieval pageants, but regular performances by professional female actors began in Europe with *commedia dell'arte*.

Institutionalizing drama in Europe

The commercial production of new plays was the other option offered by the intersection of professional and academic theatre in the mid-1550s. Until then, nearly all dramatic theatre in the West had been performed for a specific occasion, such as a religious celebration, civic festival, or a royal wedding. If the play was mediocre or failed to please on one of those occasions, no one's livelihood was at stake. Commercial dramatic theatre, however, upped the ante. Now actor-managers needed a constant flow of good, new plays or rival companies would soon surpass them with the public. *Commedia* troupes, by continuing to recycle the same dramatic material into new scenarios and performances, retained more control of their productions. In contrast, actor-managers in England and Spain looked to playwrights, whom they now had to nurture and reward, for their plots and dialog.

Renaissance actor-managers could take this gamble because several of them were already profiting from new plays that merged classical learning with the demands of popular entertainment. In Spain, actor-manager Lope de Rueda (*c*.1510–*c*.1565) gained considerable income and renown in the 1550s among popular audiences and aristocratic patrons for his classically inspired farces and comedies. No one figure brought together these two traditions with similar success in England, but the frequent mix of academics, professional actors, and aristocrats in London for performances at schools and at noble houses created an interest in classical and Italian plays in the 1560s and 1570s. By 1590, most of the prominent Elizabethan playwrights writing for professional companies had received an education that included classical training. These included Thomas Kyd (1558–1594), whose *The Spanish Tragedy* (*c*.1587) drew on the dramatic devices of Seneca to set the pattern for later revenge tragedies, and Christopher Marlowe (1564–1593), who mastered episodic plotting in such popular tragedies as *Tamburlaine*, Parts I and II (1587–1588), and *Doctor Faustus* (1588) (Figure II.2). Although few contemporary plays were in print by 1600, humanist scholarship was convincing the literate public that dramatic theatre connected their own tastes with the superior culture of the ancients.

Two companies dominated London theatre in the last ten years of Queen Elizabeth's reign (1558–1603) and during the reign of James I (1603–1625). Theatrical entrepreneur Philip Henslowe (*c*.1555–1616) backed the Admiral's Men, initially headed by the actor Edward Alleyn (1566–1626), and the Burbage family ran the Lord Chamberlain's Men. The sharing system, by which leading actors, playwrights, and financers shared in the profits, organized both troupes. In recognition of the importance of these companies,

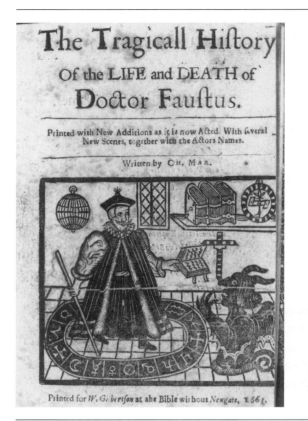

Figure II.2 Title page for a 1620 edition of *The Tragical History of Doctor Faustus*, by Christopher Marlowe. © Victoria and Albert Museum of Theatre History.

James I put the Admiral's Men under the patronage of his son (re-naming them Prince Henry's Men) and elevated the Chamberlain's Men to royal patronage (which changed them to the King's Men). Both companies, together with several minor ones, competed for plays and mounted them in outdoor and indoor playhouses as well as in "great rooms" at schools and courts. While the Admiral's Men produced Marlowe's popular tragedies, the Chamberlain's Men counted William Shakespeare (1564–1616) among their playwrights (he was also a shareholder in the company), and they controlled the rights to most of the successful plays co-authored by Francis Beaumont (*c.*1584–1616) and John Fletcher (1579–1625). Co-authorship was a common practice in the 1590–1625 period; Fletcher probably collaborated with Shakespeare on Shakespeare's last three plays.

Most Elizabethan and Jacobean spectators, like television audiences today, cared little about who wrote the play as long as it met their expectations.

Spectators wanted dramas stuffed with sexual allusions, characters disguised as someone else, and they were accustomed to such conventions as frequent direct address, as when actors delivered asides and soliloquies, and to plot developments involving incest and physical mutilations – in comedies as well as tragedies. Audiences were not disturbed by comic scenes within tragedies or mortally serious moments in comedy, and expected both genres to jump abruptly among scenes of lyricism, suspense, heroics, or grotesquerie. A good play, from their point of view, should also include several metatheatrical moments, in which the actors acknowledged the make-believe of their actions – as long as comedies ended in marriage and/or reunion and tragedies ended with a stage full of dead bodies and order restored.

The increasing prestige of well-written drama altered acting By the 1580s, performers who might have improvised their way through an evening's entertainment a generation ago were now expected to play "by the book." So important had memorization become for acting that Shakespeare in *A Midsummer Night's Dream* (1595–1596) even has the "rude mechanicals" of his subplot memorizing their lines completely before they mount their performance of "Pryamus and Thisbe" in the play-within-the-play. The expectation of the auditors and actors that a script would be played as written led, in turn, to higher standards of playwriting. Better for actor-managers and their companies to memorize and perform several plays of high quality than to have to purchase and learn many mediocre scripts that would enjoy only limited popularity.

After 1600, as more contemporary plays reached publication, the acting companies and their playwrights reaped more direct benefits from the emerging print culture. Most English companies owned the plays they performed, and they paid top dramatists good money for their scripts. The average payment per play until about 1603 was roughly six pounds, a figure that increased to ten or twelve pounds by 1613. By the 1640s, it was increasingly common for companies and professional playwrights to arrange for the publication of their dramas. Ben Jonson (1572–1637), who won applause for satirizing the follies of the time through a strong dose of classical precepts and wit, was the first English playwright to edit and publish a collection of his own plays, in 1616.

Golden Age theatre in Spain, 1590–1680

Print culture in Spain helped to sustain a vital theatre that developed near the end of the long transition from feudalism to absolutism on the Iberian

Peninsula. As several historians have noted, the joining of Castile, Aragon, and Granada to form late medieval Spain in 1492, plus the rapid success of the Spanish crown in extending its rule to the Netherlands, Austria, southern Italy, and much of Latin America in the 1500s, actually delayed the centralization of power in the Spanish monarchy. Although the royal court in Madrid sponsored theatrical performances after 1620, Spanish royalty mostly ignored the professional troupes during the formative years of Golden Age theatre. This left Spanish playwrights comparatively free to borrow from traditional regional and popular sources as well as from classical and Italian dramas for the form and content of their plays. The result was a lively theatre that, though generally aristocratic in its values, also had the freedom to criticize excessive incursions of feudal power into popular traditions. This relative freedom gradually dissipated after 1620, however, as the Spanish crown centralized and extended absolutist authority. By 1650, the Golden Age of Spanish theatre had ended.

In the 1590s, public theatres were flourishing in Madrid, Valencia, Seville, Valladolid, Lisbon, and several other cities on the Iberian Peninsula. Unlike the situation in London, Spanish acting troupes did not control their playhouses, but rented them from private capitalists or charitable institutions controlled by the Catholic Church. For most companies, this meant extensive touring and an ongoing search for residencies at aristocratic houses. The public theatres, or *corrales*, varied in size but usually included an open courtyard (*patio*) with a platform stage at one end and backstage space behind it, plus separate, raised seating on either side of the yard (*gradas*) and an elevated gallery (*cazuela*) opposite the stage (Figure II.3). Male standees occupied the *patio*, wealthier patrons (men and women) sat in the *gradas*, and the *cazuela* was reserved for women. Most staging conventions, as in Elizabethan London, were simple and traditional. The continuous stage action, with no front curtain and no breaks to change scenery, involved other characteristic elements of the popular stage, such as direct address to the audience, plots involving intrigue and disguise, stock characters, and fast-moving dialog with proverbs, wordplay, and asides.

Just as the public theatres accommodated popular and aristocratic spectators, many of the plays, too, merged the tastes and values of both groups of auditors. The history play and romantic drama, the latter known in Spain as the *comedia de capa y espada* (cloak-and-sword drama involving male honor), were two of the genres that successfully fused these traditions. Gaspar de Aguilar's (1561–1623) comedy, *The Merchant in Love* (*c.*1590s), for instance,

Figure II.3 Reconstruction of the seventeenth-century Spanish playhouse, *El Corral del Principe* (c.1697). Drawing by Carlos Dorremochea in John Allen, *The Reconstruction of a Spanish Golden Age Playhouse* (1983). © University Press of Florida.

gives his rich bourgeois protagonist the problem of deciding whether to marry for love or money. Set in Valencia at the height of that Mediterranean city's early commercial success, the play rejects the aristocracy's preoccupation with rank and examines the problematics of making money. The merchant, of course, chooses love, but comes to understand that it is acceptable for the aristocracy to harbor capitalist ambitions. Like many other romantic comedies, *The Merchant in Love* put limits on nascent capitalism in Spain at the same time that it helped the once-feudal aristocracy to adjust to changing economic conditions.

The most prolific and renowned playwright of the Golden Age, Lope Felix de Vega Carpio (1562–1635), wrote many *capa y espada* dramas among his more than 800 plays. Although a favorite of the aristocracy, Lope came from an artisan family, worked to gain more education throughout his life, and eventually became a renowned priest. Lope set his history play, *The Life and Death of King Bamba* (1597–1598), in the early middle ages and focused it on the brief rule of a peasant king in Spain. Altering much of the historical record for dramatic effect, Lope posed peasant wisdom, valor, and humility, backed by Catholic faith, against the foolish and villainous objections of a fractious nobility. Eventually God and Bamba prevail, but an aristocratic rebellion against his rule in the North of Spain leads to Bamba's death and the collusion of the nobility with invading Moors. Similar to Lope's *The Sheep Well* (c.1614), which also utilizes a peasant perspective to criticize arrogant aristocratic power, *King Bamba* calls on the Spanish nobility to draw on history and popular tradition to change their morality. The play is not anti-aristocratic, however; like *The Merchant in Love*, it validates the importance of the nobility while urging its reform. Significantly, the production of *King Bamba* followed soon after Lope's prolonged service at the court of the powerful Duke of Alba in the early 1590s.

During the reign of Philip IV (1621–1665), the Spanish monarchy asserted more control of its kingdom and colonies and also called more frequently on the theatre to bolster its absolutist claims to power. Pedro Calderon de la Barca (1600–1681) succeeded Lope de Vega as Spain's most successful playwright, but Calderon's energies were split between the public theatres and the court. Writing primarily between 1622 and 1640, Calderon continued and improved upon the previous genres. He also wrote several *autos sacramentales*, allegorical dramas that embodied Catholic ideology and often glorified the Spanish throne as the Defender of the Faith. Even his most secular play, *Life Is a Dream* (c.1636), presents the absolute power and agency of kingship as the necessary answer for a royal prince who does not know if his life at court has been a dream. By the 1630s, Calderon was spending much of his time devising court entertainments. Although he crafted the plot and dialog for *The Greatest Enchantment is Love* (1635), the lavish spectacle of the production, which involved the king and his court enjoying shipwrecks, triumphal chariots, and the destruction of a palace from their seats on gondolas, upstaged his dramatic efforts. After 1652, Calderon continued to produce *autos*, but all of his secular plays were written for the court.

Neoclassicism and print in Europe

By the 1650s, Spanish absolutism was embracing the aesthetics of neoclassicism, a mode of theatre that would soon be perfected in France. If early print culture in Western Europe raised the prestige of dramatic theatre, it also, under neoclassicism, limited the kinds of dramas that came to be acceptable to most of the literate public. By 1620, many more Europeans than before were reading printed plays and generally regarded this practice as superior to watching a live performance. In the view of most scholars – a view supported by the anti-theatrical prejudices of Plato and other ancient philosophers – the stage was, in effect, the place of bodies and mortality, while the page could attain immortality in the realm of the spirit. Even dramatists writing for the popular stage sometimes supported this view. Many of Calderon's plays celebrate the Neo-Platonic spirit over the perceived shortcomings of the senses.

This view of live performance underlay the concerns of several sixteenth-century Italian scholars who were eager to support a vibrant dramatic theatre, but fearful of its social consequences. Julius Caesar Scaliger (1484–1558) and Lodovico Castelvetro (1505–1571) used Aristotle's *Poetics* as a jumping-off point for their ideas, but set out to update and improve upon Aristotle's recommendations for good drama. Scaliger and Castelvetro synthesized the ideas of previous Italian theorists who had emphasized the need for dramatic probability, which they termed "verisimilitude." To support verisimilitude, the Italians recommended that playwrights follow three unities – place, time, and action – in constructing their dramas. In brief, a play should occur in a single setting, its fictitious time should last for no more than a single day, and its plot should encompass only one major action. Scaliger and Castelvetro reasoned that unity of place was necessary because spectators knew that the stage in front of them could not really be transformed into several actual locations. Regarding unity of time, Scaliger called for plays whose action lasted no longer than 24 hours, but Castelvetro urged that 12 hours would better serve verisimilitude. The common people attending a play, said Castelvetro, would not believe "that several days and nights had passed when their senses tell them that only a few hours have passed" (Carlson 1993:48–49).

This point of view about audience reception, of course, radically underestimated the imaginative capabilities of spectators and flew in the face of most people's actual experience in the public theatres of England and Spain. But the prejudices of early print culture, plus current beliefs about social hierarchy, supported Scaliger and Castelvetro. Educated scholars and aristocrats whose imaginations had been stretched and tested by books might be able to understand plays that violated verisimilitude, according to the sixteenth-century humanists, but the "ignorant multitude," with only their "senses" to guide them, would be lost.

French critics and theorists in the seventeenth century echoed and extended these Italian humanist prejudices to produce a body of neoclassical rules that many educated Europeans came to accept as necessary safeguards for drama on stage. Most French and Spanish scholars in the early 1600s agreed with the Italian theorists, but several popular playwrights had already voiced objections. Lope de Vega, for example, recognized the validity of the norms of verisimilitude advocated by the Italians and admitted that his plays violated them, but he forthrightly stated his intention of continuing to please his audiences rather than bowing to the theorists. Alexandre Hardy (c.1570–1632), the most popular French playwright of the 1620s, also sought the vindication of public applause over humanist praise. The dispute between the popular stage and the academic theorists came to a head in France with the production of *Le Cid*, by Pierre Corneille (1606–1684), in 1637. Believing his play was generally in accord with the norms of verisimilitude, Corneille and his friends nevertheless responded to criticism of *Le Cid*'s popular success with a defense that ignored its debt to the unities and other neoclassic rules. When the controversy threatened to get out of hand, Cardinal Richelieu (1586–1642) called on the French Academy to settle the dispute.

Le Cid and French absolutism

Richelieu, who effectively ruled France in the 1620s and 1630s behind the throne of Louis XIII, used the controversy over *Le Cid* to position the monarchy as the public arbiter of French culture. Although the French Academy had originated as a private organization of scholars, Richelieu pressured its members to adopt state support and to take as its primary goal the codification and regulation of French language and culture. Like the publication of dictionaries and grammars that attempted to standardize Western European languages in the 1600s, the French Academy was itself a product of print culture. By referring the debate over *Le Cid* to the arbitration of the Academy, Richelieu ensured that the future of French theatre would help to serve the interests of the French state.

Six months later, Richelieu's appointee, Jean Chapelain (1595–1674), delivered the verdict of the Academy. Chapelain took issue with some of the criticism leveled against Corneille, but condemned his play for breeching verisimilitude and for its lack of ethics. Even though *Le Cid* observes the unity of time, Chapelain complained that Corneille had packed too many incidents into 24 hours to sustain the play's probability. The Academy found particularly offensive the incident in Corneille's plot that involves a young woman consenting to wed the killer of her father. This the Academy viewed as transgressing the neoclassical precept of decorum. Decorum, which preserved class lines by specifying behavior appropriate for each class (only lower-class characters could act foolishly, for example), dictated that young women of the nobility must not commit immoral acts without punishment. In his decision, Chapelain had vindicated the unities, upheld decorum, and tied the purpose of dramatic theatre more firmly than had the Italian critics to the ideal of "poetic justice" – evil characters should be punished and good ones rewarded. In subsequent years, the Abbe d'Aubignac (1604–1676), a protégé of Richelieu, would codify these neoclassical rules and celebrate dramas that followed them for normalizing a socially conservative morality and glorifying the French state.

By linking dramatic construction to the power of the monarchy, neoclassicism facilitated many strategic alliances among playwrights and sovereigns in Western Europe. Louis XIV officially began his reign at the age of five in 1643 and assumed control of France in 1661. Building on the achievements of Richelieu, Louis XIV made French power and his version of absolute monarchy the envy of Europe until his death in 1715. French culture – and with it the precepts of neoclassical verisimilitude, decorum, and poetic justice – spread throughout the continent and became the European norm. The most celebrated playwright during the reign of Louis XIV, Jean Racine (1639–1699), wrote tragedies that became models of neoclassicism. In England, following the English Civil War (1642–1649), and the Commonwealth Period (1649–1660), the restoration of the monarchy with Charles II in 1660 helped to legitimize and popularize neoclassic ideals in England. John Dryden (1631–1700) was the foremost of many English playwrights who put neoclassicism on the Restoration stage. Neoclassicism remained at the center of French playwriting in the eighteenth century in the work of Voltaire (1694–1778) and others. It also informed the kinds of plays written in Germany and Spain and dictated the goals of "good" drama in Sweden, Poland, and Russia. For many literate Europeans until the French Revolution, the goals of neoclassical theatre seemed the most enlightened in the world. Print culture had helped to make them so.

The marriage of neoclassicism and French absolutism points to a larger issue in theatre history that constitutes the focus of our next chapter. Governmental power has often been used to support or limit theatrical activity. Sometimes it has served both purposes at once. Chapter 4, "Theatre and the State, 1600–1900," traces the relations between state power and major theatrical enterprises in France, Japan, and England. As we will see, these relations have varied widely, mostly due to official attitudes toward the theatre and differing historical and cultural contexts. Our case studies for this chapter examine subversive strains in Molière's comedies for Louis XIV, kabuki theatre's subversion of official culture in Japan, and sexuality in Shakespeare's comedy, *Twelfth Night*.

Scenic perspectivism in print and on stage

Print-influenced neoclassicism altered theatre architecture and scenic conventions as well as playwriting. During the seventeenth century, performances on the stages of the public playhouses were somewhat indebted to the platea and mansion arrangements of the medieval theatre, in which several mansions were always visible to spectators. (Parisian troupes continued this practice into the 1630s, using small mansions visible throughout the performance on an unframed stage.) In England and Spain, the platea-like open platforms were backed with doors and perhaps an upper level, providing a fluid, unlocalized playing area that could be whatever the lines of the actors said it was. These practices gradually gave way to the use of a series of single settings defining the place of action, organized according to the laws of perspective and framed by a proscenium arch. Neoclassic staging had already altered most entertainments at court and was changing the staging of public performances in Italy, but the commercial acting troupes of France took longer to adopt these new conventions, in part because they involved higher costs. By 1680, however, the premiere acting troupes in Paris had changed their scenic practices to the neoclassic mode. By then, the two companies in London that dominated Restoration theatre had also adopted neoclassic scenic conventions, albeit in less expensive versions.

There are many reasons for the rise and eventual triumph of proscenium staging and perspective scenery between the late fifteenth century and the first quarter of the sixteenth. By 1500, Italian painters had perfected the geometry and graphics of single-point perspective, and this mode of illustrating depth on a canvas or on walls began to influence Italian scenographers. Sebastiano Serlio (1475–1554) depicted a series of tragic, comic, and satyric settings in the second part of his *Architettura* (1545), by which time perspective scenery on wings and backdrops had been in use for performances at Italian courts for some years. To realize Serlio's conventional designs in production required a painter and carpenter to construct and hang a painted backdrop at the rear of the playing space and flank the drop with three sets of angle wings, each with painted sides that receded symmetrically toward a single vanishing point that was presumably behind the painted backdrop (Figure II.4). The stage floor was sharply raked, that is, it sloped up toward the backdrop, enhancing the effect of depth. Actors performed downstage, on an area of level flooring, not in the scenic space where they would be out of proportion to the converging lines of perspective and spoil the illusion. The vantage point of the ruler, seated in the center of the auditorium, organized the scene visually. That is, the designer figured out where in the auditorium the ruler's eyes would gaze on the scene and drew his perspective lines for painting the scenery from that single point toward the vanishing point. This meant that only one person in the temporary auditorium had a "perfect" view of the stage; from every other vantage point, the painted perspective looked skewed. For those seated at the side of auditorium the perspective was completely awry. The implicit visual demand on the other spectators in the auditorium, of course, was to imagine how the scene looked from the prince's or duke's point of view.

Figure II.4 The theatre in print: the setting for a comic scene by Sebastiano Serlio, from his *De Architettura*, 1569 edition. © Lilly Library, Indiana University, Bloomington, Indiana.

This visual power play suited the political dynamics of ruling families such as the Medici and the Farnese in northern Italy. It also served the royal absolutism of the royal courts of France, England, and Spain. By the 1610s, court entertainers in Paris were using modified versions of Serlio's designs to mount lavish ballet spectacles, which were amateur performances featuring court nobility as powerful mythological and allegorical figures. During that decade (and for 20 years more), Inigo Jones (1573–1652) designed variations on Serlian scenery for the court masques of Charles I in London – entertainments similar to the ballet spectacles in France. Jones convinced Charles I to convert two rooms at his court palace for elaborate, expensive masquing entertainments, an extravagance that angered the Puritans and helped to lead to the overthrow of the king and the English Civil War. In Spain, Italian designers worked with Calderon in the 1630s and 1640s on similar spectacles for the court of Philip IV.

Related to the prerogatives of absolutism was the popularity of building Roman triumphal arches at royal residences. The first proscenium arches, frames on the sides and top of a stage, looked like the triumphal arches of ancient Rome; most were as high as they were wide, and they usually featured some glorifying motif at the top center of the arch. As more elaborate stage machinery came into use to move scenery or to manage the ascents and descents of gods who came to earth to bless the viewing ruler's realm, the proscenium both framed the perspective scenery and masked the mechanisms on which the changing perspective pictures for the power plays depended. A permanent, structurally elaborate proscenium was in use for productions in the Uffizi Palace in Florence by 1586, designed by Bernardo Buontalenti (1536–1608). An early permanent proscenium stage, constructed in 1616 by Giovan Battista Aleotti (1546–1636) in the Teatro Farnese in the Farnese Palace in Parma, can be seen today, albeit in a reconstruction.

In addition to the influence of perspective painting, the rise of absolutist political power, and the attractions of Roman triumphal arches, theatre historians have also noted the suggestiveness of printed illustrations as a significant cause of the gradual spread of this new scenic practice. While an illustrated volume of Vitruvius's treatise on Roman architecture had been printed as early as 1486, many other books featuring scenic illustrations reached publication in the early days of print culture. More quickly than on the stage, the organization of space on the illustrated page shifted from the simultaneous representation of several images to one unified image that could take advantage of the discoveries of single-point perspective. Like printers, scenographers thought about space in graphic terms; they shaped the vision of the viewer through unity, symmetry, and the illusion of depth. By the 1550s, printers used Roman triumphal arches as a common motif to organize the title page in a book. And even when no printed symmetrical frame dominated the look of a page, the sides of its paper created a visual frame that established every page as a mini-proscenium. By the 1630s, literate Europeans had been looking for a hundred years at the pages of books and pamphlets that organized their vision according to the laws of perspective. How "natural," then, to expect that stage scenery should mirror this reality. In this sense, the development of perspective scenery and the proscenium arch may be understood as a reality effect of print culture.

Cardinal Richelieu helped to ensure the triumph of Italianate scenery in France. In the late 1630s, Richelieu instructed an architect to build him a palace housing the first theatre in France with flat-wing scenery on a raked

Figure II.5 Cardinal Richelieu's theatre in his palace (later the Palais Royal). Louis XIII converses with Richelieu (back to the viewer) during a performance, while Anne of Austria looks on. Molière's company later played in this theatre. © Bridgeman Art Library.

stage behind a permanent proscenium arch. When completed in 1641, the private theatre at Richelieu's palace featured a stage 59 ft wide by 46 ft deep and an auditorium of nearly the same dimensions (Figure II.5). Richelieu died in 1642, and his palace came under the control of the crown as the Palais Royal. In 1645, Richelieu's successor brought to the French court the Italian designer, Giacomo Torelli (1608–1678), known as the Great Sorcerer for his spectacular scenic innovations, to design for the Palais Royal. Working at a theatre in Venice in the early 1640s, Torelli had already put together the first "chariot-and-pole" system for changing scenery. In brief, this system involves flats mounted on long poles, which pass through slots in the flooring to small, 2-wheeled wagons, or "chariots," that run on tracks under the stage. Through a series of ropes, pulleys, winches, and counterweights, all of the chariots under the stage – perhaps as many as ten on both sides for each pair of five wings – could be moved simultaneously. As one flat moved into view, the flat

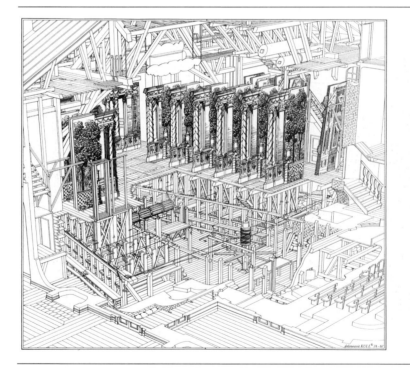

Figure II.6 Cut-away drawing by Gustaf Kull of the chariot-and-pole machinery for changing flats at the Drottningholm Court Theatre in Sweden. From Per Edstrom, "Stage Machinery," in Ove Hidemark, et al., *Drottningholm Court Theatre* (1993). © Gustav Kull, Jr.

behind or in front of it, receded offstage. The counterweighted flats and drops were also linked to painted borders hanging from the flies. Turning the master winches to which they were all linked could effect a complete scenic transformation from one setting to another in an instant. Such machinery is still in use in Sweden's Drottingholm Theatre today (Figure II.6), and such transformations are still astonishing. Productions also included special effects in perspective miniature and the ascents and descents of deities supported by complex rigging.

Torelli brought plans for the chariot-and-pole system with him to Paris and remodeled the Petit Bourbon and Palais Royal theatres in 1645 and 1646 to accommodate the new mode of scene shifting (Figure II.7). Although he did not immediately win over the French court to the new system, Torelli's innovation gradually caught on, and by 1680 its triumph in Paris was complete. By the early 1700s, court and public theatres throughout Europe were struggling to catch up with the French mode. The chariot-and-pole system

Figure II.7 Giacomo Torelli's setting for Act II of Pierre Corneille's *Andromède* at the Petit-Bourbon Theatre, 1650, in which Torelli's chariot-and-pole scene-shifting machinery was used. Engraving by François Chauveau. © Bibliothèque Nationale de France.

remained *de rigeur* among premiere theatres on the continent until the late nineteenth century. In England and in countries that followed English theatrical practice, a less expensive system was in use in which flats slid in grooves built on the stage floor and in supporting tracks behind the borders above. Scene changes required posting a scene-shifter on each flat. The English used perspective scenery too, but in relatively modest settings compared to continental practices.

Acting and print in Europe after 1700

With the arrival of a visually unified and more spectacular stage, the neoclassical theorist D'Aubignac could casually assert in 1684 that "the theatre is a place where one looks at something, not where one listens to something." Further, he asserted that its patrons are made up of "spectators or watchers, not auditors" (Peters 2000:163). D'Aubignac was primarily thinking of scenography, but his remark was increasingly true for acting as well. Actors continued to rely on their voices to express the dialog, of course, but after about 1660 they paid as much or more attention to the poses and gestures that made them visually expressive and interesting to spectators. Since the arrival of writing, the human voice had gradually declined as the chief repository of meaning in Western Europe. Where earlier music and voice had been the path to spiritual transcendence, critics now feared that mere sound could too easily seduce the other senses. Further, many commentators were laying more emphasis on the importance of gestures in human communication. One treatise written in 1644, for example, suggested that human gestures were a kind of universal alphabet of nature; preachers, actors, and orators must know this alphabet to communicate effectively. Increasingly in society, people were "reading" appearances in addition to listening to voices to understand human behavior and emotion. To be legible, a character on the stage (like a print "character" on the page) had to look right.

By the eighteenth century, actors were striving to please a print-soaked public eager to read the gestures and poses of performance. Many treatises and manuals instructed actors in the proper embodiment of their characters' "passions." Perhaps the most systematic of these was *The Art of Speaking* (1761), by James Burgh and John Walker. Despite its title, this manual offered a series of illustrated "lessons" demonstrating which pose should accompany each passion, so that the audience could understand the desired "affect." By reading *The Art of Speaking*, actors learned how to register the progression of poses involved in "Awe – Horror – Fear" with their spectators, for example

(Figure II.8). In addition, the theatre-going public praised actors who could hold these poses believably for an extended moment of stage time. Not only was it important for actors to model the right attitude, they also had to manage a believable transition from one to the next. As Gotthold Lessing explained in his *Hamburg Dramaturgy* (1767), the actor must prepare for each of his poses "gradually by previous movements, and then must resolve them again into the general tone of the conventional" (Roach 1985:73). The result in performance was a kind of garlanded effect that alternated between static poses and graceful movement as the actor used a character's lines and emotions to transition from one tableau to the next. It was crucial that each pose make an "impression" on the minds of the spectators before the actor moved on – a printing metaphor widely used in the eighteenth century to describe theatrical communication.

By all accounts, the English star David Garrick (1717–1779) mastered this style of acting better than any of his contemporaries. Garrick played an important role in sentimentalizing theatrical art during the Age of Enlightenment,

Figure II.8 The Passions classified: "Terror." From J.J. Engel, *Ideen zu Euer Mimik* (1812). © P.M. Arnold Semiology Collection, Washington University Libraries.

as the era has come to be called for the explosion of texts on everything from physics to farming that occurred between 1680 and 1789. Although the term "sentiment" now has negative connotations, the eighteenth-century public understood it in a positive light; it was a way of acting on stage and in society that united intellect, emotion, and morality. In Chapter 5, "Theatres for Knowledge Through Feeling, 1700–1900," we will examine this surprising theatre in Western Europe and developments after 1800 influenced by Romanticism, when "sentiment" came to mean cheap melodramatic tears. The case studies for the chapter begin with a cultural analysis of the printed pictures that helped to make David Garrick the model performer of his era. Next, partly for contrast, we analyze a similar genre of Indian theatre, kathakali dance-drama, in which the audience's aesthetic delight is stimulated through the actor-dancer's embodiment and conveyance of basic emotions. The chapter concludes with a case study of nineteenth-century melodrama.

Just as print culture reshaped acting and its reception in the eighteenth century, it also altered the public image of the profession. Few even thought of acting as a profession at all until print helped to elevate it in public esteem. When the public could read about actors in weekly newspapers and monthly journals and began to understand the difficulties of actor training, the past mystery and opprobrium surrounding their work began to dissipate. The press began its long love affair with actors in the eighteenth century. In addition to theatre reviews and manuals, actors' pictures appeared in printed plays, in theatre almanacs and books of anecdotes, and in engravings and illustrations by famous artists, where they usually were shown in an evocative moment of their most characteristic role. Soon after the press began to use actors, actors found ways of using the press – to puff their latest role, to create printed programs that boosted their reputations, and to write articles and memoirs that shaped the record of their performances. Without the actor-press mutual admiration society, theatrical "stars" could not have been "born." As texts and images circulated more and more widely, the stars increased the circumference of their circuits. In the 1750s, Garrick was a star in London. In the 1840s, the U.S. actor Edwin Forrest (1806–1872) could claim stardom throughout the U.S. and England. By 1900, Sarah Bernhardt (1844–1923) had performed around the world, and her printed image was recognizable on every continent.

European dramatists claim authority

The prestige and power of playwrights rose substantially between 1600 and 1900. European dramatists who published in 1600 might see little or no profit from the venture and were lucky if their names even appeared on the title page. By 1900, dramatists in the West had the legal right to bargain with publishers for enormous profits and had secured national and international copyright protection that guaranteed them remuneration for all future productions of their published plays. While print made this possible, dramatists themselves and the widening market for play readership made it happen. The rise of one historical group, however, often leads to the decline of another, and such was the case with dramatic authorship. The unauthored theatre of *commedia dell'arte* declined as the prestige of written drama increased.

The elevation of the dramatic writer from "playwright" to "author" was the first step in this development. Although the terms are used interchangeably now, they have different connotations and carried different historical meanings. Playwright, like the word "wheelwright," is a term for a craftsperson – one who makes plays for another. Author and authorship, in contrast, share the same root as "authority." One who writes for him or herself and retains some control of the product is an author. In 1600, most dramatists shared the title page of their published play with other authorities – often a printer, an acting company that employed them, a wealthy patron who subsidized the publication, and perhaps others. The only dramatists in print with real cultural authority in 1600 were the ancient Greeks and Romans. Playwrights had increased their cultural capital initially by reviewing and editing their plays before publication. By the end of the seventeenth century, many more of them were also supervising the publication of an entire collection of their dramas, not just single volumes. In the eighteenth century, the authoritative edition, corrected by the dramatist or reliant on the author's original manuscripts (if the playwright were dead), had become the accepted standard for play publication. Implicit in this institution of publication was the belief, still widely accepted today, that a printed play text could faithfully represent the intentions of a single author (for further discussion of this, see Chapter 11, "Director, Text, and Performance in the Postmodern World").

The change in the social status of dramatists and their printed plays substantially undercut the prestige of the *commedia dell'arte* troupes. As early as the 1690s, a French neoclassical critic complained that the Italian *commedia* "was not truly Drama"; instead, it was "nothing but a kind of ill-formed concert among various Actors" (Peters 2000:103). In 1738, the Italian dramatist Carlo Goldoni (1707–1793) set off a debate by advocating an increase in the authority of the playwright in *commedia* performance. Instead of crafting a scenario with some traditional business and a few speeches that a *commedia* troupe could use as it pleased, Goldoni wrote out the principal role of a play meant for *commedia* enactment. By 1743, when Goldoni authored his comic masterpiece *The Servant of Two Masters*, he left only one role to be improvised, and even wrote dialog for that one when he published the play in 1753. As the debate continued, several managers and playwrights defended the tradition of actor-dominated *commedia* and Goldoni responded with *commedia*-like plays that eliminated the half-masks, cleaned up the dialog, and sentimentalized the stock characters. Neither side won the public debate, but by 1800 many *commedia* troupes had folded and their actors were seeking work in dramatic theatres. The increasing prestige of dramatic authorship, coupled with the powerful ideology of sentimentalism, was the primary reason for *commedia*'s demise.

With the gradual shift in their status from playwright to author came more leverage with acting companies. Most companies still purchased plays outright from their authors for production in 1800, even though the troupes had lost control of publication rights. The names of acting companies rarely appeared on the title pages of plays anymore and most could no longer dictate when a play would reach print. In fact, some dramatists published their new plays before they opened at the theatre, both in the hope that play readership would generate an audience and that early publication might stop others from pirating their plays. By 1800, it had become standard practice in the Anglo-American theatre for the author to reap the profits of the third night of the performance of a new play. New playwrights could at least expect something for their efforts and celebrated authors, of course, could demand much more.

Dramatists still lacked full copyright protection for their intellectual property, however. French playwrights, though, were better off than most. In 1790, the year after the Revolution began, the new National Assembly granted production as well as publication rights to playwrights. English dramatists had to wait until 1833 for greater control over the production of their plays. Spain and the United States passed copyright laws in 1847 and 1856, respectively. None of these laws were very well enforced outside of major theatrical centers, however. Until the 1880s, it was common practice for managers to pirate plays from other theatres, make a few minor alterations, and pay nothing to the original playwrights when the play was produced. The international traffic in pirated plays was even greater because until 1886, no treaties protected the rights of non-national authors. By 1900, although dramatists continued to have difficulties collecting payments due from managers, they had won the cultural and legal battle for full copyright protection. The prestige of print had trumped business-as-usual in the theatre.

Theatre, print, and the public

Several historians have examined how print culture helped to create, sustain, and legitimate a bourgeois "public sphere" in eighteenth-century Western Europe. As literate Europeans read more about current affairs and shared ideas for improving their societies, they developed a sense of themselves as a public, with interests separate from the governments that ruled them. The newspress was especially important in forming notions of public consciousness, but so was the theatre. In fact, by 1750, many of the same people (nearly all of them male) went to the theatre, read plays, and gathered in coffee houses and salons to discuss developments in science, the arts, and current events. As the newspress and the theatre influenced each other, both helped to shape a public sphere in their countries.

After 1750, these publics increasingly thought of themselves as national audiences, with the rights of theatrical spectators. Royal and aristocratic patronage had waned, especially in England and Germany, and the public had taken its place as the major benefactors of the theatre. But what kind of public would this be? Spectators could see that some audience members formed themselves into cabals to cheer or damn a specific play or actor. Some spectators even took to rioting – typically making noise, throwing things at the actors, and breaking up some furniture – when a new management policy displeased them. While most agreed with the maxim of Samuel Johnson (1709–1784) that "the drama's laws, the drama's patrons give," many worried that the kinds of "laws" made by passion-driven or unruly spectators needed to be modified or vetoed by a higher power. Neoclassicism had attempted to set such limits, but bourgeois spectators increasingly disregarded its authority.

Most of the literate bourgeoisie looked to the power of rational public opinion expressed in print to limit behavior in the theatre. Stung by the response of a small group of critics to his *The Barber of Seville* in 1775, Pierre-Augustin Beaumarchais (1732–1799) addressed a "Temperate Letter" to the reading public. "I recognize no other judge than you," wrote Beaumarchais, "not excepting Messieurs the spectators, who – judges only of first resort – often see their sentence overturned by your tribunal" (Peters 2000:249). Although Beaumarchais might distrust, he could not dismiss the theatrical public. Indeed, he relied on this public to understand and approve his critique of the class system of pre-Revolutionary France when *The Marriage of Figaro* was produced nine years later. But like many of his contemporaries Beaumarchais believed that the reading public, less easily seduced by a cabal and with more time for rational reflection, could gradually educate the theatrical public.

Press and playhouse could work together, thought Beaumarchais, to shape an enlightened public opinion that might change the nation.

For many of the literate bourgeoisie, public opinion was becoming synonymous with a national consensus. Consequently, the theatre, for them, had an important role to play in the future of their nations. Johann Lowen, for example, expressed the hope that his little theatre in Hamburg would help to unify Germany, a language area in Central Europe but not yet a nation-state. In the mid-eighteenth century, scholars wrote histories of the German, Italian, and English theatres that linked their past dramatic heritage to national greatness. Bourgeois playwrights and columnists also began to limit their conception of the nation to the theatrical and literary public. They even posed this public in opposition to the power of the crown and to state-run monopolies to protest the policies of state-subsidized theatres. Although this conception of a public domain separate from the state prepared the French bourgeoisie for revolution, the dreadful realities of the 1790s in France shook the faith of literate Europe in the possibility of rational progress through public opinion. For most of the nineteenth century, as we will see, the idea of a primitive "folk" rather than an enlightened public shaped discussions about the nation, the press, and the theatre.

In Chapter 6, "Theatre, Nation, and Empire, 1750–1900," we examine the many ways in which the theatre shaped nationalism and its extensions in imperialism from the end of the eighteenth century through the nineteenth and into the twentieth century. In the final case study of Part II, we look at the nationalistic riots that greeted initial performances of *The Playboy of the Western World* by John Millington Synge (1871–1909) in Dublin in 1907, when Ireland was still a part of the British empire.

BMc

Key references

Listed below are all the key references for this Introduction to Part II and references for Chapters 4, 5, and 6.

Andrews, R. (1993) *Scripts and Scenarios: The Performance of Commedia in Renaissance Italy*, Cambridge: Cambridge University Press.

Barish, A. (1981) *The Antitheatrical Prejudice*, Berkeley: University of California Press.

Booth, M. (1991) *Theatre in the Victorian Age*, Cambridge: Cambridge University. Press.

Bratton, J.S. (ed.) (1991) *Acts of Supremacy: The British Empire and the Stage*, Manchester: Manchester University Press.

Carlson, M. (1993) *Theories of the Theatre*, expanded edition, Ithaca and London: Cornell University Press.

Chartier, R. (1999) *Publishing Drama in Early Modern Europe*, London: British Library.

Cohen, W. (1985) *Drama of a Nation: Public Theatre in Renaissance England and Spain*, Ithaca: Cornell University Press.

Coleridge, S.T. (1974) "Progress of the Drama [1818]," in Bernard F. Dukore (ed.) *Dramatic Theory and Criticism*, New York: Holt, Rinehart and Winston.

Cross, G. (1976) *Next Week "East Lynne:" Domestic Drama in Performance, 1820–1874*, Lewisburg, P.A.: Bucknell University Press.

Dutton, R. (1991) *Mastering the Revels: The Regulation and Censorship of English Renaissance Drama*, Iowa City, I.A.: Iowa University Press.

Eagleton, T. (1990) *The Ideology of the Aesthetic*, Oxford: Basil Blackwell.

Ellis, F.H. (1991) *Sentimental Comedy: Theory and Practice*, Cambridge: Cambridge University Press.

Elsky, M. (1989) *Authorizing Words: Speech, Writing, and Print in the English Renaissance*, Ithaca: Cornell University Press.

Fischer, S.R. (2003) *A History of Reading*, London: Reaktion Books.

Fitzpatrick, T. (1995) *The Relationship of Oral and Literate Performance Processes in Commedia dell'Arte*, Lewiston: Edwin Mellen Press.

Frederickson, G.M. (2002) *Racism: A Short History*, Princeton: Princeton University Press.

Gainor, J.E. (ed.) (1995) *Imperialism and Theatre: Essays on World Theatre, Drama, and Performance*, London: Routledge.

Gurr, A. (1996) *Playgoing in Shakespeare's London*, 2nd edn, Cambridge: Cambridge University Press.

Hays, M. and Nikolopoulou, A. (eds) (1996) *Melodrama: The Cultural Emergence of a Genre*, New York: St. Martin's Press.

Hemmings, F.W.J. (1994) *Theatre and State in France, 1760–1905*, Cambridge: Cambridge University Press.

Hill, C. (1980) *The Century of Revolution, 1603–1714*, New York: Norton.

Hobsbawm, E.J. (1962) *The Age of Revolution, 1789–1848*, New York: New American Library.

Hobsbawm, E.J. (1975) *The Age of Capital, 1848–1875*, New York: New American Library.

Howarth, W.D. (ed.) (1977) *French Theatre in the Neoclassical Era, 1550–1789*, Cambridge: Cambridge University Press.

Hudson, N. (1994) *Writing and European Thought, 1600–1830*, Cambridge: Cambridge University Press.

Kaplan, A. and Pease, D.E. (eds) (1993) *Cultures of United States Imperialism*, Durham: Duke University Press.

Lamport, F.J. (1992) *German Classical Drama, 1750–1870: Theatre, Humanity, and Nation*, Cambridge: Cambridge University Press.

Leach, R. (1999) *A History of Russian Theatre*, Cambridge: Cambridge University Press.

Leiter, S. (2002) *Frozen Moments: Writings on Kabuki, 1966–2001*, Ithaca, N.Y.: Cornell University East Asia Program.

Lopez, J. (2003) *Theatrical Convention and Audience Response in Early Modern Drama*, Cambridge: Cambridge University Press.

McConachie, B.A. (1992) *Melodramatic Formations: American Theatre and Society, 1820–1870*, Iowa City, I.A.: University of Iowa Press.

McKendrick, M. (1989) *Theatre in Spain, 1490–1700*, Cambridge: Cambridge University Press.

Nicoll, A. (1966) *The Development of The Theatre*, 5th edn, New York: Harcourt, Brace, and World.

Ong, W.J. (1988) *Orality and Literacy: The Technologizing of the Word*, London and New York: Routledge.

Orgel, S. (1975) *The Illusion of Power: Political Theatre in the English Renaissance*, Berkeley: California University Press.

Peters, J.S. (2000) *Theatre of the Book, 1480–1880: Print, Text, and Performance in Europe*, Oxford: Oxford University Press.

Roach, J.R. (1985 [reprinted 1993]) *The Player's Passion: Studies in the Science of Acting*, Ann Arbor: University of Michigan Press.

Scales, R.W. (2002) "The battle of the stages: the conflict between the theatre and the institutions of government and religion in England, 1660–1890," unpublished dissertation, City University, London.

Senelick, L. (ed.) (1991) *National Theatres in Northern and Eastern* Europe, *1746–1900*, Cambridge: Cambridge University Press.

Thomson, P. (1992) *Shakespeare's Theatre*, 2nd edn, London: Routledge.

Trussler, S. (1994) *The Cambridge Illustrated History of British Theatre*, Cambridge: Cambridge University Press.

Wikander, M.H. (2002) *Fangs of Malice: Hypocrisy, Sincerity, and Acting*, Iowa City: University of Iowa Press.

Williams, S. (1994) *Richard Wagner and Festival Theatre*, Westport, C.T.: Greenwood Press.

Wilmeth, D.B. and Bigsby, C. (1998, 1999) *The Cambridge History of American Theatre*, Vols I and II, Cambridge: Cambridge University Press.

Woods, L. (1984) *Garrick Claims the Stage: Acting as Social Emblem in Eighteenth-Century England*, Westport, C.T.: Greenwood Press.

Ziter, E. (2003) *The Orient on the Victorian Stage*, Cambridge: Cambridge University Press.

CHAPTER 4

Theatre and the state, 1600–1900

Throughout the world, relationships between governments and theatres have never been conflict-free. This is primarily because both engage in political and ethical performances, broadly understood, and their overlapping authority in these spheres often creates conflicts among theatre artists and those whom the state supports and favors. In addition to providing many important services, all governments also claim political and ethical authority and attempt to influence the views and actions of their subjects or citizens through such performances as coronations and press conferences. Although most theatres throughout history have tried to be uncontroversial, nearly all of them have presented human relationships on stage that powerful others have interpreted as questioning or even undermining their authority. When this occurs, the powerful look to the state to uphold conventional morality and/or to protect their images and interests.

Not surprisingly, then, no major theatre in history has ever escaped some measure of state regulation. In the unequal contest between the government and the stage, the state has traditionally established the laws and guidelines within which

theatre artists have been allowed to operate. But governmental policies have varied widely among different societies and over time. The primary determining factor in state regulation has been the attitude of those in power toward the theatrical arts. Where the government understood the benefits that theatre could offer to those in power – praise of their morality and authority – the state usually tried to co-opt and control theatre artists through subsidies and regulations. Many theatres in Asia and Europe before 1800 gladly accepted some initial state control in return for economic assistance. Other governments, however, viewed theatrical art as immoral, unpatriotic, or both, and attempted to contain or even destroy it. During the American Revolution (1775–1783), for example, the Continental Congress outlawed theatrical performances for both of those reasons. After 1789, the powerful in Western Europe gradually separated theatre's economic from its ethical function. From an economic point of view, most bourgeoisie believed that the entrepreneurs of the theatre deserved a free market and eventually ended state-run monopolies. Nonetheless, because the stage remained an important ethical prop for the status quo, the bourgeoisie of Western Europe continued to support various forms of state censorship after 1900.

This chapter examines three contrasting examples of state–theatre relations in different societies. Beginning with Cardinal Richelieu, the rulers of France generally understood that theatre could help to centralize the French absolutist state and the government's policy toward the most important theatres in the nation reflected this point of view. In contrast, the warlords who ruled Japan from 1600 into the 1860s strove to contain the popular kabuki theatre as though it were a plague of immorality threatening to contaminate their elite culture. The diversity of state–theatre relations in England between 1600 and 1900 reflects a mix of both attitudes. In the mid-seventh century, when those opposing theatrical entertainment as immoral gained power, they banned the theatre altogether and later passed severe restrictions to curb its influence in the eighteenth century. In both centuries, however, other Englishmen in power promoted state subsidies and regulations intended to wed theatrical performances to the political purposes of the state. After 1800, both France and England gradually abolished monopolistic control of the theatre, but continued state censorship. The case studies following this introduction help to demonstrate the effects of state–theatre relations on specific theatrical events. Performances of *Tartuffe* in France, *Chûshingura* and other kabuki plays in Japan, and *Twelfth Night* in England reflected some of the dynamics of dominant political and ethical relations in those countries. While state–theatre relations differed in other countries and at other times, these three examples explore a wide range of historical problems in this fractious relationship.

Theatre and the state in France, 1630–1675

As we saw in the Part II Introduction, Cardinal Richelieu established the power of the French monarchy in cultural matters with the French Academy's settlement of the *Le Cid* dispute in 1638. We also noted Richelieu's building of a proscenium theatre in his new palace, which opened with Italianate scenery in 1641. These followed earlier strategies of the Cardinal or the King, Louis XIII, intended to tie theatrical life in Paris to the cultural authority and largesse of the crown. When the court began to patronize the acting troupe performing at the Théâtre du Marais in the 1630s, Richelieu arranged for a subsidy for that company. Soon the crown was subsidizing the other major troupe in Paris at the Hôtel de Bourgogne. Before his death in 1642, Richelieu even attempted to raise the social status of actors in France. Traditional prejudices blamed actors for immorality (due to frequent travel, their sleeping arrangements were sometimes unconventional) and insincerity (because they could play many roles convincingly, some people supposed that they lied). A 1641 decree from the crown, pushed by Richelieu, removed some legal restrictions from acting companies and forthrightly stated the King's desire that acting as a "profession" be accorded respectability. If the crown were to gain some prestige for its support of acting companies, it was necessary to grant actors higher social status.

As other troupes in Paris vied for royal support after 1643, the new king Louis XIV and his ministers took advantage of the monarchy's position in French culture, bequeathed them by Richelieu, and continued to pull strings. A *commedia dell'arte* company from Italy under the management of Tiberio Fiorillo (1608–1694) which enjoyed the support of several influential courtiers, gained a subsidy in the middle 1640s, which was renewed from 1653 onwards. When Molière (Jean-Baptiste Poquelin, 1622–1673) and his company returned to Paris to debut before Louis's court in 1658, their path may have been paved by a courtier and fan who had served their patron in Lyon, Daniel de Cosnac, and their debut was arranged by the king's younger brother, Phillipe. Their success with a farcical afterpiece won them permission from Louis XIV to share a theatre with the Italian *commedia* troupe. Although Molière's troupe failed with performances of tragedy, they gained the King's approval with a farcical Molière afterpiece, and the actor-playwright went on to sustain the King's support with a series of farces and comedies. It was against this background of royal favor that Molière proceeded with the writing of *Tartuffe*, a play attacking the hypocrisy of holy men in high places. As we will see in a case study following this chapter, Louis suppressed the play after the comedy's premiere at court in 1664, concerned about offending Catholic fundamentalists. Remarkably, for the next five years, Molière worked on revisions and petitions to the King to lift the ban. Molière's ability to evoke laughter at the expense of absolutist practices in his final version is the subject of the first case study in this chapter.

Meanwhile, Louis XIV was extending his support to, and imposing his royal imprimatur on other kinds of theatrical entertainments. Increasing interest in Torelli's chariot-and-pole wizardry led to the popularity of "machine plays," so-called because of their instant scenic transformations from one setting to another, all in full view of the audience and accompanied by orchestral music. The "comedy-ballet" also came back into favor; Molière wrote the libretto for several, and Louis himself often paraded as the star of these entertainments in his new ballroom at the palace of Versailles. Both the machine plays and the comedy-ballet were forerunners of opera. Opera's rising popularity was recognized by Louis when he awarded a monopoly for the production of opera to one company in 1669. The monopoly soon passed to the Italian-born court composer, Jean-Baptiste Lully (1632–1687), who founded the Royal Academy of Music, later renamed the Paris Opéra. In accord with the king's wishes, Lully worked to establish the grandeur of French opera, as opposed to Italian, and found success with Paris audiences as well as the court. By the early 1670s, the crown was giving financial assistance to five operatic and theatrical troupes in Paris.

From patronage to control in France, 1675–1789

After 1675, Louis XIV and his ministers used the state subsidies they had extended to several theatres to maintain their centralized control of theatrical life in Paris. Their first significant move was the formation of the Comédie Française in 1680. When Molière died in 1673, rivalry among the Paris acting troupes led to a period of flux, with several actors leaving one company to join another. In 1679, the crown forced an end to the conflicts by ordering the two major Parisian acting troupes to combine into one – the Comédie Française. As he had already done with musical drama and the opera, Louis granted a monopoly over spoken drama in French to the new company (an exception was soon made, however, when Fiorillo's *commedia dell'arte* troupe won the right to continue to use French in their performances). Louis XIV's 1679 decree continued the traditional organization of French acting companies, by which the actors shared in the profits of the troupe, but he fixed the numbers of shares so that no new members could be admitted to the Comédie Française until an old one retired or died. The edict also regulated how actors might be elected as sharing members and the authority the members possessed in selecting plays for production. Finally, the king took control of the internal affairs of the troupe; his decree established his First Gentleman of the Chamber as the arbiter of disputes within the company. Although members of the new Comédie Française enjoyed state support and might benefit from generous pensions on retirement, they had become bureaucrats of the monarchy.

Louis XIV had enjoyed attending the theatre as a young ruler, but he grew censorious toward the stage as he aged. His suspicions were increasingly reflected in the attitudes of his ministers toward the theatre. When courtiers learned that Fiorillo's *commedia* company might be planning to perform a play that satirized the king's second wife, Louis expelled the troupe from France in 1697. Before

1700, the throne rarely engaged in direct censorship; the need for theatres to seek royal subsidies, the watchful eye of the French Academy, and self-censorship, had made direct, formal regulation of the political content of scripts mostly unnecessary. Nonetheless, Louis XIV imposed censorship in 1701 and reinforced it with another edict in 1706; these mandated that all scripts be read and approved by a censor in the police department before a public performance in Paris would be allowed. Actor-managers were implicitly allowed to produce prohibited plays in the provinces, however, where local rules and poor enforcement offered few problems. But Louis had made Paris and his nearby court at Versailles the center of France; no troupe forced to perform in the provinces could return to Paris after such disgrace.

Although royal patronage had helped to create a thriving theatre in Paris from 1630 to the early 1670s, royal absolutism after 1675 was narrowing the scope of acceptable theatre and leaving the companies that survived insular and jealous of their monopolistic privileges. After the Italians left Paris, minor troupes performing on the Paris fairgrounds outside of Paris soon stepped in to fill the gap in popular entertainment left by the Italians. The Opéra profited from its monopoly by selling to one of the troupes the right to use singers, dancers, and musicians in musical productions. Other fairground companies performed dramatic scenes, but the Comédie Française stuck to its privileges. It sued the offending actor-managers, which led them to evade the Comédie's monopoly on spoken dramatic dialog by introducing such ruses as actors performing monologues. The Comédie Française took revenge in 1706. A court ruling reinforced the Comédie's monopoly, and shortly afterwards the police tore down several booth theatres at the fairground. These conflicts among companies, of course, were a direct result of the structures that Louis XIV had put in place to extend his absolutist control of French theatre. In the early 1670s, five companies had competed for Parisian audiences and the favor of the court. By 1700 only two remained, the Comédie Française and the Opéra.

The structures enforcing state control of the stage changed little until the French Revolution (1789–99). Following the death of Louis XIV, the Italians returned in 1716 and were given a theatre, a subsidy, and the right to perform *commedia dell'arte*, reinforcing the monarchy's policy of granting a monopoly over certain genres of theatre to specific companies. This policy continued to create conflict with the fairground troupes, which generally managed to bounce back from legal restrictions with ever more ingenious means of attracting audiences. Their ongoing popularity, despite their marginal legal status, underlined the lack of variety in the state theatres (Figure 4.1). Censorship continued as well. The censors, empowered by the increasing availability of printed dramas, prohibited any play that they judged might undermine the authority of the state, which included the Catholic Church and the French aristocracy. Voltaire's *Mahomet* was banned when it seemed to grant some wisdom to Islam and suggested that Catholicism might not have exclusive access to religious truth. Pierre-Augustin Caron Beaumarchais (1732–1799) fought the censors for two years before they allowed the Comédie Française to produce his *The Marriage of Figaro* in 1784. In 1791, in the wake of the French Revolution, the new National Assembly abolished all theatrical monopolies.

Samurai warriors versus kabuki actors, 1600–1670

Civil wars wracked Japanese society from 1467 until 1590, when one group of samurai (professional soldiers) emerged victorious. In 1603, the Japanese Emperor conferred the title of *shogun* (supreme military ruler) on Tokugawa Ieyasu, thus establishing the Tokugawa shogunate, which kept peace in Japan until 1868. Desiring to end the power of Christian missionaries, the Tokugawa shoguns closed Japan to

Figure 4.1 Scene from a Parisian fair theatre play, *The Quarrel of the Theatres*, which satirized two state-supported theatres for stealing from the fair theatres: the Comédie Française (represented by the player on the right) and the Comédie Italienne (represented by the player on the left), which performed the *commedia dell'arte* repertoire and a mix of other works. From LeSage and D'Orneval, *Le Théâtre de la Foire* (1723). © Bibliothèque Nationale de France.

western influences and turned to China for much of their official culture. The samurai adopted neo-Confucian values and Chinese rituals, such as the tea ceremony, and formalized their warrior tradition in ceremonies of decorous simplicity and elegant restraint. At the same time, they attempted to isolate themselves from the merchants in the towns, whose culture they despised.

With the return of peace, the towns prospered and a vigorous new culture arose – nearly the opposite of samurai elegance and control. Vulgar, irreverent, and often lewd, the culture of the merchants burst forth around 1600 in poetry, music, and dance. At the center of their new entertainments were the

first kabuki performers, female prostitutes who danced and enacted satirical playlets and bawdy sideshows. At least as early as 1612, male prostitutes also formed kabuki troupes and competed with the women. By the 1620s, kabuki managers had established theatres linked to brothels in all of the major cities of Japan. In their sensuous dances and skits, kabuki performers often reversed gender roles and mocked samurai culture.

The popular success of kabuki annoyed the samurai rulers, but also confirmed what they took to be their innate superiority to the rowdy culture of the cities. Although the regime could have stamped out kabuki when it first emerged, Ieyasu and his warriors chose to allow it to continue within limits, fearing that a total ban would lead to worse troubles. In a revealing document from Ieyasu's rule, one samurai official stated: "Courtesans, dancers, catamites, streetwalkers, and the like always come to the cities and prospering places of the country. Although the conduct of many is corrupted by them, if they are rigorously suppressed, serious crimes will occur daily" (Shively 2002:41). This point of view, which underlay the Tokugawa shogunate's policy toward kabuki theatre for 250 years, rested on class disdain for merchants and city culture. The combination of traders and workers in wealthy towns, the samurai believed, would always breed criminality. Better for such potential criminals to be distracted and enervated by theatrical entertainment, they reasoned, than for these people to turn to "serious crimes."

At the same time, the samurai rulers worried that kabuki, if completely unregulated, would corrupt the soldiers and young men of their own class. Complaints against the kabuki performers in the 1600–1670 period centered on drunken fights among soldiers and tales of young samurai losing their fortunes and ruining their reputations by chasing after a kabuki prostitute. In 1629, the government banned females from performing in kabuki. Despite the ban, which was soon replicated in other cities across Japan, similar laws were reissued in the 1630s and 1640s, indicating that it took several years for the shogunate to eliminate this popular form of kabuki. After 1652, young male prostitutes were also prohibited from performing kabuki, again in an effort to prevent class mingling. Henceforth only older males who shaved the forelocks of their hair were allowed to perform in the plays. Apparently this change rendered the male actors less sexually appealing to other men in the audience; young samurai could not be so easily enticed – or so the government believed – by men in drag without their forelocks. This led officials to levy more rules and inspections and the actors to using scalp coverings

and wigs in an ongoing contest of regulation and innovation between the Tokugawa shogunate and the kabuki managers.

Regulating kabuki, 1670–1868

Although this conflict between the samurai and the managers continued until the end of the regime in 1868, by 1670, kabuki troupes had won enough grudging legitimacy from the regime to allow them to elaborate an art form out of this sexually enticing entertainment. After 1652, audiences in Kyoto, Osaka, and Edo began to find more enjoyment in the extended performances by the mature male actors, who now played all the roles on the kabuki stage (Figure 4.2). *Onnagata*, men who specialized in female roles, gained particular popularity among the merchant spectators. As a few star actors in the major cities sought better material, kabuki playwrights emerged to provide it. The early playwrights generally worked in teams under the direction of an actor-manager, but a few, such as Chikamatsu Monzaemon (1653–1724), gained recognition for their singular excellence. Kabuki plays, coming into print, were eagerly read by many in the merchant class, gradually boosting the reputation of playwrights within the cities, as happened in Western Europe, even though the samurai elite continued to look down on playwriting and the theatre.

In addition to limiting the number of kabuki troupes allowed to perform, the shogunate developed three major strategies to minimize kabuki's contamination of their culture. These policies, which after 1670 shifted regulation from the theatrical form of kabuki to its content and practice, continued in force until the end of the regime in 1868. First, specific laws separated theatre people from normal urban life. Actors could only live in certain districts, and their movement to other parts of town – to entertain at private parties, for example – was strictly regulated. Second, sumptuary regulations directing how different classes could dress mandated that kabuki actors could not wear clothes on stage that elevated

Figure 4.2 Kabuki actor, Kunisada Utagawa (1786–1865), in a woodcut (original in color) by a pupil of Toyokuni.
© AKG-images, London.

their status. As in other feudal societies, dress marked class and the shogunate did not allow kabuki actors to dress in costumes or carry props that rivaled the elegant attire of the samurai. Third, censorship prohibited performances that appeared to undermine the political and social hegemony of the samurai. Spectators enjoyed historical plays about samurai victories in the 1500s, for example, but the actors could not present historical characters or incidents that might be understood as criticizing the present regime. Many playwrights, however, altered historical names and cities to get around this restriction and often succeeded in evading censorship. In general, officials cracked down on the kabuki troupes when the shogunate wanted a display of righteous indignation and eased up when political pressure relaxed.

Occasional scandals and theatre closings, however, reminded the kabuki managers how precarious their situation might suddenly become. In 1714, the shogun discovered that one of the ladies of his castle in Edo was having an affair with the star actor, Ikushima Shingôrô (1671–1743). In addition to banishing the lovers and the others implicated in the crime from his capital, the shogun closed Ikushima's theatre, one of the most popular in Edo, confiscated its assets, and demolished the building. For the rest of the Tokugawa period, Edo had only three major theatres instead of the four that had flourished before the scandal.

As in the France of Louis XIV, the Tokugawa samurai controlled the theatre through regulations, censorship, and licensing restrictions. While in France, the carrot-and-stick policy provided subsidies and theatre buildings and even attempted to raise the status of actors, in Japan, the shogunate segregated the theatre from other urban activities and kept the official status of actors near that of thieves and prostitutes. The two political absolutisms differed in their aims. The French crown wanted a theatre that would legitimize its interests and values. The Japanese shogunate sought to protect itself and its values from theatrical corruption. Ironically, many of the results were similar. Most prominent among these similarities, perhaps, was both governments' impact on dramatic form and theatrical convention. Without the restrictions of monarchy and shogunate, neither neoclassic theatre nor kabuki would have developed as they did. Both genres, in fact, might not have existed at all.

Theatre and the state in England, 1600–1660

Within this 60-year period, English state policy toward the stage swung wildly from legal protection to attempted elimination to modified state control. By 1600, the English crown had accorded legitimacy to theatre companies in London. Despite opposition from the Common Council of the City of London, Elizabeth I (1553–1603) granted royal patents to some troupes and provided legal protection to actors, who previously had been subject to arrest if they were unconnected to a royal or aristocratic household. New laws also exempted English actors from sumptuary regulations; unlike kabuki players, they could wear the garments of the aristocracy on stage. Intent on stamping out the last vestiges of the Catholic cycle plays to reinforce Anglican authority throughout England, Elizabeth may have seen the professional theatre as a substitute for these popular community productions. The crown's granting of prestige and protection to professional troupes led to a theatrical building boom in the late 1570s. By 1580, four outdoor theatres ringed the city of London; six more playhouses, indoor as well as outdoor, would be built by 1600.

But royal preferment came with a price. In the 1580s and 1590s, the crown had given the authority to license all plays and playhouses in the London area to the Master of the Revels, the office traditionally responsible for court entertainments. After 1603, with the ascension of James I to the throne, the Master of the Revels was also empowered to license the publication of plays, and, later, all acting companies. These laws, in addition to leading to occasional heavy fees and bribery, also entailed some censorship. Unlike French dramatists in the 1700s, however, English playwrights simply had to avoid inflammatory political and religious issues; they were not expected to overtly reinforce the absolutist values of the regime to the extent that the French were. Within this mix of royal preferment, light regulation, and tight competition, William Shakespeare emerged as the premiere playwright of the Chamberlain's Men. Our third case study in this chapter focuses on the performance of Shakespeare's *Twelfth Night* around 1600.

This flourishing theatrical life came to an end in 1642, when the English Parliament closed all London theatres. Intended initially as a temporary safeguard against civil strife, the 1642 act was later broadened and extended by the Puritans. Led by Oliver Cromwell (1599–1658), opponents of the monarchy incited a Civil War, beheaded King Charles I, and declared a Commonwealth that lasted until 1660. The Puritans banned professional theatre for three main reasons. First, they associated the stage with the expensive and lavish masques that Charles I had enjoyed at court; to oppose the theatre was to oppose royal absolutism in the eyes of many Puritans. Second, they voiced religious objections, partly linked to the rise of print culture. Believing that the revealed Word of God as printed in the Bible was revealed truth, the Puritans feared that base mimicry and spectacle would corrupt people's reason, teach them to delight in illusion and debauchery, and turn them away from the biblical path to salvation. Further, the Bible specifically forbade transvestism, a regular part of the pre-1642 theatre. Boy actors played all of the female roles and many plot and character devices of the stage involved varieties of gender bending. Finally, the Puritans believed that the theatre incited immoral and illegal behavior. Ordinary people, already inherently depraved (according to the Puritans), would be tempted to robbery, sodomy, and even murder if they watched or even heard such behavior discussed on the stage. Puritan anti-theatrical prejudice in England went far beyond the animosity that the Japanese samurai felt for kabuki. In fact, the Tokugawa shogunate had nothing against theatrical performance as such and continued to enjoy productions of noh plays during their rule.

Patents, censorship, and social order in England, 1660–1790

Although some productions occurred during the Commonwealth period, regular performances by professional companies did not return until 1660, with the Restoration of Charles II to the throne. While living in exile at the court of the French monarch, Charles had come to appreciate the control that Louis XIV was exercising over French theatre, opera, and ballet. Charles II did not want to pay the direct theatre subsidies that allowed the French throne to enjoy entertainments that reflected its absolutist goals, but he did believe that he needed the stage to legitimate his fragile hold on power. Before his return to the throne he awarded a royal patent for producing theatre to Thomas Killigrew (1612–1683), a minor playwright who had followed the King into exile. Charles II soon compromised Killigrew's monopoly by awarding a second patent to William Davenant (1606–1668), also a playwright and theatrical entrepreneur, who would soon prove better able than Killigrew to fulfill the King's theatrical ambitions. By December of 1660, Killigrew and Davenant were the only men allowed to produce plays in London, an unprecedented

theatrical monopoly in England (though not, of course, in France). Charles II also decreed that English companies should now employ women as professional actors, which he would have seen on the French stage. Called the "merry monarch" for his sexual affairs, Charles extended his royal prerogatives to taking actresses of his choice as new bedmates.

For the next twenty years, the desires and values of Charles and his aristocrats dominated the English stage. Charles had wanted a theatre in which he could entertain foreign dignitaries. Davenant's plans for a new playhouse in Dorset Garden so impressed him that he spent one thousand pounds of the royal treasury to have it completed. Much more lavish than the rival Drury Lane theatre, which housed Killigrew's company, Dorset Garden was also equipped with the necessary backstage facilities to stage continental opera. For ten years after its opening in 1671, the king used Dorset Garden as an extension of his royal power, even though it remained primarily a commercial operation. Restoration tragedies, such as John Dryden's (1631–1700) *Indian Queen* (1664) and his two part *The Conquest of Granada* (1669–1670) followed neoclassical patterns and focused on the royal heroes and heroines supposedly of great soul, caught in endlessly involved conflicts between love and duty to the state. Restoration comedies, such as Dryden's *Marriage à la Mode* (1672) and William Wycherley's (1640–1715) *The Country Wife* (1675) played to a coterie audience of fashionable London, and featured witty language and titillating sexual intrigue among the beautiful and privileged. The new female actors were an instant hit (and the boy-actor convention died out). Several women achieved artistic stature, including Nell Gwynn (1650–1687), who became Charles's mistress, and Ann Bracegirdle (1663–1748), both of whom excelled in comedy, and tragedian Elizabeth Barry (1658–1713). A new law (passed as a sop to the Puritans) made it illegal to produce plays that offended "piety and good manners," but had no real effect. By 1680, it seemed to some that the

English theatre was going the way of its French absolutist cousin.

The political crisis of the 1680s, however, cut short the drift toward absolutism in England. This led in 1688 to increased power for Parliament and less overt support and control by the crown over the theatre. As in France, fairground theatres were attracting popular audiences in England and draining spectators from the aristocratic playhouses. The patent troupes, however, lacked the legal power of the Comédie Française; the English crown did not attempt to enforce their apparent monopolies on theatrical production. After 1688, the theatres at the Hounslow, Southwark, and Bartholomew fairs continued to compete with the patent playhouses, sometimes mounting productions that challenged royal and aristocratic rule. When in 1695 the legal validity of the patents expired, the English throne, which no longer claimed absolute political authority, did not renew them.

By 1730, the English merchant class was replacing the aristocracy as the dominant group in both the government and at London playhouses. No more approving of the fairground theatres than the monarchy had been, the merchants also tried to shut them down, but without success. Theatrical licensing was allowed to slide as well, with the consequence that four unlicensed theatres were operating in London in 1730. By the middle of the decade, there was regular traffic between the fairs and the London theatres. London actors performed frequently at the fairs, and theatre managers borrowed rope dancers and jugglers for entre-act entertainments and incorporated into their plays the political jibes that were common at the fairs. Most Londoners were enjoying the political openness of the playhouses, including the political satires.

Prime Minister Robert Walpole (1676–1745), however, was not among them. Following a theatrical attack on his political manipulations, Walpole rushed the Licensing Act of 1737 through Parliament. The act strengthened the censorship exercised by the Lord Chamberlain (to whom the Master of the Revels reported) by requiring companies to submit all scripts for approval before performing them. It also limited to two the theatres authorized to perform plays – Drury Lane and Covent Garden in London. Ever since John Gay (1685–1732) had attacked him in *The Beggar's Opera* nine years before, Walpole had been the butt of much theatrical satire, and the Prime Minister hated being laughed at. Requiring prior approval for all plays put an end to these attacks on him, and it also helped Walpole with the royal family, whose troubles had led to some theatrical ripostes as well. The 1737 act quickly transformed London playhouses from arenas of debate and political dissension into models of decorum and false consensus. Not coincidentally, the act also enriched the office of the Lord Chamberlain because the two licensed theatres had to pay handsomely for the "privilege" of holding a monopoly on the production of regular drama. Walpole had succeeded in pushing the bill through primarily because others in the governing classes also preferred censorship to derisive laughter.

Despite its short-term success, the 1737 act proved unwieldy over time. Designed to protect Walpole and the monarchy, the act made no provisions for theatre outside of London, and troupes and towns in the rest of the country ignored its strictures. Its numerous loopholes also allowed fairground managers and other theatre entrepreneurs to produce plays for lower-class patrons that encouraged a range of antisocial behavior. This led the governing classes to pass the Disorderly Houses Act of 1751, a new strategy in social control that put the onus for restraining the masses on those who owned and operated theatres. After 1751, all places for entertainment of any kind within a twenty-mile radius of London had to display a license that certified that the managers took responsibility for the good conduct of their patrons. The local constabulary might revoke the license if order were not maintained. Intended to cut down on the rioting that sometimes accompanied lower-class theatre, the 1751 act effectively acknowledged that the Licensing Act of 1737 could not restrict all forms of theatre in the London area. It also moved theatrical regulation toward the Japanese model. Like the samurai, the English governing classes had come to recognize that lower-class "immorality," from their point of view, was inevitable. The 1751 law admitted that it would be more effective to make managers responsible for the behavior of popular audiences than to try to dictate the form and content of their entertainments.

Theatre and the state in England and France, 1790–1900

When the French National Assembly ended all theatrical monopolies in 1791, it marked the end of one era and the beginning of another. The bourgeoisie who triumphed in the first phase of the French Revolution believed in the classic liberal principle of free markets without governmental interference. They abolished most restraints of trade upheld by the old regime, including theatre monopolies. The 1791 act also recognized a difficult truth: monopolies had not worked to restrict the theatres to approved genres and to conservative social-political values. In France, several fairground troupes had grown so popular that they established permanent theatres and operated year-round. Prohibited from performing regular dramas and operas, they developed pantomimes with minimal dialog set to music and comic operas involving new (sometimes satirical) lyrics set to popular tunes.

Similar genres had arisen in England to get around the Licensing Act of 1737. English pantomime, which had emerged from the *commedia dell'arte*, flourished on gags, spectacle, and subversive humor (see the case study in Chapter 7 for a brief history of English pantomime). Burletta, a satirical operatic sketch similar to French comic opera, spread quickly among several theatres after 1740. Following the French Revolution, gothic plays and melodramas gained popularity in London and several new

theatres arose to fill the demand for them. By 1820, the two-theatre monopoly provision of the 1737 act was in tatters.

At the same time, the social prestige of theatre among the governing classes had never been higher in England. Since the mid-eighteenth century and the popularity of Garrick, newspapers, memoirs, illustrations, and numerous other print media had kept a theatre-hungry public attuned to the latest stars, hits, and scandals. The English bourgeoisie recognized the theatre not only as a site of glamor and celebrity, but also as a business where star performers and dramatic authors could make a profitable living. Although many members of Parliament supported a bill to abolish the monopoly held by the two patent theatres in the 1830s, a similar bill did not pass until 1843. The Theatre Regulation Act of 1843, like the 1791 act of the French National Assembly, allowed any licensed company to produce theatre of any kind. It kept censorship alive, however, by leaving unchanged the authority of the Lord Chamberlain who could refuse to license public performances of plays that violated political and moral norms.

In France, the 1791 act had eliminated censorship as well as monopolies, but both were soon restored. Fearing subversion, the revolutionary government during the Reign of Terror re-instituted censorship. Napoleon returned France to monopolistic theatre soon after. By 1807, the French Empire had granted state support and genre monopolies to four theatres: The Comédie Française (for regular tragedy and comedy), the Opéra (for grand opera), the Odéon (for lesser drama) and the Opéra-Comique (for light opera and comic ballet). These restrictions remained in force until 1831, when a new bourgeois government loosened some of the regulations. As in England, however, the unsupported theatres continued to provide most theatrical innovation. The tide of nineteenth-century liberalism gradually turned against monopolistic control in the theatre in France, too. An 1864 French law removed all remaining mandates linking specific genres to certain theatres, although it did allow for continuing state support of the four Parisian theatres noted above.

France also continued state censorship through the end of the century. Recognizing that censoring plays had led to several flourishing *avant-garde* movements that opposed its values, however, the French bourgeoisie relented and ended censorship in 1905. In England, state censorship through the Lord Chamberlain's office continued until 1968. Long after the governing classes of France and England had abandoned attempts at direct control of the theatre, both had continued to restrain the range of political and ethical values that productions might embody and profess.

BMc

Key references

For further references for this chapter, see the Key references at the end of the Introduction to Part II.

Shively, D.H. (2002) "Bakufu versus Kabuki," in S. Leiter (ed.) *A Kabuki Reader: History and Performance*, Armonk, N.Y.: M.E. Sharpe.

CASE STUDY: Molière and carnival laughter

Carnival laughter . . . builds its own world versus the official world, its own church versus the official church, its own state versus the official state.

Mikhail M. Bakhtin

This case study uses the concept of carnival folk humor proposed by Russian critic, Mikhail M. Bahktin (1895–1975), to reveal a deep connection between the comic Molière and the Molière whose plays were sometimes very controversial, especially his *Tartuffe* (1664–1669), which is of special interest here. It will benefit the reader to read one of Molière's short plays, such as *The Precious Damsels* (1659) or *Love's the Best Doctor* (1665), as well as one of his other five-act verse comedies, such as *The School for Wives* (1659), *The Miser* (1668), or *The Imaginary Invalid* (1673). (Molière [1622–1673] was the stage name of Jean Baptiste Poquelin.)

Molière's full-length verse comedies are regarded as the cornerstone of French drama. They have been staples in the repertoire of the Comédie Française, France's national theatre, for over three centuries and are revived often in the classically-oriented theatres of Great Britain, the United States, and Canada. Molière served Louis XIV as playwright, actor, and courtier for fifteen years, from his court debut in 1658 to his death in 1673. During those years, his theatre company enjoyed many successes in the company's public theatres in the Salle de Petit Bourbon, attached to the Louvre palace, and, later, in the nearby Palais Royal (Figure II.5). Molière also devised, on the King's command, complimentary court pageants. Molière, like his friend, the poet and fabulist La Fontaine, was a good "swimmer in the seas of patronage" (Scott 2000:189), although Molière's relations with the Sun King seem to have cooled over the years.

But Molière was very unlike the court literati in important ways. He was an actor, after all, who, while excelling in the leading roles of his own comedies, suffered the social stigma attached to the profession. Some of his satires on the fashionable and foolish made him powerful enemies. Most importantly for this study, his plays and his performances were strongly influenced by the popular comic theatre traditions of 1) French farce, which had roots in the medieval theatre; 2) the *commedia dell'arte*, which had plots and character types similar to French farce; and 3) the kind of street medicine show that Molière put on stage in his *Love's the Best Doctor* (1665), in which hawkers sold potions said to cure anything (Gerry McCarthy's *The Theatres of Molière* provides a good introduction to them). Molière knew them well even before Louis XIV assigned his company to share a royal theatre with an Italian company that specialized in *commedia dell'arte* pieces and the old French farces. Bakhtin finds what he calls the "carnivalesque" spirit in all of these traditions (Figure 4.3). This case study suggests that the carnivalesque spirit is at work in Molière's plays and was doing profound cultural work that, in the case of *Tartuffe* especially, an absolutist church had to suppress. We know that the Parisian literati characterized his plays as mere "bagatelles" – trifles, or, short pieces of light verse, but the carnivalesque in them goes deeper.

Figure 4.3 In this farce at a country carnival (staged in the centre of the painting), a husband is cuckolded by a monk. The painting (original in colour) is "Village Festival in Honor of St. Hubert and St. Anthony," by Pieter Brueghel, the younger, (1564?–1637), © Fitzwilliam Museum, Cambridge University.

INTERPRETIVE APPROACH: Mikhail M. Bakhtin's concept of the carnivalesque

Mikhail M. Bakhtin's concept of carnival folk humor was developed in his analysis of the evolution of the novel, but it is useful to theatre studies. Writing in the former Soviet Union between 1919 and the early 1970s and barely escaping Stalin's infamous purges of the 1930s, Bakhtin was little known in the West until the publication in English of his *Rabelais and His World* (1968), his rich study of *Gargantua* and *Pantagruel* by François Rabelais (c.1490–1553). His work has been internationally recognized since as contributing to the century's investigations into the production of meaning in language. In the 1920s Bakhtin was criticizing formalist, psychological, and early structuralist approaches to language and literature for closing off considerations of the social energies within them. His idea of language as a naturally dynamic, even subversive force runs counter to more pessimistic western theories of language as a construct of dominant ideologies, perpetually imprisoning our consciousness.

In his own Marxist account of language as based in material reality – in speech as a social event, he stressed that meaning occurs at that borderline where individual consciousness and the daily social world meet creatively, in a continuously reciprocal, dialogic process. In his subsequent works on the novel, Bakhtin saw this form as a vital, liberating genre because it includes popular languages from everyday reality, "unofficial" languages as opposed to "epic" literature's singular language. He saw epic literature as the "official voice" of dominant value systems, characterized by the representation of, and reverence for an absolute past, eternalized and closed, and by finalized characters. The novel, by contrast, engages the present, and its multiple voices insure that its structure is always open-ended, even ambivalent. Meaning is not over determined. In some ways, Bakhtin's ideas also anticipate theories of reception (for reception theory, see the Chapter 3 case study on kutiyattam).

Bakhtin sees the "culture of folk carnival humor" (Bakhtin 1984:3–5) as an elemental force, nurtured by a thousand-year tradition of folk humor, from satyr plays to medieval fools, liberating language and literature from the "official" ecclesiastical and feudal cultures and surging into the renaissance. For Bakhtin, the carnivalesque spirit found its expression in the clowns, fools, farces, and *commedia dell'arte* seen in the medieval and early modern marketplaces. He located it in the comic hawking of medicine show barkers, the cries of Parisian street merchants, the roaring curses and obscenities of the market and workplace, and in written parodies. In these, he argued, language had a material base – concrete and sensuous – close to the earth, to daily labor, to bodily functions. The culture of folk humor found opportunities for expression in popular festivals such as those of Mardi Gras, city carnivals of feasting and drinking, or the medieval feast of fools, in which Catholic church rituals were travestied – festivals at first authorized by the Church and then banned, but

▷

▷

which continued outside of it. Such festivals often came with agricultural seasons – harvests or winemaking – and were linked with renewal, the future, and hopes of "a more just social and economic order, of a new truth" (ibid.:81).

Carnivalesque humor reveled in life's fecundity, in sexuality and all the irrepressible life forces of the material body; its humor was full of images of copulating, defecating, dying, and birthing, always expressive of life's regenerative processes. Images of excessive eating and drinking were common (the clowns of early German farces, Hanswurst and Pickelherring, are named after folk foods). Images of the body, from nose to phallus, and lower bodily functions were writ large and grotesquely in carnival folk humor; such representations were not about the individual body/ego but about the regenerative body of the people.

Given this celebration of regenerative forces, carnival folk humor in effect laid open the short-lived nature of power; it was full of symbols of "the gay relativity of prevailing truths and authorities" (ibid.:11). It was naturally hostile to "all that was immortalized and completed" (ibid.:10,12). In contrast with official feasts that reinforced stability, hierarchy, and unchanging norms, values, and prohibitions, the festivals where carnival humor prevailed "celebrated temporary liberation from prevailing truth and established order; they marked the suspension or inversion of hierarchical rank, privileges, norms, and prohibitions." All were equal during carnival festivities. Carnival presented "a world inside out," or a bottoms-up world, in its "parodies and travesties, humiliations, profanations, comic crownings and uncrownings" (ibid.:11,411). Carnival humor, with its obscenities and topsy-turvey world erupts as a counterpoint to the oppressive, rigid controls of the ruling class. Applying Bahktin to Shakespeare, we may say that carnivalesque humor is manifest in such characters as Falstaff, Mistress Quickly, Sir Toby Belch, the Porter in *Macbeth*, and the Fool in *King Lear*. For Bakhtin, the works of Rabelais, Shakespeare, and Cervantes are all enriched by the resulting "dialogic interaction" in them between official and unofficial language and between popular and humanist consciousness. Parody – the comic imitation of another's socially typical speech, behavior, thinking, or deepest principles – was an important strategy for Bakhtin. Carnival parody uncrowned the old order and simultaneously made a place for the new, which it also upended. It was not terminally negative like modern satire, in which the satirist places himself above the object of his mockery. Like other forms of carnivalesque humor, parody was an expression of "the wholeness of the world's comic aspect; he who is laughing also belongs to it" (ibid.:12). Carnival laughter was festive laughter; it mocked in order to revive. All in all, carnival humor offered the possibility for social change, "a new outlook on the world, [a means] to realize the relative nature of all that exists and to enter a completely new order of things." "Carnival is the people's second life," Bakhtin writes (ibid.:34,8).

Bahktin's idea of the carnivalesque opens not only to the study of plays but to a wide spectrum of performative activities, from banqueting to pageantry to mock crownings in

▷

▷ which the orcinary order of life is overturned (see Michael Bristol's *Carnival and Theatre* [1985] which applies Bakhtin's theory to early modern English theatre). Bakhtin did not think the popular-festive spirit was compatible with the footlights – polite proscenium theatre – high art, text-contained, domesticated. He makes only a passing allusion to Molière, seeing the age of Louis XIV in general as one of "abstract and rationalist utopianism." The popular-festive comic traditions were no longer appreciated or even understood amid the dominant mode of neoclassicism, which served to reinforce absolutism. However, this case study argues that there are strains of those traditions in Molière which come alive as we view them in the light of Bakhtin's concept of the carnivalesque. His ideas also open to considerations of the actor's performances not merely as an ornamentation of a text, but as an embodiment of a whole force-field of social energies. This essay's application of Bakhtin's theory draws especially on *Rabelais and His World* (1984), and the essays published under the title, *The Dialogic Imagination: Four Essays* (1981).

KEY QUESTIONS

1   Where do we see in a given play or performance a suspension or inversion of hierarchical rank, privileges, norms, and prohibitions, or comic crownings or uncrownings, a topsy-turvy world? Are there any implicit critiques of power in the humor?

2   Where do we find comic images of the body, of excessive eating or drinking, or of copulation, defecation, or other bodily functions?

3   Where do we do find dialogic interaction between "official" and "unofficial" language?

4   What multiple meanings are available? Where are the ambivalences?

Elements of carnival humor are arguably present throughout Molière's work, early, middle, and late. While Molière scholarship has recently benefited from theatre studies, it is still often occupied with showing how his five-act verse comedies meet the literary high-genre requirements of "comedies of character" or "comedies of manners," or demonstrating an evolving literary sophistication in his work. Surely as important is the fact that Molière never abandoned the kind of disruptive comic elements that are in the spirit of the carnivalesque.

As Gerry McCarthy has noted (even without reference to the carnivalesque), "We see a resurrection of the cruder structures of the farce at moments when a tidy chronology would show Molière's genius to be at the height of its powers" (McCarthy 2002:209).

Molière's early one-act farce, *The Precious Damsels* (*Les Précieuses ridicules*, 1659) has many attributes of the carnivalesque. It is a broad parody of the affectations of the salons of fashionable court women (*précieuses*) who were setting the protocols for aristocratic manners, courtship, language, and literature.

Two affected young women turn away two potential suitors for lacking faddish manners and language. The young men then contrive a hoax. They send their valets, Mascarille and Jodelet, to visit the young women in the guise of fashionable courtiers, and the foolish women take them to be genuine. This is not yet in the scale of the carnivalesque. But enter Molière, the actor. Molière played Mascarille, who comes in disguise as a marquis. A surviving account tells us that Molière's costume was a hyperbolic parody of a courtier's apparel. His powdered wig was so large that it swept the area around him every time he made a bow; on his head he wore a tiny hat. His lace collar was huge and so were his breeches, the pockets of which sprouted colored tassels. He wore six-inch heels on his beribboned shoes and was carried onstage in a sedan chair by porters, whom he tried to avoid paying (Dock 1992:53; Molière 1971:I, 1008). The scale of exaggeration here is beyond satire; it has the overflow of the carnivalesque about it. It is a festive undoing, a parodic uncrowning of established order writ large on the body. Bakhtin's theory here allows us to value performance as something more than an accessory to a literary text. Molière's Mascarille is a larger-than-life comic icon who bursts the seams of both salon decorum and the neoclassical rules for plays that required rationalized representation (verisimilitude). While his marquis represents an original departure from the stock characters of the *commedia dell'arte*, he functions in the same iconic way: the bold extravagance of the figure testifies to a force of elemental comic energy that explodes the world of over-rationalized drama. Without this kind of elemental comic force, without the precedents of the *commedia dell'arte* and old French farces, it is hard to imagine this performance. Equally, without such precedents, it is doubtful that Harpagon in *The Miser* would break through the proscenium plane as he does in Act IV when he accuses the audience itself of stealing his missing money.

In the original performance of *The Precious Damsels*, a more traditional comic icon was also on stage with Molière. Jodelet (Julian Bedeau), Paris's most famous actor of old French farce and Italian comedy, played the other valet who impersonated an old viscount. Known as a good-natured clown, Jodelet always wore clown-white face make-up (probably a vestige of old farce's flour-faced millers). Mascarille tells the young women, "Don't be surprised at the Viscount's looks. He just got out of bed from an illness that left him so pale" (Molière 1957:23). Jodelet had recently left a rival theatre company, and Molière had jumped at the chance to hire him. Jodelet would have brought with him plays written for him by Paul Scarron, whose parodies Bakhtin cites often, and who influenced Molière. The two comedians go through some ribald jokes involving the lower anatomy under the guise of talking about old war wounds and then call in musicians for a dance, typical *commedia dell'arte* business. Their masters enter to put an end to the deception and the play, beating and stripping their valets of their clothes. No one gets to lord it long in carnival humor. Bakhtin speaks of thrashings and clothes-changing as part of the cycle of crownings and uncrownings in carnival humor in which the reign of the clown-made-king is ended by thrashing and stripping him of his robes (Bakhtin 1984:197).

Such analysis could be extended through most of Molière's comedies, but a sampling must suffice here. Two obvious instances of the parodying of "official" language occur in *The Would-be Gentleman* and *The Imaginary Invalid*. In the first, a servant dupes Monsieur Jourdain into believing that a long, burlesque ceremony, conducted in an amalgam of pseudo-Latin and pseudo-Turkish, is conferring on him the noble title of "mamamouchi." In *The Imaginary Invalid*, in which Molière satirizes the medical profession (as he does in at least five other plays), an elaborate ceremony ends the play that parodies medical practice and its degree-conferring. It travesties the profession's Latinate language, and its conferring on a dunce of a new doctor the right to slash, purge, bleed, and kill his patients at will. The mocking of the "official" language suggests that it has no more truth-value than any other language.

Carnival humor's uncrownings of authority can take the form of cuckoldry. A wife's sexual deception of her husband is an uncrowning of domestic authority (and a parodic crowning with horns) (ibid.:241). Cuckoldry is commonplace in medieval farces and the *commedia dell'arte*. Cuckoldry or near-cuckoldry is a feature of several of Molière's plays, most notably *The School for Wives*, *Don Juan* (1665), and *Amphitryon* (1668). In the *School for Wives*, the foolish Arnolphe has had his prospective young wife raised in the country in convent captivity on the theory that she will be too ignorant to know how to be unfaithful to him, a proposition the play gaily unravels. Carnivalesque sexuality often erupts in this play. Arnolphe, justifying to a doubtful friend his expectation of success in his training of Agnes, says he was delighted when Agnes once came to him much troubled to ask, "In absolute and perfect innocence, / If children are begotten through the ear!" (Molière 1957:37). Earlier in the same scene, when the zealous Arnolphe is fantasizing about his control of his prospective young wife, a *crème tarte* figures as a salacious sexual reference (Molière 2001:5; Molière 1971:I, 548). These and several other such moments have the comically subversive merit of suggesting that strong sexual forces are surging just below the surface of Arnolphe's selfish, rational social engineering. Predictably, such bawdiness disturbed decorous court audiences, but Molière went on to mock them further in his *Critique of the School for Wives* (1663), one of several episodes in the year-long controversy over the play.

In another variation on carnival humor's upside-down world, the servants in Molière are often wiser than their masters and mistresses (much like those in Plautus's comedies, from which Molière borrowed directly for his *Amphitryon* and *The Miser*). Dorine in *Tartuffe* and Toinette in *The Imaginary Invalid* challenge their masters' delusions to a degree that borders on comic domestic anarchy. In *Don Juan*, Sganarelle

challenges his master about his seductions: "Do you think because you are a gentleman and wear a fashionable wig, because you have feathers in your hat and gilt lace on your coat and flame-colored ribbons . . . that you can do as you like . . . ?" (Molière 1953:204). Street-smart underclass characters in Molière frequently are foils to the self-deluding bourgeoisie. In many of the plays, folk wisdom comes from the servants in the form of proverbs, Molière mining another vein of popular culture.

Let us bring the carnivalesque lens down last on Molière's *Tartuffe*, in which a clergyman preaches holiness but practices seduction, almost with impunity. It was his most controversial play and, ultimately, the most profitable in his lifetime. Molière first staged it as part of Louis's lavish entertainments at Versailles in 1664, in a version now lost. The king enjoyed it but suppressed it in deference to the outrage of a sect of zealously devout Catholics. The play has many strains of popular folk humor inherited from farce and the *commedia dell'arte*, including Tartuffe's near sexual overpowering of Orgon's wife on top of the table under which Orgon is hiding (Figure 4.4). But let us focus here on one profound example of carnival humor in the play.

In the comic spectacles of popular festivals, travesty – the mocking appropriation of the costumes and insignia of authority and identity – was typical. Travesty suggests a slippage between the ideal and reality, between symbol and truth, between the sign and what it signifies – an effect which, for Bakhtin, nourishes positive social change. Molière's plays are full of imposters and poseurs, such as his affected courtiers, his bourgeois would-be gentleman, and all of his mock doctors. Disguised in the vestments and language of authority, such imposters create comic havoc. *Tartuffe*, as a sexual predator in the guise of a devout, creates more. Molière's play, like the theatre art itself, raises the question of whether we can ever know where the performance of the self ends and a true self begins. Taken seriously, a question about the stability of our knowledge of truth is not one an

Figure 4.4 Orgon catches Tartuffe (left) in the act of trying to seduce his wife in Act 4 of Molière's *Tartuffe*. Engraving by François Chaveau from the 1669 edition of the play.
© Bibliothèque Nationale de France.

absolutist church or state can long entertain. Molière's play could be seen not only as irreverent but as a strike at the heart of the church's authenticity. It is this, perhaps more than the sexuality, that would account for the deep wrath of the powerful conservative cabal who insisted that the King, who had been Molière's protector in controversies up to this time, suppress the play. One Catholic curate raged in print against *Tartuffe*, saying the author was "a demon . . . dressed like a man," that Molière had held Christ's church in contempt, and that he should be burned at the stake as a foretaste of what he would surely suffer in hell (Molière 1971:I, 1143–1144) When Molière tried to produce a revised version in

1667, the Bishop of Paris closed it down, threatening the excommunication of anyone who performed or read it.

A very persistent Molière finally got his play to the public stage in 1669 in the version that survives today. The ending probably represents his revising process and has been the subject of much debate. The ending's last-minute intervention of the emissary from Louis XIV to save Orgon and his home from Tartuffe's grasp was available to be read as an obsequious compliment to the omniscience of Molière's sovereign and patron. But this last act dénouement was also available to be read as an ironic *Deus ex machina*, which is to say a carnivalesque parody of power, an unmistakable *coup de théâtre* by a master of theatrical artifice. At the very least, two language zones, as Bakhtin would call them, were in play in the ending – the official and the unofficial – and two different reception possibilities. The result is the kind of dialectic in which Bakhtin found the gay ambivalence that subverts orthodoxy.

In their ribald humor and theatrical artifices drawn from street theatre traditions, Molière's plays, at least momentarily, critiqued decorum and absolutist control. Whether instinctively or consciously, Molière persisted in deploying carnivalesque humor throughout his career as if his integrity as both artist and citizen depended on it.

GJW

Key references

Bakhtin, M.M. (1981) *The Dialogic Imagination, Four Essays by M.M. Bakhtin* (ed. M. Holquist; trans. C. Emerson and M. Holquist), Austin: University of Texas Press.

Bakhtin, M.M. (1984) *Rabelais and His World* (trans. H. Iswolsky), Bloomington, Indiana: Indiana University Press.

Bristol, M.D. (1985) *Carnival and Theatre*, New York: Methuen.

Dock, S.V. (1992) *Costume and Fashion in the Plays of Jean-Baptiste Poquelin, Molière*, Geneva: Editions Slatkine.

Gaines, J.F. (ed.) (2002) *The Molière Encyclopedia*, Westport, C.T.: Greenwood Press.

McCarthy, G. (2002) *The Theatres of Molière*, New York and London: Routledge.

Molière [Poquelin, J.B.] (1971) *Oeuvres completes* (ed. G. Couton), Paris: Gallimard. [Scholarly French edition of all the plays and related documents referred to in this study. English translations of the plays discussed here follow below.]

Molière (1953) *Molière, Five Plays*, trans. J. Wood, Baltimore: Penguin Books. [Includes *Don Juan, The Miser*, and *The Would-Be Gentleman*.]

Molière (1957) *Eight Plays by Molière*, trans. M. Bishop, New York: Modern Library. [Includes *The Precious Damsels* (*Les Précieuses ridicules*), *The School for Wives* (*L'École des femmes*), *The Critique of the School for Wives* (*La Critique de l'École des femmes*), *Tartuffe*, and *The Would-Be Gentleman* (*Le Bourgeois gentilhomme*).]

Molière (1984) *Tartuffe* [video recording of the Royal Shakespeare production, directed by Bill Alexander, with Antony Sher as Tartuffe.]

Molière (1993) *Tartuffe*, trans. R. Wilbur (1961), in W.B. Worthen (ed.) *The HBJ Anthology of Drama*, Fort Worth: Harcourt Brace Jovanovich. [Includes English translations of Molière's important preface and other documents.]

Molière (2001) *The Misanthrope, Tartuffe, and Other Plays*, trans. M. Slater, Oxford: Oxford University Press. [Includes *School for Wives* and *Critique of the School for Wives*.]

Scott, V. (2000) *Molière, A Theatrical Life*, Cambridge: Cambridge University Press.

CASE STUDY: Kabuki and bunraku: Mimesis and the hybrid body

"Why can't a woman be more like man?" sings Professor Henry Higgins in Lerner and Lowe's *My Fair Lady*, echoing the musical's source play, *Pygmalion* (1913), by George Bernard Shaw (1856–1950). When Higgins meets the Cockney flower-seller, Eliza, he does not see a "woman"; he sees only a dirty, squalling member of the working class. When he successfully teaches her how to sound and act like a member of his own class, he becomes aware of (and disturbed by) her gender. His comic, lamenting song demonstrates that social class and gender are constructed from behaviors such as diction, vocal quality, grammar, clothing, hair style, bodily adornment, walking, and deportment. Higgins has, in effect, created a "hybrid body," filled with "mimetic excess."

The history and aesthetics of Japan's kabuki theatre (and its related puppet form, bunraku) are filled with "hybrid bodies" and "hybrid cultures.' The word kabuki originally derives from the verb *kabuku*, "to tilt or slant dangerously to one side.' Around the beginning of the seventeenth century, it referred to shocking, counter-cultural people, including actors, who roamed Edo (present-day Tokyo). Today, however, when kabuki is considered a "classical" art form, the word itself is now written differently, using Chinese characters meaning "song-dance-skill."

INTERPRETIVE APPROACH: Mimesis, hybridity, and the body

In kabuki, especially as it developed during the Tokugawa era (1603–1868), we can see cultural constructions of class and gender that demonstrate how "the concept of hybridity stresses the productive nature of cultural integration as positive contamination" (Gilbert and Lo 1997:7). Gilbert and Lo were discussing hybridity in colonized societies; as we shall see, the Tokugawa shogunate's creation of a closed, supposedly unchanging social order had effects similar to those that colonialist rule has.

In his *Mimesis and Alterity: A Particular History of the Senses*, Michael Taussig (1993) shows how colonizing Europeans who viewed native people as "childish" or "primitive" were mistaken. Taussig maintains that the Europeans (deeply imbued with Platonic ideas) failed to understand that when native peoples wore foreign costume items, mimicked European song and dance, or created religious effigies of the white man, they were attempting to incorporate the colonizing Other into their souls and their society. They were actually negating the threat while celebrating the wonder of Otherness by using "mimetic excess" (including parody) to work out a concept of their own identity. Taussig suggests this strategy may be more common that we think. "Mimetic excess provides access to understanding the unbearable truths of make-believe as foundation of an all-too-seriously serious reality. . . . [Mimetic excess is the power] to become any Other and engage the image with the reality thus imagized" (255). Such a concept complements the idea of hybridity as "productive contamination."

In writing about mimesis (imitation), European and American theorists inevitably begin with a discussion of Plato and his distrust of imitation. Although Catholic missionaries (with their fondness for neo-Platonic idealism) were active in Japan beginning in the mid-sixteenth century, their influence waned with the establishment of the Tokugawa shogunate, until all foreigners were banned in the mid-seventeenth century. It is important to understand that kabuki developed in isolation, unaffected by the outside world.

▷

▷ **KEY QUESTIONS**

1   What are the images on stage of a gender, race, class, or nationality? Do those represent you? Who is not represented? Are there any instances of productive or positive contamination?

2   What are some examples of parody and "excessive mimesis" in contemporary performances in music, television, or film? What is the effect? Do they serve a positive purpose?

3   If you were acting in a play, would you need to "see yourself" in the character in order to understand that character? Put another way, how might a Brazilian teenage boy go about understanding Juliet in Shakespeare's *Romeo and Juliet*?

Hybrid culture in Tokugawa Japan

Woodblock prints from around 1600 depict Okuni (d. 1610), the female temple dancer/prostitute who originated the performance style eventually called *kabuki*. She is dressed outrageously in male Portuguese garb and wears a Christian cross around her neck and a samurai's double swords at her waist (Figure 4.5). Wearing items belonging to the opposite gender, to foreigners, to Christians, or to the samurai class was forbidden. Does Okuni's scandalous mimicry suggest some influence by the West?

The Tokugawa rulers, guided by neo-Confucianism, insisted on society divided according to hereditary class. Each class was permitted garments and adornments appropriate to them and forbidden to others. For example, only samurai, the highest class, could wear the double swords. Next in the hierarchy were the farmers, followed by artisans and craftspeople. At the bottom were the merchants, thought to contribute nothing to society, because they merely traded items grown or made by others. These three lower classes wore only cotton garments of blue and brown, with little or no pattern. Outside and above the class system were the Imperial family, the nobility, and Buddhist and Shinto priests. They could wear colored silks, embroidered and elaborately patterned. Outside and below the class system were hereditary outcasts, sorcerers, prostitutes, beggars, and actors, all forbidden to wear the trappings of those "inside society."

However, this inflexible hierarchy was turned upside-down in reality during a long period of peace. Money could be spent on leisure instead of war. The *daimyô* (feudal lords) actually became poor because they were forced to maintain two households: in their home province and in the new capital of Edo. Unemployed samurai (*ronin*) became bandits or lived secretly among the merchants. In contrast, the despised merchants became rich. They secretly defied the law by wearing extravagant silks and bold colors beneath their simple cotton kimonos. Seeking identity, they mimicked the external markers of the aristocracy. As the "mimetic excess" of many kabuki plots demonstrates, the merchants embraced the virtues and values once appropriate to the samurai and feudal lords but which these upper classes no longer possessed. They became "cultural hybrids," mimicking and incorporating the look and behavior of "the Other," not unlike Eliza Doolittle or colonized peoples who practice "productive . . . cultural integration."

In the early Edo era, political opposition, rebelliousness, and the desire for excitement resulted in unruly gangs of youth, originally from all classes. Gang members sported outrageous costumes, wild

Figure 4.5 Detail from a painting showing Okuni, the Japanese female temple dancer/prostitute who originated the performance style eventually called kabuki, probably in the late sixteenth century. Note the Christian cross and double samurai swords. Other images show her in male Portuguese garb.
© Tokugawa Reimeikai Foundation.

hairdos, large and extravagantly decorated swords, and four-ft long tobacco pipes. Like Okuni, they resisted legal dress codes and performed "mimetic excess." These counter-cultural people were termed *kabuki-mono*. As long as people performed and dressed outrageously, whether on stage or off, order could not be maintained.

Unlike Europeans opposed to theatre, the neo-Confucians did not suggest that stage acting, cross-dressing, or imitation were inherently evil; rather, they feared class mingling and social rebellion. Most of kabuki's patrons were merchants. Samurai and aristocrats, including high-born women, were forbidden to attend, but they flagrantly broke the law. Sometimes they came in disguise; in some periods, they were forced to sit behind screens where they were "invisible." Actor/aristocrat love affairs became public scandals. The 1715 "Ejima affair"

between a court lady and a kabuki actor resulted in one theatre being torn down and others closed; those involved were imprisoned or exiled – one was even executed.

Draconian regulations failed to destroy kabuki. Instead, kabuki actors and managers devised creative solutions to remain in business and to entertain the patrons. Attempted censorship and control actually gave birth to innovations, such as more attractive costumes and wigs, better scripts, and the creation of the *onnagata*, a term meaning "female form," which designates the male actor who specializes in female roles.

Imaging "Woman"

When women were banned from kabuki in 1629 (replaced by boys, who were banned in 1654), adult male actors performing female roles appeared.

Female characters in kabuki include not only such "ideal women" as heroic princesses, virtuous wives, and glamorous courtesans, but also ugly, elderly women, stupid peasants, betrayed lovers, mothers driven mad by the death of a child, vengeful ghosts, demons, traitors, bandits, and prostitutes, among others. The *onnagata* does not need to appear "beautiful" or even typically "feminine." He speaks in a created falsetto rather than a realistic voice. The *onnagata* does not need to be "believable" as a woman (as we might expect a Judy Garland impersonator to be a realistic, believable imitation of the original). Rather, he must be a skillful performer, creating a pleasing staged image of "woman." Today, however, some popular *onnagata* also perform realistic women in films and on stage. For example, the kabuki *onnagata*, Bandô Tamasaburô V (b. 1950), also excels in roles such as Blanche DuBois in Tennesse

Williams's *A Streetcar Named Desire* and Shakespeare's Lady Macbeth.

The playwright Chikamatsu Monzaemon (1653–1725), best known for deeply moving domestic tragedies such as *Love Suicides at Sonezaki* (*Sonezaki Shinjû*), maintained that "beauty lies in the thin margin between the real and the unreal." He felt too much realism was repulsive; audiences would prefer the tension created by the actor's doubleness, an awareness of opposites in the same body (actor/character, male/female). For example, he advised the *onnagata* to kneel with the upstage knee slightly raised, although this might differ from how a real woman would kneel, because it would be aesthetically pleasing.

Chikamatsu's contemporary, the great *onnagata*, Yoshizawa Ayame I (1673–1729), maintained that the successful *onnagata* must behave like a woman on

Figure 4.6 The well-known Japanese male actor, Onoe Baiko, in the *onnagata* (female) role in *Fuji Musume* (*The Wisteria Maiden*). He was considered one of the finest *onnagata* of the twentieth century. Reproduced from the Grand kabuki theatre program, Japanese American Theatre, tenth anniversary season, 16–19 September, 1993, Los Angeles.

stage and in real life, even in private and even if he is married with children. He must practice a female's outward behavior and inner thoughts: by eating, walking, and gesturing like a woman. Even at the public bath, Ayame would use the women's section. No one objected, and no one was fooled. The *onnagata*'s body and character are neither imagined ideals nor imperfect copies. His aesthetic appeal results from being a "hybrid" that incorporates both genders within a single body through "mimetic excess."

In a famous scene from the 1825 *Yotsuya Ghost Stories* (*Tôkaidô Yotsuya Kaidan*), the corpses of a man and a woman are nailed to either side of a door that has been thrown into the river. As the man responsible for their deaths walks along, the door bobs up and down in the water, tossing and turning so that we see first the bloated, decaying body of the woman, then the man, and so on. Hybridity and mimetic excess are here doubled, because both dead bodies (male and female) are played by the same actor, an *onnagata*. Kabuki audiences love such "tricks" of quick bodily transformation. Another trick is called *hikinuki*, a spectacular onstage costume shift that reveals a character's inner nature, often in

the midst of a complex dance. In the kabuki version of the noh play, *Dôjôji* (see the case study on the noh play in Chapter 3), stage assistants unobtrusively pull out threads basting a costume together, then whip off the outer garment to reveal a totally different kimono, suggesting various aspects of the character's nature.

A more complex type of hybrid body is represented by the kabuki actor who impersonates a bunraku puppet. Bunraku developed at the same time as kabuki and shares many of the same plays. Bunraku puppets were three to four ft tall and are manipulated by three adult men (Figure 4.7). Like the boy actors of Elizabethan England, they rivaled adult male kabuki actors in popularity. The puppets performed as much like live kabuki actors as possible, and one type of kabuki acting developed in which the actors copied the movement of puppets.

In this special style of puppet imitation (*ningyô buri*), the kabuki actor appears to be a limp doll brought to life and manipulated by visible, black-robed stage attendants, who act as though they are puppet manipulators. The actor's "live" body mimics the lifeless (but mechanized) carved doll to create a

Figure 4.7 Japanese bunraku puppets. The head manipulator, without mask, controls the doll's head and right arm. The secondary manipulator, with face covered, controls the left arm. If needed, a third controls the feet. [Source: *Bunraku: The National Theatre of Japan*, December 1994, p.7. Published by Japan Arts Council, Tokyo.]

new hybrid body. A famous *ningyô buri* dance in *Yaoya Oshichi* features Oshichi, the greengrocer's daughter, as she climbs a fire tower. The play is based on the true story of a love-sick girl who was executed for committing arson. Mimetic excess in this performance means that the live, male *onnagata* actor mimics the dance of a mechanical bunraku doll; in the bunraku version, the doll mimics an imaginary *onnagata*. Both the performing male body and the bunraku doll mimic a once living woman.

Merchants incorporating samurai

Just as the *onnagata* represents a successful hybrid of opposite genders, the Tokugawa era kabuki plays represent the way in which the code of the samurai (no longer practiced but still valued) became incorporated into the bodies and souls of the merchants.

The merchant class was beginning to imagine its new, self-created identity, just as colonized peoples mimic and incorporate the dress and behaviors of the colonizers in a process that results in independent national identity. The two plays considered below use the technique of *mitate*, in which the playwrights substitute a past historical, literary or legendary "world" for the present. They did so because censorship forbade the depiction of current events and criticism of the samurai.

Sukeroku: Flower of Edo (1713) is staged in *aragoto* (rough-house) style featuring striking, non-realistic makeup, hugely exaggerated costumes, extreme vocal patterns, and powerful gestures that are based on images of *Fudô*. *Fudô* is the patron deity of a Buddhist-Shinto sect of mountain ascetics, whose rituals include terrifying demon-quelling dances.

Figure 4.8 Danjûrô XII as Sukeroku, the commoner who is an aristocrat of the past in disguise, in the kabuki play, *Sukeroku: Flower of Edo*. Here, Danjuro is seen striking the *mie* pose. [Source: *Kabuki*, January 1995, Kabukiza Theatre program, Tokyo, p.20.]

Nothing in kabuki so clearly demonstrates "mimetic excess" as this *aragoto* style. At climactic moments, an *aragoto* actor may toss his head, raise his leg and stamp his foot, pose with open, outreached hand, grunt, and freeze his face in a cross-eyed grimace. Such "punctuation" in acting is called *mie* (Figure 4.8). In these moments, the expressive body of the outcast actor incorporates both the Buddhist-Shinto deity and samurai warrior, suggesting to the merchant audience that they, themselves, partake of such hybrid identity.

Sukeroku is a rowdy commoner in love with a gorgeous courtesan who refuses the advances of the evil samurai, Ikyû. The action takes place in Yoshiwara, Edo's "pleasure district," where theatre, tea-houses, and brothels were located. In Sukeroku's danced entrance on the *hanamichi* (a rampway extending from down stage right through the audience to the back of the auditorium), he wears a purple headband (a color permitted only to the upper classes), suggesting disdain for society's rules. Like the merchants' ideal self, he is brave, clever, funny and a great lover. However, this contemporary surface is revealed as false.

Sukeroku is in disguise, and the time is not the present. He is actually one of the Soga brothers, historical samurai who avenged their murdered father in 1193. He typifies both the pluck of the Edo townsman and the abandoned ideals of the ancient samurai. Sukeroku comically insults and picks fights with samurai; when Ikyû finally draws his sword, Sukeroku recognizes it as his father's, proving that Ikyû is the murderer. A hybrid commoner-samurai, Sukeroku has inherited the values and behaviors that the ruling samurai no longer possess.

This issue was not always treated so lightly. *Chûshingura: The Treasury of Loyal Retainers* (1748) was based on events that took place between 1701 and 1703. A young, untutored *daimyô* failed to bribe an elegant samurai, who mercilessly taunted him until the samurai drew his sword while in Edo castle and wounded his tormentor. In punishment, he was ordered to commit *seppuku* (suicide by disembowelment), his lands were confiscated, and his family line was to be stamped out. However, his former retainers (now *rônin*, masterless samurai) attacked and murdered their lord's tormentor, aware that for this act of loyalty, they would be condemned to death.

Their deeds polarized society. Some people insisted they should not be punished, because they had only obeyed their obligation to their lord rather than succumbing to *ninjô* (human emotion). Others demanded their deaths. As a compromise, the *rônin* were permitted to commit *seppuku* and were buried along with their lord.

The rapid publication of materials dealing with the incident and subsequent trial insured that the general population was well informed. Here were *rônin* acting in accordance with the code of *bushidô* (the way of the warrior), seemingly a lost value. Twelve days after the mass suicide, the first play based on the vendetta was staged, set (like *Sukeroku*) in the medieval world of the Soga brothers. Nevertheless, the government closed it after only three performances. Over the years, many other versions appeared. Finally, the 1748 version, set in yet a different historical era, became the standard. The censors were appeased since the outer form of this version of the play did not violate the law, and audiences understood the real subject.

Just as the performance of the *onnagata* demonstrates how gender images were constructed through "hybridity" and "mimetic excess," so plays such as these permitted the primarily merchant-class audience of the Tokugawa era to create a new social identity that incorporated the colonizing "Other."

CFS

Key references

Brandon, J.R. (1975 [2nd ed. 1992]) *Five Classic Kabuki Plays*, Honolulu: University of Hawaii Press.

Brandon, J.R. and Leiter, S.L. (eds) (2002–2003) *Kabuki Plays on Stage*, vols 1–4, Honolulu: University of Hawaii Press.

Brazell, K. (ed.) (1998) *Traditional Japanese Theatre*, New York: Columbia University Press.

Dunn, C.J. and Bunzô, T. (1969) *The Actors' Analects*, New York: Columbia University Press.

Ernst, E. (1956) *The Kabuki Theatre*, New York: Grove.

Gilbert, H. and Lo, J. (1997) "Performing hybridity in postcolonial monodrama," *Journal of Commonwealth Literature*, 32(1):5–19.

Keene, D. (trans.) (1961) *Four Major Plays of Chikamatsu*, New York and London: Columbia University Press.

Keene, D. (trans.) (1971) *Chûshingura: The Treasury of Loyal Retainers*, New York and London: Columbia University Press.

Kominz, L. (1997) *The Stars Who Created Kabuki: Their Lives, Loves and Legacy*, New York: Kodansha.

Leiter, S.L. (ed.) (2002) *A Kabuki Reader: History and Performance*, Armonk, N.Y. and London: M.E. Sharpe.

Ortolani, B. (1995 [revised edn]) *The Japanese Theatre: From Shamanistic Ritual to Contemporary Pluralism*, Princeton: Princeton University Press.

Taussig, M. (1993) *Mimesis and Alterity: A Particular History of the Senses*, London and New York: Routledge.

CASE STUDY: Shakespearean sexuality in *Twelfth Night*

Sexual desire has been a perennial subject of theatrical performance. Even during periods when only actors of a single sex appeared on the stage, audiences have applauded plays in which the anxieties, illusions, and expected pleasures of sexual desire took center stage. During the theatrical renaissance of the early modern period in England (1590–1642), cross-dressed boys between the ages of eight and eighteen performed all of the women characters. Nonetheless, the comedies, satires, and tragedies of numerous playwrights, including John Ford, Ben Jonson, and William Shakespeare, featured boys playing women involved in a range of sexual relationships, including conventional romance and marriage, potential lesbian affairs, prostitution, and even incest. The performance of Shakespeare's *Twelfth Night* at the Globe Theatre in London allowed audiences to explore, enjoy, and agonize about a range of sexual desires, including the desire for same-sex love.

The homoerotics of patriarchy

Most people in early modern England judged sexual urges and actions by patriarchal standards. Patriarchal ideology, the belief that males in superior social and political positions had an inherent right to their authority, generally elevated the expression of male over female sexuality. A man's desire for a woman or for another man could be more ennobling than a woman's desire for a man. Patriarchy, however, needed women as a means of cementing alliances and accumulating property through marriage, as well, of course, as ensuring male heirs. The result was a social system and a dominant ideology that tied sexuality to class hierarchy and allowed for homoerotic acts that solidified the patriarchal order.

Within some early modern institutions – the church, the school, the household – same-sex love initiated by men in superior positions was not uncommon. Male teachers often formed liaisons with male students, and a master might act on his desire for a male apprentice living in his household without raising the neighbors' eyebrows. Likewise, powerful women might form homoerotic relationships with ladies-in-waiting or servants in their households. When these relationships threatened the procreation of patriarchy, however, society persecuted them. Although few instances of lesbianism ever came to court, men convicted of "sodomy" were imprisoned or hung. In most of these instances, "sodomy" was broadly seen as an act that threatened the social order – not just sexual morality but the hierarchy of class and gender.

INTERPRETIVE APPROACH: Queer theory

The general acceptance of homoerotic love in early modern England raises significant questions for contemporary readers and critics. Most westerners today draw a sharp distinction between hetero- and homosexuality and understand sexual orientation as key to a person's identity. Shakespeare's contemporaries, however, did not think about sexuality in these ways. For most Elizabethans, there was nothing unnatural about a man desiring both women and other men; if he acted on these desires, he was not a "homosexual," a confused "heterosexual," or even a "bisexual," since identity was not tied to sexual expression. Of course there were many people then, as now, who preferred same-sex or opposite-sex intimacy and practiced it exclusively, but they did not classify themselves according to their sexual orientation. Most social and literary historians recognize that the homo-hetero binary used to categorize modern sexuality derives from the late nineteenth century and should not be read back into the sexual practices of early modern England.

How, then, might we explain the homoeroticism of Shakespeare's England? Recent work by historians and critics in the field of "queer studies," so named to alter a formerly negative term into a positive one, has explored our critical assumptions about sexual desire and expression. Much of this scholarship rests on the ideas of Michel Foucault, whose three-volume *History of Sexuality* developed the contention that sexuality, like notions of insanity, varies from one culture to another; sexual expression is tied to culture, not nature. In other words, as Bruce Smith argues, we can distinguish between sex, the bio-chemical urge experienced by all humans, and sexuality, the cultural expression of that urge: "Sexual desire animates human beings in all times and places, but the forms that desire assumes, the objects to which it is directed, change from culture to culture, from era to era" (Smith 1991:3). The normal sexuality of one era may seem foolish, unethical, or inexplicable to people in another time or culture. Thus, culture channels male and female sexual desires toward a hierarchy of approved objects and away from objects deemed inappropriate or immoral.

Drama historian Mario DiGangi deploys a useful vocabulary to discuss these possible couplings. Drawing on the assumptions of Foucault and his own knowledge of renaissance sexual practice, DiGangi makes some helpful distinctions in his *The Homoerotics of Early Modern Drama*. He uses the term "sexuality" to refer to the social organization and erotic meanings and practices of sexual expression in the renaissance, but denotes as "homosexual" only those "sexual acts between people of the same sex." DiGangi continues,

▷

▷ "Because the phrase 'homosexual desire' seems to ground erotic desire in a core sexual identity, I reject it in favor of 'homoerotic desire,' which to my mind signifies only a relation and not a causality" (DiGangi 1997:3–4). To this list of useful terms might be added "heteroerotic desire," to distinguish it both from the "homoerotic" type as defined by DiGangi and from sexual desire generally, which could take either form.

Interpreting the history of sexuality as it pertains to theatrical performance or to similar human practices, then, will involve attempting to answer the following questions.

KEY QUESTIONS

1   How did the historical culture construct sexuality?

2   Toward what kinds of approved objects did the culture direct hetero- and homoerotic desire?

3   How did the culture's sexuality intersect with other practices and ideologies?

Homoerotic desire and the boy actors

The convention of boy actors cross-dressed to play women's roles had been the norm in play productions throughout medieval Europe. This changed on the continent during the sixteenth century with the widespread touring of *commedia dell'arte* troupes, the first professional theatres to cast women in female roles regularly. Slowly, other continental theatres also began employing women actors, but English companies did not.

Historians and critics have suggested several reasons for the continuation of cross-dressed boys on the English stage. Fear of female sexuality probably played a part, although powerful men on the continent would have been no less wary of a woman's desire and procreative ability than the patriarchs of England. Then, too, few *commedia* troupes crossed the channel to perform in London; English audiences, consequently, had little familiarity with the possibilities of women on stage. Further, the practice

of boys dressing as women was a theatrical convention of proven and continuing effectiveness. Even after the banning of all religious plays in 1559 and their complete suppression in the 1570s, boys continued to play female roles in secular mummers plays and medieval farces as well as in school productions at boys schools, such as Eton. In fact, plays written specifically for and performed by all-boy troupes were enormously popular in London after 1576. From 1600 to 1608, an all-boy company at the Blackfriars Theatre, an indoor playhouse more exclusive and prestigious than the outdoor theatres, did better business on average than any of the adult companies in London.

The popularity of the boy companies suggests a fourth reason for the continuation of boy actors in female roles: they may have provided a safe, conventional means of exploring the pleasures and anxieties of homoerotic desire on the stage – safe in most ways, at least. The Master of the Revels, a censor appointed by the royal household to guard against religious and political subversion in all dramas performed by licensed troupes, did not forbid plays on the basis of sexual suggestiveness, homoerotic or otherwise. Puritan critics of the stage, however, repeatedly pointed to the dangerous eroticism of beautiful boys. Opposed to any public displays of sexual desire, homo or hetero, Philip Stubbs, for example, singled out the "whoredome & unclennes" induced by the boy players in 1582: "[For proof], but marke the flocking and running to Theaters and curtens . . . to see Playes and Enterludes, where such wanton gestures, such bawdie speaches; such laughing and fleering; such kissing and bussing; such clipping and culling; such wickinge and glancinge of wanton eyes, and the like is used, as is wonderfull to behold. These goodly pageants being done, every mate sorts to his mate . . . and in their secret conclaves (covertly) they play the Sodomits, or worse" (Brown 1990:250). Although their fear of the theatre made the Puritans biased reporters, Stubbs's description, echoed in less overheated phrases by more objective observers, does suggest that the boy actors were trained to make themselves objects of sexual desire on the stage.

The adult companies of renaissance England generally employed four to six boys, both for female roles and for roles of their own age and sex. As in other master–apprentice relationships in early modern England, the boys lived in the household of the company member under whom they served, and the company paid the master a small fee for the boys' services. The Lord Chamberlain's Men, the company for which Shakespeare wrote and in which he had a financial share, probably employed four boys in the early 1600s, when they produced *Twelfth Night* at the Globe. Historians know little about the acting style of adults on renaissance stages and less about the techniques used by boys to impersonate women. The skimpy evidence does suggest that the boys playing major female roles attempted to fully embody the voice, movements, and emotions of their characters rather than merely indicate them. That Shakespeare wrote such complex psychological portraits as Juliet

(*Romeo and Juliet*, 1594–1595), Rosalind (*As You Like It*, 1599), and Cleopatra (*Antony and Cleopatra*, 1606–1607) also suggests that his company had boy actors who could play these roles believably. For their part, spectators probably focused on either the female characters or the boy underneath during different moments of the performance. And Shakespeare, like other renaissance playwrights, frequently reminded his auditors of the sexual incongruity between the two.

Twelfth Night at The Globe

Early modern audiences in London could attend an outdoor, public playhouse most days of the year, except for the Christian season of Lent and for periods of intense heat (and possible plague) during the summer months. For Londoners, a trip to The Globe took them across the River Thames beyond the reach of a city government dominated by Puritans and into an area populated by taverns, brothels, bear-baiting arenas, and other playhouses. The theatres south of the Thames, like others north of the city, drew audiences of all classes. Apprentices, journeymen, soldiers, and others paid a penny for admittance into the yard of the playhouse, where they could stand to watch the show on the thrust stage, roughly four to six ft high (Figure 4.9). For an additional penny, merchants and their families, courtiers of both sexes, foreign travelers, and others might purchase a bench seat in one of the three-tiered galleries that surrounded the yard and the stage. If the Lord Chamberlain himself came to enjoy the troupe he sponsored, he and his retinue might sit in a lord's room behind and above the stage platform, an excellent location to see and be seen. Although the Globe could hold perhaps 2,500 spectators, the average crowd for most performances was probably around 600.

When *Twelfth Night* began near two o'clock in the afternoon, the audience heard the musicians – probably six instrumentalists in an elevated gallery – playing melancholy music as Duke Orsino and his

Figure 4.9 A 1596 drawing of the interior of the Swan Theatre, London, probably generally similar to the nearby Globe Theatre. Note the figures in the gallery above the two stage doors; this area may have been used as a Lord's Room and as an acting space. The only picture of the interior of a professional Elizabethan theatre, it was copied from a lost original by a Dutch visitor, Johannes DeWitt, by his friend to whom he sent it, Arend von Buchell. From E.K. Chambers, *The Elizabethan Stage* (1923). Buchell's drawing is in the Bibliotheek der Rijkuniversiteit, Utrecht.

court entered through the two doors at the rear of the stage. Music would have played a significant role in establishing the various moods of the comedy and the auditors' attitudes toward its major characters. No doubt the spectators also noted the lavish costumes worn by the Duke and his court, costumes which gave important information about the social class and gender of these and other characters (including the cross-dressed boys) at their entrance. A throne-like chair, placed center stage for the Duke, was all the scenery needed to establish the setting of the first scene.

Twelfth Night tells the story of two shipwrecked twins stranded in the fairy-tale land of Illyria. They eventually find their rightful, aristocratic place by marrying into the two powerful households of the country. In order to secure her livelihood, Viola dons male attire and apprentices herself to Duke Orsino as his page. Unknown to Viola, Sebastian, her twin brother, survived the wreck and also is seeking his fortune in Illyria. He is initially helped by Antonio, whose apparent homoerotic desire shapes their relationship. The plot focuses on Viola, who is soon caught up in the romantic intrigues of the two households. Duke Orsino is trying to gain the hand of the Countess Olivia, who disdains his love. When Viola, in male disguise as Cesario, goes to woo her as the Duke's agent, Olivia falls in love with "him," not realizing Cesario/Viola's sex (Figure 4.10). Viola, meanwhile, is "desperate" for the Duke.

The character relationships in the secondary plot reflect the sexual "madness" of the major characters. Olivia's uncle, Sir Toby Belch, gulls Sir Andrew Aguecheek into believing that Olivia loves him. Knowing that Olivia's steward, Malvolio, also loves the Countess, Sir Toby and his friends trick Malvolio into believing that she wants to marry him. Malvolio's attempts to confirm Olivia's love land him in prison for his "madness." After Viola (costumed the same as her twin brother, Sebastian) refuses to help Antonio, he also falls into a kind of "madness." Next, Olivia assumes Sebastian is Cesario and promptly marries the amazed lad. In the end, the twins finally appear together on stage, the mistaken identities are resolved, and Viola reveals her male disguise. The Countess reaffirms her marriage to Sebastian, and the Duke, affectionate throughout with Cesario/Viola, pledges to wed her.

Staging homoeroticism

The double marriage at the end of *Twelfth Night* is a conventional comic ending that satisfies patriarchal values, but it does not resolve the homoerotic relationships hinted at and, arguably, even established during the play. The ending promises that both family households, once threatened by the narcissistic self-love of their heads and by eventual, childless dissolution, can flourish in the future. Threats to the aristocratic position of both families, such as Malvolio's desire for the Countess, have been averted or punished. In the case of Orsino's love for Viola, however, the Duke remains attached to the image of Viola as a boy. He even calls her "Cesario" in his final speech, perhaps reflecting his ongoing attraction to Viola's boyish role.

The marriage of the woman to the boy in Olivia's – now Sebastian's – household, may be based

Figure 4.10 Interior of the reconstructed Globe Theatre, London, which opened in 1997. Shown is a scene from an all-male production of *Twelfth Night*, with Mark Rylance as Olivia and Michael Brown as Viola/Cesario. Photo by John Tramper, © Shakespeare's Globe Picture Archive.

on a firmer heteroerotic desire, but ambiguities remain here as well. Olivia's former love for Cesario, a girl in boy's clothing, continues to shadow her attraction to her new husband, costumed identically to his sister. And Sebastian's past homoerotic relation with Antonio may influence his marriage to Olivia. Sebastian's greeting to Antonio when they are reunited is: "How have the hours racked and tortured me / Since I have lost thee" (5.1.211–212 – all citations are from Greenblatt 1997). This might suggest that Antonio would be a welcome guest in Sebastian's new household. In short, the ending guarantees the reproduction of patriarchy, but it does not rule out the continuation of homoerotic desires and alliances. At the same time, however, the finale puts potentially disruptive homoeroticism under the control of patriarchy. Olivia's covert desire for other women, evidenced in her attraction to Viola/ Cesario, is now channelled into a marriage with Viola's twin. And Sebastian's homoerotic desires must now take second place to his marital responsibilities with Olivia.

Considered from a theatrical, rather than a simply dramatic point of view, the action of *Twelfth Night* allowed the audience even more opportunities to identify with homoerotic attractions. While dramatically the ending presents two opposite-sex couples united in wedlock, theatrically an adult male actor (who played Orsino) held the hand of a cross-dressed boy actor (Viola), while near them on stage two boys (Olivia and Sebastian) also posed as a heterosexual couple. Shakespeare frequently reminded his audience that boy actors were playing all the female roles by having Viola disguise herself as Cesario. This triple-level gender confusion entailed a boy actor playing a girl playing a boy. Shakespeare gave Viola several lines of dialog that underscored these multiple layers of sexual identity: "I am not that I play" (1.5.164) and "Disguise, I see thou art a wickedness" (2.2.25), for example. The script also required the boy actor playing Viola/ Cesario to change his voice in order to separate his two roles. Thus, every time the actor shifted from high-voiced Viola to boy-voiced Cesario (probably the boy-actor's natural intonation), auditors were reminded of the boy actor underneath Viola and behind all the other female roles.

The intimate scenes between Viola/Cesario and Olivia – they are alone together on stage three times – consequently carried multiple homoerotic charges that may have created anxiety and pleasure in Shakespeare's audience. (For a modern all-male production, see the photograph in Figure 4.10.) Dramatically, Olivia's love for Cesario hinted at same-sex desire among two women, because of audience knowledge of Viola's disguise. Theatrically, one boy actor (Olivia) flirted with another boy actor, while the second boy (Viola/Cesario) demurred to profess his love for a man (Orsino). How could the need for patriarchy to reproduce itself find a way through the maze of homoerotic possibilities presented in the drama and theatre of such scenes? Shakespeare set up the situation and then relied on the comedy of "time" – "O Time, thou must untangle this, not I" (2.2.39) – to untie the knot, resolving in the end only the audience anxieties about the fate of these patriarchal families.

Some of this is speculative. What Elizabethan audiences made of these homoerotic possibilities can never be known with certainty, of course. Some may have understood but ignored the homoerotic enticements of the performance while a few of both sexes may have come to the theatre chiefly to be aroused by them. Given their familiarity with both homo- and heteroerotic desire, most early modern auditors probably feared for and enjoyed the performance of both sexualities. Clearly, the Lord Chamberlain's Men put both on stage in their Globe production of *Twelfth Night* in the early 1600s.

BMc

Key references
Brown, S. (1990) "The boyhood of Shakespeare's heroines: notes on gender ambiguity in the sixteenth century," *Studies in English Literature*, 30:243–264.

Casey, C. (1997) "Gender trouble in *Twelfth Night*," *Theatre Journal*, 49(May):121–141.

DiGangi, M. (1997) *The Homoerotics of Early Modern Drama*, Cambridge: Cambridge University Press.

Greenblatt, S. (gen. ed.) (1997) *The Norton Shakespeare*, New York and London: W. W. Norton and Company.

Howard, J.E. (1988) "Crossdressing, the theatre, and gender struggle in early modern England," *Shakespeare Quarterly*, 39:418–440.

Jardine, L. (1992) "Twins and Travesties: Gender, Dependency, and Sexual Availability in *Twelfth Night*," in S.

Zimmerman (ed.), *Erotic Politics: Desire on the Renaissance Stage*, New York and London: Routledge.

Shapiro, M. (1994) *Gender in Play on the Shakespearean Stage: Boy Heroines and Female Pages*, Ann Arbor, M.I.: University of Michigan Press.

Smith, B.R. (1991) *Homosexual Desire in Shakespeare's England: A Cultural Poetics*, Chicago and London: University of Chicago Press.

Thomson, P. (1992) *Shakespeare's Theatre*, London: Routledge.

CHAPTER 5

Theatres for knowledge through feeling, 1700–1900

As noted in the Introduction to Part II, European print culture began to change around 1700 with the regular publication and broad dissemination of periodicals – newspapers, magazines, journals, and other time-sensitive publications. Unlike books in the eighteenth century, which were printed "for the ages," periodicals were the websites and listservs of their day, intended to bring current news to a broad readership with common interests. Where early book culture generally helped to legitimate absolutism, periodical culture after 1700 enabled the new bourgeoisie to solidify its values and to enlarge the arena of public discourse. Periodical culture, in turn, helped to legitimate a sentimental theatre that embraced the morality and feelings of the emerging middle class.

"Sentimental" is a term assigned in modern times to describe eighteenth-century drama and theatre. It is shorthand for the belief of eighteenth-century playwrights, actors, and spectators in Europe that human nature was innately good and that both personal and social bonds would thrive if individuals were true to their innate virtues, their moral sentiments, resisting selfishness and exercising benevo-

lence, a regimen in which reason was to assist. For them, a sentimental play (or poem or novel) evoked feelings of sympathy, joy, and sorrow for worthy others; it allowed genteel spectators (or readers) to test and broaden their own virtuous instincts. The theatre was seen as an especially effective school for emotionally kindling the public's moral consciousness by revealing the virtuous feelings innate in humankind – most especially the middle class. As we shall see, a significant school of moral philosophy endorsed this aesthetic point of view in the eighteenth century. Sentimental theatre chose middle-class figures rather than royalty as its heroes, endorsed benevolent paternalism instead of royal absolutism for its ethics, and reconfigured the traditional neoclassical forms of tragedy and comedy to accommodate its point of view. Bourgeois sentimentalism challenged aristocratic neoclassicism in the theatre throughout Europe during the 1700s.

The French Revolution (1789–1799) marked the end of genteel sentimental culture, both in the theatre and elsewhere. The Revolution re-channeled much of the emotional fervor and moral earnestness of sentimentalism into melodrama, a broad-ranging genre that eventually gained popularity with all classes and came to dominate nineteenth-century theatre. As we will discover, the chief difference between nineteenth-century melodramas and eighteenth-century sentimental plays was their understanding of evil. Where sentimental theatre optimistically assumed that evil characters might reform, most melodramas – drawing on popular perceptions deriving from the French Revolution – divided humanity into good and evil types. Melodrama fostered the belief that evil people would always conspire against the innocent. Like the sentimental theatre before it, melodramatic theatre was fundamentally bourgeois in orientation, although it sometimes embraced other values.

This chapter, then, primarily examines major changes in European middle-class theatre oriented toward gaining knowledge through feeling from 1700 to 1900. To some extent, the shift from sentimental to melodramatic theatre in Europe mirrored actual changes in bourgeois values and in the bourgeoisie itself. In the early 1700s, the emerging bourgeoisie, a small group of merchants and investors living in large cities, adopted sentimentalism to distinguish itself from the aristocrats who dominated urban life. After 1800, a much larger and more fragmented bourgeoisie was trying to salvage what it could from the French Revolution and protect itself from radical and reactionary conspiracies above and below. Although sentimental theatre had become more sophisticated and diverse, many in the bourgeoisie embraced melodrama as more suited to their psychosocial and ethical needs. By the early twentieth century, when the bourgeoisie had become masters of the Industrial Revolution and the major governing class in Western Europe and the United States, playwrights of melodrama, like the previous artists of sentimental theatre, had broadened the appeal of their genre to gain more respectability and success. By then, however, a few middle-class artists and spectators were rejecting melodrama for the aesthetics of modernism, as we will see in Part III.

Included in this chapter are case studies on David Garrick, the premiere English star of the mid-eighteenth century renowned for his portrayal of sentimental roles, and a case study examining changes in nineteenth century melodrama, which gradually altered to embrace the materialism of its mid-century bourgeois spectators. Placed between these two, is a case study on India's kathakali dance-drama, a relevant contrast to the ways that feeling and knowledge were configured in western sentimental and melodramatic theatre.

Sentimental drama in England

Sentimental theatre first flourished in London. After 1688, merchants, traders, and investors gained more power in England, where problems of religion and royal succession undercut attempts to establish absolutism on the French model. Grown rich on colonial domination, expanding domestic markets, and the international slave trade, the top tier of the English bourgeoisie sought a government that would protect and expand its interests. They, and other middle-class men and women, also sought periodicals that would provide important news, keep them up-to-date on current trends in fashion and the arts, and justify their emerging cultural values.

They found such reading material initially in two periodicals, *The Tatler* and *The Spectator*, edited by Joseph Addison (1672–1719) and Richard Steele (1672–1729). The editors of both weekly journals, which began publication in 1709 and 1711, respectively, strove to create the sense of a benevolent community among their readers. They published pieces advocating mutual trust and self-disclosure within circles of families and friends, and they invited letters-to-the-editor to foster such a circle of affection within their readership. In contrast to aristocratic culture, which emphasized a hierarchical order and the public projection of social status, Addison and Steele underlined the importance of social bonds and fellow-feeling in public communications, especially in print. As the models for hundreds of subsequent periodicals, *The Tatler* and *The Spectator* broadcast the principles of sentimental culture in the early eighteenth century. The form as well as the content of the new periodicals thus underwrote the legitimacy and increased the reach of bourgeois sentimentality.

English sentimental culture drew on the precepts of "moral sense" philosophy. Liberal thinkers of the age distinguished their ideas from those of previous philosophers, who had advocated absolutism. Thomas Hobbes (1588–1679), for example, had argued that a strong monarchical government was necessary to control the problems created by rapacious individual interests. In contrast, John Locke (1632–1704) urged that free individuals in a state of nature might form civil governments that could channel competing interests toward socially beneficial results. Locke, immersed in print culture, also believed that people were like blank pieces of paper when they were born, awaiting the "imprint" of their parents and society. Later "moral sense" philosophers built upon Locke's premises to argue that humanity had an inherent sense of right and wrong and would generally choose the right for its natural beauty and worth. A bad environment, however, could "impress" other values on children, they believed. According to moral sense philosopher, Adam Smith (1723–1790), all people had within them an "ideal spectator of our sentiments and conduct" (Kramnick 1995:287), who, awakened by social pressure, would ensure that each person do his or her moral duty. In addition to friendly conversation and the sight of strangers in distress, watching the right play could awaken that "ideal spectator" in the mind and steer the playgoer toward affection and beneficence. For the moral sense philosophers, morality was inherent and natural; doing the right thing required emotional sensitivity, but no abstract reason.

In the English theatre, early advocates of sentiment found temporary allies among the Puritans. Puritan attacks on the wickedness of the London stage increased in the 1690s, culminating in Jeremy

Collier's *A Short View of the Immorality and Profaneness of the English Stage* in 1698. Beginning with the neoclassical precept that "the business of plays is to recommend virtue and discountenance vice," Collier cited several comedies from the aristocratic Restoration era for "their smuttiness of expression; their swearing, profaneness, and lewd application of Scripture; their abuse of the clergy; and their making their top characters libertines and giving them success in their debauchery" (Collier 1974:351–352). Collier's attack aroused indignation in some, struck home for others (a few playwrights even apologized), and led to controversies that continued into the next century. Even before Collier's *Short View*, however, some playwrights were already softening Restoration cynicism and arranging sentimental endings for their plays. In *Love's Last Shift* (1696), for instance, actor-playwright Colly Cibber (1671–1757) celebrated several characters for their inherent goodness and featured a rakish hero, Loveless, who gladly repents of his compulsive woman-chasing in the last act. While Cibber was writing popular variations on this formula in the first decade of the eighteenth century, playwright George Farquhar (1678–1707) took several of his dramatic characters and conflicts out of London into the more sentimental air of the English countryside.

In *The Tatler* and *The Spectator*, Richard Steele campaigned for moves replacing Restoration comedy, with its cynical wit and erotic interest, with comedy reflecting the new values, and he carried this out in his own very popular play, *The Conscious Lovers* (1722). Its plot centers on young Jack Bevil, who has hidden a mysterious female stranger in rooms that he is paying for, even though he has promised his father that he will wed a girl of his father's choosing. Although Jack loves the beautiful stranger, Indiana, whom he treats with courteous respect, he obligingly prepares to marry his father's choice. Then, a rich businessman who suspects Jack of duplicity, decides to investigate the relationship between Jack and his mysterious beauty. This sets up a recognition scene in which Indiana is discovered to be the long-lost daughter of the rich businessman. Jack can now marry Indiana, who is suddenly rich, and still obey his father's command. A secondary hero is found for the other girl. In the course of his plot, Steele tests the worthiness of both heroines and, for the modern reader, stretches dramatic credibility with Jack's forbearance and virtue. Eleven years before in *The Spectator*, Steele had announced his belief that "A man that is temperate, generous, valiant, chaste, faithful, and honest, may, at the same time, have wit, humour, mirth, good breeding, and gallantry" (ibid.:392). He created Jack Bevil partly to prove his point. *The Conscious Lovers* drew sympathetic tears as well as laughter from English audiences for the rest of the eighteenth century.

Notions of sentiment altered tragedy as well as comedy during the 1700s. Early in the century, Nicholas Rowe (1674–1718) wrote several tragedies featuring pathetic heroines that partly broke the mold of neoclassic tragic form. With *The London Merchant* (1731), however, playwright George Lillo (1693–1739) crafted a tragedy that dispensed completely with the idealized aristocratic heroes and constraining unities of neoclassicism. Its apprentice-hero, George Barnwell, is enticed by an evil woman, Millwood, who tempts him into stealing from his bourgeois master. Barnwell eventually murders his rich uncle for his money. Throughout the play, Lillo contrasts the optimistic and benevolent sentiments of the merchant, Thorowgood, with Millwood's deep-rooted resentments (based, interestingly, on her misuse by men). Despite Thorowgood's attempts to save him, a repentant Barnwell dies on the gallows – but not before Lillo props him up as an example of the destructiveness of wanton sexuality. *The London Merchant* achieved surprising popularity and inspired several imitations. Real-life London merchants, who expected the morality of the play to produce wholesome and profitable results, sent their own apprentices to see the show during the Christmas season for the next hundred years.

Watching *The Conscious Lovers*, *The London Merchant*, and other sentimental plays, spectators generally expected to immerse themselves in the feelings of sentimental heroes and those with whom they sympathized. The objects of sympathetic concern in sentimental plays ranged from slaves, to the poor, to distraught heroines, all the way to general pity for suffering humanity. According to sentimental aesthetics, exposure to such feelings on stage would spark a sentimental response in the genteel viewer, who might then use this response to improve his or her own sensitivity and morality. Like *The Tatler* and *The Spectator*, sentimental plays sought to evoke a benevolent community in the audience. Neoclassicism, in contrast, generally kept spectators at a greater emotional distance and involved them more typically in feelings of awe, disdain, and suspense rather than sympathy, pity, and generous good humor.

By the end of the eighteenth century, the battle between sentimentalism and neoclassicism on the London stage had resulted in more pathos in tragedy and more wit and laughter in comedy. The success of several minor genres – ballad opera, pantomime, burlesque, and comic opera – also influenced the development of comedy, mostly by turning it away from sententious moralizing. By the 1790s, the neoclassical tragedies that had dominated the repertory were fading in popularity, and most new comedies had made their peace with a less didactic mode of sentimentalism. Even comic playwrights who professed a dislike for sentimentalism still bowed to most of its precepts. In *She Stoops to Conquer* (1773), Oliver Goldsmith (1730?–1774) derives the central comedy from a mother's love for her foolish son and arranges a sentimental ending for the lovers. Richard Brinsley Sheridan (1751–1816), parliamentarian, theatre manager, and playwright, tweaks the excesses of sentiment and derides those who pose behind a sentimental mask in *The School for Scandal* (1777). But he comes down firmly on the side of paternalistic benevolence and morality in wedlock. By 1780, the bourgeois morality behind sentimentalism had made its way into the dominant culture of England.

Sentiment on the continent

Until the 1789 Revolution, neoclassicism and its absolutist values were more firmly entrenched in France than England. The major French playwright of the eighteenth century, Voltaire (Francois-Marie Arouet, 1694–1778), added significant complexities in plot and characterization to his tragedies, for example, but did not break with neoclassical precepts. Pierre Carlet de Chamblain de Marivaux (1688–1763) injected subtle expressions of feeling into his love comedies, but his heightened prose style kept his plays much less sentimental than Steele's. Nonetheless, sentimental comedy, called *comédie larmoyante*, enjoyed a brief run of popularity in the 1730s and 1740s, with *The False Antipathy* (1733) and other plays by Pierre Claude Nivelle de La Chaussée (1692–1754). In the 1750s, Denis Diderot (1713–1784) urged the adoption of "middle" genres between comedy and tragedy that would encompass sentimental notions of morality and domesticity. As editor and chief writer of the *Encyclopédie*, the first modern compendium of knowledge and a triumph of Enlightenment culture, Diderot argued for a type of comedy emphasizing tears and virtues, domestic tragedy centered on bourgeois family problems (*drame*), and more realistic dialog in all plays. Diderot won many readers throughout literate Europe. A few *drames* based on Diderot's ideas saw production in some French theatres, but the actors at the Comédie Française saw little in the new genre that would advance their careers, and interest in it faded in France. Although the country had a large bourgeoisie by the middle of the eighteenth century, state monopolistic practices retarded the growth of a sentimental, bourgeois theatre in France until after the Revolution.

Despite an early crusade for neoclassicism, by 1780 sentimentalism had taken a firmer hold in the German theatre. Beyond a few court theatres and occasional visits from *commedia dell'arte* troupes, public theatre was in its infancy in Germany at the beginning of the eighteenth century. Still recovering from the devastations of the religious wars, German society could afford little more than performances by fairground troupes, which were nonetheless enjoyed by peasants, workers, burgers, and aristocrats (Figure 5.1). Although these troupes acted a variety of genres, the star of most of them was the clown, who generally performed a character called Hanswurst. This fun-loving, hard-drinking, and often devilish figure combined attributes from several previous clown-figures seen in Germany, including medieval fools, Falstaffian figures (introduced by English actors who played in Germany during the English Civil War), and Harlequins (known to German audiences from *commedia* tours). Within this context, two reformers, Johann Christoph Gottsched (1700–1766) and Caroline Neuber (1697–1760), used their combined companies to introduce several neoclassical innovations into the German theatre after 1727. Gottsched translated and adapted French plays into German, and Neuber staged them and polished their troupe's performance style. Although the Gottsched-Neuber company made some allies among the German aristocracy, they never found a large audience for their neoclassic plays in Leipzig and Hamburg, their primary sites for performance. Both had hoped to banish Hanswurst and the kind of theatre he represented from the stage, but Hanswurst plays at fairground theatres remained popular when their troupe broke in two in 1739.

The turn to sentimentalism in Germany came with the popularity and influence of Gotthold Ephraim Lessing (1727–1781). Lessing was one of the first writers in Germany to make his living from his pen and he gained success as much from his criticism as his plays. Influenced by Diderot, he advocated domestic tragedy in his writings in the 1750s and used these ideas for his middle-class play, *Miss Sara Simpson* (1755), which enjoyed wide popularity.

Figure 5.1 Painting by Joseph Stephan (1780) that includes strolling players and their audience in a market square in Munich. © Bayerisches National-museum, Munich, Photo courtesy The Deutsches Theatermuseum.

By 1759, Lessing was attacking Gottsched and French neoclassicism and advocating Shakespeare as a better model for German theatre. The literary advisor of the Hamburg National Theatre for a short time, Lessing used his *Hamburg Dramaturgy* (1767–1769) to offer a non-neoclassical interpretation of Aristotle's *Poetics* and to urge the writing and production of more sentimental plays. He put this criticism into practice with *Minna von Barnhelm* (1767), a romantic comedy that unites lovers from two sides of a recent war that divided Germany. Like his model Diderot, Lessing was critical of aristocratic privilege and morality and attacked both in his next influential drama, *Emilia Galotti* (1772). Although Lessing did not intend *Nathan the Wise* (1779) for the stage, his dramatic demonstration of the wisdom of toler-ance and understanding among representatives of Judaism, Islam, and Christianity became one of his most widely-produced plays in the German theatre.

Together with other playwrights and companies after 1750, Lessing had helped to ensure that German drama would gravitate more toward sentimentalism than neoclassicism for the rest of the century.

Acting in the eighteenth century

Although actors performed both sentimental and neoclassical plays during the century – and neces-sarily adapted their playing styles to suit each type of production – a gradual change from grand rhetoric toward everyday speech and from heroic to more homey emotions occurred between 1700 and 1790. Acting remained idealized and presentational by today's standards, with performers striking poses, playing directly to the spectators, and inviting applause in the middle of scenes. Nonetheless, the new emphasis on affecting audience emotions grad-ually pushed playing style toward more intimacy and vulnerability. This was possible, in part, because after about 1760 the actors reclaimed the full stage from spectators who had been sitting on a part of it since the beginning of the century. Voltaire and Garrick effected this reform in France and England, respectively, and the relative ease with which they removed stage spectators reflected the increasing social status of actors in Europe.

Several significant performers after 1740 embodied the audience's increasing interest in sentiment. On the London stage, for example, Charles Macklin (1699–1797) altered the traditional clownish interpretation of Shylock in *The Merchant of Venice* to emphasize the character's domestic affections and fierce ambition. In the 1770s, Friedrich Ludwig Schröder (1744–1816) performed the major plays of Lessing and Shakespeare with his company in Hamburg, Germany, with greater attention to his characters' emotions than had been common in the past. At the Comédie Française in the 1750s, Madamoiselle Clarion (Claire-Josephe-Hippolyte Leris de la Tude, 1723–1803) challenged the traditional rhetorical force of French heroic acting by adopting more conversational tones for her tragic roles. Henri-Louis Lekain (1729–1778) followed in her footsteps in the 1760s and garnered applause for his more restrained style in neoclassical tragedy. Because leading actors usually chose their own costumes during this time, Macklin, Schroder, Mlle Clarion, and Lekain also won acclaim for their costuming innovations, which generally shifted stage dress from lavish toward domestic.

The eighteenth-century bourgeoisie, many of them new to the pressures of social performance, welcomed these and other actors as models for enacting their own emotions in public life. This social anxiety, plus genuine curiosity about the actor's craft, prompted a wide range of investigations into stage performing, the first general outpouring of interest in acting since classical times. Among the most significant of these were reflections by Aaron Hill (1685–1750), an English playwright and critic

who published them in his theatrical journal, and *The Paradox of the Actor*, written by Diderot in 1773 (and published posthumously in 1830). Both dealt creatively with problems that still concern actors today.

Hill examined the process used by actors for producing emotion and based his conclusions on the mechanistic assumptions about the body that Cartesian philosophy had made popular among many literate Europeans. Denouncing those who advocated mere rhetorical technique, Hill depicted a three-step process that involved the will operating the body almost as though it were a computer game. First, the actor's imagination was to generate an image of the body expressing a specific emotion. Or, as Hill put it in a poem in *The Prompter*, deploying a print metaphor to capture his Cartesian idea: "Previous to art's first act – (till then, *all vain*) / Print the *ideal pathos*, on the *brain* . . . " (Roach 1985:81). Next, the actor was to allow the "impressions" of the emotion in his mind to play out in his face. Third, facial expression would impel what Hill took to be the "animal spirits" of the mind and nerves to affect and shape the muscles, so that the actor would fully embody the emotion he had first imagined and thus could speak and act accordingly. In the end, wrote Hill, "the *mov'd* actor *Moves* – and passion shakes" (Roach 1985:81). Hill's ideas are similar to modern theories that assume that the actor's mind can trick the body into automatically producing the necessary emotions for a role.

Diderot also built his ideas upon mechanistic Cartesian assumptions, but broke with Hill (and most other acting theorists of his time) to argue that emotion actually got in the way of good acting technique. Like Hill, Diderot believed that the actor must use observation, imagination, and rehearsing to create an inner model of the character, but this preparation provided the basis for enacting an illusion of that character, not embodying the figure's actual emotions in performance. From Diderot's point of view, actors who relied on spontaneity and emotion rather than study and technique reduced the character to themselves, undercut the illusion of the character's emotional life for the audience, and compromised the range of characters they could create. In *The Paradox of the Actor*, Diderot praised performers who could marry a flexible vocal and physical technique to a perfect conception of the role and its emotional dynamics, thus enabling them to present their character in exactly the same way at every performance. Aware that enacting even the illusions of various emotions would tend to involve the actors in experiencing them directly, Diderot drew on Enlightenment science to argue that actors could effectively separate their minds from their bodies and control themselves on stage, much as a puppeteer controls a puppet. As we will see, Diderot's cool-headed, self-manipulative actor might be compared to the ideal actor of Meyerhold and Brecht in the twentieth century.

Diderot held up Mlle Clairon and David Garrick as exemplars of his theory. He had watched Garrick perform a parlor entertainment in which the great actor shifted his facial expressions instantly to embody a wide range of characters, much to the amazement and delight of his Parisian hosts. Diderot published his *Observations on Garrick* in 1770, and it is clear that the English star significantly influenced his thoughts on acting. Garrick's conscious creation of images of himself through engravings is the focus of our first case study in this chapter.

Feeling and knowledge in Kathakali dance-drama

While David Garrick delighted Parisian parlor audiences with the plasticity of his ability to shift among emotions, performers in Kerala, India developed a highly popular form of dance-drama called kathakali in the sixteenth century that pleased audiences with measured changes in emotion. Kathakali literally means "story" (*kathā*), "dance" or "play" (*kali*). Like other forms of Indian performance, kathakali playwrights often adapted their dramas from episodes in

the Indian epics (the *Mahabharata* and *Ramayana*) or from stories about Lord Krishna. Wealthy rulers and land-holders in Kerala usually sponsored the productions, which were performed by all-male companies of actor-dancers accompanied by percussionists and vocalists and generally lasted an entire night. The actor-dancers developed and still use a highly physicalized style of performance based on traditional martial arts to play a variety of roles, which included kings, heroines, peasants, male and female gods and demons, and even animals. Although singers vocalized all of the third-person narrative and first-person dialog in the play texts, the actor-dancers deployed a complex language of gesture and expression to communicate the emotions and actions of their characters.

To be able to embody these states of being/doing, kathakali performers trained their bodies, eyes, and facial muscles with techniques derived from kutiyattam (see Chapter 3) to a point where they were capable of instantaneous shifts from one expressive state to another. The training of the kathakali actor evolved so that he learned to direct his passions partly by controlling his breath. In the famous play *Nalacaritam* (*First Day*), by Unnayi Variyar (c.1675–1716), for instance, the performer playing the male hero, Nala, must progress from reflection to sorrow to pain in one scene of the drama. Reflecting about his unrequited love for the beautiful heroine of the play, the traditionally-trained actor who played Nala would initially embody *cinta bhava*, the state of reflecting, through an interior psycho-physiological process that infused his facial expression with contemplation and hope. When the vocalist, following the script, sang that Nala's "mind was pained by sorrow," the actor took a quick breath and moved his right hand to his chest as his eyes looked up to the sky. Then, after his slow exhalation of breath, the traditional actor would have allowed his eyes to trace a line downward to the ground as he heaved a deep sigh. Kathakali actors still use these techniques to perform *Nalacaritam*. Although Indian actors in the eighteenth century described their artistry in terms that would have puzzled Diderot, the emphasis on technique and repeatability and the understanding of the body and breath as the basis of emotion may be compared in general to Diderot's notions of acting.

The reception of kathakali by a Kerala audience differed substantially from the response of Europeans to sentimental theatre in the eighteenth century. Like most other traditions of Indian dance-drama, kathakali drew on the aesthetics of *rasa*, literally "flavor" or "taste." Kathakali actor-dancers working with *rasa* aesthetics as a goal would strive to provide their spectators with a variety of "tastes" or dominant states of emotion. The actor playing Nala above, for example, was expected to take as long as he needed to embody the emotions of reflection, sorrow, and pain, partly to allow the spectators to savor his artistry. Unlike the aesthetics of sentimental response, the aim for the spectator was not simply to immerse his or her self in the same emotions as those experienced by sympathetic characters, but to respond to the different "flavors" offered by the performers so as to achieve a heightened, non-ordinary aesthetic state. In India, unlike the West, the terms for "reason" and "emotion" do not connote opposing states of mind and feeling. Tasting the *rasas* of dance-dramas over time refined the spectator's ability to appreciate not only the arts of drama, dance, music, and poetry, but also life as it is experienced.

Clearly, the social, cultural, and economic conditions of Kerala produced a very different theatre than that of Western Europe in the eighteenth century. European bourgeois spectators, for whom time was fast becoming money, would not have sat through an all-night performance in which the experience of a variety of emotions was the primary source of pleasure. In India as in China, the merchant class had not become a bourgeoisie and did not question the traditional Indian union of emotion and reason. Nor had Kerala and the rest of India yet shifted from a manuscript to a print culture. Rather, kathakali developed in response to a change in traditional Kerala culture, the growth of religious devotionalism to Vishnu, one of the three primary Hindu deities. These vast historical and cultural differences help to explain the major disparities between Kerala and Europe in the eighteenth century. While some similarities in acting preparation and presentation are apparent between kathakali performance and European acting, these can be partly explained on the basis of the broad similarities that all humans share in experiencing emotion.

The Progeny of Krishna case study below provides a detailed example of one of kathakali's popular plays in which the performance of emotional states occurs within the context of Indian *rasa* aesthetics.

Changes and challenges in sentimentalism

Although the French Revolution would shatter genteel sentimentalism irreversibly in Europe, there were several cracks in the sentimental vase before 1789. At one extreme of eighteenth-century sentimentalism was the cult of sincerity that drew its ideas from Jean-Jacques Rousseau (1712–1778). In his writings, Rousseau criticized Enlightenment rationalism and celebrated natural, sincere, authentic humanity, unencumbered by social masks. These ideas eventually led Rousseau to damn the theatre because acting necessarily trades in what he took to be duplicitous role-playing. Despite Rousseau's antitheatrical prejudices, his ideas carried wide influence in the theatre and culture of his time, both before and after the Revolution, and shaped the work of several playwrights.

Rousseau's extreme version of sentimentalism fired the imagination of a young generation of German playwrights, loosely grouped together as the Storm and Stress movement. Friedrich Maximilian Klinger's (1752–1831) *Sturm und Drang* (1776), which posed Rousseau's natural, sentimental humanity against the restrictions of rationality, gave the movement its name (Figure 5.2). Not all in this rebellious generation of playwrights embraced Rousseau, but most rejected Lessing's synthesis of sentimental and Enlightenment values and challenged conventional social norms. Recognizing the natural sexual desires of young soldiers, for example, Jacob M.R. Lenz's (1751–1792) *The Soldiers* (1776) advocated state-sponsored prostitution. Although many Storm and Stress plays, including *The Soldiers*, never made it past German censorship and into performance, several circulated in print. Three plays from this movement, however, gained some productions and are still in the standard German repertory: *Goetz von Berlichingen* (1773), by Johann Wolfgang

von Goethe (1749–1832), and *The Robbers* (1782) and *Fiesko* (1782), by Friedrich Schiller (1759–1865).

Another German playwright, Friedrich von Kotzebue (1761–1819), avoided the dramatic and social excesses of the Storm and Stress movement, but popularized its rejection of rationalism and its general embrace of Rousseau. Kotzebue's first hit, *Misanthropy and Repentance* (1787) – a pot-boiler stuffed with Rousseauian sentiments, pathetic situations, comic relief, romantic love, and moral didacticism – set the formula for his later successes. Several of Kotzebue's more than 200 plays retained popularity for the next 70 years in translations and adaptations in Russia and the United States as well as in Western Europe. Among his most successful plays

Figure 5.2 A scene from Friedrich Maximilian Klinger's *The Twins*, a Storm and Stress play, in a contemporary engraving by Albrecht. © Osterreichische Nationalbibliothek, Vienna.

were *The Stranger*, *Pizarro in Peru*, and *Lovers' Vows* (to use their English titles). Kotzebue explored the democratic potential of Rousseau's philosophy in theatrical terms. Where most previous sentimental plays had invited middle-class audiences to test their sentimental feelings and ethics within a genteel and rational framework, Kotzebue's dramas appealed to a wider audience by encouraging them to believe that all people, with or without enlightened reason, were already natural, ethical, and authentic human beings. By downplaying rationality and democratizing sentiment, Kotzebue's plays anticipated a significant aspect of nineteenth-century melodrama.

Gothic thrillers anticipated another. Sentimentalism had never arrived at an adequate explanation for evil. If human nature were essentially good, as the moral philosophers, Rousseau, and most other Enlightenment thinkers believed, sentimentalism could not explain the perseverance of evil in the world. Gothicism, popular first in novels and then on stage after the mid-1790s, explored this shortcoming of sentimentalism in English and American theatres. At the center of the gothic thriller was the hero-villain, usually a remorseful but still passionate figure who rules female captives and fights ghosts from his past in a crumbling castle. Although these hero-villains struggle in proper sentimental fashion to reform, most go to their deaths without renouncing their desire for lust and revenge. In such plays as *The Castle Spectre* (1797) and *Blue Beard* (1798), gothicism offered no complete answer for the evil of such protagonists, but it did fix images of horror that fascinated audiences – all the more so because the spectators' sentimentalism could not explain the evil they witnessed. Gothic thrillers continued to be popular on English-language stages well into the 1820s.

Melodrama and the French Revolution

While inherent excesses and problems with sentimentalism laid the groundwork for melodrama, the shock of the French Revolution provided a more general cause for its emergence and its immense popularity during the nineteenth century. In 1789, many Europeans looked to France as the most prosperous and civilized country in the world. The bourgeoisie who read periodicals and shared the values of the Enlightenment welcomed most of the first stages of the Revolution, such as the Declaration of the Rights of Man, the abolition of state monopolies, and the attempt to separate the French Catholic Church from the power of Rome. With the beheading of the King and the Reign of Terror (1792–1795), in which Enlightenment principles were deployed to justify revolutionary slaughter, however, many literate Europeans saw the utopia they had hoped for in France slide into chaos and horror. The political turmoil, civil strife, and international wars of the late 1790s brought more confusion, and many Europeans were relieved when Napoleon emerged as a strong leader in 1799. Although Bonaparte's rule ensured stability in France, his imperial ambitions soon brought parts of the Revolution to the rest of Europe and engulfed the entire western world in intermittent warfare until 1815.

How were Europeans to come to terms with what was happening in France and Europe during the revolutionary era of 1789–1815? Conspiracies, prompted by individual villainy, provided perhaps the easiest answer and many people adopted this melodramatic explanation because it left them free of complicity and guilt. The dynamic of the Revolution itself and the wars that followed enjoined Europeans to make absolute distinctions between friend and foe, hero and villain, "us" and "them." In addition, the Revolution (coupled with Rousseauian thinking) had induced a desire for utopia, the conviction that naturally good people might create a society in which evil could be banished from the world. Revolution and war degraded the value of enlightened reason, which many believed had led to The Terror, and elevated nature and intuition as better guides to morality and possible utopia.

Consequently, in the wake of the Revolution, melodrama retained the moral urgency and appeal to natural feelings of late eighteenth-century sentimentalism, but simplified its ethics. The first melodramas presented a world in which a traditional utopia of order and happiness was just around the corner if only the good people used their intuition to root out and banish the bad people from society. This was effectively the plot of *Coelina, Or the Child of Mystery* (1800), by Guilbert de Pixérécourt (1773–1844), which was soon translated and adapted by Thomas Holcroft (1745–1809) for the English stage as *A Tale of Mystery*. Significantly, the original and the adaptation embrace different political points of view, an early indication of the flexibility that would help to keep melodrama on the boards (and, later, on film and television screens) for a long time. While Pixérécourt's version emphasizes the restoration of absolutist values in a French village, it also bows to the superior intuition of commoners and the utopian hope of regaining a past free of bourgeois greed. In his English adaptation, Holcroft, a political radical, emphasized utopian possibilities and the honesty of the common people and erased most of Pixérécourt's reactionary Catholicism.

Melodramatic spectacle

The demands of melodrama, plus improved technology, led to an expansion of theatrical spectacle. In 1800, painted flats, rigged for chariot-and-pole or wing-and-shutter changes, remained the dominant mode of scenic representation in Europe. On the London stage, Philippe Jacques DeLoutherbourg (1740–1812) had expanded the possibilities of this mode of staging through the addition of ground rows masking the bottoms of flats and drops, better lighting, attention to the unity of design, and other reforms. But the basics of perspectival illusionism had changed little for a hundred and fifty years. Part of the appeal of melodrama, however (and another similarity tying it to the culture of the French Revolution) was its interest in hiding nothing from

the public. Where neoclassical and sentimental theatre generally kept violence offstage, melodrama reveled in physical combat and spectacular calamity.

The melodramatic mandate to show all tested the limits of the illusionist stage and kept inventors and technicians busy throughout the nineteenth century. Several early melodramas set in exotic lands demanded the construction of practical land bridges and waterfalls. As the size of stages expanded to accommodate the increased demand for spectacle, playwrights called for more three-dimensional scenic units – fortresses that could collapse in an explosion and a mountain up which a horse and rider could ascend to near the top of the proscenium, for example. A craze for nautical melodramas in the 1840s led several theatre managers to invest in huge water tanks, expensive pumps, and partly-rigged ships and cannons. As candlelight changed to gaslight for general theatrical illumination after 1825, the possibilities for spectacle skyrocketed. Now the auditorium could be partially darkened to increase the on-stage effectiveness of steamboat explosions and erupting volcanoes. By the 1880s, sinking ships, steaming trains, and galloping horses – the latter done with treadmills and revolving scenery – stretched the ingenuity and endurance of technicians and stagehands (Figure 5.3). All of these devices and effects, of course, would later be taken over, improved upon, and eventually digitized by Hollywood in the next century.

Melodrama gains spectators

Although some audiences initially rejected melodrama as obvious and crude, the genre proved flexible and diverse enough to overcome most objections to it by the 1880s. Working-class spectators, attending the theatre in increasing numbers after the 1820s, enjoyed plays like *The Carpenter of Rouen* (1837) that pitted plebeian avengers against decadent aristocrats. Temperance and abolitionist melodramas like *The Bottle* (1847) and *Uncle Tom's Cabin* (1852) converted some sober, even antitheatrical Protestants to playgoing. After 1840, many star-struck playgoers

Figure 5.3 1890 print showing the mechanics for staging a horserace, which involved a moving panorama and treadmills, using electric motors, at the Union Square Theatre in New York. From George Moynet, *La Machinerie Théâtrale* (1893). © Bibliothéque Nationale de France.

enjoyed their favorites in melodramatic spectacles. Charlotte Cushman (1816–1876) gained prominence and legitimacy in her performance as a cross-dressed Romeo in Shakespeare's tragedy, but audiences knew her best from her electric performance as the preternaturally prophetic old woman in the melodrama, *Guy Mannering*, which she played for much of her long career. English star Henry Irving's (1838–1905) most famous role was Mathias in *The Bells*, a haunted figure who robbed and murdered to gain success early in his career (Figure 5.4). As we will see in the next chapter, melodrama mixed easily with romantic drama and also organized the dramatic plots of many nationalistic war plays.

After 1850, many melodramatists incorporated aspects of the well-made play into their plots. French playwright Eugène Scribe (1791–1861) pioneered the form, which was later perfected by Victorien Sardou (1831–1908). In brief, the plot of the well-made play depends on a secret, known to a few characters and the audience, on which the fate of many – perhaps an entire nation – hangs. Through the clever manipulation of chance and circumstance, all of which must appear logical and plausible, the playwright leads the audience to an "obligatory scene" in which the secret is revealed and the characters must resolve their conflicts. Dion Boucicault (1822–1890) was one of the first dramatists to successfully merge melodrama and the well-made play, thereby lending melodrama much more flexibility than before. In the last case study following this chapter, we examine Boucicault's alterations to melodramatic form and the changes to bourgeois values they reflect.

Figure 5.4 Henry Irving in his production of *The Bells* at the Lyceum Theatre, London, 1871. © V&A Images, Victoria and Albert Museum.

The combination of melodrama and the well-made play shaped many successful dramas at the end of the nineteenth century. Several English playwrights linked the two to dramatize social problems among them Henry Arthur Jones (1851–1929) whose *Mrs. Dane's Defense* (1900) examined the scandal of "the woman with a past." In London and Paris, Victorien Sardou's *Robespierre* (1899) painted a melodramatic picture of The Terror during the French Revolution, using over three hundred actors. In New York, *The City* (1909) by Clyde Fitch configured the moral adjustments necessary for urban life as melodramatic problems with individual solutions. These productions used the conventional realism of the era to reinforce their melodramatic messages (on the rise of realism, see the Introduction to Part III). As had sentimental theatre before it, the melodramatic stage had become a part of the dominant culture of the bourgeoisie.

BMc

Key references

For further references for this chapter, see the Key references at the end of the Introduction to Part II.

Collier, J. (1974) "A Short View of the Immorality and Profaneness of the English Stage" [1698], in B.F. Dukore (ed.) *Dramatic Theory and Criticism*, New York: Holt, Rinehart and Winston.

Kramnick, I. (ed.) (1995) *The Portable Enlightenment Reader*, London: Penguin.

Roach, J.R. (1985 [reprinted 1993]) *The Player's Passion: Studies in the Science of Acting*, Ann Arbor: University of Michigan Press.

CASE STUDY: Theatre iconology and the actor as icon: David Garrick

Theatre is a transitory art that thrives in the air of that brief, vanishing cultural moment that a performer and audience share. Past performances cannot be hung in a museum or replayed from a score. To appreciate performances of the past, theatre historians turn to several kinds of primary sources, among them, pictorial representations, which pose both intriguing opportunities and problems. This case study offers examples of interpretive *iconological* analysis of such images, here informed by cultural studies. Iconology is used here, following Erwin Panofsky (1955), rather than "iconography." The latter term has been more associated with the work of documentation, such as results in a catalog of paintings, prints and sculptures on the same subject (say David Garrick), or in a survey of the visual vocabulary conventionally used in art across the ages of, for example, a particular biblical prophet or Hindu god. This case study discusses four pictorial representations of the famous English actor, David Garrick (1717–1779), with particular emphasis on the relation between these images and two culturally important issues of the eighteenth century: moral sincerity and England's quest for a national identity. Garrick was a significant – and richly signifying – figure in the English people's construction of their personal and national identity.

As a gifted actor, manager, and playwright, Garrick dominated the British stage and became a focal point in British culture across the mid-century. In his debut, he astonished London as Shakespeare's Richard III in a small, unlicensed theatre in 1741. His first biographer, Thomas Davies, wrote: "Mr. Garrick shone forth like theatrical Newton; he threw new light on elocution and acting; he banished ranting, bombast, and grimace, and restored nature, ease, simplicity, and genuine humor" (Davies 1780:I, 43). All of fashionable London turned out to see him; poet Alexander Pope went three times. Garrick became the leading actor at Drury Lane Theatre, where, within a few years, he won extraordinary acclaim for his performances in his signature roles, tragic and comic, including Hamlet, King Lear, Macbeth, Archer in *The Beaux' Stratagem* (1707) by George Farquhar (1678–1707), and Abel Drugger in Garrick's own adaptation of Ben Jonson's *The Alchemist* (1743). As artistic manager of Drury Lane from 1747 to 1776, Garrick was especially dedicated to Shakespeare, staging 26 of the plays and playing leading roles in 14. With his 1769 Shakespeare "Jubilee," he made Stratford-upon-Avon a site for literary pilgrimages, capping his promotion of Shakespeare as the national poet. He framed his dedication to Shakespeare and to the national and moral agendas as one and the same.

His successes derived from the combination of his genius in the role – on stage and off – as the new "natural man" of reason and moral sensibility. Easy and graceful in motion, with a quick intelligence, Garrick planned his performances meticulously, offering a model of the century's scientific ideal of the rational soul governing the mechanical body. He blended his physical and vocal grace with the virtue and manner of the Lockean "natural man," which is to say, the self-possessed man of vital moral sympathy, in whose bosom was the potential for the virtue and the benevolence toward others that the new social order required (see Chapter 5 on "sentimentalism"). Garrick (born of a relatively poor family) thus offered the persona of a gentleman by nature more than by title, a persona seen in some of the key plays of the period, such *The Beaux' Stratagem*. This made him an appealing figure for an England still negotiating its transition from an old social order, which had its roots in the concept of a divinely ordained, absolutist monarchy, toward a relatively democratized monarchy and a new social order based on civic and personal virtue. The middle, merchant class saw itself as the national moral and economic foundation of this new social order.

Garrick is an ideal figure for iconological studies; portraits of him have been the subject of many articles and exhibitions. The number of engraved portraits of him in the British Museum is exceeded only by those of Queen Victoria. The painting of him as Richard III by William Hogarth (1697–1774) is perhaps the most famous portrait of a western actor ever done (Figure 5.5). Among other major English artists who did portraits of him, in his roles or in private life, were Joshua Reynolds, Thomas Gainsborough, Johann Zoffany, Benjamin Wilson, Nathaniel Dance, and Angelica Kauffmann. Louis François Roubiliac did neoclassical busts of Garrick in marble and bronze, and images of him appeared on porcelain dishes, silver tea caddies, enameled boxes, and medallions. Garrick was arguably the West's first modern commodified celebrity.

He himself did much to bring that about. He commissioned many paintings and prints of himself in performance and circulated them. Visiting Paris in 1764 as England's most famous actor, he wrote back urgently requesting prints for distribution to friends and fans. He also commissioned portraits of himself in his off-stage role of the natural gentleman, a role that straddled old and new ideas of class.

Moreover, he conceived his performances with a visual acuity that intersected perfectly with trends in English art (Garrick was a knowledgeable collector) and theatre. Garrick was among the first of a younger generation of actors with a freer physical style and more appeal for the eye than had been in the case of the older, declamatory school, which emphasized classical, rhetorical music for the ear. He was, as Michael Wilson has suggested, also well aware

Figure 5.5 *Mr. Garrick in "Richard III,"* engraving by William Hogarth and Charles Grignion, 1746, based on Hogarth's painting. The print was being printed and sold throughout most of David Garrick's career. There were many other paintings and prints of him in the role. © Gary Jay and Josephine S. Williams.

of the visual lexicon of painters of the time for portraying the passions. Applying this knowledge to his acting, Garrick brought a visual legitimacy to the stage that aligned performance with the long dominant legitimacy of the literary drama. Hogarth expert Ronald Paulson makes a key point about Hogarth's painting of Garrick as Richard III: "If Hogarth tended to make his painting look like a play, Garrick made his play look like a painting" (Paulson 1992:III, 250). Maria Ines Aliverti nicely observes that in Garrick's era, "actors affect the art and practice of making portraits . . . because they create images that generate portraits" (Aliverti 1997:243). Garrick might be described as an iconic actor in his acute use of visually arresting poses, which he planned carefully. He then reified these images in paintings and prints – the visual media of his time. By commissioning paintings and prints of them, he advanced his career and his performances into the national social consciousness. Today, this kind of self-conscious use of the media is familiar in almost every corner of the world. Garrick's entrepreneurialism might be compared to that of many modern stars, such as Prince, Madonna, or Michael Jackson.

INTERPRETIVE APPROACH: Cultural studies and theatre iconology

Theatre iconology is used here to denote the interpretive analyses of theatre and performance-related pictorial representations, such as prints, paintings, and photographs, to better understand the theatre of the past, and, in this case study, to understand the cultural forces that shaped the images. In recent scholarship, pictorial sources are being used with an awareness that any representation of performance will itself be the product of many forces at play in the culture of the time. Such images are as valuable, perhaps more so, for what they can tell us about the social formations in which actor and audience, painter and viewer participated as they are as literal depictions of performance.

Analyzing images in this way will involve, as Christopher B. Balme notes, the interpretive task of "uncovering the semantics of a painting's 'sign language' and its relation to the larger social formation" (Balme, 1997:193). To uncover what Balme calls "the semantics of a painting's 'sign language'" is to approach the work as a cultural phenomenon in which there are underlying, tacit conventions and codes. A picture presents us with an inherited system for making meaning within a particular culture. While pictorial representations may aspire to the general truth-level of myth, as Roland Barthes notes (Barthes 1973:117–174), they are always constructions of reality, embedded with value choices. The cultural historian's task may involve some demystification in order to understand the cultural forces at work in a pictorial representation. Among the sign-systems in a painting to be considered are the usual compositional ones: choice, size, and placement of the main figure and its spatial relation to other figures, the relation between the figure(s) and their environment, or their clothing, gestures, or postures – but as matters revealing social relations. (The discussion below of Hogarth's *David Garrick as Richard III* offers examples of this kind

▷

▷

of analysis.) Such analysis draws on the field of semiotics, which began with the study of language but expanded to consider how meanings inhere in all kinds of human endeavor, from the use of colors in military uniforms to the rules for social rituals or athletic games. (See the case study on Brechtian theatre following Chapter 9 for more on semiotics.) Not only the painting or print itself, but the circumstances of its production and distribution also can tell us what cultural work it was doing. For example, the analyses here point to the fact the Garrick images were produced in response to a new market for accessibly-priced prints of popular actors. This is a symptom of middle-class economic development to which enterprising artists responded, a variation on print capitalism. Garrick's acting choices were influenced by the eighteenth-century media, as we shall see.

The analysis of a painting and print representing a performance may also involve examining it in relation to all the other theatrical primary sources on the performance, such as eyewitness accounts and promptbooks (play texts annotated by those involved in the production), or other related paintings and prints. The analysis of such visual resources requires some understanding of the conventions of the art. Portraits of actors in Garrick's day reveal more about individual personalities than did those in the preceding period, which were in the French neoclassical mode that monumentalized actors. To take an eighteenth-century example from Japan, the study of kabuki theatre using the contemporary color prints of kabuki actors would need to consider the conventions of this special genre of *ukioy-e* woodcuts. Also, artists derive some of their compositional vocabulary from the works of other artists, as will be seen in the discussion of Hogarth's composition below. Artists of Garrick's time drew on a widely published illustrated book that offered a science of archetypal facial expressions of emotions (horror, anger, surprise, grief), *Methode pour apprendre à dessiner les Passions* (*A Method for Learning to Delineate the Passions*) by Charles Le Brun (1619–1690), President of the French Academy. Both Hogarth and Garrick knew the work. In Hogarth's painting, *Mr. Garrick as Richard III* (Figure 5.5), Garrick's expression of horror and amazement is closer to Le Brun's sketch of an archetypal expression of horror than to a likeness of Garrick. Denis Diderot described Garrick doing a demonstration of Le Brun-like expressions when Garrick visited Paris in 1764 (Diderot 1957:32–33) (compare Figure II.8.).

Iconological studies may also look at scenery, costumes, and staging arrangements. Pierre Louis Ducharte's *The Italian Comedy* (1929) draws on 259 prints, paintings, and drawings as sources for the costumes, properties, and poses typical of each of the stock characters of the *commedia dell'arte*. Martin Meisel's *Realizations* (1983). explores relations between nineteenth-century fiction, painting, and drama.

Some key questions that could be asked in analyzing any pictorial representation of a performance are below.

▷

▷
KEY QUESTIONS

1   How does the image correspond to other primary sources on this production – promptbooks, eyewitness descriptions?

2   Why was this subject of special interest?

3   What are the circumstances of its production – Who did it? Who commissioned it? Who benefited?

4   What cultural ideals of the time did it reinforce (or critique)? How does it compare with the conventions of other works of the time? What does it reveal about class, gender, or race?

5   If any stories travel with this picture, what might lie behind their construction?

Thirty Garricks

One comic color print made in England in the mid-nineteenth century serves both as an amusing index to the Garrick image industry and as an insight into the English fascination with him. *Garrick and Hogarth or The Artist Puzzled* (1845) by R. Evan Sly was based on an amusing anecdote about a Hogarth-Garrick skirmish that appeared in a London newspaper several years after Garrick's death (Figure 5.6). Reportedly, every time Hogarth thought he had captured Garrick's likeness in a painting session, the actor mischievously changed his expression (by all accounts, Garrick's expressive face was famously mobile, never at rest, even offstage). Discovering the trick, Hogarth drove Garrick from his studio in a hail of brushes (Paulson 1971:285–286). Sly used a clever mechanical device to capture the mercurial Garrick face. He placed a rotating wheel on the back of the print so the viewer can change the face of Garrick on Hogarth's canvas and the face on the seated actor, bringing into view thirty different likenesses of Garrick – which are, in fact, caricatures of other artists' portraits of him. The faces in the sketches on the floor – caricatures of other Hogarth's works – also change (you can see this print in color and all the thirty likenesses on the Folger Shakespeare Library's website on Garrick: <www.folger.edu/garrick>). The dog at left, whose knowing look at

the viewer heightens the joke on Hogarth, is Sly's borrowing from a Hogarth self-portrait with his dog, Pug (1745).

The anecdote that Sly's print illustrates is the kind of lore about celebrity actors of which the public in any era is fond. The public often wants to get a fix on the "real" identity of the actor who so ably constructs different personas. The print also might be seen as a joke on two famous image-makers. However, its main subject is the protean★ Garrick.

The tale on which this print was based was probably an embellished one; its construction and repetition (there was a Gainsborough version) suggests some complexity in the fascination with Garrick. Behind the tale and the print was a paradox: the figure who had become a national exemplar as a natural gentleman was an actor, a very adroit member of a profession that was historically suspect, morally and socially. Eighteenth-century English audiences with a hunger for outward signs of interior moral sincerity were enthralled with a talented professional who was skilled in creating meticulous semblances of sincerity. Could an actor be a natural, virtuous gentleman? The question went to both class and morality. Horace Walpole seems to have been

★From the Greek myth of Proteus, a sea god who could change shapes at will.

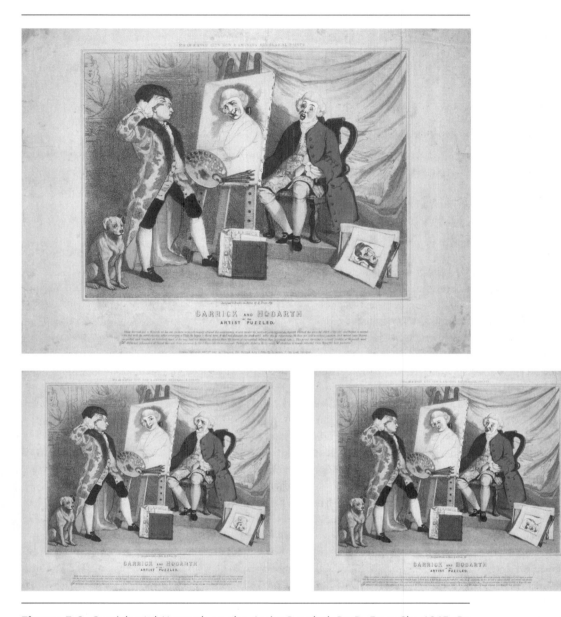

Figure 5.6 *Garrick and Hogarth or the Artist Puzzled*. By R. Evan Sly, 1845. By rotating a wheel on the back of Sly's print, the face on Hogarth's canvas and the face on the seated actor can be changed, bringing into view 30 different likenesses of Garrick. (Available in color at <www.folger.edu/garrick>.) The print is based on an eighteenth-century anecdote that is evidence of the public fascination with the protean Garrick. © The Trustees of the British Museum.

sniping at Garrick for class jumping when he warned his friend, Sir Horace Mann, the British Envoy in Florence, "Be a little on your guard, remember he is an actor" (Shawe-Taylor 2003:11.) Morally, the English had been through a war against the art and the whole theatre profession, led by the 1698 book by the cleric, Jeremy Collier, *A Short View of the Immorality and Profaneness of the English Stage*. Collier had accused the theatre of threatening the moral welfare of the nation. Joseph Addison (1672–1719) and Richard Steele (1672–1723) had then set out the moral majority program for a national theatre of virtue in their newspapers and provided plays for it (see Chapter 5). Appealing as Garrick was, in this moral climate the fascination with his face-changing skill betrays some anxiety about both the class and moral center of the actor: could an actor be the paradigm of the sincere, natural, virtuous man? In addition, there was not only Garrick the meticulous actor, but Garrick the adroit manager of many media images of himself – prints and paintings. The late twentieth century offers an instructive comparison. The American public was similarly intrigued when an attractive Hollywood actor became the President of the United States and a spokesperson for the conservative right. Was Ronald Reagan acting or was he sincere? How much of the public impression of him was the result of clever management of his image in the media? David Garrick managed to perform his roles and himself successfully. Sixty-six years after Garrick's death, Sly's print could still play broadly with the legend of the famous image-maker.

Four Richards III

In Hogarth's *Mr. Garrick as Richard III*, there is Garrick and more. Garrick debuted in 1741 in the Shakespearean role, as compelling a protean character as any in western drama. Plotting his ascent from Duke of Gloucester to King of England, Richard vows (in an earlier Shakespeare play that includes him), to deceive everyone like a good actor and to kill anyone between himself and the throne:

Why I can smile, and murder whiles I smile,
And cry 'Content' to that which grieves my heart,
And wet my cheeks with artificial tears,
And frame my face to all occasions.
[. . .]
I can add colours to the chameleon,
Change shapes with Proteus for advantages,
And set the murderous Machiavel to school.
Can I do this, and cannot get a crown?
Tut, were it farther off, I'll pluck it down.
(*Henry VI*, Part 3, 3.2:182–195,
in Greenblatt 1997)

His deception and murders bring him to the throne, but they finally result in his overthrow and death in battle at the hands of the decent Earl of Richmond, Henry Tudor.

Hogarth's painting represents the moment when, on the night before the battle, Richard wakes in his tent from a dream in which he has been visited by the ten souls of those he killed, including his king, his brother, his two young nephews, and his wife. Awaking terrified, he cries out, "Give me another horse! Bind up my wounds! / Have mercy, Jesu! – Soft, I did but dream. / O coward conscience, how doest thou afflict me?" (*Richard III*, 5.5.131–133). The adaptation of the play by Colley Cibber that Garrick used stressed Richard's villainy heavily, and, in this scene, Cibber added the ghosts' demand that Richard "wake in all the hells of guilt," which he does, though he goes on to fight to his death.

For a mid-eighteenth-century English audience, this anguished recognition of his sins by this, the most evil of men, would have been a critical moral turn, and Garrick turned it into a moral awakening of great visual power, meticulously arranged. Arthur Murphy, a contemporary playwright and Garrick biographer, wrote, "His soliloquy in the tent scene discovered *the inward man* [italics added]," a code phrase in England's age of moral sensibility signifying the natural, inner potential for good in humankind.

Hogarth renders Richard's expression of horror in the wide eyes that stare out over the shoulder of the viewer of the portrait and in the outstretched arm and extended fingers. However, Hogarth does not render Garrick's face with portrait particularity, nor is the figure and costume in the natural mode of that in his earlier theatrical paintings of *The Beggar's Opera* (1728–1729). Rather, the painting of Richard III is rendering the theatrical moment in the grand manner of history painting, a genre in which Hogarth had worked in the previous decade. Hogarth took his general composition from Le Brun's *Tent of Darius*; the voluminous flowing robes and other fabrics were painterly strokes to convey nobility. The painting's huge size – over eight ft long and six ft high – is in the mode of history painting, and here it magnifies and ennobles the figure of King Richard. This Richard is, then, a combination of four Richards III: the Richard of Garrick – meticulous master of the morally iconic moment, the Richard of English history, the Richard of Shakespeare, the great national poet (which Garrick was promoting in his playhouse), and the Richard of Hogarth, by then the great English artist. Each

presence complements the other. Together they constitute a national narrative aspiring to the status of myth. The buyer, Thomas (William?) Duncombe, paid two hundred pounds for the painting, more than had ever been paid to an English painter for a portrait (Paulson, 1992:3, 256–257). The engraving that followed shortly after served the interests of both Garrick and Hogarth. Painting and print inspired a new vogue of theatrical portraiture. Analyzing the work and its cultural valences today, we can see not only a vestige of Garrick's iconic performance but the ways in which the image was speaking from, and to the English people's construction of their national identity in the eighteenth century.

Two rivals, two prints

Many other of Garrick's performances resulted in images suitable for framing, including those of his Hamlet and Lear, considered briefly here (Figures 5.7, 5.8). James McArdell did mezzotints★ of him in these roles. Published in 1754 and 1761, respectively, they

★The mezzotint represented a new kind of engraving technology in which a special tool created surface texturing on the paper that allowed inking in gradations of shading and subtle chiaroscuro effects.

Figure 5.7 *Mr. Garrick in Hamlet*, mezzotint by James McArdell, 1754, after a painting by Benjamin Wilson, depicting Hamlet's encounter with his father's ghost. © The Folger Shakespeare Library, Washington, D.C. Folger Art file G241 no. 94.

Figure 5.8 *Mr. Garrick in the Character of King Lear*, mezzotint, hand-colored, by James McArdell, 1761, after a painting by Benjamin Wilson. With the mad Lear in the storm scene are Kent (Astley Bransby) and Edgar (William Havard). The Fool is missing because he was cut from Nahum Tate's sentimental adaptation. Neoclassicism dictated that comedy and tragedy should not be mixed. © Gary Jay and Josephine S. Williams.

were based on paintings (both lost) by Benjamin Wilson (1722–1788). (Zoffany also painted the same scene from Hamlet.) Both images seem to aspire to the effects of Hogarth's hugely successful portrait of Richard III. Both advance Garrick's moral agenda. Collaboration among actor, painter, and printmaker on both is very probable. Also, in both instances, Spranger Barry, the "silver-tongued" actor who was a close competitor of Garrick, was playing these same roles at the rival theatre, Covent Garden, at about the time that each of the Garrick images was published. Garrick may have had McArdell do these prints to imprint Garrick's triumph in these roles in the public mind.

Garrick took special visual care with both scenes. He was proud of the scene from Hamlet, performing it in private for friends. He reportedly used a mechanical wig that he could manipulate to make his hair rise in fright, the better to capture scientifically Hamlet's horror and the actor's rational mastery of his craft. The effect seems to be apparent in McArdell's print (Figure 5.7). The print is corroborated by a detailed description of the scene by Georg Christoph Lichtenberg who saw a performance. Garrick's sentimentalized Lear, seen in Figure 5.8, is frail and vulnerable in the storm scene. Garrick's performance was of a piece with the Nahum Tate adaptation that he used. Lear is the sentimentalized father of the family whose demise is tragic in the domestic sphere, where eighteenth-century Britain had now relocated its national moral center. Tate has Cordelia live to marry Edgar, assuring succession to the throne and a stable future for kingdom and family more than Shakespeare's play does. Both of McArdell's prints were among those Garrick sought supplies of for distribution to friends in Paris.

In summary, this case study provides examples of theatre iconology that reads pictorial representations not only for what they might tell us as depictions of performance but for what they tell us about the social formations in which the actor and audience, and painter and viewer all participated. Garrick's performances and the making of the theatrical images of him are parts of a large historical picture, albeit one in which his uses of the media of his time are very recognizable today.

GJW

Key references

Aliverti, M.I. (1997) "Major portraits and minor series in eighteenth century theatrical portraiture," *Theatre Research International*, 22:234–254.

Balme, C.B. (1997) "Interpreting the pictorial record: theatre iconography and the referential dilemma," *Theatre Research International*, 22:190–201. [This issue is devoted to articles exploring different possibilities and problems in pictorial analysis.]

Barthes, R. (1973 [1st ed. 1957]) *Mythologies*, London: Paladin.

Davies, T. (1780) *Memoirs of the Life of David Garrick, Esq* (2 vols), London: Thomas Davies

Diderot, D. (1957) *The Paradox of Acting* [*c.*1778], trans. W.H. Pollock, New York: Hill and Wang.

Greenblatt, S. (1997) *The Norton Shakespeare*, New York and London: W.W. Norton and Company.

Highfill, P, Jr. and Burnim, K.A. (eds) (1978) *A Biographical Dictionary of Actors, Actresses, Musicians, Dancers, Managers, and Other Stage Personnel in London, 1660–1800*, vol. 6, Carbondale: Southern Illinois University Press. [The Garrick entry includes an annotated iconography of Garrick portraits.]

Lennox-Boyd, C. and Shaw, G. (1994) *Theatre: The Age of Garrick*, London: Christopher Lennox-Boyd. [English Mezzotints from the Collection of the Hon. Christopher Lennox-Boyd, published in conjunction with an exhibition at the Courtauld Institute Galleries.]

Mander, R. and Mitchenson, J. (1980) *Guide to the Maugham Collection of Theatrical Paintings*, London: Heinemann and the National Theatre. [Somerset Maugham's collection, which he gave to London's National Theatre, includes several important Garrick paintings.]

Panofsky, E. (1955) "Iconography and Iconology: An Introduction to the Study of Renaissance Art," in E. Panofsky, *Meaning in the Visual Arts*, New York: Garden City.

Paulson, R. (1971) *Hogarth: His Life, Art, and Times* (2 vols), New Haven and London: Yale University Press.

Paulson, R. (1992) *Hogarth* (3 vols), New Brunswick: Rutgers University Press.

Shawe-Taylor, D. (2003) *Every Look Speaks, Portraits of David Garrick*, Bath: Holbourne Museum. [Catalog for the Exhibit at the Holbourne Museum of Art, Bath, England.]

Wilson, M.S. (1990) "Garrick, iconic acting, and the ideologies of theatrical portraiture," *Word and Image* 6, 368–394.

CASE STUDY: Kathakali dance-drama: Divine "play" and human suffering on stage

This case study illustrates and discusses issues of ethnographic research into performance. It is based on ethnographic fieldwork on kathakali dance-drama. The fieldwork was conducted in Kerala, India where the author lived for approximately seven years between 1976 and 1983. In order to understand kathakali training and performance from the actor-dancer's perspective, the author underwent intensive training eight hours a day at the Kerala State Arts School, traveled with touring companies, and attended numerous performances. The author conducted interviews with actors, students, administrators, and audience members.

INTERPRETIVE APPROACH: Ethnography and history

Ethnography is one of the primary research methods developed by anthropologists during the nineteenth century and later used by folklorists, sociologists, and, most recently, by those studying performance. Ethnography involves fieldwork usually carried out by living in the community that is the site of research, conducting numerous interviews with people involved in the subject of research, and active engagement in learning what one is studying.

Early studies of non-western performance were often ahistorical, reflecting and projecting onto non-western cultures and peoples a romantic view, including assumptions that they were "unchangeable," or "eternal." Ethnographers have sought to correct that but also have recently embraced history, and historians have begun to embrace ethnography. Both are concerned with providing complex and detailed descriptions of socio-cultural processes and events, and with giving voice to the people involved in these processes and events. Performance ethnographers must develop non-leading, open-ended questions in order to properly conduct their field research. The ethnographer might ask performers or their teachers questions such as the following: "How does the teacher attempt to correct the student so that her/his technique comes to be as correct as possible? How is the experience of acting/performing described? What is the optimal state of awareness of the performer when she or he is giving a 'good' performance?"

Kathakali – an overview

Kathakali dance-drama is a distinctive genre of South Asian performance. It developed during the sixteenth and seventeenth centuries in the coastal region of southwest India known today as Kerala State. The term kathakali combines "story" (katha) and "dance" or "play" (kali). The vast majority of the plays performed in this style of Indian dance-drama are adaptations of episodes from the Indian epics (*Mahabharata* and *Ramayana*) or stories from the *purāṇas* – encyclopedic collections of traditional stories and knowledge. The active repertory includes approximately 60 plays of the 500 authored over the years. Traditionally, performances took place either at the courts of Kerala's rulers, on the grounds of wealthy land-holding families, or as part of Hindu temple festivals. The main "season" lasted from January through April/May and might have been attended by several thousand people. Today, performances are also held throughout the year, inside theatres in towns and cities, and under the sponsorship of cultural organizations, with as few as 50, mostly male, connoisseurs attending.

On a bare stage using only a few stools and properties, three groups of performers collectively create kathakali performances: traditionally all-male companies of actor-dancers, who enact each character in a story, and the percussionists and vocalists who accompany them. The actor-dancers use a highly-physicalized style of performance based on traditional martial arts to play a variety of roles including kings, heroines, demons, demonesses, gods, animals, and priests. A few characters, such as the Midwife in *The Progeny of Krishna*, are drawn from everyday life. The local audience can easily identify each character type, having learned to read the basic make-up and costume codes. The actor-dancers create their roles using a repertory of dance steps, choreography, a complete gesture language for literally "speaking" their character's lines, and expressive use of the face and eyes to communicate the internal states (*bhava*) of the characters.

The percussion orchestra consists of three different types of drums, each with its own distinctive sound and role in the ensemble. The singers vocalize the entire text, including third-person narration as well as first-person dialog, and also keep the basic rhythms with hand-held brass cymbals.

Performances traditionally begin at dusk, and it requires an entire night to perform a thirty-page drama. Texts are composed in the local language of Malayalam, but they make extensive use of Sanskrit, the ancient poetic language of India that produced a long history of well-patronized court poetry and drama, recorded in the *Nātyasastra*. While unique, kathakali developed its conventions and aesthetic of performance from many sources, especially kutiyattam – the tradition of performing Sanskrit

dramas in temple theatres discussed in the Chapter 3 case study.

Since the 1960s, kathakali has become known through many international cultural exchanges. While there is a long history of experimentation with content and technique in kathakali, recent performances have prompted new arguments about change. Controversial experiments have included adaptations on the subject of Adolf Hitler at the end of World War II and leftist kathakali dramas such as *People's Victory* (1987). A kathakali *King Lear* was performed throughout Europe and at international theatre festivals such as Edinburgh, Scotland in 1989 and at Shakespeare's Globe (London) in 1999.

The pleasures of *The Progeny of Krishna*

In 1993, the author was working as a performance ethnographer with V.R. Prabodhachandran Nayar, a life-long appreciator of kathakali and Professor of Linguistics at the University of Kerala. The first collaborative project was a translation of *The Progeny of Krishna* (*Santānagōpālam*) – a kathakali drama, authored by Mandavapalli Ittiraricha Menon (*c.*1747–1794). The author had selected *The Progeny of Krishna* as the first play for this translation project for all the "wrong" reasons, in literary terms. Prabodhachandran Nayar explained as both a linguist and appreciator of good Sanskrit and Malayalam poetry that *The Progeny of Krishna* simply "isn't great poetry. There's too much repetition, and the vocabulary is meagre. It's just not rich!" What connoisseurs of kathakali appreciate most are passages with rich poetic imagery for performers to interpret. In this respect, as a text on the page, *The Progeny of Krishna* cannot compare to the four plays authored by the Raja of Kottayam (*c.*1645–1716): *The Killing of Baka*, *The Killing of Kirmira*, *The Flower of Good Fortune*, and *The Killing of Kalakeya*. These are considered formative in the history of kathakali, as is Unnayi Variyar's (*c.*1675–1716) much heralded *King Nala's Victory*. These plays are included in the required syllabi of Malayalam literature courses, but *The Progeny of Krishna* is considered such "bad" poetry that Prabodhachandran Nayar had never read the text.

Prabodhachandran Nayar, however, knew the text-in-performance by heart, and might be heard humming the well-loved, if simple language set to appropriate musical modes (*ragas*). Moreover, he cherished a life-long set of memories of *The Progeny of Krishna* in performance (Figure 5.9). He had seen performances in family house compounds and local temples, sponsored by childless couples hoping in this way to secure future progeny and he had seen performances earlier in the century of the renowned actor-dancer, Krishnan Nayar, whose genius (along with Kunju Nayar) left its stamp on the way today's actors perform the main role of the Brahmin.

At performances of *The Progeny of Krishna* at village temples that the author observed in 1993, many levels of appreciation and pleasure were clearly experienced by audiences. Among those with the most nuanced level of appreciation was the 78-year-old Ganesha Iyer, who explained to the author:

> From six years of age I was taken to see kathakali performances by my father and older brothers. I've read all the plays, can appreciate performances, and point out all the defects! But real appreciation requires critical study and drawing on knowledge of actors and other experts.

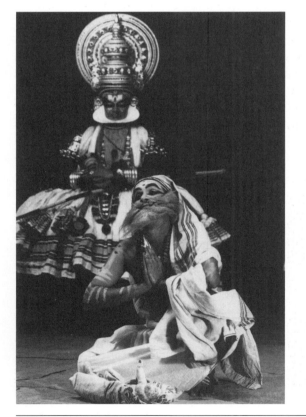

Figure 5.9 *The Progeny of Krishna*, Scene 2. With the body of his eighth son lying before him, the Brahmin (M.P. Sankaran Namboodiri) pours out his tale of woe at court. Arjuna in green (*pacca*) make-up observes in the background. Photo © Phillip B. Zarrilli.

Known as "kathakali mad," connoisseurs like Ganesha Iyer used to travel far and wide during the festival season to attend as many performances as possible by their favorite actor-dancers. The ideal connoisseur is knowledgeable in Sanskrit, culturally sophisticated in the nuances of each poetic text, able to read kathakali's gesture language through which the actor's "speak" their lines, and able to appreciate and appraise each performer's style and approach to performing particular roles. Today a connoisseur is known as a *rasika*, "taster of *rasa*," or *sahṛdaya*, one whose heart/mind (*hṛdaya*) is able to respond intuitively to a performance.

Educating actor-dancers

The all-day formal training of a kathakali actor/dancer traditionally began at the age of seven, but today begins somewhere between ten and 16. The entire performance vocabulary is broken down into small units for individual mastery. Starting in the early morning hours, students undergo a rigorous training regimen designed to render their bodies flexible, balanced, and controlled. Originating in the indigenous martial art, *kaḷarippayaṭṭu* (kah-lah-rip-pay-YA-too), the regimen requires a series of gymnastic full-body exercises (Figure 5.10), including kicks, jumps, and massage for the entire body given through their teacher's feet and hands. They also do exercises for the eyes, eyebrows, facial muscles, wrists, and hands. All these components are reassembled as students learn the nine codified facial expressions, 24 root hand gestures through which to speak the text, a variety of dance steps set in rhythmic cycles, the coordination of movement of the eyes with the hands, set pieces of choreography, and then roles in the repertory. By the end of the minimum of six years of formal training, students will have been introduced to all the basic roles in the repertory and should be able to learn new roles as required for performance. Mastery only comes after lengthy stage experience, with most "star" actors gaining recognition, if at all, only after at least twenty years of experience on stage and in life.

Figure 5.10 One of kathakali's psychophysical training exercises, intended to render the actor's bodymind supple and flexible. Photo © Phillip B. Zarrilli.

The most accessible aspect of kathakali performances is its popular epic/mythic stories. Kathakali performances traditionally served as a pleasurable form of education, not just for connoisseurs but for people from all walks of life, inasmuch as "Myths are not written by gods and demons, nor for them; but they are by, for, and about men. Gods and demons serve as metaphors for human situations" (O'Flaherty 1976:8). Therefore, performances also may be appreciated by those with little or no education in kathakali's nuances. It does not require specialist knowledge to be interested in *The Progeny of Krishna*'s drama of a couple's love and loss of their children, to have empathy for the main character of the Brahmin, or to enjoy the beautiful musical modes to which the text is sung. Audiences laugh raucously at the Brahmin's all-too-human foibles, they experience a sense of devotion for Krishna, and they feel a sense of affirmation knowing that human suffering is subsumed within the workings of Lord Vishnu's cosmic "play." If from a literary and poetic point of view *The Progeny of Krishna* was the "wrong" play to translate, from the perspective of the author as a performance ethnographer, *The Progeny of Krishna* was a good play to translate because it allowed the author-observer to explore the wide popular appeal this play has in performance.

Introduction to *The Progeny of Krishna* and its playwright

Kathakali owes its birth to the powerful, wealthy ruling lineages of Kerala who were interested in the performing arts and had sufficient resources to patronize a company, all of whom were traditionally from castes serving the ruler. Following the ancient tradition of royal authorship, kathakali's first dramas were written by the ruler of Kottayam in northern Kerala. Other authors were court poets, like Mandavapalli Ittiraricha Menon, who served as court poet for Kartikatirunal Maharaja, ruler of the large southern kingdom of Travancore. Born to a poor family, Ittiraricha Menon received a traditional education in Sanskrit literature. He came to the ruler's attention in 1763. At court in the city of Thiruvananthapuram, now Kerala's capital, he composed his two kathakali plays, *The Progeny of Krishna* and *King Rugmamgada's Law*. He was so successful that the ruler awarded him the highest honor possible – a gift of a gold bracelet.

Both plays were probably first performed either within the palace compound or as one of many performances given annually as part of a festival at the nearby main Hindu temple, Sri Padmanabhaswamy Temple. The main deity in this temple is Lord Vishnu in his reclining form, known as Padmanabha. Vishnu is considered the "preserver." Along with Brahma "the creator," Siva "the destroyer" and forms of the goddess, he is one of the four major Hindu deities. Lord Krishna is one of the ten incarnations of Vishnu. As reflected in *The Progeny of Krishna*, there was a very close relationship between rulers and the main local temple. Kings were held responsible for upholding the cosmic order of the universe by protecting and preserving the social order. This responsibility is reinforced in the ritual calendar of the temple when the reigning monarch carries the sword representing the deity's power in annual processions to the nearby Arabian Sea where Lord Vishnu's image is bathed.

Given the close ties between temple and state, it is not surprising that both Ittiraricha Menon's plays focus on devotion to Lord Vishnu. In *King Rugmamgada's Law*, this takes the form of a test of the king's devotion, while in *The Progeny of Krishna* the devotion of a simple brahmin is tested. Brahmins were learned in Sanskrit, serving as priests, scholars, and grammarians. They are considered "priests" and therefore "highest" among the categories into which people are born. Plays based on the life of Krishna are adapted from stories in the *puranas*. The *Bhagavata-Purana*, the source of the story dramatized in *The Progeny of Krishna*, dates between the fifth and tenth century. The story was originally told to illustrate how Vishnu is the greatest deity in the

Hindu pantheon, especially in his incarnation as Krishna.

Both of Ittiraricha Menon's plays stage the notion of "divine play" or *lila*. A fundamental concept in a Hindu understanding of the world, "divine play" means that when god wants to act in the world by taking one of many forms (incarnations), such as Rama or Krishna, he does not do so out of any need or lack, but "by a free and joyous creativity that is integral to his own nature. He acts in a state of rapt absorption comparable to that of an artist possessed by his creative vision or that of a child caught up in the delight of a game played for its own sake" (Hein cited in Sax 1995:13). The child-like nature of "divine play" is reflected in the character of the Brahmin in *The Progeny of Krishna*.

The Progeny of Krishna – the play

Kathakali actor, Margi Vijayan, told the author that he thought *The Progeny of Krishna* was accessible and popular not only because its language was relatively simple, but also because it was "a very simple play." Connoisseur G.S. Varyar echoed this, saying the play "has an everyday (*lōkadharmî*) aspect." *The Progeny of Krishna* enacts the very human dilemma faced by a simple Brahmin householder and his wife. They have suffered the loss of all nine sons born to them. The original play is composed in twelve scenes, each of which is briefly summarized below:

Scene 1: The greatest martial hero in the Mahabharata epic, Arjuna, returns after the Pandavas' victory over their evil cousins, the Kauravas, in the battle of Kurukshetra, to visit Krishna's court. Krishna blesses Arjuna, and then convinces him to stay awhile and share his company.

Scene 2: A Brahmin householder unexpectedly bursts into the Council Hall carrying the body of a dead child. He pours out his woeful tale of loss (Figure 5.9):

This grief is unbearable for me.
I am not one who has committed any deed prohibited to brahmins.
Why this result! Oh son, Siva! Siva!

Alas, what you see here is my dear child lying with his eyes having turned upward.
Thus eight boys are lost and gone due to the fault of our arrogant king!

Lord Krishna, the object of the Brahmin's anger, not only turns a deaf ear, but literally walks away, exiting the stage. Arjuna is moved by the Brahmin's tale, and rushes forward to offer his help. He promises that he will protect his next child. The Brahmin is skeptical of Arjuna's brash promise:

When Vishnu, the master of the worlds and
protector of the good, heard of my sorrow,
He did not move (even an inch).

But, quite surprisingly, without thinking even
a little why this was so,
You, Fool, have ventured into this!

To convince the Brahmin, Arjuna vows that he will throw himself into a pit of fire if he does not protect the baby.

Scene 3: At home, the Brahmin's Wife (which is how she is known) hears his news, but at first remains philosophical as she asks, "Is it possible for even those who are accomplished to turn away fate?" Putting his trust in Krishna, he convinces his wife that their fate is about to change with Arjuna's help.

Scene 4: The time has come for the Brahmin's Wife to give birth. The joyous and nervous father calls the Midwife from the village to care for her (Figure 5.11).

Scene 5: The Brahmin rushes to tell Arjuna, who builds a delivery house of arrows to

Figure 5.11 In *The Progeny of Krishna*, Scene 4, the Brahmin's Wife (Margi Vijaykumar), in pain as the time for her delivery draws near, is helped by the village midwife (Margi Suresh). Photo © Phillip B. Zarrilli.

protect them. The Midwife and Brahmin's Wife enter. Arjuna guards the entrance as the Brahmin paces nervously outside. When the Wife delivers a ninth son, it immediately vanishes! At first the Brahmin faints. When he revives, he turns his fury on Arjuna, taunting him

> Fool! What happened to your highly accomplished skill?

> Oh best among dunces, what is the use of this tent of arrows with all its "pomp and circumstance?"

Finally, he commands him to leave, "Go! Go! Go!"

★*Scene 6*: Arjuna travels to the abode of the god of death, Yama, and angrily demands the return of the Brahmin's son. Yama says he has not taken any of the sons, and sends him in search of Krishna.

★*Scene 7*: Arjuna next goes to the god of thunder and rain, Indra's heavenly world, to demand the return of the Brahmin's sons. He too tells him to seek out Krishna.

Scene 8: Arjuna searches all the worlds, but does not find the missing sons. Acting on his vow, he is about to jump into the fire pit when Krishna saves him, humbling Arjuna's pride.

Scene 9: Krishna and Arjuna set out for Vaikuntha, the heavenly abode, but along the way they encounter the darkness of Mount Lokaloka. Krishna releases his great weapon to dispel the darkness so they may continue their journey.

Scene 10: Krishna and Arjuna arrive in Vaikuntha where they encounter the wonders of the heavenly abode.

Scene 11: Mahavishnu greets Krishna and Arjuna, expresses his delight with their presence, and reveals the following:

> Only to make you come here itself, did I bring that
> best among Brahmin's children here with delight.

Vishnu entrusts all nine sons to them to return to the Brahmin and his wife.

Scene 12: Arjuna and Krishna arrive at the Brahmin's house where he and his wife are still in mourning. After recounting his journey through the heavens, Arjuna requests the parents to receive "with delight" all their sons being returned "by the compassion of the Lord [Vishnu]!" Overjoyed, the couple receives each of the nine children (Figure 5.12), and give their blessings to Krishna and Arjuna.

When a drama like *The Progeny of Krishna* has been performed for over 200 years, the performance ethnologist may ask a number of questions about changing texts, changing audience tastes and expectations, and changing performance conditions.

Figure 5.12 With his seventh son on his shoulders, the Brahmin dances with joy at his return. At his left is his wife (Sajan) and behind her several other children. Arjuna is on the right. Photo © Phillip B. Zarrilli.

Text and performance, past and present

Over the past 40 to 50 years, most kathakali texts, including *The Progeny of Krishna*, have been edited and shortened from what was once an all-night performance to a now more typical three-and-a-half to four-hour performance. There are several practical reasons for this change:

■ For town audiences at performances sponsored by cultural clubs made up of connoisseurs, perform-ances are often shortened to allow people to return home by the last available modes of public transportation.

■ Full productions are expensive to mount, and with the waning of court patronage, costs must be reduced. *The Progeny of Krishna* is much more expensive to mount because it requires five addi-tional actors playing divine roles, each with elab-orate make-up and costumes. The edited version only requires four actors, plus village children.

■ Throughout the twentieth century, there has been an increasing emphasis on featuring star performers in roles popular with connoisseurs. Rather than performing a single play in its entirety, all-night programs often feature three shortened plays with three different star per-formers. The edited version keeps the focus much more on the star actor playing the role of the Brahmin – a character who does not appear in any of the scenes cut from the full-length version.

As exemplifed in *The Progeny of Krishna*, what is edited from a performance both reflects and shapes audience taste and expectations in a changing socio-cultural landscape. Of the original twelve scenes, the five cut (★ above) are Arjuna's search for the chil-dren (Scenes 6 and 7), and his journey with Krishna to Vishnu's heavenly abode (Scenes 9–11). These five scenes emphasize the overarching point of view of the *original* story: that Vishnu is "the greatest" of all the gods and that his own inscrutable, capricious divine play, *lila*, is manifest not only in his incarnation in Lord Krishna, but in his own "play." (He brings the Brahmin's children to Vaikuntha in order to necessitate a visit by Krishna and Arjuna.) As described by Krishna in Scene 10, these scenes reveal the wonder and glory of Vishnu's abode:

> Please look with delight at Vishnu's home.
> . . . all eyes have begun to swim and play
> in the immense waves of this
> ocean of ambrosia!
>
> In the center of this ocean of milk is a
> wonderful world called Vaikuntha . . .
>
> [It is] the prosperous Goddess Lakshmi's
> playhouse where there is no grief,
> and where all people are immersed in pleasures!

With these scenes cut, the dramatic narrative does not focus nearly as much on the cosmic dimensions of Vishnu's "divine play," but more specifically on the Brahmin's "everyday" human dilemma, Arjuna's prideful attempt to resolve that dilemma, and the joy and devotion that comes with Krishna's gracious return of the children. Because the five scenes cut are all briefly summarized by Arjuna at the begin-ning of Scene 12 when he reports to the Brahmin, the narrative continuity of the story is not broken. Indeed, in its shortened version, the pace of *The Progeny of Krishna* is decidedly up-tempo, in keeping with the Brahmin's sense of urgency about his very human situation. As we shall see below, in the hands of the great twentieth-century actor, Kunju Nayar, the style of playing the lead role of the Brahmin came to emphasize his endearing humor, popularizing a shortened production's focus on the Brahmin's human dilemma. The focus on star performers like Kunju Nayar developing the human side of this role reflects a major historical shift from an earlier emphasis on the larger cosmological drama of Vishnu's "divine play."

Everyday concerns: male progeny and the suffering of the pious and innocent

Childlessness, and in particular, lack of male progeny, bursts upon the stage with the Brahmin's dramatic entrance in Scene 2. This is perhaps the worst dilemma that can befall traditional Hindu males. As kathakali actor, Vasu Pisharoti, explained, "the greatest loss one can suffer is to lose a child." Children "are the only form of *physical* permanence. They are the links of the eternal chain of rebirths . . . in contrast with (and often at the sacrifice of) the setting free or Release (*moksa*) of the eternal soul" (O'Flaherty 1988:73).

The point of view assumed in *The Progeny of Krishna* is that inherent in a set of Sanskrit texts, *Dharma Sastras*, which provide an idealized model of how society should be organized and one's duties within that order. According to this religious and social ideal, the [male] brahmin passes through at least the first two of the four "stages of life" open to him – student, householder, forest dwelling hermit, and renunciant. In the play, the Brahmin is attempting to fulfill the two most essential duties of householder through which society is preserved – offering sacrifices and raising sons. Although release from the cycle of rebirths is the ultimate goal, "for most people, householder life was the limit of their present existence: they married, raised a family, carried out their social duties, performed their prescribed rituals, and ended life as householders, hoping that they had prepared the way for a better future birth" (Hopkins 1971:81). Of these, the householder role, was considered most important, because, of the four stages,

> it alone leads to the production of offspring and the support of society. . . . Every Brahmin was said to be born with a triple indebtedness: to the sages, to the gods, and to his ancestors. He

became free of these only when he had satisfied the sages with celibacy, the gods with sacrifices, and his ancestors with a son.

> (ibid.:82, 77)

The tragedy that befalls the Brahmin and his Wife is exacerbated by the apparent injustice of their situation since they are faultless. The Brahmin is described as "pious," "noble," "good," and "best among brahmins." *The Progeny of Krishna* dramatically raises the question that confronts all families – why the pious and innocent suffer.

In a study of how Malayalis interpret such a situation, villagers shared thoughts that echo the Brahmin's Wife's view that their suffering is divinely ordained, that is, it is their fate (*vidhi*):

> Sometimes really good people suffer. . . . What is to happen will happen. One cannot prevent it. It is called [fate] *vidhi*. . . . *Vidhi* means the happenings in life which are beyond one's control, e.g., the sudden death of a young person.

> (Ayrookuzhiel 1983:123, 126–127)

For pious, upright individuals like the Brahmin and his Wife, they suffer not from some sin committed in the past but from a present fate over which they have no control. Innocent people also suffer. It cannot be that they have done something wrong. It may be "what is written on their foreheads" (ibid.:129). The everyday concerns with childlessness and suffering in *The Progeny of Krishna* are part of the play's popular appeal to kathakali's broad-based audiences.

Kathakali make-up and costume categories

Costuming and make-up are part of the process which "transforms" the actor into idealized, archetypal character types, each of which is individualized by the dramatic context and the choices actors make playing each role. Costumes and make-up for these archetypes have evolved from several sources: kutiyattam, ritual performances, local artistic conventions, and conventional daily dress. There are seven basic archetypal costumes and make-ups, of which the first three below appear in the short version of *The Progeny of Krishna*:

(1) "Green" (*pacca*) archetype (Figure 5.9): These are the divine figures like Krishna and Vishnu in *The Progeny of Krishna*, and epic heroes such as Arjuna. They are upright, moral, and ideally full of a calm inner poise – "royal sages," modeled on the hero of Sanskrit drama whose task is to uphold sacred law. A white frame sets off the green base of the face makeup, reflecting this type's basic inner refinement. The stylized mark of Vishnu is painted on the forehead with a yellow base and markings of red and black. The soft curving black of the eyebrows and black underlining of the lower lids extends to the side of the face, framing the eyes. The lips are brilliant coral red. The outer jacket is red and the lower skirt is white with orange and black stripes. Most characters in this class wear the highly-jeweled medium size crown like Arjuna. Krishna wears a special vase-shaped crown with a short tuft of peacock feathers on top, a blue upper garment, and skirt of bright mustard-yellow.

(2) "Radiant" (*minukku*): includes both idealized female heroines such as the Brahmin's Wife, and spiritually-perfected males including brahmins, holy men, and sages. The base make-up is a radiant yellow-orange. Costumes are close to traditional everyday dress. For female roles, men don a long-sleeved upper garment, a white lower cloth, and suggest a traditional female hairstyle by wrapping a colorful cloth around a false top-knot worn slightly to the left of the head. Holy men wear the typical saffron yellow and a special crown, while brahmins, like the main role in *The Progeny of Krishna*, wear a simple lower cloth as well as an upper cloth tied over the head.

(3) "Special" (*tēppu*): a catch-all class of approximately eighteen characters, including the comic Midwife in *The Progeny of Krishna*, as well as special bird-style make-ups and costumes such as Hamsa (a goose).

Other categories include: (4) the orange-red "ripe" (*pazhuppu*) type for four divine characters: Brahma, Shiva; (5) "knife" (*katti*) make-up for arrogant and evil demon-kings like the ten-headed Ravana; (6) "beard" (*tati*) characters including the divine/higher "white beard" for the valorous chief of the monkeys, Hanuman, the "red beards" for the evil, vicious, and vile demons, and "black beards" for evil schemers; and (7) "black" (*kari*) for demonesses.

Everyday characters

Another reason for the popular appeal of the play is its everyday characters. Connoisseur G.S. Varyar explained that the Brahmin in *The Progeny of Krishna* is "more everyday" than most major kathakali characters. In part this is due to the Brahmin's costume and make-up, which is relatively close to how brahmins traditionally dressed in Kerala with a grey beard, simple wrapped cloth, sacred thread, and beads. It is also because of the way in which the role of the Brahmin is enacted today.

One way senior actors develop roles is to create a mini-scene not in the original dramatic text that allows the actor to elaborate some aspect of the drama – the mood of a scene, a character's state of mind, or a story which provides further information on the situation. Toward the conclusion of Scene 2 actor Kunju Nayar developed a small scene which elaborates the Brahmin's mistrust of Arjuna's vow that he will throw himself into the fire. This interpolation helped crystalize Kunju Nayar's style of acting the Brahmin, and made the character popular.

Kathakali actor, Vasu Pisharoti, explained that in the Kunju Nayar tradition of playing the role, the Brahmin is "typical" of his social type because "he's very very innocent. Because of his innocence, he lashes out, terribly angry, against the ruler and loses control." His innocence comes from qualities traditionally understood to be determined at birth, which leave him uncorrupted. When he enters the scene he is filled with the anguish of sorrow over the loss of his eighth son. But his sorrow (the dominant emotional state) is tinged with anger over the death of yet another son. He moves back and forth between expressing pathos and anger. But immediately after becoming angry, he regrets it. Another actor, Nelliyode Vasudevan Namboodiripad, explained that "Since the Brahmin is so innocent, he shows everything in the extreme. If he is happy, he will be extremely happy . . . . So at last, when he sees all his children together, he is very happy, and he can't control his happiness! It's like a person winning the lottery!"

The Kunju Nayar tradition of playing the role also involves an important element of endearing humor. When Pisharoti's Brahmin reacts to the thunderous sound of Arjuna's first arrow shot, he shouts, "My ears are broken!" Improvising, he adds, "I'm only familiar with the sounds of worship – the ringing of the bell." The Brahmin's innocent piety creates humor. As G.S. Varyar explains, "the enjoyment of a really good performance . . . is seeing the wide gamut of emotions through which [the Brahmin] passes. [It] is what makes the play unusual . . . [and] popular."

Although the Brahmin is a familiar character, by no means is he a caricature. M.P. Sankaran Namboodiri explains how the actor must keep within the bounds of "what is appropriate" (aucityam-bōdham) to the type – a fundamental concept guiding the acting of all major roles. In contrast is the minor role of the Midwife, which is intentionally played as a caricature; she is one of the most "everyday" (lōkad-harmī) roles in the repertory. Like other caricatures, kathakali's are created by carefully copying easily identifiable stereotypical behaviors of particular groups of people within the society at large. The Midwife is played as a buck-toothed, hunchbacked old village woman. Her portrayal never fails to elicit a good-humored response from the audience.

Responding to *The Progeny of Krishna*

Kathakali actor Vasu Pisharoti recollected how, at the age of thirteen or fourteen, "tears fell unconsciously from [my] eyes" while watching Kunju Nayar play the Brahmin in a performance of *The Progeny of Krishna*. Although he knew the story and had seen it performed before, on this particular night the performance "touched and pierced my heart/mind. It is a special feeling . . . . I cried and so did many other people in the audience." Such an overtly empathetic response is unusual, and is occasioned either by the Brahmin's moments of pathos, and/or by the occasion of overwhelming joy that concludes a good performance – a moment when joy, wonder, grace, and devotion are melded as parents and children are united and the Brahmin's suffering is ended.

In productions of *The Progeny of Krishna* today, the roles of the Brahmin's eight oldest children in *The Progeny of Krishna* are not played by young kathakali actors, but rather by children from the community where the performance is being held. Ideally, the organizers of the performance gather eight volunteer children, male *or* female, from families attending the performance, ideally of different heights and ranging from 4 year-olds to 15 year-olds. They are then arranged onstage from oldest/tallest to youngest/smallest. This ideal casting reflects the fact that Vishnu had taken all of the children to his heavenly abode where they had been living fully and joyfully with their heavenly father (Vishnu) and mothers (Lakshmi and Bhuumi Devi) until they were taken by Arjuna and Krishna to rejoin their parents of birth.

Naturally, the spectator/actor relationship is altered with village children rather than young kathakali actors playing these roles. The audience is usually abuzz with conversation and commentary throughout the opening of the final scene as Krishna serves as an onstage stage-manager for the children, arranging them from tallest to shortest, prompting them about how to hold their hands to pay proper respects to their parents, and when to go forward to Arjuna to be given to their parents. Much of this is improvised by the actors playing Arjuna and the Brahmin. Once the children have been brought forward, given the predominant mood of the Brahmin's abundant joy, the improvisations are often uproariously funny.

The author-enthographer was unable to determine precisely when it became common for village children to play these roles instead of young kathakali actors, but this convention brings the larger religious context of the play *into the performance text*. Krishna's grace is not an abstract theological/cosmological construct, but becomes part of the village's progeny here and now. In *The Progeny of Krishna*, the "everyday" has the potential to take on the sense of being *this* particular day for these particular people. This phenomenon reflects an increasing emphasis in popular Hinduism today on the immediacy of devotion to Krishna, rather than on the larger cosmology of "divine play."

Among connoisseurs, the same performative moments that brought tears to Pisharoti's then young eyes are often experienced and interpreted as a subtler internal resonation or "vibration" "within the mind" – signs of actualizing an aesthetic experience of "tasting" known as *rasa*. As Ganesha Iyer explained,

> When the actor enacts certain states (*rasas*), they are able to create a sympathetic motion in my heart. When he enacts a sorrowful aspect, I do not experience sorrow, but appreciate his expression of sorrow. . . . I experience sympathetic vibration. But in some people, they may experience this as a *real* emotion. . . . When a very sorrowful scene is enacted, some may weep. . . . This difference may be due to having a more intellectual appreciation, and not emotional.

The aesthetic experience Ganesha Iyer describes is part of an Indian cultural understanding of what happens when one's sensibilities are developed through education, whether as a spectator or practitioner learning yoga or a martial art. According to this paradigm, one's sensibilities begin at the grossest, physical, most external level, and through a gradual process of education and disciplined training one moves toward a subtler, more refined internal mode of appreciation and action.

How has the West read and interpreted non-western performance?

Discussions of kathakali have often described it as a "classical" art, and privileged the educated point of view of the connoisseur and his "theater of the mind." This point of view suggests that kathakali is an art of the elite to the exclusion of the everyday and the mundane. Although kathakali was traditionally, and still is, of greatest interest to those castes/classes involved as performers and patrons, and whose view of the world is best reflected on stage, it has never been a dance-drama appealing only to an elite. When kathakali is discussed exclusively as a "theatre of the mind," the discourse disparages the simpler pleasures and broad popular appeal of a play like *The Progeny of Krishna*, which, at least when Kunju Nayar performed the Brahmin, was able to bring tears to the eyes of some among his audiences.

If kathakali is classified, as some in the West have, as "classical," or "traditional," these labels imply that kathakali is relatively fixed and unchanging, rather than a dynamic reflection of socio-cultural and political/economic processes. Such labels also say something disturbing about the West. In 1976, Edward Said identified this kind of ahistorical process of projecting onto cultures of the Middle East and Asia what the West desires them to be as "orientalizing" the "Other" (see the Chapter 11 case study, "Global Shakespeare" for a further discussion of "Orientalism"). In the nineteenth century, German philosopher, Friedrich Hegel (1770-1831), represented Europe as open to change and development, but Asia as more or less static and unchangeable. The view of India in particular as unchangeable and absolutely different allowed the British to justify their colonization of India: they could provide the rules of reason and bureaucracy which Indians (ostensibly) could not provide for themselves. This legacy of India as the "absolute other" is discernable still in the West's continuing romance with India as the "mystical" or "spiritual Other." The degree to which such mystification has affected traditional Indian performance, especially performances designed for western tourists, is witnessed in P.K. Devan's tourist kathakali performances in the port city of Kochi-Ernakulam in central Kerala. Devan touts kathakali as a 2,000 year old "ritual art" (see Chapter 12 on "Tourism"). This representation of kathakali reflects a western desire to encounter India as that "other" magical place of antique "ritual" spirituality, rather than to see kathakali, as we have here, as a genre that continued to change, responsive to dynamics

in culture, in the late twentieth century. To give one more example of this, contemporary experiments involving kathakali have included Iyyemgode Sreeddharan's 1987 play, *People's Victory*, where Karl Marx met Imperialism on the kathakali stage, a play that reflected the fact that Kerala State, when formed in 1957, had the first democratically-elected communist government in the world (Zarrilli 2000: Chapter 10).

PZ

Key references

Ayrochuzhiel, A.M.A. (1983) *The Sacred in Popular Hinduism: An Empirical Study in Chiralla, North Malabar*, Madras: The Christian Literature Society.

Bollard, D. (1996 [1st edn 1980]) *A Guide to Kathakali*, 3rd edn, New Delhi: Sterling Paperbacks.

Hopkins, T.J. (1971) *The Hindu Religious Tradition*, Encino, C.A.: Dickenson Publishing Co.

Inden, R. (1986) "Orientalist constructions of India," *Modern Asian Studies*, 20:401-446.

Jones, C.R. and Jones, B.T. (1970) *Kathakali: An Introduction to the Dance-Drama of Kerala*, New York: Theatre Arts Books.

Nair, D.A. and Paniker, K.A. (eds) (1993) *Kathakali: The Art of the Non-Worldly*, Bombay: Marg.

O'Flaherty, W.D. (1976) *The Origins of Evil in Hindu Mythology*, Berkeley: University of California Press.

O'Flaherty, W.D. (1988) *Other People's Myths*, New York: Macmillan.

Said, E. (1978) *Orientalism*, New York: Pantheon.

Sax, W.S. (ed.) (1995) *The Gods at Play: Lila in South Asia*, New York: Oxford University Press, citing Norvin Hein (1972) *The Miracle Plays at Matuura*, New Haven, Yale University Press.

Zarrilli, P.B. (1984) *The Kathakali Complex: Actor, Performance, Structure*. New Delhi: Abhinav.

Zarrilli, P.B. (2000) *Kathakali Dance-Drama: Where Gods and Demons Come to Play*, New York and London: Routledge. [Includes translations of *The Progeny of Krishna, King Rugmangada's Law, The Flower of Good Fortune*, and *The Killing of Kirmira* by V.R. Prabodhachandran Nayar, M.P. Sankaran Namboodiri, and Phillip B. Zarrilli.]

Audio-visual resources

Introduction to Kathakali Dance-Drama, 20 minute color videotape introducing Kathakali in context, London: Routledge, 2000.

The Progeny of Krishna, 3½ hour documentary of complete performance in Kerala, India. [For rental only from: Centre

for Performance Research, 8H Science Park, Aberystwyth, Wales, SY23 3AH, U.K., or Centre for South Asia, Film Distribution Center, University of Wisconsin-Madison, Ingraham Hall, Madison, W.I. 53706

The Killing of Kirmira, 3½ hour document of complete performance in Kerala, India. London: Routledge, 2000.

CASE STUDY: Theatre and hegemony: Comparing popular melodramas

Melodrama in history

The Titanic sinks, the police arrest a murderer, and aliens threaten to conquer the earth! These are three examples of stories that make good melodrama, a popular dramatic form during many historical eras that continues to terrify, reassure, and propagandize audiences today. Briefly defined, melodrama allows spectators to imaginatively experience an evil force outside of themselves, such as a greedy person, a rapacious criminal, or a vast conspiracy. Consequently, melodrama dramatizes social morality; it names the "good guys" and "bad guys" in our lives and helps us to negotiate such problems as political power, economic justice, and racial inequality. It may also point audiences beyond their present circumstances to transcendental sources of good and evil.

Because melodrama can help audiences to identify new types of virtue and vice, it is often in demand during periods of rapid historical change. Melodramatic plays flourished, for example, in fifth-century B.C.E. Athens, seventeenth-century England, and eighteenth-century Japan. Melodrama rose to prominence again in nineteenth-century Europe and the United States, first in response to the American and French Revolutions (1776, 1789) and later as a means of coping with the vast economic and social changes caused by the Industrial Revolution. As we will see, two very different kinds of melodrama spoke to people's need for a new social morality in the wake of each of these

transformations. By comparing these types of plays, we can trace significant changes in the practical ethics of western societies during the course of the nineteenth century.

Comparing popular melodramas

To compare the social morality of two kinds of melodrama using only one play of each type, the historian needs to be sure that she or he is comparing dramas that were popular in their time and broadly representative of many similar plays. Both *Coelina, or The Child of Mystery* (1800) by Guilbert de Pixérécourt and *The Poor of New York* (1857) by Dion Boucicault fit these criteria. *Coelina* achieved nearly 1500 performances in France during the first 30 years of the century. English, German, Dutch, and Italian adaptations also flourished. In 1857, Boucicault adapted *Les Pauvres de Paris*, already a popular melodrama in Paris, as *The Poor of New York*. Following the play's success in New York, Boucicault re-tooled the melodrama for theatres in other cities by keeping its basic plot but altering local references. Over the next fifteen years, the drama resurfaced as *The Poor of Liverpool*, *The Poor of the London Streets*, *The Streets of Dublin*, and similar titles for other industrial cities in the British Empire and the United States. Both *Coelina* and *Poor*, then, enjoyed international success for a significant period of time.

Both dramas are also broadly representative of two types of nineteenth-century melodrama. The success of *Coelina* and other plays by Pixérécourt spawned dozens of melodramas with similar plots and characters. Similarly, other playwrights at mid-century repeated the formula of Boucicault's melo-dramas to gain success. Like writers and producers of television melodrama today, theatre people in the nineteenth century strove to reproduce plot situa-tions, character types, and significant themes that had worked in the past. The result were two distinct types of melodramatic entertainment, each involving over a hundred plays: providential melodrama, popular from roughly 1800 to 1825, and materialist melo-drama, successful from around 1855 to 1880.

Providential melodrama

Coelina is a typical *providential* melodrama. The setting for these kinds of plays is usually timeless and uni-versal, as in a fairy tale. *Coelina* occurs before the Revolution of 1789 in a village in rural France that has changed very little since the Middle Ages. Like other providential melodramas, the agent of evil in *Coelina* is a single villain, alienated from the social institutions that provide order in this society of hard-working peasants and small shopkeepers. Truguelin, the "monstre" of *Coelina*, scorns the Catholic faith, flees from the King's law, and attempts to use his fam-ily to advance his greedy ambitions. When Coelina, the heroine of the play, refuses to marry his son, Truguelin has her driven from her home and perse-cutes her and her true father to gain her inheritance.

Providential melodramas, however, always assure the audience that God watches over innocent good-ness and His power will ensure a happy ending. In *Coelina*, nature works in conjunction with the Almighty, causing Truguelin to crumble in fear at a thunderstorm, a symbol of the Final Judgment that awaits him. Unlike the villain, the natural innocence of Coelina and her father, whose identity is unknown to her, gives them insight into Truguelin's machinations and draws them together to protect each other. Like other providential melodramas, the play ends with the villain banished from the stage and the good characters returned to the rural utopia from which they started (Figure 5.13). No original

Figure 5.13 This advertisement depicts a scene from Pixérécourt's *The Forest of Bondy*, still popular in 1843 when this print was published. For this providential melodrama, a dog was trained to jump at the throat of the actor playing the villain, the killer of the dog's master. © Harvard Theatre Collection.

sin stains the virtue of good characters in providential melodrama; eliminate persecuting villainy, *Coelina* promises, and Paradise can be regained.

Materialist melodrama

The Poor of New York by Boucicault differs significantly from *Coelina* and its providential spin-offs. Instead of a fairy-tale-like setting, *materialist* melodrama places the action within time-bound, historical realities – the streets, mansions, and tenement rooms of a depression-wracked New York in *The Poor of New York*. In this materialist world, the institutions of liberal, bourgeois government and society provide order and justice. The villain of *Poor*, Gideon Bloodgood, violates their codes when he ignores legislated laws, breaks with sound business practices, and attempts to use his money to gain social respectability. The financial "panics" of 1837 and 1857 and the economic depressions that follow frame the plot of Boucicault's play. When a rich depositor dies in his bank in 1837, Bloodgood steals the money rightfully due to the Fairweather family, and the plot of the melodrama examines the consequences of this theft, its discovery, and the eventual restitution of the money 20 years later. As in a well-made play, the plot of *Poor* hinges on a secret known to the audience but not to most of the characters (who stole the money?), which is finally revealed at the end of the play. The social world of *Coelina* ensured worldly justice through idealized hierarchical institutions – the Church, the autocratic state, and the patriarchal family. In *Poor*, the actual, historical institutions of the United States in the 1850s have taken their place.

Gone from productions of *The Poor of New York* were appeals to Providence and the expectation that the Almighty would restore a utopian paradise to characters of virtue. Where natural instincts, heroic action, and God's grace could reveal the "mysteries" of *Coelina*, the characters of Boucicault's play inhabit a denser, more impenetrable world. For much of the play, the Fairweathers do not know that Bloodgood is the primary cause of their distress; it takes a detective-like figure, Badger, to reveal his villainy. (Indeed, the detective, a figure with specialized knowledge of the mysteries of the industrial city, first gains prominence as a dramatic character in materialist melodramas.) In addition to man-made villainy, chance causes much of the evil in materialist melodrama. Characters in *Poor* may be wealthy one day and poor the next, as happens to one of the heroes as a result of the "panic" of 1857. While the ending of providential melodrama banished evil from the stage to rejoice in the return of a traditional utopia, materialist melodrama, more fatalistic than utopian, typically allows villains to reform and rejoin society. Thus, the Fairweathers forgive Bloodgood and his daughter, both of whom also suffered from mistakes and accidents, and the ending celebrates the reconciliation of these two families. Chance, not providential design, structures much of the action of materialist melodrama (Figure 5.14).

The code of bourgeois respectability regulates class relations in this type of play. Although the Fairweathers are middle class, they have less money during the 1857 depression than the Puffys, a working-class family characterized as Irish-American. Nonetheless, the Puffys, temporary landlords of the Fairweathers, treat the middle-class family as their "betters," even sacrificing their own welfare to feed and house them. Bloodgood and his daughter have the wealth to claim upper-class status in the play, but lack sentimental affection. Because bourgeois respectability looked askance at rich people whose pretentiousness led them to believe they deserved special privileges, the action of *Poor* snubs the Bloodgood's social ambitions. By the final curtain, the Bloodgoods and Fairweathers are on the same social plateau, while the Puffys are placed below them in social status. The social hierarchy of *Poor* is less steep and has fewer gradations than that of *Coelina*, which began at the top with the Church and the King, descended to landed gentry, made a place for royal officers, and bottomed out with tradesmen and peasants.

Figure 5.14 In the "Water Cave Scene" from *The Colleen Bawn* by Boucicault, a servant misunderstands his master's wishes and tries to kill the peasant girl his master has secretly married. Many materialist melodramas featured similar scenes of high emotion and scenic illusionism. From an acting edition of the play. [Source: Brockett and Hildy (2003), *History of the Theatre*, p.346.]

Two Major Types of Nineteenth-Century Melodrama

Providential (popular 1800–1825)	Materialist (popular 1855–1880)
Timeless, universal setting	Time-bound, historical setting
Autocratic institutions ensure order	Liberal, bourgeois institutions ensure order
Natural innocence glorified	Social respectability honored
God ensures happy ending	Chance puts happy ending at risk
Return to utopian paradise	Acceptance of material status quo

Why did the successful formula for melodramatic entertainment change so radically between the 1820s and the 1850s? Where popular theatre is concerned, the answer can never be limited to the changing intentions of playwrights and other artists in the theatre. Certainly Boucicault and those working with him after 1855 wanted to write and produce different kinds of plays than had Pixérécourt and his fellow artists, but both groups of theatre-makers, eager for popular success, were primarily responding to their audience. Why, then, did audience tastes for melodramatic theatre change in this thirty-year period from an embrace of providential plays to materialist ones? Contrary to popular belief, matters of taste are primarily social and historical in origin, not individual. People enjoy certain types of melodramas (and melodramatic films, songs, and DVDs today) because their performances represent their hopes, fears, and beliefs about social morality. These enjoyable feelings and ideas – present in both the content and form of any theatrical performance – are shaped by social and historical experience. Certain kinds of plays attain popularity because they appeal to the values and emotions of specific social groups, often groups able to exercise significant power in their historical societies.

One way for historians to understand the changing popularity of types of melodramatic plays in the nineteenth century is to use the concept of cultural hegemony. From this point of view, the popular formula for melodramatic theatre changed from providential to materialist because the 1850s audience sought different definitions and assurances about social morality than had previous spectators in 1800.

INTERPRETIVE APPROACH: Cultural hegemony

Italian Marxist Antonio Gramsci (1891–1937) believed that those with social, economic, and political power also exert widespread influence on the culture dominating their society. The kinds of stories told in fiction, movies, and plays, for example, typically limit how most people in a society understand their lives and their potential for changing the power relations that enfold them. Told that "the Almighty" or "the economy" determines their place in society, for example, many people will not challenge the structures of the status quo. Gramsci's ideas, modified and elaborated by later theorists and historians, have shaped many investigations of popular culture and the persuasiveness of its ideological limitations.

Theatre historians can begin to apply the notion of cultural hegemony to understanding a specific period of theater history by asking and answering the following:

KEY QUESTIONS

1   **Which social groups had the most power in that historical period?**

2   **When these powerful groups attended the theatre, what kinds of plays did they enjoy?**

3   **How did performances of these kinds of plays position these spectators to understand their power and privilege? Did these plays legitimate or undercut the power relations of the status quo?**

4   **What other, less powerful social groups enjoyed these plays of the dominant culture? How might their enjoyment have helped to convince these spectators that the status quo was necessary and just?**

In addition to examining the hegemonic role of plays, theatre historians can also draw on Gramsci's ideas to relate acting style, theatre architecture, and all other aspects of theatrical events to questions of social power and cultural domination. Further, historians can use the concept of cultural hegemony to compare two historical types of the same genre of drama and the reasons for the success of each in related periods of theatre history.

Melodrama and cultural hegemony

During the first decade of the 1800s, the social groups with the most power in France applauded the rise of Napoleon and his restoration of political and social order after a decade of revolutionary turmoil. These reactionaries also renewed their faith in Christianity and the traditional authority of the Catholic Church, which began to recoup much of the power it had lost in the 1790s. At the same time, these powerful groups, especially significant factions of the bourgeoisie and many in the military, had come to accept the sentimental and utopian promises of the Revolution. That is, they believed that natural intuition was a better guide to morality than reason and continued to hope for a society in which evil could be banished from the world. These reactionaries applauded many different kinds of entertainment in Parisian theatres and throughout the West, but they were especially fond of the providential melodramas of Pixérécourt and his imitators. And no wonder – these plays induced nostalgia for the authoritarian order of the *ancien regime* and complimented their audiences on their inherent innocence and spiritual wisdom. Although many working-class groups in Europe and the United States also applauded providential melodrama, the genre undercut values supporting the kinds of reforms that might have benefited them.

By the 1850s, the capitalist revolution in Western Europe and the United States had created an international middle class with very different desires and anxieties than the post-revolutionary groups of the early 1800s. Like the earlier social groups, however, many Americans and Europeans responded to the economic revolution of the nineteenth century in contradictory ways. Many embraced the apparent efficiency of the contracts, train schedules, and increasingly complex manufacturing processes of industrial capitalism. The belief that man's rational mind could control the material world for the betterment of all undercut the need for religion and undermined traditional, hierarchical forms of authority. The new bourgeoisie, however,

Figure 5.15 Poster for Byron's melodrama *Across the Continent* (c.1870) showing a train crashing through ethnic minorities and dispersing fighting workers. © New York Public Library. Rephotographed from Richard Moody, *Dramas from the American Theatre, 1762–1909.*

also attempted to brake the steam-powered forces of nineteenth-century capitalism through the code of respectability. Respectability taught that profits alone were no guarantee of social status; the respectable also needed sentimental affection and correct manners, behavior that could get in the way of simply making money. Consequently, just as providential melodramas helped powerful social groups early in the century to craft a new morality in the wake to the French Revolution, so did materialist melodramas assist the new bourgeoisie in forging a social morality that would benefit their class in the 1850s. Arguably, this kind of melodrama was even more antithetical to working-class interests than the providential kind because it rendered fundamental reform unthinkable in a chance-ridden world (Figure 5.15).

Melodrama continued to change after the 1880s, when the materialist plays written by Boucicault and his imitators went out of fashion. And the concept of cultural hegemony continues to be a useful way of understanding the effects of their popularity. Which social groups benefit from current conceptions of "good guys" and "bad guys" in detective stories on television today? What is the social morality behind the popular genre of disaster films? By understanding how these dramas help to legitimate or undercut the values of powerful social groups, we can begin to answer these questions.

BMc

Key references

Brooks, P. (1984) *The Melodramatic Imagination: Balzac, Henry James, Melodrama and the Mode of Excess*, New Haven: Yale University Press.

Gramsci, A. (1971) *Selections from the Prison Notebooks of Antonio Gramsci*, Hoave, Q. and Nowell-Smith, G. (eds), New York: International Publishers.

Heilman, R. (1968) *Tragedy and Melodrama: Versions of Experience*, Seattle: University of Washington Press.

McConachie, B. (1992) *Melodramatic Formations: American Theatre and Society, 1820–1870*, Iowa City, I.A.: University of Iowa Press.

Pao, A.C. (1998) *The Orient of the Boulevards: Exoticism, Empire, and the Nineteenth-Century French Theater*, Philadelphia: University of Pennsylvania Press.

Redmond, J. (ed.) (1992) *Melodrama*, Themes in Drama, No. 14, London and New York: Cambridge University Press.

CHAPTER 6

Theatre, nation, and empire, 1750–1900

As we have seen, the French Revolution and the Napoleonic wars led to major changes in European culture and its theatre. In addition to inciting a need for the black-and-white morality of melodrama, the revolutionary era also inflamed European nationalism. Unlike earlier European wars, much of the combat between 1795 and 1815 involved citizen-soldiers who believed they fought to defend people like themselves, not to advance the interests of a king or emperor. As in subsequent wars involving nation-states, the bloodshed of the revolutionary era required justification, and the ideologies of nationalism provided ready answers. Consequently, the rise of melodrama and nationalism in the theatre after 1800 were linked. Like melodrama, nationalism defines and separates a moral group of people from others who are unethical and dangerous. In both kinds of contests, spectators, voters, and combatants come to believe that the "good people" must prevail over the "bad people," or chaos and immorality will triumph. The blood-stained logic trumpeting nationalistic goals through melodramatic means sustained hundreds of theatrical productions during the nineteenth century and still pervades many Hollywood melodramas today.

After 1800, nation-states increasingly combined the ideology of nationalism with the political authority and military might of the state. This combination was relatively new in world history. The idea that a people, a nation, loosely united by a common language or culture, has an inherent right to its own geographical and political state would have seemed absurd to most of humanity before 1700. As historian Benedict Anderson notes, the imagined fellowship that undergirds nationalism has to be invented and continuously reaffirmed. Nations, as gatherings of strangers, must both build upon and surpass the affiliations that draw people together as families and neighbors. According to Anderson, a nation is "an imagined political community – and imagined as both limited and sovereign" (Anderson 1991 6). That is, the nation and its accompanying state is limited with regard to its territorial expanse and sovereign in terms of its ability to take independent political action within its boundaries and against other countries.

Print culture was one of the major factors leading to the construction, success, and proliferation of nation-states, notes Anderson. The success of print in Europe involved the standardization of national languages and facilitated communication among groups that shared that language. In effect, says Anderson, print allowed the literate classes of each European country to imagine the existence of other readers like themselves as they read their books, newspapers, and journals. Print gave more power to the laws and procedures emanating from the capitals of nation-states and enabled their bureaucrats to prevail over officials tied to local customs. The increasing legitimacy of the nation-state sparked an interest in national histories, and the dissemination of printed histories, in turn, increased the imagined coherence of nation-states.

Nationalists in England and France were the first successfully to transform their countries into national "imagined communities," and this development gave their bourgeoisie and political leaders a decided advantage in international politics and economics over other countries during the nineteenth century. Although the wars against Napoleon had inspired nationalists throughout Europe to form their own nation-states, the peace of Vienna in 1815 restored most of the pre-1789 borders to the map of Europe. Despite some commonalities of language and culture, Italy and Germany remained divided into small states, and the Austrian Empire encompassed a patchwork of national cultures, including Polish, Hungarian, and Czech in 1815. During the century, Cavour, Garibaldi, and a series of short wars brought most of Italy under one rule (in 1861). A decade later Bismarck, the Prussian army, and more wars united most German-speaking lands within the German Empire (in 1871). Meanwhile, cultural nationalism, a belief in the uniqueness and greatness of one's language-based culture, flourished within European nations that could not yet claim their own state. Only after the Great War (1914–1918) and the dissolution of several European empires could cultural nationalists climb to political power within the new nation-states of Ireland, Czechoslovakia, Poland, Hungary, Finland, and several others.

While nationalism helped the rulers of old and new nation-states to solidify their authority at home, it also emboldened many of them to seek empire abroad. It is no accident that European and American imperialism flourished alongside nationalism during the long nineteenth century, from 1789 to the start of the Great War. While imperialism, the conquest and exploitation of a geographic area and its people by another power, has been a fact of world history since ancient times, the success of nation-states and print culture speeded its advance in the nineteenth century. The first countries to develop into nation-states, England and France, also became the first imperial powers to dominate the globe. The standardizations, efficiencies, and imaginative leaps enabled by print that had helped to transform their countries into modern nations also worked to transform much of the world into areas for their exploitation. Behind the western drive for empire were economic goals, as competing national economies vied for raw materials, cheap labor, and new markets. In contrast to earlier European colonialism, imperializing nations in the nineteenth century justified their dominance by a belief in their inherent cultural and political superiority. Nationalism, often joined with a racialized sense of "the white man's burden," fueled western imperialism.

The belief in racial and/or cultural superiority led to imperialistic adventures against others close to home as well as overseas. By 1890, England had incorporated Scotland and Wales into Great Britain, which at its peak occupied and administered a quarter of the globe. From its core around Moscow, Russia had established its power over many diverse peoples from Finland to the Ukraine to the eastern tip of Siberia. Many historians now regard the westward expansion of the United States, which involved the decimation and removal from their lands of most of the indigenous tribes and the purchase and annexation of other lands, as a form of imperialism. By 1914, after "the scramble for Africa," ongoing European depredations in Asia, and the United States's success in the Caribbean and Pacific, the European imperial powers and the United States controlled 85 percent of the land mass in the world.

This chapter examines the kinds of theatre that followed from and helped to legitimate western nationalism and imperialism from 1750 to 1900 (actually 1914). As we will see, nationalism was profoundly indebted to romanticism, a movement in the arts linked to the cultural dynamics of the French Revolution. After tracing the rise and proliferation of nationalistic and imperialistic theatre in Europe and the United States during the nineteenth century, we turn to a case study that centers on cultural nationalism and the rejection of imperialism in Ireland. One faction of cultural nationalists rioted to protest the work of another when the Abbey Theatre produced *The Playboy of the Western World* in 1907.

Romanticism and the theatre

The French Revolution fragmented European literate opinion into four major political-cultural camps: liberals clung to Enlightenment principles of rationality and hoped for a return to moderation; conservatives rejected the rationalistic excesses of the Revolution and looked to national traditions for stability; radicals, believing the Revolution had not gone far enough, continued to work against despotic regimes; and reactionaries rejected all aspects of the Revolution and yearned for a return to a Catholic and absolutist Europe. These political-cultural positions on the Revolution had hardened by 1815 and the smaller European Revolutions of 1830 and 1848 kept them alive. Although the positions changed over time, their general orientations would shape European politics and culture into the 1870s.

Within the orientations left by the French Revolution, romanticism grew best in radical and conservative soil. In the theatre, as in literature and music, romanticism prized the subjectivity of

genius, looked to nature for inspiration, elevated strong emotions above reasonable restraint, and often sought to embody universal conflicts within individual figures. Initially, romantic theatre shared the radical utopian hopes of the revolutionaries, but later romantics, especially after the fall of Napoleon in 1815, turned pessimistic and conservative. In Germany after 1815, for example, romantics Christian Dietrich Grabbe (1801–1836) and Georg Büchner (1813–1837) wrote pessimistic plays about history's ironies and life's absurdities, but found few companies willing to produce them. Most of their best work, *Jest, Satire, Irony and Deeper Significance* (1822) by Grabbe, and *Danton's Death* (1835) and *Woyzeck* (1836) by Büchner, would await discovery and production in the twentieth century.

In another sense, however, the political-cultural orientations left by the Revolution could not contain the intense subjectivity of romanticism. In the music of Beethoven and the poetry of Wordsworth, romanticism marked a new point on the continuum of cultural modes for gaining knowledge about the self. In medieval and early modern times, western culture taught humans to look primarily to external entities – the feudal order, the Church, the logic of absolutism – for self-understanding. Beginning with the Protestant Reformation and moving to the Enlightenment, to sentimentalism, and then to romanticism, western culture increasingly invited humans to discover purpose and understanding from within. The romantic movement from 1790 to 1850 marked a new step in this 500-year development in the West from external institutions to internal subjectivity – a development epitomized by the gradual shift from the Catholic confessional to the Freudian couch.

The theatre of the early 1800s, however, lacked many of the means that later avant-garde artists would use to explore subjectivity in the twentieth century. Primarily reliant on poetic dialog and the human voice, romantic poets who turned to the stage too often wrote plays that relied on monologue instead of action aimed at involving an audience. Several of the great English romantic poets tried playwriting, for example, but Wordworth's *The Borderers* (1796), Keats's *Otho the Great* (1819), and Shelley's *The Cenci* (1819) either failed to gain production or to move spectators in performance.

The principles of romanticism, however, broke the hold of neoclassicism in theatrical criticism and shaped a new generation of European critics and audiences. Romantic criticism began primarily with August Wilhelm Schlegel (1767–1845), a devotee of Shakespearean production in Germany, who sharply distinguished between neoclassical and romantic theatre. According to Schlegel, Shakespearean dramatic form was organic – it germinated and flowered from within, like a plant – unlike neoclassic plays, in which unity was achieved externally and mechanically. Schlegel's ideas influenced a whole generation of English romantic critics, primarily through the work of Samuel Taylor Coleridge (1772–1834). Like Schlegel, Coleridge advanced the concept of organic unity and dismissed the neoclassical unities of time and place as mechanical. In France, Victor Hugo (1802–1885) emphasized Schlegel's belief that dramatic genres are primarily distinguished by their distinctive moods. Hugo claimed that romantic plays, for example, combined sublime with grotesque moods. These and other romantic critics emphasized the power of the imagination, in readers of poetry and spectators as well as dramatists and actors. The reader's engagement in the fiction of a good poem will involve what he called "that willing suspension of disbelief that for the moment that constitutes poetic faith," and Coleridge's happy phrase sums up his idea about the spectator's imaginative engagement in a theatre production (Coleridge 1974:588; 1989:306). By 1850, romantic criticism, aided by the ongoing proliferation of scholarly works, journal articles, and newspaper reviews through print, had helped to alter audience expectations at the theatre.

Romanticism, with its emphasis on individual genius, also energized European acting and star power. Although each star crafted a public image to convey the impression that his or her talent was unique, star acting during the romantic era shared many attributes: close attention to the individualizing details of characterization, sudden bursts of powerful emotion, and the display of eccentric behavior. Ludwig Devrient (1784–1832), who performed in Berlin and Vienna from 1804 into the early 1830s, was known for his novel interpretations of Shakespearean roles. Edmund Kean (1787–1833) electrified London audiences with his eccentricities and raw emotionality. Between the mid-1830s and 1850, the passionate outbursts of Frederick Lemaître (1800–1876) and the emotional power of Rachel (1821–1858) dominated the French stage, where romanticism came late.

Romanticism, history, and nationalism

Arguably, romanticism's primary influence on nineteenth century theatre sprang from its advocates' fascination with national history. When most Enlightenment thinkers looked at history in the eighteenth century, they tried to deduce universal principles about human behavior from the past that they could apply to all nations in the present and future. Romantic historian J.G. Herder (1744–1803), however, denied that this was possible. In his *Ideas on the Philosophy of the History of Mankind* (1784), Herder argued that every historian's understanding of the past was necessarily subservient to a *Volksgeist*, the spirit of a national people. Not even well-trained historians could transcend their particular *Volksgeist* to write universal history because the history of each national people was unique, said Herder. Although Enlightenment notions of the potential universality of historical interpretation remained dominant in much of the West for the rest of the century, Herder's ideas about history and later modifications to it shaped most discussions about cultural nationalism during the nineteenth century. Napoleon's armies had conquered in the name of universal

Enlightenment principles, and Europeans oppressed by the French looked to Herder and his followers to justify their nation's opposition to French imperialism. Although Herder himself never argued that one nation or racial group might be superior to others, several of his later disciples claimed that his historicism justified their nationalistic and/or racialized superiority. In general, Herder's legacy animated historians and others to search for the origins of their nation's *Volksgeist*, to explore what they took to be the unique features of their "imagined community," and to celebrate their own national heroes. Many of Herder's ideas continue to be influential today.

The mix of romanticism, historicism, and nationalism inspired by Herder played out primarily in conservative ways in many countries in nineteenth-century Europe. In England, theatre artists began working with historians to mount more accurate productions of national historical plays, principally the dramas of Shakespeare. This was a part of the movement known as antiquarianism, which aimed to immerse spectators in the spirit of past and exotic cultures through an accurate rendering of their details. In Shakespearean theatre, antiquarianism began with Charles Kemble's (1775–1854) production of *King John* in 1823. James Robinson Planché (1796–1880) based his costuming of Kemble's actors on scrupulous research into medieval dress, an innovation welcomed by Kemble's bourgeois audience. Planché, a leader in antiquarianism, costumed subsequent Shakespearean productions with attention to historical detail and provided managers with extensive information on the banners and insignia of medieval heraldry (Figure 6.1). William Charles Macready (1793–1873), who dominated the English stage from the 1830s into the early 1840s, popularized the goals of antiquarianism by aiming consistently for historical accuracy in costuming, props, and painted scenery for his major productions. Perhaps the highpoint (or lowpoint) of English antiquarianism came in the 1850s, with the Shakespearean productions of Charles Kean (1811–1868). Aware that many in his respectable audience were interested in historical accuracy, Kean

Figure 6.1 Print of J.R. Planché's 1824 design for the King's costume in Charles Kean's production of Shakespeare's *Henry IV*. From Planché's *Costume of Shakespeare's King Henry IV, Parts I and II* (1824). © Lilly Library, Indiana University, Bloomington.

printed lists in his programs of the sources he and his designers had consulted in putting together his productions. Kean even subjected Shakespearean comedy to his pedantry, claiming, for instance, that the tools depicted as a part of Peter Quince's workshop in his production of *A Midsummer Night's Dream* were all copied from discoveries at a Roman ruin. Under antiquarianism, Shakespearean productions in England became a means of honoring the genius of the national poet and a conservative understanding of the national past.

In France, revolutionaries staged nationalistic, open-air festivals to celebrate the victory of the people in the 1790s, but Napoleon revived neoclassicism and the theatrical institutions of the old regime soon after he became emperor. After 1815, with the return of the monarchy, reactionaries blocked the rise of romanticism in France. Nonetheless, by 1830, Victor Hugo had announced the goals of a romantic theatre in his preface to his historical play *Cromwell* in 1827, and romantic productions

had already achieved some success at the Comédie Française.

The reactionaries took their stand in 1830 at the Comédie's production of Hugo's *Hernani*. Hugo put together an alliance of conservatives and liberals to support his romantic *Hernani*, which intentionally violated many of the rules of neoclassicism. After an initial three nights of calm, a shouting and shoving match raged for the remaining 36 performances between the romantics and the reactionaries in the audience, drowning out the actors (Figure 6.2). In the end, most of the Parisian press hailed the romantics as the victors, chiefly for outlasting their opponents, and the romantics mounted many more productions in the 1830s and achieved widespread respectability. French romanticism on the stage mixed easily with melodrama, both in the generally liberal plays of Hugo and in the conservative costume dramas of Alexandre Dumas *père* (1802–1870), such as *Henri III and His Court* and his adaptation of *The Three Musketeers*.

Figure 6.2 Contemporary illustration of the *Hernani* riots, showing the audience and the final scene of Hugo's play at the Comédie Française in 1830. Bibliothèque Nationale, Paris.

European cultural nationalists in nations without major states (that is, most of the lands in Germany, Italy, and several language groups in the Austrian and Russian Empires) wrote plays and sponsored national theatres to celebrate what they believed was their people's unique culture and glorious past. This tradition began in Hamburg in 1765, when actor-manager Konrad Ackermann (1712–1771) joined with the critic Johann Friedrich Löwen to found the short-lived Hamburg National Theatre (1765–1769). Later troupes in other German cities also announced their plans for a theatre that might unify the many distinctive dialects and traditions of an imagined "German people" and several dramatists attempted such a synthesis in their plays.

Friedrich Schiller (1759–1805), a celebrated historian as well as a playwright and director, was the most ambitious, complex, and talented of the early German cultural nationalists. Following his early plays during the Storm and Stress movement and his tenure as a professor of history at the University of Jena, Schiller returned to the theatre in 1799 as a playwright at the Weimar Court Theatre. Like Goethe, the director at Weimar, Schiller had reassessed his earlier embrace of Storm and Stress anarchy and his late plays reflect an interest in classical restraint and Enlightenment morality. *Mary Stuart* (1800), for instance, demonstrates the guilt and emotional isolation Queen Elizabeth I of England must face despite her triumph over her rival for the throne, Mary Stuart, who achieves tragic sublimity in defeat. In *The Maid of Orleans* (1801) and *William Tell* (1804), Schiller investigates the role that moral independence must play in the fight for religious and national freedom. Although later German nationalists often pointed to William Tell as the model of the Germanic hero who would unite the nation, Schiller's nationalism was firmly tied to the universal principles of the Enlightenment, not to Herder's historicism. Indeed, the "Weimar classicism" that Schiller and Goethe achieved in their productions at the Weimar Court Theatre remained

a model of Enlightenment restraint against the xenophobia that more fervent German nationalists expressed during the nineteenth century.

German attempts to establish national theatres and write national history plays set the precedent for later cultural nationalists in the Austrian and Russian empires. As a result of three land-grabs by Russia, Austria, and Prussia, Poland had ceased to exist as a sovereign state by 1795, but Polish nationalists throughout the nineteenth century pushed for a return to independence and mounted two major revolts against the occupying powers. Many prominent theatre artists were also nationalists, among them Wojciech Boguslawski (1757–1829), who worked to develop a repertory of nationalistic dramas during his intermittent tenure as Director of the National Theatre in Warsaw from 1783 to 1814. While in exile, two of Poland's outstanding poet-playwrights, Adam Mickiewicz (1798–1855) and Juliusz Slowacki (1809–1849), wrote romantic plays that gained substantial influence as texts but could not be produced until the twentieth century. Several Magyar-language plays in the 1840s dramatized the plight of Hungarian peasants, and Magyar cultural nationalists partly succeeded in gaining legitimacy for their heritage within the Austrian empire, which became the Austro-Hungarian empire in 1867. In Prague, Bedrich Smetana (1824–1884) composed nationalistic operas about his native Czech lands and rallied public support for a national theatre, which opened in 1881. Cultural nationalists in Finland pushed for more independence from Russia in the last decades of the nineteenth century. National poet Aleksis Kivi (1834–1872) celebrated the Finnish qualities of his peasant hero in *Cobblers on the Heath* (1875), while he and others pushed for a Finnish-language national theatre, finally established with a new building in 1902. For the most part, these cultural nationalists followed in Herder's conservative footsteps in their assumptions about the organic uniqueness and potential greatness of their imagined national communities.

Nationalism and imperialism in theatre in the United States

Herder's romantic legacy had some influence on U.S. nationalism, but Enlightenment universalism was a more dominant strain. As in the French Revolution, Americans had fought against their oppressors on the basis of the Enlightenment values of political liberty, individual freedoms, and the rights of private property. Rather than supposing that their values were unique, most Americans, like French liberals, believed that their Enlightenment precepts represented the aspirations of all humankind. The legacy of Puritanism, which preached that America might separate itself from the decadence of Europe and lead the world to salvation, reinforced American self-righteousness and the claim of moral exceptionalism. Given this point of view, few Americans understood their conquest of other peoples and their incorporation of western lands into their nation as imperialism. Instead, most viewed their nineteenth-century wars with England, Mexico, Spain, and with dozens of Native American tribes as expanding the area of freedom, even when these wars increased the territory in which chattel slavery was legal. American exceptionalism justified American conquests as victories for democracy and justice.

In the period between the American Revolution (1776–1783) and the Civil War (1861–1865), many U.S. playwrights embraced and enhanced the theme of American exceptionalism. Royall Tyler (1757–1826) used English sentimentalism to sharpen the differences between decadent Europeans and virtuous Americans in *The Contrast* (1787), the first significant American comedy. Manager-playwright William Dunlap (1766–1839) found that he had to revise his neoclassical tragedy *André* (1798), which valued enlightened reason over narrow-minded nationalism, into the more overtly patriotic, *The Glory of Columbia: Her Yeomanry* (1803), to make it acceptable to his spectators. American plays on the Revolution, the War of 1812, and the Mexican War typically joined melodrama to nationalism to celebrate the exceptional bravery and resourcefulness of American manhood. A virtuous people fighting to free themselves from decadent oppressors dominated the plots and sentiments of many romantic melodramas, including *Metamora* (1829), *The Gladiator* (1831), and *Jack Cade* (1835), vehicles crafted to boost the appeal of American-born star Edwin Forrest (1806–1872). Several dramatists in the 1830s and 1840s wrote plays that racialized Native Americans, usually depicting them as either noble representatives of a dying race or uncivilized savages, fit for destruction by advancing whites. American exceptionalism continued as a dominant theme in U.S. comedies. *Fashion* (1845), for example, by actor-playwright Anna Cora Mowatt (1819–1870), depicts a foppish European foiled by the Yankee character, Adam Trueman, his name redolent of originary innocence and integrity.

After the Civil War, many playwrights simply assumed the exceptional superiority of the U.S. to Europe and sought a racialized "American identity" in the contrast with non-white ethnic groups in the West. In plays like *Across the Continent* (1870), *Horizon* (1871), and *Davy Crockett* (1872), American dramatists mixed marauding Indians, comic Chinese, and white love-interests in melodramatic pot-boilers to celebrate the telegraph, the Gold Rush, the transcontinental railroad, and other extensions of U.S. power. Several later plays, including *The Girl of the Golden West* (1905) and *The Great Divide* (1906), used the West as the appropriate setting to explore what they took to be the white essences of American gender roles. Like many western playwrights on both sides of the turn of the century, several American dramatists marked their superiority to other peoples and nations in racial terms.

This new emphasis continued in the Civil War plays that gained popularity from the late 1880s through 1900. Tellingly, the commercial theatre rarely engaged the dramatic possibilities of the Civil War until the failure of Reconstruction had settled the fate of black citizens in the U.S., and even then the plays ignored the issue of slavery that had divided the Union. Bronson Howard (1842–1908), the first U.S. citizen to make his living solely as a dramatist, penned *Shenandoah* for the New York stage in 1888. Its emphasis on romance – four love-interests across the battle lines – drove home the need for reconciliation between whites in the North and South. Other popular Civil War melodramas, such as *Secret Service* and *The Heart of Maryland* (both 1895), offered a similar mix of romance, sensation, and conventional villainy in well-made melodramas. The need for national unity based on whiteness implicit in these plays evaded and abetted the racism that was increasing against black citizens and many groups of foreign immigrants. Many post-Civil War plays helped to unite white Americans for racism at home and imperialism abroad, which flourished during the Spanish-American War (1898), the repression of Philippine independence, economic exploitation in China, and numerous U.S. incursions into Latin American countries to protect American interests.

Nationalism and imperialism on the Russian stage

Before the 1820s, neoclassicism dominated the Russian theatre. Tsarina Catherine II (1729–1796) imported the French theatrical system and French plays, built neoclassical theatres, and even wrote her own plays on the French model. Sentimentalism also enjoyed some success with the Russian nobility and small middle class that constituted most audiences; Kotzebue's plays continued to be popular throughout the nineteenth century, for example. Alexander I (1777–1825) imposed censorship on printed as well as performed drama and a monopoly on theatrical production, which lasted until 1882. As such laws had done in France before the Revolution, these severely restricted theatrical expression, fostered cynicism about the regime, and spawned numerous ways to evade imperial regulations.

Napoleon's invasion of Russia in 1812 sparked a patriotic response in the theatre, which the

absolutist regime turned to its own purposes. The fight against France boosted the popularity of V.A. Ozerov's (1769–1816) neoclassic history play, *Dmitry of the Don* (1807), which reminded the Russian nobility of their victory against the Tartars in 1380.

Tartars, Turks, and Moslem tribesmen, the historic foes of the Russian empire in its drive to extend its power from Moscow south to the Black Sea and east to China and Alaska, would recur as frequent villains in many nineteenth-century historical epics and melodramas. By the 1830s, neoclassicism had yielded to romanticism in the Russian theatre, but imperial censorship favored the reactionary romantic plays of N.V. Kukolnik (1809–1868) and N.A. Polevoi (1796–1846). Kukolnik's *The Hand of the Almighty Has Saved the Fatherland* preached the divine right of the Tsars to rule the Russian empire. He followed this 1833 piece with other historical epics depicting heroic and paternalistic Tsars and noblemen, picturesque and grateful serfs, and exotic Moslems in need of Russian Christianity. N.A. Polevoi (1796–1846) blended sentimentalism into Kukolnik's reactionary world of nationalism and imperialism with such epics as *The Grandfather of the Russian Fleet* (1838). These and similar plays helped to justify the Tsar's declaration of war against Turkey in 1853 in another attempt at imperial expansion. However, the Crimean War (in which France and England joined Turkey to defeat Russia) punched holes in the image of Russia advanced by the reactionaries and led to some reforms.

Liberal and radical romantics in Russia such as Alexander Pushkin (1799–1837) had also turned to history for inspiration. But the radical politics of his *Boris Godunov* (1825), a sprawling masterpiece, kept it out of publication until 1831 and off the stage entirely until 1870. Censorship eased somewhat in the 1850s, allowing the staging of poet Mikhail Lermontov's (1814–1841) *Masquerade*, inspired by Shakespeare's *Othello*. His *The Spaniards*, however, a play about the Inquisition written in 1830 to expose the repression of Tsar Nicholas I's reign (from 1825–1855), was not published until 1880 and was never performed during the nineteenth century. Russian comic satirists A.S. Griboedov (1794–1829) in *Woe from Wit* (1824) and Nikolai Gogol (1809–1852) in *The Inspector General* (1836) had more success with their attacks on individual bumblers, embezzlers, sycophants, and hypocrites, but their generally conservative politics offered little offense to the ideology of the regime. It would not be until later in the century that playwrights could examine Russian history and publish their dramas without propagandizing for absolutism. In his trilogy of plays about three Russian feudal monarchs, *The Death of Ivan the Terrible* (1864), *Tsar Fyodor Ivannovich* (1868), and *Tsar Boris* (1870), Aleksei Tolstoy (1817–1875) focused on the psychological and ethical ramifications of political rule. Most Russian historical plays, however, like many operas and ballets popular with the regime, continued to fuse together Tsarist rule, Christianity, patriotism, and imperialism until the Russian Revolution of 1917.

Orientalism on the European stage

When Russian artists and imperial administrators looked at Tartars, Turks, and various non-Christian others within the Russian Empire, they tended to depict them as indolent, exotic, devious, and irrational – and in need of civilization. In this, the Russians shared with other imperial powers an orientalist vision of the world to the east and south of Europe. (For a discussion of "orientalism," see the case study, "Global Shakespeare," in Chapter 11.) The romantic antiquarianism that reshaped Shakespearean productions on the London stage excited a similar interest in orientalism for English audiences, which followed in the wake of British imperialism in the Middle East. English imperialists gained influence and control in many Moslem countries, including Egypt, the Sudan, and Pakistan, and they won increasing concessions from the Turkish

Ottoman Empire, which stretched from the Balkans through Turkey to the Arabian peninsula and to present-day Iran before 1914.

The romantic star Edmund Kean excited substantial interest in the lures of "the Orient" on the London stage during the 1810s and 1820s. Kean performed Turkish kings, Saracen warriors, Arab princes, half-Greek-half-Turk heroes, and other roles in plays set in the Middle East. In addition, he specialized in exotic figures from many lands, including a Moorish Othello and what critics termed an "oriental" Shylock. Through various make-ups, costuming, physicality, and accents, Kean racialized these roles to such an extent that his critics claimed that he embodied the spirit of each exotic people he portrayed. Several of Kean's star vehicles, including a stage adaptation of *The Bride of Abydos* (1827), a romantic poem by Lord Byron, centered on episodes set in a harem. These scenes not only allowed for parades of female beauty in skimpy attire, but encouraged the western imperialist dream of rescuing exotic maidens from evil Moslem rulers.

The London Exhibition of 1851, the first of many world's fairs to present the non-western world as a marketplace open for western tourists and capitalists, added to the desirability of "oriental" lands. As in many U.S. melodramas about western expansion, late-Victorian plays about British triumphs in the Middle East often celebrated the technology that made imperialism possible. London audiences watching *Freedom* (1882), for example (in which the British invade Egypt to quell the slave trade and save the daughter of a British financier from sexual slavery in a harem), were assured that the steamships, railroads, and international trade that the white men will bring to the brown people of Egypt more than made up for the unfortunate deaths of a few Egyptians. One of the key figures in *Khartoum* (1885) is a newspaper reporter who uses the telegraph and other new modes of communication to tell English imperialists about the dire circumstances in the Sudanese city. The melodrama actually reversed General Gordon's loss of Khartoum to rebeling Islamic tribesmen the year before. Like later adaptations of *Around the World in Eighty Days* and dozens of other imperial plays, these two well-made melodramas presented British domination as the march of white progress and civilization. London theatre managers used the techniques of realism and antiquarianism for these plays to assure their audiences that their knowledge of the "primitive" cultures around the globe was geographically accurate and anthropologically correct.

Theatre riots

Although the new fields of geography and anthropology helped imperialists to fix and classify the peoples they were subjugating, these disciplines rarely predicted "native" opposition. In Europe, many stateless cultural nationalists carried the fight against imperial domination into the theatre by fomenting riots. Theatre riots in the West have a long history, only partly connected to the dynamics of nationalism and imperialism. From the renaissance through the nineteenth century, audiences rioted for many reasons – to protest an increase in ticket prices, to take sides in feuds between actors, and to denounce the perceived undermining of their status, in addition to rejecting slurs against their national identity and protesting what they took to be signs of imperial arrogance. Sometimes these causes worked together, as when anxiety about higher ticket prices, lower status, and national identity led to 67 days of rioting at the Covent Garden Theatre in London in 1807. A feud between a British and an American actor, William Macready and Edwin Forrest, was the initial cause of the Astor Place riot in New York City in 1849, but protests against English domination and class privilege also fueled the disturbances. Although the Astor Place Opera House was privately owned, social custom understood all playhouses as a part of the public sphere and consequently an available site for public protest.

Theatre riots in the eighteenth and nineteenth centuries, like most contemporary riots in marketplaces, at worksites, and elsewhere, usually involved noisemaking and fighting, but little property damage and few deaths. Aware that most people considered rioting a legitimate form of social protest, local elites and the constabulary generally let a riot run its course and only intervened if excessive damage or any deaths occurred. Rioting waned in the major theatre capitals of the West after 1850, largely because of better policing, the dimming of house lights during performances, and the increasing privatization of cultural life under bourgeois authority.

Occasional riots continued in provincial theatres and at the margins of European empires. Before Ireland gained independence in 1922, it was a part of the British Empire. Our case study following this chapter examines the cultural nationalist, anti-imperialist riots that greeted the first week of the Abbey Theatre's production of *The Playboy of the Western World*, by John Millington Synge, in Dublin in 1907.

BMc

Key references

For further references for this chapter, see the Key references at the end of the Introduction to Part II.

Anderson, B. (1991) *Imagined Communities: Reflections on the Origin and Spread of Nationalism*, 2nd edn, London and New York: Verso.

Coleridge, S.T. (1974) "Progress of the Drama [1818]," in Bernard F. Dukore (ed.) *Dramatic Theory and Criticism*, New York: Holt, Rinehart and Winston.

Coleridge, S.T. (1989) *Biographia Literaria* [1815–16], Chapter 14, in D.H. Richter (ed.) *The Critical Tradition*, New York: St. Martin's Press.

CASE STUDY: The *Playboy* riots: Nationalism in the Irish theatre

Background to the riots

In 1900, many factions in Dublin had conflicting views on the future of Ireland, which had been a part of the British Empire for over 300 years. Some groups hoped that the colonial status of Ireland could be improved with no major changes to the status quo. Others urged a political union with Great Britain, in which the Irish might share in the limited democracy of English subjects. A small minority argued for an immediate revolution against British rule. Several groups looked to a revival of one or several aspects of Irish culture – its mythic heroes, hardy peasants, Catholic tradition, or its Gaelic language – as the key to eventual national independence. Catholic and Protestant groups favoring cultural nationalism often were pitted against each other. Many Catholics among the nationalists elevated peasant tradition and strict Catholic morality as the essence of Irishness. Cultural nationalists of Protestant descent, whose families had typically emigrated from England to acquire land and rule the country, also wanted eventual independence. Many of them, however, looked to Ireland's pagan past, before Catholic conversions and English invasions, as a tradition that might unite all Irish people.

Despite their historical and political differences, several groups of cultural nationalists helped to launch the Irish National Theatre Society (INTS) in Dublin. Under the management of actors Frank and W.G. Fay (1870–1931 and 1872–1947), the company opened with a 1902 performance of *Cathleen ni Houlihan*, by William Butler Yeats (1865–1939) and Lady Augusta Gregory (1852–1932), and moved into a refurbished theatre (courtesy of an English heiress) on Abbey Street in Dublin in 1904. As the first President of the INTS, Yeats, whose family was Anglo-Irish, initially fostered plays that sought to bridge the differences among the cultural nationalists. *In the Shadow of the Glen*, a one-act play by John

Millington Synge, however, riled the anger of many Catholic patriots in 1903. Synge's play features a peasant heroine who leaves a loveless marriage to gain freedom with a poetic tramp. From Synge's point of view, his protagonist, named Nora to point up her similarity to Ibsen's heroine in *A Doll House*, was justified in sacrificing bourgeois respectability and Catholic morality to embrace a Celtic spirit that will lead to her true liberation.

By the time the Abbey announced its upcoming production of *The Playboy of the Western World*, Yeats had already presented a second Synge play at the Abbey, and Catholic nationalists were losing patience with the INTS. Backed by English money, Yeats had altered the governance of the INTS, making it less democratic and concentrating power in the hands of Anglo-Irish writer-directors. A few disaffected members had left the Abbey to form their own theatre, which sought to produce more Gaelic plays. Now Yeats, who was always suspect among the Catholics for his Anglo-Irish roots, was trumpeting another play by Synge, a dramatist known by the nationalists to harbor anti-Catholic sympathies. Catholic nationalists who went to the opening of *The Playboy* at the Abbey Theatre in January of 1907 expected the worst.

The *Playboy* riots

The first two acts of Synge's comedy proceeded without incident, although the action probably aroused some nationalist ire. On stage Synge's protagonist, Christy Mahon, arrived at a "shebeen" (a small tavern) in County Mayo in western Ireland and told the group of villagers that he had hit his father over the head with a shovel and killed him. Instead of turning him in to the "peelers" (the English police), the villagers celebrated his act of rebellion against an oppressor and praised Christy as a hero. Their adoration transformed the young man, who changed from a shy and fearful peasant into "the playboy of the western world" in the villagers' estimation. By the end of Act II, Christy had won prizes at a local fair and the heart of Pegeen Mike, daughter of the local publican. In addition, however, Synge's two acts had revealed another male character, a pious Catholic peasant, as a coward. He also characterized an Irish peasant woman, Widow Quinn, with a lustiness that affronted respectable nationalists. The comedy of the situation may have kept nationalist anger temporarily in check.

For some in the audience, comedy turned to grotesquerie at the start of Act III. The elder Mahon, supposedly dead, wandered into the shebeen with a bloody bandage on his head. Christy's heroic killing of his father, his youthful rebellion against authoritarian tradition, abruptly lost its glamor. Synge rubbed salt in the nationalist wound by having Christy pursue his father and kill him "again" to win back Pegeen's affections. Several of the spectators groaned, hissed, or shouted. Then Synge exposed the hypocrisy of the peasants, who had initially praised the patricide. They turned on Christy, tied him up, and vengefully tortured him resulting in more hisses and jeers from the nationalists. When Old Mahon returned "from the dead" a second time bloodier than before, a full-scale riot broke out. Scattered audience members cheered for the play trying to counter the catcalls from the nationalist patriots. This led to more noise and occasional fights among the spectators. Although Synge's play ended in a comic reconciliation between father and son, the ending was mostly lost on the patriotic spectators, who continued their tumult.

The Playboy riots, initially spontaneous, hardened into organized protests and continued for a week in the theatre. As one eyewitness later recalled, "The first-night demonstration had set up prejudices and currents of feeling." In the course of the week, "Some, hearing that the peasant was maligned in the play, came to hiss; others, in order to protect, as they thought, the challenged freedom of the theatre, came to support. Still others, hearing the peasant was maligned, came to applaud the maligners" (Levitas 2002:127). To quiet the house, co-manager W.G. Fay called in police protection, which eventually reached 50 English officers. Synge and Gregory dismissed them for fear of exacerbating things, and, although the uproar subsided, Irish patriots from several factions condemned the theatre for resorting to British imperial power to shield the INTS. Newspaper coverage of the nationalist rioters and the theatre's response ran the gamut of political opinion, with a number of editorialists finding much to blame on both sides (Figure 6.3).

Explaining the riots

Any explanation for the riots and the responses they provoked must put these events in the context of British colonial power and Irish aspirations for independence. Historians agree that while Yeats, Synge, and the nationalist rioters at the Abbey all opposed imperialism, they and the groups they represented had had diverse experiences with British oppression and sought very different solutions to the problem of Irish nationhood. It is clear that conservative, Catholic patriots and their allies in the press initiated and sustained the rioting. But historians differ as to the relative importance of the factors that set them off in the performance.

In his recent book *The Politics of Irish Drama*, Nicholas Grene examines four causes of the rioting without taking a position on their relative importance. First, he notes that portions of Synge's dialog (Acts 2 and 3) referring to a woman's undergarment, known then as a "shift" (a chemise) – scandalized conservative members of the audience. In tandem with the suspiciously loose sexual morality of some of the female characters in the play, this affront to the purity of Irish Catholic womanhood roused the anger of the patriots. Second, Grene points to Synge's indictment of his peasants' casual acceptance of crime. The English had long condemned the Irish as a lawless people, and Synge's comedy, which showed peasants glorifying a patricide, seemed to

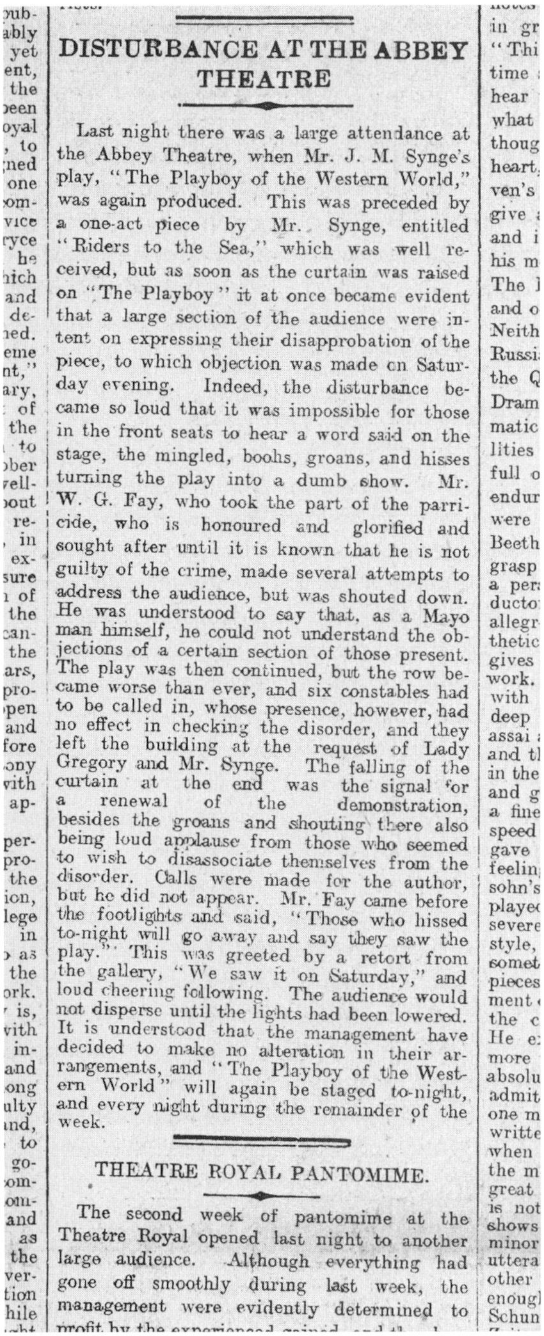

DISTURBANCE AT THE ABBEY THEATRE

Last night there was a large attendance at the Abbey Theatre, when Mr. J. M. Synge's play, "The Playboy of the Western World," was again produced. This was preceded by a one-act piece by Mr. Synge, entitled "Riders to the Sea," which was well received, but as soon as the curtain was raised on "The Playboy" it at once became evident that a large section of the audience were intent on expressing their disapprobation of the piece, to which objection was made on Saturday evening. Indeed, the disturbance became so loud that it was impossible for those in the front seats to hear a word said on the stage, the mingled, boohs, groans, and hisses turning the play into a dumb show. Mr. W. G. Fay, who took the part of the parricide, who is honoured and glorified and sought after until it is known that he is not guilty of the crime, made several attempts to address the audience, but was shouted down. He was understood to say that, as a Mayo man himself, he could not understand the objections of a certain section of those present. The play was then continued, but the row became worse than ever, and six constables had to be called in, whose presence, however, had no effect in checking the disorder, and they left the building at the request of Lady Gregory and Mr. Synge. The falling of the curtain at the end was the signal for a renewal of the demonstration, besides the groans and shouting there also being loud applause from those who seemed to wish to disassociate themselves from the disorder. Calls were made for the author, but he did not appear. Mr. Fay came before the footlights and said, "Those who hissed to-night will go away and say they saw the play." This was greeted by a retort from the gallery, "We saw it on Saturday," and loud cheering following. The audience would not disperse until the lights had been lowered. It is understood that the management have decided to make no alteration in their arrangements, and "The Playboy of the Western World" will again be staged to-night, and every night during the remainder of the week.

THEATRE ROYAL PANTOMIME.

The second week of pantomime at the Theatre Royal opened last night to another large audience. Although everything had gone off smoothly during last week, the management were evidently determined to profit by the experience gained and the

Figure 6.3 Newspaper article from the *Daily Express* of January 1907 describing audience response to Synge's *Playboy of the Western World*. © National Library of Ireland.

confirm this negative stereotype. Third was the locale of the play. Synge had set *The Playboy* in the West of Ireland, an area celebrated by the nationalists for its pure Irish peasant culture, uncontaminated by British rule. Yet Synge's western peasants seemed to be more immodest, murderous, and vengeful than the typical Irish lackey of English power. Finally, Grene notes that the comedy parodied and profaned Catholic belief. With sympathetic characters denouncing piety, deriding priests, and asking blessings for murderers, *The Playboy* seemed to turn Catholicism upside down.

Most critics agree that each of Grene's four causal factors played some role in sparking the rioting that occurred. But historians are usually uncomfortable with a mere listing of several factors; they try to locate one or two fundamental causes to explain an event. What was the most important reason for *The Playboy* riots? Might this reason enable the historian to fold other causal factors, including the four mentioned by Grene, into a broader explanation?

The search for an overarching cause often sends the historian back to the primary documents of the event for clues. In this case, two comments from contemporaries offer suggestive evidence. According to W.G. Fay, the actor who played Christy at the Abbey in 1907, Synge's play angered the nationalists because it mounted "a deliberate attack on the national character" (Ayling 1992:144). In a letter to the editor of a newspaper in Dublin, a spectator who had attended *The Playboy* during the week of rioting wrote: "Sir, if Mr. Synge wishes to turn the 'Sinn Fein' howlers [that is, the Catholic nationalists] into an applauding claque, he need only write a play portraying the Irish peasant as a flawless demi-god. . . .' (Kilroy 1971:54). Together, these comments imply that "the national character" of Ireland, an idealized image of a male Irish peasant, was at stake for the Catholic patriots who rioted. If these clues to the puzzle of causality are to yield an understanding of a fundamental cause of the rioting, however, the historian needs a valid approach to the abstraction, "national character."

INTERPRETIVE APPROACH: Cognitive linguistics

When writers, speakers, dramatists, and others use of the term "national character," they generally invoke social stereotypes, ideal cases, salient examples, and other kinds of prototypical categories. This occurred as well in *The Playboy*. Synge painted one male character negatively as a social stereotype of the pious Catholic, for instance. He carefully crafted Christy Mahon to emerge by the end of Act II as an ideal case of the young, rebellious Irishman. Synge also used Christy to suggest several salient examples – actual people who had performed similar deeds that were well known to the audience. In a widely publicized case in 1898, a son had murdered his father in a violent rage, and Synge's dialog drew attention to this parallel with his protagonist. Each of these kinds of categories – social stereotypes, ideal cases, and salient examples – became possible prototypes of the Irish national character for the audience responding to the world of the play. Other categories with possible relationships to nationalism also abound in *The Playboy*: typical examples (such as the garrulous publican), paragons of morality (the strict village priest), and submodels of an ideal Ireland (all of the County Mayo peasants).

▷

▷

Cognitive linguists study such categories and their use in everyday discourse. This kind of linguistics is a part of the wider field of cognitive studies, which has already provided the basis for one of our previous interpretive approaches. In the case study on classical Greek theatre (Chapter 2), we used an approach within cognitive studies to gain historical understanding of the spatial dynamics of the initial performance of *Oedipus the King*. Here, cognitive linguistics can help us to understand how Synge's mix of characters and categories helped to provoke the riots that greeted his play.

According to cognitive linguist George Lakoff, the mental processing of people, things, and events into categories is natural and inevitable. As humans evolved over thousands of years, they relied on categories to simplify information about the world, make quick judgments, and store knowledge. As a result, the need to categorize became a part of humankind's in-built mental equipment. Humans invariably think in terms of typical examples, ideal cases, submodels, and stereotypes. This does not mean that some consequences of categorizing are inevitable, however. People have the ability to complicate and overturn initial racist and sexist stereotypes, for example, through other modes of categorizing.

Through experimentation, Lakoff and other cognitive linguists have found that some examples in all categories will appear to be more central to that category than others. People identify a robin, for instance, as closer than a penguin to the essence of the category "bird." Similarly, some versions of the color red will register in human experiments as more prototypical of "redness" than other shades. All categories, then, have their prototypes, those best examples that tend to be perceived as more typical of the category than others. As we have already seen, humans often use several kinds of prototypes to specify their categories – ideal cases, social stereotypes, salient examples, paragons, submodels, and typical examples.

Humans process the notion of "national character" through these same prototypical categories. In any performance that raises questions about the "national character" of a people, especially for an audience vitally concerned with defining who is "inside" and who is "outside" of that category, spectators will examine the cast of characters for those who exemplify one or another of its prototypes. Once spectators have been guided to select a character or group of characters as a social stereotype, a paragon, or any other prototype of the nation, they will make generalizations about other members of that nation on the basis of that best example. This is what Lakoff and others term a "prototype effect" (Lakoff and Johnson 1999:40–45). If a play (or a novel or a poem) presents an ignorant drunkard as a national stereotype, for example, others who identify as members of that nation will likely be outraged by the portrait because the "prototype effect" leads them to take it as an insult to themselves.

Because prototypical characters on stage exert immense power over the imaginations of their audience, historians can deploy these ideas about categorization to seek the cause

▷

▷ of *The Playboy* riots. It is clear that Synge's characters represented several kinds of national prototypes for the Catholic cultural rationalists in the audience at the Abbey Theatre in 1907. What response did the production of *The Playboy* seek to evoke toward these prototypes, how might the nationalists have felt about these responses, and did their rioting result from indignation triggered by prototype effects? Questions about such categorizations could be asked of many controversial theatrical events that engage issues of national identity.

Recall that Grene noted four major causes of the riots. From the point of view of cognitive studies, each of these explanations may be linked to a prototype effect that would have annoyed, embarrassed, and/or angered nationalist spectators. Two of Grene's causes are tied to *The Playboy's* attack on Irish Catholicism. A close reading of the play reveals several male and female Catholic characters set up as typical examples of the Irish nation. All of them have character flaws arguably related to their Catholicism – cowardice and blaspheming for the men and confusion about healthy sexuality for the women Christy's love interest, Pegeen Mike, for example, first rejects Catholic strictures about romance and then furiously embraces them when torturing Christy. Grene also pointed to Synge's satire on Irish peasant culture. While the nationalists glorified the prototype of the heroic peasant of Western Ireland, *The Playboy* revealed these paragons of Irishness as lawless avengers. If the peasants of Synge's County Mayo were typical examples and submodels of a heroic, Catholic nation, the cognitive logic of the prototype effect reduced all of the nationalists in the audience to immoral, worthless fools.

The ripple effects of Christy Mahon's unmasking as the ideal representative of young Ireland must have been especially galling for the nationalists. Having gradually inflated his heroic balloon over two acts, Synge pinched it to make it squeal for much of Act III, and then popped it at the end. All that Christy's slaying of his father had come to

represent – righteous youth against repressive age, the present breaking free from the past, even Ireland refusing submission to English imperialism – all painfully petered away with the appearance of Old Mahon and Christy's comic attempt to kill him "again." When toward the end of Act III, Pegeen told Christy "there's a great gap between a gallous story and a dirty deed" (Synge 1964:129), few in the increasingly boisterous audiences would have heard the words spoken by the actress. Nevertheless, Pegeen's memorable line underscored the prototype effect that upset the Catholic patriots. Within *The Playboy*, the speech reduced Christy's attempt on his father's life from an adventurous tale to a murderous attack. On the national political scene, Synge had exposed the Catholics' heroic image of themselves as a dangerous fraud. In the end, Christy and his father simply return to their narrow, repressive life together; Christy is neither a "playboy" nor a Christ figure (as his name implies) for the salvation of Ireland.

BMc

Key references

Ayling, R. (ed.) (1992) *J.M. Synge: Four Plays*, Casebook Series, London: Macmillan.

Grene, N. (1999) *The Politics of Irish Drama: Plays in Context from Boucicault to Friel*, Cambridge: Cambridge University Press.

Kilroy, J. (1971) *The "Playboy" Riots*, Dublin: Dolmen Press.

Lakoff, G. (1987) *Women, Fire, and Dangerous Things: What Categories Reveal About the Mind*, Chicago: University of Chicago Press.

Lakoff, G. and Johnson, M. (1999) *Philosophy in the Flesh: The Embodied Mind in Western Thought*, New York: Basic Books.

Levitas, B. (2002) *The Theatre of Nation: Irish Drama and Cultural Nationalism, 1890–1916*, Oxford: Clarendon Press.

Synge, J.M. (1964) *The Playboy of the Western World*, in W.A. Armstrong (ed.) *Classic Irish Drama*, Harmondsworth: Penguin.

Swettenham, N., "Categories and Catcalls: Cognitive Dissonance in *The Playboy of The Western World*," in *Performance and Cognition* (forthcoming).

PART III

Theatre in modern media cultures, 1850–1970

Edited by **Bruce McConachie**

Theatre in modern media cultures, 1850–1970

INTRODUCTION: HISTORICAL CHANGES AFTER 1850

Between 1850 and 1970, immense economic, political, and cultural changes altered theatregoing for much of the world's population. These changes included the expansion of capitalism in the Industrial Revolution, the ravages of imperialism across the globe, the calamity of the Great War (1914–1918), the Russian Revolution in 1917, the rise of totalitarianism, World War II (1939–1945), the Holocaust, nuclearism, the emergence of new nations from imperial domination after 1945, and the cold war. These major markers only begin to sum up the alterations that rocked the world over these 120 years.

These crises were compounded by slower changes that altered the lives of millions. Improving technologies revolutionized transportation from wood-and-sail to steel-and-steam power, culminating in the petroleum-driven technologies of the automobile and airplane. Massive emigration and immigration, not only across nations and oceans but from countrysides to cities, resulted in a sharp rise in urbanization. In 1800, only seventeen cities in Europe had a population of 100,000 or more; by 1890, there were 103 cities with populations exceeding 600,000. Paris, Berlin, London, and Vienna had already surpassed a million. So had Tokyo, which burgeoned as a result of Japanese imperial policies favoring urbanization and the rapid industrialization of the country after its opening to the West in 1868. The new technologies of the age – locomotives, steamships, steel mills, power plants – stood out sharply in these urban cityscapes.

New modes of communication – the telegraph, photograph, and telephone early on, and film, radio, and television by 1950 – also proliferated. By 1920, the dominant medium of communication in the West had shifted from printing to photography and its many spinoffs in magazines, picture albums, slides, and films. For much of the rest of the world, however, where the printed word had barely altered customary forms of orality and writing, both print and photography revolutionized perceptions of reality for those people who had access to them. In India, for example, the widespread dissemination of photographs and printed material in English led to the popularity of western forms of spoken drama that differed significantly from India's dance-drama. While new modes of visual communication gradually altered the dominance of print and reshaped "the real" for people living in the West, new modes of audiophonic communication – media meant for the ears, such as the telephone, the phonograph, and the radio – offered more inward and immaterial experiences.

Twentieth-century theatre to 1970 would have been very different without the perceptual realities for artists and spectators that were established by photography, radio, and film. This introduction focuses primarily on the ways in which the dominance of photography and film transformed the theatre in Japan and the West between 1850 and 1970. Secondarily, we will examine how the reality effects of the new audiophonic media shaped theatrical responses that conflicted with those of the dominant visual media. Subsequent chapters and case studies in Part III will discuss important ramifications and developments of this media context in three areas of theatre history during the 1850–1970 period: popular entertainment, the avant-garde, and political theatre.

Photography and audiophony in the theatre

Many of the tensions in modern theatrical practice after 1900 can be traced to conflicts between the kinds of realities induced by photographic and audiophonic modes of communication. Henry Fox Talbot invented photography in 1839 and, by the 1860s, photographic studios were flourishing in all the major cities of Western Europe and North America. According to historians of the medium, most westerners believed that the photograph did not merely *represent* reality, as might a painting or a work of literature; the photo actually transcribed the real. Talbot, in fact, claimed to have "discovered" photography, much as a physicist might claim to have discovered a new process in nature.

Indeed, the optics and chemistry of photography clearly distinguish it from most other art forms. Although a human being must point the camera and develop the film, the material world plays a central role in photography because without physical objects and light, no photographic image is possible. For this reason, photography tends to validate a materialistic understanding of reality. People immersed in a world of orality, writing, or print could imagine spiritual and mental realities without material form. Viewers of a photograph, however, were induced to believe that the real world "out there" was limited to what they could see with their eyes or to what a camera might take a picture of.

Photographs were ubiquitous in Japan and the West by 1900. By the turn of the century, the police were taking mug shots, tourists used new Kodaks to snap their travels, war correspondents and junior officers photographed battles, and Queen Victoria had translated herself and the objects of her reign into thousands of photographic images. While photography validated the material solidity of these realities for contemporary witnesses, others tried to use photography to prove the existence of an immaterial, spiritual realm. So persuasive, objective, and "real" was the photographic image that many enthusiasts accepted the validity of "spirit photography," images ostensibly produced on photographic plates by spirits from beyond the grave.

Most Japanese, Americans, and Europeans, however, simply accepted the straightforward materialism that photography seemed to validate. The long-term cultural consequences of this acceptance were immense. In 1850, many still believed in transcendent and immanent realties that were not material, such as a Christian God or a Spirit dwelling inside every person, guiding them toward the Right and the True. Photography was not alone in undercutting such faith; new scientific developments, especially the theory of evolution advanced by Charles Darwin and others, also questioned the reality and effectiveness of immaterial forces. The rise of European socialism, based in Karl Marx's materialist view of history, and the proliferation of products emanating from industrial capitalism also led westerners to wonder about the existence of realities that could not be seen or photographed. Photography unsettled political loyalties as well; suddenly a photo of a monarch or emperor made it apparent that the ruler had a body just like everybody else. The materiality of photography, together with other historical forces, helped to level political hierarchies, erode religious faith, and advance capitalist consumerism. By 1970, most westerners and many people across the globe perceived a much more material world than anyone imagined possible in 1850.

At the end of the nineteenth century, however, audiophonic media were challenging the implicit materialism of photography. The telephone and phonograph, invented in 1876 and 1877, separated the human voice from the materiality of the body. Writing, print, and photography had made it possible for people to communicate across distances, but these audiophonic inventions carried the intimacy and immediacy of the human voice on invisible sound waves that lacked the tangible concreteness of previous media. In the past, "hearing voices" had been a sign of religious possession or mental instability, and these traditional attributes clung to the affects of the new audiophonic media. Audiophonic modes of communication revived interest in religion, altered musical composition, and played on age-old fears of "others." It also inspired belief in the new psychoanalytic techniques of Sigmund Freud and his followers. Freud, in fact, understood phonographic recording as a metaphor for part of the work of the analyst. He advised psychoanalysts to transcribe all of the vocal language mistakes of the patient in order to understand her or his psychological problems. Convinced that sound revealed the immaterial realities of the unconscious mind, Freud urged the accurate recording of patient vocalizations as the first step in a psychoanalytic session.

The rapid rise of radio broadcasting throughout the West after 1920 ensured that notions of reality that could not be photographed would continue to entrance the public. On popular radio broadcasts in the United States, for example, listeners willingly suspended their disbelief to accept the reality of ghosts, immaterial visitors from outer space, and shadowy detectives who could see into the minds of villains through a kind of psychoanalytic x-ray vision. Disembodied voices worked their way into other media as well, relating flash-backs in films and narrating major events in early television series. Although "the talkies" and television generally relied on visual codes deriving from photography for communicative coherence, audiophonic cues (musical, vocal, and special effects) continued to shape these media in significant ways. While most films and television programming effectively blended visual and audiophonic codes, the conflict between the materiality of the photographic and the immateriality of the audophonic continued beneath the surface of their signs and sounds.

Spectacular bodies on the popular stage

Photography and its materialist reality effects had an immense influence on popular entertainment from 1850 until 1914 and the start of the Great War. Popular audiences have always enjoyed spectacular bodies – bodies that are meant to be looked at – but the proliferation of photographic bodies after mid-century excited this interest even more so. At the same time that western and Japanese imperialists, driven by the need for raw materials and new markets, were conquering native peoples around the world, their photographers were publishing images of "primitive" types ripe for exploitation. Photography was as much a tool of imperialism as were print media, steam ships, high explosives, and machine guns. The Japanese annexation of Korea in 1910, for instance, was preceded by numerous photographs depicting a corrupt and backward Korean people in need of Japanese civilization. A 1910 Japanese play, *Korean King*, represented all of Asia in the same way; the play suggested that other Asians would welcome Japanese imperial conquest as progress. In a related development, the American minstrel show had white performers "blacking up" to embody childish images of American blacks (see the case study, Chapter 7). The minstrel show spread from the United States, where it originated in the 1840s, throughout the British empire. In many instances, minstrelsy helped to confirm the racism that justified imperialist oppression.

Other spectacular bodies – strongmen, burlesque queens, contortionists, exotic dancers, and "freaks" of all kinds – peopled the variety stages of all the major cities in Europe and North America (Figure III.1). While these types of entertainment were hardly new, they did draw new audiences, often

Figure III.1 U.S. vaudeville star Eva Tanguay, in a publicity photo for a 1908 performance in Kentucky. © Special Collections, University of Iowa Library, Iowa City.

a mix of working-class and bourgeois spectators, into huge auditoriums for vaudeville, burlesque, music hall, and other forms of variety theatre before the Great War. Likewise, musical comedy and revue flourished before the war, forms of entertainment that had developed from both popular and elite genres and relied on spectacular bodies as well as music for their success. Ever since the "burlesque extravaganzas" of the 1850s – concoctions of music, parody, dance, melodrama, and spectacle – the chorus girl had offered her own spectacular body as an element of sexual allure on the popular stage. Although Florenz Ziegfeld's (1869–1932) musical revues, which began in 1907, sought to glorify the "American Girl," the thousands of choristers that danced across western stages before the Great War received more salacious looks than social esteem from male spectators. Photographs of chorus girls and other spectacular females of the theatre (or of women pretending to theatrical art), in various states of undress, were popular pornographic items after 1850.

Photography also widened the public appeal of theatrical stars. By the 1860s, it was common for stars to arrange for the sale of small pictures of themselves, typically costumed as a favorite character, at their performances. Photographic images splashed on posters and throughout newspapers after 1900 told the public that their favorite star was in town. It helped make possible the great era of international stars who toured from Tokyo to St. Petersberg between 1875 and 1914. Eleanora Duse (1858–1924) and Tommaso Salvini (1829–1915) from Italy, Henry Irving (1838–1905) and Ellen Terry (1847–1928) from England, Kawakami Otojirô (1864–1911) his wife Kawakami Sadayakko (1872–1946) from Japan, Edwin Booth (1833–1893) and Richard Mansfield (1857–1907) from the United States and Sarah Bernhardt (1844–1923) from France performed (in their native languages) before millions of fans. International starring on this scale had not been possible before telegraphs, railroads, and steam ships allowed agents to schedule theatres, plan mass publicity campaigns, and transport their precious cargoes to the desired site on the right night with efficiency and economy. Photography, among several other technologies, made the international star a possible and very profitable commodity.

Chapter 7, "Theatres of Popular Entertainment, 1850–1970," relates the rise and immense popularity of theatrical diversions for urban spectators, then its gradual diminishment after the Great War as film, radio, and television captured the audience that had patronized these kinds of entertainments. The chapter includes sections on urban carnivals, variety theatre, the English music hall, musical comedies, and revues. It also features case studies on blackface performance in the United States and British pantomime. As we will see, these popular genres primarily offered their audiences the materialist delights induced by the modern world's love of photography.

The rise of realism in the West

Perhaps the major impact of photography on western theatre after 1850 was the rise of stage realism. Since the 1830s, the romantic interest in history and exotic cultures had excited audience interest in authentic costuming and properties for historical melodramas, Shakespearean productions, and escapist spectacles. Photography focused a similar interest on more mundane realities, especially the ways in which contemporary dress and domestic lifestyles marked class, regional, and economic differences among various populations. This led to a greater demand for realism in costuming and stage properties. Early nineteenth-century managers in the West often required actors to purchase their own costumes, a costly expense for women actors especially, and a practice that defeated the possibility of uniformity in costuming style. By the 1880s, however, most producers purchased costumes for their entire casts to ensure a measure of authenticity for contemporary as well as historical and exotic productions.

Scenically, antiquarian and most other kinds of romantic productions in the 1850s continued to rely on flats and backdrops, painted in perspective, to evoke the illusions of interior and exterior space. The scenic artists of romantic and melodramatic productions occasionally deployed three-dimensional scenery, but stages rigged for chariot-and-pole or wing-and-drop changes were ill-equipped to handle such practical units on a regular basis. Interior stage settings before mid-century rarely looked like real rooms. The flats did not enclose stage space and the actors could not use most of the two-dimensional furniture painted on the canvas walls. Although the "box set," which offered the illusion of three walls with realist doors and windows, was introduced on the London stage in the 1830s, it, together with real furniture, was not in regular use until the 1890s.

The fifty years between 1870 and 1920 witnessed a revolution in western stage technology. The demand for scenic spectaculars put increasing pressure on the conventional means of changing scenery. Many theatres added "cuts" in the stage floor through which flats could be raised and lowered and extra room in the "fly" space above the stage, all to accommodate more two-dimensional, changeable scenery for melodramatic and exotic spectacles. Electrical stage lighting, however, which began in the late 1870s and was mostly complete by 1900, made two-dimensional illusionism appear unreal. Further, electrical illumination heightened the differences between black-and-white photographs, the new measure of "the real," and the conventions of painted scenery, which now looked quaintly superficial and immaterially flimsy by comparison. This led theatre architects and managers to abandon the older systems of scene changing, dominant in the West since the seventeenth century, for a flat stage with clear access from the wings. The elevator stage was one method of shifting three-dimensional units and real props and furniture. The 1879 Madison Square Theater in New York, for example, rigged elevators for two complete stages, one above the other, to allow one stage be to changed while the other stage served as the playing area. Scrapping the chariot-and-pole or wing-and-groove systems (see Chapter 2) and increasing storage space offstage for furniture and three-dimensional units were more typical, however. Henry Irving, for instance, had his workers rip out the grooves for sliding flats to allow for the "free plantation" of scenic units at his Lyceum Theatre in London. Other innovations to set and manipulate three-dimensional realities followed. Before the Great War, several German theatres installed elaborate turntables to wheel on the cumbersome materiality of stage realism. Concave, plaster cycloramas upstage were lighted to give a variety of outdoor realist illusions.

Playwrights after 1850 gradually adapted their techniques to the new interest in realism. Some, like Dion Boucicault, pasted realist effects over conventionally melodramatic contrivances, as in the *Octoroon* (1859), when a photograph taken by accident eventually reveals the murderer of a slave boy. On the English stage, productions of the plays of Thomas W. Robertson (1829–1871) set the standard for domestic realism in the late 1860s. Written to reveal character through the actors' handling of realist stage properties, Robertson's "cup and saucer plays" (as they were called), such as *Society* (1865) and *Caste* (1867), also pointed the way toward a less declamatory style of acting (Figure III.2). In Vienna, Ludwig Anzengruber (1839–1889) turned the peasant play, formally a romantic piece meant to evoke nationalistic pieties, toward realist purposes in the 1870s. Alexander Ostrovsky (1823–1886) popularized realist playwriting in Moscow. His *The Thunderstorm* (1859) and *Enough Stupidity for Every Wise Man* (1868) demonstrate a realist handling of melodrama and comedy and keen attention to the details of middle-class life.

Realist producer-directors

Audience interest in photorealism led to a demand for specialists with the power to ensure realist illusion in all of the facets of a theatrical production.

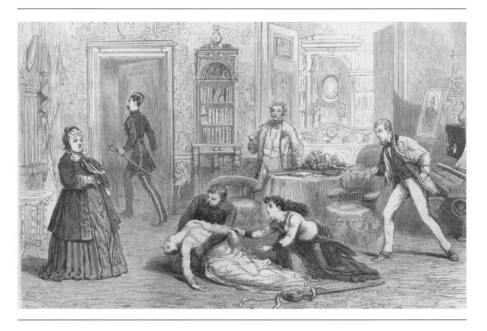

Figure III.2 1879 print illustrating a scene from Tom Robertson's *Caste*, at the Prince of Wales Theatre, 1879. © Enthoven Collection, V&A Images, Victoria and Albert Museum.

On the Anglo-American stage, several stars, such as William Gillette (1857–1937) and Herbert Beerbohm Tree (1853–1917), made their fortunes by augmenting their star appeal with realist effects. Gillette's star vehicle, *Sherlock Holmes* (1899), set the famous detective in the midst of properties, costumes, and scenery that looked as though they had been whisked from Victorian London into the United States. In Tree's technologically-advanced new theatre, his London production of *A Midsummer Night's Dream* in 1900 featured real flowers and mechanical birds in the forest scenes, together with fairies with battery-operated glow lamps. By its revival in 1911, there were live rabbits. Several realist playwrights, such as Victorien Sardou and George Bernard Shaw (1856–1950), also played a major role in mounting productions of their dramas. By 1900, however, a new figure had emerged as a specialist in staging realism, the producer-director. In central and eastern Europe, where subsidized theatrical institutions predominated, a few strong producers championed realism in the repertories of several state- and city-supported theatres. In Western Europe and the United States, by contrast, some producers gradually wrested economic control of commercial theatrical production from the stars, which allowed them to shape both the economic and the artistic fortunes of their productions.

Georg II (1826–1914), the Duke of Saxe-Meiningen (an independent duchy in Germany before 1871), was the first of several producer-directors to exercise near total control over his productions. The Duke himself designed all of the costumes, scenery, and props, even insisting on genuine materials and period furniture to ensure a look of historical authenticity. When the Meiningen company toured throughout Europe between 1874 and 1890, it set new standards for the aesthetic integration of realist productions. What chiefly astonished spectators was the unity of theatrical effects achieved by the company, especially in ensemble acting. Most members of Saxe-Meiningen's company played both leading roles and supernumeraries; there were no stars stealing the limelight or supernumeraries wandering through crowd scenes in awkward befuddlement. For the first time on a European stage, individuals with their own character traits who spoke intelligible lines made up a mob, and the mob itself was choreographed to move with a level of reality and power that audiences had never witnessed before (Figure III.3). The Duke achieved these effects by rehearsing his company for several months, frequently with full sets and costumes, until he believed his productions were ready for

Figure III.3 A crowd scene in the Duke of Saxe-Meiningen's staging of Shakespeare's *Julius Caesar* at Drury Lane Theatre, 1881. © V&A Images, Victoria and Albert Museum.

the public. By 1890, the Meiningen troupe had given over 2,500 perform-ances of 41 plays and the Duke had demonstrated how an authoritarian producer-director could integrate realist productions.

Several realist producer-directors in the West followed in the wake of Saxe-Meiningen. Perhaps the most influential was André Antoine (1858–1943), who founded and directed an avant-garde company, the Théâtre Libre, in Paris in 1887. For many of his productions Antoine directed his actors to observe the realist convention of the "fourth wall," the imaginary wall across the prosce-nium opening enclosing an interior room in a box set in which actors performed and which spectators observed, ostensibly as if neither knew of the other's presence. Within this convention, furniture along the line of this "wall" might face up stage, and actors could occasionally deliver their lines with their backs to the audience. For several of his later productions of French classical plays at the state-subsidised Théâtre Odéon, Antoine used the conventions of realism in a meta-theatrical mode to re-create the theatrical conditions of a typical seventeenth-century playhouse. He placed costumed actors playing spectators on the stage and hung chandeliers over them, for example, to frame historically accurate productions of Molière's comedies, acted and designed to match the style of the period. Antoine's produc-tions toured widely in Western Europe and, like Saxe-Meiningen's, shaped a generation of theatre artists.

Konstantin Stanislavsky (1863–1938) and Vladimir Nemirovich-Danchenko (1858–1943) brought high standards of realist production to Russia after the founding of the Moscow Art Theatre (MAT) in 1898. Although Stanislavsky wielded less direct power than did similar producer-directors, he carried substantial authority in the company due to his membership in the Moscow business elite, his connections to wealthy patrons, and his growing eminence as an actor and director. The MAT established its reputation for realism by producing the four major plays of Anton Chekhov (1860–1904), *The Seagull* (1896), *Uncle Vanya* (1899), *Three Sisters* (1901), and *The Cherry Orchard* (1904). Stanislavsky staged these plays with scrupulous attention to the realities of Russian provincial life on which they are based and worked toward ensemble playing and a "fourth wall" performance style with the MAT company (Figure III.4). After 1906, Stanislavsky began working on a "system" that would help actors toward a more complete commitment to the realities of their characters – work he would continue for the rest of his life. (Stanislavsky's system is the subject of a case study in Chapter 8.)

Figure III.4 V.S. Simov's 1898 naturalistic design for Act I of the Moscow Art Theatre's production of Anton Chekhov's *The Seagull*. © The Society for Cooperation in Russian and Soviet Studies, London.

Despite the immense success of the MAT's productions of his plays, Chekhov disliked several of Stanislavsky's staging choices. In part, he was skeptical that photographic reality could reveal very much about human experience. In *The Three Sisters*, for instance, there is a moment near the end of Act 1 when a minor character takes a flash photo of all of the major characters in the play. The on-stage picture seen by the audience in Stanislavsky's production was the same as that supposedly taken by the actors: the illusion of real people dressed in contemporary clothes in a real room with real lighting, and posing, as most in the audience had often done themselves, for a transcription of their reality. Here, it seemed, were the real lives of the Prozorov sisters and their friends in all of their material specificity. Photographs, however, freeze the flow of life in a static pose, and Chekhov's characters change immeasurably over the several months of action in *The Three Sisters*. In recognition of human mutability, Chekhov's plot arranges to have all of Fedotik's photos burned up in an offstage fire in Act 3. By Act 4, the snapping of photos has become a sour joke. As we will see, Chekhov was not alone in questioning the reality of photo-like effects on the stage.

The rise of realism in Japan

Samurai warlords had isolated Japan from nearly all western influences for over two hundred years until 1868, when an internal revolution forced renewed contact and commerce. In the 1870s, theatrical reformers eager to embrace western ideas pushed stage realism as an antidote to what they saw as irrelevant traditions. As in the West, the photograph became the new measure of the real for the reformers in Japan. At first, a few reformers attempted to modernize kabuki by making it more contemporary in subject matter and characterization. Ichikawa Danjûrô (1839–1903), for example, appeared in white tie and tails instead of traditional Japanese dress in 1872 to inaugurate a new theatre that he promised would cleanse kabuki by presenting its historical plays with as much realism as possible. In a series of productions that paralleled antiquarian Shakespearean performances in the West, Danjûrô produced kabuki history plays with authentic-looking costumes, properties, and scenery.

Later reformers sidestepped these initial attempts at altering kabuki to push for western models of playwriting and production. Kawakami Otojirô (1864–1911), for instance, produced *shimpa* – literally "new style" – dramas that adapted nineteenth-century western dramatic forms to Japanese tastes in such plays as *The Sublime*, and *The Delightful Sino-Japanese War* (1894). Like Sardou's historical melodramas in Paris, Kawakami's production of his play used photographically-authentic military uniforms and make-up to depict realist battle scenes. When Kawakami produced *The Geisha and the Knight* (1900) while on tour in the United States, the desire of U.S. audiences to see females playing female roles prompted him to allow his wife, Sadayakko (1872–1946), a former geisha and thus a trained dancer, to perform the major female role. She continued to do so in subsequent tours of Europe, to great critical acclaim. Sadayakko's presence on the international stage challenged the exclusion of women from female roles and professional actor training in Japan. Japanese traditionalists demanded that acting remain a male preserve; they were joined by some advocates of reform who believed that women could never attain the same level of artistry and reality on stage as men. Because Osanai Kaoru (1881–1928) believed it would be too difficult to train female amateurs for his new Free Theatre, he and his collaborator, kabuki actor Ichikawa Sadanji (1880–1940), suggested that the male *onnagata* actors (specialists in female roles) learn to play modern women in western-style, realist plays.

Leading literary critic Tsubouchi Shôyô (1859–1935), however, argued that the appearance of men in women's roles could never match the expectations established by realist representation. Tsubouchi had translated all of Shakespeare's plays and introduced the western realist novel to Japan in his 1885 book, *Shôsetsu shinzui* (*The Essence of the Novel*). Like critics and theorists in the West influenced by the reality effects of photography, he believed that stage images and sounds, including scenery and dialog as well as characterization, must represent material reality as accurately as possible. In 1906, Tsubouchi founded a Theatre Institute in his Literary Arts Society to train actors and mount private productions of *shingeki* – literally, "new theatre." There, Tsubouchi experimented with modes of performance that both broke free from the traditions of kabuki and moved beyond the imitative qualities of *shimpa*. In Tsubouchi's production of *Hamlet* in 1911, one of his students, Matsui Sumako (1886–1919), became the first professionally-trained woman actor to perform in Japan. Later in that year, Matsui performed her most famous role, Nora in *A Doll House*, with another *shingeki* troupe. By 1930, *shingeki*, featuring women in female roles, had become the perferred style for the production of comedies and dramas based on contemporary life.

Avant-garde theatres in the West

In the West and Japan, realism had become the default mode of playwriting and production for contemporary theatre by the 1920s; most artists and spectators expected representations of material, photographable reality when they created or witnessed a theatrical production. This did not mean that the entire stage had to look like a photograph, of course. Artists and spectators were already adjusting their sights and expectations to accommodate "stylized," "minimalist," and "psychological" realisms, in recognition that the stage was better suited to the depiction of partial material realities rather than an entire "slice of life." With few exceptions on mainstream stages, however, these reality effects were entirely materialist in orientation. Individual characters under realism might profess a belief in an external god or in an immanent spirit, but these unphotographable realities were not represented on the realist stage. The transition to a secular, materialist stage had been especially rapid in Japan, where (with few exceptions) *shingeki* had forthrightly banished the gods of noh and the highly theatrical kabuki.

Not surprisingly, the rise of realism led to several reactions. For some, the naturalists, the focus on external realities in stage realism did not go far enough. The naturalists of the 1880s and 1890s wanted the theatre to depict the material forces of biological evolution and social environment that they believed totally determined human life. Others, the symbolists, rejected the materialism of the realists and naturalists and urged that the theatre attempt to concretize spiritual realities that photographs generally overlooked. Perhaps influenced by the new audiophonic media of the telephone and the phonograph, symbolist playwrights and directors of the 1890s looked to unseen, often aurally manifested forces that they believed shaped human fate. The conflict between the naturalists and the symbolists was the first of many similar clashes between 1880 and 1935 that animated the many movements of the international avant-garde.

In Chapter 8, "Theatres of the Avant-Garde and Their Legacy, 1880–1970," we survey the major avant-garde movements, beginning with naturalism and symbolism and considering much of the experimental work of artists in Germany, France, and Russia, the centers of avant-garde activity in the first half of the twentieth century. As this chapter will show, avant-garde energies often drew on the implicit immaterial reality effects of audiophonic media to challenge the materialism of the realist stage. Although the fractious political realities of the 1930s dispersed the international avant-garde, its legacy continued after World War II and shaped experimental work in the theatre through to 1970. The actor training programs of Stanislavsky and Meyerhold, the legacy of avant-garde thinking in a play by Eugene O'Neill, and Samuel Beckett's theatrical minimalism are the subjects of case studies included in this chapter.

The Great War as a turning point in world theatre

Many Europeans have continued to call World War I the Great War because they have come to understand that the 1914–1918 conflict was a significant turning point in the world as well as in European history. This is not only because of the immediate devastation it wreaked on lives, wealth, and established political power. It led to the Russian Revolution (1917–1921), precipitated the decline of western imperialism, and was an indirect cause of the rise of fascism and the world-wide economic Depression of the 1930s. In these ways, the Great War undermined western bourgeois culture and introduced new realities and possibilities undreamed of before 1914. The 1910s and 1920s also marked other turning points unrelated to the political and economic consequences of the Great War. Competition from silent films led to the decline of all forms of popular theatrical entertainment during those decades; the arrival of the "talkies" in 1927 accelerated this trend. Other changes in the 1920s – the growing importance of the radio, records, and telephones; the widespread electrification of homes and apartments; and the rise of psychologism and consumerism – separated everyday western reality in this decade from the reality of most lives before the war.

Even before the sound era of the movies, theatre and film artists borrowed extensively from each other, a mutual give-and-take that shaped the reality effects of both media. Until about 1915, most of the influence ran from theatre to film, as film entrepreneurs borrowed variety acts, scenic conventions, modes of storytelling, acting styles, and musical underscoring (played by musicians during the screening) from the popular stage. In the early days of film, most theatre artists looked down on the movies as a paltry entertainment for the lower classes; few believed that film had anything to teach them. By the end of the Great War, however, when better technology had led to a much wider range of shots, locations, and editing possibilities, and when mass distribution was attracting the middle classes for feature-length films, the balance had shifted. Throughout the 1920s and into the 1960s, when film and radio were the two dominant forms of mass entertainment, the reality effects of film had more of an influence on the stage than the other way around.

One result of the ubiquity of film after the war was to popularize some of the innovations that the theatrical avant-garde had been pushing since the 1890s. Several artists had advocated that the theatre move away from the mere reproduction of reality in scenic and lighting effects to allow a more fluid use of theatrical space. Through jump-cuts, pans, and tracking shots, film could easily take spectators into numerous places, and audiences began to expect the same kinds of flexibility while watching a play on stage. Consequently, many theatre designers and directors after 1920 began to use lighting instruments almost as though they were cameras in order to heighten an actor's presence, gain design flexibility, and speed playing time. Some dramatists moved closer to the kinds of scripts increasingly favored by filmmakers – short scenes with more action and less dialog, dramatic development across many locales, and the revelation of dramatic meaning through "montage," a rapid sequence of thematically-related scenes or images. In cities where artists could work easily in both media, such as Berlin, Paris, and Moscow, the crossover effects of film on the theatre were especially pronounced. Avant-garde artists in each of these cities – German expressionists, French surrealists, and Russian constructivists – moved toward a filmic orientation to the theatre after 1920.

While these film-influenced techniques pulled the theatre away from the old conventions of stage realism, film remained a moving "picture" and generally kept the imagination of the audience tethered to the literal, material world that still photography had reproduced. In most films, characters were even more immersed in their material surroundings than in any realist stage play. At the same time, however, filmic materialism was more dynamic in its camera movements and emotional affects than the materialism of pre-1900 photography. In general, film realism pushed stage realism in two contradictory directions – a continuing demand for material authenticity in the stage environment coupled with new pressure to speed scenic changes and heighten realist acting effects. By the 1940s, as subsequent chapters will show in greater detail, most realist theatre in Japan and the West had bowed to these constraints.

After the Great War, some filmmakers also ventured beyond realism. Their use of abstract scenery and lighting influenced theatrical direction and design. In Berlin, for example, German expressionists working in both film and theatre experimented with the manipulation of light on human bodies and faces in the midst of three-dimensional abstract forms to produce startling shifts from terror to joy. These possibilities had been present in most theatres since the 1890s, but the legacy of two-dimensional, pictorial scenery and lighting for general illumination or special effects retarded their exploration. The conventional means of effecting a change of mood on the non-realist pictorial stage, in productions of ancient Greek tragedy or Wagnerian opera, for example, was to bring on new painted scenery that, together with the acting, told the audience how to feel. But long scene shifts were already problematic by 1914 and the emerging conventions of abstract scenery and lighting in film made this pictorial mode of communicating emotions in the theatre seem increasingly awkward and unbelievable.

Before the Great War, two visionaries in the theatre, Adolphe Appia (1862–1928) and Edwin Gordon Craig (1872–1966) had urged that adjustable electric lighting could effect a radical break from the tradition of pictorial atmosphere by fusing the image of the moving actor with sculpted scenery. Eager to perfect a scenic equivalent to the soaring, myth-driven music of Richard Wagner (1813–1883), Appia published *The Staging of Wagner's Musical Dramas* in 1895 and *Music and Stage Setting* in 1899. In these and later works, Appia argued that the aesthetic unity of opera depended on synthesizing all of the stage elements – crucially the music, scenery, lighting, and performers. Because actor-singers worked in three dimensions, the setting must too; the contradiction of actors and two-dimensional painted flats destroyed the aurally-induced mystery of Wagner's music, Appia stated. This led him to recommend steps, platforms, vertical columns, and other non-realist three-dimensional units for scenery (Figure III.5). Influenced by the "eurythmics" movement after 1906, Appia emphasized musical rhythm as the key to aesthetic coherence. (Eurythmics, begun by Emile Jacques Dalcroze [1865–1960], trained students to exercise their bodies by moving to a variety of musical rhythms.)

Figure III.5 Adolphe Appia's design for Christoph Willibald Gluck's opera, *Orpheus and Eurydice*, 1913, at Hellerau. © 3D Visualization Group, School of Theatre Studies, University of Warwick.

For Appia, audiophonic communication was the proper basis for artistic unity and the key to true reality. Most theatre practitioners ignored Appia's ideas before 1914, but his precepts exerted significant influence after the war when German expressionist experiments with sound, scenery, and light gave his ideas new cogency.

Unlike Appia, Gordon Craig's visionary statements about the need to revolutionize the stage were harder to ignore because he never ceased to publicize them. In a series of books beginning in 1905 and in a periodical, *The Mask*, which he edited sporadically between 1908 and 1929, Craig argued for aesthetic and atmospheric coherence through designs that integrated the actor with three-dimensional, abstract set pieces through the bold use of light and sound. Unlike Appia, Craig favored a single setting for an entire performance to evoke the spirit of the play, with minor changes effected through the movement and dynamic lighting of towering, vertical screens. Craig also urged that the theatre – which he believed was an individual, not a collective art – must bow to the control of a master-artist. Influenced by Wagner's call for stage production as a *Gesamtkunstwerk* (a total, synthesized art work) and by Friedrich Nietzsche's desire for a superman who could bear the burden of life's contradictions, Craig sought a total artist of the theatre who could combine playwriting, designing, and directing. At one point, Craig, despairing of the intransigence of stars and the materiality of actors' bodies, suggested that live performers should be replaced by large puppets – *Übermarionettes* that would more easily evoke spiritual realities and would be easier to control. Like Appia, Craig prefigured the film era of theatrical art, advocating flexibility of lighting and abstract scenery, and pushing the stage director toward the role of auteur, a figure who would control all the elements of a production – just like some film directors.

Shakespeare and film in England

The development of new conventions for staging the plays of Shakespeare in England demonstrates how these pressures from film played out in one national culture. Artists and spectators in 1930s England were eager to enjoy the dramas of their national poet, but Shakespeare in realist style, a problematic mix of authentic stage environments and poetical speech, now seemed cumbersome and unbelievable, mostly because of the movies. Before 1914, a few scholars and artists had advocated a return to Elizabethan playing conventions, but fascination with photorealism had kept most of Shakespeare's plays anchored to a reproduction of their historical milieux. Scholar-director William Poel (1852–1934) produced Shakespeare on an Elizabethan-like stage (placed behind a regular proscenium, however) at the turn of the century. This allowed the continuous playing that Shakespeare had intended without the long pauses for scene changes typical of the pre-1914 period. In a few productions just before the war, H. Granville Barker (1877–1946), who bridged the avant-garde and the commercial theatre worlds in London, used suggestive scenic pieces, draped curtains, and metaphorical props and costumes to keep the Shakespearean action moving in performances that emphasized simplicity and poetry. Most critics scoffed at Poel and Barker, but their ideas undergirded many later reforms.

After the war, London's "Old Vic" Theatre gradually became the home of the most respected Shakespearean productions in England (Figure III.6). There, a succession of directors incorporated several of the innovations of Poel and Barker that moved the staging and scenery away from the clutter of realism,

Figure III.6 The Old Vic production of Shakespeare's *The Tempest*, 1934, with Charles Laughton as Prospero. © V&A Images, Victoria and Albert Museum.

but generally maintained historical authenticity for costuming and props. Tyrone Guthrie (1900–1971), artistic director of the Old Vic from 1937–1945, deployed Appia-like settings of ramps and platforms, rapid movement by actors, and quick light changes to lend Shakespearean productions the speedier rhythms and heightened contrasts of the cinema. Directors Barry Jackson (1879–1961) in Birmingham and Terence Gray (1895–1986) at the Cambridge Festival Theatre used similar techniques that moved Shakespeare into the film age during the 1920s and 1930s. By 1940, actors John Gielgud (1904–2000), Sybil Thorndike (1882–1976), Laurence Olivier (1907–1989), and others had developed energetic playing styles that emphasized the psychology of their characters rather than their realist situations. Olivier's success in filming several Shakespearean plays – notably his *Henry V* (1944) and *Richard III* (1955) – confirmed the popularity of a more cinematic acting style for Shakespeare on the stage. For spectators attuned to the reality effects of the movies, Guthrie's, Olivier's, and others' mix of dynamic open staging, authentic-looking costumes and props, and a more natural, psychological playing style – all reforms initiated at the Old Vic – rejuvenated Shakespearean production in the 1930s and 1940s.

Lyrical abstraction and the radio in France

Although film was also popular in France between the wars, the reality effects of the radio probably played a greater role in altering the culture of that national theatre. On the one hand, it is difficult to separate the reality effects of film and radio; although film is a predominately visual medium, sound has played an increasingly important role in establishing the believability of any film sequence. By the mid-1930s, films were borrowing extensively from the microphone effects, musical conventions, and dialog devices of radio. Soon, the traffic in all types of sound effects was traveling both ways, especially between radio plays and dramatic films. On the other hand, radio listening by itself produces reality effects that can be distinguished from those of "talking pictures." By hiding the human body that produces sounds – typically a body in a studio in front of a microphone – the radio privileges the mental over the physical, the abstract and general over the historical and specific. In addition, radio drama favors distinctive, emblematic sounds, including those sounds produced by the human voice; the actual sounds of real people talking on a crowded street would confuse the radio listener with too much noise. Finally, good radio drama plays on the imagination, creating a space in the listener's mind that is more intimate than the space of any theatrical stage or film screen. This combination of reality effects from the radio pressured the theatres of all modern national cultures in the 1930s and 1940s to create performances in intimate spaces involving emblematic characters in conflicts that centered on universal themes.

Several directors and playwrights in France from the 1930s through the 1950s bowed to the reality effects of radio and drew on their heritage of Racinean tragedy and the comedy of Molière to fashion a distinctive theatre of lyric abstraction. In France, as elsewhere in Europe, radio broadcasting was principally a state-run monopoly. Radio France began in 1922, and by the 1940s most households were listening to a mix of music, public affairs, sports, and radio drama for several hours a day. As the French made the radio a part of their everyday activities, its reality effects began to transform French culture.

At the center of the early years of this transformation in the theatre was the work of Jacques Copeau (1879–1949). Like Granville Barker, Copeau, who was a critic turned producer-director, eliminated realist details to emphasize the work of his actors. At his small theatre, the Vieux Colombier, Copeau produced several plays with minimal realism for audiences of only 400 people before 1914. He resumed productions at the Vieux Colombier for a short time after the war and later served at the Comédie Française, the prestigious national theatre, from 1936 until 1940. Copeau and his successors charged the type characters and generalized themes of the French classics with a fresh, lyrical energy. He applied this style to Shakespearean productions and modern plays as well (Figure III.7). Directors who modeled their artistry on Copeau's – a group that included Louis Jouvet (1887–1951) and Charles Dullin (1885–1949) – emphasized adherence to the details and rhythms of the script and strove to invest their stylized costumes and minimalist scenery with symbolic significance. After World War II, two of Dullin's students, directors Jean-Louis Barrault (1910–1994) and Jean Vilar (1912–1971), continued to refine this tradition. As the head of the Théâtre National Populaire in the 1950s, Vilar demonstrated that the lyric abstraction deriving from Copeau could succeed with a popular audience.

French playwrights influenced by this style tended to write allegories in which the general problems of humanity predominated over historical or psychological concerns. The first major playwright to work in lyric abstraction was Jean Giraudoux (1882–1944), who collaborated closely with Jouvet to stage his plays. These included *The Trojan War Shall Not Take Place* (1935), *Ondine* (1939), and *The Madwoman of Chaillot* (1945). Jean Anouilh (1910–1987), also following this style, wrote light comedies with fairy-tale-like resolutions, such as *Thieves' Carnival* (1938), and dark allegories, the most famous of which was *Antigone* (1943), composed during the German occupation of France. Joining

Figure III.7 Stage of the Vieux Colombier, as adapted for Shakespeare's *Twelfth Night*. Redrawn from *Theatre Arts Magazine*, 1924.

Anouilh after the war in this playwriting style were Marcel Achard, Albert Camus, and several others.

Anouilh's *Waltz of the Toreadors* (1952) provides a ready example of lyric abstraction that demonstrates its ties to the reality effects of radio. Like Molière, Anouilh uses the structure of farce to explore a serious theme – the depredations of time in the case of *Waltz*. The play's chief representative of foolish old age is a French general still in love with a mistress who returns, after many years, to discover that she would rather fall in love with the general's young male secretary. The general is upset, but finally resigns himself to the triumph of fiery passion over cooling embers. Emblematic characters, a universal theme, an appeal to an imagined past, intimate staging, and an action that verges on allegory help to mark this lyrical confection as a product of the radio age.

Psychological realism in the United States

Political and economic pressures, a legacy of realist theatre, plus the reality effects of film and radio led to psychological realism in the United States, a major trend by mid-century that significantly differed from the predominant style of early postwar France. Although the roots of this style date from the late nineteenth century and include many of the plays of Eugene O'Neill (1888–1953), the kind of theatre that O'Neill's plays hint at could not have flourished on the stage without acting, directing, and design practices to support it. Beginning in the 1920s, new approaches to these theatrical practices, informed by film and radiophonic techniques, gradually transformed the production of realist plays in the United States. By the 1950s, "method" acting, psychologically-attuned directing, and fluid scenography produced a theatre of psychological realism that became a distinctive national style before achieving international popularity. Without these theatrical innovations, the plays of Tennessee Williams, Arthur Miller, and others could not have succeeded during the early years of the cold war. Without the effects of film and radio on the culture, the production and popularity of psychological realism in the American theatre would not have occurred. The widespread popularity of psychological realism throughout the world, in filmic as well as stage media, attests to the formative influence of radio and especially film on the period 1945–1970.

In the U.S. of the 1930s, Harold Clurman (1901–1980), Stella Adler (1903–1992), Lee Strasberg (1901–1982), and other members of The Group Theatre in New York applied what they took to be Stanislavsky's precepts about acting to their work on realist plays. Although their understanding of Stanislavsky was incomplete, the actors and directors of The Group forged a "method" that helped them to empathize with their stage characters. After the war, when Strasberg, Adler, and several former members of The Group began teaching acting to professionals in New York, versions of the "Method" shaped the backbone of their work. Primarily through psychological techniques, "method" acting marries the personality of the actor to the character she or he is playing; when the actor and the character are a good match, "method" acting can generate explosive and intimate performances. During the 1950s, "method" actors Marlon Brando (1924–2004), Geraldine Page (1924–1987), Ben Gazzara (1930–), and several others became icons of popular culture for their realistically psychological performances on stage and screen. The believability of "method" acting for spectators drew on the typecasting and close-up shots that were already a part of filmmaking in Hollywood. Although the "method" was developed as a technique for the stage, it is no accident that it continues to inform the work of many film actors, including Dustin Hoffman and Al Pacino.

While the influence of Appia and Craig on the New Stagecraft Movement during the decade of the Great War had moved some U.S. stage design away from the dictates of literal realism, most scenic and lighting designs for dramatic productions in the 1920s and 1930s continued to emphasize the massiveness of realist rooms and exteriors. Lee Simonson (1888–1967), Boris Aronson (1900–1980), Jo Mielziner (1901–1976), and a few other designers of Broadway productions, however, drew on European ideas to discover more abstract solutions for staging realist plays. At the same time, the pressure from film to create quickly-shifting scenic effects was also moving realism away from three-dimensional units toward more light-weight, lyrical designs. This led Mielziner, especially, toward the fanciful use of color and soaring vertical lines in scene designs that left rooms without ceilings and substituted transparent walls made of painted scrim for the apparent solidity of regular stage flats.

Consequently, when playwright Tennessee Williams turned to Mielziner to design his "memory play," *The Glass Menagerie*, in 1945, the designer knew that he could regulate the flow between the scenes of narration in the present and the scenes of memory in the past through the manipulation of scrim and lighting. When lit from the front, scrim can give the illusion of a solid wall. Illuminated from behind as well, the wall of scrim becomes transparent, allowing spectators to see objects and actors through a gauzy grain. Mielziner's painterly, soft-edged designs nicely complemented the psychological realism of Williams's plays. He designed seven productions for Williams between 1945 and 1963, including *A Streetcar Named Desire* (1947) and *Cat on a Hot Tin Roof* (1955).

Although Mielziner's use of lighting and scrim to shift from one locale or atmospheric affect to another allowed for the kind of scenic transformation that film could accomplish through jump cuts in the editing room, the lighting-and-scrim shift also borrowed from what radio producers called a "segue," a sound transition, in a radio drama. By the 1940s, many popular radio serials used a musical or vocal bridge that faded in and faded out to move from one scene to another. At times, the segue moved the listener inside of the narrator's head, where he or she could share intimate thoughts with the listener or take the listener into a daydream or flashback scene.

The principal of the radio segue shaped playwriting as well as design on the postwar American stage. "Inside of His Head" was Arthur Miller's initial title for *Death of a Salesman* (1949), which deploys several radio-drama techniques to tell the story of the dreams of success that push salesman Willy Loman to his death. Mielziner's design for *Salesman* used his lighting-and-scrim shift to move spectators inside of Willy's head, where they could see the world from the perspective of Miller's Everyman figure (Figure III.8). Audiences familiar with the "voice-over" convention of radio drama – a narrator taking the listener directly to a new episode in the plot – had no difficulty following Willy's vocal transitions from present time and place into his daydreams located

Figure III.8 Jo Mielziner's setting for Arthur Miller's *Death of a Salesman*, 1949. Photo, Peter Juley & Son. © The Smithsonian Institution, Washington, D.C.

in the past. Many radio plays divided the internal psychology of the protagonist into different voices and sounds so that the split desires of the main character could be dramatized. Miller, who had written radio plays in the early 1940s, achieves a similar effect in *Salesman* by dividing the voices of Willy's conscience among characters who encourage him to live, like the off-stage voice of his wife near the end of the play, and those, like his rich older brother (a figment in Willy's mind), who urge him to kill himself for the insurance money. Directly shaped by the techniques as well as the reality effects of radio drama, *Death of a Salesman* was a milestone in American psychological realism.

Salesman was directed by Elia Kazan (1909–2003), the premiere director of psychological realism in the U.S. from the late 1940s through the 1950s. During those years, Kazan also enjoyed a successful career in Hollywood and brought several of the techniques of film directing to his work in New York. Kazan had been a member of The Group in the 1930s and, like several of his cohorts, taught "method" acting after the war. He used this psychological approach to work with actors in his stage productions, which included Miller's *All My Sons* (1947) and Williams's *Sweet Bird of Youth* (1959), and in such films as *On the Waterfront* (1954) and *East of Eden* (1955). Both the stage and film versions of Williams's *A Streetcar Named Desire* were directed by Kazan (1947, 1951). Kazan carefully coached his actors through "method" techniques and used the actors' edgy, high-strung psychological rhythms to shape their stage movements and the camera shots and editing choices for his films. By modifying filmic techniques, Kazan was also able to employ versions of the close-up and the "over-the-shoulder shot" for his stage productions. Kazan's success helped to ensure that the style of psychological realism would unite the film screens and the theatrical stages of cold war America. Given the widespread influence of film on the postwar imagination in the West and Japan (and the power of Hollywood's distribution system), it is not surprising that filmic images of psychological realism achieved international renown.

Theatre and politics

Politically, the U.S. theatre in the 1950s was the culmination of liberalism, one of the two major political orientations of the modern era. The other was democratic socialism, which rivaled liberalism in the West after 1890 and triumphed in several western nations after World War II. Authoritarian communism, a third political option, gained power in Russia and elsewhere after the Revolution of 1917, but did not enjoy wide support where its ideology was understood. Although twentieth-century politicians sometimes denied it, all three political orientations were based in materialism, the primary reality effect of still and moving pictures. Liberalism and socialism spilled out from Europe, where they had originated, to influence political conflicts in the rest of the world. After the Great War, anti-imperialists began to turn these discourses against Britain, France, Japan, the U.S., and other imperialist powers in order to gain independence for their countries. This struggle culminated in the 1960s, when many of the nations of Africa and other formerly colonized territories gained political freedom (although many continued in economic relationships that perpetuated their problems).

Chapter 9, "Theatres for Reform and Revolution, 1880–1970," discusses these developments as they shaped world theatre. The chapter considers theatrical versions of liberalism and socialism before the Great War and traces the impact of the Russian Revolution on European theatre. It examines theatres of anti-imperialism and significant changes in German and Japanese theatre after World War II. It describes the theatre of the cold war, and notes the breakdown of liberalism and socialism in 1968, when students and workers worldwide rioted against their governments. The chapter includes case studies on Ibsen's realist plays, social drama in Kerala (India), and Bertolt Brecht's direction of his play, *Mother Courage and Her Children*.

The continuing power of print

The increasing importance of new technologies of communication in shaping theatre and its reality effects during the twentieth century diminished but did not eliminate the power of print in modern culture. On the one hand, spectators immersed in photography, film, and radio by 1950 had come to expect scenery and acting on stage that reflected the representational possibilities of these media. The scenic and acting conventions at the high water mark of print culture on the stage in the late eighteenth century – flats painted in perspective and acting that presented stock poses to be read – now seemed artificial and even unbelievable to twentieth-century audiences.

On the other hand, print retained significant power in the theatre, especially through dramatic authorship. Because the market for published plays remained strong, many playwrights, including Bernard Shaw, Eugene O'Neill, and Bertolt Brecht, wrote dramas meant for the reading public, not simply scripts intended as raw material for theatre artists. Several dramatists, such as Brecht and Samuel Beckett, sought to extend the power of authorship beyond the usual royalty rights and copyright restrictions. Brecht, who directed many of his plays, published detailed "model-books" of his productions, complete with photographs, to instruct future directors and designers in mounting his dramas. Beckett took the next step in extending the authority of dramatists, refusing to allow productions of his dramas that violated his published stage directions (see Chapter 11). These playwrights and others drew their authority from the continuing power of the printed word in the twentieth century.

Critics, publicists, interviewers, and others who mediated between performance events and the public also relied primarily on print during the 1850–1970 period. Because modern culture involved an increasing number of options for dramatic entertainment – from plays and variety shows in the 1850s to theatre, film, radio, and television by 1970 – consumers of these media sought information about local dramatic offerings. Consequently, publicists, critics, and other mediators gained substantial authority during the period, including the power to make or break a new play and to construct the public image of a dramatist, star, or theatre company. Most of these mediators worked through print, although radio commentators and television advertising played a role late in the period. The importance of print in secondary and university education should also be emphasized here. The enormous growth of public education in the 1850–1970 period put play texts in front of millions of students. This may have helped create future audiences, but it also reinforced the notion that the "real" play was on paper, not on stage (see Chapter 11). Indeed, print continued to be so much a part of people's daily lives that it was nearly invisible.

BMc

Key references

Listed below are the key references for this Introduction to Part III and for Chapters 7, 8, and 9.

Adams, B. (1997) *E Pluribus Barnum: The Great Showman and U.S. Popular Culture*, Minneapolis: University of Minnesota Press.

Bailey, P. (1998) *Popular Culture and Performance in the Victorian City*, Cambridge: Cambridge University Press.

Block, H. (1963) *Mallarme and the Symbolist Drama*, Detroit: Wayne State University Press.

Booth, M. (1991) *Theatre in the Victorian Age*, Cambridge: Cambridge University Press.

Braun, E. (1982) *The Director and the Stage*, New York: Holmes and Meier.

Braun, K. (1996) *A History of Polish Theater, 1939–1989*, Westport, C.T.: Greenwood.

Brockett, O.G. and Findlay, R. (1991) *A Century of Innovation: A History of European and American Theatre and Drama in the Late Nineteenth Century*, 2nd edn, Needham Heights, M.A.: Prentice-Hall.

Burger, P. (1996) *Theory of the Avant Garde*, trans. M. Shaw, Minneapolis: University of Minnesota Press.

Cole, T. and Chinoy, H.K. (eds) (1963) *Directors on Directing*, Indianapolis: Bobbs-Merrill.

Davis, T. (1991) *Actresses as Working Women. Their Social Identity in Victorian Culture*, New York and London: Routledge.

Deak, F. (1993) *Symbolist Theatre: The Formation of the Avant-Garde*, Baltimore: Johns Hopkins University Press.

Drain, R. (ed.) (1995) *Twentieth-Century Theatre: A Sourcebook*, London: Routledge.

Gordon, M. (1987) *Dada Performance*, New York: PAJ Publications.

Green-Lewis, J. (1996) *Framing The Victorians: Photography and the Culture of Realism*, Ithaca, N.Y.: Cornell University Press.

Hobsbawm, E. (1987) *The Age of Empire, 1875–1914*, New York: Pantheon.

Hodge, A. (ed.) (2000) *Twentieth-Century Actor Training*, London: Routledge.

Innes, C. (1993) *Avant-Garde Theatre, 1892–1992*, London: Routledge.

Johnston, B. (1992) *The Ibsen Cycle*, rev. edn, University Park, P.A.: Penn State University Press.

Kahn, D. and Whitehead, G. (eds) (1992) *The Wireless Imagination*, Cambridge, M.A.: MIT Press.

Kift, D. (1996) *The Victorian Music Hall: Culture, Class, and Conflict*, trans. R. Kift, Cambridge: Cambridge University Press.

Kirby, M. (1971) *Futurist Performance*, New York: PAJ Publications

Kittler, F. (1999) *Gramophone, Film, Typewriter*, trans. G. Winthrop-Young and M. Wutz, Stanford: Stanford University Press.

Kuhns, D.F. (1997) *German Expressionist Theatre*, Cambridge: Cambridge University Press.

Levenson, M. (ed.) (1999) *The Cambridge Companion to Modernism*, Cambridge: Cambridge University Press.

Makinen, H., Wilmer, S.E. and Worthen, W.B. (eds) *Theatre, History, and National Identities*, Helsinki: Helsinki University Press.

May, L. (1980) *Screening Out the Past: The Birth of Mass Culture and the Motion Picture Industry*, New York: Oxford University Press.

Mayer, D. and Johnson, S. (2002) *Spectacles of Themselves: Popular Melodramas Which Became Significant Silent Films*, Westport, C.T.: Greenwood Press.

McConachie, B. (2003) *American Theater in the Culture of the Cold War: Producing and Contesting Containment, 1947–1962*, Iowa City, I.A.: University of Iowa Press.

Milling, J. and Ley, G. (2001) *Modern Theories of Performance: From Stanislavski to Boal*, Houndmills, Basingstoke, Hampshire: Palgrave.

Murphy, B. (1992) *Tennessee Williams and Elia Kazan: A Collaboration in the Theatre*, Cambridge: Cambridge University Press.

Patterson, M. (1981) *The Revolution in German Theatre, 1900–1933*, Boston: Routledge and Kegan Paul.

Powell, B. (2000) *Japan's Modern Theatre: A Century of Change and Continuity*, London: Japan Library.

Roediger, D. (1991) *The Wages of Whiteness: Race and the Making of the American Working Class*, New York: Verso Press.

Rudnitsky, K. (1988) *Russian and Soviet Theatre: Tradition and the Avant-Garde*, London: Thames and Hudson.

Schumacher, C. (ed.) (1996) *Naturalism and Symbolism in European Theatre*, Cambridge: Cambridge University Press.

Segel, H.B. (1987) *Turn-of-the-Century Cabaret: Paris, Barcelona, Berlin, Munich, Vienna, Cracow, Moscow, St. Petersburg, Zurich*, New York: Columbia University Press.

Senelick, L. (1989, 1992) *Cabaret Performance: Europe 1890–1940*, 2 vols, New York: PAJ Publications.

Senelick, L. (1997) *The Chekhov Theatre: A Century of the Plays in Performance*, Cambridge: Cambridge University Press.

Styan, J. L. (1981) *Modern Drama in Theory and Practice*, 3 vols, New York: Cambridge University Press.

Szalczer, E. (2001) "Nature's dream play: modes of vision and August Strindberg's re-definition of the theatre," *Theatre Journal*, 53 (March):33–52.

Taylor, D. (1991) *Theatre of Crisis: Drama and Politics in Latin America*, Lexington, K.Y.: University Press of Kentucky.

Versenyi, A. (1993) *Theatre in Latin America: Religion, Politics, and Culture from Cortes to the 1980s*, Cambridge: Cambridge University Press.

Walker, J. (2005) *Expressionism and Modernism in the American Theatre: Bodies, Voices, Words*, Cambridge: Cambridge University Press.

Willett, J. (1988) *The Theatre of the Weimar Republic*, New York: Holmes and Meier.

Williams, R. (1969) *Drama from Ibsen to Brecht*, New York: Oxford University Press.

Wilmeth, D.B. and Bigsby, C. (eds) (1999) *The Cambridge History of American Theatre, Volume II: 1870–1945*, Cambridge: Cambridge University Press.

Wilmeth, D.B. and Bigsby, C. (2000) *The Cambridge History of American Theatre, Volume II: Post World War II to the 1990s*, Cambridge: Cambridge University Press.

Worthen, W.B. (1992) *Modern Drama and the Rhetoric of Theater*, Berkeley: University of California Press.

CHAPTER 7

Theatres of popular entertainment, 1850–1970

Although scholars disagree on a definition, we may define "popular" theatre as stage entertainment that appeals to cross-class audiences in complex societies through commercial means. In this sense, popular theatre reaches a broader audience than "elite" or "working-class" entertainment and relies on performance and marketing strategies that "folk" theatre cannot deploy. Popular entertainments may draw on class-based or folk traditions of theatre, but these are typically transformed in the commercial move to generate as big an audience as possible. Because theatre relies on live actors who cannot be distributed like the images of filmed, televised, and digitized performers, popular theatre never became "mass" entertainment of the kind we have today; even the most famous international stars could not be seen by an entire population.

In the days before radio and sound film, however, the popular stage had an impact similar to that of mass media today. After 1850, concentrations of urban populations drawn to cities by industrialization led to the development of major businesses devoted to popular theatre. As theatrical entrepreneurs professionalized and commercialized their operations, new forms of production, presentation, and publicity emerged that altered the cultures of Japan, India, China, and the West. Popular theatre often reflects and shapes the ideologies of large populations – ideologies of nationalism, racism, and capitalism, for instance. Studying the popular stage has become increasingly important for historians. Further, the popular entertainment industries of the nineteenth century shaped the ways we produce and enjoy films, television, and digital diversions today.

Promoting popular entertainment

P.T. Barnum (1810–1891) was the first impresario of popular theatre on either side of the Atlantic to shape modes of publicity and promotion in ways that both attracted huge urban crowds and made popular entertainment respectable. Though now remembered chiefly as a circus owner, Barnum was best known in the 1850s as a tireless promoter of his "museum," the American Museum in New York City. Before museums were public institutions, private businessmen owned and operated them for a profit. In addition to featuring several exhibits of natural history, fine art, and mechanical wonders,

Barnum also touted such "freaks" of nature as the "Feejee Mermaid" (supposedly half-fish, half-human) and the "What Is It?" (a black man presented as an evolutionary "missing link" between humans and animals) to his astonished customers (Figure 7.1). He outfitted the dwarf Charles Stratton in bourgeois elegance as the gentleman, "Tom Thumb," and even arranged for Tom's introduction to Queen Victoria. Barnum both challenged his spectators to see through his "humbugs" and also fed them with illusions of omnipotence; if a dwarf could meet the queen, anyone could.

Further, Barnum's promotions made upper-class culture available to the millions and convinced them that they would enjoy it. In 1850, he organized and publicized the American tour of the Swedish soprano Jenny Lind, a renowned opera star, and pocketed

huge profits. Barnum also recognized that the claim of moral instruction sold tickets to urbanites anxious about their respectability. In the Lecture Room of his Museum – actually a small theatre, but renamed so as not to offend the antitheatrical prejudices of the straightlaced – Barnum banned liquor and advertised his presentation of pleasing variety acts and moralistic melodramas, such as *The Drunkard*, for respectable families. Later promoters of popular entertainment learned many of the tricks of their trade from Barnum.

Urban carnivals and optical delights

Barnum and his imitators after 1850 extended the form of the medieval carnival into the new urban environments. These entertainments featured such

Figure 7.1 Henry Johnson as Barnum's "What Is It?" Photograph by Mathew Brady (c.1872). [Source: *Freak Show* (1988), Robert Bogdan, University of Chicago Press.]

traditional delights as animal acts and fire-eaters, together with the new mechanical innovations of merry-go-rounds and ferris wheels. When produced in tandem with a world's fair, which began with the Crystal Palace Exhibition in London in 1851 and culminated in the St. Louis International Exposition of 1904, urban carnivals became potent entertainments to legitimate the capitalist-imperialist order of the pre-1914 era. Light entertainment acts in carnivals spilled over into traveling circuses, Wild West productions in the United States, and similar tent shows in Europe. The economics of such ventures depended on telegraphs and railroads connecting these entertainments with urban masses eager for diversion; traveling troupes of entertainers on this scale had not been possible before 1850.

Optical and mechanical entertainments also flourished in the newly-industrialized cities. Peepshows and freak shows had long been popular, but the nineteenth century also introduced urban viewers to "panoramas" and "dioramas" that told dramatic stories through long, unrolling cylinders of painted canvas or artfully-lighted tableaux that revealed historical battles and other fashionable spectacles. This type of entertainment also included "magic lantern" exhibitions, which featured projections of photographic images and painted glass slides onto a screen. Influenced by the immense popularity of photography, these optical shows prepared the public for "moving" pictures. In fact, many of the first films of the 1890s were shown in the same venues that staged magic lantern exhibitions and variety acts.

Variety theatre

One major form of popular entertainment that proliferated after 1850 was variety theatre. Variety is simply a series of light entertainments unconnected by any overriding theme, story, or major star. Since the renaissance, theatre in western cultures had often incorporated singers, acrobats, performing animals, and other acts as a part of an afternoon or evening of entertainment, usually featuring such "turns" between the acts of a regular drama. As the demand for these diversions increased, however, showmen worked up formulas and found venues in which they could string together a series of such "numbers" without providing a regular play as the main attraction. Variety took numerous forms after 1850. One was the blackface minstrel show, which began in the U.S. and quickly spread to Europe and to European colonies. The first case study in this chapter explores the pleasures of racialized entertainment in afterpieces, minstrelsy, and musical comedies in the U.S. between 1830 and 1910.

Another form of variety was the burlesque show, which began with female performers doing a parody, or "burlesque," of a popular play or work of literature. Eventually the parodic elements dropped out of the formula, and, by 1900, the typical burlesque show in England and the U.S. featured a male comic, several comic sketches, dance acts and musical pieces, plus scantily-clad females in all of the numbers. The striptease, now identified as the central act of a burlesque show, did not make its appearance in the U.S. until the 1920s. Other kinds of variety theatre in the U.S. included dime museums (which continued the traditions of Barnum's American Museum into the 1890s), medicine shows (variety acts used to sell patent medicines), and concert saloons (which peddled beer and food along with entertainment in New York and other large cities in the 1850s).

The concert saloon was actually a worldwide phenomenon of industrializing cities that led to the most resilient and significant form of popular variety theatre, the music hall. Although "music hall" is an English Victorian term, it may be used to designate any type of variety that features a series of unconnected entertainments on an indoor stage. Music hall entertainment, lacking the coherence of "blacked up" white performers or the presence throughout of a male comic and pretty girls, typically had even less aesthetic unity than a minstrel or burlesque show. In the U.S., this form of variety was called vaudeville; in Germany, *Singspielhalle* and in Russia, *myuzik-kholl*. The French initially called them *café chantants* and eventually *café concerts*.

In France, as in most western countries, *café chantants* began in taverns in the eighteenth century. These large taverns and their entertainers quickly gained mass popularity, especially in Paris after 1789, when the National Assembly abolished the licensing of public amusements. In response to Napoleon's reimposing theatrical regulations, however, the *café chantants* altered their formulas for performing in order to continue to operate. By the 1870s, the *café concerts* – long halls with a high stage at one end in which spectators could smoke and drink while enjoying the acts – had replaced them. By 1900, similar commercial venues for variety entertainment had emerged in Moscow, Berlin, Madrid, Sydney, Rio de Janiero, and in hundreds of other cities where newly urbanized workers, their families, and some members of the middle class sought diversion and camaraderie.

English music hall

In England, the music hall lasted longer than similar forms of variety in other countries and probably had a more enduring effect on the national culture. Already by 1850, the Star Music Hall in Bolton, a textile-manufacturing center in the North, boasted a capacity of 1500 and performances ranging from singers and acrobats to full-stage, patriotic spectacles. In 1866, London had over 30 large music halls and more than 200 smaller ones; a few of the larger halls seated over 3000 spectators. Most English music halls in the 1870s provided entertainment, food, and drink to a predominately working- and lower-middle-class audience. During the 1880s, some music hall entrepreneurs, seeking higher profits through increased respectability, opened new halls in middle- and upper-class neighborhoods. By the 1890s, many halls, even in working-class neighborhoods, no longer allowed patrons to eat and drink

while watching the show, and they also featured more homogenized acts that would not offend Victorian tastes. Over the next twenty years, several booking syndicates, which signed variety acts for tours of the entire British Isles, eliminated the last vestiges of local control and further standardized music hall entertainment. The halls reached their high point of popularity around 1910, when competition from silent films began to erode their numbers. In the 1930s and 1940s, the radio, which brought many former music hall entertainers into English homes "for free," cut even deeper into their popularity. The widespread enjoyment of television in the 1950s delivered a deathblow to the English music hall.

Until the 1890s, the English music hall provided an alternative, both in its environment and its entertainment, to the strictures of Victorian life for many working-class families. While many music hall songs sentimentalized romantic love, others delighted in sexual pleasure, a taboo subject for proper Victorians, and several derided the entanglements of marriage, a major prop for Victorian respectability. In songs and comic sketches, policemen, government clerks, and other figures of authority provided frequent butts for music hall humor. The music hall generally remained culturally conservative. Entertainers might poke fun at factory discipline and lambaste politicians caught up in scandals, but they usually applauded English victories in war and the racism that accompanied English imperialism. A favorite comic character of the pre-1890 era, for example, was the *lion comique*, a loquacious, preening, and bibulous lower-class swell, who enjoyed relating his latest adventures in comic song and swagger (Figure 7.2). Amidst the acrobats, magicians, performing animals, and human "freaks," early music hall variety preserved aspects of traditional English customs that provided workers and others with strategies for enduring and occasionally countering a culture that oppressed them.

Although gentrification and standardization drained the class-based vitality from music hall entertainment after 1890, its anti-Victorian legacy had

THE GREAT COMIC SONG WRITTEN & SUNG BY
GEORGE LEYBOURNE.
MUSIC BY
ALFRED LEE

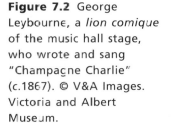

Figure 7.2 George Leybourne, a *lion comique* of the music hall stage, who wrote and sang "Champagne Charlie" (c.1867). © V&A Images. Victoria and Albert Museum.

wide ramifications in the twentieth century – from satiric popular songs and a scandal-mongering penny press to the electoral success of socialism in English politics. The rhythms and pleasures of music hall entertainment also influenced the dramatic works of several significant playwrights, including John Osborne, Harold Pinter, and Samuel Beckett. Because prominent music hall entertainers often appeared in productions of Christmas pantomimes in England, music hall songs and humor also shaped changes in this traditional form of amusement. The popular form of British pantomime is discussed in a case study following this chapter.

Theatrical revues

Revues flourished on western stages for mostly bourgeois audiences between 1900 and 1930. This genre of variety theatre featured many of the same kinds of turns as music hall, although revues usually excluded circus, animal, and freak acts, lavished more money on dance and design numbers, and often organized themselves around a unifying theme. As in many other forms of variety, Paris led the way with spectacular revues at the Folies-Bergère and elsewhere in the 1880s that involved dancing girls and glamorous tableaux. Florenz Ziegfeld (1869–1932) popularized revues in the United States with his lavish Follies, staged yearly between 1907 and 1931. The "follies," "shows," "scandals," "vanities," and "revues" of these years in U.S. entertainment typically featured top talent, from Eddie Cantor (1892–1964) to Bert Williams (1874–1922), and exciting music, by the likes of George Gershwin (1898–1937) and Irving Berlin (1888–1989). The legacy of these spectacular revues may be seen in the films of Busby Berkeley and the night club acts at Las Vegas. Revues flourished on the London stage from 1912 into the 1960s, often on a more intimate scale than their U.S. models, with such performers as Noel Coward (1899–1973) and Beatrice Lillie (1895–1989). In Germany and Austria, high-priced variety shows often ended with spectacular revues. After the Russian Revolution, several playwrights and companies in many nations took up the revue form to push their politics. The work of several of these groups is discussed in the forthcoming chapter on theatre and politics.

Because the revue has a long history as an international genre, it is not surprising that its formula continues to shape a wide variety of entertainments around the world. One contemporary example is *Takarazuka*, performed by all-female troupes in Japan. Begun in 1914, this form of light entertainment rests chiefly on music, dance, and parody and appeals to many groups of Japanese, from conventional housewives to gay couples. Female *Takarazuka* actors play all of the roles, and their spectators enjoy the gender ambiguity and idealizations of masculinity embodied in their performances of men. *Takarazuka* scripts, which often foreground gender disguise, range from historical romances set at the time of the French king Louis XIV to spectacular productions of *Gone with the Wind*. With two major theatres and five permanent touring companies in Japan today, *Takarazuka* remains a successful form of revue entertainment.

Popular melodrama and comedy

Along with variety and revue entertainment, popular audiences in the industrialized world enjoyed genres of theatre that had long been successful with urban audiences. By 1914, the theatre capitals of the West – preeminently London, Paris, New York, and Berlin, but also Milan, Vienna, Moscow, and Madrid – featured several theatres devoted to melodramas

and comedies for cross-class, popular audiences. These centers also launched touring productions of popular shows that played in circuits around a country, a region, or – in the case of London, Paris, and Madrid – around the world to far-flung populations of English, French, and Spanish speakers in colonies and former colonies. In addition, by the Great War, several regional centers of popular theatrical activity had emerged in many countries that mixed local and touring productions. In Glasgow, for example, a local poll counted 29,000 theatre seats available in 1906, most of them in auditoriums dedicated to music hall, pantomime, and touring troupes performing popular comedies and melodramas. After the unification of Germany in 1871 and its subsequent rapid industrialization, the population of Munich quadrupled by 1914, by which time the city hosted over forty theatres. A mix of privately-owned and publicly-supported theatres performed a wide variety of shows to mostly popular audiences in this southern German city. By the Great War, Buenos Aires in Argentina boasted over 30 theatres, the majority booked by touring companies out of Madrid and elsewhere. The most popular form of entertainment in Buenos Aires, provided by both local and international companies, was the *genero chico*, one-act skits written as comedies or melodramas presenting familiar characters, local color, and light satire.

In India, a form of melodramatic popular theatre emerged that combined English and South Asian conventions of production to present traditional Indian stories to different language groups in India. Called Parsi theatre, after the religion of its initial entrepreneurs, this type of touring entertainment used proscenium stages throughout India for lavish productions with declamatory acting, orchestral support, and spectacular costumes and scenery. Beginning in northern India in the 1860s, the first troupes performed in Gujarati or English and played to urban audiences of Parsis and Europeans. The companies broadened their appeal in the 1870s by introducing Urdu-language dramas that incorporated the romance of Urdu poetry and Hindustani music. Many Parsi companies were playing in Hindi and performing fairy romances and mythological material from traditional Hindu epics as well as occasional adaptations of Shakespearean plays by 1914. Although males initially played all women's parts, female actors began to appear in the 1870s, and many Parsi shows continued to feature both males and females in women's roles. Actors from several Indian ethnic groups, including many Anglo-Indians, had become Parsi stars by the 1920s, when hundreds of Parsi companies were touring India. The introduction of Indian sound films in 1931, which incorporated most of Parsi's spectacular romantic and melodramatic elements, led to the form's rapid decline.

Musical theatre

While film, radio, and later television were eliminating the audience for most forms of popular stage entertainments in India, Japan, and the West, in China, *jingxi* (or Beijing Opera) survived longer as a popular art form, in part because electricity and film were not widespread in China until the 1950s. *Jingxi* can be traced to 1790, when performers from several Chinese provinces gathered in Beijing and fused together their different theatrical traditions to celebrate the emperor's birthday. Since then, other regional forms were added until, by 1900, *jingxi* had synthesized the major traditions of Chinese musical theatre. In performance, *jingxi* relates mostly romantic and melodramatic stories through a mix of song, stylized speech, spectacular dance, pantomimed action, and sometimes acrobatics. The orchestra for *jingxi*, which introduces all major characters and often comments on the stage action, consists primarily of string and percussive instruments. *Jingxi* features lavish costumes, make-up, and hairpieces, but typically involves few set pieces and little scenery. Instead of scenic transformations, new locations are signaled by a narrator and through conventions of dance and pantomime, which can indicate such diverse places and activities as a throne room or traveling by boat.

Several dozen troupes were performing *jingxi* in the major cities of China by the 1920s. In that decade, *jingxi* star, Mei Lan-Fang (1894–1961), formed his own troupe, initiated a new category of *jingxi* entertainment, toured to Japan and the U.S., and later influenced Meyerhold and Brecht while appearing in the Soviet Union. *Jingxi* remained popular through the war against Japan and the founding of The People's Republic of China in

Figure 7.3 Photograph of actors from the Beijing Opera in full costume performing *Pop-Eye*, a *jingxi* play, in Berlin. © AKG-Images. Ullstein Bild.

1949. During the 1950s, Chairman Mao Zedong infused *jingxi* with Communist propaganda.

In the West, where musical theatre traditionally meant opera, light operatic entertainment (operetta) emerged in the nineteenth century in Vienna, Paris, and London to amuse mostly bourgeois spectators. Out of that, with injections from the popular stage, came musical comedy. In London in the 1890s, musical comedies challenged and soon replaced operetta in popularity – including the delightful, "topsy-turvy" concoctions of William S. Gilbert (1836–1911) and Arthur Sullivan (1842–1900). While there is no firm distinction between operetta and the musical, pre-1914 musicals typically featured a book with a girl-gets-boy love story, songs that could be marketed by the popular music industry, and a chorus line of beautiful women. Indeed, the first important impresario of musicals was George Edwardes (1852–1915), who made his initial reputation through shows highlighting the Gaiety Girls chorus at his Gaiety Theatre in London. At one time before the Great War, Edwardes had over a dozen companies touring in Great Britain, the U.S., India, and Australia.

A variety of musicals flourished with popular audiences on U.S. and English stages from 1895 to 1930. Several, such as Victor Herbert's (1859–1924) *Babes in Toyland* and Franz Lehar's (1870–1948) *The Merry Widow*, reminded spectators of the lightly satiric comedy or the soaring musical tones of operetta. Others, like George M. Cohan's (1878–1942) *Little Johnny Jones*, made a splash with catchy tunes, wise-cracking humor, and polished dancing. Some, such as *A Chinese Honeymoon*, were close to revues. London saw a run of musicals with "girl" in the title – *The Earl and the Girl*, *The Girl in the Taxi*, *The Shop Girl*, and *The Quaker Girl*, for example. In New York, African-American artists wrote and performed in several successful musicals, from *A Trip to Coontown* in 1898 to *Shuffle Along* in the 1920s. These London and New York musicals,

as their titles suggest, had to accommodate contemporary beliefs about racial and gender roles to win popularity.

After 1920, innovation in musical theatre shifted from London to New York and several changes occurred in the years before 1970 that marked the growing sophistication of the form. By 1920, with the production of *Sally*, composer Jerome Kern (1885–1945) and librettist Guy Bolton (1884–1979) had perfected the small-cast musical, which relied on contemporary situations and fresh musical styles rather than elaborate production values. Kern also wrote the music for *Show Boat* (1927), the first musical to recognize the effects of American racism. George and Ira Gershwin, Cole Porter, Lorenz Hart, Marc Blitzstein, and others also broadened the scope of the musical stage by including political satire, adult sexuality, and capitalist oppression in some of their shows. After 1943 and the success of *Oklahoma*, the musical dramas of Richard Rodgers (1902–1979) and Oscar Hammerstein (1895–1960) set the formula for successful musicals – lush, often exotic melodies, challenging choreography, books with relatively complex characters and serious subjects, and less emphasis on pretty girls and snappy jokes. The postwar American theatre produced several hit musicals within this general formula, each of which ran for over two years on Broadway and toured to major cities throughout the English-speaking world: *South Pacific*, *The King and I*, *My Fair Lady*, *West Side Story*, *Fiddler on the Roof*, *Gypsy*, and *Cabaret*, among others. By the 1950s, however, few working-class families in New York, London, Toronto, and Sydney were attending these shows or other professional productions. Except for specialty events like the Christmas pantomime, the era of large-scale popular theatre had ended in the West.

BMc

Key references

For further references for this chapter see the Key references at the end of the Introduction to Part III.

CASE STUDY: "Blacking up" on the U.S. stage

White people "blacking-up" to play street rowdies, circus clowns, and African-American characters – both on stage and off – is a long tradition in western performance; it dates from at least the middle ages and perhaps before. Although often racist in intent and effect, the blackface mask served a variety of other purposes within popular entertainment in the U.S. during the nineteenth and early twen-tieth centuries. At times, even African-American performers darkened their complexions to entertain commercial audiences. This case study examines instances of blackface performance in three related genres of popular entertainment on U.S. stages: the comic afterpiece, the minstrel show, and early musical comedy.

INTERPRETIVE APPROACH: Reification and utopia in popular culture

According to cultural historian Fredric Jameson, many forms of popular and mass entertainment, including films, music videos, and stand-up comedy today, pull the spectator in two contradictory directions. On the one hand, the performance offers a utopian vision of liberation and bliss to the spectator that would require revolutionary change in the social order to be sustained. On the other hand, commercial productions also involve the audience member in reifying – that is, transforming into objects – the performers and the entertainment they have provided. Popular performance, then, induces the hope for radical change and the desire to consume the "thing" that provides the entertainment. Much contemporary music, for example, both inspires hope for a utopia of satisfaction and manipulates the listener into making purchases that reinforce the status quo. Like other forms of popular culture, including blackface performance, its consumption induces revolutionary and reactionary desires simultaneously.

The theatre historian applying Jameson's understanding of popular culture to blackface performances in the U.S. would begin by asking the following:

KEY QUESTIONS

1   How did performances of blackface induce revolutionary utopian desires in its spectators?

2   How did blackface performances induce their spectators to settle for the repressive values of the status quo?

As we will see, each of the major genres of blackface entertainment persuaded its spectators to embrace very different notions of utopia and repression in the course of its popularity on U.S. stages between 1830 to 1910.

"Jump Jim Crow"

Thomas Dartmouth Rice (1806–1860), a white actor, was performing minor roles in the frontier theatres of the Mississippi valley when he invented or stole from a slave – the historical record is unclear – the song and dance that would make him famous:

> Come listen all you galls and boys,
> I'm just from Tuc-ky hoe;
> I'm goin' to sing a leetle song,
> My name's Jim Crow.
>
> Weel about and turn about,
> And do jis so;
> Eb'ry time I weel about,
> I jump Jim Crow.
>
> (Lott 1994:23–24)

Dressed in rags with burnt cork covering his face and neck, Rice performed several verses of the song, jumping with agility and variety on each chorus (Figure 7.4). When he performed his "Jim Crow" dance as a part of a comic afterpiece at the New York Bowery Theatre in 1832, the young, mostly male working-class audience gave him a tumultuous reception. Rice wrote several one-act plays that featured his Jim Crow character and his famous dance, and he performed them successfully at the end of a regular evening's entertainment for the next twenty years. Like similar mythic characters from the Southwest, Jim Crow boasted that he could outfight, outeat, outlie, and outsex anyone else. Rice's dance was a variation on the shuffle, a dance done by lower-class blacks and whites to lively fiddle music in the taverns, dancehalls, and brothels of northern cities.

Drawing on Jameson's understanding of utopia and reification, we may speculate that Rice's "Jim Crow" afterpieces animated his male spectators to

Figure 7.4 Thomas Dartmouth Rice performing "Jim Crow," at the Bowery Theatre, New York, 1833. © the Museum of the City of New York.

dream of political and physical liberation. The verses of his song celebrated working-class victories over social and economic oppressors, and they were taken up by mobs destroying symbols of elite privilege during urban rioting in the 1830s and 1840s. His rough-music and violent gyrations probably reminded Rice's spectators of their own raucous parades through town during holidays, when they blackened their faces to entertain and alarm friends and enemies with scurrilous antics and the noise of tin kettles and cow bells. This European tradition dated from medieval mummers plays at Christmastime and continued into the nineteenth century. Like "Jump Jim Crow," these cacophonous spectacles encouraged traditional male forms of merrymaking and celebrated the rights of the common man. Applauding T.D. Rice, however, also meant cheering for the anarchy and aggressiveness of his performance. Blacking up, making noise, and dancing foolishly evoked traditional utopian notions of plebeian male solidarity, but it also cut against progressive possibilities for workingmen in the 1830s. During this decade, when trade unions and workingmen's parties sought collective bargaining and the ten-hour day, "Jump Jim Crow" turned workers away from productive political action and towards revelry and riot. Jameson's theory and the historical evidence suggest that Rice's performance encouraged a utopian dream of traditional freedom but undercut practical, progressive reform.

Happy Uncle Tom

By the 1850s, blackface performance had grown from occasional afterpieces by Rice and others into full evenings of entertainment, presented by an all-male minstrel troupe of four to ten performers. Dozens of minstrel companies played throughout the urban northeast, paying top salaries to their headliners and composers, among them the popular songwriter Stephen Foster. White performers borrowed much of their material from slave festivities in the South, including musical instruments (the banjo and bones), slave dances ("patting juba"), and the comic exchanges typical of corn-shucking rituals on a plantation. Minstrel shows usually featured jokes and musical numbers, specialty acts, and a concluding one-act comedy, parody, or farce. While some of the verses of Rice's song in the "Jim Crow" afterpieces called for the abolition of slavery, most minstrel troupes of the 1850s pandered to groups of white urban males who needed to be assured of their racial superiority. In general, minstrels portrayed black characters as inept fools, grotesque animals, or sentimental victims. The mythic Old South of the minstrel stage was peopled by kindly white masters, Earth Mother mammies, boastful Zip Coons, feminized old uncles, and "yaller gals" (played by a male in drag), light-skinned slaves whose beauty and allure motivated romantic songs and incidents of victimization.

The racism of 1850s minstrelsy was especially apparent in the skits that parodied the contemporary success of performances of *Uncle Tom's Cabin*. Full-scale stage adaptations of Harriet Beecher Stowe's anti-slavery novel appeared soon after its publication in 1852; some of them were nearly as abolitionist as her book. Minstrel one-acts based on the novel, however, derided or ignored Stowe's abolitionism. One typical version, titled "Happy Uncle Tom," depicted Stowe's exemplar of self-sacrificing morality and vigorous spirituality as a decrepit old uncle, meant to be laughed at for his grotesque jigs and foolish dialog. Like many minstrel parodies of the 1850s, "Happy Uncle Tom" delivered its audience to a never-never land of domestic warmth, sentimental love, and easy power in which "whiteness" provided the ticket to fun. For the Irish immigrants and rural newcomers who constituted much of the audience for pre-Civil War minstrelsy, "Happy Uncle Tom" temporarily took them out of the dangerous cities of the 1850s to a plantation utopia in which they could indulge their nostalgia for a lost home.

At the same time, however, by assuring them that their "whiteness" made them superior to the fools on the minstrel stage, parodies like "Happy Uncle Tom" exacerbated the tensions between these spectators and the free blacks of northern cities. In the 1850s, the American business class exploited this split between Irish immigrants and African-American workers to the detriment of both "races." (Most Americans racialized the Irish as well as blacks for much of the nineteenth century.) On the basis of Jameson's theory and the history of American racism, it might be argued that the racial fragmentation of the American working class partly derived from minstrel entertainment, contributing to riots, undermining working-class solidarity, and perpetuating race-based inequities and repressions for the next hundred years.

Abyssinia

Before the U.S. Civil War (1861–1865), black performers had occasionally appeared on the minstrel stage, but white minstrels, eager to distinguish their true "race" from the blackface they performed, had discriminated against free entertainers of color to avoid any confusion that might harm their reputations. After 1865, however, black minstrel troupes proliferated, as African-American performers sought entry into the flourishing entertainment industry. They needed the work, but minstrelsy was usually the only path open to them in the white-controlled business. This created a double bind for black performers. Once on the minstrel stage, African-American entertainers had to conform to white stereotypes of their "race" to please predominately white audiences. To increase their success in this highly competitive field, black troupes often advertised themselves as truthful delineators of authentic plantation life. The result was that an entire generation of black performers helped to perpetuate and confirm racist fantasies and stereotypes in mainstream American culture. Composer James Bland, for instance, elaborated the myth that African-Americans really longed to return to slavery in his song, "Carry Me Back to Old Virginny," and Billy

Kersands (c.1842–1915), a popular Jim Crow in minstrel skits, played on the belief that blacks were creatures of primitive appetites.

The rise of vaudeville in the U.S. gradually displaced minstrelsy as the dominant form of variety entertainment in the 1880s. As minstrel troupes splintered and dispersed, individual blackface acts, performed by entertainers of both "races," enjoyed newfound popularity on the vaudeville stage. African-American Bert Williams (1874–1922) had begun in minstrelsy where he learned the necessity of blackening his light complexion to please white audiences. In vaudeville, Williams teamed up with George Walker (c.1873–1911), another American of color, who generally played a fast-talking, free-spending dandy to Williams's slow-moving, melancholy "Jonah man," so-called because disaster always befell him. The success of the duo (aided by Walker's business acumen) propelled them into a series of all-black musical comedies produced in New York between 1900 and 1908.

Williams and Walker faced a social and cultural world more hostile to black equality and ambition than at any time since slavery. In New York, African Americans were excluded from most restaurants and hotels and rigidly segregated in theatres and other places of public amusement, if allowed in at all. While the traditional minstrel show had generally depicted blacks as primitive and foolish, the "coon acts" and razor songs popular in vaudeville around the turn of the century added the stereotype of the "dangerous nigger," a marauder eager to stab and rape. Middle-class white fears of black potency and violence would soon reach their dubious acme in 1915 with *The Birth of a Nation*, D.W. Griffith's racist film celebrating the rise of the Ku Klux Klan as the protector of white womanhood in the South after the Civil War.

Williams and Walker had billed themselves as "Two Real Coons" in vaudeville, and their first musicals on Broadway stayed within the narrow range of American racist beliefs. With *In Dahomey* in 1903,

Figure 7.5 The cast of *In Dahomey*, 1903: Hattie McIntosh, George Walker, Ada Overton Walker, Bert Williams, and Lottie Williams. © Billy Rose Theatre Collection, New York Public Library for the Performing Arts, Astor, Lenox and Tilden Foundation.

however, Williams and Walker moved part of the setting of their comedy to Africa to poke gentle fun at white American ways and to locate a utopian space for black dreams. This idea was more fully realized in 1906 with *Abyssinia*, a lavish production capitalized by white businessmen, featuring music by Will Marion Cook and Alex Rogers. Their songs laughed at wealthy Americans and allowed the pair to protest their designation as "coons." The plot for the musical has Rastus Johnson (Walker) winning the lottery and taking his family and friends, including Jasper Jenkins (Williams), to Europe and Africa. Thinking he is an American prince, the Emperor of Ethiopia invites Rastus and his friends to a feast. Comic misadventures, onstage camels and donkeys, and exotic dances

and romances soon follow before the pair bid farewell to their African hosts.

Abyssinia kept Williams and Walker in their stock, minstrel-derived roles, but, by changing the locale of the show, the duo induced black spectators to imagine a place where people of color ruled and where African Americans might be treated (at least temporarily) with respect and even honor. Seated in the segregated second balcony of a Broadway theatre, black audience members might imagine a utopian space for their hopes. On the other hand, the musical did not seriously challenge white racist beliefs; to do so would have doomed it at the box office. The whites that predominated in the audience and controlled the space of the auditorium could dismiss the production's utopian possibilities and laugh at the racial clowning. Seen through the lens of Jameson's theory, it is likely that *Abyssinia* induced utopian desire for some blacks and confirmed racist beliefs for many whites.

Blackface acts continued to amuse white audiences into the 1950s, when African-American activism and cold war concerns gradually exposed the racism under the burnt cork. Until then, however, some of the premiere performers of popular entertainment on stage and screen paraded their talents in blackface – including Al Jolson, Eddie Cantor, Mickey Rooney, and Judy Garland.

BMc

Key references

Boskin, J. (1986) *Sambo: The Rise and Demise of an American Jester*, New York: Oxford.

Cockrell, D. (1997) *Demons of Disorder: Early Blackface Minstrels and Their World*, New York and Cambridge: Cambridge University Press.

Jameson, F. (1979) "Reification and utopia in mass culture," *Social Text*, 1:130–148.

Krasner, D. (1997) *Resistance, Parody, and Double Consciousness in African-American Theatre, 1895–1910*, New York: St. Martin's Press.

Lott, E. (1994) *Love and Theft: Blackface Minstrelsy and the American Working Class*, New York: Oxford University Press.

Roediger, D. (1991) *The Wages of Whiteness: Race and the Making of the American Working Class*, London: Verso.

Toll, R.C. (1974) *Blacking Up: The Minstrel Show in Nineteenth-Century America*, New York: Oxford University Press.

Woll, A. (1989) *Black Musical Theatre from Coontown to Dreamgirls*, Baton Rouge, L.A.: Louisiana University. Press.

CASE STUDY: British pantomime: How "bad" theatre remains popular

An overview of "panto"

By early December each year, commercial production companies, repertory theatres, and amateur dramatic societies are rehearsing their annual contributions to a unique British form of popular theatre that accounts for up to 20 percent of all live performance in the United Kingdom annually – pantomime. Pantomime has existed on the British stage since the early eighteenth century. During the 1870s, the basic content (fairy tales and folk legends) and the formulaic set of conventions that characterize today's "pantos" crystallized. They have remained flexible enough to be quickly adapted to current public tastes, fashions, and events. Each Christmas season over 200 pantomimes run concurrently throughout the United Kingdom. In a given year you might attend commercial productions of *Jack and the Beanstalk* at the King's Theatre (Edinburgh) or *Snow White and the Seven Dwarfs* at the Birmingham Hippodrome, repertory productions of *Mother Goose* at the Oldham Coliseum or *Peter Pan* at the Wimbledon Theatre (greater London), or an amateur cast in *Cinderella* at the village hall in New Quay, Wales.

Pantomime defies political correctness, good taste, literary merit, and critical disdain. Like the evil villain such as the wicked Witch in *Snow White* or Captain Hook in *Peter Pan* who, by tradition, make the very first entrance of any character from the "dark" (evil) left side of the stage to the discordant tones of the orchestra and the resounding "boos" of the audience, pantomime productions return each year to "haunt" theatre critics who ignore, decry, or simply tolerate this annual national popular entertainment. Writing for the *Independent* in 1999, Dominic Cavendish admitted:

It's hard for an adult — let alone a reviewer — to admit that they have actually enjoyed an example of this maligned art form. And not at the arm's-length distance of ironic approval, or vicariously, through the gurgling delight of other people's children . . . but closely involved, experiencing a state of wonder. It's a shock to say it, but *Peter Pan* at Wimbledon Theatre induced such a state.

Pantomime thrives on caricature, "bad" jokes, slapstick comedy, and pratfalls. It includes cross-dressing, with a woman playing the heroic "principal boy" role and a male comedian in skirts playing the "dame." Other conventions are its sentimental romance, easily recognizable popular songs, incidental music supporting the visual action throughout the performance, and, depending on the size of the budget, sumptuous costumes with spectacular scenic transformations and as large a dance chorus as possible. Pantomime embraces its diverse popular audience, occasionally retains its old satirical edge, and ignores the proscenium arch by using the entire theatre as its performance space. It engages the audience in occasional shouting matches and often takes time out from the dramatory story to bring some children onstage for a sing-along, cheap gags, and prizes of candy for them to take home as a Christmas treat.

To help convey some of the flavor of the "panto," we offer the following excerpt from scene 5 of *Aladdin*, by Derek Dwyer and Merlin Price. The setting is Widow Twanky's cottage (see Figure 7.6). As the curtain opens, the Dame is washing the laundry while impersonating Julie Andrews in *The Sound of Music*.

Figure 7.6 Dan Leno in *The Widow Twankey*, 1896. © V&A Images. Victoria and Albert Museum.

DAME: (*Sings*) The house is alive, with the piles of washing! The socks, vests and knickers, from a thousand homes! An' I wish they'd stayed there. Oooh, I hate washing! Don't you just hate washing? (*Repartee with audience*) I tell you, working in a laundry is no job for someone with a delicate sense of smell (*sniffs armpits*). Oooooh!

Enter Wishee and Washee [her sons].

DAME: Ah, there you are, you two. Now that you're unemployed, and your brother seems to be living on a different planet since he peeked at the princess, you'd better give me a hand with this laundry. If we finish early, I'll take you all to the park this afternoon for a picnic.

WISHEE AND WASHEE: Great, mum.

WASHEE: What do you want us to do then?

DAME: Well, you can take the washing off the spin drier.

WISHEE: But mum, we haven't got a spin drier.

DAME: Oh yes we have. Hold this. (*Dame hands ends of washing line to Wishee. Takes off cardigan to reveal bundles of clothes wrapped round her. She twirls round and all clothes come off pegged on to washing line. Hands other end to Washee.*) There you are. Hang that lot up.

There are two types of "pantos," those produced by commercial companies and those done by the subsidized theatres. Commercial pantomimes are mass-produced by large production companies, each running between five and fifteen pantomimes each season. Commercial pantomimes tend to stay with established, conventional practices, and are most likely to feature television and entertainment personalities in key roles to attract large audiences. In order to recoup the huge initial costs of a production, a new production will be recycled for performances in different regional theatres – running up to ten years. To keep costs down, the rehearsal period is usually only one week, plus a production week. Given the minimal rehearsal period, actors, musicians, and dancers must rely on their experience with the received conventions of pantomime.

In contrast, repertory pantomimes are produced by subsidized companies, such as the Oldham Coliseum or Theatre Royal Stratford East (London). Depending for their success more on the strength of the actors, their scripts are specially written for their own local/regional audiences and therefore may have more satire relevant to current issues than commercial pantos. Because pantomime is so much a part of the Christmas holiday season, most regional theatres depend on their pantomime income to subsidize much of the remainder of their year's repertory season.

Whatever the critics think of pantomime, it is to popular entertainment what Shakespeare is to today's literary theatre – an inescapable part of the British national cultural landscape. It brings into the theatre a more inclusive audience than any other form of theatre today, with three generations of a family often attending a performance together. For the overwhelming majority of children, it is their first, and perhaps only experience of live theatre, and for the majority of people, it will be their only annual visit to the theatre.

The early history of British pantomime

Since its first introduction on the London stage as "night scenes" or "Italian night scenes" in the early eighteenth century, what came to be known as British pantomime has been a theatrical chameleon, its performers and producers constantly changing its form, content, and conventions as necessary for its survival and continued popularity. The word pantomime is derived from the Greek, meaning "an imitator of things." During Roman Imperial rule, troupes of mimes (*mimi*) presented variety performances including dance, music, acrobatics, and skits, and solo pantomime (*pantomimus*) emerged as a somewhat more refined performance in which a silent performer of great beauty and skill mimed all the characters of a drama using a series of costumes and masks to the accompaniment of an orchestra.

Pantomime reemerged in fifteenth-century Italy as part of the *commedia dell'arte* tradition. When illegal fairground performances of *commedia* were suppressed in Paris in 1702, a number of performers from the *commedia* tradition sought work in London. Thus some of *commedia*'s non-verbal comic scenes were set to music and dance, and performed with a few of the key *commedia* characters in a transposed English context as "Italian night scenes" – one small part of a full evening's bill of theatre lasting late into the evening.

By 1716 the dance master at London's Drury Lane Theatre, John Weaver, created *The Loves of Mars and Venus* featuring dancers impersonating Roman gods. It was advertised as a "new Entertainment in Dancing after the manner of the Antient Pantomimes" (of Rome). To rival it, John Rich (1692–1761), dancer, actor, and manager at the rival Lincoln's Inn Fields theatre, created his own pantomime with characters from Roman mythology, magically transformed in the second part of the performance into characters in a knockabout comedy. Rich, known by his stage name, Lun, further developed and popularized this earliest form of British pantomime as "Harlequinades" – spectacular performances in which the *commedia* character, Harlequin, magically underwent self-transformation, or transformed the scenery with a touch of his magic sword or wand.

The success of Rich's productions led the eminent actor, David Garrick, to produce his own pantomimes at Drury Lane. It was in Garrick's productions that the hero, Harlequin, first began to speak. His multi-colored costume of various colored patches also became a literal map for portraying his emotions. Touching red meant love, blue was truth, yellow indicated jealousy, and, to become invisible, Harlequin pointed to a black patch, disappearing in order to work his magic.

By the 1780s and 1790s, the content of the Harlequinade began to change as folk and nursery tales were enacted during the first part of the entertainment. In 1789, in a production of *Robinson Crusoe* loosely based on Daniel Defoe's novel, Harlequinade characters appeared, including the clown, Pantaloon, as well as Harlequin and Columbine. Whatever the tale, as it was concluding, the Fairy would transform the characters, whether Robinson Crusoe or Jack the Giant Killer, into well known Harlequinade characters. By 1800, a pantomime was part of an evening of theatre, and, by the mid 1800s, the elaborate and spectacular scenic changes and tableaux – such as the revelation of Cinderella's coach, often complete with a team of live ponies – became the most important part of these early pantomimes. Before photography and film were invented, pantomime's spectacles offered some in urban audiences their first glimpse of the countryside, Scottish moors, or foreign temples.

Beginning with his *Jack and the Beanstalk* (1844), E.L. Blanchard began to give increasing importance to the fairy tales and folk legends in pantomime. Between 1852 and 1888, Blanchard authored all of Drury Lane's pantomimes, establishing the style of rhyming verse and topical wit that came to characterize the genre in the late nineteenth century.

Other conventions still found in today's pantomime were also introduced. In 1852, Miss Ellington became one of the first "principal boys" playing the Prince in *The Good Woman in the Wood* at the Lyceum Theatre. By the 1860s, both the "principal boy" and "dame" roles were becoming well established, further eroding the appearance of Harlequin and the Clown.

By the 1870s the introduction of Music Hall stars on the pantomime stage brought changes to pantomime plots and dialogs as the Music Hall artists brought along their own material. One of the earliest Music Hall stars appearing on the pantomime stage was G.H. MacDermott in the 1870 production of

Herne the Hunter at the Grecian Theatre. Female Music Hall stars began to monopolize the playing of "principal boy" roles as they titillated Victorian audiences with their displays of thigh as well as ankle, and the public wanted to see its favorite comedian playing the dame role.

Between 1879 and 1895, Augustus Harris (1851–1896) produced the most spectacular full-length pantomimes ever staged, making use of the newest scenic inventions, and discovering the great comic genius of Music Hall star, Dan Leno (Figure 7.6). The role of Mother Goose was created for Leno at Theatre Royal Drury Lane in 1902.

With the demise of Music Hall, other variety stages produced pantomime stars, only to be replaced by the stars of new twentieth-century media as each developed – radio, television, and then film stars have all found their way onto the pantomime stage.

Pantomime and its audiences

In order to remain popular, British pantomime has been chameleon-like in changing to communicate with its audiences. Using phenomenology, we will explore how pantomime simultaneously communicates through several performance modes or registers in order to entertain its multiple audiences.

INTERPRETIVE APPROACH: Phenomenology and history

Phenomenology as a European philosophical movement was inaugurated by Edmund Husserl (1859–1938). In the first edition of his *Logical Investigations* (1900–1901), he announced the need for a method that would describe how we encounter, experience, think about, and come to "know" the world. As a way of doing philosophy by providing a close description of a particular phenomenon, Bert O. States applied the method to the essential materials of the theatrical event such as sound, sight, movement, and text in his *Great Reckonings in Little Rooms: On the Phenomenology of Theater* (1985). In a subsequent essay (1995), States provided a description of the three modes through which the audience encounters the actor in performance: self-expressive, collaborative, and representational modes.

1   In the "self-expressive mode," we encounter the actor operating in the first person, speaking as an "I." This is the actor operating at her most virtuosic, openly displaying her artistry, as in an operatic solo where the soprano does not "disappear" into her role, or when the superb mime artist, Marcel Marceau, ascends an invisible stairway. In dramatic theatre, the self-expressive mode is also evident when the artistry of the actor commands our attention, thereby providing part of our pleasure in appreciating a particular actor's interpretation of a role, such as Laurence Olivier's portrayal of Hamlet.

2   In the "collaborative mode," we encounter the actor addressing the audience in the second person, as "you." A variety of theatrical conventions, such as the comic aside, are employed to directly address the audience so that the distance between actor and audience becomes a collaborative "we," engaging us directly in the world of the play.

3   In the "representational mode," the actor speaks in the third person, conveying the dramatic narrative. Even if the actor does not tell a story, the performance is "about" something.

▷

> These three "pronominal modes" can serve as points of reference for analyzing how a particular theatrical event makes meaning and experience within a particular historical context or period. Within the conventions of contemporary realist dramatic theatre, the actor's self-expressive artistry ideally "disappears" into the role, thereby serving the representational mode. In contrast, the *commedia dell'arte* operated primarily in the collaborative and self-expressive modes, communicating directly with its audience through the display of the actor's improvisatory skills within a particular "mask," or role. Pantomime remains popular by operating between and among all three modes.
>
> Of any performance in the theatre then, whether in kathakali, western opera, Shakespeare, kabuki, or a realistic play, we may ask:
>
> **KEY QUESTIONS**
>
> 1 **Where are the moments of the self-expressive mode, when the artistry of the artist, overtly or otherwise, commands our attention?**
>
> 2 **Where are the moments when the actor directly addresses the audience, seeking its collaboration?**
>
> 3 **Where do we see the representational mode in which the actor is conveying the dramatic narrative?**

In pantomime, each actor plays a character in the unfolding drama of the adapted fairy tale so that the actor is always operating, at least nominally, within the representational mode through which the dramatic story is conveyed to the audience. For young children, the tale may be both dramatic and "magical." Whoever plays a character is usually accepted at face-value as that character. The collaborative mode comes directly into the foreground when the entire audience is called upon to become part of the action by shouting, "he's behind you" whenever the evil, "baddie" is about to capture his innocent prey in a chase scene.

For adults in the audience, the well-known story is simply a pretext for the enjoyment of some of the self-expressive and collaborative modes of acting "invisible" to younger children. When popular stars of the entertainment world play a particular role, they are intentionally cast by the director, not to disappear into the role as would a dramatic actor, but to play the role as/through their public persona, underscoring the importance of the self-expressive mode. When a fly-by-night, untrained personality from the reality television show, *Big Brother*, such as Jade Goody, a tabloid-labeled "dimwit," performs in a panto, she will do no more than re-present and reinscribe her (short-lived) public persona in the role in order to attract an audience wanting to see Jade Goody.

Like a hungry fairy who must be satisfied each year, pantomime consumes popular cultural icons and fashions like Jade Goody only to spit them out

Figure 7.7 Sid and Babs (Barbara Windsor) in *Carry on Abroad.* © Acquarius Fox/Rank/Rogers Cult Images.

as soon as they are no longer flavor of the month. In the years when the Spice Girls were the most popular girl band in the U.K., they were conspicuously present as the Ugly Sisters in productions of *Cinderella*, only to be jettisoned in favor of Brittany Spears's Ugly Sister in another year.

But when a seasoned professional actress and entertainer such as Barbara Windsor appears in a panto, something much more complex can take place. Barbara Windsor is best known for playing highly sexualized, dumb-blonde roles in the hugely popular "Carry On" films of the 1960s and 1970s (Figure 7.7), and more recently was institutionalized as the pub-bar matron in the long-running U.K. television soap, *EastEnders*. But early in her career, she gained valuable on-stage acting experience with Joan Littlewood's famous experimental Theatre Workshop. As a well-known star, when she appears in a version of *Cinderella* as the Fairy-godmother, at the level of representation for the children, she creates "magic" as she transforms the pumpkin into a coach, or transforms "Cinders" from her ashen-covered servant role into the beautiful young girl with whom

the Prince falls in love. But for the parents and grandparents in the audience, who are old enough to have experienced Windsor during her youthful film career, she is simultaneously debunking the myth of female beauty and youth represented by Cinderella by simply being herself – a gracefully aging, feisty woman with a sharp, self-deprecating, satirical sense of humor about her past as a sexualized object. The appearance of major and minor stars and personalities like Windsor and Goody exemplifies the importance that the contribution of the self-expressive mode plays in contributing to British pantomime's ability to constantly re-fashion itself through the self-expressive, collaborative, and representational modes of expression.

PZ

Key references

States, B.O. (1985) *Great Reckonings in Little Rooms: On the Phenomenology of Theater*, Berkeley: University of California Press.

States, B.O. (1995) "The Actor's Presence: Three Phenomenal Modes," in P.B. Zarrilli (ed.) *Acting ReConsidered*, London: Routledge.

CHAPTER 8

Theatres of the avant-garde and their legacy, 1880–1970

"Avant-garde" was originally a French military term referring to the forward line of soldiers – those leading the charge into battle. Likewise, avant-garde artists thought of themselves as the front ranks of artistic progress, fighting bourgeois propriety to expand the boundaries of the possible. Avant-garde movements generally consisted of small groups of artists and spectators who reinforced each other in their rebellions against middle-class conventions and established cultural institutions, and in their desires for utopian change. Most movements published manifestos to proclaim their ideology and to elevate their work over that of conventional artists and rival avant-garde groups. Beginning with the naturalists and followed soon after by the symbolists, international avant-garde movements proliferated in the theatre between 1880 and 1935. While some of these movements flamed out within a few years, others burned for two decades or longer. Some were quickly forgotten, but several had a significant impact on twentieth-century theatre. Although some of the innovations that we now recognize as theatrical modernism began in avant-garde movements, the more important legacy of the avant-garde was its

insistent challenge to conventional modes of making and enjoying theatre.

Avant-garde theatre did not exist before 1880. Innovative artists in earlier decades and centuries might have rejected the prevailing norms of artistry, but they did not form movements, write manifestos, and attempt to set the terms by which their art should be understood. The rise of an international avant-garde in the late nineteenth century in all of the arts (including the theatre) has partly to do with artists being cut free from traditional obligations of patronage and a new struggle for economic survival, plus a bourgeoisie unsure of its own artistic values. Technologies new to the period also empowered avant-garde theatre artists – not only photography and recent audiophonic inventions, but electricity and the electrical illumination of the theatre.

Without electricity, the avant-garde might not have flourished at all. Electric lights opened up an immense range of new visual effects that Appia, Craig, the new directors, and all of the avant-garde movements exploited. Electricity also powered new dynamics between theatre artists and audiences in general. With electrical illumination came the full dimming of house lights during performances, which left audiences, for the first time in theatre history, in the dark. When spectators could no longer communicate with each other during performances, theatregoing shifted from a generally social to a much more private experience. Increasingly, modern audiences after 1880 no longer interrupted the show to correct the actors, applaud at random, or start a riot if the production displeased them. Diminished forms of audience participation continued during the variety acts of the popular stage. Avant-garde artists could anticipate that most of their spectators came to the theatre for moments of emotion and insight that would be experienced privately, not primarily socially. While some avant-garde movements attempted to shock bourgeois spectators into an awareness of the sociality of performance, most used their new found power to experiment with new theatrical forms meant to access the imaginations of individual spectators as a means of challenging their expectations and values.

From the point of view of the avant-garde, much in the modern era needed challenging. With the decline of traditional religious faith and the rise of anthropological understanding came an unsettling relativism. As the philosopher Martin Heidegger noted, modern people were the first to realize that their worldview was only one of several ways of perceiving reality. Perhaps, as some linguists and philosophers were beginning to affirm after 1900, this relativism was absolute; maybe there was no position beyond human language and experience that allowed for objective truth.

Complementing this cultural relativism was the recognition that human subjectivity was much more complex and irrational than people had realized. If human nature were chiefly sexual in orientation, bourgeois society was reduced to little more than a clanking, voracious, and ridiculous machine for sexual repression; this, in more scientific language, was the pessimistic conclusion of Freud's *Civilization and Its Discontents* (1930). Similar insights led some

to look to "primitive," usually colonial "others," for images of sexual liberation. Some modernists such as Friedrich Nietzsche hoped that the realm of aesthetics, previously understood as an embellishment of social life, provided the best model for how to live a vital if fatalistic life. Avant-garde artists in the theatre, like avant-garde modernists such as James Joyce, Pablo Picasso, and Igor Stravinsky in the other arts, struggled with these themes in their work.

It is no accident that "avant-garde" is a French term. Since the eighteenth-century Enlightenment, French culture had provided public forums for debates among the intelligentsia, a recognized elite of artists, academics, critics, philosophers and others, on topics ranging from the nature of art to the nature of being. This tradition spread to other national cultures strongly influenced by France or containing a significant level of public debate about the arts, notably Italy, Germany, Poland, and Russia. In England and the U.S., in contrast, few theatre artists felt that it was their responsibility to publicly contest the relative merits of each others' plays and productions. Consequently, although avant-garde artists were active in all of the major cities of the West between 1880 and 1930, most of the major avant-garde movements of theatrical modernism originated in France and French-influenced cultures. Given the felt need to debate new artistic experiments in public, these movements typically generated many manifestos, essays, and public letters that stated the utopian hopes of each new movement but were often vague about the details of theatrical realization. In studying the avant-garde, it is important to distinguish between public debates and theatrical practices.

Naturalism on stage

The gradual shift toward realism in playwriting and production after 1850 reached its apogee in the West in the movement known as naturalism. While absolute distinctions between realism and naturalism are probably impossible, the former may be understood as a general style that remains pervasive today, while the latter can be seen as an avant-garde movement that gained substantial influence in the theatre between 1880 and 1914 and then disbanded. Committed naturalists joined Emile Zola (1840–1902), their leader, in asserting that heredity and the environment were the primary causes of human behavior. Influenced by Darwinian notions of evolution and an approach to reality that claimed scientific objectivity, Zola argued in *Naturalism in the Theatre* (1881) that plays must demonstrate the effects of these materialist causes. Like the general shift toward realism, naturalism was influenced by photography. "You cannot claim to have really seen something until you have photographed it," wrote Zola (Sontag 1977:87), with characteristic overstatement, in 1901. Where realist playwrights, directors, and designers relied on photo-like stage effects for a variety of reasons, however, the naturalists believed that an accurate rendition of external realities was only the necessary starting point for an exploration of materialist causation.

Although Zola strove to meet his announced goals for the movement in the dramatization of one of his novels, *Thérèse Raquin* (1873), the plays of Henri Becque (1837–1899) more fully realized Zola's naturalist ideals in France. Becque's *The Crows* (1882) and *La Parisienne* (1885) nearly abandon conventional plotting to present everyday situations in which rapacious characters prey on the weak and a "respectable" wife sleeps with other men to advance her husband's career. German theatregoers interested in radical reform applauded the early plays of Gerhart Hauptmann, which included *Before Sunrise* (1889) and *The Weavers* (1892), a play with a group protagonist about the exploitation and rioting of Silesian workers in 1844. In Russia, Maxim Gorky, who participated in the revolutions of 1905 and 1917, wrote several naturalist plays, including *The Lower Depths* (1902), which centered on tramps and impoverished workers living in a flophouse in

Moscow. Like most naturalist plays, *The Lower Depths* dramatized a photographic "slice of life," with all of its banality, cynicism, sentimentality, and violence.

State censorship throughout much of Europe before 1914, however, made it difficult for most naturalist playwrights to get their plays produced. The authorities objected to the offensive language of much naturalist dialog and feared the political implications of the dramas. To avoid censorship, producers in several countries interested in naturalism (and in other censored plays) organized independent theatres on a subscription basis for members only. In Paris, for instance, André Antoine began the Théâtre Libre in 1887 when the censors refused him permission to produce a short season of new plays, which included an adaptation of a Zola novel. One of his early productions was Henrik Ibsen's (1828–1906) *Ghosts* (1881), which many believed to be the epitome of stage naturalism. His Théâtre Libre also produced several of Becque's plays, *The Power of Darkness* (1888) by Russian novelist Leo Tolstoy (1828–1910), and *Miss Julie* in 1893, by the Swedish dramatist August Strindberg (1849–1912).

Antoine's theatre provided a model for other free theatres. Also organized as a private club to escape censorship, the Freie Bühne (Free Stage) in Berlin produced predominately naturalist plays by Ibsen, Becque, Tolstoy, and others and created the first audience for Hauptmann's dramas. The Independent Theatre, modeled on the other "free" theatres on the continent, opened in London in 1891 with a production of *Ghosts* and continued until 1897, mostly showcasing naturalist plays. Because the free theatres of Berlin and London employed actors who rehearsed and performed in the midst of other professional commitments, neither the Freie Bühne nor the Independent Theatre could mount the kind of fully-integrated productions that marked the success for the Théâtre Libre, where Antoine relied on trained amateurs. Nonetheless, all three theatres played a significant role in introducing Europe to the possibilities of stage naturalism.

Symbolism and its influence

After 1900, many theatre artists moved beyond the ideology of naturalism; some, like Hauptmann, openly rejected it for symbolism. The symbolists urged viewers to look through the photo-like surface of appearances to discover more significant realities within – spiritual realities that the naturalists had ignored. Seeking to advance a theatre of immanent spirituality, Gustave Kahn wrote the first manifesto of theatrical symbolism in 1889. The early symbolists, who also included the French poet Stephane Mallarmé (1842–1898) and Belgian playwright Maurice Maeterlinck (1862–1949), drew inspiration from the myth-laden music dramas of Richard Wagner, the spiritual insights of Fyodor Dostoevsky, the gothic mysteries of Edgar Allan Poe, and the imagistic poetry of Charles-Pierre Baudelaire.

The Théâtre de l'Oeuvre, begun in Paris in 1893 and run by Aurélien Lügne-Poë (1869–1940) – he added the "Poe" to his name in honor of the American author – became the center of symbolist performance in Western Europe. Lügne-Poë opened his theatre with Maeterlinck's *Pelléas and Mélisande*, written in 1892. Like other of his early plays, including *The Intruder* (1890), *Pélleas and Mélisande* evokes a mood of mystery through multiple symbols, eerie sound effects, and ominous silences; with little overt action, *Pélleas and Mélisande* relies as much on sound as sight. Lügne-Poë produced Maeterlinck's play on a semi-dark stage with gray backdrops and gauze curtains separating performers and spectators. In accord with the symbolists' desire to foreground the aurality of language, the actors chanted or whispered many of their lines and moved with ritual-like solemnity. Maeterlinck's symbolist plays mystified and irritated many spectators, but they also fascinated some. In his theatre, Lügne-Poë also experimented with synesthesia in an attempt to engage all of the senses (including taste and smell) in the theatrical experience. Although the Théâtre de l'Oeuvre produced plays in many styles and from many periods (including translations of Sanskrit dramas from India)

until its demise in 1929, it continued to be known for its symbolist works.

The symbolist theatre of the 1890s in Paris directly and indirectly influenced the efforts of several other artists interested in elevating the implicit immaterial realities of audiophonic communication over the materiality of the photographic. Symbolism exercised its major impact on European playwriting between 1890 and 1910. In Germany, the so-called neo-romanticism of Hugo von Hofmannsthal (1874–1929) had strong affinities with symbolism. Von Hofmannsthal invited a meditative response from audiences with a group of short, poetic plays in the 1890s, including *Death and the Fool* (1893) in which allegorical characters speak a highly imagistic language. Oscar Wilde (1856–1900) in England is best known for his social comedies, but his "Aesthetic Movement" had much in common with the aims of the symbolists and his one symbolist drama, *Salomé* (1893), was eagerly produced by the Théâtre de l'Oeuvre. As a young man, the Irish poet William Butler Yeats (1865–1939) saw several productions at the Théâtre de l'Oeuvre and returned to Dublin to help start the Abbey Theatre in 1904, where he hoped that his own symbolist plays would awaken the Irish public to the grandeur of their past. Yeats despised realism and wrote several poetic dramas based on Celtic myths in the first decade of the century, then turned to the noh drama of Japan after 1917 as a partial model for his plays. In their symbolist work, these playwrights called for simple, evocative sets and relied primarily on the sounds and meanings of their poetic language to involve and inspire the audience.

Two other centers of symbolist production emerged before 1914, Moscow and St. Petersburg. In Moscow, Valery Briusov (1873–1924) initiated the turn to symbolism in Russia in the 1890s and later argued that the naive lyricism of Russian folk drama was superior to naturalist dialog for the symbolist stage. Vyacheslav Ivanov (1866–1949) led the St. Petersburg symbolists with manifestos calling for a theatre in which actor-priests would facilitate the creation of mythic dramas with audience-congregants, primarily through the chanting of archaic language. Stanislavsky produced several symbolist pieces at the Moscow Art Theatre, but Vsevolod Meyerhold (1874–1940) had more success with symbolism at Vera Kommissarzhevskaya's (1864–1910) theatre in St. Petersburg. Meyerhold's production of *Hedda Gabler*, for example, ignored Ibsen's realist stage directions and deployed bold colors and sculpted, repetitive movements to evoke the claustrophobia of Hedda's world.

Symbolism flourished in cabarets as well as regular theatres. Avant-garde artists and "bohemians," university-educated members of an urban youth culture of the bourgeoisie, constituted the primary participants and spectators for cabaret entertainment, which emerged in Paris in the 1880s. After 1900, cabarets in several of the major cities of the continent – in Le Mirliton in Paris, Motley Stage in Berlin, the Kathi Kobus in Munich, The Green Balloon in Krakow, The Stray Dog in St. Petersburg, and the Cabaret Voltaire in Zurich – hosted many of the avant-garde movements of the twentieth century. Performances at these cabaret venues might include puppet dramas, poetry readings, ballads and art songs, monodramas, satirical and literary tableaux, and occasionally even the staging of one-act plays. With the level of talent ranging from amateurish to outstanding, the cabarets provided a hot-house environment for many who would later become major innovators in the theatre, including Max Reinhardt and Frank Wedekind in Germany and Nikolai Evreinov and Meyerhold in Russia. In some respects, the evocation of spiritual realities central to symbolist ideology flourished more imaginatively in the performance art of the cabarets than in the fully-mounted productions of symbolist theatre.

Strindberg and the expressionists

By the 1890s, August Strindberg had achieved an international reputation as a writer of historical epics and naturalist plays. After 1898 (and a difficult period of mental instability the dramatist called his "Inferno"). Strindberg strove for a theatre that he hoped might synthesize the materialism of naturalism with the spirituality of the symbolists. His post-Inferno plays, notably *To Damascus* (a trilogy, 1898–1901), *A Dream Play* (1902), and *The Ghost Sonata* (1907), attempted to embody the experience of mythical journeys and spiritual dreams. Not surprisingly, theatre artists before 1914 had difficulty realizing Strindberg's quest to merge external details and internal realities in theatrical images and sounds that would lead spectators toward both material and spiritual truths. Later productions of Strindberg's post-1900 plays were more successful, and the plays were widely read, exerting a significant influence on the European avant-garde, especially on a movement later termed German expressionism.

While writing his naturalist plays Strindberg had experimented with photography, and similar experiments preceded and informed his post-Inferno dramas. Strindberg's belief in the materiality of spiritual presence in the universe led him to attempt "spirit photography," which involved leaving a photographic plate exposed to the elements and then developing it to reveal (ostensible) traces of this "spirit." Like many others in his time, Strindberg believed that human vision was limited and imperfect; he hoped that photography might reveal spiritual realities undetected by the eye. This belief underlies *A Dream Play*, for example, which posits a disjuncture between an eternal world of abstract justice and the subjective, human world of pain and struggle, where eternity is a shadowy dream. The protagonist, Indra's Daughter, journeys from the eternal world into the subjective realm and gradually loses her identity as the illusions of humanity draw her into the mire of human visuality. To establish his dream world on the stage, Strindberg suggested the use of light, projections, and screens, techniques that derived from photography.

He was more successful in finding visual metaphors for his synthesis of materialism and spirituality in *The Ghost Sonata* (1907), written to be produced at the Intimate Theater in Stockholm. There, Strindberg, like Copeau at the Vieux Colombier, hoped that the combination of few spectators and simple staging would produce a theatre of spiritual and material insight. In *The Ghost Sonata*, which makes vision a central motif of the action, scenic surfaces are pierced, removed, and turned around to reveal the psychological tricks and inevitable shortcomings of human perception. As in many symbolist dramas, *Dream Play* and *Ghost Sonata* also make significant use of sound to suggest spiritual presences. The former involves several passages of ethereal music and invites singing, chanting, and reciting poetry from its actors, while the latter features a singing milkmaid and a transformed figure in a closet who squawks like a parrot. Unlike most

symbolists, Strindberg never posited the superior reality of Platonic abstraction or spiritual transcendence over the concreteness of the material world. Instead, like the expressionists whom he influenced, Strindberg sought the realm of the spiritual in the material.

Expressionism emerged as an avant-garde movement in the German theatre around 1910. Art critics had been using the term since the turn of the century to denote a non-realist painting suffused with the subjective emotions of the artist, and this general connotation was conferred on the new theatrical movement. Indeed, early German expressionist plays called for such anti-realist techniques as grotesquely-painted scenery, exaggerated acting and movement, and "telegraphic" dialog, so named because it copied the abbreviated, mechanistic quality of a telegraph message (Figure 8.1). These features were evident in several early expressionist

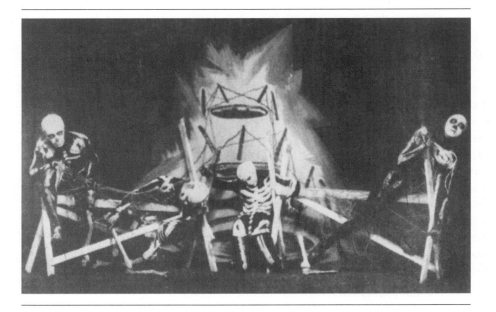

Figure 8.1 Contemporary print of a scene from the 1919 expressionist production of *Transfiguration* (*Die Wandlung*), by Ernst Toller (1918). © Oskar Fischel, *Bildernerische der Scene* (1931), Abb. 125. Photo courtesy Deutsches Theatermuseum München.

plays, including Walter Hasenclever's (1890–1940) *The Son* (1914) and *From Morn to Midnight* (1916), by Georg Kaiser (1878–1945).

While both plays invite spectators to view the distorted dramatic action through the fevered eyes of the protagonist (who also represents much of the author's point of view), neither play ignores the very real material factors of the external world that constrain the protagonist's spiritual longings. The younger generation's revolt against the restraints of bourgeois society in *The Son*, in fact, acknowledges that the title character cannot realize his subjective world of utopian hope without killing his father and all he represents. Like Strindberg, the early expressionists explored the tensions between spiritual desires and material constraints. Although censorship before and during the Great War prevented most expressionist plays from reaching the stage, expressionism flourished in Germany immediately after the war. This development will be explored in the next chapter.

Retrospectivists and futurists

The response of the Russian avant-garde to the standoff between naturalism and symbolism took a different turn than that of Strindberg and the expressionists, mostly for political reasons. In 1905, radicals led a revolution to overthrow Russian autocracy. Although the revolution was suppressed, subsequent reforms led to a loosening of Tzarist restrictions on the arts and spurred new avant-garde movements more interested than before in radical reform. The cabaret culture of St. Petersburg and Moscow that had nurtured symbolism in the 1890s turned toward a movement known by several names but generally understood as cultural retrospectivism. Aleksandr Blok (1880–1921), earlier hailed as a major symbolist poet and dramatist, now rejected symbolism for what he believed was its empty mysticism and decadence. Meyerhold, too, moved beyond symbolism after 1905. His 1906 production of Blok's tragifarce, *The Puppet Show*, combined *commedia*

dell'arte comic techniques with grotesque effects to underline Blok's absurdist vision. In addition to its satirical intent, the aim of this production, and of cultural retrospectivism in general, was to recover older forms of theatre as a means of injecting their playful energy into contemporary life. Life ought to be as inventive and spontaneous as a puppet show, the retrospectivists believed.

Nikolai Evreinov (1879–1953) was the major proponent of retrospectivism. He drew on Nietzsche's image of the superman and Henri Bergson's vitalism (a spiritualized notion of evolution that avoids Darwinian determinism and materialism to allow for self-perfection) to propose that the artist-hero transform his own life. In a series of manifestos, essays, and plays, Evreinov urged the production of monodramas that would externalize the consciousness of the protagonist. He co-founded a theatre in St. Petersburg to explore his ideas and later served as artistic director at the Maly Theatre in Moscow where he directed harlequinades, pantomimes, and satirical monodramas. After the Bolsheviks took power in the 1917 Revolution, Evreinov merged his retrospectivism with Communism, and in 1920, he wrote and directed the Soviet mass spectacle *The Storming of the Winter Palace* with a cast of 10,000. Retrospectivism, begun as an avant-garde movement, moved into the mainstream after the Revolution.

The 1917 Revolution also advanced the agenda of the Russian futurists. Futurism had begun in Italy with the publication of "The Founding and Manifesto of Futurism" by F.T. Marinetti (1876–1944) in 1909. It damned the art of the past, including museums, concert halls, and conventional theatre, and, contrary to symbolism, called for artistic forms that would exalt the speed and dynamism of the machine age. Earlier than most avant-garde artists, Marinetti embraced the revolutionary potential of film to transform the theatre. More manifestos followed, and soon Marinetti was producing "Futurist evenings" that included poetry readings, art displays, and theatrical skits. Some skits were little more than conventional cabaret sketches, but others explored themes and conflicts that were anti-realist, alogical, and abstract. Marinetti also experimented with performer-spectator dynamics, usually in an attempt to outrage bourgeois audiences. Because Marinetti glorified war as a necessary source of modern energy, interest in futurism declined in Italy with the mounting devastations of the Great War.

The Russian Revolution, however, energized the futurists of the new Soviet Union. Like its Italian counterpart, Russian futurism scoffed at the idealizing mysticism of the symbolists and looked to the machine and to film as a metaphor for the transformation of mankind. Soon after the Revolution, Vladimir Mayakovsky (1893–1930), leader of futurism in Russia, aligned the movement with Bolshevism and went to work to create effective propaganda for the struggling regime. With Meyerhold, Mayakovsky co-directed his play *Mystery-Bouffe* (1918), which depicts the establishment of a paradise on earth. His later plays, *The Bedbug* (1929) and *The Bathhouse* (1930), on the other hand, are sharply critical of the utopian dreams of communism, a position that probably contributed to Mayakovsky's suicide in 1930. Other futurists flourished briefly in Leningrad (the former St. Petersburg), where Daniil Kharms (1905–1942) used moving scenery to disrupt conventional dramatic plotting and regulate the rhythms of his actors. Although Stalinist persecution decimated the Russian futurists after 1930, their desire to merge man and the machine had already shaped many productions in the early Soviet Union. Futurism would continue to play a significant role in Eastern European theatre for much of the rest of the twentieth century.

Meyerhold and constructivism

Like many in his generation of theatrical artists, Vsevolod Meyerhold had journeyed from naturalism, to symbolism, and into retrospectivism and

futurism in the years before 1917. Meyerhold welcomed the Revolution and led members from most factions of the avant-garde into active collaboration with the Bolsheviks. While holding several leadership positions in the new government, Meyerhold also continued his theatrical experiments, which included a system of actor training known as biomechanics. In the first case study of this chapter, Meyerhold's biomechanics is contrasted with Stanislavsky's program of actor training. Biomechanics became the basis for Meyerhold's constructivism, the final avant-garde movement of his career. Constructivism would also end the phenomenal success of the Russian avant-garde in the 1905–1930 era.

Partly a synthesis of retrospectivism and futurism, constructivism sought to energize audiences with actors and designs that demonstrated how human beings could use their emotions and machines to produce engaging art and a more productive life. Meyerhold collaborated with Lyubov Popova (1889–1924) on a constructivist set for *The Magnanimous Cuckold* (1922), for instance, that used platforms, ramps, slides, ladders, and three moving wheels to suggest a mill that had been transformed into a huge mechanical toy (Figure 8.2). As the actors performed in biomechanical rhythms, the wheels of the mill turned to complement their timing. The production fused the clowning of retrospectivism with the mechanical rhythms of futurism. During the 1920s, Meyerhold applied his constructivist style to several plays that pushed communist propaganda, to Mayakovsky's grotesque futurist dramas, and to a range of Russian classics. In one scene of his constructivist production of Gogol's *The Inspector General* in 1926, fifteen officials popped out of fifteen doors around the stage to offer a bribe to the man they took for an inspector. As these examples suggest, Meyerhold drew inspiration from filmic techniques. "Let us carry through the 'cinefication' of the theatre, let us equip the theatre with all the technical refinements of the cinema," he wrote in 1930 (Meyerhold 1969: 254).

Figure 8.2 Lyubov Popova's constructivist set for Vsevolod Meyerhold's production of *The Magnanimous Cuckold*, 1922, by Fernand Crommelynck. The ramps and machinery provided a practical playground for biomechanical acting. © Society for Cooperation in Russian and Soviet Studies, London.

Increasingly out of favor with Stalin and tethered by the dictates of socialist realism, an official policy that required artists to celebrate the victories of the communist state in a mode of heroic realism, Meyerhold lost his theatre in 1938. In 1939, he was arrested and by the end of 1940 he was probably dead. With him died the last hope of the Russian avant-garde during the Stalinist era. After Stalin's death in 1953 and the 1956 "thaw" in the cold war, however, the ideas and images of Meyerhold's constructivism began to emerge. They influenced theatrical practice throughout the world, especially in England, Germany, and Eastern Europe.

Dadaists and surrealists

Artist-refugees, most of them French, initiated dada in a cabaret in neutral Zurich in Switzerland during the Great War. The dadaists (who apparently chose their name randomly by opening a dictionary) rejected the rationality that they believed had led to war. They were partly inspired by Alfred Jarry's (1873–1907) *Ubu Roi*, a scandalous success in 1896 at the Théâtre de l'Oeuvre, which depicted a decadent, war-mongering bourgeois anti-hero. In cabaret sketches that experimented with chance orderings of sounds, simultaneous poetry, and movement pieces, the dadaists mocked the absurdity of western notions of logic and harmony. Tristan Tzara (1896–1963), their principal spokesman, wrote several manifestos to provide some ideological unity for their anarchistic goals.

After the war, some of the dadaists moved to Berlin while Tzara and others went to Paris where they met André Breton (1896–1966) and his circle, who were experimenting with "automatic writing." Breton believed that chance, spontaneity, and the unconscious might lead a writer into a dreamlike state in which he or she could discover the source of aesthetic truth. For a short time, Breton's group joined with the dada artists, but in 1924 Breton issued a manifesto proclaiming his allegiance to "Surrealism," which separated dada from the psychoanalytic aims of his own group. Breton took the new name from Guillaume Apollinaire (1880–1918), whose 1903 play *The Breasts of Tiresias* had been subtitled a "*drame surrealiste*." Although the 1924 manifesto was heavily indebted to Freud and mostly apolitical, Breton's next manifesto in 1929 embraced communism. Suspicious of theatre and eager to make surrealism more militant, Breton denounced many former colleagues after this manifesto, including all of those who wished to use Surrealism on stage.

Before Breton's rejection of the theatre, however, other influences had helped to shape theatrical surrealism. Chief among them was the work of Luigi Pirandello (1867–1936), a controversial Italian dramatist whose philosophical plays validated artistic vision over the illusory qualities of everyday life. *Six Characters in Search of An Author* (1921), for example, uses the convention of a play-within-a-play to explore the differences between the flow of real life and the idealized stability of artistic creation. In *Henry IV* (1922), Pirandello focused on the impossibility of distinguishing reality from illusion and the effect of time on human perception. Although his melodramatic plays have little in common formally with most of the works of the surrealists, Pirandello provided some philosophical justification for the subjective visions of the surrealists.

The theatrical surrealists had mounted only a dozen performances by 1929, but their emphasis on spontaneity, shocking effects, and psychological imagery affected the experiments of many artists. French playwright Jean Cocteau (1892–1963) and Spanish dramatist Federico Garcia Lorca (1898–1936)

were the most significant inheritors of surrealism in the theatre before World War II. Several of Cocteau's plays inject surrealistic images and associations into plots based on ancient Greek myths. In *Orpheus* (1926), for example, a horse talks "horse sense" and a glazier, because he works with windows and mirrors, becomes a kind of psychoanalyst whose insights allow him to float in the air. Garcia Lorca's surrealistic vision was generally darker than Cocteau's. In *Blood Wedding* (1933) and other plays, Lorca deploys surrealistic images in language, design, and action to depict a tragic conflict between passion and death. dada and surrealism had a direct influence on cabaret entertainments in Paris, Prague, Krakow, and Budapest between the wars and inspired some of the writers who later became identified with the "theatre of the absurd" after World War II. The indirect influence of surrealism can be seen in the work of many theatre artists after 1935, including Jean Giraudoux in France, Emilio Carballido in Mexico, Tennessee Williams in the U.S., and Terayama Shûji in Japan.

Breton had appointed Antonin Artaud (1896–1949) his first director of research for surrealism in 1924, but then kicked him out of his coterie two years later. In response, Artaud, together with playwright Roger Vitrac and Robert Aron, founded the Théâtre Alfred Jarry, which staged surrealistic productions for two seasons. Artaud struggled to start other theatres and wrote manifestos for most of the 1930s. Psychiatrists declared him insane in 1937, and Artaud spent much of the rest of his life in mental hospitals until his death in 1949.

Artaud's substantial reputation and influence on world theatre rest not on his few productions or psychological difficulties, however, but on his manifestos, published in 1938 under the title *The Theatre and Its Double*. Writing in the tradition of Rousseau, who believed that civilization had corrupted mankind, Artaud argued for a theatre that would return modern humans to primitive mysteries through their bodies. Artaud urged theatre artists to reject the dramatic masterpieces of the western tradition – in fact, to throw out all text-based theatre – and embrace instead performance involving music, dance, and spectacle. He had witnessed a Balinese dance troupe performing in Paris in 1931 and believed that their "primitive" rhythms and chants held the key to transformative theatre. In the mystical and impassioned essays of *The Theatre and Its Double*, Artaud conjured a kind of theatre that could unite an entire audience and purge them of their rational restraints and individual freedoms. He proposed what he called a "theatre of cruelty," an emotionally-extreme experience, which would work through the bodies of its spectators to purify them of their civilized repressions. Although Artaud expected that such an experience would free its participants from violence, conformity, and anxiety, critics have noted similarities between his invocation of a "Theatre of Cruelty" and the fascist rallies that were occurring in Europe at the same time. *The Theatre and Its Double* had little influence on theatrical practice during Artaud's life. In the English, American, and Japanese theatre of the 1960s and 1970s, however, Artaud's visions inspired a generation of artists. His theory and influence are discussed further in Part IV.

Institutionalizing the avant-garde

A few directors from avant-garde groups, such as Meyerhold and Artaud, worked in both avant-garde and mainstream theatres. Although most avant-garde directors rejected the institutionalization of their innovations, this did not stop other directors who were committed to bourgeois cultural institutions from borrowing extensively from the avant-garde to shape their own productions. These successful directors and their institutions helped to introduce modernism to many playgoers during the twentieth century. Modernism in the theatre may be generally defined as those modes of production and reception that rely on modern technologies to deal critically with the photographic and audiophonic reality effects of the early twentieth century. Modernists

often built upon the innovations of the avant-garde in their productions. Modernist theatre often involves such themes as the search for a modern self, the relation between humans and machines, and the ravages of economic change. By 1940, modernism had triumphed in the major theatres of the West and Japan. Some critics and historians believe that modernist concerns continue to dominate much of world theatre.

The group of mainstream directors who turned western theatre toward modernism before 1940 include several of those already discussed in the introduction to Part III, such as Barker and Guthrie in England and the disciples of Copeau in France. Perhaps the most important popularizer of the avant-garde in the early twentieth century was Max Reinhardt (1873–1943), whose work set an important precedent for other commercial directors. Believing that no single style suited all plays and theatrical occasions, Reinhardt directed naturalist, symbolist, and expressionist plays in Germany and Austria in a variety of spaces, often to wide public applause. He incorporated the innovations of Appia, Craig, and others in lighting and design and sought out new training techniques for his actors. Reinhardt was able to embrace such eclecticism because he worked closely with his collaborators while insisting on final artistic control and also maintained a significant degree of stage illusionism. That is, his actors generally used realist props and costumes and typically did not acknowledge the presence of the audience. His production of Wedekind's *Spring's Awakening* in 1906, for example, featured frilly transparent curtains (of the kind that proper bourgeoisie used to dress their windows) over much of the proscenium opening and created innovative lighting effects, but kept his actors behind the proscenium (Figure 8.3). After the Great War, Reinhardt staged many of his productions in churches and extra-theatrical settings, such as public squares. Reinhardt's success exerted an immense influence in German-speaking theatre between 1910 and 1925.

Figure 8.3 Karl Walser's rendering of his design for a scene from Reinhardt's production of Wedekind's *Spring's Awakening*, 1906. © Max Reinhardt Archive, State University of New York, Binghamton.

Several other pre-1940 directors followed Reinhardt's lead, adapting avant-garde techniques to mainstream productions. As Director of the Odéon, Firmin Gémier (1869–1933), an early proponent of bringing theatre to all of the French people through tent productions, produced and directed an eclectic mix of modernist styles in the 1920s. In Germany, Leopold Jessner (1878–1945), Director of the Berlin State Theatre from 1919 until 1933, incorporated new design principles into several of his productions. These often featured Appia-inspired flights of stairs, non-realist lighting, and symbolic costuming. In the U.S., the Theatre Guild brought European modernist theatre to audiences from 1919 into the 1930s, operating with a broad subscription base. Philip Moeller (1880–1958), who generally worked

in a style of modified realism, was the Guild's chief director. Several directors of international renown followed in the wake of Meyerhold's avant-garde experiments in the 1920s and early 1930s in Russia. After Nikolai Okhlopkov (1900–1966) was appointed Director of the Realistic Theatre in Moscow in 1932, he ignored the proscenium stage and began to mount scenes for his productions throughout the auditorium, in the aisles and on a raised bridge above the audience. Not surprisingly, the speed and realism of film influenced many of these directors. Okhlopkov, for instance, moved his productions around the auditorium to achieve filmic montage, and Moeller eventually left New York to work in Hollywood. Through the influence of these directors and their institutions and the adoption of similar innovative practices elsewhere, modernism gradually altered mainstream theatre throughout the West.

The end of the avant-garde

Surrealism was the last of the major international avant-garde movements. The political problems that fragmented theatrical modernism into a series of national theatre cultures after the Great War eventually killed the international thrust of the avant-garde as well. Before the war, the plays of Ibsen and Maeterlink and the ideas of Craig and Stanislavsky had traveled easily throughout the West; emerging theatre artists had often looked to international figures as their models. After the war and the 1917 revolution, the international utopian ambitions of Russian communism fueled the avant-garde movements within the Soviet Union in the 1920s and animated the French surrealists to link their Freudianism with communism. But the worldwide economic depression of the 1930s turned many citizens toward their own nations and away from the international scene. And Stalinism and fascism had already deadened most international utopian hopes in Europe by the outbreak of World War II in 1939. As we will see in the next chapter, utopian hopes revived in the 1960s, but the radical theatre artists of that era rarely shaped their disparate aesthetics into international movements. Many of these groups, in fact, disdained the kinds of discipline and leadership that had sustained such movements in the past. Further, the political realities of the cold war, both worldwide and within national cultures, undermined the international and utopian aspirations of innovative artists.

The avant-garde legacy in the United States

Although theatrical innovation flourished for much of the twentieth century in the U.S., no major avant-garde movements based on the European model emerged to challenge American bourgeois culture. (Some scholars suggest that the U.S. did have its own brand of avant-garde theatre, more popular and democratic than the European movements.) Nonetheless, European modernism had a formative influence on significant elements of American playwriting, directing, and design from the Great War through to 1970. As already noted in the Introduction to Part III, Stanislavsky's work influenced American acting and directing, and the artists of the New Stagecraft Movement borrowed liberally from Appia and Craig in the 1920s and 1930s. In addition, Freudian surrealism shaped the more grotesque plays of Tennessee Williams, and Arthur Miller used some of the techniques of German expressionism.

Actually, expressionism was a home-grown style (though not an avant-garde movement) in the U.S. before American artists and audiences had seen much of it from Germany. American expressionists Eugene O'Neill (1888–1953) and Elmer Rice (1892–1967) used the term "expressionism" to refer to the expressive culture movement, a broad-based program in the U.S. that sought to counter anxieties about new technologies by drawing on the performing arts. Rice's best-known play, *The Adding Machine* (1923), depicts the recycling of a mechanized and alienated bourgeois boob, Mr. Zero, who refuses possible freedom to float from a pointless office job adding up figures, through death, to eventual reincarnation as another cowardly office worker. Sophie Treadwell (1885–1970), another U.S. expressionist, demonstrates the need for a middle-class woman to rebel against her robotic life in *Machinal* (1928). Treadwell's protagonist murders her husband, an act which eventually sends her to the electric chair. O'Neill wrote two major "expressionist" plays, *The Emperor Jones* (1920) and *The Hairy Ape* (1921), the first a peeling-away of the layers of civilization in the mind of a black man and the second about a working-class loner struggling to find a group where he feels he "belongs."

Although O'Neill knew little about expressionism in Europe when he wrote *The Emperor Jones* in 1920, he, more than any other U.S. dramatist of the decade, had studied many of the works that shaped the European avant-garde movements, and he went on to experiment with their ideas in his plays. In addition to reading Ibsen and Strindberg, O'Neill had studied Nietzsche and knew the work of Freud. Many of his realist plays, preeminently *Long Day's Journey Into Night* (1939–1941), echo and extend the psychological penetration of Ibsen's masterpieces. Strindbergian views about the pitfalls of marriage recur in *Welded* (1922–1923) and *Desire Under the Elms* (1924). Nietzschean despair grounds the desperation of the drunks who inhabit Harry Hope's bar in *The Iceman Cometh* (1946). In *The Great God Brown* (1926), O'Neill borrowed from Freud to put his actors' faces behind masks in order to depict the social masks that hide the "true" psychological self. The second case study in this chapter examines O'Neill's *Desire Under the Elms* (1924) as a part of the discourse of popular psychology during the 1920s.

The avant-garde legacy in France, 1945–1970

Although the avant-garde had fragmented before World War II, this did not stop theatre critics and the public from identifying innovative dramatists and other theatre artists as members of new avant-garde movements after 1945. When critic Martin Esslin published *The Theatre of the Absurd* in 1961, which focused chiefly on a group of Parisian dramatists who shared a general sense of the metaphysical absurdity of the human condition, the designation of this "movement" stuck. Many journalists and others were soon referring to Samuel Beckett (1906–1989), Eugene Ionesco (1912–1994), Jean Genet (1910–1986), Arthur Adamov (1908–1971), and others as "absurdists" and treating their work as part of an avant-garde movement. In truth, many of these artists did not know each other, professed no utopian or international aspirations for their art, published no manifestos together, and agreed on no common principles.

While the early plays of Ionesco and Adamov share some common ground, the dramas of Genet and Beckett were strikingly unique. Like dada skits, the farces and tragicomedies of Ionesco and Adamov typically feature cartoon-like, bourgeois figures in inane situations who mouth platitudes and nonsense. While Ionesco's early one-act plays attack language and logic, his later ones, such as *Rhinoceros* (1960) and *Exit the King* (1962), mourn social conformity and the despair that comes with a knowledge of death. Adamov's *The Invasion* (1950), *Parody* (1952), and *All Against All* (1953) show the influence of Strindberg and surrealism on his work. Persecuted, morally bankrupt characters are driven to destructiveness in these seriocomic plays. In 1955, with *Ping-Pong*, however, Adamov abandoned this mode of absurdism for a form of playwriting that advocated Marxism as the antidote to an irrational world. Most of Genet's plays, including *The Balcony* (1956), *The Blacks* (1959), and *The Screens* (1961), explore the link between theatricality and power and the impossibility of moving beyond social roles to effect radical change. Genet's interest in ritual, sexuality, role-playing, and excess locate his plays in the tradition of Pirandello and Artaud, even though their performances did not lead to the kind of cathartic release that Artaud had envisioned.

Perhaps the most famous of the Parisian "absurdists" was Samuel Beckett, an Irish playwright living in France who wrote in both English and French. Heidegger and James Joyce were major influences on his work. Our final case study in this chapter centers on Beckett's theatrical minimalism.

Theatrical innovation in Latin America, 1930–1970

Traditional European forms of drama dominated professional theatrical life in the countries of Latin America from colonial times until the 1930s. During the same period, native peoples continued to perform some of their ritual dramas, even though the Catholic Church succeeded in suppressing most of them. Latin American creoles and criollos (people of European descent acculturated in the Americas), however, generally looked to Spain or Portugal, the ruling colonial powers of most of the region until the early nineteenth century, for models of professional theatre. By 1900, they were importing plays, actors, and traveling companies from the Iberian Peninsula for a range of entertainments, from opera to vaudeville. Argentine playwright Florencio Sanchez (1875–1910) was the first to popularize a form of drama that was distinctly Latin American. His domestic comedies, called *costumbristas*, poked fun at the foibles of the rising bourgeoisie and dealt specifically with Argentine culture. Sanchez was also the first significant Latin American playwright to embrace naturalism.

The European avant-garde began to have a major impact on Latin American theatre after 1930, especially in Argentina and Mexico. The People's Theatre in Buenos Aires produced the expressionist plays of Roberto Arlt (1900–1942), whose dramas were also influenced by Pirandello's interest in illusion, dreams, and the grotesque. A few independent theatres flourished in Buenos Aires in the 1930s, producing the work of Cocteau, Synge, O'Neill, and Pirandello, as well as several new national dramatists. In 1932 in Mexico City, Xavier Villaurrutia (1903–1950) co-founded the Teatro Orientación to produce modernist plays using the directorial ideas of Reinhardt, Stanislavsky, and others. Villaurrutia's own dramas, especially his five short *Profane Plays* (1933–1937), show the influence of Giraudoux.

Several theatres in many Latin American countries embraced modernism after Word War II. With the production of *The Bridal Gown*, by Nelson Rodrigues (1912–1981) in 1943, modern expressionist theatre emerged in Brazil. After the war, the Teatro Brasileiro de Comédia imported several Italian directors to direct modernist European plays and similar works by some Brazilian dramatists. New playwrights and directors in the Chilean theatre of the 1950s turned primarily toward realism and

theatre of the grotesque. *The Toothbrush* by Jorge Diaz (1930–), for example, is a Beckett-like, two-character play about miscommunication. Experimental groups drawing on the European avant-garde also flourished in Honduras and Guatemala. Several Mexican playwrights and theatres began incorporating indigenous and mestizo (mixed heritage) influences with modernist techniques. The magical realist plays of Emilio Carballido (1925–) in the 1950s and 1960s, for example, combined forms and ideas from the miracle plays of Catholic and mestizo tradition with the character complexities of psychological realism. In *I Too Speak of the Rose* (1965), Carballido used a metaphorical rose to explore the process of human creativity. His *The Golden Thread* (1955) probes existential questions in a dull provincial setting alive with elements of the fantastic. While modernist imports and experiments continued in Latin America through the 1960s, leftist political theatre predominated in many countries after 1955. These developments are discussed in the next chapter.

Theatrical innovation in Eastern Europe, 1955–1970

Following the death of Stalin in 1953 and the "thaw" in the cold war in 1956 when Soviet Premier Khrushchev denounced Stalinism, major theatrical artists emerged in Russia, Poland, and Czechoslovakia. Russian theatres remained under state control (the general pattern throughout continental Europe), but state censors exercised fewer restrictions; they allowed plays by Brecht, Miller, Ionesco and many non-communists to be performed and also encouraged new Soviet playwrights. As in the West, plays urging governmental reform and featuring generational conflict became popular. The Moscow Art Theatre (MAT), long the home of socialist realism, lost influence to new companies, such as the Theatre of Satire, which revived Meyerhold's constructivism in its production of Mayakovsky's *The Bedbug* in 1954. Director Nikolai Okhlopkov (1900–1967), who had experimented with placing spectators in the midst of playing areas for actors in the 1930s, renewed his work. At the Gorky Theatre in Leningrad, director Georgi Tovstogonov (1915–1989) staged new productions of Russian classics, using cinematic techniques to heighten their contemporary significance. Oleg Efremov (1927–), director of the youth-oriented Contemporary Theatre in Moscow, mounted realist plays with minimalist sets in productions that directly challenged the encrusted realism of the MAT.

Polish theatre underwent a similar transformation after the "thaw." Between the wars, formism, led by Stanislaw Witkiewicz (1885–1939), had been a major avant-garde theatrical movement in Krakow, seeking to introduce fantastic psychology and action. Tadeusz Kantor (1915–1990) continued the kinds of futurist experiments that the Formists had begun; in spectacles often inspired by the plays of Witkiewicz, he treated his actors as props in grotesque and disturbing tableaux. Jerzy Grotowski (1933–1999) worked toward an intimate theatre of psychological and spiritual transformation by creating arresting images that altered traditional actor–audience relationships. In several productions of *Akropolis* (1904), by symbolist playwright Stanislaw Wyspianski (1867–1907), Grotowski placed the play's mythical charcters in the gas chambers and body ovens of a German concentration camp (Grotowski's work is further discussed in Chapter 11). By the mid-1960s, Polish theatre was among the most innovative in Europe. In addition to Kantor and Grotowski, playwrights such as Slawomir Mrożek (1930–) were turning Ionesco-like absurdism toward political satire and directors like Josef Szajna (1922–) were discovering ironic and grotesque meanings in their imagistic stagings of Polish and European classics. International modernism, strongly inflected by specifically national styles and contents, had triumphed in Poland by 1970.

In Czechoslovakia (a single nation-state until 1992, when it divided into the Czech Republic and Slovakia), directors and designers after 1950 also drew on the legacy of futurism to shape disturbing productions that relied on technological innovations and vivid images. Prague director Otomar Krejca (1921–) collaborated with designer Josef Svoboda (1920–) on western classics in which the sets and the lighting became dynamic elements of their productions. Svoboda worked with another director, Alfred Radok (1914–1976), to fuse live acting and projected film in a theatre called Laterna Magika, which gained international applause in 1958 at the Brussels World's Fair. Svoboda developed other stage technologies and materials, including rapidly-moving platforms and new uses for plastics and mirrors. Among the many innovative playwrights in Czechoslovakia was Vaclav Havel (1936–), resident playwright during the 1960s at the Balustrade Theatre, which performed his ironic farces aimed at the bureaucratic and ideological double-think of communist Prague. After the Russians invaded the country in 1968, Havel was imprisoned and many directors and designers were forced to resign. The invasion was a setback for Czech artists eager to use their modernist innovations for nationalistic purposes.

Theatrical innovation in South and Southeast Asia, 1950–1970

Once India gained independence from British rule in 1947, the building of a modern, secular nation-state began in earnest under the leadership of Prime Minister Jawaharal Nehru, whose cultural policy of "unity within diversity" guided developments in theatre, drama, and dance. National and regional cultural policies followed two tracks in the 1950s – the promotion and appreciation of both the traditional Indian performing arts and modern forms of theatre and drama. As in much of the West, however, the immense success of cinema with the middle class cut into the potential audience for modern theatre in India. Further, the continuing popularity of mixed modes of theatrical communication – productions that relied on song, dance, and pantomime as well as spoken dialog to carry the story of the play – retarded the influence in India of the European avant-garde, which, for all of its diversity, was primarily based in dialogic communication. Not surprisingly, perhaps, several professional theatres in India after 1950 continued to produce Parsi melodramas, the popular, pre-realist-style plays that could accommodate the many modes of traditional Indian theatrical communication.

Nonetheless, European modernism shaped a part of postwar Indian theatre, especially among the many amateur troupes that flourished in all of the major cities. Some of these groups continued the social drama and anti-colonial drama movements begun before Indian independence (see Chapter 9) while others focused their energies on producing the plays of the European avant-garde and their postwar legacy. In addition to adapting some of the modern classics by Pirandello, Brecht, and Beckett to Indian life, they produced Indian playwrights who wrote in a modern mode. These included Mohan Rakesh (1929–1972), whose work in radio and film laid the groundwork for the economical realism of many of his plays, and Vijay Tendulkar (1928–), whose realist plays attacked the hypocrisies of middle-class Indian life. When he became the Director of the National School of Drama in 1962, Ebrahim Alkazi (1925–) began a three-year training program in the fields of modern acting, directing, and stagecraft. International modernism flourished at the National School during the 1960s and culminated in the formation of a professional repertory theatre in New Delhi in 1968. Alkazi's strict professionalism raised the standards of many of the amateur theatres.

Other South Asian countries with strong indigenous traditions of theatre also selectively adapted modern western practices. The imperialism of France brought modern theatre to Vietnam, and it began to flourish among Vietnamese playwrights, directors, and audiences after the end of French colonialism in 1954. In the Philippines, modernism was evident in the repertories of a few companies in the 1950s and in such play titles as *Portrait of the Artist as a Filipino* (1952), by Nick Joaquin (1917–). Modernism also shaped several theatres in Jakarta, Indonesia that played to predominately wealthy audiences in the 1950s. W.S. Renda (1935–) studied abroad and returned to Indonesia to direct a few plays by Ionesco before drawing on the politically-radical theatre of the West to found the *Bengkel* (Workshop) Theatre in 1967. Renda's workshop trained a generation of Indonesian directors and playwrights to confront the policies of Suharto's dictatorial government. Among them was playwright Arifin Noer (1941–1996), whose dramas used poetry, metaphysics, and psychology to challenge Indonesian society in the 1960s and 1970s.

The avant-garde and political theatre

Much of the political theatre of the West in the 1960s had strong roots in avant-garde traditions. In fact, beginning with naturalism, many avant-garde movements expressed socialist views, although a few, such as the Italian futurists, embraced fascism. The anti-bourgeois stance of modernist theatre continued to turn many innovative artists toward radical politics after 1935, when the international avant-garde fragmented. The next chapter discusses these developments, plus the intersection of politics with more conventional means of making theatre in the 1880–1970 period.

BMc

Key references

For further references for this chapter, see the Key references at the end of the Introduction to Part III.

Esslin, M. (1969) *The Theatre of the Absurd*, rev. edn, New York: Anchor Books.

Meyerhold, V. (1969) *Meyerhold on Theatre*, trans. and ed. E. Braun, New York: Hill and Wang.

Sontag, S. (1977) *On Photography*, New York: Delta Books.

CASE STUDY: Selves, roles, and actors: Actor training in the West

Stanislavsky and Meyerhold

Two primary modes of training actors, the psychological and the sociological, dominated in the West between 1920 and 1970. The psychological mode, which emphasized the actor's immersion in a stage character, began in the Moscow Art Theatre (MAT) under Konstantin Stanislavsky, and later flourished in the U.S. (Figure 8.4). Deriving primarily from Stanislavsky's interest in naturalism, the psychological approach to actor training continues to inform most training methods for film and television acting in Hollywood. Vsevolod Meyerhold initiated a modern version of the sociological mode, which involves the actor demonstrating the character to the audience. The sociological mode underlay Meyerhold's constructivist experiments with actors, and it later provided the basis for Brechtian performance. Both approaches have deep roots in western culture but also similarities to many non-western modes.

Stanislavsky began experimenting with the possibilities of a systematic approach to actor training in 1906 when he experienced difficulties with his own acting work at the MAT. In 1912, he set up the First Studio at the MAT to test his ideas and gradually convinced his reluctant acting company to try them. Stanislavsky continued to modify and improve his "system," as he called it, until his death

Figure 8.4 The Moscow Art Theatre production of Maxim Gorky's *The Lower Depths*, 1902, with Stanislavsky as Satin (center). © Society for Cooperation in Russian and Soviet Studies, London.

in 1938. This "system," however, varied widely over his professional life and was not systematized at his death. By 1938, Stanislavsky had approved the final drafts for only two of the books that would bear his authorship, *My Life in Art* and *An Actor's Work on Himself*. The translation of the latter book into English as *An Actor Prepares* omitted and misrepresented many of Stanislavsky's precepts, leading later practitioners of the American "Method" to misunderstand some of Stanislavsky's ideas. Despite these difficulties, the Stanislavsky "system" and its U.S. spin-off as "the Method" became the dominant model for the psychological mode of actor training.

Meyerhold joined the MAT as a young actor, but left in 1906 to explore movement-oriented methods for staging symbolist dramas. Before the Revolution, Meyerhold worked in several theatres and in cabaret in St. Petersburg, exploring and developing his ideas for the actor-puppet, a performer who could combine the arts of characterization, singing, dancing, and acrobatics with precise physical and vocal expression. In 1921, he named these concepts and practices "biomechanics" to denote their fusion of biology and machinery and began teaching them systematically to his students in a new Soviet school for actors. Like Stanislavsky, Meyerhold extended and perfected his approach to acting through practice and writing; by 1930 his ideas and exercises were virtually complete. The Russian Blue Blouse troupes first demonstrated simplified versions of some of Meyerhold's performance ideas to other theatre artists in the West. Gradually, as directors from Germany, France, and the United States made their way to Moscow to witness Meyerhold's bold productions in the 1920s and early 1930s, his ideas for actor training began to attain an international following. His sociological mode of actor training had a major impact on Brechtian aesthetics.

Comparing actor training programs

Comparing different modes of actor training is not an easy task. Because most training programs teach actors how to work on themselves and how to engage with a stage role, a description of the exercises for both kinds of preparation, noting similarities and differences, might appear to be a straightforward means of comparison. But assumptions about the self and about the process of characterization may be unstated or elusive. After all, ideas of the self vary, even within the same culture, and actors' notions of what constitutes a stage role have shifted from one historical period to another. Finally, acting programs always assume that actors have certain responsibilities to the audience. These assumptions, too, are culturally and historically situated. For these reasons, it is helpful to adopt a scholarly language that approaches neutrality when comparing two training programs and then use this relatively neutral terminology to pose the same questions of both practices.

One scholarly approach distinct from any of the conventional orientations to actor training is cognitive psychology. A cognitive psychological approach can help theatre scholars answer the following questions:

1 What notion of the actor's self is embedded in a particular program of training? What are the distinctive aspects of this self for the actor and what kinds of exercises help the actor to prepare her/himself to perform on stage?

2 What is the definition of character in this program of training? How is the self of the actor to become the character on stage? Which exercises prepare the actor for this transformation?

3 How does a particular training program understand the actor–audience relationship? What should actors attempt to do to and for their spectators?

INTERPRETIVE APPROACH: Cognitive psychology

Cognitive psychology is a part of the larger field of cognitive studies, which has already provided us with two interpretive approaches – to classical Greek theatre and the *Playboy* riots.

In *Philosophy in the Flesh* (1999), George Lakoff and Mark Johnson devote a chapter to the several ways humans experience themselves. Drawing on cross-cultural psychological and linguistic experiments, they point out that there is no single version of the self in any world culture; evolution and social interaction have equipped humans with several Selves. All cultures, however, recognize a distinction between what Lakoff and Johnson call the "Subject" and the "Self": "The Subject is the locus of consciousness, subjective experience, reason, will, and our 'essence,' everything that makes us uniquely who we are . . . . The Selves consist of everything else about us – our bodies, our social roles, our histories, and so on" (Lakoff and Johnson 1999:268). Conditioned by culture and history, Subjects can operate a variety of metaphorical Selves. One is the "physical-object self" (ibid.:270–274). When people say, "I've got to get myself moving," or think that they have "lost control" of themselves, they are treating the Self as a physical object. Another is the "locational self" (ibid.:274–277), as in "I was beside myself," which understands the Self as a place one can be in or out of. "She's a Kentuckian," "He's down to earth," and "I'm all over the place today" are other examples of the locational Self. One significant variation on the locational Self is the contained self (ibid.:282–284); people who speak of a "true Self" within the shell of an "outer Self," for example, locate the Self as a container with an inside and outside. In "the social Self" (ibid.:277–280), the Subject treats the Self as another person; "she takes care of herself" and "I disappointed myself" are examples. In all of these cases, the Subject conceives of the Self as a metaphor for a person's inner life.

The "multiple Selves metaphor" (ibid.:280–281), which extends the social Self metaphor to other people, is especially relevant to acting. By projecting themselves imaginatively onto others, people may come to identify their values and feelings with those of others. Lakoff and Johnson recognize that this commonly occurs in two ways, advisory and empathetic projection: "In one, what we call Advisory Projection, I am projecting my values onto you so that I experience your life with my values. In the other type, Empathetic Projection, I am experiencing your life, but with your values projected onto my subjective experience" (ibid.:281). When a person says, "If I were you, I'd punch him on the nose," Advisory Projection is operating. "I feel your pain," on the other hand, is an example of Empathetic Projection. The difference is a matter of the direction of projected values and feelings – Self onto other (Advisory) or other onto Self (Empathetic).

Cognitive psychology and actor training

Lakoff and Johnson's conclusions about the Subject's notions of various Selves are especially useful for understanding the processes of acting. Their conclusions can help us answer the questions posed above about Stanislavsky's and Meyerhold's training programs for actors. Before moving into this analysis, however, it is important to underline one general conclusion about all acting, regardless of the mode of training, implicit in Lakoff and Johnson's cognitive point of view. For any acting to occur, all actor-Subjects working up a characterization must rely on their "social Selves," described above. This is because the actor rehearsing a play in order to embody a role must transfer what is on the page of the script into the Self; s/he must create another Self, the Self of the role, that exists apart from the everyday Self of the performer. In the cognitive understanding of the social Self, there are potentially many Selves that all people, including actors, can perform. Every actor, whether trained in Stanislavskian, Meyerholdian, or any other mode, draws on this potential to create many roles. How actors do this – and the relationship they craft between the actor-Subject and the created role-Self – varies widely, however.

A cognitive analysis of the "system"

Reading Stanislavsky's "system" through the lens of Lakoff and Johnson's cognitive psychology will give us a basis for comparing it to Meyerhold's "biomechanics." A review of Stanislavsky's language in his exercises for the actor's development of his/her concentration, imagination, and communication reveals that his "system" primarily depends on a locational conception of the Self. From a cognitive point of view, the actor-Subject works on a Stanislavskian notion of the Self that is a container. Simply put, the role-Self contains the intentions of the character, plus specific physical, emotional, and interpersonal attributes. Actors playing characters attempt to fulfill their roles' intentions and overcome their obstacles within the "given circumstances," as Stanislavsky termed them, of their characters' situation. Actors must learn through analysis, concentration, and imagination how to contain the world of their characters within themselves. Metaphors of containment are also apparent in Stanislavsky's "rays of energy" and "circles of attention" exercises. Influenced by yoga, which he practiced most of his adult life, Stanislavsky believed that people communicate both verbally and non-verbally through rays of energy that can be controlled by the Self. In one exercise, he urged actors to absorb energy from their surroundings and send it out again, through the fingers of their extended hands, to others in the room. According to Stanislavsky, actors in performance can sharpen their concentration by imaginatively dividing the stage and the auditorium into concentric circles of increasingly larger circumference that ripple out from the Self. Inside the first circle may be some furniture and other characters of great significance to the actor's role. The next circle might include the rest of the setting and the others on stage. The largest circle takes in the audience and the entire auditorium. Stanislavsky taught that actors must restrict themselves to the smallest possible circles necessary for the moment-to-moment performance of their roles in order to retain a sense of themselves as private people, despite their public exposure on the stage. In both of these acting exercises, Stanislavsky placed the Self of the actor at the center of rays of energy and concentric circles. As in the actor's Self, each of the circles is a container with an inside, an outside, and a boundary between them.

In terms of the actor's work on the character, Stanislavsky recommended that the actor-Subject primarily engage with the created role-Self through empathetic projection. That is, the actor must understand the feelings and values of the character and empathize with this created Self to such an extent that the actor sees the circumstances and actions of the character through that character's eyes and reacts accordingly. For example, in an exercise Stanislavsky termed "affective cognition," he recommended that actors visualize distinct moments in the lives of their characters so that these images would trigger affective, empathetic responses to the characters they were playing. In general, Stanislavsky's understanding of characterization was similar to that of many nineteenth-century novelists; like them, he saw characters as complex human beings with many attributes, feelings, and unconscious desires with whom readers could be invited to empathize. Stanislavsky's famous "magic if" – which might be paraphrased as, "if I were this character in the midst of the circumstances of this scene, what would I do?" – depends on empathy. Once the actor had begun to understand her/his character from the character's point of view, Stanislavsky required actors to analyze the script for the character's intentions and physical actions and to "score" them as a composer might develop a melody. Rehearsing the intentions and actions of the character ensured that the actor in performance would not depart from his/her empathetic involvement with his role to play directly for applause or become distracted by off-stage circumstances.

As an artist of the theatre, Stanislavsky understood that spectators could engage with actors playing roles in a number of ways. In cognitive terms, spectators could distance themselves from actor-characters, objectify and laugh at them, or engage in advisory as well as empathetic projection with them. Several of Stanislavsky's best productions, however, established an empathetic bond between actors and spectators. For the 1909 MAT production of *A Month in the Country* by Ivan Turgenev (1818–1883), Stanislavsky was able to direct actors trained in the techniques of his First Studio to empathize with their characters through close attention to the conflicts between their inner lives and their social facades. In one scene in which a young mother is attracted to the tutor of her son, Stanislavsky directed the actor to heighten the contrast between her inner desires and her outward distraction. By playing the role-Self in this way, the actor pulled the audience into the problems of her contained character and induced them to empathize with her plight.

A cognitive approach to biomechanics

Meyerhold's understanding of acting and his program for actor training differed substantially from Stanislavsky's. Regarding his conception of the actor's Self, Meyerhold primarily held to a notion of the physical object Self, not the locational Self. Most of Meyerhold's biomechanical exercises to prepare the actor's sense of him/herself for the stage involved the actor-Subject consciously moving his/her own physical body. Meyerhold's syllabus for his new acting school in 1921, for example, required his students to learn gymnastics, fencing, juggling, a variety of dances, and several other physical skills, plus anatomy and physiology so that the students would understand the potential of their bodies. During the 1920s, Meyerhold frequently compared his biomechanics to the industrial time-and-motion studies of Frederick W. Taylor; both were designed to increase the physical efficiency of the actor or worker. Meyerhold also perfected more complex movement exercises that he called *études*. In his "Shooting from the Bow" *étude*, for example, the actor pantomimes a series of rhythmic movements that suggest running toward a quarry, shooting an imaginary arrow, and celebrating the kill. The exercise involves a thorough workout of the muscular tension and release appropriate for each movement. The actor-Subject's ability to manipulate him/herself, understood as a physical object, is fundamental to all of this training (see Figure 8.5). After an intense regimen of this program, the Meyerholdian actor-Subject is ready for characterization. While Stanislavsky urged actors to empathize with their roles, Meyerhold, from a cognitive point of view, primarily taught advisory projection: Actors should use their own reason, values, and emotions as the basis for characterization. As Meyerhold saw it, a character in a drama was not a

Figure 8.5 The "meat mincer" setting, designed by Varvara Stepanova, in Vsevolod Meyerhold's 1922 production of *The Death of Tarelkin*, by Alexander Sukhova Kobylin. Stepanova referred to her set pieces as "acting instruments", designed to enable vigorous physical limitation. © University of Bristol Theatre Collection.

fully rounded, complex individual who had a kind of existence apart from the actor's body and imagination, as might a character in a novel. Rather, for Meyerhold, a playwright's characters were little more than social types. In one of his syllabi for an acting workshop, Meyerhold listed 17 set roles for men and women, such as the fop, the heroine, the moralist, the young girl in love, the clown, the matchmaker, and the guardian, that were similar to the kinds of types traditionally played by actors.

Like the great French actor Constant-Benoit Coquelin (1841–1909), Meyerhold believed that it was the actor's responsibility to flesh out these types, to embody them with actions and emotions appropriate to their social roles. He gave his actors mask exercises in which each froze her/his face into a social mask and explored movements appropriate to their expression. Meyerhold went beyond Coquelin and other traditionalists, however, and emphasized that actors could play several types within the same character and even momentarily break from one of these types – throw in an action that contradicted and commented upon the social role they were playing. From Meyerhold's point of view, a successful production presented a series of discrete, self-contained units of action, and the role played by an actor within these units need not add up to a consistent characterization. A "character" was a bundle of related movements and sounds grounded in the body of one actor, not a coherent, contained individual. How this worked is best seen in one of Meyerhold's most famous productions, *The Magnanimous Cuckold* (1922). In Fernand Crommelynck's tragi-farce, a village miller, Bruno, is infatuated with his lovely young wife, Stella, but so doubtful of his own sexual appeal that he believes Stella must have a lover. So he forces her to sleep with every man in the village to discover who the lover is. As previously noted in the introduction to this chapter, the Meyerhold-Popova set for the play suggested the machinery of a miller's windmill, but also created a series of movement possibilities for the performers in the production (Figure 8.2). Maria Babanova, a small, radiant, energetic actor, played Stella as a series of related types. According to one eyewitness report,

> [Babanova's] performance is based on rhythms, precise and economical like a construction. . . . The role develops, strengthens, matures without restraint – violently, yet according to plan. One moment, she is talking innocently to a little bird, the next she is a grown-up woman, delighting in the return of her husband; in her passion and devotions, she is tortured by his jealousy. And now she is being attacked by a mob of blue-clad men, furiously fending them off with a hurricane of resounding blows.
>
> (quoted in Braun 1995:182)

Igor Ilinsky also deployed several character types to depict Bruno; he even undercut his most prominent characterization of the miller with clowning. As a fellow actor stated,

> Bruno . . . stood before the audience, his face pale and motionless, and with unvarying intonation, a monotonous declamatory style, and identical sweeping gestures he uttered his grandiloquent monologues. But at the same time this Bruno was being ridiculed by the

actor performing acrobatic stunts at the most impassioned moments of his speeches, belching, and comically rolling his eyes whilst enduring the most dramatic anguish.

> (ibid.:183–184)

Where Stanislavsky primarily taught his actors how to induce an empathetic response from an audience, Meyerhold mostly wanted spectators to engage with actors through objectification and advisory projection, that is, to understand actor-characters as laughable, sexual, or pitiable physical objects or to project their own values onto a role-playing performer. In the example from the *Magnanimous Cuckold* above, Babanova-Stella's physical presence excited affection, desire, and admiration, by turns, from the audience. Meyerhold apparently allowed some empathetic involvement with her. When she fought off the advances of other men, the audience probably took her values as their own, for example. He mostly encouraged spectators to see her as a physical object. In the action noted above for Ilinsky-Bruno, the actor's belching no doubt undercut the pontificating of his character's speech. Such a situation encourages the audience to identify with the actor at the expense of the character he is ridiculing by championing the actor and laughing at the character through advisory projection.

Although these are complicated responses to describe from a cognitive linguistic point of view, it is important to keep in mind that they happened quickly in the theatre. Where a Stanislavsky-trained actor might need several scenes to involve an audience in the complexities of her or his character, the Meyerhold-trained performer could deftly sketch a type for the audience with a few rhythmic movements, quickly draw them in to the character's situation, and provoke the desired response within the action unit.

By the end of a production, the ideal ensemble of Meyerholdian actors will have created a series of actions that challenge the spectators to make use of what they have learned through their responses. While Stanislavsky thought of audiences as similar to novel readers, bringing individual, psychological responses to what they saw and heard, Meyerhold conceived of spectators as a group of filmgoers whose social responses would help to transform the new Soviet nation. For Meyerhold, these were not Hollywood filmgoer-consumers, as movie audiences would later become, but self-conscious viewers aware of the construction of film montage and meaning. (The famous film director Sergei Eisenstein, an early student of Meyerhold's, claimed that he had learned his understanding of montage from Meyerhold's inventive juxtaposition of action units in his productions.) Rather than creating an illusion on the stage, Meyerhold sought to create a kind of carnival in the entire auditorium, and often had his actors breaking the illusion of the fourth wall or even running through the playhouse to engage spectators directly. Meyerhold trained his actors not only to play social types, but also to become social models and inspirations for social actions that might move Russia toward a communist utopia.

Conclusion

Can an actor use training methods from both Stanislavsky and Meyerhold to join the psychological and sociological modes together in performance? From the point of view of cognitive psychology, there is no reason these methods could not be fused. Human beings have the natural capacity to understand themselves both as a container and as a physical object. Subjects perform both kinds of Selves in everyday life and can do so on the stage. Since the 1960s, in fact, many actor training programs have moved toward the integration of these modes. These include the movement-based work of Jacques LeCoq (1921–1999) in Paris, Tadashi Suzuki's (1939–) psychophysical regimen for actors in Japan, and the actor-as-facilitator model that was developed and applied by Brazilian Augusto Boal (1931–).

BMc

Key references

Benedetti, J. (1988) *Stanislavski: A Biography*, London: Methuen.

Braun, E. (1995) *Meyerhold: A Revolution in Theatre*, Iowa City, I.A.: University of Iowa Press.

Carnicke, S.M. (1998) *Stanislavsky in Focus*, London: Harwood.

Hodge, A. (ed.) (2000) *Twentieth-Century Actor Training*, London: Routledge.

Lakoff, G. and Johnson, M. (1999) *Philosophy in the Flesh: The Embodied Mind and Its Challenge to Western Thought*, New York: Basic Books.

Leach, R. (1989) *Vsevolod Meyerhold*, Christopher Innes (ed.) Directors in Perspective Series, Cambridge: Cambridge University Press.

Milling, J. and Ley, G. (2001) *Modern Theories of Performance: From Stanislavski to Boal*, New York: Palgrave.

Stanislavski, K. (1948) *An Actor Prepares*, trans. E. Hapgood, New York: Theatre Arts Books.

CASE STUDY: Discoursing on desire: *Desire Under the Elms* in the 1920s

"Amazing New Discoveries About Love," trumpeted a magazine advertisement for a 1922 book, *Psychoanalysis and Love*, by Andre Tridon. According to the ad, "[Tridon] shows part of what love is, why there are so many different kinds of love; just what characteristics about certain types of people attract others and why; why love sometimes expresses itself in abnormal ways; what is behind the mask of modesty." As a bonus, Tridon's book supposedly explained "why love often drives people to the most extreme acts, why it sometimes leads to sensational crimes" (Pfister 1995:91). To underline the primitive nature of sexual desire, the ad printed an illustration of a bare-chested caveman with a club approaching a frightened but aroused cave woman. Popular culture had discovered Freud. Tridon's titillating book was one of thousands of films, articles, photographs, stories, novels, and purported explanations that circulated the "new" revelations of pop psychology in American culture during the 1920s.

Two years later, the Experimental Theater in New York produced a play with striking affinities to Tridon's book. Like *Psychoanalysis and Love*, Eugene O'Neill's *Desire Under the Elms* explored "why certain types of people attract others," why this love often expresses itself "in abnormal ways," and how such love might lead "to sensational crimes" (Figure 8.6). In O'Neill's play, a son is attracted to his father's young wife, the two of them begin an affair in a room haunted by the memory of the son's mother, and the young wife ends up killing the child

produced by their love. Although the play is not set among cave dwellers, O'Neill does suggest that primitive sexual passions on a New England farm in the 1850s drew the two lovers together – desires just as natural, potent, and irresistible as in prehistoric times. In retrospect, *Psychoanalysis and Love* might almost have been written as an advertisement for *Desire Under the Elms*.

How is the theatre historian to explain the many similarities between this piece of pop psychology and one of the best plays of a celebrated American playwright? Did O'Neill read *Psychoanalysis and Love* before writing *Desire*? This is unlikely and there is no evidence that he did. Was he influenced directly by Freud or one of his several disciples? Here the evidence is stronger, but not conclusive. On the one hand, O'Neill had personal contact with three psychoanalysts, professed adherence to Karl Jung's notion of a "collective unconscious," and admitted to reading two of Freud's books, *Totem and Taboo* and *Beyond The Pleasure Principle*. In a 1926 interview

Figure 8.6 Old Cabot (Walter Huston) looks down on Abbie (Mary Morris), who is comforting Eben (Charles Ellis) in the 1924 production of Eugene O'Neill's *Desire Under the Elms*. © Museum of the City of New York.

about the success of *Desire Under the Elms*, O'Neill stated that he wanted the play's dialog "to express what [the characters] felt subconsciously"(Pfister 1995:61). On the other hand, O'Neill always objected when his contemporaries suggested that he had simply transferred the findings of psychoanalysis to the stage. Subsequent critics have rightly noted that many factors may have influenced the playwright. Greek mythology, the works of Nietzsche, and O'Neill's family history as well as psychoanalysis are likely influences on *Desire*, for example. But such personal influences will not fully account for the form and content of any drama. Further, the influences on an author's product probably play a very small role (if any) in shaping the effect of a drama among audiences when it is staged. Most of the thousands of spectators who applauded *Desire* in New York and on tour in the 1920s knew no psychoanalysts and had not read Freud.

Rather than chasing down the evidence of various influences on a playwright's work, some critics and historians have turned to discourse theory to understand the relationship between a popular play and the culture of its time. As we will see, discourse theory understands historical causality differently than conventional notions of influence allow. Instead of trying to explain the text of *Desire* as the end product of many personal experiences in the background of the author, discourse theory places all cultural texts on the same level of analysis and inquires into the larger historical reasons for their creation and success. To answer why Tridon's *Psychoanalysis and Love* and O'Neill's *Desire Under the Elms* gained popularity in the 1920s, the critic-historian using discourse theory must look for the common assumptions about truth and knowledge embedded in both of these texts. In explaining popular texts, discourse theory privileges the assumptions and rules that generate shared knowledge in a specific historical era, not the individual experiences or beliefs of an author.

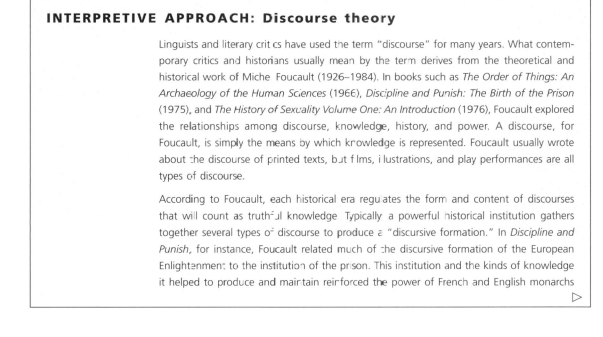

INTERPRETIVE APPROACH: Discourse theory

Linguists and literary critics have used the term "discourse" for many years. What contemporary critics and historians usually mean by the term derives from the theoretical and historical work of Michel Foucault (1926–1984). In books such as *The Order of Things: An Archaeology of the Human Sciences* (1966), *Discipline and Punish: The Birth of the Prison* (1975), and *The History of Sexuality Volume One: An Introduction* (1976), Foucault explored the relationships among discourse, knowledge, history, and power. A discourse, for Foucault, is simply the means by which knowledge is represented. Foucault usually wrote about the discourse of printed texts, but films, illustrations, and play performances are all types of discourse.

According to Foucault, each historical era regulates the form and content of discourses that will count as truthful knowledge. Typically a powerful historical institution gathers together several types of discourse to produce a "discursive formation." In *Discipline and Punish*, for instance, Foucault related much of the discursive formation of the European Enlightenment to the institution of the prison. This institution and the kinds of knowledge it helped to produce and maintain reinforced the power of French and English monarchs

▷

▷

in the eighteenth century. For Foucault, truth is always relative; it is embedded in historical discourses and linked to power.

Dominant discursive formations, which Foucault termed *epistemes*, regulate a wide range of social practices in their historical culture. By shaping what is thinkable in a given society, *epistemes* set mental boundaries in matters of status, gender roles, racial definitions, and even sexual relations. Sexuality, for Foucault, is less a matter of biology than discourse. Like other discourses, the discursive construction of sexuality has become a resource for the control of populations living within its terms and rules. Psychiatry, advertising, and rock stars, for example, have gained power from the modern discourse on sexuality. Not all discursive formations current in a culture, however, work within the dominant *episteme*. Modern medicine, psychoanalysis, and educational practices may have produced what is understood as knowledge about sexuality for the last eighty years, but older discourses, such as the texts of Christian and Judaic tradition, have not disappeared. Their definitions and prohibitions continue to influence cultural conversations about sexuality.

Nevertheless, Foucault emphasizes that *epistemes* tend to undermine and take over the older discourses of a culture. In his *History of Sexuality, Volume One*, for instance, Foucault notes that confession has become a mode of truth telling in the modern era that links the traditional Christian act of confession to the kinds of confessions patients are expected to make to their psychiatrists. This discourse also operates to give credibility to the "confessions" appearing in such mundane discourses as newspaper advice columns and soap operas. "Confession," in all of its forms, is now a part of the dominant discourse of sexuality and works within the contemporary *episteme*. At both the popular and elite levels of culture, confession is considered a path to truth.

KEY QUESTIONS

1   In a given institution – religious or educational, for example – where do we find special vocabularies, special terms of hierarchy perhaps, that help the institution maintain its power?

2   How would you characterize the discourse about a particular racial and/or religious group in our time – western discourse about the Muslim world, for example?

3   How did this come about? Who controls this? (You will find some help on western views of the "Orient" in the Chapter 5 case study on kathakali dance-drama and in the Chapter 11 case study, "Global Shakespeare.")

The historian adopting discourse theory to understand the success of O'Neill's *Desire Under the Elms* in the 1920s might raise these questions:

1 What operations govern the primary discourse of O'Neill's play? How is this discourse expressed in the plot, characters, and themes of *Desire*?
2 How does the play's primary discourse fit within one of the discursive formations at work in the U.S. in the 1920s?
3 Was this discursive formation dominant in the 1920s – a part of the culture's *episteme*?
4 What other discourses at play in the culture of the time impacted on the production and reception of *Desire*?

Psychoanalysis and *Desire*

From what has been discussed so far, it is evident that a generally Freudian orientation to human identity and sexuality is the major discourse of *Desire Under the Elms*. Psychoanalysis understands human identity as divided into a conscious mind and the more powerful realm of the unconscious, where primitive drives and desires can overcome conscious control. This discourse maintains that culture and civilization impose restraints and taboos that encourage individuals to repress their unconscious desires and stifle their emotional fulfillment. To counter repression and attain mental health, popular advocates of these Freudian notions urge people to delve into their past to reveal unconscious motives, confess their past problems and deep desires, and find ways to act with greater freedom in the future. While there may be some good advice in these ideas, a Foucauldian approach to psychoanalysis must recognize that its truths cannot be absolute and universal, that psycholanalysis, as a discursive practice, can also be controlling, limiting.

As in many advice columns, popular films, and other examples of psychoanalytic discourse in the 1920s, *Desire Under the Elms* suggests that unconscious passions and complexes can easily overtake conscious control. What Freud termed an Oedipal complex – in popular terms, the desire to kill the father and sleep with the mother – stalks the younger male characters in *Desire*. All three of old Cabot's sons hate their father and play out variations on copulating with their "mother." In an early scene, his two older sons, who have visited the same prostitute in town as their father, plot to get out from under Cabot's repressive control. When they finally gain their psychological release from the power of the father, they dance around him like wild Indians, performing a symbolic killing of the old farmer. From the start, Abbie, Cabot's new wife, is attracted to Eben, the youngest son, but he scorns her for taking the place of his mother, whose loss continues to obsess him. Abbie meets Eben in the front parlor of the farmhouse, where the ghost of his mother continues to haunt him. There, Abbie effectively takes the place of Eben's "Maw," and the two of them consummate their passion.

Popular Freudianism also shapes the gender roles of *Desire*. The males of *Desire* are the prime movers of the plot, and this accords with Freud's own generally Victorian understanding of men being naturally more active and aggressive than women. Old Cabot brings home a new wife, the two older sons rebel and leave, Eben impregnates Abbie, and Cabot throws a party to celebrate the birth of what he believes is his son. But Abbie is far from passive; she takes an active role in seducing Eben and eventually kills their baby when she (wrongly) believes that he is planning to abandon her. In the Freudian discourse of the play, however, Abbie, because she is a woman, is closer to nature and less aware of her actions than the men in the play. Abbie, in fact, is much like the elms that "bend their trailing branches down over the roof" of the Cabot farmhouse, as O'Neill states in his stage directions. "[The elms] appear to protect and at the same time subdue. There is a sinister maternity in their aspect, a crushing jealous absorption" (O'Neill 1973: 2) (Figure 8.7). When she first appears, Abbie's "sinister" qualities are paramount;

Figure 8.7 Mordecai Gorelik's design for the revival of *Desire Under the Elms* at the ANTA playhouse, New York, 1952.
[Source: In *From Script to Stage: Eight Modern Plays*, Ralph Goodman (ed.) (1972), R & W Holt.]

her possessiveness about the farm and "absorption" with her sexuality drive her initial intentions. From a popular psychoanalytic point of view, her id (unconscious desire) dominates her superego (conscience). Only after she learns the mutuality of love with Eben does she begin to break free from what O'Neill understands as her natural, unconscious impulses.

Abbie and Eben effect this cure in good psychoanalytic fashion through mutual confession. Despite their fears and anxieties, Abbie and Eben play patient and therapist for each other, gradually building a relationship of trust and love out of their initial lust. Abbie temporarily relapses into unconscious jealously when she kills their baby without asking Eben, but she confesses her act and Eben forgives her. By the end of the play, both are more conscious of their past lives and have accepted responsibility for their actions. They know they are going to jail and determine to wait for each other until their release. In contrast, *Desire* pities those who refuse to confess, to let go of past repressions. Even at the end of the play, Old Cabot takes pride in the repressive life he has led and the possessions, especially the farm, that his repressions have helped him to acquire. And Cabot

suffers – justly, according to the discourse of the play – for the repressions that drive this possessiveness. For Abbie and Eben, however, *Desire* ends on a note of affirmation, despite a past of adultery and murder. They have worked through their psychological problems and found love through confession. For them, the play acts like a long therapeutic session: complexes, repressions, and neuroses are recognized and exorcised through a dramatic version of the "talking cure," as Freudian psychoanalysis has been called.

Competing discursive formations

The historian using Foucauldian discourse theory, then, may conclude that *Desire Under the Elms* operates within the discursive formation of popular psychoanalysis common in the U.S. during the 1920s. That accounts for the similarities among the play and such pop psychology treatises as *Psychoanalysis and Love*. But was this discursive formation dominant in the 1920s? Was it part of the culture's *episteme*? In this regard, the historical evidence of the censorship of the play suggests that the Freudian construction of sexuality evident in the play was not yet dominant in the national culture.

O'Neill, Kenneth Macgowan (1888–1963), and Robert Edmund Jones produced *Desire* in 1924 as a part of their Experimental Theater, Inc., which had evolved out of the Provincetown Players. Under Jones's direction and design, the play scored an initial success with audiences and critics. When the producers moved the show from the Greenwich Village Theater to a Broadway playhouse in 1925, however, a local district attorney, responding to spectator complaints, found the play obscene and ordered it closed. Opposing voices in the press and from prominent citizens, however, helped to convince a grand jury that there was nothing objectionable in O'Neill's drama, and the production continued. *Desire* had less luck in Boston. There, a censor's demand for numerous revisions led to the banning of the play and the closing of the production. In Los Angeles, the police initially arrested the entire cast of the road company production, but soon allowed them to continue performing while the trial took place. The production eventually closed before the completion of the court case.

In contrast, productions of the play in New York in the 1950s and 1960s met with no calls for censorship. Harold Clurman (1901–1980) directed the 1952 revival, which starred Karl Malden as old Cabot. George C. Scott and Colleen Dewhurst riveted audiences in the 1963 production, directed at the Circle in the Square Playhouse by Jose Quintero (1924–). Why was *Desire* banned in Boston and attacked elsewhere in the 1920s, but met with respect and enthusiasm by audiences after mid-century? Part of the answer to this complex question has to do with anxieties about respectability in Boston and elsewhere, with different productions with different actors that emphasized different aspects of the play, and with the weakening of local censorship in the U.S. during the twentieth century.

Discourse theory also suggests another response to this question about audience reception. It may be that the discursive formation that gave knowledge and power to O'Neill's reliance on a Freudian construction of sexuality was not yet a dominant formation in the U.S. in the 1920s. Artists, critics, and bohemians in Greenwich Village might embrace Freudian ideas for the freedom they seemed to give them over Victorian strictures. Advertisers and others could use Freudian notions to suggest that consumption of the right products provided a ticket to sexual excitement and emotional fulfillment. But when the apparent license of Freudian sexuality ran directly into Christian tradition and Victorian respectability, many Americans in the 1920s may have balked.

There is little doubt that the discourse of *Desire* privileges psychoanalytic release over traditional morality. While it is true that Abbie and Eben will pay for their crimes at the end of the play, O'Neill arranges the rhetoric of his drama to induce the audience to pity the old father for his continuing repressions and to rejoice in the emotional release that confession has brought to the lovers. The ending reverses the conventional rhetoric of poetic justice, in which audiences could feel good when some characters were rewarded for upholding morality and others were damned for committing crimes. No wonder some spectators in the 1920s were confused and a few called for censorship.

Why, then, did the play succeed with audiences in the 1950s and 1960s? Again, several explanations are possible, but Foucauldian theory suggests another approach to this question. Perhaps the Freudian construction of sexuality, a significant but not yet dominant discourse in U.S. culture in the 1920s, increased in power to become part of the culture's *episteme* by the 1950s. To explore this hunch, the historian would need to investigate many more primary and secondary sources in cultural history than this case study can accommodate. But there is suggestive evidence to support this explanation. In the 1950s and 1960s, more Freudian psychoanalysts were practicing in the U.S. than ever before (or since), and Freudian explanations for human behavior were embedded in a range of powerful discourses and institutions, from business management to the operations of the CIA. Given the dominance of this discursive formation, U.S. audiences during the early cold war may have had little difficulty embracing the truths that O'Neill's dramatic Freudianism had to offer.

BMc

Key references

Foucault, M. (1980) *The History of Sexuality, Volume One*, New York: Vintage.

Herman, E. (1995) *The Romance of American Psychology: Political Culture in the Age of Experts*, Berkeley: University of California Press.

Manheim, M. (ed.) (1998) *The Cambridge Companion to Eugene O'Neill*, Cambridge: Cambridge University Press.

McConachie, B. (2003) *American Theater in Culture of the Cold War: Producing and Contesting Containment, 1947–1962*, Iowa City, I.A.: University of Iowa Press.

O'Neill, E. (1973) *Three Plays: Desire Under the Elms, Strange Interlude, Mourning Becomes Electra*, New York: Random House.

Pfister, J. (1995) *Staging Depth: Eugene O'Neill and the Politics of Psychological Discourse*, Chapel Hill: University of North Carolina Press.

CASE STUDY: Beckett's theatrical minimalism

Beckett in brief

Samuel Barclay Beckett was born near Dublin, on Good Friday, 13 April, 1906. The second son of a well-to-do Protestant family, he received his B.A. in Modern Literature (French and Italian) from Trinity College, Dublin in 1927. He taught two terms at Campbell College, Belfast, in 1928, and from 1928–1930 was Lecturer at École Normale Supérieure, Paris. There he published his first poem, *Whoroscope*, and met James Joyce. After two years (1930–1932) of teaching at Trinity College, Dublin, and the publication of his single major work of criticism, *Proust* (1931), Beckett moved to Paris permanently and turned his attention exclusively to writing, publishing a short story collection, *More Pricks than Kicks* (1934), and his first novel, *Murphy* (1938). From 1942–1945 he was active in the French resistance movement. Beckett's major period of creative work in Paris from 1946–1950 resulted in a trilogy of novels in French, *Molloy*, *Malone Dies*, *The Unnamable*, and his first two plays, *Eleutheria* and *Waiting for Godot* (*En attendant Godot*). Beckett increasingly turned his attention to writing for the stage, radio, television, and film. He was awarded the Nobel Prize for Literature in 1969. Beckett died in 1989.

A chronology of first productions and publications of Beckett's plays for stage, radio, and television

1952   *En attendant Godot* published (Paris)

1953   World premiere: *En attendant Godot* (Paris)

1954   *Waiting for Godot* published in English

1955   English premiere: *Waiting for Godot* (London)

1957   BBC radio: *All That Fall*. World premiere: *Fin de partie* (*Endgame*) and *Acte sans paroles I* (*Act Without Words I*) (Paris)

1958   World premiere: *Krapp's Last Tape* (London)

1961   World premiere: *Happy Days* (New York)

1962   BBC radio: *Words and Music*

1963   World premiere: *Spiel* (*Play*) (Germany)

1964   Makes *Film* with Buster Keaton in New York, directed by Alan Schneider

1965   World premiere: *Come and Go* (Germany)

1966   BBC television: *Eh Joe*

1972   World premiere: *Not I* (New York)

1976   BBC radio broadcast: *Rough for Radio*. World premieres: *That Time* and *Footfalls* (London). Beckett directs *Footfalls*

1977   BBC television: *Ghost Tri* and . . . *but the clouds*

1979   World premiere: *A Piece of Monologue* (New York)

1981   World premiere: *Rockaby* (New York), *Ohio Impromptu* (Ohio)

1982   World premiere: *Catastrophe* (Avignon Festival). Süddeutscher Rundfunk television: *Quad*

1983   Süddeutscher Rundfunk radio: *Nacht und Traume*. World premiere: *What Where* (New York)

The performative writer on four Beckett plays

In *"faint diffuse light,"* Speaker stands *"well off centre downstage audience left"* with white hair, white nightgown, white socks in Beckett's *A Piece of Monologue* Two meters to his left is a *"standard lamp, skull-sized white globe"* – the source of the faint diffuse light illuminating Speaker. At the extreme right on the same level, and barely visible is the foot of a white pallet bed. Ten seconds before Speaker begins, the lamp is gradually illuminated so that the stark whiteness of Speaker and the foot of the pallet bed stand out against the black void of the remainder of the theatrical space – that "black beyond." Into this void, Speaker, standing still throughout the twenty minutes it takes to deliver the monologue, conjures a life – his life – between birth and death:

> Birth was the death of him. Again. Words are few. Dying too . . . So ghastly grinning on. From funeral to funeral. To now. This night. Two and a half billion seconds.
>
> (Beckett 1984:265)

The monologue is spoken, continuously, without the wide range of vocal inflections common in realist acting, that is, "without color" as Billie Whitelaw describes it, a noted British actor known for her work in Beckett. The incessant stream of words is not Speaker's everyday voice, but his consciousness. It speaks in one moment from the outside as an observer – "birth was the death of *him*" – and then, from the inside in this moment – " . . . *now. This night.*" Speaker describes the room in which he stands, now, speaking before us as he conjures past, present, and the not yet:

> In the room dark gaining. Till faint light from standard lamp. Wick turned low. And now. This night. Up at nightfall. Every nightfall. Faint light in room. Whence unknown. None from window. No. Next to none. No such thing as none.
>
> (1984:265)

The worlds Beckett creates are the "black vast" of life, reflecting the bleak aftermath of the horrors of World War II, and more. His entire body of work reduces action, words, and settings to a minimum in order to express only what *must* be said into that unbearable silence or darkness. When Beckett began to write creatively after moving to Paris, he chose to do so in French in order to force himself to be spare in his writing. In his earliest produced play, *En attendant Godot*, first performed in 1953 in Paris, two men, Vladimir and Estragon, must perpetually occupy themselves while waiting for Godot in a barren landscape – a road with a single, forlorn tree. Although a small boy, and a master (Pozzo), and his servant (Lucky) come, and then depart, Godot remains an absence, never arriving. Vladimir and Estragon attempt to fill the void of their waiting with music-hall-like patter. The numerous silences must be filled not only by the characters, but by the expectant audience (Figure 8.8).

So minimal is the action in some of Beckett's later plays, like *A Piece of Monologue* (1979), *Not I* (1972), and *Ohio Impromptu* (1981), that they are virtually single image, still-life paintings. Reflecting his interest in art, Beckett describes setting and lighting precisely; his sets are almost formal compositions in a proscenium frame. The unique hues of each painting are provided by the cadences, tones, and quality of the spoken words animating the still-life. Reflecting his love of music, Beckett orchestrates his speeches with periods, question marks, and sometimes " . . . " to indicate those momentary pauses in thought when consciousness reflects on itself.

In *Ohio Impromptu* two men, Reader and Listener, are identically dressed in long black coats, and have long white hair. Mirror images of each other, their heads bowed and propped on their right hands so that their faces are hidden, they sit on white chairs at a white table, with only a "worn volume" open before Reader and a single (shared?) wide-brimmed black hat before them. One "last time" Reader tells "the sad tale" – Listener's tale. The quietude is broken only when Listener signals Reader with a rap of his left-hand knuckles on the table. With "nothing . . . left to tell," Reader closes the book. After five seconds of silence, the two figures, virtually frozen for fifteen minutes, "*Simultaneously . . . lower their right hands to table, raise their heads and look at each other. Unblinking. Expressionless. Ten seconds. Fade out*" (ibid.:288). It is as though they have "turned to stone" before us.

In *Not I*, all that is visible on the "*stage in darkness*" is Mouth – the illuminated lips of a female mouth located about eight feet above stage level – and the barely illuminated shadowy figure of Auditor dressed "*in a loose black [robe], with hood.*" Once

Figure 8.8 Samuel Beckett's *Waiting for Godot*, directed by Roger Blin, at the Théâtre Récamier in Paris, 1970. Photo by Roger Pic. © Bibliothèque Nationale, Department ASP, Paris.

Mouth, seemingly afloat in a sea of black above the audience, begins her non-stop twenty-five minute monologue ". . . out . . . into this world . . . this world . . . tiny little thing . . . " the only movements are the three times Auditor raises his arms "in a gesture of helpless compassion" (ibid.:215). Auditor and audience witness the incessant ravings of Mouth's consciousness – a "steady stream" of words that can't be stopped (ibid.:220).

The formal minimalism of Beckett's plays keeps the audience's focus on these few, sparse elements. As Beckett said of James Joyce's work, concerns with pattern, form, and detail make the work "not *about* something . . . [but] *that thing itself*" (quoted in Kalb 1989:3). Form becomes content; content is form. For example, the form and content in *A Piece of Monologue* plays between "birth" and "death."

Speaker's ' birth " can *only* become his death. From as early as *Waiting for Godot* in 1952, Beckett's concern with the "sure reality" of death is not with "death as an *event*" but rather with "dying as a *process*" (Worton 1994:70). And the process of dying is nowhere more clearly present than in language itself. Words given birth in a physical act of speaking die as they are spoken. "Stands there staring beyond waiting for first word. It gathers in his mouth. Birth." (1984:268). Just as the word, "birth," gathers in the mouth to be born, only to "die," so too with light and sight. At the moment something is illuminated it "fades," and is "gone."

INTERPRETIVE APPROACH: Performative writing

The relationship between form and content in Beckett's work focuses attention on the limits and possibilities of language, speech, and memory by creating "plays" that are not "dramatic" in the conventional sense of the term. Beckett's plays are "performative" rather than "dramatic" in that their minimalism creates fragments, and not "whole" or "complete" plots or characters. Thus, they challenge conventional notions of interpretation and meaning. In *Not I*, there is *only* Mouth, no body, and the incessant stream of words pouring forth. Do these words pour out of or into a/the void? There is no single or final answer to this or other questions. Rather, form and content invite a surplus of meanings.

Rather than being mimetic, Beckett's plays are evocative and metonymic, that is, they gain their effect in performance by suggestively conjuring absence through a partial or incomplete presence. In *Not I*, Mouth and its rushed fragments of thought conjure a life, body, subject, memory . . . but *whose*? Who is this "she! . . . SHE!"??? Thought, language, representation, subjectivity, and meaning all *fail* to provide us with answers. Therefore, Beckett's work offers us "dramatic" writing and performance *in extremis*.

The "failure" of thought, language, representation, subjectivity, and meaning as they are conceived in objectivist thought and modernism has led some scholars, such as Herbert Blau (1982) to attempt an alternative approach to scholarly writing, an approach that shares some of the characteristics of Beckett's non-dramatic "dramas." Since we can no longer assume that there is a single master narrative or interpretation, writing "performatively"

▷

▷ is a self-aware way of approaching the act of writing and thought as an "inquiry into the limits and possibilities of the intersections between speech and writing" (Phelan and Lane 1998:13). Like Beckett's plays, performative writing does not attempt to reach closure, but rather to enter wounds, or black holes. Parts of this case study, particularly the first section, are written in a semi-performative style, rather than discursively, to reflect this mode of thought.

"Make sense, who will"

When Beckett's work began to be performed with *En attendant Godot* in 1953, it challenged all the prevailing expectations of a well-made play, with psychologically-grounded characters. It forced directors, actors, critics, and scholars to think freshly about both what constitutes the structure of a Beckett play, as well as how to perform those tasks that constitute roles that are not psychologically motivated.

Beckett rejected many early interpretations of his work, especially when *Waiting for Godot* was interpreted as a Christian allegory or symbolic of contemporary concerns with the announcement of the "death of God." Beckett once remarked that if he knew who Godot was, he would have said so. The attempt to define and interpret Godot is part of an ongoing problem with certain modes of interpretation. The desire to know what Godot signifies tells us more about those desiring a stable world with fixed references, than about the potentially moving experience of absence an audience can have when watching a production of *Waiting for Godot*.

Reactions to first productions of Waiting for Godot

En attendant Godot opened on 3 January, 1953 in Paris at Théâtre de Babylone, directed by Roger Blin. Beckett scholar James Knowlson summarizes the responses:

> Reactions to the first performances were very mixed . . . [A]t first numbers dropped off after the first night . . . . But its success was assured when it became controversial, for it surprised and shocked many conventional theatregoers. Beckett was told about an incident when the curtain had to be brought down after Lucky's monologue as twenty well-dressed, but disgruntled spectators whistled and hooted derisively. During a stormy intermission, the most irate protestors came to blows with the play's supporters, then trooped back into the theatre only to stomp noisily out again as the second act opened with the same two characters still waiting for Godot as they had been at the beginning of act one. . . . As *Godot* became the talk of theatrical Paris, the character of the audiences changed, and it became the play that everyone simply had to see.
>
> (Knowlson 1996:350)

Even worse was the American opening night of *Waiting for Godot* on 3 January, 1956 at the Coconut Grove Playhouse in Miami. Featuring American comedian Bert Lahr (as Estragon), the production was hyped in advance as the "laugh hit of two continents," almost guaranteeing, says Knowlson, that it would flop. "The audience left in droves at the intermission" (ibid.:378).

▷

▷   Quite in contrast was the response of prisoners to the play when it was performed at San Quentin penitentiary in 1957, directed by Herbert Blau:

> [W]hat had bewildered the sophisticated audiences of Paris, London, and New York was immediately grasped by an audience of convicts. As the writer of "Memos of a first-nighter" put it in the columns of the prison paper, the *San Quentin News*: "The trio of muscle-men, biceps overflowing . . . parked all 642 lbs on the aisle and waited for the girls and funny stuff. When this didn't appear, they audibly fumed and audibly decided to wait until the house lights dimmed before escaping. They made one error. They listened and looked two minutes too long – and stayed. Left at the end. All shook . . . " It was an expression, symbolic in order to avoid all personal error, by an author who expected each member of his audience to draw his own conclusions, make his own errors. It asked nothing in point, it forced no dramatized moral on the viewer, it held out no specific hope. . . . We're still waiting for Godot, and shall continue to wait.
>
> (Esslin 1969:1–2)

Just as problematic have been some of the labels used to describe Beckett's work. When Martin Esslin wrote his seminal book, *The Theatre of the Absurd*, in 1961, he devised the concept of the "absurd" as a complex interpretive tool – referring to the absurd condition of meaninglessness in human existence – to discuss the works of Beckett and other playwrights such as Eugene Ionesco (1912–) and Jean Genet (1910–1986), whose plays did not fit conventional categories. Since then the "absurd" has been used as an unfortunate, totalizing category that allows work that is "different" to be dismissed.

While Beckett's work was dismissed early in his career, by the time he died in 1989, his nineteen plays were regarded as modernist masterpieces, and productions of *Waiting for Godot* and *Endgame* in particular had become theatrical standards. The Dublin Gate Theatre produced the entire canon for audiences in New York and London (1999), and during 2000 all 19 were filmed.

Who should control a play's production?

Beckett's concern with precision is reflected in his attempts to assert control over productions that did not conform to his stage directions. He forced the closure of several productions. Arguably the most controversial was American experimental theatre director JoAnne Akalaitis's production of *Endgame* for the American Repertory Theatre in Cambridge, Massachusetts in 1984, in which the setting was a subway, apparently after a nuclear holocaust. This production greatly distressed Beckett. It is discussed in Chapter 11 in the context of the changes in the role of the director and the idea of the unstable "text" that characterize postmodern theatre. Beckett did occasionally give permission for adaptations or experiments to those whom he knew personally, and he even ignored "transgressions." The latter was the case with well known American experimental theatre company, Mabou Mines, and its 1976 production of an adaptation by Lee Breuer and Thom Cathcart of Beckett's short prose work, *The Lost Ones* (Figure 8.9). David Warrilow, an actor in many of Beckett's plays, acknowledges it was done "against the rules" and without Beckett's permission (Kalb 1989:220). The claustrophobic world of the story was staged for a small number of spectators who removed their shoes to enter a black cylindrical space. It was peopled only by the narrator, Warrilow,

Figure 8.9 David Warrilow in the Mabou Mines' production of *The Lost Ones*, by Samuel Beckett. © New York Public Library. Photo: Richard Landry.

and 205 one-half inch tall miniature figures, who were made to ascend and descend miniature ladders or to inhabit the various "niches or alcoves" in a cylindrical wall. Visiting the company while in Berlin on tour, Beckett examined the setting for the production of *The Lost Ones*, but never saw a performance. Having heard positive reports from his trusted friends, Beckett "came to accept that Lee Breuer's adaptation worked outstandingly well in its own terms. After learning about it, he told his agents that they should go on refusing all adaptations as a matter of course without even consulting him, but stressed that Mabou Mines' productions were exceptions to the rule" (Knowlson 1996:556).

Beckett's theatrical minimalism, exemplified in *Not I*, *Ohio Impromptu*, and *The Lost Ones*, questioned the limits of language and memory, and the expressive possibilities of both in form as well as content, thereby helping focus attention on the performer's body, experience, and consciousness. Consequently, Beckett's plays arguably contributed to the transition from the concerns of modernism, toward the kind of fragmentation, parody, and pastiche that are characteristic of what is now known as post-modern theatre and performance, attributes that also characterize experiments in performative writing.

PZ

Key references

Beckett, S. (1984) *The Collected Shorter Plays*, New York: Grove Press.

Beckett, S. (1986) *Samuel Beckett: The Complete Dramatic Works*, London: Faber and Faber.

Ben-Zvi, L. (ed.) (1990) *Women in Beckett: Performance and Critical Perspectives*, Urbana: University of Illinois Press.

Blau, H. (1982) *Take up the Bodies: Theatre at the Vanishing Point*, Urbana: University of Illinois Press.

Blau, H. (1994) "Herbert Blau," in L. Oppenhein (ed.) *Directing Beckett*, Ann Arbor: University of Michigan Press.

Esslin, M. (1969) *The Theatre of the Absurd*, Garden City, N.J.: Anchor Books.

Juliet, C. (1995) *Conversations with Samuel Beckett and Bram van Velde*, Leiden: Academic Press.

Kalb, J. (1989) *Beckett in Performance*, Cambridge: Cambridge University Press.

Knowlson, J. (1996) *Damned to Fame: The Life of Samuel Beckett*, New York: Simon and Shuster.

Knowlson, J. (gen. ed.) (1992–1999) *The Theatrical Notebooks of Samuel Beckett*, vols 1–4, London: Faber and Faber.

McMullan, A. (1993) *Theatre on Trial: Samuel Beckett's Later Drama*, New York: Routledge.

McMullan, A. (1994) "Samuel Beckett as Director: The Art of Mastering Failure," in J. Pilling (ed.) *The Cambridge Companion to Beckett*, Cambridge: Cambridge University Press.

Phelan, P., and Lane, J. (eds) (1998) *The Ends of Performance*, New York: New York University Press.

Pountney, R. (1988) *Theatre of Shadows: Samuel Beckett's Drama 1956–1976*, Gerrards Cross: Colin Smythe.

Ricks. C. (1993) *Beckett's Dying Words*, Oxford: Clarendon Press.

Whitelaw, B. (1995) *Billie Whitelaw . . . Who He?* New York: St. Martin's Press.

Worth, K. (1999) *Samuel Beckett's Theatre: Life Journeys*, Oxford: Oxford University Press.

Worton, M. (1994) "*Waiting for Godot* and *Endgame*: Theatre as Text," in *The Cambridge Companion to Beckett*, Cambridge: Cambridge University Press.

Zarrilli, P.B (1997) "Acting 'at the nerve ends': Beckett, Blau, and the Necessary," *Theatre Topics*, 7(2):103–116.

CHAPTER 9

Theatres for reform and revolution, 1880–1970

This chapter examines the political culture of the modern theatre from 1880 to 1970. Although our interest will occasionally narrow to plays with a specific political "message," most of this chapter focuses on general questions of political orientation and the different responses of the stage to the problem of the role of the individual in modern society. Two major political orientations offered significant answers to this problem between 1880 and 1970: liberalism and socialism. Many successful plays continued to espouse varieties of conservatism during these years and some were reactionary, but these orientations offered little insight into what most understood as the modern condition. Neither liberalism nor socialism, however, now means what most westerners understood by these terms during this 90-year period.

Regarding liberalism, the right of individuals to pursue their interests unrestrained by aristocratic privileges or state regulations, had been the banner of liberal reformers since the French Revolution. As noted in Part II, these ideas derive from the premises of John Locke and the rationalism of several Enlightenment thinkers during the seventeenth and

eighteenth centuries. The bourgeoisie throughout Europe had largely secured these rights by 1850, but continued to guard them against excessive state power from above and the clamor for more democracy and better living conditions from below. From the liberals' point of view, the laws of the marketplace, if unimpeded, would guarantee economic progress and social justice. Classical liberalism was meritocratic rather than democratic; under liberalism, individuals must earn their social status and economic security through their talents and efforts, not by voting for them.

Nineteenth-century socialists, on the other hand, argued that blindly following the laws of the capitalist market might produce some progress in the short term, but guaranteed the long-term oppression of the working class. By 1890, socialist political parties with a base in the working class were electing representatives in all industrial countries with a modicum of democracy. In Germany and the Scandinavian countries, the socialists claimed more voters than any other national party by 1914. Even in the United States, despite ethnic and racial animosities that fragmented working-class solidarity, the socialists polled almost a million votes in 1912. Socialists throughout the world drew on Marx's arguments about the inherent class conflict between workers and capitalists, but often differed on the question of revolution. Most argued that political and economic reform might alter the capitalist system to produce more economic justice, while a minority believed that only violent revolution could secure the rights of the proletariat. Although Marx had urged socialists to build an international movement, most socialists before the Great War worked within the politics of their nation-states, a shortcoming that disabled socialist pacifism in 1914.

As we will see, the general political orientations of liberalism and socialism took many specific forms as they played out in various societies, nations, and institutions, including the theatre. The discourses of liberalism and socialism also spilled out from Europe and influenced political struggles in the rest of the world. Two momentous events further shaped the historical dynamics of the political culture of the modern stage around the world: the ideological fallout from the Russian Revolution of 1917, when radical socialists seemed to many to have gained control of a European nation, and the ongoing struggle against imperialism, which received an enormous boost from the moral and economic disarray of Europe after the Great War.

Liberalism in the theatre, 1914–1930

Liberalism was the underlying but often unacknowledged ideology of much European theatre after 1850, informing the materialist melodramas of Dion Boucicault and the realist comedies of Tom Robertson, among many other popular genres. In these plays, as in much of nineteenth-century culture, sympathetic figures rarely argued directly for liberalism; rather, liberal freedoms were simply taken for granted as the way things were or ought to be. Naturalism, however, challenged the principles of liberalism. If environment and heredity determined human actions, belief in an individual's ability to act as a free agent in society, a core liberal conviction, was a deceit and a delusion. By the late nineteenth century, it was evident to many of the bourgeoisie that the material conditions of social life were compromising liberal individualism.

Although many condemned the plays of Henrik Ibsen for their apparent radicalism, discerning liberals applauded the Norwegian playwright's dramas for preserving a role for individual freedom in the face of naturalistic determinism. Two early romantic plays in Ibsen's career, *Brand* (1865) and *Peer Gynt* (1867), celebrate the individual's search for liberal self-fulfillment. Brand is a symbolic Everyman who struggles to transcend earthly fragmentation and live up to the idealistic claims of his imagination. Peer Gynt is the comic opposite of Brand, a figure who prefers indirection and compromise to Brand's pursuit of perfection. In effect, Peer's futile life confirms the superiority of Brand's flaming idealism. In both plays, Ibsen recognized that the pursuit of self-fulfillment through transcendence, a liberal ideal, was both necessary to strive for and impossible to achieve. As we will see in the first case study of this chapter, this notion of liberal tragedy informed Ibsen's later realist plays.

Assuming the possibility of substantial individual freedom, liberals often depicted unnecessary social constraint as its evil opposite. The individual-versus-society conflict was a common liberal theme in many dramas after 1880; a few plays even sparked some liberal reform measures. John Galsworthy's (1867–1933) *Justice* (1910), for example, which depicted the cruelty of solitary confinement, helped to reign in the use of that punishment in British prisons. In *Damaged Goods* (1902), Eugène Brieux (1858–1932) campaigned against the ignorance and fear that led to the spread of syphilis in France. His liberal sermonizing set the stage for health reform in France. More often, politically contentious liberal plays stirred up some discussion but did not change the status quo. In *A Man's World* (1910), by U.S.

playwright Rachel Crothers (1878–1958), the protagonist struggles to find a place for herself and a child (not biologically her own) that she is raising, only to discover that the man who wants to marry her has fathered and abandoned that child. Crothers's play takes a strong stand against the double standard, which allowed society to wink at a man's promiscuity but condemned a woman for the same social sin. Her liberal feminism, however, was too radical for most theatregoers in the U.S., and she modified her position in later plays.

Socialism in the theatre before 1914

Socialism offered women playwrights in Europe a firmer orientation than liberalism for opposing bourgeois patriarchy. Many first-generation feminists became socialists, although this position rarely led to commercial success. Elizabeth Robbins (1862–1952), who premiered two of Ibsen's female heroes

on the London stage, however, won modest renown with *Votes for Women* (1907) and contributed to the eventual triumph of women's suffrage in Great Britain. One of the earliest and most radical socialist feminists was Minna Canth (1844–1897), whose naturalistic depictions of Finnish life shocked Helsinki audiences in the 1880s. Her *Children of Misfortune* (1888) depicted the diseases, drunkenness, crimes, and death that degraded the lives of unemployed workers, with special attention to unemployment's effect on working-class women and children. Earlier, in *The Worker's Wife* (1885), Canth portrayed the legal subjugation of working-class women by their husbands. Like Zola and many of his followers, Canth joined avant-garde naturalism to political socialism (Figure 9.1).

Canth's dramas, however, underline a problem with naturalism for socialist writers. Naturalists could point out the pitiable circumstances of working-class lives, but their ideology left them with

Figure 9.1 Emile Zola's naturalistic *The Earth*, directed by André Antoine at the Théâtre Antoine in Paris, 1902. © Bibliothèque Nationale, Paris.

no clear means of taking action against these oppressions. If heredity and environment were all-determining, individual and collective action to correct social problems had little chance of success. Socialists eager to push for the gradual reform of capitalist society and the minority of socialists who clamored for immediate revolution against it had to find a way out of naturalistic determinism.

While various socialist writers approached this problem with different degrees of success, George Bernard Shaw's (1856–1950) solution was ultimately the most significant for the 1880–1914 period of the theatre. Shaw became a socialist in 1882 and soon after joined the Fabian Society, a group of journalists, professionals, and others who campaigned to end capitalist oppression by gradualist, political means. Shaw's first plays in the 1890s carried Fabianism into the theatre by attacking slum-landlordism, capitalist profits from prostitution, and the idiocy of armies and war. In *Man and Superman* and *Major Barbara* (both performed in 1905), Shaw dramatized a political philosophy that undercut the stultifying determinism of naturalism and promoted active engagement with the complex realities of modern industrial society. Through *Major Barbara*, Shaw's audience learned that social conscience without economic power is useless and, finally, unethical. Further, *Man and Superman* demonstrated that all the political power in the world cannot alter material reality unless it works in conjunction with evolutionary force. Shaw's Fabian vitalism, his conjuring of a life force that could animate individuals to push humanity toward evolutionary progress, trumped the despair inherent in the naturalist perspective. While this philosophy and the plays that embodied it may no longer seem politically relevant, Fabian vitalism did change political discourse in England before 1914. Shaw's efforts helped to lay the groundwork for the political triumph of socialism in England. Further, Shaw's comedies from this period continue to startle playgoers with their combative debates and acute social analyses.

Theatricalizing the Russian revolution

The apparent victory of radical socialism in Russia in 1921, following the Revolution and the civil war, sharply altered the political dimensions of western theatre. Only later would democratic socialists discover that the Russian communists despised democracy and instituted many forms of political oppression, including mass starvation and slave labor camps, to maintain their authoritarian rule. In the afterglow of the Revolution, however, the short-term sacrifice of some democratic rights seemed to many European socialists a small price to pay for the opportunity to transform an entire society and economy. With the example of Lenin and the Bolsheviks in front of them, the question of whether individuals and small groups of revolutionaries could break free from naturalistic constraints to radically alter the course of history had been answered. Despite the setbacks caused by the Great War, eager socialists renewed revolutionary action in Eastern and Central Europe and nearly toppled some postwar liberal regimes, including the fragile German state. Although liberal governments were soon established in the nations of the former German and Austro-Hungarian empires, a new, revolutionary form of Russian theatre soon spread from the Soviet Union to socialists around the world.

To teach illiterate peasants and workers the basics of communism, the Bolsheviks organized Blue Blouse troupes, named for the color of workers' shirts, and sent them around the country. A collection of short skits legitimating the radical changes brought by the Revolution, these Blue Blouse revues were called "living newspapers" because they taught communism through speech, music, gestures, and spectacle. In style and ideology, the Blue Blouse revues were anti-naturalistic; they asserted that workers and peasants, despite the past degradations of heredity and environment, could take control of their lives and effect radical change. By 1927, more than five thousand Blue Blouse troupes were active in the Soviet Union.

As we have seen in the previous chapter, the 1920s also witnessed the brief triumph of Meyerhold and the Russian avant-garde in the new Soviet Union. In retrospect, it is clear that Lenin, Stalin, and other communist leaders needed the avant-garde in the early 1920s to stabilize their regime internally and to give it credibility and influence outside of Russia, especially since the initial foreign policy of the Soviets was to foment international revolution. In line with this policy, the communists funded futurist and constructivist theatres, invited theatre people from abroad to witness the exciting innovations of the Soviet avant-garde, and occasionally sponsored tours of Soviet troupes to other nations. After the mid-1920s, however, when hopes for international revolution had dimmed, Stalin and his bureaucrats began tightening the funding and freedoms of the avant-garde. They squeezed out and eventually eliminated those who would not conform to the narrow political and aesthetic constraints of "socialist realism," a mix of realism and communist party propaganda.

The influence of the revolution in the West

The transformation of German expressionism was perhaps the most immediate impact of the Revolution on theatre outside of Russia. As we have seen, early expressionistic plays had tended to be liberal or anarchist in orientation. Optimism about the imminent overthrow of conventional German society in the wake of German defeat in the war and revolution in Russia, however, turned expressionism toward utopian socialism. Georg Kaiser's politics now embraced pacifism in his anti-war play *Gas* (1918), which took the poison gas used by troops in the Great War as a metaphor for the spread of social corruption. In the same year, Ernst Toller (1893–1939) advocated a Soviet-like revolution in Germany in *Transfiguration* (1918) (Figure 8.1). Other expressionists joined the generational rage that had fueled several pre-war plays to a more general

call to overthrow the whole bourgeois order. Revolutionary fervor was short-lived in German expressionism, however. Kaiser ended *Gas II* (1920), his sequel to the 1918 play, with the apocalyptic destruction of the world to indicate his growing despair with politics. Toller, a more overtly socialist writer than Kaiser, ironized his disillusionment with socialism in *Hurrah, We Live!* (1927).

The extremes of expressionism and its evident failure to inspire Germans to change their political and social institutions led to a counter reaction. After 1924, as the worst of the postwar inflationary spiral subsided and the new Weimar government began to exert its authority, socialist theatre artists experimented with more dispassionate and objective means of inducing audiences to alter their society. In 1927, Russian Blue Blouse troupes visited Germany, where German-language troupes had been performing the Russian-inspired revues for several years. At Berlin's Volksbühne, director Erwin Piscator (1893–1966) expanded on the techniques of the Blue Blouse troupes to teach straightforward lessons about socialism that emphasized that the working class could exercise power. Piscator used situations of class conflict, film clips of historical scenes, and a panoply of on-stage technological devices to create dramatic history lessons in socialism. Piscator termed his plays documentary "montages," in recognition of his debt to the artistry of film. Like Bertolt Brecht (who borrowed several of his techniques), Piscator fled Germany with the Nazi's rise to power in 1933, but returned after the war.

By the early 1930s, spurred on by the worldwide Depression, Blue Blouse troupes were agitating for revolution and spreading communist propaganda throughout the industrial West. In English, Blue Blouse revues came to be called "agit-prop" plays, short for agitation and propaganda. (The term derives from the Department of Agitation and Propaganda, established by the Soviet Communist Party in 1920.) Agit-prop theatre generally involved stereotypical characters and a chorus of workers in class-conflict situations. Relying on bold gestures, mass chants and tableaux, emblematic props and costuming, most agit-prop pieces were written to be performed by amateur workers' theatre groups in union halls and at factory strikes. Amateur Blue Blouse agit-prop theatre proliferated in the early 1930s in the United States, Canada, England, France, Sweden, and Austria. Germany remained a leader in this theatre movement until 1933, when the Nazis began closing down their troupes.

In addition to amateur theatre, international communism influenced many left-wing theatre artists and groups after 1920. In Ireland, Sean O'Casey (1880–1964) wrote socialist plays for production at the Abbey Theatre. His Dublin trilogy, *The Shadow of a Gunman, Juno and the Paycock*, and *The Plough and the Stars* (1923–1926), presents incidents in the Irish fight for independence from the anti-heroic view of people living in the Dublin slums. In Mexico, Carlos Diaz Dufoo's popular play *Father Merchant* (1929) focused on the socioeconomic relationships of a poor Mexican family. In the U.S., a few socialist plays, such as John Howard Lawson's (1895–1977) *Processional* (1925) and *Inter-*

nationale (1928), departed from the conservative consensus in the 1920s. Socialist hopes also shaped the "living newspapers" of the Federal Theatre Project (FTP) in the United States. The U.S. government organized and funded the FTP in 1935 to create jobs for out-of-work theatre professionals. The living newspapers, which derived from the Blue Blouse form and dramatized such social and economic problems as housing, agriculture, and electrical power through large-cast shows, were among the FTP's most distinctive productions (Figure 9.2). However, the U.S. Congress, fearing the influence of communism in the nation, shut down the FTP in 1939. In England, the agit-prop tradition shaped many socialist troupes, including Joan Littlewood's (1914–2002) Theatre Workshop.

Theatres of anti-imperialism, 1900–1960

In addition to its influence in the West, the Russian Revolution also speeded revolts against imperial domination. By 1914, the imperial powers – chiefly England, France, the Netherlands, Germany, the United States, and Japan – had occupied crucial

Figure 9.2 *Triple-A Plowed Under*, a 1936 "living newspaper" production by the U.S. Federal Theatre Project about the Agricultural Adjustment Act. From Mordecai Gorelik, *New Theatres for Old* (tenth printing, Samuel French, 1952).

islands in the Caribbean and Pacific, solidified their control in most of South Asia, extracted sizeable chunks from the Ottoman and Chinese empires, and carved up nearly all of Africa. Although rebellions against foreign capitalists and merchants had occurred before 1914, nationalistic movements in India, China, and elsewhere gained more leverage against the imperial powers during and shortly after the Great War, when the combatants in Europe needed their help. The war in Europe, however, emboldened Japanese imperialists, who saw the decline of European power in China and the Pacific as a chance to expand their hegemony. The triumph of the Bolsheviks in Russia inspired nationalists in the colonized countries, in part because they, like Marx, identified imperialism with capitalism. If workers in one country had destroyed capitalism, nationalists might destroy imperialism in their own.

Many educated colonials also worked against imperialism after 1914 because they saw widening differences in standards of living, democratic rights, and literacy between the populations of their own countries and those in Japan and the West. In per capita income alone, the developed countries surpassed the rest by 2:1 in 1880. By 1914, the ratio was 3:1 and it rose to 5:1 by 1950. While most westerners enjoyed some individual and political rights, slavery and various forms of serfdom persisted in many parts of the colonial world. Literacy increased rapidly among both sexes and all classes after 1850 in Europe, Japan, and North America, but remained a privilege of the social and economic elite in most areas of Africa, Asia, and Latin America. Although the imperial powers generally believed they were civilizing and improving their subjects, the realities of empire bred racism, exploitation, and degradation.

Revolution against the imperialists had begun in China in 1911 and continued through the 1920s. Led by Dr. Sun Yat-sen, the Nationalist Party fought against western-backed warlords to unify the nation. Sun's politics, like those of many anti-imperialists, mixed liberalism and socialism, but emphasized nationalism above both. For a few years during the 1920s, the Nationalists collaborated with Russian-based communists to purge China of foreign imperialists, an alliance that was revived in 1937 when China refused further Japanese incursions and declared war on Japan. The victory over Japan in 1945 finally ended a century of foreign domination. The Chinese communists, who won the civil war against the nationalists in 1949, benefited throughout this period from the perceived alliance between communism and anti-imperialism.

The development of Chinese theatre between 1914 and 1950 followed the political fortunes of the country. As in Japan, western realist theatre had been introduced before the Great War and began to flourish in the 1920s with the founding of modern theatres, an increase in translations of western plays, the establishment of new training centers for actors, and the eventual casting of women in female roles. *Jingxi* (Beijing Opera), however, remained the dominant genre throughout China. Several communist troupes emerged in the 1930s to protest Japanese imperialism; their "living newspapers," modeled on the Soviet example, appealed to thousands in the countryside and in cities unoccupied by the Japanese. Following China's declaration of war in 1937, nationalists and communists used theatre to rally patriotic support against the Japanese.

Within communist-controlled areas of the country, Chinese artists developed a new form of theatre based on the fusion of *jingxi* and *yangge*, an ancient rice-planting song. Featuring 20 to 30 dancers accompanied by drums, flute, and other instruments, *yangge* plays typically involved disputes among villagers over abusive social practices and village ethics, performed in a question-and-response pattern. One *yangge* drama, *The White-Haired Girl* (1944), formed the basis for the emergence of a new national drama called *geju*, or song-opera, which flourished after the communist victory in 1949. By the 1960s, state-sponsored *geju* performances featured thousands of professional and amateur performers, integrated the music and dance traditions of several minority groups within China, and both embodied and propagated Mao Zedong's ideology of strength through collective effort. More than a thousand performers staged *The East Is Red* in 1964, for example, a nationally famous spectacle.

In India, the introduction of western-style spoken drama spawned two closely related theatrical movements in the late nineteenth century. The first, anti-colonial drama, resisted English culture and British rule. This began with an 1872 production of *Indigo Mirror* (*Nil Darpan*), by Calcutta playwright Dinabendhu Mitra (1830–1873), which focused on the plight of peasant workers oppressed by British indigo planters. In 1905, the British banned a later anti-imperialist play, *Sirajuddaula* by Bengali playwright Girish Chandra Ghosh (1844–1912), for inciting Indian nationalism. Anti-colonial nationalism intensified in India after the Great War and the Russian Revolution and reached a peak during World War II. In 1943, The Communist Party of India founded the Indian People's Theatre Association (IPTA), which established regional centers throughout the country to produce anti-colonial plays. Perhaps its best known production was Bijon Bhattacharya's (1917–1978) *New Harvest* in 1944, which incited anger against British failures to help the starving during a Bengali famine that killed more than three million. The IPTA celebrated the independence of India from colonial rule in 1947.

The second type of spoken play popular in India was social drama, which criticized the inequalities of India's traditional socio-economic system. Our second case study, "Social Drama in Kerala," traces the development of this form of liberal protest theatre in southwestern India from the late nineteenth century through the 1960s. Several local peoples' theatres, such as the Little Theatre Group in Calcutta, continued to produce social drama after 1970.

Anti-imperialist theatre flourished in many colonized countries after World War II and helped to liberate them from external political domination. We will examine some of these theatres in Part IV.

Postwar theatre in Japan and Germany

Unlike the Great War, World War II (1939–1945) had little major impact on the national theatres of most countries in the West. No such continuity existed for the national theatrical cultures of Germany and Japan, however. The advent of Nazism in 1933 closed left-wing and avant-garde theatres in Germany, silencing or scattering into exile many of Germany's best theatre artists. Japanese ultranationalists began restricting democratic rights and censoring all forms of Japanese theatre soon after the seizure of Manchuria from China in 1931. In 1940, the Japanese government closed two left-wing *shingeki* troupes and imprisoned their leaders. Until its defeat in 1945, Imperial Japan censored all theatrical productions and even turned performances of traditional noh plays to patriotic purposes.

After the war in the Pacific, U.S. occupational forces helped to rebuild Japanese theatres, but censored productions that they believed would retard the growth of constitutional democracy in Japan. Because many kabuki plays celebrated the values of revenge, feudalism, emperor worship, and the subjugation of women, kabuki theatre in general was suppressed, while the western-derived, realist *shingeki* was allowed to flourish. The most popular *shingeki* playwright of the postwar era was Mishima Yukio (1925–1970). Like several other of his plays, *The Deer Cry Pavilion* (1956) featured romantic intrigue and psychological intensity. Mishima, an ultranationalist who despised western liberalism and longed for a return to samurai values, also adapted the stories of noh plays into *shingeki*, using modern settings and psychology Kinoshita Junji (1914–) moved beyond the realist constraints of *shingeki* in several folktale dramas of the 1950s, but returned to realism in 1970 with *Between God and Man*, one of the few dramatic attempts to come to terms with Japanese war crimes.

Although *shingeki* remained the dominant style in the 1950s, many Japanese artists came to believe that its realist, materialist conventions could not adequately explain their nation's defeat, the postwar occupation of Japan, and the shock and devastation of Hiroshima and Nagasaki. Anti-*shingeki* artists began to collaborate after Japanese radicals and workers staged mass protests in 1960 against the ratification of the United States–Japan Mutual Security Treaty. During the 1960s, some of these artists wrote and directed plays that fused traditional Japanese and international modernist elements. Betsuyaku Minoru's (1937–) *The Elephant* (1962), for instance, deals with the horrors of nuclear contamination in a style inspired by kyogen forms and Beckett's *Waiting for Godot*. Several plays in the 1960s and 1970s feature mortals who are transformed into gods as a means of explaining a disgraceful past and formulating a plan for the future of Japan. In Akimoto Matsoyo's *Kaison, the Priest of Hitachi* (1965), for example, a young man escapes from his historical burden of war guilt into mythic time to become Kaison, a twelfth-century warrior. By the late 1960s new companies, such as *Tenjō Sajiki*, the Situation Theatre, and the Black Tent Theatre, were experimenting with forms of staging and actor–audience relationships that had traveled a long way from the realist conventions of *shingeki* (See Chapter 11).

In East and West Germany after 1945, local governments quickly rebuilt their playhouses as a matter of civic pride, but a national German theatre emerged more slowly. Until the mid 1950s, the Berliner Ensemble was the only German theatre with an international reputation. Soon after Bertolt Brecht established the Ensemble in 1949, it became the most influential socialist theatre of the postwar era. Working as both playwright and director, Brecht exposed the contradictions of capitalism and explored theatrical means of animating audiences to political action (Figure 9.3). In his theoretical writings, Brecht attacked what he took to be Aristotelian dramatic theory and called for a mode of performing that differed sharply from Stanislavsky's "system." "Brecht Directs Mother Courage" is the final case study of this chapter.

Brechtian theatre had its origins in Piscator's documentary theatre of the 1920s and early 1930s, which, in turn, partly derived from Schiller's close attention to historical dynamics in his Weimar Classicism dramas. In the 1960s, a new generation of German theatre artists also looked to the documentary tradition of the German stage to question their parents about the Holocaust and the Nazi past. Several socialist playwrights, including Rolf Hochhuth (1931–) and Peter Weiss (1916–1982), used documentary devices to expose the extent to which thousands of ordinary Germans, not just the Nazis in command, had been responsible for the extermination of millions of Jews, Slavs, Gypsies, and other minorities. A firestorm of controversy swirled around Hochhuth's play, *The Deputy*, when it opened in 1963. The play drew on documentary evidence to suggest that many German Catholics and even the Pope himself had condoned the slaughter of European Jewry. In *The Investigation* (1965), Peter Weiss used dialog taken directly from official transcripts of the investigations into the Auschwitz extermination camp. In their lack of spectacle, both *The Deputy* and *The Investigation* suggest that emotion-laden pictures of the Holocaust, whether photographs or films, would detract from the necessity to probe Germany's guilty past; to understand an event of such magnitude and to prevent a recurrence of the attitudes that fostered it requires close attention to the logic and morality of its perpetrators. Other German documentary plays of the 1960s used similar methods to focus audience attention on English war crimes, European imperialism, the development of the hydrogen bomb in the U.S., and the U.S. war in Vietnam. This socialist "theatre of fact," as it was called, generally shunned complex media effects to rely on the theatre's oldest weapons, the actor's voice and the moral imagination of the audience.

Figure 9.3 Helene Weigel singing as Mother Courage in Brecht's staging of *Mother Courage and Her Children* in Berlin, 1949. From the Willy Saeger Archive. © the Deutsches Theatermuseum.

Although some of the techniques of the "theatre of fact" departed from the general aesthetic approach of the Berliner Ensemble, Brechtian and documentary German theatre shared the same general moral and political point of view in the 1960s. The Berliner Ensemble was located in East Berlin, but many socialist artists in both East and West Germany looked to the productions of the Ensemble as a model for their work. In addition to Brecht's plays, the Berliner Ensemble regularly produced the dramas of Shakespeare and the German classics. Brecht's death in 1956 and his wife Helene Weigel's assumption of the leadership of the Ensemble did not diminish the influence of Brechtian theatre (and may even have enhanced it). In East Germany, the work of playwright Heiner Müller (1929–1995) and director Peter Palitzsch (1918–) (who began with the Ensemble and later

moved to West Germany) derived from, but went beyond Brecht. In the West, playwrights Tankred Dorst (1925–) and Peter Handke (1942–) joined Hochhuth and Weiss in their embrace of Brechtian politics. In postwar Germany, Brechtian theatre crossed the cold war divide.

Theatre and the Cold War

The political antagonism between the two victorious superpowers of World War II, the Soviet Union and the United States, quickly hardened into a world-wide ideological struggle between authoritarian socialism and liberal capitalism. Other nations of the world were pressured to align themselves with Russia or the U.S.; a few like India remained neutral, but most succumbed to military might, economic power, and/or diplomatic leverage. Although the mix of alliances and nuclear terror that emerged by the early 1950s prevented another world war, both superpowers injected their influence and sometimes their troops into regional and civil wars, which proliferated under the general stalemate of the cold war. By the 1960s, most politicians and much of the population in both Russia and the U.S. viewed all conflicts within and beyond their borders – whether nationalist, anti-imperialist, ethnic and racial, or even gender-based – through the "us-versus-them" lens of the cold war.

The cold war stifled innovative theatre in both the Soviet Union and the U.S. The ideology of socialist realism, plus censorship and control, kept most Soviet theatre within the boundaries of cold war communism, even after the death of Stalin and the "thaw" in international relations that eased internal repression in 1956. While approving of Brecht's Marxism, the Soviets kept Brechtian theatre at arm's length; they recognized that its anti-militarism and democratic socialism subverted their authoritarian power. Although U.S. theatre artists generally thought of themselves as apolitical, self-censorship and the reigning authority of the market in theatrical capitalism restrained criticism in the 1950s and most of the 1960s. Under cold war liberalism, most productions supported notions of individual success, consumer choice, and corporate power, while accepting limits on democracy and on the power of the government to change patterns of economic inequality and traditional racist behavior. These liberal values were apparent in most light-hearted musical comedies and in the intense psychological dramas that relied on "method" acting for their success. A few playwrights dissented from this liberal consensus, notably Tennessee Williams, with his attacks on homophobia and consumerist values, and Lorraine Hansberry (1930–1965), whose portrayals of African-American life owed more to international socialism than to the liberal civil rights movement that had begun to change U.S. society. By the late 1960s, several radical groups that rejected cold war liberalism – such as the Living Theatre, the San Francisco Mime Troupe, and the revolutionary Black Arts company in Harlem – were also flourishing on the margins of the dominant culture.

Despite American and Soviet pressure on other countries to shape their culture and society according to the ideological dictates of either superpower, many theatre artists sought an alternative to this rigid binary. Brechtian theatre emerged for many as a means of both opposing the international power of American militarism and capitalism and of building a democratic, rather than an authoritarian socialism at home. Following the influential European tour of the Berliner Ensemble in 1956, English playwrights John Arden (1930–) and Edward Bond (1934–) joined with director Joan Littlewood and others to improve the democratic socialism that had begun to flourish in the United Kingdom after the war. Italian Giorgio Strehler (1921–1997) and Finnish Ralf Langbacka (1932–) directed productions of Brecht's plays to influence socialist theatre and politics in Italy and Finland. In the late 1960s, Nigerian playwright Femi Osofisan (1946–), together with other playwrights and left-wing critics in Nigeria, borrowed heavily from Brecht to shape a post-colonial, class-based critique of Nigerian politics and economics in their plays and essays. After 1956, artists in the Soviet bloc of Eastern Europe also began exploring Brechtian aesthetics in the hope of moving their societies toward more democratic practices. These included playwrights Vaclav Havel in Czechoslovakia and Slawomir Mrozek (1932–) in Poland.

In Latin America, long dominated by U.S. interests, Brechtian theatre was especially influential during the 1960s. Argentinean playwright and director Osvaldo Dragun modeled many of his short plays in the 1950s and 1960s on Brecht's dramas to point up the sacrifice in human dignity demanded by capitalist economics. Brechtian theatre influenced several Mexican playwrights and directors, Luisa Josefina Hernandez (1928–) among them, whose *Popul Vuh* (1966) dramatized the traditional sacred book of the Mayan people. Brecht's model of socialist theatre also inspired several directors and playwrights in Colombia in the 1960s. Enrique Buenaventura (1925–) led the charge, staging Brechtian productions, writing plays with revolutionary messages, and helping to reorganize the university theatre movement in Colombia for radical purposes. Although the authorities suppressed the collective theatre movement Buenaventura had helped to begin, its legacy continued in Bogotá and other major cities, with radical street theatre and plays that dramatized Colombia's oppressive history. In São Paulo, Brazil, the Arena Theatre modified its use of Brechtian techniques to search for a specifically Brazilian stage language for social criticism. International activist Augusto Boal (1931–) joined Arena in 1956, wrote and directed several politically-radical plays, and began experimenting with participatory forms of theatre. Boal broke from the master playwright-director tradition (that included Brecht) to create theatre with the audience. The Brazilian military dictatorship forced Boal into exile in 1971, and he soon published *The Theatre of the Oppressed* (1974), which laid out his techniques for directly involving and empowering spectators. Both Buenaventura and Boal would have enormous influence in the New Popular Theatre movement in Latin America during the 1970s and 1980s.

1968 and its consequences

In 1968, groups of students and workers in several cities, many supported by radical theatre troupes, mounted demonstrations and rebellions against the cold war order. In New York and Paris, students and others rioted to protest U.S. military intervention in Vietnam and French acquiescence to U.S. policies. In Tokyo and Mexico City, there were violent demonstrations against the political and economic imperialism of the U.S. In Prague, Czechoslovakia, workers and students first celebrated their apparent liberation from Soviet oppression and then battled tanks in the streets when Warsaw Pact troops invaded to restore Russian hegemony. Although these demonstrations and rebellions lacked international coordination, they did express widespread opposition to American and Russian militarism and imperialism. They also expressed the hope, inflected differently in each society, for more democratic and peaceful alternatives to the cold war system of international order. Immediate military and political realities sparked the protests, but they also reflected dissatisfaction resulting from the rising expectations of the postwar economic boom and the growing distance between the ideals of both liberal and communist societies, and the realities of everyday life under both systems.

Despite the utopian hopes of many of the protesters, few major political and economic changes occurred, primarily because the structures and mindset of the cold war impeded substantial change. The Soviet Union tightened its control over Eastern Europe, and the U.S. reasserted its hegemony in Japan and Latin America. In several countries south of its borders, the U.S. subverted democratic socialism and replaced it with repressive dictators in the 1970s and 1980s. In these decades, many theatre activists with international reputations – including Vaclav Havel, Augusto Boal, Enrique Buenaventura, and the artists of the Living Theatre – were arrested or repressed. In the wake of 1968, the U.S. and Eastern Bloc governments increased their grants to innovative theatre artists, partly as a means of controlling their politics. The cold war would continue for another 20 years before the Soviet Union collapsed, from both internal and international pressures.

In the long run, reaction in the West against the perceived excesses of 1968 helped to undercut commitment to the goals of liberalism and socialism, the twin anchors of western politics for 90 years. After a brief progressive interlude in the 1970s, this response led to more reactionary politics in the West and Japan. Influenced by capitalist marketing techniques, populations began to view themselves more as consumers and less as citizens, a necessary self-definition for political involvement in both liberal and socialist societies. Linked to consumerism was the rise of identity politics – the individual's identification with a traditional racial, ethnic, or social group – which debilitated the rational calculation inherent in liberal politics and dispersed the class-consciousness necessary for democratic socialism. As we will see in Part IV, the initial hopes aroused by 1968 animated many theatre groups toward radical politics. Many theatre and performance artists began to take up social justice issues. By the last decade of the century, those included issues raised by globalization.

BMc

Key references

For further references for this chapter, see the Key references at the end of the Introduction to Part III.

CASE STUDY: Ibsen's *A Doll House*: If Nora were a material girl

INTERPRETIVE APPROACH: Cultural materialism

The following analysis of Ibsen's *A Doll House* represents the critical approach known as cultural materialism. The term was suggested by British critic Raymond Williams in his studies of modern drama (Williams 1977:1–7).

"Cultural" is used here not in reference to the arts and literature or the aesthetic appreciation of these but as the cultural anthropologist uses it – to point to all those social practices through which a society expresses its understanding of itself. The cultural materialist looks at literary works as social practices, to be read as representations of social formations and the structures beneath their surfaces, structures that serve the interests of power. In this approach, aesthetic evaluations of art take a back seat to concerns with oppressive social structures.

"Materialism" derives from (but is not now limited to) the economic and cultural theories of Karl Marx and Friedrich Engels. A society's thinking and institutions are said to be determined by its basic economic organization, its material production. These materialist forces are considered the real determinants of social conditions in human history, as opposed to any "idealist" or airy philosophies. One of Marx's famous tenets, first offered in 1859, was: "It is not the consciousness of men that determines their being, but, on the contrary, their social being that determines their consciousness" (Marx 1950:328–329). In any given historical society, the social formations, the social practices, and the human consciousness in general that arise from its economic, material basis may be described as constituting an "ideology." In the Marxist critique of modern capitalist economies, those who control the means of production (the "bourgeoisie") determine the values and laws and control all institutions, rather than the working class. All social practices are seen as constructed to

▷

▷

sustain this ruling class and its interests. Many in the West today reject such determinism because of their belief in individual freedom and potential. Marxism has long been suspect in the United States because it is the basis for socialist thinking and for communism, known chiefly in the failed, totalitarian version of the former Soviet Union.

Today's materialist criticism represents developments germane to but well beyond early Marxism. Today's materialist critic seeks to understand how literature is both a product of, and a participant in a wide range of social formations and practices, from a society's language to its constructions of gender, race, ethnicity, or nationhood. The materialist typically draws on many other kinds of approaches, such as language studies, psychological criticism, or feminist criticism, usually in tandem with considerations of economic and class structures.

The cultural materialist urgently wants to make the point that any ideology, like language itself, is not based in some divinely-ordained truth but is a cultural construct that can be challenged as such. This is important because an ideology that serves those in power in a society is likely to have so pervasively shaped each individual's mental picture of lived experience as to seem "natural" rather than culturally constructed. Michel Foucault wrote of institutionalized "discursive formations," structures that determine the field of available knowledge, which function automatically, but which have such power that individuals cannot think or speak without obeying the unspoken "archive" of rules and constraints. Codes for class membership would be an obvious example, but many formations run deeper. Much of what is taken as western knowledge of sexuality is determined by a nexus of forces, including religions. The western idea of an "author," Foucault points out, carries with it expectations that lead to a desire for the power to establish immortal, stable truths (see the Chapter 8 case study. "Discoursing on Desire" for more on Foucault). To take an example from the area of gender discourse, many men feel entitled to "hit on" women or to gaze at them in flagrant sexual perusal. These presumed entitlements flow out of a large, supportive apparatus of oppressive, gender-related practices – an ideology – in which men assume they have the power to treat women as "naturally" subordinate to them. When women say of men who hit on them, "They just don't get it!," they are saying, with frustration, that such men are so much the product of this ideology that they are hardly conscious of the larger implications of their treatment of women. (For more on the concept of ideology, see the next case study, "Social Drama in Kerala, India.")

This raises the issue of individual agency: if men and women are so deeply conditioned by the ideology, can either escape it? Recognizing when art and literature are reinforcing such an ideology is one way to begin to escape its effects. Some materialist critics have written appreciations of the ways in which complex art critiques such ideologies.

Raymond Williams has shown how the ideology of liberal humanism operates in modern liberal tragedy (realism). Williams notes that Arthur Miller's plays immerse us in the private

▷

▷ world of an individual, such as Willy Loman in *The Death of a Salesman*. Willy embodies the liberal humanist dream of self-fulfillment, a dream that omits any consideration of material limitations. Seeking that fulfillment in a flawed society that he cannot change, the hero ultimately destroys himself. The liberal dream of self-fulfillment inevitably leads to the death of the hero as the last attempt at verifying the self. At this point, Williams writes, "liberal tragedy has ended in its own deadlock." In this liberal humanist vision, "we are all victims" (Williams 1966:103–105).

Cultural materialism's practitioners do not rule out considerations of transcendent truth and beauty in literature, but they do foreground issues of social justice believing that traditional humanistic, aesthetic criticism has been impotent if not complicit in the face of social oppression. Materialist studies of literature may be seen today as part of the whole field of cultural studies.

In general, in studies of literature and art, cultural materialist critics ask:

KEY QUESTIONS

1   What ideologies are inherent in the subject or the form of the work?

2   How does the work, in effect, *consolidate* or reinforce dominant social values of a society?

3   Where in the work are they *subverted* or *resisted*, if at all?

In the mid-1890s, an enterprising canned foods company in Paris, Compagnie Liebig, was offering playing-card size color illustrations of scenes from well-known plays ("*tragédies célèbres*") to purchasers of its canned products, such as corned beef. One card depicted the last scene in *A Doll House*, in which a forceful Nora is telling her startled husband why she is about to leave him (Figure 9.4). In an oval frame above the scene, with its realistically detailed living room, is the stern-faced image of Ibsen; below is a picture of one of the company's products. On the reverse is a play synopsis and advertising for Liebig ("Capital: 25 million francs").

How is it that an enterprising capitalist company in France could appropriate a play that, when it premiered in 1879, had shocked audiences in Scandinavia, Germany, and England with its story of a wife abandoning her husband and children? The controversy had even caused Ibsen to write an alternative, sentimental ending in which Nora, after looking in on her children one more time, falls to her knees, unable to leave. Ibsen despised this ending but preferred to do it himself when a German actress threatened to provide her own ending in which Nora did not leave (revisions that softened the ending were done as recently as 1976). How could Ibsen's controversial play help the Liebig Company get its corned beef into the kitchen of every good French housewife?

First, by the early 1890s, progressive playgoers in Paris, Berlin, and London had seen more of Ibsen's plays, thanks in large part to the visionary producers

Figure 9.4 In the mid-1890s, a canned food company in Paris, the Compagnie Liebig, offered this pocket-size trading card, depicting the final scene from Ibsen's *A Doll House*, with the purchase of one of its products. © Gary Jay and Josephine S. Williams.

André Antoine, Otto Brahm, and J.T. Grein. They had created private producing societies to stage the controversial plays of the new realists and naturalists in small, low-budget theatres that, being private, were free from government censorship. Courageous actresses had undertaken *A Doll House* in commercial venues in the late 1880s and early 1890s, including Janet Achurch, Eleonora Duse, and Elizabeth Robins in London, and Minnie Maddern Fiske in New York. In 1894, about the time that Liebig issued its advertising cards, *A Doll House* was performed in a commercial production in Paris that had some popular success, due to the appeal of the popular young actress, Gabrielle Réjane. In her Nora

there were strong notes of eroticism and fear, and, in the end, she was an unbroken, rebellious woman who was freeing herself. Her director, Herman Bang, wrote that for Réjane, "the play became a work about revolt" (Marker and Marker 1989: 60–61). French male critics were not threatened though. They found Nora's behavior both sexually indelicate and too extreme for the circumstances; one saw in Nora "a kind of intellectual hysteria" peculiar to Scandinavian women (Marker and Marker 1989:62; Shepherd-Barr 1997:30–31).

But the reason Liebig was comfortable about appropriating Ibsen's play probably goes deeper than Ibsen's increasing visibility. Inherent in its advertising is what British cultural materialists have called "liberal humanism," and liberal humanism has cordial relations with capitalism.

The myth of liberal humanism

The term "liberal humanism" is used to describe the notion that every individual has the potential, unimpeded by any material barriers, to achieve self-fulfillment. For those who subscribe to this, life is a kind of divinely-ordained game plan that rewards spunk. However, such an account of reality obscures or omits the material conditions that limit the scope of individual agency. Spunk may count for little if you are a female in a male-dominated business. Like television commercials, such an account comes with no label warning you that your dreams of economic autonomy may be illusory. The dream of driving your off-road SUV over a rocky mountain trail to a secluded beach is in stark contrast with your daily commute in it through urban traffic to the job that allows you to make the payments on it. A complex social formation will disguise the material realities, just as they are disguised by Christmas illusions in the Helmer household.

The myth of liberal humanism is inherent in Nora's miraculous transformation from a child-like wife, imprisoned in a Victorian culture where she has long been infantilized by her father and husband, into a budding, self-reliant intellectual, who leaves her home, husband, and three small children to take charge of her own destiny. This transformation, we are to believe, occurs over three days, during the Christmas of 1879. There is, finally, not much ideological difference between Ibsen's liberal humanist dream of Nora's autonomous leap toward liberation and self-realization and the promise in Liebig's advertising cards, in which Liebig's product is associated with self-fulfillment, such as going to the theatre promises.

To be sure, Ibsen unfolds with sophisticated craft the material circumstances entrapping Nora. In the first scene, we see Nora as a homemaker and blissful shopper. Her responsibilities are to please her husband, buy Christmas gifts for her children, and ready the tree. Raised by her father – the absence of her mother is never explained – and by her nanny, Anne Marie, who now tends Nora's children, Nora still seems emotionally childlike at times, secretly eating her macaroons. Torvald refers to his wife in trivializing diminutives, as "my little squirrel," and his "little lark" (Ibsen 1978:125–126). She has long since known how to play upon her sexuality and take advantage of the inconsequentiality men assign to her, as she does when she manipulates her husband for the extra money that she will use to pay off her secret loan. She takes pride in having saved Torvald's life when his health broke from overwork. She may believe she has "worked the system," but it is she who is being worked by ideologies long in place. Her husband is sovereign in the household; on his side are the full force of tradition, state law, and scriptural passages on wifely obedience by St. Paul (*Ephesians*, 5:22–33). What marginal power Nora has she derives from the ways a male-dominated culture constructs her: she is sexualized on the one hand and idealized on the other, subject in both to the pleasure and convenience of men. Male-constructed capitalist and domestic formations encircle her. The play takes place during Christmas, a traditional Christian family feast day. In the setting of the premiere production in Copenhagen in 1879, a copy of Rafael's portrait of the Madonna and child hung over the fireplace, reinforcing the "natural" order of things (Figure 9.5).

Were Nora a material girl of the 1870s, that is, were she an actual person functioning within all the social formations of the time, she would have had no access to an education or job-ladder that would have trained *her* to head a bank. In the male world of business, it was unthinkable to hire a woman to manage other people's property or money. As a married woman in Norway in 1879, she could own property only jointly with her husband. Mrs. Linde observes in Act I, "a wife can't borrow money without her husband's consent" (Ibsen 1978:135),

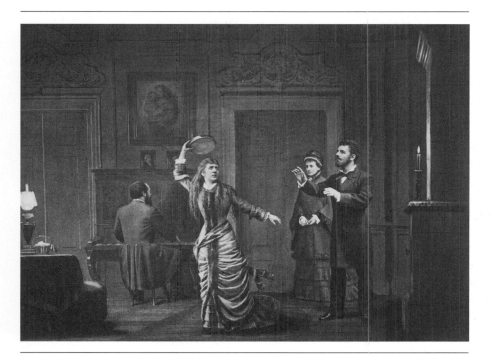

Figure 9.5 Nora dancing the tarantella, with Rafael's portrait of the Madonna and Child in the background. From the premiere production of *A Doll House* in Copenhagen, 1879. At the piano, Dr Rank (Peter Jerndorff), Nora dancing (Betty Hennings), Mrs Linde (Agens Dehn), and Helmer (Emil Poulsen). © Teatermuseet i Hofteatret, Copenhagen.

and that was typical. Ibsen's Nora was able to provide security for the secret loan that saved her husband's life only by forging her then-dead father's signature.

Krogstad knows how to ruin Nora. Desperate in the face of his blackmail, she briefly considers suicide but has not the courage. She resorts to sexually tantalizing the dying Dr. Rank, trying to extract money from him (the silk-stocking scene in Act 2 – once omitted by some translators). Beneath the painting of the Madonna and Child, she raises her tambourine and dances the tarantella wildly, desperate to distract Torvald from seeing Krogstad's letter (Figure 9.5). When the truth is finally revealed that Nora forged her father's signature for the loan to save Torvald's life, Torvald shatters her last

desperate illusion. So far from understanding that her subterfuge was for his sake, Torvald explodes in rage about the loss of his honor. The "miracle" Nora hoped for did not happen and never could have. To his credit, Ibsen has revealed a great deal about Nora's material circumstances.

But not all. He gives Nora her famous exit. He asks us to believe that Nora evolves in this crucible of three days and three acts to the point that she can sit her husband down for the famous Act 3 discussion and begin it with three shattering insights, "I've been your wife-doll here, just as I was Papa's doll-child. And in turn the children have been my dolls" (ibid.:191). Nora comes to this famous discussion having done nothing less than deconstruct her social identity. For Ibsen's Nora, and for all the real Noras at the time of Ibsen's play, one could only grant this kind of overnight progress if one subscribed to the gospel of liberal humanism. True, as feminist critic Annelise Maugue writes, Ibsen's play had important symbolic value for women: "Nora's action, her improbable departure, symbolized this necessary change in attitude" (Maugue 1993:523). Late nineteenth-century feminists admired the play and predicted that it would have reformative effects. But Annelise Maugue adds the important material point that, on the whole, Nora's leaving "is precisely the step that real women could not imagine, let alone take."

Had Nora been a real woman in Victorian Norway, it would have been very difficult for her to have supported herself on the other side of Torvald's door. Ibsen's Nora has earned some money of her own with "odd jobs – needlework, crocheting, embroidery and such," and with copy work, as she tells Mrs. Linde. But, as Torvald's pet, she has had no experience with basic account-keeping; when Mrs. Linde asks her how much of the 250 pound loan she has managed to pay off, Nora replies: "These accounts, you know, aren't easy to figure. I only know I've paid out all I could scrape together" (Ibsen 1978:137). Job prospects for real Noras were poor. Census data for four French cities at the end of the nineteenth century show that one out of every two women was single, widowed, or divorced, and therefore seeking employment. In England in 1851, 40 percent of the women who were working were domestic servants; 22 percent were textile factory operatives. The typical weekly wage for working-class women in the Victorian era was a little over twelve shillings, well below the very comfortable middle-class income to which Ibsen's Nora is accustomed. In the cotton mills of Glasgow and Manchester, staffed largely by women and children, average wages were between eleven and twelve shillings a week. A London shirtmaker told an interviewer in 1849 that her normal hours were from five in the morning

until nine at night, and in the summer she often worked "from four in the morning to nine or ten at night – as long as I can see." Still she was barely able to support herself (Yeo and Thompson 1972: 122–123). The low wages – not the hard work – drove many such women to prostitution.

Ibsen does bring into focus briefly the economic circumstances of two other women within his play. Mrs. Linde married her husband not for love (which astonishes Nora) but because her mother was bedridden, and she had two younger brothers to support. Now widowed, she seeks a clerical job, which she gets only through Nora's strenuous intercession with Torvald. The nurse to the Helmer's children, Anne-Marie, had to give her own illegitimate child away in order to get employment: "A girl who's poor and who's gotten into trouble is glad enough for that" (Ibsen 1978:155). Nora hears this in a conversation with Anne-Marie at the point when she is glimpsing the unspeakable consequences of Krogstad's blackmail. But when she walks out the door, she will be subject to the same employment conditions. In the late 1870s, courageous women were leading movements in Europe and the U.S. to improve women's working conditions and change the laws, but Nora would not have benefited from them for another decade. Ibsen's Nora has no ties to such a sisterhood, nor would she have thought to seek them.

Even for those women who had more intellectual resources than the real Noras, circumstances were not much different, as is clear in Ibsen's own *Hedda Gabler* (1890). One could find no more relevant and poignant example than the real-life case of the woman on whom Ibsen based Nora. Laura Kieler (then Petersen) wrote a novel called *Brand's Daughters* that was a sequel to Ibsen's play, *Brand* (1866). She visited him in Dresden in 1871, and they apparently came to know each other very well. Ibsen called her his "lark" and encouraged her to write more (Meyer 1971:443). After she married, her husband became ill with tuberculosis, and she was advised to take him to a warmer climate to save his life. To do so, she secretly obtained a loan (on the security of a friend). Her husband survived, but two years later Laura sent a manuscript to Ibsen, written hastily under the pressure of needing to pay off her loan, begging his help to get it published. Ibsen judged it a poor work and declined. Laura then burned the manuscript and forged a check to pay off the loan. When the forgery was discovered, she told her husband what she had done. She suffered a nervous breakdown, and her husband had her committed to an asylum. Ibsen biographer Michael Meyer writes: "After a month, she was discharged . . . and for the children's sake, begged her husband to take her back, which he grudgingly agreed to do" (Meyer 1971:445; see also 634–635). In his liberal humanism, Ibsen had his Nora take "precisely the step that real women could not imagine, let alone take." Not to examine the ideology embedded in the play is to risk perpetuating it.

The very form of modern realistic tragedy perpetuates the ideology, as Raymond Williams has shown. Realism purports to be clinically life-like, providing a transparent window on events. But realism hides its craft-wise operations. With its selective focus, its exposition planted as unobtrusively as possible, its appearance of real time, its linear sequences of cause and effect action that lead (seemingly) to a third act crisis, and its careful construction of credible character psychology, realism does everything it can to make us unaware that its representation of life is anything but "natural." Realism in effect keeps you inside the ideology of the middle-class world that it represents. With its focus on character psychology, it is not a mode well suited to showing how social formations have been constructed or how they might be dismantled. It is not that realism would do so if it could; it cannot do so and still meet the requirements of the form. Williams has shown that modern liberal tragedy as a whole, from A Doll House through Arthur Miller's Death of a Salesman (1949), tracks the individual

struggling toward the fulfillment of desire but ultimately defeated, a victim of social formations that are never addressed (Williams 1966:87–105; 1969: 331–347). There are final rites of sympathy for the victim, but the materialist argues that it is not enough to leave the theatre having feasted on empathy and fatalism. Williams shows the inherent contradictions between all the talk of social reform in modern liberal tragedy and the invisible limitations of the form. Williams's one-time student, Terry Eagleton, summarizes the argument:

> The discourse of the play may be urging change, criticism, rebellion; but the dramatic forms – [that] itemize the furniture and aim for an exact "verisimilitude" – inevitably enforce upon us a sense of the unalterable solidity of this social world, all the way down to the color of the maid's stockings.
>
> (Eagleton 1983:187)

The end of A Doll House leaves both Nora and Torvald Helmer grasping for understanding of what has destroyed their marriage. Torvald is nearly speechless as his wife closes the door behind her. Ibsen's American translator, Rolf Fjelde, preferred the title A Doll House to the more common A Doll's House as the translation of Ibsen's title, Et Dukkehjem, because the title without the possessive points not just to Nora but to the entire household – husband, wife, servants, and the whole set of social formations to which all are subject (Ibsen 1978:121).

In the context of the struggle for women's rights in the West in recent decades, Ibsen's play has had special interest for many directors and actresses, but they have run headlong into the problem of whether Nora's leaving is any liberation at all (Figure 9.6). The answer of Austrian playwright and Nobel prize winner, Elfriede Jelinek, is understandable. In the late 1970s, she wrote a sequel to Ibsen's play, entitled What Happened After Nora Left Her Husband, or Pillars of Society. In it, Nora works in a factory, marries an

Figure 9.6 In Henrik Ibsen's *A Doll House*, Nora (Caitlin O'Connell) has just returned home from Christmas shopping. Both Nora and her husband, Torvald (Richard Bekins), were in anguish at the end of this 1991 production of Baltimore's Center Stage, directed by Jackson Phippin, designed by Tony Straiges. © Center Stage.

industrialist, is forced to become a high-class prostitute, and then turns to anarchism, which fails. At the end, she is back in her stifling home with Torvald, who clearly will soon become a Nazi.

Ibsen was a pioneer reformer in bringing substantive ideas to the theatre. It is not to detract from his achievement that the materialist critic stresses the importance of understanding the limitations of the old liberal humanism and the mode of realism as we find them in *A Doll House*.

GJW

Key references

Eagleton, T. (1983) *Literary Theory, an Introduction*, Minneapolis: University of Minnesota Press.

Foucault, M. (1972) *The Archaeology of Knowledge*, New York: Pantheon Books.

Foucault, M. (1969) "What is an Author?" in H. Adams and L. Searle (eds) (1986) *Critical Theory Since 1965*, Tallahassee: Florida State University Press.

Ibsen, H. (1978) *A Doll House*, trans. R. Fjelde, in *Henrik Ibsen, The Complete Major Prose Plays*, New York: Farrar Straus Giroux.

Marker, F.J. and Marker, L.L. (1989) *Ibsen's Lively Art*, Cambridge: Cambridge University Press.

Marx, K. (1950) "Preface" to *A Contribution to the Critique of Political Economy*, in K. Marx and F. Engels, *Selected Works*, Vol. 1, London: Lawrence and Wishart.

Maugue, A. (1993) "The New Eve and the Old Adam," in G. Fraise and M. Perrot (eds) *Emerging Feminism from*

Revolution to World War, Vol. 4 of G. Duby and M. Perrot (gen. eds) *A History of Women in the West*, Cambridge: Harvard University Press.

Meyer, M. (1971) *Ibsen, a biography*, Garden City, N.Y.: Doubleday & Company.

Shepherd-Barr, K. (1997) *Ibsen and Early Modernist Theatre, 1890–1900*, Westport, Connecticut, Greenwood Press.

Williams, R. (1966) *Modern Tragedy*, Stanford: Stanford University Press.

Williams, R. (1969) *Drama from Ibsen to Brecht*, New York: Oxford University Press.

Williams, R. (1977) *Marxism and Literature*, Oxford: Oxford University Press.

Yeo, E. and Thompson, E.P. (eds) (1972) *The Unknown Mayhew*, New York: Schocken Books. [Henry Mayhew was a journalist famous for his *London Labour and the London Poor* (4 volumes, 1861–1862)].

Audio-visual resources

A 1973 Paramount film of the play, directed by Patrick Garland with Claire Bloom and Anthony Hopkins, is available in a video recording.

CASE STUDY: Social drama in Kerala, India: Staging the "revolution"

There once was a time like this. A time when human lives burned in the 'test fires' of social change.
Tooppil Bhaasi (1924–1992),
playwright and director, Kerala.

This case study examines the complex relationship that drama, theatre, and related public events played in "staging" the social, economic, and political revolutions that helped transform "old" Kerala, India of the late nineteenth century from a feudal, hierarchically-ordered social system into today's "new" Kerala – often called a "model" of social development. I consider theatre both in the narrowly-defined sense of the performance of dramas whose content is overtly political in that they stage a social crisis or revolution, and in the broad sense of related "theatres" of public events in public spaces. Rallies, meetings, marches, protests, and even publications stage a "revolution" in individual and social consciousness in the streets, meeting halls, libraries/reading rooms, and paddy fields. During certain historical periods, public events collectively reflect not some "frozen cultural ideals, but . . . the turbulence that wracks social order during that time and place. . . . [I]t becomes a direct extension of ongoing or emergent struggle that co-opts any and all venues for their conflicts" (Handelman 1990:60). Theatre performances become one public arena for the staging of conflict.

INTERPRETIVE APPROACH: Politics, ideology, history, and peformance

Janelle Reinelt raises several important questions about writing histories of theatre when she asks, "what is the relationship of politics [and ideology] to culture? How does social change result in cultural change – or can various cultural practices initiate or precipitate change?" (1996:1). The old rationalist view of politics or ideology as conscious, well-articulated systems of belief is no longer adequate for analyzing the complex relationship between

▷

▷ how we think, feel, and relate to the material realities of our human condition. A more complex view of "politics" assumes that all forms of cultural practice are "political" in that they are not neutral. The term "ideology" is now understood to encompass both implicit as well as explicit ideas, theories, and assumptions that inform the human subject's consideration and interpretation of his/her condition. Consequently, ideologies constantly shape and (re)form our consciousness of, and relationship to the world. (For more on ideology, see the preceding case study, "Ibsen's *A Doll House*.") Cultural theorist Terry Eagleton argues that what is most important is the place of intersection where ceaseless negotiation takes place, where the possibility exists for a transformation in what and how one thinks, believes, understands, and relates to the world. Eagleton explains that:

> there is one place above all where such forms of consciousness may be transformed almost literally overnight, and that is in active political struggle. . . . When men and women engaged in quite modest, local forms of political resistance find themselves brought by the inner momentum of such conflicts into direct confrontation with the power of the state, it is possible that their political consciousness may be definitely, irreversibly altered. (1991:223–224)

This case study examines how theatre and drama played an active role in helping generate shifts in individual and socio-political consciousness at a local level in Kerala, India during the last century.

The socio-economic system of "old" Kerala

The Malayalam-speaking coastal region of south-western coastal India today, known as the state of Kerala, is a very small geographical region (15,000 square miles), but with a population of approximately 30 million (larger than Canada's, but Canada's land mass is more than 250 times greater). It has the highest density of people per square mile of any state in India. From the eighth century when Hinduism displaced Buddhism and became the dominant religion of Kerala, a highly stratified, hierarchical socio-economic order was gradually established in which people were born into particular *jātis* – actual or potential networks determined by blood ties and marriage. (The Portuguese gave the problematic name "caste" to these kinship lineages.) One's identity was understood to be determined at birth, and

one's standing within a local hierarchy was determined by one's relative "purity" or "pollution" within the entire network of relationships. One's role and work within society were also established by birth into a particular *jāti* (see Table 9.1).

The interlocking system created a complex, permanent set of restrictions and rights, as well as service obligations. Strict rules governed what types of clothes you wore, what temples or shrines you might enter, and those you touched and those with whom you ate, socially interacted, or married. To take food from someone born into a lower *jāti*, or to be touched by an untouchable at the bottom of the scale would be polluting, requiring a process of ritual cleansing for the higher born. Kerala became notorious for the distance that untouchables were required to keep away from a pathway or road when a high-ranking Namboodiri was traveling.

TABLE 9.1 Brief summary of main *jātis*

Categories	Occupation	Kerala name
Non-polluting jātis		
[Brahmins]	Priests/Landholders	Namboociri Brahmins not born in Kerala
[Kshatriyas]	Ruling/landholding royal lineages	Samantars titled Nayars
	High-caste temple servants/performers of *kutiyattam*	Ambalavasis
	Smaller landholders	Nayars (upper ranking)
[Vaisyas]	Artisans/traders	Kammalans [some Syrian Christians and Muslims]
[Sudras]	Middle ranking retainers: soldiers, cooks, barbers, scribes, funeral priests, washer- men, performers of *kathakali*	Nayars (lower ranking)
Higher-polluting jātis		
	Coconut workers	Tiyyas/Izhavas, Thandans
	Tenant farmers	Chovans
	Laborers/astrologers	Kaniyans
Lower-polluting jātis		
[Harijans/Untouchables]	Farm/menial workers	Pulayas or Cherumans
[Tribal peoples]	Farmers/workers	

Only the highest-ranking groups and temples had the right to own land, thereby the right to permanent wealth through agricultural production, or to have such luxuries as a permanent tiled roof. Everyone else living on the land did so only with the permission of those whom they served; therefore, they were subject to eviction. Namboodiri Brahmins were considered most pure, and therefore at the top of the hierarchy. They usually served as priests at large, wealthy temple complexes set within walled compounds – such as the Vadakkun-nathan (Siva) Temple described in Chapter 3, in which entry was restricted to the 'non-polluting' castes. Some Namboodiri Brahmins were also land-lords of large properties. High-ranking princely families (Samantans and royal Nayar lineages) were said to be charged with protecting "brahmins and cows,' that is to say, the social order. Like Namboodiris, lower-ranking castes such as scribes, teachers, barbers, washers, and ritual specialists, as well as retinues of soldiers, served their kingdoms and/or large extended households. Very low-caste farm laborers (Pulayas or Cherumans) were virtually born into servitude to the land and family on whose behalf they would till the paddy-fields, giving to their "lord" a fixed percent of their crop at harvest.

Although inheritance passed along matrilineal lines in some castes (Nayars), and patrilineal lines in others (Namboodiris), absolute power remained concentrated in the hands of the eldest male member of each extended family. Known as the *kārṇavan*, this powerful male figure made all decisions within an extended family such as the right to evict tenant-laborers or arrange marriages.

One obligation of the wealthy landholding castes and temples was to patronize the full set of traditional performances woven into the annual Hindu festival calendar. As discussed in a Chapter 3 case study, *kutiyattam* was offered annually in certain high-caste temples as a visual sacrifice to the main deity, and therefore attendance was prohibited to all "polluting" castes. Kathakali dance-drama (Chapter 5 case study) was patronized by the high-caste princely and landholding families, but performances when held outside temples were open to a relatively wide spectrum of people.

Toward a new Kerala: Social consciousness and social drama in Kerala's "revolution"

Effectively under British colonial rule since 1790, by the nineteenth century Kerala was governed either by direct British rule in Malabar (north), or indirectly through the princely states of Cochin (central) and Travancore (south). Like all India's princely states, the rulers had some independence, but paid taxes and answered to British authority. During the nineteenth century, the idea that it might be possible to re-imagine and reform the old systems of marriage, caste inequalities, or land-distribution, was gradually brought to public awareness through education, the founding of caste-specific reform organizations, journalism, new forms of literature such as the novel and short stories written in the local language (Malayalam), and public protests. Imagining the possibility of a fundamental change within one's socio-economic circumstances has the potential to shake the foundations of one's vision and one's understanding of one's place in the world. One must even re-imagine what that world is and how it is constituted. Along with issues of social reform, the movement toward independence gained momentum and was formalized when the Indian National Congress was founded in 1885, with its share of adherents in Kerala.

Some progressive changes were instituted by a few British and Indian administrators, such as banning compulsory labor and establishing wage-based labor service to the government. While traditional forms of education serving the high-castes such as Namboodiri study of the traditional sacred texts (*Vedas*) continued, new forms of education were introduced throughout the nineteenth century. These included English-language missionary schools and colleges preparing (primarily) Nayars and Christians for administrative service. By the late nineteenth century many Malayalam-language government schools opened, and, in 1902, lower-grade education in Malayalam was mandated. During 1911–1912, caste restrictions in government schools were abolished.

A Hindu religious and social reform movement developed under the leadership of three major public figures. Chattampi Swamikal (1853–1924) who, as a Nayar, rebelled against high-caste Namboodiri dominance on behalf of his own community as well as the lower-caste Ezhavas, wanted all to play an important role in building a new society. His counterpart among the Ezhavas was Sri Narayana Guru (1856–1924) who consecrated a number of shrines offering open entry for all, even the lowest-caste Hindus. The "untouchable" Pulayan, Ayyankali (1866–1941), staged a protest in 1893. He illegally traveled in a bullock cart along a public road when he should have walked, calling out his presence to any high-caste persons so they could avoid coming too close to him. All these reformers established communal organizations dedicated to the cause of social reform and improvement of their own rights and privileges, and those of other lower castes. Even within the high-caste Namboodiri communities, social reform organizations were established to examine their own problems and to re-examine their role within the larger socio-economic system.

Alongside the growth of education, the publication of O. Chandu Menon's (1847–1899) social novel, *Indulekha* (*Crescent Moon*) (Malayalam, 1889), radicalized new literary forms. It follows the development of romantic love between Madhavan and

Indulekha, both members of a joint extended family, the Poorvarangil, who represent the aspirations and attitudes of the then new generation of high-caste Nambooridis receiving an English education. The novel focuses on the tension between conservative forces of tradition in the old order, and the reformist values represented by English education.

Eventually, dramas were staged as one more tactic for moving ideas about social reform into the public domain. *Indulekha* itself was often staged. But it was the 1929 production of *From the Kitchen to the Stage* by V.T. Bhattathirippad Namboodiri, which among other things focused on the tremendous problems caused by arranged marriages, that propelled serious social drama into the forefront of the reform movement. This was one of the first spoken dramas that did not attempt to appeal either to middle-class audiences or to the towns and that was without the broad appeal of the popular, formulaic Tamil-language music-dramas, intended for entertainment. E.M.S. Namboodiripad provides the following account of the original production, staged at the Convention of the Welfare Association at Edakkunni in 1929:

> The reason for its success was nothing but the fact that the actors "lived" their roles, and in portraying the characters they were virtually projecting nothing but their own actual lives . . . women who had never before in their lives attended a meeting or heard any speech, much less seen a drama [witnessed the play]. The idea of fighting polygamy, opposing old persons marrying young girls, and also the idea of love marriage began to be seen by Namboodiri women as possibilities. . . . The transformation that this one, single drama brought about in the minds of the Namboodiri women in so short a period could well be equated with that obtained through the medium of meetings and newspaper propaganda for more than a decade.
> (Namboodiripad 1976:98–99)

By 1930, Kerala's own progressive literary movement was widely recognized as social issues dominated the writing of novels, short stories, drama, and even some poetry. K. Damodaran's play, *Rental Arrears (Pattabakki)*, had a similar impact to that of *From the Kitchen to the Stage*. Banned for a time by the British authorities, it was performed for mass audiences throughout the rural Malabar district. It focuses on the eviction of tenant-laborers from the land. Kuttunni, the young male mainstay of the family, has been forced by its extreme poverty to become a petty thief, trying to steal food for his younger siblings. Caught red-handed and jailed for six months, his sister has no choice but to sell her body to get enough food to feed her younger brother. The play concludes with Kuttunni announcing to his sister, "If poverty is to disappear, then the government we have today must change. . . . We should refashion the social structure!"[1]

The use of drama and education for raising social issues continued with the founding in 1948 of the Kendra Kala Samithi in Kozhikode (Malabar), under the leadership of literary figures such as S.K. Pottekkat, P.C. Kuttikrishnan, and N.V. Krishna Varier. This grass-roots movement centered on the establishment of village libraries and reading rooms, each of which was not only to promote mass literacy and reading, but also was charged with staging one drama each year for which there would be local and district competitions. This movement set the stage for the emergence of Kerala's pre-eminent social dramatist – Tooppil Bhaasi (1924–1992).

Tooppil Bhaasi and the Kerala People's Arts Club

Toopil Bhaasi was born in Vallikkunu, a typical agri-cultural village in south central Kerala, India and part

---

1 It should be noted that the Malayalam translation of Ibsen's *Ghosts* in 1934–1935 by A. Balakrishna Pillai did not inspire dramas of social reform within the progressive movement for performance in both rural and town contexts so much as it did dramas of individual characters and dramatic tension for town consumption.

of the old Travancore kingdom. He received his lower school education in a Sanskrit School, and went on to pass his examination in traditional Indian medicine (Ayurveda). However, Bhaasi never pursued a career in medicine. Rather, like many other young men receiving an education during this turbulent period in Kerala and in Indian history, Bhaasi became a student activist and leader, working in the student congress movement as part of the national drive toward independence from British colonial rule. He later joined the communist movement. By Indian Independence Day (15 August 1947), he was temporarily in the Allappuzha jail. He was arrested for his activities of organizing low-caste agricultural workers, protesting against the hoarding of food grains and black-marketeering by wealthy land-holders, for the cultivation of waste land, and for attempting to overturn the hierarchical caste system, that is, seeking to replace the old Kerala social and economic order with progressive social-democratic models. Between 1946 and 1952, while the Communist Party of India was advocating active and sometimes violent revolutionary struggle, Bhaasi and other activists were forced to live in hiding because some of their activities were declared illegal. While in hiding, in 1952 he wrote his first play, *You Made Me a Communist*, and it was almost immediately produced by the Kerala People's Arts Club (KPAC).

Founded in 1950 by a group of committed student activists at the Law College in Ernakulam Town, KPAC began to produce dramas as one means of raising socio-political issues. The group first used shadow puppets and then staged the political drama, *My Son is Right*. But it was their production of Bhaasi's *You Made Me a Communist* that launched KPAC onto the path toward becoming Kerala's most visible contemporary theatre company. *You Made Me a Communist* enacts the struggles of agricultural laborers and poor peasants for a better life by focusing on how Paramu Pillai, a conservative farmer, makes the decision to become a communist. The play

focuses on his change in socio-political conscious-ness and calls for the revolutionary overthrow of landlordism. With its very loose structure, and with characters who burst into one of its singable thirteen songs at unexpected moments during the course of the story, *You Made Me a Communist* swept across the length and breadth of Kerala. Dr. Radhakrishnan of the Gandhi Centre, New Delhi, recalled his experience of it :

> Even though a child, I could sense the excite-ment! There were nights when KPAC had more than four performances. From one place, they went on moving for months on end. . . . KPAC became a very powerful social inspira-tion for people to fight against social injustice and for their rights. It gave them the feeling that anybody, irrespective of their low birth, [could be] equal.

There can be no doubt that there was a decided sense of "eventness" to attending a performance of *You Made Me a Communist* in 1952–1953. It was not simply a dramatic representation of a fictionalized story and its characters, but part of an unfolding and evolving socio-political revolution as it was happening. Journalist, essayist, playwright, and activist Kaniyapuram Ramachandran explained both the timeliness and excitement generated by this interrelationship between stage and life in Bhaasi's early social dramas, and in *You Made Me a Communist* in particular:

> The fourth element of drama is the audience; and the audience is the fourth character. That dividing line between stage and audience was simply erased! What they saw there was their real lives! The workers, agricultural laborers, people coming onstage and speaking their own dialects and ordinary language – not literary language. The ultimate aim is to make the audience part of the experience. There is no

detachment, but attachment. So with the social issues in the play – it was all so relevant. At the end of a performance the entire audience would come to its feet. So, *You Made Me a Communist* wasn't a drama at all! The social relevance of the play made people forget everything when they saw it. It was a drama for the people, by the people. It gave people what they wanted to see at the right time. It was a magic wand. The audience was like a mental vacuum that sucked up what was given. . . . In 1951 it was so apt! It was the medicine that the patient was waiting for. People were ready for that message of social change.

Bhaasi always wanted the audience to first understand his plays. They should be clear and straight. He was speaking to the heart, and not the intellect. He used to talk to the emotions, and through the emotions, people would change their thinking.

(Interview with the author 1993)

The impact of the production of this play on the Malayalis was remarkable. So important was it for the spread of the communist point of view from 1952 to 1954 that some commentators have suggested that without it the emergence of the first democratically-elected communist government to the newly established state of Kerala in 1957 would never have happened.

Since 1952, *You Made Me a Communist* has been performed well over 2,000 times and continues to be part of KPAC's active repertory of social dramas. Bhaasi went on to become one of Kerala's most important playwrights, providing KPAC with a series of highly popular social dramas, including *The Prodigal Son* (1956) in which a wayward, selfish rowdy is transformed into a champion of the low castes. His *Aswameetam* (1962) explores the social stigma of leprosy. His political satire, *Power House* (1990) focuses on the irresponsible behavior of a government institution – the Kerala State Electricity

Board. *Memories in Hiding* (1992), which won the Kerala Best Play Award, was his final play.

Like *You Made Me a Communist*, *Memories in Hiding* examines the radical change in consciousness of a poor tenant farmer, Ceenan, and re-examines the consequences of the real-life Suranad Revolution in central Travancore (1949–1951) in which Bhaasi took part, and during which a number of agitators and police died. Ceenan is the head Pulayan, an agricultural tenant-laborer who works for a landlord. Like his father before him, he has served this "lord" (*tampuran*) as a "slave" – a translation of the Malayalam *adiyan*, implying servitude for someone of higher status. Pulayans like Ceenan were tenant-laborers who in effect were considered the "property" of their landlords and therefore functioned virtually as slaves (Figures 9.7, 9.8). The moment of his radicalization comes when, after several generations of quiet servitude, the landlord refuses to assist Ceenan in seeking the release of his son who has been falsely arrested for the killing of local police in the Suranad rebellion. Ceenan announces:

> Tamburaan! (*He stares at the landlord and stands up straight. The landlord is puzzled by the expression on his face. Nannu Nayar becomes afraid. Ceenan stares at him for a moment. In a firm declaration:*)
> I no longer have a Tamburaan! I am no longer a slave!!
> (*Stares at him, and slowly walks out, exiting*).
> (Bhaasi 1996:55)

From its nineteenth-century realities as a hierarchically-ordered, feudal social system ridden with caste and class conflicts, with high birth and infant mortality rates, Kerala was gradually transformed into a turn-of-the-twentieth-century social democratic state with radical reductions in population growth and infant mortality rates. Illiteracy was virtually eradicated, and there was extensive land-reform, with the redistribution of considerable land

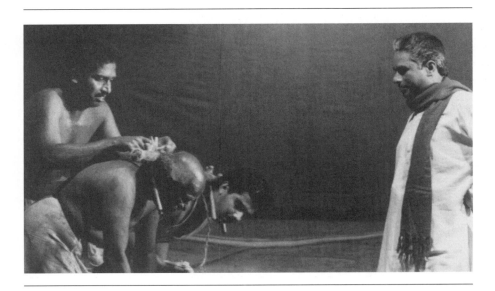

Figure 9.7 In a 1993 production of *Memories in Hiding* by Toopil Bhaasi, in Thiruvananthapuram, Kerala, the Landlord (right with scarf) forces Teevan to yoke together his father, Ceenan, and Paramu Naayar to plough a paddy field. Photo © Phillip B. Zarrilli.

Figure 9.8 In *Memories in Hiding*, the jailed Paramu Naayar shouts defiantly near the end: "Our voices will be heard even after we die. They are the voices of revolution." Photo © Phillip B. Zarrilli.

to the landless. This transformation of Kerala in just over 100 years into a new model of social development in which many previously dispossessed peasants and communities were enfranchised has taken place peacefully within a democratic framework and without the outside assistance of neo-liberal global institutions such as the International Monetary Fund (IMF) or World Bank (Parayil 2000:1–15). Along with numerous modes of public performance and the eradication of illiteracy, spoken drama and theatre have clearly played an essential role in redefining individual, social, and political awareness in contemporary Kerala.

PZ

Key references

Bhaasi, T. (1996) *Memories in Hiding*, trans. J. George and P.B. Zarrilli, Calcutta: Seagull.

Eagleton, T. (1991) *Ideology: An Introduction*, London: Verso.

Handelman, D. (1990) *Models and Mirrors: Towards an Anthropology of Public Events*, Cambridge: Cambridge University Press.

Namboodiripad, E.M.S. (1976) *How I Became a Communist*, Trivandrum: Chinta Publications.

Parayil, G. (ed.) (2000) *Kerala: The Development Experience*, London: Zed Books.

Reinelt, J. (ed.) (1996) *Crucible of Crisis: Performing Social Change*, Ann Arbor: University of Michigan Press.

CASE STUDY: Brecht directs *Mother Courage*

In the fall of 1948, Bertolt Brecht returned with his wife and entourage to the Russian-occupied section of war-torn Berlin, where he hoped to establish a theatre. Formerly working as major writer and director in the theatre of Weimar, Germany, Brecht had been forced to flee in 1933, when Hitler came to power. Returning from exile after 15 years, he could not be sure of his reception by the Soviet and German communists who now controlled the institutions of culture in what would soon become East Berlin. Although a Marxist, Brecht favored a kind of theatre that was very different from the socialist realism promoted by Stalin's commissars of culture.

Brecht brought with him a script of *Mother Courage and Her Children*, which he had written in 1939, and photographs from a Zurich production of the play in 1941, staged when he was living in Finland. He and his wife, Helene Weigel (1900–1971), decided to gamble their theatrical future in Soviet-occupied Berlin on a production of *Mother Courage*. If the show were successful with Berlin spectators and the critics, Brecht and Weigel might gain enough leverage with the communists to wrench a subsidy from the new government and start their theatre. If not, they knew they would have to continue their travels to find another theatrical home.

A chronology of Brecht's career

1898   Born in Augsburg, Germany, to a middle-class family.

1918   Serves briefly in the German army as a medical orderly.

1922–1928   Establishes himself as a director and writer in Berlin with several productions, including *A Man's a Man* and *The Threepenny Opera*.

1928–1933   Broadens his work to include radio and film, joins the Communist Party, writes several short didactic plays, including *The Measures Taken*.

1933–1938   Flees Germany with his entourage to live and work in Scandinavia.

1938–1941   Threatened by the Nazis, Brecht works in Finland, then travels across the Soviet Union to the United States. Brecht completes drafts of several major plays, including *Mother Courage and Her Children* and *The Good Person of Setzuan*.

1941–1947   Works in Hollywood on several plays, including *The Caucasian Chalk Circle*. Co-directs an English-language version of his *The Life of Galileo Galilei*. Lies about his communist connections to the House Un-American Activities Committee and hastily flees to Europe.

1948–1949   Premiere of *Mother Courage* in Berlin (11 January 1949). Brecht and Weigel found the Berliner Ensemble.

1950–1956   Directs and adapts his and others' plays at the Berliner Ensemble. Ensemble tours to Paris and London. Brecht dies and Weigel continues to lead the Ensemble (until her death in 1971).

As the timeline of Brecht's career suggests, the playwright-director was caught up in most of the major political crises of the twentieth century – the Great War, the German response to the Russian Revolution, the rise of Nazism, World War II, and the cold war. To help theatre spectators to navigate such dangerous waters, Brecht developed a kind of socialist theatre that engaged them in a careful reading of their political options. Aware firsthand of the persuasive charisma of politicians, the dangerous emotions of patriotism, and the callous manipulations of economic power, Brecht sought to educate, entertain, and empower his audiences with dramatic lessons in social, political, and economic relationships.

When the Berliner Ensemble appeared in Paris in 1955, the French critic Roland Barthes commented:

> Whatever our final evaluation of Brecht, we must at least indicate the coincidence of his thought with the great progressive themes of our time: that the evils that men suffer are in their own hands – in other words, that the world can be changed; that art can and must intervene in history; ... that, finally, there is no such thing as an 'essence' of eternal art, but that each society must invent the art which will be responsible for its own deliverance.
>
> (Barthes 1972:38)

Barthes is well known for his work in semiotics, a method of analysis that critics and academics were beginning to use in the mid-1950s for insights into many fields across the humanities and social sciences. Since that time, many critics have used semiotic analysis to understand theatrical performances.

INTERPRETIVE APPROACH: Semiotics

Most theories of semiotics, including Barthes's, derive from the work of French linguist Ferdinand de Saussure (1857–1913). Saussure emphasized the language-like character of all signs, which in the theatre includes the words, objects, physical actions, and all of the other signifying practices that occur in performance. According to Saussure, there is no evident connection between either the sound or the written expression of signs and their

▷

▷

meanings; the word "tree" and our understanding of actual trees in nature is an arbitrary relationship. Similarly, for Barthes and other semiologists, there is no fixed relation between signifiers on the stage and what they signify to us in the performance. Spectators interpret a piece of scenery in relation to other signifiers they know, not because there is any inherent meaning in the scenic unit's combination of wood, muslin, glue, and paint. Consequently, according to semiotics, spectators look for differences among signifiers on stage to make sense of their experience in the theatre.

For semioticians, everything on stage that is presented to spectators is a sign of something else. In traditional theatre, the conventions of artistic performance and audience expectation have established and coordinated these signs. In the modern and contemporary theatre, playwrights, directors, and other artists must carefully organize the signs and sign systems of their productions. To continue with the example of scenery, if a designer were to place flats with furniture painted on it (an eighteenth-century convention) next to three-dimensional pieces of furniture (as occurs in most realist settings), spectators would likely experience confusion between these two different sign systems for scenery. Spatial relationships between people on a stage convey meaning; two people facing each other but on opposite sides of the stage probably will be seen as emotionally separated from one another. Contemporary directors usually work to see that an entire production uses a consistent sign system, including the gestures of the actors. The mostly small gestures of everyday life in realistic theatre would be inconsistent with the broad, pantomimic gestures of nineteenth-century melodrama. Modern theatre artists seek to coordinate all of the sign systems in a production, including lighting, set design, costuming, properties, and sound effects, as well as acting.

The director is also expected to present the audience with a clear hierarchy of signs in the moment-to-moment rhythms and pictures of her or his production. Directors "tell" spectators where to look on the stage and shape their response by the manipulation of signs. For a storm and shipwreck scene presented in a minimalist theatrical style, for instance, the director might begin with sound and lighting effects focused on a ship's mast, follow it with a blackout and a transition to soothing music, and end with the entrance of stumbling actors clothed in wet, ragged costumes. In such a sequence, the director would need to coordinate all of the sign systems of the production and also highlight specific signs to tell the story. A knowledge of semiotics can assist directors in unifying their productions and also help critics to describe and analyze the coherence (or incoherence) of a performance.

Some questions one would ask in a semiotic analysis of any production would be the following.

▷

▷
KEY QUESTIONS

1   Taken together, what do the components of the setting signify – form, color spectrum, texture, definition of spaces – about the world in which the play takes place?

2   In what ways do the actors convey meaning by gesture or their use of space and how do these signs relate to other signs on stage?

3   What does the rhythm of sequences of action signify?

When Brecht began rehearsals for *Mother Courage and Her Children* in 1948, he had a poorly-equipped theatre, insufficient funds, and many actors and designers with whom he had never worked before. The audience, Brecht knew, would be struggling to survive a cold winter in a postwar Berlin that remained mostly a pile of rubble. How is the theatre historian to understand the effectiveness and success of the production that emerged from this inauspicious beginning? In addition to analyzing the critical reviews and the demographics and desires of the audience, the historian can examine Brecht's script and his directorial choices as they were recorded in the production book and in rehearsal photos, to assess the semiotics of the production.

Mother Courage on stage

As a playwright, Brecht set *Mother Courage and Her Children* during the Thirty Year's War (1618–1648) that ravaged Germany, destroying whole cities and killing nearly half of the German population during the historical era of the Protestant Reformation. Between 1624 and 1636, the years encompassed by the play, Mother Courage struggles to support herself and her three adult children by selling supplies to both Protestant and Catholic armies from a wagon that she and her children haul behind them. The drama focuses on the conflict between war profiteering and maintaining a family, between capitalist economics and family survival. As Mother Courage pursues business as usual, the war pulls each of her children into the ongoing conflict and eventually it kills them. For over 12 years, Mother Courage haggles while her children die. Although Courage learns nothing from her struggle, Brecht wanted the audience to understand that capitalistic wars must be abolished if families are to survive.

As a director, Brecht tried to induce spectators both to grapple with the historical specifics of early capitalism during the Reformation era and to apply what they learned to their present situation in 1949 Berlin. In this regard, he deployed scenography and lighting primarily to point to his universal themes, not to literally depict the historical situation of seventeenth-century Europe. On either side of the stage were large frames illustrating the general implements of warfare, such as muskets, tenting, and broadswords, while upstage was an enormous, semi-circular cyclorama that covered the entire back wall of the theatre. Into this mostly open stage space, Brecht placed occasional three-dimensional scenic units as necessary for the action, such as cannon, a half-ruined parsonage, and other set pieces, plus Mother Courage's wagon.

Three sign systems for the production

From the success of the Zurich production, Brecht decided that Courage's wagon, the chief symbol of her business enterprise, would constitute the main scenic unit for nearly all of the 12 scenes in the play. The stage was fitted with a revolve, a rotating circular platform, on which the wagon could move when pulled by Courage and her children. This occurs frequently in the play to indicate that they are traveling as they follow various armies across Europe. When pulled in the opposite direction from the rotating stage, of course, the characters and the wagon simply move in place; for 12 years, in effect, Courage and her business appear stuck on a treadmill. In addition to using white light to illuminate the actors, Brecht worked with his designers to create images on the cyclorama that would indicate the carnage caused by war. Through scenery and lighting, then, Brecht and his designers created a non-realist sign system to indicate the Universal History that underlined the general horror of war – stage images as relevant to his 1949 audience as to the historical situation of the play.

In contrast, the costumes and props used by the actors were historically specific. Photographs of the production show costumes that suggest the actual dress of seventeenth-century Germans, ranging from different military uniforms to regional varieties of peasant work clothes. In addition, the designer distressed the costumes appropriately to suggest their wear and tear over the 12 years of the play's duration. This meant that occasional new clothes, such as a colorful hat and red boots given by an aging colonel to his prostitute-mistress, stuck out on stage in comparison to the drab grays and earth-tones of most of the other clothing. Brecht instructed his property master to keep in mind the hand-crafted nature of the properties used by the characters, such as eating implements, washing buckets, and cookware. The sign systems of these naturalist costumes and props for *Mother Courage and Her Children* were designed to pull the audience into a realist illusion of Specific History.

But never for long. Brecht continually reminded his spectators that they were in a theatre. At the top of each scene, a sign suspended from the flies told

the audience in large block letters where, in Europe, the scene was set. Each scene began and ended with an actor, in full view of the audience, drawing a half curtain across the proscenium opening. Throughout, the spectators could see the lighting instruments, which were not masked from view. Whenever the small orchestra in a side box on the stage played some of Paul Dessau's music for the production, a musical emblem was lowered from the flies. Unlike the conventions of most musical comedy, where the music seems to arise out of the emotional situation, Brecht used music to break the dramatic illusion. Dessau's difficult, often atonal and haunting music reminded spectators of their present circumstances, sitting in a theatre and watching a play that had something to tell them about rebuilding their society and culture. Brecht intended this sign system of music and stage machinery to evoke the Theatrical Present, where the actual work of the stage production might suggest the work to be done beyond the playhouse.

The semiotics of Brechtian acting

Brecht involved his actors in all three of his major sign systems – those of the illusion of Specific History, non-realist Universal History, and the Theatrical Present. Simply standing on stage in their naturalist costumes made the actors signs of the social reality of seventeenth-century Europe. Much of the speech uttered by the actor-characters also placed them realistically in the sign system of Specific History. Some of Brecht's dialog and many of his songs, however, point to generalizations about social and economic behavior that indicate truths about all history. Several major characters in the play speak in parables that display the hard-bitten wisdom of peasant life, for instance, and the songs often contrast foolish religious faith to the material demands of survival. In enunciating these truths, the actors either spoke or sang within the signs of Universal History or worked directly with spectators in the auditorium. An actor might even begin a line of dialog within the sign system of Universal History and then throw the end of it to the Berlin audience, shifting abruptly into the sign system of the Theatrical Present.

The actors' gestures and movements also played out across the three sign systems. Brecht coined the term "gestus" to denote an actor's ability to present a way of standing or moving that signified the social position of her or his character in Universal History. In the production of *Mother Courage*, actors could even separate themselves momentarily from the character they were playing to indicate to the audience Brecht's understanding of the social position and action of their characters. That is, the actors could create the persona of "the Brechtian actor" to comment directly, within the signs of the Theatrical Present, on the usefulness and morality of the social role of their characters.

Semiotics in action

From a semiotic point of view, Brecht deployed the three sign systems of his production with ingenuity and fluidity in directing *Mother Courage*. Further, he used spatiality and rhythm, the theatrical tools unique to the director's art, to underline significant turning points in the story of the play. In the first scene of the drama, two army recruiters lure Eilif, Courage's oldest son, away from the family and bribe him to enlist. For the start of this scene, Brecht placed the family in a tight knot center stage and close to the wagon to emphasize their unified stand against the recruiters' threat. As the recruiters chipped away at the family's unity, Brecht dispersed the family members across the stage. Eventually, one recruiter lured Eilif some distance from Courage, whose back was turned as she bargained with the other recruiter over the price of a belt, leaving Eilif to be filled with thoughts of heroism by the recruiter and join the army, leaving the family.

Mother Courage's loss of her third child, Katrin, is the emotional climax of the play. To warn the towns-people and save their children from an imminent and deadly secret attack, Katrin climbs

onto the roof of a peasant's house near the town and begins beating a drum (Figure 9.9). The attacking soldiers, who cannot reach her (she pulls her ladder up after her), try to bribe her to stop. They even begin destroying her mother's wagon, left in Katrin's care, but she continues drumming to alert the town to defend its battlements. Finally, the soldiers bring a large musket, set it up on its forked holder, and shoot her. As Katrin is dying on the roof, the sounds of cannon and alarm bells from the town indicate that she has succeeded and the children of the town will survive. Brecht's use of rhythm and spatiality made this a powerful scene for his Berlin audience. Katrin's intermittent but progressively louder and longer drumming was the primary rhythmic element, while her vertical isolation on the rooftop gave the sign of her resistance spatial focus and dominance in the scene.

Semiotic critics like Barthes praised the clarity and unifying effects of Brecht's direction of *Mother Courage and Her Children*. In his organization of the sign systems and his deployment of specific signs at significant moments in the production, Brecht encouraged his 1949 audience to apply Courage's Specific History to their own Theatrical (and socio-political) Present. The link uniting past and present was through Universal History, Brecht's Marxist understanding of the ongoing dynamics of economics and power. Brecht used the signs of Universal History to provide some distance and insight for his spectators, rendering their past and present worlds strange and unusual for them, thus preparing them to accept his own vision of events. The term Brecht used to describe this effect on spectators was *Verfremdungseffekt*, Brecht's German neologism (sometimes mistranslated as "alienation effect") for a Russian phrase first used by the Meyerhold aesthetician, Victor Shklovsky.

Conclusion

Whether Brecht's Berlin audience read his signs and sign systems for *Mother Courage* as the director-

Figure 9.9 Katrin, Mother Courage's daughter, beats her drum to warn the townspeople, in Scene 11 of the 1949 production of Brecht's *Mother Courage*. © Deutsches Theatermuseum, Berlin.

playwright seems to have intended them cannot, of course, be known. For Brecht and Weigel, however, their gamble had paid off; the success of the production led to the founding of the Berliner Ensemble in 1949, a company that soon emerged as a leader in postwar Europe on both sides of the "Iron Curtain" of the cold war.

While this analysis of the 1949 production suggests that Brecht involved his spectators in interpreting meanings within three distinct sign systems during performances, and used rhythm and spatiality to focus audience attention on meaningful signs at climactic moments, other analyses might come to different conclusions about Brecht's semiotic direction of the play. No semiotician-historian, however, would deny that Brecht's complex yet coherent use of signs helped to ensure the success of *Mother Courage and Her Children* in 1949.

BMc

Key references

Aston, E. and George, S. (1991) *Theatre as Sign-System: A Semiotics of Text and Performance*, London: Routledge.

Barthes, R. (1972) *Critical Essays*, trans. Richard Howard, Evanston, I.L.: Northwestern.

Brecht, B. (1972) *Mother Courage and her Children*, in R. Manheim and J. Willett (eds) *Bertolt Brecht: Collected Plays*, vol. 5, New York: Random House.

Elam, K. (1980) *The Semiotics of Theatre and Drama*, London: Routledge.

Fuegi, J. (1987) *Bertolt Brecht: Chaos, According to Plan*, Directors in Perspective, Cambridge: Cambridge University Press.

Thomson, P. (1997) *Mother Courage and Her Children*, Cambridge: Cambridge University Press.

Willett, J. (1964) *Brecht on Theatre*, London: Methuen.

PART IV

Theatre and performance in the age of global communications, 1950–present

Edited by **Gary Jay Williams**

Theatre and performance in the age of global communications, 1950–present

INTRODUCTION: COLONIALISM, GLOBALIZATION, MEDIA, AND THEATRE

Today all cultures are border cultures.

Néstor García Canclini

The landing of United States astronauts on the moon in July 1969, watched by an estimated one billion people on television screens around the world, was taken by many not only as a dramatically new technological triumph by humankind and as a landmark media event but as symbolizing a new era and a new kind of global consciousness. A few years later, NASA's famous "blue marble" color satellite photos, circulating on global television, showing planet earth floating in space, reinforced the euphoria.

From a wider cultural perspective, and in historical perspective, we can see that the image of the U.S. planting its flag on the moon in an imperial space race with the Soviet Union, came in a decade when many nations were trying to break from long histories of colonial subjugation by imperial nations or partitioning by the rival superpowers. Most of them were struggling with the political and economic instabilities that were the legacies of imperialism. Those struggles – in Angola, Biafra, Uganda, Nigeria, the Dominican Republic, Argentina, Nicaragua, the Balkans, South Asia, and Southeast Asia (to name a few) were often accompanied by wars, bloody coups, terrorism, mass killings, poverty, and starvation, all of which provoked migrations. The moon landing also came at a crisis point in the relations between the Soviet Union and the United States, who had cast themselves as nuclear gladiators vying to determine the future for all humankind. It came at the peak of demonstrations in major world capitals against the U.S. intervention in South Vietnam. It came as waves of internal cultural change were sweeping across nations on almost every continent, including the wave of communist China's Cultural Revolution, political protests by the Left in Japan, and civil rights demonstrations in the United States. It came as new globalization processes were beginning to gather momentum, sped by space technology. The moon landing of 1969 was, considered in the light of these events, a dramatic performance of national identity of an older kind, bred in World War II and the cold war. It came at a time when the world was moving into a very different era, in which identities of almost every kind – national, ethnic, racial, religious, tribal, and sexual – would be challenged and reassessed.

This final section of *Theatre Histories* focuses especially on the way theatre and performance artists have given expression to both the cultural disjunctures in the era and the struggle for new communities, twin offspring of events in the last half of the twentieth century and the beginning of the twenty-first. Theatre artists were staging the experiences of displacement and alienation, and the dialectic between traditional communities and next-generation communities. These phenomena and their expression in theatre are not entirely new in human history. One thinks of Euripides's *Medea* (431 B.C.E), in double bondage as a powerless woman and a foreigner in the patriarchy of ancient Greece; or of the warrior in the Japanese kabuki play, *Sanemori* (seventeenth century), who saves an enemy child and then defects to the opposing side; or of the Jewish Shylock in Christian Venice in Shakespeare's *The Merchant of Venice*. Of course, the development of nations and cultures historically has always involved cultural interactions, with trade, migrations, assimilations, and cross-fertilizations being the rule, not the exception. What has been new in millennium globalization is both the rapidity, the immense scale, and the horizontality of the transnational engagements. In this era, large numbers of people were – and still are – migrating from rural areas to cities and from nation to nation. Prices for jet travel became affordable enough that middle-class families in economically-developed nations traveled internationally, frequently. (Chapter 12 takes up the issue of tourism and "performance," broadly understood.) Frequent interactions with other cultures have become commonplace and not just among the wealthy and educated, but at a variety of social levels. As one anthropologist has observed, "Today all cultures are border cultures."

Communication technologies have played key roles in accelerating the process. Between the 1950s and the last decade of the century, radio, film, television, satellite television, video cassettes and compact disks, and finally the Internet's web of communication brought a steadily increasing number of ordinary people into new cultural negotiations daily. By the early years of the new century, there were over 500 million users of the Internet worldwide. It connected university classrooms in Manchester and Tokyo, living rooms in New Delhi and New York, coffee houses in Kabul and Berlin, and broker-ages in New York and Geneva. Satellite television shaped perceptions of events world wide, and sometimes altered political processes. The death of the cold war in 1989 became a telegenic reality when television carried images of people tearing down the wall separating East and West Berlin and toppling of statues of Lenin. Kenneth Branagh's film of *Hamlet* (1996) echoed this reality effect when it ended with the toppling of a statue of Claudius, after the death of the corrupt ruler at the hands of Hamlet. World television was on hand again to capture the opening of the borders in Hungary in 1988, an event that signaled the disintegration of totalitarian communist power in the Soviet satellites, soon to be followed by the collapse of Russia's communist govern-ment. When cameras watched a statue of Saddam Hussein being pulled down in Baghdad after the U.S. invasion of Iraq in 2003, the event seemed like an replay of a convenient telegenic reality.

However, there are many times when the uses of the global media also offer a new/old lesson for thinking about theatre and performance in a world both fractured and newly interconnected. Anthropologists and sociologists are finding that, in the process of globalization, the global media are often sites where the disjunctures between cultures are played out. So too, as we will show in this Introduction, are theatre and performance. We will examine examples of the way the cultural disjunctures have played out in the electronic media and then consider parallels in the work of theatre and performance artists. We will focus especially on postcolonial theatre and performance, especially in African nations, where artists have dealt with the issues of cultural displacement and quests for cultural identity common amid globalization.

We offer first a brief sampling of some of the conversations between new media technologies and theatre/performance, which will help prepare the way for the work of this Introduction and the chapters to come.

Media and theatre: All in the family

Media technologies had some obvious impacts on the forms, styles, and techniques of the theatre. In the realm of theatre as popular entertainment (Broadway and London's West End are two major demarcations of this), producers responded to the expectations of audiences increasingly accustomed to the escalating spectacles of film and television. Scenic spectacularism became a star performer in big-budget American and British musicals, such as *The Phantom of the Opera* (1984). For audiences accustomed to home audio systems and rock concert amplification, musicals began to equip actors with wireless microphones and to digitally balance and distribute blends of singers and orchestras. British and Broadway musicals were recycled into films, CD soundtracks, DVDs, and touring shows for international audiences. There has been no business like show business for the repackaging of its own mythologies, from *Showboat* (1927) through *Chorus Line* (1975) to *42nd Street* (1980). Broadway's domestic situation comedies, especially those by Neil Simon, were often almost indistinguishable from television's "sitcoms," in which couches were major characters.

More significantly, although realism remained the major mode in both theatre and film, both mediums were exploring new expressive possibilities (as we saw in the Introduction to Chapter III, Jo Mielziner's setting for Miller's *Death of a Salesman* has roots in radio and film). By the 1970s, verbal language no longer occupied the central, dominating place in either medium that it once had. As film became sophisticated in visual storytelling and in visual explorations of complexities and ambiguities, it became less reliant on dialog. Film (and even some television dramas) began developing stories in non-linear ways or creating visual sequences (with the technical help of digitization by the 1990s) that allowed thematic or symbolic associations and multiple readings. Some developments may have served short attention spans or the thirst for violent spectacle, but they also suggest a shift in cultural sensibilities – less dependence on verbal language alone, on the truth-value of language (the dark side of this is discussed in Chapter 11), and on linear continuities. They suggest a trust (especially in the U.S.) in expressiveness of a less rational, more atavistic kind. Toward the end of the century, spectators were becoming increasingly nimble with multi-focal representation, associational experiences, and multiple available meanings. The rapidly increasing use of computers may have meant that spectators were becoming more visually sophisticated; any glimpse of software programming languages also makes apparent the constructedness of language. On the other hand, as computerization took on the role of rationalized data-processing and the function of a memory-keeper of infinite capacity, perhaps spectators were seeking theatre and film experiences involving more instinctive and emotional processing, as alternatives to scientized knowledge. Also, by the end of the century, a person living in a technologically-advanced nation was being exposed to, and negotiating over 1600 commercial messages a day from all media.

Many serious theatre and performance artists moved away from the once-primary and sacred verbal text, challenging its dominance and expanding the expressive range of the stage. These developments, and their cultural and theoretical backgrounds, are the subject of Chapter 11 and its companion case studies. As we will see, Jerzy Grotowski's "poor" theatre of the 1960s was in part a spiritual revolt against a spiritless commercial theatre, with its elaborate scenic trappings. Tadashi Suzuki's *The Trojan Women* (1974) imaged contemporary Japanese suffering and confusion, disrupting the conventional elevations of humanistic renderings of Greek tragedy. Peter Brook's *Orghast* (1971), was an arrangement of musical phonemes and fragments of ancient languages, intoned by the actors along with ancient music. The imagery in the films of directors such as Japan's Kurosawa Akira and Sweden's Ingmar Bergman challenged theatre directors and designers. Peter Brook was directly influenced by Kurosawa's film version of *Macbeth, The Throne of Blood*. Many western theatre artists turned eastward to the performance languages of kabuki, noh, kathakali, Balinese dance drama, and other theatre forms. Multi-media theatres of visual and aural landscapes and choreographed movement were created by many artists internationally, including Ping Chong, Robert Lepage, Pina Bausch, Robert Wilson, Richard Foreman, and Ah Min Soo, leading to what has been called "theatre of images" (see Chapter 11). Directors in Germany, Japan, France, the United States, and elsewhere were deconstructing Shakespeare and the ancient Greek tragedies (Chapter 11). Theatres in world capitals were exporting "intercultural productions" meant to cross all language barriers and culture borders. Performance artists found ways to use their own bodies as performance instruments and their own lives as subjects, straddling boundaries between art and life; a rich vein of performance art opened in the Americas. Both the spiritual abyss and the emotionally volatile and destructive forces beneath the surfaces of language was probed even in the realms of realism in the plays of British playwright Harold Pinter (1930–) and U.S. playwrights Sam Shepard (1943–) and David Mamet (1947–). *Angels in America* (1992), the two play, prize-winning epic by Tony Kushner (1956–) is often rich in language but, more significantly, almost cinematic in its collage of scenes representing multiple, conflicting strands of American life during the first stages of the AIDS crisis in the late 1980s. The play juxtaposes scenes in non-linear, associative sequences to represent the lives of gay men suffering from AIDS amid the intellectual and moral shallows of both American liberalism and conservatism, traditional Jewish family life in New York City, and prophecies of the Church of Jesus Christ of the Latter Day Saints. Kushner also talks back to the film medium when the chief character makes a self-conscious reference to the play's chief spectacle – the appearance of an angel above him – as being "Very Spielberg" (Figure IV.1). The ironic allusion is, of course, to Steven Spielberg (1947–), director of such film spectaculars as *E.T.: The Extra-Terrestrial* and *Raiders of the Lost Ark*. In 2003, Kushner's play, one of the few intellectually serious plays on Broadway in the last decades of the twentieth century, was made into a film, directed by Mike Nichols, for the cable movie channel, H.B.O. The crossover is not surprising. The borders between all mediums and genres grew increasingly permeable in the era.

Figure IV.1 The appearance of the angel in the final scene of Tony Kushner's *Angels in America: Millennium Approaches*, directed by George C. Wolfe, with Stephen Spinella as Prior Walter and Ellen McLaughlin as the angel. Photo © Joan Marcus.

Globalization, media, theatre, and performance

The globalized landscape has become familiar. Globalization is the computerized transnational network of banks that put A.T.M.s on every street corner in every wealthy city in the world. It is Japanese Toyotas manufactured in Tennessee, Nike shoes made in Southeast Asia, and computers made in China using U.S. Microsoft programs. It is the rock musical, *Bombay Dreams* and India's "Bollywood" films for international audiences. It is the increasing flow of migrants from rural areas to cities and across borders and the resulting diasporas. It is Hispanic maids in New York luxury hotels, walled Verizon technical parks in India, and domes for Vedic meditation rising at Maharishi University in Iowa cornfields. It is international theatre festivals and corporate-sponsored, international blockbuster art exhibitions. It is our anguished experience of seeing televised images of the abject poverty of a diseased, dying child in Rwanda alongside stories of the wealth and greed of Enron corporation executives. Not only can world affairs no longer be framed in terms of a center (The West) and a periphery (the Rest) in the manner characteristic of cold war discourse. The ways in which cultures are now engaging with each other have fundamentally changed the ways in which communities are, and will be imagined. In his study of globalization's effects and the responses to it, anthropologist Arjun Appadurai puts a critical question: "What is the nature of locality as a lived experience in a globalized, deterritorialized world?" (Appadurai 1996:52). Of course, the habit of thinking of the term "culture" in any singular sense, as if it were some singular, autonomous mode of beliefs and behaviors, in isolation and in stasis, is not one that a long view of history will support at any time.

Globalization has required us to think of a plurality of cultures, in motion and constantly interactive. Appadurai has characterized today's globalized world in terms of transnational cultural flows of peoples, money, goods, and technologies, rather than in terms of static nations (Appadurai 1996:27–47). By the early 1990s, over 100 million people were living outside their country of origin, a 100 percent increase in three years. Appadurai sees a continuing process of disjunctures between these cultural flows. He and other scholars have provided evidence that these often play out in the electronic global media. This argument is more complex than the usual view that the capitalist media – mostly American – is advancing imperialism by other means, poisoning other cultures with corrosive fantasies of a consumer culture.

Similarly, many theatre artists have created works that give expression to the cultural disjunctures and the imagining of new communities. Playwrights, theatre groups, and performance artists have taken up such globalization issues as the exploitation of Third World nations by wealthy, technologically-advanced nations; the loss of national and cultural identities to the consumer marketplace; and the anxious assertion of new identities – including radical religious identities. We will see some of these issues in the works of theatre artists in postcolonial African nations which have endured, and are enduring similar cultural transitions. Kenyan Playwright, Ngugi wa Thiong'o (1938–) has written of the "cultural bomb" of globalization. Its effect, he believes, is to "annihilate a people's belief in their names, in their languages, . . . in their heritage of struggle, in their capacities. It makes them see their past as one wasteland of non-achievement, and it makes them want to distance themselves from that wasteland" (Thiong'o 1986:3). We will see some theatre groups working at the grassroots level to deal with the issues by creating new communities.

The media: Power and resistance

Examples of the way the cultural disjunctures have played out in the electronic media offer instructive parallels to the works of theatre artists. Néstor García Canclini, an Argentinian-born anthropologist who fled political persecution to live in Mexico, writes of the two-way circulation of cultures between Mexico and the United States:

> If there are more than 250 Spanish language radio and television stations in the United States, more than fifteen hundred publications in Spanish, and a high interest in Latin American literature and music, it is not only because there is a market of twenty million "Hispanics". . . . It is also due to the fact that so-called Latin culture produces films like *Zoot Suit* [based on a 1978 play by Luis Valdez] and *La Bamba*, the songs of Rubén Blades and Los Lobos, aesthetically and culturally advanced theaters like that of Luis Valdez, and visual artists whose quality and aptitude for making popular culture interact with modern and postmodern symbolism incorporates them in the North American mainstream.
>
> (García Canclini 1995:231)

To be sure, these scholars and others have rightly warned against the power of media controlled by governments and megacorporations. In 2004, Italy's Prime Minister, Silvio Berlusconi, had nearly total control of Italy's mass media, including the three most powerful television networks and the leading newspaper. In his videocracy, Berlusconi could squelch any opposition, usher in laws favorable to his holdings, and enjoy near-immunity from prosecution for corruption. The global corporation of the politically conservative magnate, Rupert Murdoch, controls various media in Australia, the United States, the United Kingdom, and Asia. America's AOL-Time Warner is the fourth largest corporation in the globalized world.

But there is plentiful evidence that the effects and uses of the media are not always controllable by corporations or governments, as James Lull argues in his *Media, Communication, Culture*. Two domestic television serials in China were widely recognized as contributing to social unrest in the late 1980s (Lull 1995:123). The famous televised image of a lone young man confronting a line of government tanks in Beijing during the student protests in Tiannemen Square in 1989 was shown by the communist government as evidence of the military's use of restraint. Everywhere else – and satellite television assured that it was seen everywhere else – it was read as a symbolic act of defiance of an oppressive regime. Public perception/reception is not wholly controllable.

Nor are the uses of the media. In 1992, the beating of Rodney King, a black motorist, by four white Los Angeles police officers was captured by a private individual on video tape. With U.S. commercial television networks airing the tape repeatedly, the scene became an indelible symbol of continuing, invidious racial discrimination in the United States In 2004, digital photos of the abuse of Iraqi prisoners by Americans in a Baghdad prison were revealed by a conscience-troubled American soldier who delivered them to an officer on a compact disc, and they soon made their way to a website on the World Wide Web, adding fuel to the controversy over America's pre-emptive invasion of Iraq. Soon after, a Jordanian theatre director created a popular production called "A New Middle East," which included recreated scenes of the abuse. On the other side of the Iraqi war, Islamic terrorists created international fear with videotapes of their beheadings of kidnapped captors from nations involved in the war. The terrorists assured the global dissemination of the horrific images by providing the tapes to the Arab-language satellite television channel, Al Jazeera.

In Brazil in 1992, the telegenic President, Collor de Melo, was impeached for corruption due to the impact on the public of the televised appearance before congressional committee of a singularly honest motor pool driver, who defied the system and testified about delivering bribes. In Mexico City, the host of a popular television morning show for several years was Brozo the Clown, created by comedian Victor Trujillo. On the channel owned by

Televisa, a media conglomerate, Brozo read the news, interviewed guests in greasy clown makeup and a tattered costume, and generally presided with foul language. He appealed to the many poor citizens in the capital city who shared his disrespect for the hypocrisy of corrupt politicians and the solemnities of conventional news coverage of them. On one show, Brozo exposed a powerful legislator by airing a secretly filmed video tape that revealed him stuffing his briefcase and coat pockets with bribe money. A similar lack of trust of media news and politicians may be behind the results of a recent poll in the United States showing that young television viewers were getting most of their news from comic talk shows, including that of the widely popular satirist, Jon Stewart, on the cable channel, Comedy Central.

Theatre, performance, resistance

Many theatre artists, too, have given resilient expression to the difficulties and possibilities of living in a world both globalized and culturally fractured. Their work has aimed, among other things, at exposing corruption; capturing the cultural confusions of the nomadic experience; satirizing racial, ethnic, or gender stereotyping; and fusing disparate performance traditions. The remainder of this introduction describes two kinds of theatrical works at the cultural borders, chosen deliberately for the disparate methods and geographies they represent: an example of performance art in the work of Guillermo Gómez-Peña (1955–) and selected theatrical works of artists in postcolonial African nations.

Guillermo Gómez-Peña is a prolific performance artist and writer who was born in Mexico and came to the United States in 1978. As with Appadurai and García Canclini, migration and the nomadic experience are central features of the era for Gómez-Peña. He is, by his own account,

> a nomadic Mexican artist/writer in the process of Chicanization, which means I am slowly heading North. . . . I make art about the misunderstandings that take place at the border zone. But for me, the border is no longer located at any fixed geopolitical site. I carry the border with me, and I find new borders wherever I go.
>
> (Gómez-Peña 1996:5)

He has created performance events, solo and often in collaboration with Coco Fusco (1960–) and Roberto Sifuentes (1967–), that often have focused on the Latino experience in the United States and have been designed to make audiences more aware of the ways in which national and cultural identities are constructed.

Performance art

Performance art may be compared to the avant-garde movements of the early twentieth century, such as dadaism, that broke from self-contained aesthetic expression to call into question the very ways in which art is classified, or framed as art. The point of both, in part, is to demystify high art and call attention to the social processes that "confirm" art as art. Performance art has taken many forms, from solo work to large spectacles, but it always seeks to break through that separation of art and life that is characteristic of conventional art. Performance artists often use their own bodies as performance instruments and their own lives as subjects. Their interest is not in written dramatic texts but embodied expression. Performance works are often done outside of theatres, on roofs, in shop windows, in airports, lobbies, or street corners – rejecting the usual performance venues. The works may use video, dance, sculpture, painting, or music. Performance art is inhabited by theories of performativity that insist that all social realities are constructed, that "every social activity can be understood as a showing of doing," as Richard Schechner writes (Schechner 2002:140). Performance artists often have taken up social or political concerns, exposing, for example, the ways in which our notions of race, gender, and national or ethnic identity have been constructed.

The figures in Gómez-Peña's early performances included a Mexican poet/detective (Mister Misterio), a burned-out ballerina who is his friend, an Aztec princess working as a cabaret singer, a wrestler shaman, and an androgynous Maori warrior opera singer. They are all hybrid creations of an ironic trickster probing the cultural collisions that globalization brings about. As an outsider dealing with dominant American cultures, Gómez-Peña has not only acutely chronicled border collisions and cultural hybrids but has attempted to provoke spectators to critically assess and alter habitual and harmful concepts of race, nationality, ethnicity, and gender. In a "performance photo essay" on the Web (http://www.pochanostra.com), Gómez-Peña demonstrates, with an interactive test, the dangers of ethnic profiling in the post 9/11 era. In 1994–1996, Gómez-Peña and Sifuentes collaborated on the *Temple of Confessions*, in which they displayed themselves in an exhibit in Plexiglas booths, as if relics or scientific specimens. They were advertised as the last living saints from a "border region." Spectators were invited to confess their "intercultural fears and desires" to them. In Scottsdale, Arizona, in the southwestern United States, hundreds of spectators "confessed" their fantasies and fears about Mexicans, Chicanos, and other peoples of color. Gómez-Peña describes spectators seeking an intimate connection with him and expressing emotions ranging from guilt to anger, and from tears to sexual desire. Schechner has suggested the performance event revealed people's "sense of resigned desperation" in the face of the inevitability of globalization and their need for human interaction to counter its alienating and homogenizing effects (Schechner 2002:261).

Theatre in postcolonial African nations

In postcolonial African nations undergoing cultural transitions, theatre artists have given expression to similar kinds of tensions. Under the pressure of independence movements, European powers withdrew from their 50 African colonial territories between the mid-1950s and the mid-1970s, after nearly a century of humiliating domination, leaving legacies of deep poverty, political instability, and ethnic wars. Indigenous peoples have tried since to forge cultural and national identities in the nations that European powers artificially created and in which they suppressed local languages and customs. After independence, indigenous theatre artists began to reclaim tribal myths and performance practices and, at the same time, develop new, often politically-themed works that assessed the damage or critiqued the new regimes. A number of African playwrights have been imprisoned for such works. Bertolt Brecht's plays, designed to provoke audiences to critique their socio-economic conditions, have been influential in several postcolonial African nations.

Nigeria, which gained its independence from Britain in 1960, is rich in performance traditions, such as the Yoruba peoples' masquerade festival, *Egungun*, and it has been rich in theatre critical of both its colonial rulers and those after. Hubert Ogunde (1916–1990) drew on Yoruba myths for his anti-colonial plays before independence, which authorities banned, and for his *Yoruba Awake!* (1964), written after independence and also banned. Wole Soyinka (1934–), Nigeria's best-known playwright and winner of the Nobel Prize for Literature in 1986, has written plays drawing on his Yoruba heritage and probing events before and after independence, including his *Death and the King's Horseman* (1975) and *Madmen and Specialists* (1971). The latter is a bitter, if enigmatic play inspired by Nigeria's civil war, during which Soyinka was detained without trial, and after which he went into exile. He returned to stage his *Opera Wonyosi* (1977), a Nigerian amalgam of *The Beggar's Opera* (1728) by John Gay (1685–1732) and Brecht's *Threepenny Opera* (1928). It satirizes a self-proclaimed African emperor and the Nigerian middle class. Nigerian writer Femi Osofisan (1946–), influenced by Marx and Brecht, has been critical of Soyinka's sometimes abstruse metaphysics. Osofisan's plays reflect both his own aesthetic interests and his passionate advocacy of social justice. His *Once Upon Four Robbers* (1980) satirized the Nigerian military government. He adapted *The Government Inspector* (1836) by Nikolai Gogol (1809–1852) to satirize the ruling elite. His *The Chattering and the Song* (1976), is a notable example of the attempts of Nigerian dramatists to use traditional performance modes (including dance and music), myth, and folklore to explore modern class polarities in the country.

In Sierra Leone, independent since 1957, Thomas Decker has promoted theatre in Krio, an urban, English-based Creole language that developed in the interchange among freed slaves in Freetown, their European colonial masters, and the indigenous people of the region. Krio theatre serves a wide cross-section of society and has inspired a number of playwrights, including the radical, Yulisa Amadu Maddy (1936–). His play, *Big Berrin* (1976), the title of which means "big death," is critical of the plight of the urban poor and resulted in his imprisonment. In Ghana, the Concert Party theatre, a major, long-lived form that mixes many elements, including American black vaudeville and African story-telling traditions, usually concludes with a play designed to provoke audiences to think about current issues.

Not long after Angola's independence (1975), the Xilenga-Teatro in its capital city of Luanda, staged a work derived from the oral performance traditions of the Tchokwe people. An adaptation of Brecht's *The Caucasian Chalk Circle* by Henrique Guerra was produced in 1979.

In South Africa, where blacks suffered under the British colonial legacy of apartheid policies that relegated blacks to separate, inferior living and working conditions, theatre artists since the 1960s have created politically controversial productions. One of the most fertile sources has been the Market Theatre in Johannesburg (1976), whose productions have included *Sizwe Bansi Is Dead* (1972) and *The Island*, collectively created through improvisation by Athol Fugard, John Kani, and Winston Ntshona. *Sizwe Bansi Is Dead* is about a man who obtained the "pass," a document necessary for black men to work in South Africa, by taking on the identity of a dead man. It has had wide success in Africa, the U.S., and elsewhere. It inspired other collectively created works, including *Woza Albert!* (1980), by Barney Simon, Mbongeni Ngema, and Percy Mtwa, which is about the reactions of the white government and the black community to the return of Jesus to South Africa (Figure IV.2). Several of the realist plays of Athol Fugard (1932–) have become well known outside South Africa, including his *Boesman and Lena* (1969), and *Master Harold and the Boys* (1982), an autobiographical play about a white boy's relationship with his black fellow-worker, which the boy destroys through biases learned from apartheid.

The Theatre for Development movement has been successful in several African nations. As we will see in Chapter 10, its community-based efforts involve theatre activities in which local residents participate. Typically, a leader guides local performers in identifying a local problem. They create, through improvisation and role-playing, a short play that highlights the problem and sometimes suggests a solution. The play is then performed for local audiences – in a marketplace or a church – followed by community discussion and planning. Such works may take up health care relating to the AIDS epidemic, literacy, or agricultural practices. Some of these democratically created

Figure IV.2 Percy Mtwa and Mbongeni Ngema in the "pink-nose" mimicry scene in *Woza Albert!*, by Percy Mtwa, Mbongeni Ngema, and Barney Simon, directed by Barney Simon, at the Market Theatre, Johannesburg, South Africa, 1982. Photo © Ruphin Coudyzer, The Market Theatre.

performances seek to raise community consciousness about human rights. Kenyan writer, Ngugi Thiong'o (cited above), collaborated with a community at Kamiriithu to create an influential production for the movement, entitled, *I'll Marry When I Want* (1977). Performed in the Kikuyu language, the piece used traditional ritual, song and dance to tell a story of the betrayal of the people by Kenyans allied with foreigners. The Kenyan government suppressed the work, and Ngugi was fired from his university position. The Theatre for Development movement parallels the work in Brazil of Augusto Boal (1930–), who describes similar methods in his *Theatre of the Oppressed* (1975). Penina Mlama (1948–), who has written plays in Swahili dealing with social justice issues and has been active in community-based theatre in Tanzania, describes her strategies in her *Culture and Development: The Popular Theatre Approach in Africa* (1991) (see Chapter 10 for other examples of this movement).

With globalization and all of its attendant tensions and possibilities, we have thought it important in our final chapter in *Theatre Histories* to deal with a wide variety of performances at the borders and intersections of cultures. Chapter 12 and its case studies deal with cultural negotiations in performances as diverse as shamanistic ceremonies for tourists, Ariane Mnouchkine's *Les Atrides*, and ethnic tourist performance in a small town in Wisconsin.

GJW

Key references

Appadurai, A. (1996) *Modernity at Large, Cultural Dimensions of Globalization*, Minneapolis: University of Minnesota Press.

Banham, M., Hill, E. and Woodyard, G. (eds) (1994) *The Cambridge Guide to African and Caribbean Theatre*, Cambridge and New York: Cambridge University Press.

Byam, L.D. (1999) *Community in Motion, Theatre for Development in Africa*, Westport, Connecticut, and London: Bergin and Garvey.

Cole, C.M. (2001) *Ghana's Concert Party Theatre*, Bloomington: Indiana University Press.

García Canclini, N. (1995) *Hybrid Cultures, Strategies for Entering and Leaving Modernity*, trans. C.J. Chiappari and S. López, Minneapolis: University of Minnesota Press.

García Canclini, N. (2001) *Consumers and Citizens, Globalization and Multicultural Conflicts*, trans. George Yúdice, Minneapolis: University of Minnesota Press.

Gómez-Peña, G. (1996) *The New World Border*, San Francisco: City Lights Books.

Gómez-Peña, G. (2000) *Dangerous Border Crossers: The Artist Talks Back*, London: Routledge.

Gorman, L., and McLean, D. (2003) *Media and Society in the Twentieth Century, A Historical Introduction*, Oxford: Blackwell Publishing Ltd.

Kellner, D. (1995) *Media Culture, Cultural Studies, Identity and Politics between the Modern and the Postmodern*, London and New York: Routledge.

Kruger, L. (1999) *The Drama of South Africa*, London and New York: Routledge.

Lull, J. (1995) *Media, Communication, Culture, A Global Approach*, New York: Columbia University Press.

Nordenstreng, K. and Schiller, H.I. (eds) (1993) *Beyond National Sovereignty, International Communication in the 1990s*, Norwood, N.J.: Ablex Publishing Co.

Schechner, R. (2002) *Performance Studies, an Introduction*, New York and London: Routledge.

Thiong'o, N. (1986) *Decolonizing the Mind*, London, Portsmouth, Nairobi, Harare: James Curry (London), Heineman (Portsmouth), EAEP (Narobi), Zimbabwe Publishing House (Harare).

CHAPTER 10

Rich and poor theatres of globalization

Since the 1970s, globalization has tended to push theatrical production in two opposite directions. On the one hand, large theatrical institutions caught up in the globalization process – many national theatres, international festivals, and corporations producing mega-musicals – have expanded, and their costs have escalated. On the other hand, many artists around the world have dedicated themselves to local and regional theatrical institutions that have fought the incursions of western capital and cultural homogenization in their economies and local cultures. Many grassroots theatres in developing regions – often operating on very small budgets – have opposed the imperialism, political dictatorships, loss of economic control, and deteriorating social conditions that have accompanied cold war divisions and globalization in their countries.

If a large map were scaled to contrast the economic importance of all of the theatres in the world in the year 2005, the theatrical capitals of the West and Japan, plus a few other cities with large festivals, would take up most of the room on what would be a very skewed drawing. Squeezed into odd pockets and corners of this funny map, however, in

parts of Africa and in the inner cities and underdeveloped areas of western countries, for instance, would be many small but vibrant centers of theatrical activity. Such a map would also show many medium-range theatrical economies, in regional centers throughout the West and in most of the large cities of the rest of the world. This chapter ignores the medium-sized theatres to focus on the rich and poor extremes. It surveys some salient examples of big-budget theatre in Western Europe and North America, then turns to select instances of low-cost troupes in Africa, Latin America, and the Pacific, as well as to some poorer theatres in the backyards of the West. The primary burden of this chapter is to investigate how these particular kinds of theatres were altered by and responded to the cold war era and to the processes of globalization that have dominated since.

National theatres in the international marketplace

The postwar economic boom that lasted into the mid-1970s inspired many advocates of national theatres in the West to push for the realization of their dreams through massive building projects and increased budgets and repertories. In the United Kingdom, two major institutions vied for financial support from the government, the National Theatre and the Royal Shakespeare Company (RSC). The National opened a three-theatre complex in 1976 on the banks of the Thames in London that cost over $32 million to construct. In 1982, the RSC, which had been producing Shakespeare in the countryside at Stratford since 1961, also opened two new playing spaces in London, at the Barbican, making it the largest theatrical institution in the world. By the mid-1980s, both companies had expensive theatres to maintain and needed big budgets to fill their several stages with many actors and impressive scenery and costumes.

At stake in the success of both companies was the international theatrical prestige of the United Kingdom. Both theatres strove to produce the best of classical and contemporary theatre and boasted world-class companies and artistic directors. Peter Hall (1930–) replaced Lord Laurence Olivier as director of the National in 1973, and Trevor Nunn (1940–) managed the RSC from 1968 until 1986. For the government to allow either company to flounder was unthinkable. Although both companies had begun as national ventures to celebrate English theatre for English audiences, international tourism, global criticism, and high aesthetic expectations had put both in the world's limelight.

Controversy surrounded the London operations of both theatres from their inceptions. Fringe companies in the U.K. argued that the tax-generated sums spent on constructing the National should have been spread around to support many smaller groups. Hostility increased when the government revealed that a quarter of the Arts Council's drama budget in 1975–1976 had gone to the National, much of it for operating costs. Critics attacked the poor design of the Barbican complex, especially its huge mainstage and inadequate second space, and the RSC eventually abandoned its London site. The artistic directors

and supporters of both companies fought back, but even several outstanding productions from both companies could not quiet the controversies. Meanwhile, both the RSC and the National struggled to meet their massive budgets, often by resorting to smaller shows, shorter seasons, and extensive touring and residencies. The RSC departed from its primary mission to produce the plays of Shakespeare and his contemporaries by mounting large money-makers, including *Nicholas Nickleby* (1980) and *Les Miserables* (1985). In the face of shrinking subsidies and smaller audiences, the Arts Council for England published a paper in 1999 announcing new priorities for all state-subsidized theatres. The National and the RSC are still adjusting to these new demands, which include more educational initiatives and innovative productions. Both companies have been caught in the crunch between national budgetary constraints and international expectations.

A somewhat similar conflict faced the major theatres of Berlin after German reunification in 1990. During the cold war, both Germanys lavished large subsidies on several theatres in East and West Berlin, which became international showplaces for the rival cultures of the two superpowers. In the western half of the city, the Schiller Theater offered a repertory of bourgeois classics and contemporary plays from Western Europe and the United States. West Germany also located yearly festivals in Berlin that were designed to display the best West German productions to the world. In East Berlin, the Berliner Ensemble, the Volksbühne, and the Deutsches Theater, once the center of Max Reinhardt's theatrical enterprises, flourished on the international scene during the 1970s and 1980s.

After 1990, a newly unified Germany could no longer afford the costs of maintaining several world-class theatres in Berlin. In part, this was due to the fact that state subsidies in Germany typically covered about 80 percent of all operating costs. German theatre artists wanted their governmental bodies to maintain this level of support. The competition for spectators and subsidies, plus major reorganization in several companies, forced the closing of the Schiller Theater and several others. The Berliner Ensemble continued, but a new company modified its ties to the traditions of Brechtian production. To enhance the reputation of Berlin as a center for global performances, Theatertreffen, the festival that show-cases the best German productions of each year, increased its international productions. Like London, Berlin remains a center of globalized theatre, but the price of an international reputation limits the number of Berlin theatres that can maintain it.

The conflict between national and international priorities also played out in Canada, at the Stratford Festival. Begun in a town named after Shakespeare's birthplace in the province of Ontario in 1953, the Stratford Festival is now the largest repertory company in North America and heavily subsidized by the Canadian government. Though not an offi-cial national theatre, it is widely recognized as the theatrical flagship of Canada.

In his *Shakespeare and Canada*, Canadian historian Ric Knowles points out several ironies that have dogged the Stratford Festival since its begin-nings. Many Canadians understood the initial success of the Festival as a marker of Canada's maturity as a nation-state, despite the fact that Stratford rested on the authority of a famous English playwright and borrowed most of its actors and its artistic director (Tyrone Guthrie) from the country that had once ruled it as a colony. From the late 1960s through the 1970s, Stratford struggled to find a more "Canadian" identity with the appointment of a Canadian artistic director and more Canadian actors and plays. Nonetheless, the Canadian Left criticized the Festival for failing to recognize and incorporate the variety of Canadian nationalisms that had begun to prolif-erate and for confirming the status of Stratford as a high-art venue for the privileged. During the 1980s and into the 1990s, many Canadian playwrights and directors targeted "Shakespeare" at Stratford for satiric attack and reappropriated the Bard's plays for

their own uses. Black Theatre Canada produced a "Caribbean" *A Midsummer Night's Dream* in 1983, Skylight Theatre did a native-Canadian *The Tempest* (1987), and Theatre Under the Bridge staged an urban *Romeo and Juliet* (1993), literally under a bridge in downtown Toronto.

By the 1990s, the Stratford Festival still drained tax dollars from the Canadian people but had cut or compromised most of its national responsibilities to Canadians and looked to multinational corporate sponsors, international consumers, and global criti-cism for its legitimacy and prestige. Knowles exam-ines Stratford during the 1993 season and concludes that globalization had triumphed over national prior-ities. According to Knowles, the emphasis on aging sensualism in *Antony and Cleopatra* suited the consumerist fantasies of its audience, as did the conservative construction of black street culture for the 1993 *A Midsummer Night's Dream*. Other produc-tions that year included *The Mikado* and *The Importance of Being Earnest*, both old standards attrac-tive to the aesthetic predispositions of its mostly upper-class customers, many of whom were from the U.S. Fourteen pages of the souvenir program listed the individual and corporate donors for the season, and multinational companies got their names printed on the tickets for each show they sponsored. Knowles concludes that "Shakespeare at Stratford in 1993 was constructed and read as an intercultural, multinational, and historically transcendent product, presented for the pleasure of a privileged and cultur-ally dominant group of consumers for whom 'glob-alization' meant market access, and for whom cultural production was undertaken for the benefit and advantage of those who could afford it" (Knowles 2004:54).

International festivals

Although "festival" is a part of the Stratford's name, it might more properly be called a repertory theatre. Festivals may be better defined as invited gatherings of several theatre companies in a limited area for a limited time, usually less than a month. For theatre-goers, festivals typically offer the opportunity to see a number of critically acclaimed productions in a few days. For producers, invitational festivals are a chance to re-run their best shows, usually with low production costs and excellent publicity. Because many festivals invite small companies as well as large ones, some marginalized and experimental troupes have an opportunity to play to festival audiences. Transnational festivals also contribute to theatrical globalization. They tend to internationalize aesthetic trends and provide an important showcase for directors with global reputations. The fringe festivals that have grown up around some of the more prominent internationals also provide a chance for a few troupes to emerge as globally known companies.

Several festivals emerged after World War II that were designed to bring high culture to the common people. This was the goal of Jean Vilar, who founded the Avignon Festival in southern France in 1947. During the 1950s, Vilar also directed the Théâtre National Populaire (TNP), and the two institutions coordinated their efforts to decentralize French theatre and open it up to popular audiences. By 1963, the Avignon was attracting over 50,000 spectators for French theatre. Vilar, who had left the TNP to devote all of his time to the Festival, added new spaces and brought in younger directors.

Although several of Vilar's productions and the ones he championed at Avignon had challenged the French status quo, the radical Living Theatre from the U.S. led demonstrations in 1968 against what they called his "reactionary" leadership of Avignon and demanded that the Festival open its doors to all comers at no admission charge. The next year, several French-language troupes began offering fringe performances at Avignon, outside of the official program. These unofficial groups proliferated in the 1970s and 1980s – amateur and professional troupes performing everything from edgy minimalism to fully-staged classics – and gradually created a second Festival, called Avignon Off.

In 1994, the official Festival began to internationalize its offerings, although French-language productions still predominated. Avignon now boasts over 500 productions throughout the month of July, with most of them at the Avignon Off. French subsidies and corporate sponsorship, however, have elevated the official Festival to the status of global culture. As at the Canadian Stratford Festival, jet-set playgoers, the French elite, and international critics can enjoy high-priced theatrical fare at Avignon that does little to challenge their values. Although the fringe continues to dominate in sheer number of performances, by a ratio of about 10:1, few fringe productions are attended by these global players. A similar ratio has emerged at the Edinburgh Festival, which officially recognized its fringe festival as a separate operation much sooner than did the organizers of the Avignon. Most view the Avignon as a success, but its two-track festival, the official Avignon for the international elite and the Avignon Off for others, was clearly not what Vilar (or the Living Theatre) had in mind.

Perhaps the biggest drawback of international festivals is the decontextualization of their performances. Most festival productions begin in a different city with a local audience, one that might not share the interests and concerns of the national and international spectators attending the festival. Many directors and companies get around this problem by mounting well-known plays for festival spectators – the plays of Shakespeare, Beckett, and Chekhov, for example. When the DuMaurier World Stage festival in Toronto invited Brazil's Grupo Galpo, a street theatre troupe, to perform in 1998, however, the results were disorienting for most of the audience. Few Toronto spectators could understand the conventions of the neo-medieval biblical pageant that the Grupo had reshaped for their radical political purposes. The production, thrust out of its normal context in the villages of Brazil, became mostly an exercise in exotic tourism (see Chapter 12 on theatre and "tourism"). Not all festival productions suffer this level of decontextualization, of course, but those that veer very far from the expectations of international audiences risk the most.

Despite such tensions between the local and the global, international festivals have increased. The Vienna Festival in Austria, begun soon after World War II like the Avignon and the Edinburgh, has long featured companies from Russia and Eastern Europe. Its popularity, coupled with the ongoing success of the Bayreuth and Salzberg festivals, which date from before the war, has helped to foment the international festival spirit in other German-speaking areas. The Bonn Biennale, for example, got underway in 1992 and the Ruhr Triennale began in 2002. Many other cities around the globe now sponsor one or more international festivals. As nation-states have lost power in the globalization process, large cities have gained it, and hosting an important festival boosts a city's international reputation. These cities include Montreal, Toronto, Los Angeles, Mexico City, Buenos Aires, Wellington (New Zealand), Sydney, Melbourne, Singapore, Hong Kong, Tokyo, Athens, Rome, Paris, London, and Dublin, to name some of the most prominent. In addition, world-class cities have been hosting the Theatre Olympics, an international festival with more than 150 productions lasting over two months since the first one in Athens in 1995.

Mega-musicals

Producing musicals is now a global business. Composers, directors, and producers design musical spectaculars like Andrew Lloyd Webber's (1948–) *The Phantom of the Opera* as franchise operations that several companies can run for years in all the major cities of the English-speaking world. The scope and scale of these productions have led to several innovations. As costs and investment time continue to rise, producers have found ways to share their risks with non-commercial theatres. Moreover, the multinational corporation is taking the place of the individual producer in marketing mega-musicals.

(Producers typically formed short-term corporations in the past, but the global corporate players of today are long-term firms, with investments in a range of products.) *Phantom* and its offspring have been called mega-musicals for their lavish production values, enormous investments, high ticket prices (most tickets in New York cost $100 in 2004), and potential for huge profits.

The transition to risk sharing and corporate production for mega-musicals began in the 1980s. When London producer Cameron Mackintosh (1946–) teamed up with Lloyd Webber to produce *Cats* in 1981, the lush pop music and lavish spectacle of this dance-based production outclassed most of the other musical offerings in London and New York, and the show began an international run that lasted over 20 years. Mackintosh followed with other musical hits in the 1980s – *Les Miserables* (1985), *Phantom* (1986), and *Miss Saigon* (1989). Significantly, *Les Miserables* began at the publicly funded RSC, where Trevor Nunn staged its initial run. He and Mackintosh franchised the production, contractually obliging other producers of *Les Miserables* to mount it as near as possible to the original, with the result that both Mackintosh and the RSC profited nicely from the arrangement. Following his work with Mackintosh, Lloyd Webber formed a corporation, Really Useful Group, to produce his next musicals, which have included *Sunset Boulevard* (1993) and *The Beautiful Game* (2000).

More corporations entered the mega-musical business in the 1990s. In Toronto and New York, Livent produced two musical splashes, including *Ragtime* (1996, Toronto), before ending in bankruptcy The Walt Disney Corporation began producing on Broadway in 1994 and renovated a theatre on 42nd Street to house *The Lion King* (1998) and future productions. In the West End, Disney co-produced *Mary Poppins* with Mackintosh in 2004. Clear Channel Communications, a corporation with major investments in radio and television, also began developing mega-musicals (usually with other producers), but its major interest, in corporate lingo, is "feeding the road": creating musical products that supply its road companies with profitable fare. To ensure these profits, both conglomerates primarily feature "family entertainment," such as *Rugrats – A Live Adventure* (1998). Although this economic constraint does not rule out significant artistry – *The Lion King* won six Tonys, one for best musical – it does limit the financial risks.

Disney and other producers are also contracting to develop Broadway musicals with not-for-profit theatres in the U.S. When the non-profit regional theatre movement in the U.S. began in the late 1960s, companies in Chicago, Minneapolis, San Francisco and elsewhere looked primarily to European theatres and classical plays for their models, not to commercial Broadway. Few even produced musicals on a regular basis until the 1980s. The success of *A Chorus Line* (1975) at the New York Public Theatre (NYPT) and its transfer to Broadway for a 15-year run, with the resulting transfer of millions to the NYPT, however, permanently altered the non-profit landscape. The La Jolla Playhouse in San Diego has transferred several musicals to New York, including *The Who's Tommy* (1993) and many revivals. Disney opened an initial version of its *Aida* (1998) at the non-profit Alliance Theatre in Atlanta. Even the Guthrie Theatre in Minneapolis, the model of the classically-oriented regional theatre, has played the mega-musical game; in 1999, Mackintosh took his production of *Martin Guerre* to the Guthrie to prepare it for a Broadway opening. Once indifferent to each other's fortunes, the non-profits and the commercial theatres of the U.S. are now cooperating in the hope of milking musical cash cows. The second case study in this chapter looks at U.S. regional theatres in relation to niche marketing.

In 2000, a mega-musical in New York cost about ten million to produce and roughly $400,000 per week to run. With a possible weekly gross of around $800,000, most musicals must play for a year and a half before they break even. After two years

in New York and with the "Broadway" label affixed to its price tag, a mega-musical can begin a run in the international market; in 2003, ten versions of *The Lion King* were playing around the world. To explore how Broadway became the launching pad for mega-musicals and similar entertainments, the first case study in this chapter examines the history of Times Square.

Radical theatre in the West after 1968

While heavily financed theatres that played mostly to western consumers were adjusting to globalization after 1970, other theatre groups operating on shoe-string budgets opposed many of the changes that were altering the lives of disempowered peoples during the same decades. As noted in Chapter 9, the uprisings of 1968 awakened a sociopolitical consciousness in a new generation of theatre artists who were eager to help those oppressed by the cold war system of global power and the elites and governments within each country that supported it. Influenced primarily by democratic socialist ideals, these radical artists recognized the disparities in power caused by class, racial, and/or regional differences and hoped to forge an alternative culture that might help workers, peasants, and others to oppose capitalist power. To connect with this new audience, these troupes typically performed in parks, community centers, popular demonstrations, village squares, churches, and similar gathering places. Although much of this radical theatre began in the West, it had more political effectiveness in developing countries.

In the U.S., three radical troupes, The San Francisco Mime Troupe, El Teatro Campesino, and The Bread and Puppet Theatre were already in operation before 1968. Actors interested in exploring the traditions of *commedia dell'arte* had started the Mime Troupe in 1959, which reorganized as a theatre collective in 1970 and moved toward Marxist politics and Brechtian theatre. Its productions during the

1970s used comic-book stereotypes and fast-action farce to excoriate U.S. imperialism in Vietnam, push for women's rights, and expose the lies of local right-wing politicians. Luis Valdez (1940–), who briefly apprenticed with the Mime Troupe, began El Teatro Campesino in 1965 to support a farm workers strike in California. Several of Valdez's early plays contrasted poor Mexican-Americans with their rich white employers, celebrated Chicano culture, and urged the recognition of a separate territory in the Southwestern U.S. for a Chicano homeland. When Valdez began exploring the mythic basis of social injustice in the mid-1970s, however, many of his Latin American admirers criticized him for confusing social analysis with religious mysticism. Peter Schumann (1934–) founded The Bread and Puppet Theatre Company in 1961 and began aligning his puppet parades with anti-war demonstrations in 1964. For the next thirty years, the puppet heads of his peasants, washerwomen, and workers, plus his bad-guys like King Herod and Uncle Fatso (a capitalist-exploiter), figured in many demonstrations against war, homelessness, nuclearism, and the World Bank on the eastern seaboard of the U.S.

Bread and Puppet toured Europe in 1968, followed by El Teatro Campesino the next year. Their broadly satirical productions influenced many European theatre artists. Two major companies emerged in France, le Théâtre Populaire de Lorraine and Lo Théâtre de la Carriera, which pushed for the recognition of the unique culture of southern France and decried the region's industrialization by Parisian "imperialists." The events of 1968 led to the founding of several theatres in West Germany, most notably the Grips Theatre, which produced radical plays for children and youth in Berlin. In Spain, several theatres opposed dictator Francisco Franco and his repressive regime during the early 1970s, despite rigorous censorship. These included Els Joglars in Barcelona, troupes pushing for Basque independence in northern Spain, and Tabaño in Madrid, which mocked Spanish consumerism,

authoritarianism, and the Catholic church in several productions.

The theatres of John McGrath (1935–2002) and Dario Fo (1926–) represent the highpoint of radical, post-1968 theatre in Europe. Both had succeeded professionally in the entertainment business before turning to radical theatre. McGrath chose the name for his theatre, "7:84," from a statistic published in 1966 in *The Economist*, which stated that 7 percent of the population of Great Britain owned 84 percent of the capital wealth. For McGrath and his company, 7:84 underlined the need to develop socialist alternatives to the capitalist system that dominated English and Scottish lives. Following the start of 7:84 in 1971, McGrath quickly adapted his theatre to the tastes of British working men and women by including broad humor, catchy tunes, and identifiable locations. His two companies toured to working-class halls and pubs throughout the 1970s with such plays as *The Cheviot, the Stag, and the Black, Black Oil* (1973), which demonstrated that capitalists' desire to profit from North Sea oil was simply one more episode in the long exploitation of the Scottish poor by the English rich.

In 1968, Dario Fo and his playwright-actor wife, Franca Rame (1929–), broke from the commercial theatre to establish a theatrical cooperative, which soon produced *Mistero Buffo* (1969), a one-person show (with Fo as court jester) that satirized Catholicism. *Accidental Death of an Anarchist* followed in 1970, a farcical attack on police corruption (Figure 10.1). During the 1970s and 1980s, Fo continued his explorations of Italian folk drama, including *commedia dell'arte*, wrote several more plays, and expanded his repertoire of theatrical clowning. Rame wrote and performed feminist pieces, such as *All Bed, Board, and Church* (1977), which excoriated Italian patriarchy. Fo and Rame performed at many rallies for progressive causes and in culturally-deprived zones, often donating the proceeds to radical political movements. These proceeds might be quite substantial; in the mid-1980s, Fo often

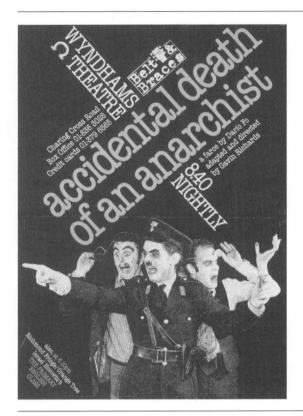

Figure 10.1 Poster for
*Accidental Death of an
Anarchist*, by Dario Fo.
© V&A Images, Victoria
and Albert Museum.

attracted over 10,000 spectators per performance. In 1997, he was awarded the Nobel Prize for Literature.

These radical theatre artists of the post-1968 generation were only the most prominent of the several thousand artists and their troupes in Western Europe and North America that used theatrical means in an attempt to change the direction of politics and economics of their nation-states toward more egalitarian versions of democratic socialism in the 1970s and 1980s. They targeted non-theatre audiences of agricultural or industrial laborers, often worked in collectives and created plays collaboratively, and generally incorporated many elements of folk and popular culture without, however, bowing to commercial tastes or values. Most troupes struggled financially, and several turned to governmental funding to support their work. Although these

groups could claim many strategic successes, the movement as a whole had little impact on the shape and direction of western society. Measured in terms of the democratic socialism favored by most of these artists, the West was clearly less progressive in 1990 than it had been in 1968.

Critics have pointed to several reasons for the failure of radical theatre to transform western society and culture. Accepting governmental funding may have compromised their goals. Many artists left the movement to work in commercial entertainment, and some companies maintained a superior attitude toward their audiences instead of working with them to produce what they wanted and needed. While these shortcomings within the movement probably played some role, other factors were likely more important. After World War II, most workers relied on their unions and socialist or democratic political parties to improve their lives; they did not build alternative institutions in opposition to capitalism. Even the Communist party in Italy was working within the system by the 1970s, and Dario Fo had to break his ties with them in order to present his more radical theatrical visions. Consequently, radical theatres found little support within the ongoing secular institutions of working-class life. Further, the ideological constraints of the cold war, perpetuated by western nation-states and the commercial media, limited the options that workers and others imagined as practical for themselves. It was one thing to cheer the radical socialist vision of the Mime Troupe or 7:84 at a weekend performance, but quite another to act on those beliefs in the union hall or at the voting booth. Finally, with increasing globalization, workers and others were defining themselves less in class, racial, or regional terms than as consumers, and this reorientation of primary identity undercut their commitment to radical politics. Although many theatre troupes in the West clung to the utopian hopes of the late 1960s, their audiences were moving toward other values and identities.

Post-1968 radical theatre in developing nations

In contrast, radical theatre companies in the developing world after 1968 found audiences that were more responsive to their politics. Several troupes grew out of institutions that already opposed the politics, unions, and culture of the dominant society, and these companies maintained their ties to alternative institutions during their theatrical work. Further, many theatre artists and their audiences lived under oppressive governments and faced a difficult choice between servile poverty and the dangers of active opposition. Apolitical consumerism, the default choice of many westerners, was simply not an option for many people in developing countries during the 1970s and 1980s. Several non-western theatre companies chose active opposition to their

national regimes and helped their oppressed countrymen toward better lives and political liberation.

Many theatre troupes in Africa aroused their audiences to oppose the legacies of imperialism, racist policies, and state-sponsored oppression. In South Africa, for example, the Peoples' Experimental Theatre performed plays in the 1970s that undermined the apartheid regime. *Shanty*, by Mthuli ka Shezi (1947–1972), demonstrates the need for solidarity among three characters representing the major groups of non-whites: "Black," "Indian," and "Colored," as defined by the apartheid government. The play dramatizes the beliefs of the Black Consciousness Movement in South Africa, headed by activist Steve Biko and others. In Eritrea, on the horn of Africa, the Eritrean People's Liberation Front (EPLF) produced several plays in the 1970s and 1980s as a part of its struggle for independence from Ethiopia. The EPLF staged some of these plays and many variety shows near the front lines of military combat as a morale booster for the troops, one-third of whom were female. *If It Had Been Like This* (1980), by Afewerki Abraha, transcends the usual fun of troop entertainment to explore one of the goals of the Eritrean struggle, equal rights for women. Reversing the usual gender roles, the farce shows a man cleaning house, preparing food, and suffering the beatings of his wife when she returns from work, after drinking and carousing with another man. Afewerki's send-up of normal gender roles in eastern Africa led to mixed responses among the soldiers, but left no doubt that feminism would be a part of the ELPF's fight for independence.

Perhaps the most successful radical theatre in the developing world was the Philippine Educational Theatre Association (PETA), a network of community-based theatres that fought against the dictatorship of Ferdinand Marcos from 1967 until its fall in 1986. During the 1970s, PETA members combined improvisational exercises, values from Catholic liberation theology, and the radical educational ideas of Paolo Freire (a Brazilian educator who also influenced Augusto Boal) to train themselves in theatrical skills and community organizing. Core groups of facilitator-organizers moved from Manila and other cities into the countryside to educate villagers in anti-imperialism and democratic socialism through theatrical activities and performances. In most of the companies, facilitators helped locals to write and direct scripts that analyzed their social, economic, and political conditions and suggested solutions. PETA's widespread local bases and popularity gave it enormous resilience in the face of Marcos's attempts at suppression and the official opposition of the Catholic Church. By 1986, nearly 300 local theatres, run by fishermen, peasants, students, industrial workers, and others, comprised the PETA network.

After the fall of the regime, PETA shifted its emphasis from anti-imperialism and socialism to examining and protesting the effects of local, national, and global policies on everyday lives. In addition to many touring productions for youth and village audiences, PETA has a repertory company that mounts large productions in the courtyard of a former Spanish fort in downtown Manila. Recent productions include *Domestic Helper* (1992), about Filipina maids who must work abroad to support their families back home, and *1896*, staged in 1996 to mark the centennial of the Filipino revolution against Spain (Figure 10.2). In 1995, PETA collaborated with the San Francisco Mime Troupe on a musical satire about elections in the Philippines. Most of PETA's financing now comes from external

Figure 10.2 Performance of *1896* (1995) by PETA, the Philippine Educational Theatre Association, a network of community-based theatres that fought against the regime of Ferdinand Marcos from 1967 until its fall in 1986. Libretto by Charley de la Paz; music by Lucian Leteba; directed by Soxie Topacio © PETA.

NGOs (non-governmental organizations) and from local contributions and fees. These fund a wide range of projects, from local workshops, to a school for people's theatre, outreach and touring programs, and direct subsidies for theatrical and video activities.

Theatres for development

Given its present educational and community-building goals, PETA has become an example of a theatre for development as well as a radical political theatre. The term "theatre for development" (TFD) originated in Botswana, Africa in the mid-1970s to describe performances intended to help communities address their difficulties with health, agriculture, literacy, and similar problems. The basic model, as it emerged in a series of conferences and workshops, involved theatre activists researching a community problem, creating a play through debate and improvisation, presenting the piece to the community, and following the performance with discussion and community planning. Well-funded by NGOs, this model spread throughout English-speaking Africa in the 1980s, as we saw in the Introduction to Part IV. Many theatre and community leaders, however, criticized the early phase of TFD for its crude modernization ideology, its failure to involve community participants, and its blindness to local customs and political power struggles. Most present versions of TFD now incorporate these criticisms and have remained an important strategy for activists seeking theatrical means to improve the lives of many Africans.

Soon after the Cuban Revolution in 1959, Castro and his deputies began to use a type of theatre for development to transform Cuba. Although influenced by the success of the Blue Blouse troupes in the Soviet Union after the Russian Revolution, the Cuban radicals also drew on the examples of Buenaventura in Colombia and Boal in Brazil. In 1969, the Castro regime sent a company of professionals from Havana who had been performing modernist works into the Escambray region, roughly in the center of the island, where counterrevolutionary groups had been fighting in the early 1960s. Their job was to work with the traditional small farmers and peasants of the region and prepare them for the collectivization that the regime planned to introduce. Mixing revolutionary propaganda with participatory techniques and developmental strategies, the Teatro Escambray succeeded with the local population and became a model for Cuban revolutionary theatre by the mid-1970s.

Nuevo Teatro Popular

The combination of radical political theatre and theatre for development exemplified by the Teatro Escambray exerted wide influence in Latin America during the 1970s and 1980s. In part, this was because Cuba had repelled U.S. intervention and countered U.S. imperialism with policies that encouraged national revolutions. Cuba also welcomed dissident radicals and exiled revolutionaries from all of Latin America and encouraged them to apply the lessons of Teatro Escambray and other Cuban success stories to their own nations. Some of these theatres pushed for a Cuban-style revolution, but many more worked toward versions of democratic socialism. In Mexico, where over 200 theatres joined socialist politics to community development, this movement was called Nuevo Teatro Popular (New Popular Theatre), a term that can be applied to the movement as a whole.

Throughout Latin America, Nuevo Teatro was nearly as various as it was huge, embracing amateurs and professionals, performing in agit-prop and realistic styles, drawing urban intellectual and village peasant audiences, and ranging widely among aesthetic and political priorities. Some of the more prominent companies included the Teatro Experimental de Cali from Colombia, El Galpon in Uruguay, Grupo Octubre from Argentina, and the CLETA (Centro Libre de Experimentación Teatral y Artística) alliance in Mexico. Each of these groups, in turn, influenced dozens more in their regions.

These Nuevo Teatro companies helped to empower peasants and workers in Colombia, Peru and Mexico, worked against repressive dictatorships in Brazil, Argentina, and Uruguay, and supported democratic socialist regimes in Chile and Nicaragua.

In their *Latin American Popular Theatre* (1993), Judith Weiss and her co-writers point to several factors that made Nuevo Teatro a movement and not just a series of similar theatrical efforts. First, these radical troupes drew from a common tradition of Brechtian theatre and politics, often via the work of Buenaventura and Boal, even though their productions varied widely in style. Second, Spanish-speaking groups in several nation-states shared many of the same directors, actors, and playwrights, sometimes because exile from one country would force a theatre artist to work in another. Third, several theatres gained funding from the same international NGOs (Inter Pares and OXFAM, for example) for their community development work. Fourth, most troupes conducted research into the social and economic circumstances of their audiences, and all sought substantive spectator feedback. Finally, the major troupes met regularly in festivals and conferences to compare their best work and to workshop new strategies. Not surprisingly, Cuba took the initiative in this regard, promoting significant hemispheric meetings of theatre artists and troupes in 1964 and 1967.

Since 1990, with the end of the cold war, the decline of Cuba, and the fall of most dictatorial governments in Latin America, the Nuevo Teatro movement has lost steam. Fewer theatres now do this kind of work; the traditional organizing and theatrical strategies of Nuevo Teatro do not always speak to the new realities of globalization. Nevertheless, many troupes have made a successful transition to the globalization era. The Yuyachkani company in Peru, for example, began moving away from Marxist theatre in the 1980s in response to the mass killings of indigenous and rural mestizo populations by the Maoist revolutionaries in Peru known as The Shining Path. In such pieces as *Contralviento*

(1989) and *Adios Ayacucho* (1990), Yuyachkani – the name translates roughly as "I am remembering" in Quechua – affirmed the need to remember the victims of these genocides and to understand the trauma they have caused. Performing primarily to sophisticated audiences in Lima, Yuyachkani invites its spectators to experience indigenous points of view and to broaden their vision of what it means to be a Peruvian in their multilingual and multiethnic country.

In Chiapas, the southern-most area of Mexico, two related theatre companies are also raising questions about national identity that are directly related to the dynamics of globalization. As men lose traditional positions in farming and women migrate to the cities to support their families, globalization is pulling apart indigenous Mayan communities. In response to these and other problems in Chiapas, Lo'il Maxil and La Fomma work with Mayan populations to improve literacy, raise political awareness, and pressure the Mexican government to provide better options. Lo'il Maxil (Tzotzil for "Monkey Business") is closely allied with the Zapitista movement, which has been negotiating with the government for a degree of self-rule in Chiapas since their armed uprising in 1994. Lo'il Maxil's *De Todas Para Todas* (*From All, For All*), initially produced in 1994, for example, celebrates a rural Mayan community that is robbed of its lands, banished to the jungle, and then takes up arms to reclaim its heritage. Significantly, the ending of the play recommends negotiation with the Mexican government, not the continuation of armed rebellion. La Fomma is an acronym in Spanish that stands for "Strength of the Mayan Women." In addition to producing plays aimed at assisting women with a variety of new social problems, their dramas target the neo-liberal economic policies of Mexico that have forced the separation of Mayan family members. Other plays, such as *Hechame la Mano* (*Lend Me a Hand*) (2001), explore the dangers for women of participating in the international tourist trade.

Community-based theatre since 1990

Lo'il Maxil, La Fomma, and most other theatres with roots in Nuevo Teatro Popular are now considered part of a worldwide phenomenon that U.S. theatre scholars and others have called community-based theatre. Though not a coordinated movement, community-based theatres around the world share several features in common. Drawing on the legacy of Nuevo Teatro Popular and other theatres that mixed political agitation and developmental strategies, community-based theatres also depend upon ongoing dialog between artists and spectators and explore ways of maximizing the agency of a local audience. Unlike those earlier theatres, however, the political beliefs of artists committed to community-based work are not oriented to revolutionary action or democratic socialism, but grow out of their commitment to a local community or social group. Although most espouse leftist values, some are motivated by a conservative desire to preserve the past or to pursue neo-liberal notions of community development. Not surprisingly, these political differences often relate to competing definitions of the term "community," which may encompass one or several regional, racial, or ethnic groups, but usually involve excluding some groups as outsiders. Community-based theatre's commitment to a "community" has been both a strength and a weakness, energizing some groups for self-improvement and progressive change and limiting the social, political, and aesthetic reach of others. For those communities caught up in problems related to globalization, community-based theatre has primarily led to smart tactics and long-term adjustment or resistance, but also to parochialism and nostalgia.

There are thousands of community-based theatres around the globe. In Western Europe and North America, community-based artists and facilitators have focused much of their attention on empowering marginalized groups, celebrating the useable past of a community, and helping people to energize communities that have been damaged or destroyed. With regard to this third goal, Roadside Theatre in the United States works with Appalachian citizens to restore pride in their past culture (among many other projects). The LAPD (the Los Angeles Poverty Department) helps to generate a sense of community among the residents of Skid Row in Los Angeles. In Toronto, Ground Zero has been more interested in empowerment than community building; it has facilitated the political agency of several groups, including indigenous tribes and unionized hospital workers. While facilitator Ann Jellicoe (1927–) has helped several communities in England to celebrate their histories, Swamp Gravy, located in a small town in Georgia in the U.S., draws on local tradition and African-American Christianity to bridge the racial divide in the American South. Several companies work toward all of the goals noted above. Stut Theatre in Utrecht, The Netherlands, recently devised a production involving Dutch, Turkish, and Moroccan young people and their parents to recognize the needs of the two marginalized groups and encourage intercultural understanding.

Community-based theatres in other parts of the world also incorporate these goals, as well as pursuing aims that demonstrate more commitment to social and economic transformation. Nos do Morro (Us from the Hillside) produces theatre for the poor citizens who live in the hills above the rich beaches of Rio de Janeiro in Brazil. The theatre serves as a local community center that provides participatory entertainment and occasional intervention to help the workers, street children, and dispossessed of the area. Like PETA in the Philippines, Jodrikdrik in the Marshall Islands trains squads of young people to lead outreach programs using theatrical techniques that help other youth adjust to the many problems that globalization is bringing to the islands, including AIDS, increasing alcoholism, and the disruption of traditional culture. The Kawuonda Woman's Group shows the continuing influence of Theatre for

Development programs in a small village in Kenya. When the women dramatize one of their stories for the village, they typically rehearse them in the midst of doing the laundry or picking coffee beans, and they perform their short scenes within a circle of dancers and singers to demonstrate their female solidarity. The artists leading Aguamarina in Costa Rica model their work on the socialist politics of Nuevo Teatro in the rest of Spanish-speaking America. One of their recent pieces, created collaboratively with local fishermen, examined the problem of industrial trawlers that fish Costa Rican waters and saturate the local market with cheap produce.

Many of the artists involved with these community-based theatres have adopted savvy strategies to moderate or resist some of the effects of globalization that are changing the lives of the populations they assist. The United States media, especially television programming and films, now saturate the lives of young people around the globe; global media are fast replacing traditional cultures as a common point of reference in most societies. Jodrikdrik on the Marshall Islands recognizes this fact and encourages their participants to mix island traditions with popular songs and media genre from the U.S. in their annual talent show, called, appropriately, *Showtime!* Nos do Morro in Rio has found film and television work for several of the young actors who have performed on its stage. Other community-based theatres, including PETA, la Fomma, and Aguamarina, have helped their participants to organize collectives to maintain the economic viability of traditional crafts in competition with international corporations.

The pressures of globalization are also changing the organizational strategies of community-based work. Yuyachkani in Peru maintains its company identity, but also facilitates the work of individual members to pursue projects related to company goals. Ground Zero in Toronto has abandoned the notion of a theatre company altogether. Its founder, Don Bouzek, now works with temporary alliances of funders, clients, and artists to produce theatre pieces that will advance progressive causes and alliances in Canada. Scholars of contemporary interventionist theatre Alan Filewod and David Watt argue that such "strategic ventures" (Filewod and Watt 2001: *passim*), involving like-minded artists and activists collaborating together on specific projects, provide the best strategy for transforming communities in the global future.

BMc

Key references

Adler, S. (2004) *On Broadway: Art and Commerce on the Great White Way*, Urbana, I.L.: Southern Illinois University Press.

Boon, R. and Plastow, J. (eds) (1998) *Theatre Matters: Performance and Culture on the World Stage*, Cambridge: Cambridge University Press.

Erven, E. van (1988) *Radical People's Theatre*, Bloomington, I.N.: Indiana University Press.

Erven, E. van (1992) *The Playful Revolution: Theatre and Liberation in Asia*, Bloomington, I.N.: Indiana University Press.

Erven, E. van (2001) *Community Theatre: Global Perspectives*, London: Routledge.

Filewod, A. and Watt, D. (2001) *Workers' Playtime: Studies in Theatre and the Labour Movement in Australia, Canada, and the United Kingdom, 1970–1997*, Sydney: Currency Press.

Fischer-Lichte, E. (1997) *The Show and the Gaze of Theatre: A European Perspective*, Iowa City, I.A.: University of Iowa Press.

Haedicke, S. and Nellhaus, T. (eds) (2001) *Performing Democracy: International Perspectives on Urban Community-Based Performance*, Ann Arbor, M.I.: University of Michigan Press.

Kershaw, B. (1992) *The Politics of Performance: Radical Theatre as Cultural Intervention*, London: Routledge.

Knowles, R. (2004) *Reading the Material Theatre*, Cambridge: Cambridge University Press.

Knowles, R. (2004) *Shakespeare and Canada: Essays on Production, Translation, and Adaptation*, Bruxelles: Peter Lang.

Underiner, T. (2004) *Contemporary Theatre in Mayan Mexico: Death-Defying Acts*, Austin: Texas University Press.

Weiss, J.A. with Leslie Damasceno, *et al.* (1993) *Latin American Popular Theatre: The First Five Centuries*, Albuquerque, N.M.: University of New Mexico Press.

Wilmer, S.E. (2002) *Theatre, Society, and The Nation: Staging American Identities*, Cambridge: Cambridge University Press.

CASE STUDY: The vortex of Times Square

Shopping on Broadway

On every Saturday night in 2002, tourists to New York City who had attended the musical *42nd Street* at the Ford Center emerged from the darkness of the auditorium into the crowd to blink at the bright lights of the real 42nd Street. Instead of the "naughty, bawdy, gaudy, sporty" 42nd Street of the musical, those tourists soon encountered stores in the Broadway-42nd Street area with the brand names of American mass culture – The Gap, McDonald's, and Toys "R" Us, among many others. Where the musical is overtly nostalgic, appealing to the desperate hope for show-biz fame celebrated in Busby Berkeley's 1933 musical film (on which the

stage musical is based), the Times Square district today pulsates with contemporary culture. The hope for commercial success still remains, of course; crowds gather around a Turkish master of spray painting, a young black man breakdancing, and a few Chinese calligraphers who will print your name for a price. Other salesmen inside the stores offer Coke, Kellogg, Samsung, Proctor and Gamble, General Electric, Sprint, and Nike products (to name a few). Times Square has meant many things to many people in the past hundred years, but now it is principally about shopping. Indeed, squeezing through the crowds along Broadway or 7th Avenue between 42nd and 48th streets at 11:00 pm on a Saturday

Figure 10.3 Traffic and advertising signs along the Seventh Avenue side of Times Square at night, December 2004. Photo © Bruce McConachie.

night, tourists soon get the feeling that they are careening inside an enormous reflecting bowl of American pop culture and celebrating their identities as consumers of familiar products, which are dressed up and dancing in the computer-controlled megawatts of over five hundred illuminated signs (Figure 10.3).

The meeting of actors and spectators in a space dedicated to performance is only one part of theatre-going. In all historical eras, spectators have traveled to the sites of performances and re-emerged into the environment in which their theatres were located.

The ecology of theatre districts has directly shaped spectators' expectations and memories of perform-ance events. Throughout history, buildings or places set aside for public performances have often been sited at important crossroads, near centers of power, sometimes overlooking a central city square. (At other times, as in Elizabethan London and Tokugawa Tokyo, significant theatres were located at the margins of power.) The location of a state-supported playhouse or of a commercial theatre district within a city can tell the historian much about the role of the theatre in that society and culture.

INTERPRETIVE APPROACH: Vortices of behavior

In *Cities of the Dead: Circum-Atlantic Performance*, historian Joseph Roach describes theatre districts and other urban areas dedicated to performance as "vortices of behavior." The word "vortex" usually means a whirling mass of water, but it can also refer to a kind of whirlpool situation that draws everything toward its center. According to Roach, theatre districts create metaphorical whirlpools that pull performers and audiences together into the same space, where they transform everyday behavior into performances that nurture and validate their culture. States Roach:

> The vortex is a kind of spatially induced carnival, a center of cultural self-invention. . . . Into such maelstroms, the magnetic forces of commerce and pleasure suck the willing and unwilling alike. Although such a zone or district seems to offer a place for transgression, for things that couldn't happen otherwise or elsewhere, in fact what it provides is far more official: a place in which everyday practices may be legitimated, "brought out into the open," reinforced, celebrated, or intensified. When this happens, what I will be calling condensational events result. The principal character-istic of such events is that they gain a powerful enough hold on collective memory that they will survive the transformation or the relocation of the spaces in which they first flourished.

(Roach 1996:28)

Roach implicitly invites the student of theatre history to locate such vortices of behavior in the past and present, to note how everyday behaviors are celebrated and intensified within them, and to focus on those "condensational events" that have emerged from the "mael-strom." As their name implies, condensational events condense, conflate, and compact certain practices in such a way that they can "travel" to other locales for re-performance

▷

▷ by other actors. Perhaps the most widely recognized "condensational event" associated with Times Square over the years has been the dropping of a giant, illuminated ball at midnight on 31 December to mark the start of the New Year. That event first occurred in 1907 and it has been widely imitated and re-performed ever since.

Following Roach's ideas, it ought to be possible to write a brief history of Times Square by examining the major condensational events that emerged from this vortex of behavior. Several of these events of course, have been theatrical in nature. Broadway-Times Square (the two terms are nearly interchangeable) has initiated thousands of plays, revues, and musicals that have toured the country, endured the blunderings of countless amateur productions, and switched media to be recycled as film and television re-makes. Other condensational events of the Times Square area, however, have not always supported the commercial stage – or have supported light entertainment but not heavier dramatic fare. A history of the Broadway district as a vortex of behavior, then, might also comment on the effects of condensational events on the expectations and memories of theatregoers – the mental images the district has generated that have shaped the hopes and dreams of patrons walking to and from the theatre.

In using this approach for any historical period, the historian of theatre and culture would ask such questions as these:

KEY QUESTIONS

1   How did the entertainment district of a historical period operate as a vortex of behavior?

2   Within this vortex, which everyday behaviors were celebrated and intensified? Which behaviors emerged as condensational events?

3   How did these condensational events travel through the culture in several media and to other locales?

The Broadway vortex, 1904–1960

Times Square got its name in 1904. The owner of the *New York Times* newspaper, Adolph Ochs, pulled some strings at City Hall and asked that the old Longacre Square be re-named Times Square in honor of his newspaper, which had just relocated there. In 1904, Times Square was one of the fastest growing areas in metropolitan New York. The subways had opened that year, and the station at 42nd and Broadway, a major junction in the new system, was soon pouring thousands of New Yorkers into the district every day. The moguls of the commercial stage, who had concentrated their theatres ten blocks south in Herald Square, saw the opportunities of the new district and began to open new playhouses. By 1910, there were 40 first-class theatres and nearly as many vaudeville and burlesque houses in and around Times Square. Restaurateurs also took advantage of the increased traffic and soon several "lobster palaces" were catering to the pre-show and post-show trade. Led by such tunesmiths as Irving Berlin and dance celebrities Vernon and Irene Castle, popular ragtime music was rousing New Yorkers out of sedentary spectating and swirling them into the new "dance craze." To feed the craze, entrepreneurs opened dozens of dance halls and nightclubs in the Times Square area before 1914. Not all was top hats and ball gowns, however. Saloons, cheap hotels, and whorehouses jammed the side streets east and west of Broadway for the gamblers, chorus girls, longshoremen, waiters, and newspapermen who lived in the district, and the tourists and elite who came to play.

Perhaps the most important condensational event of this historical period, and one that would epitomize the vortex of Times Square for the next hundred years, was the instant success of the spectacular sign. Advertising billboards had long been popular, but it was only after 1890 that they began to be powered by electricity. O.J. Gude, already a leading adman in New York at the turn of the century, perfected the first generation of electric signs. The first of Gude's "spectaculars," as the new signs were called, depicted the Heatherbloom Girl in a short, illuminated drama that showed a rainstorm whipping at the dress and petticoats of the light-bulb-outlined giantess and revealing a glimpse of her stockinged calf. Gawkers gathered for hours on the street below in 1905 to watch the recurring scene. Condensed versions of this potent mix of product placement, sexual titillation, and electricity would continue to circulate through American culture and come to dominate the advertising pitches of global culture by the end of the century.

While Gude's spectaculars illuminated Broadway as "The Great White Way," the image of the chorus girl led to condensational events of whiteness of another kind. Florenz Ziegfeld began producing his annual *Follies* in 1907. By 1920 he and his designers, with the help of hundreds of "girls," had perfected the Follies fashion model of *haute couture*. Sexy, sophisticated, but wholesome and always white, this image gained cultural dominance. She paraded into fashion runways, beauty pageants, car shows, and football half-time events for the next 50 years (Figure 10.4).

Although the ambience of the Times Square vortex in the early days validated most of the theatrical activity on Broadway, there were exceptions. Before 1914, even serious dramatic offerings at high-priced theatres rarely taxed the mind or criticized the status quo. This began to change in the 1920s, however, as the productions of the new American modernist theatre mixed it up with the revues, musicals, murder melodramas, and sex farces on Broadway. The theatre of Robert Edmund Jones, Elmer Rice, and Eugene O'Neill had little in common with the froth and fun of Times Square in the "roaring" twenties. Nineteen of O'Neill's plays gained production on Broadway between 1920 and 1934. At the same time, the Theatre Guild was staging many of the playwrights of European modernism, including Shaw, Kaiser, and Pirandello. By most terms of comparison, Ziegfeld's Broadway was incompatible with *Desire Under the Elms*.

In contrast, the plays of George S. Kaufman (1889–1961) and others who practiced deflating farce and witty repartee fit right in to the ambience of 1920s Times Square. This was the era of *The Smart Set*, *The New Yorker*, and the wits of the Algonquin Round Table. The image of Kaufman, Dorothy Parker, Alexander Woollcott, Edna Ferber, Robert Benchley, Harpo Marx, and others sitting around their reserved table at the Algonquin Hotel and trading wisecracks emerged as a condensational event that put Times Square on the map as the home of quick wit, backbiting innuendo, and modern irony and aplomb. Kaufman's plays, including *Dulcy* (1921), *Merton of the Movies* (1922), and *Beggar on Horseback* (1924) – all co-authored with Marc

Figure 10.4 Publicity photo-collage showing the see-through runway for Ziegfeld's *Midnight Frolic*, produced on the roof of the Amsterdam Theatre between 1913 and 1927. © Museum of the City of New York.

Connelly (1890–1980) – recycled the sparkle and snap of the Algonquins for middle-class distribution. This brand of wisecracking irreverence also made it into many movies, most memorably the early films of the Marx Brothers – Chico (Leonard) (1887–1961), Harpo (Adolph Arthur) (1888–1964), and Groucho (Julius Henry) (1890–1977). Their *Cocoanuts* and *Animal Crackers* succeeded first as stage productions (1925 and 1928) and later joined *Monkey Business* (1931) and *Duck Soup* (1933) as films to parody the powerful, send up sexual propriety, and celebrate release from middle-class restraints.

The rise of film viewing, the decline of live entertainment, and the Depression of the 1930s led to a major shift in the environment of Times Square. By the late-1930s, the Broadway vortex still boasted opulent signs, black-tie openings, and glamorous nightclubs, but dime museums, peep shows, and flea circuses had also moved in. Sleaze and eccentricity

were replacing the swank and style of the 1920s, as the elite found other playgrounds in the city. Mr. and Mrs. Middle-Class America had decided that they would rather watch films than live theatre, and the growth of film production led to the transformation of numerous Broadway playhouses into movie theatres. It also brought many of the delights of the Coney Island amusement park into downtown Manhattan. Film audiences, however, still liked to see their stars live and the Hollywood moguls accommodated this profitable desire by creating film premiere nights at the movie palaces of the nation – on Broadway. The event of the opening night, no longer restricted to the elite and condensed for radio and newsreel consumption by the masses, circulated widely in the culture. It continues to command media attention.

On 14 August, 1945, the date that Japan surrendered to the Allies to end World War II, Times

Square became the center of the nation's joyful celebration. All the media of the day broadcast sounds and images of strangers hugging, kissing, and sobbing. By 10:00 pm on that evening, two million people had flocked to the Broadway district, the largest gathering in the history of Times Square. A *Life* magazine reporter shot the photo that would condense and memorialize this event for the nation – a sailor in his dress blues scoops an unsuspecting nurse off her feet and plants a joyful kiss on her lips. This image of Times Square as the center of national celebration underwrote the ecology of the district from 1945 through the early 1960s. Although at odds with the serious plays of Arthur Miller, Tennessee Williams, and others who continued and enhanced U.S. theatrical modernism, the image was congenial to the upbeat musicals of Rodgers and Hammerstein, Kander and Ebb, and Lerner and Lowe. As in the musical *Guys and Dolls* (1950), set in a half-mythical Times Square of night clubs, gambling dens, and Salvation Army shelters, the Great White Way of the postwar era seemed to be the home of benevolent eccentricity. Its seedy but romantic urbanity continued to buoy the nation's spirits through the anxious era of the cold war. The electrified signs of the times, now mostly designed by Douglas Leigh, were bigger and more inviting than ever. Perhaps his most successful "spectacular" was an enormous image of a satisfied Camel smoker who blew perfect smoke rings (made of steam) out his mouth every four seconds.

Times Square goes global

By the 1970s, the Broadway district had sunk into sleaze and crime. Pornography, drugs, and prostitution had been a part of the area since its beginnings, but these problems began to drive out legitimate businesses in the early 1960s. The clientele for these activities remained largely middle class, but now Times Square was servicing the middle-class "deviants" of the nation, not just in New York. Worse, the crime rate rose to one of the highest in the city – not just victimless crimes but frequent muggings, rapes, and murders. Several national images and condensational events emerged from Times-Square-as-hell-hole during the 1960s and 1970s. These were perhaps best captured with the release of the film *Taxi Driver* in 1976, in which Robert DeNiro plays a deranged taxi driver who goes on a killing rampage against the hookers, hustlers, and assorted crazies in this urban heart of darkness.

The businessmen and politicians who ran New York understood that the Broadway district could not be allowed to rot forever. It was too centrally located and still generated enormous tourist dollars. But they dithered until the 1990s over plans for its renewal. Luckily for them, the crime rate declined, and New York City gradually dug itself out of its fiscal hole. Promoters floated several plans for the area in the 1980s, one involving an indoor mall with aerial walkways and another the erection of four enormous office towers straddling Times Square. In the 1990s, local investors, city bureaucrats, and global conglomerates, aided by a change in the ideology of urbanity, gradually overcame these earlier schemes. A 1978 epic-marking manifesto by Dutch architect Rem Koolhaas celebrated "Delirious New York" for the surfaces of its neon signage and pop glamour. New zoning laws honored this altered ideology and began to require the signs of the Broadway district to continue to burn brightly. Each sign facing the Square now had to produce a minimum LUTS (Light Unit Times Square) reading. The real estate moguls of New York who owned much of the land in the Broadway district soon found global corporations, including Disney and Clear Channel Communications, to rent, renovate, and rebuild their properties.

By 2000, Disney and Clear Channel controlled much of Broadway. Not only had Disney renovated its own theatre and begun producing shows, but also, as the owners of ABC and ESPN, it rented space and employed thousands of others in the area. Clear Channel funded productions for its national subscription series of mega-musicals. Viacom, the owner of MTV, many of the Times Square "spectaculars," and the Viacom Building at 45th and Broadway, was also a player. The actual investment in live theatre by these three global conglomerates was only a small percentage of their total revenue. Most of Clear Channel's money came from radio stations, for instance; its Theatrical and Family Division generated less than 10 percent of its revenues.

The future of Broadway theatre (?)

Will these and other global corporations continue to be interested in supporting live theatre on Broadway? While no one can say, the Times Square vortex will likely remain an important launching pad for world entertainment. Its smile-button commercialism is no longer particularly friendly to live theatre that does not conform to the mega-musical formula, however. In December of 2004, only one non-musical drama was playing on Broadway – *Gem of the Ocean*, by August Wilson (1945–). The reduction of straight plays in Times Square to two or three per season is now taken for granted.

More significantly, perhaps, the ambiance of Times Square forcefully reminds all theatregoers that theatrical spectating is itself old fashioned and may soon be outmoded. Traveling to a separate place for entertainment, sitting in a seat for most of the time, and responding with laughter and polite applause may still have its pleasures, but how much longer can it compete with the delights of direct participation in the newer media of communication? In 2003, *Total Request Live*, MTV's version of the old *American Bandstand*, broadcast every afternoon from a second story studio overlooking Times Square. People gathered in the street below to look through the glass wall, wave at the bands in the studio, and occasionally provide cheering backup on television when a rock star waved back. Like "reality TV," these are the kinds of condensational events that the vortex of

Times Square is now producing. Of course, *Total Request Live* appeals mostly to teens, but will they become theatregoers when they reach forty? Although the materiality of Times Square is not about to disappear into virtual space, the chance of participating in its mediated image may be becoming more important for many than the physical reality of being there.

Broadway has always been a vortex of contrasts, however, and live theatre is a necessary part of the mix for many. In 1980, roughly 60 percent of spectators for Broadway shows came from the New York metropolitan area. By 2000, most spectators, around 56 percent, came from elsewhere, and the total theatregoing population had increased by nearly two million people in 20 years. Approximately twelve million audience members came to a Broadway show in the 2000–2001 season. During that year, theatre in the Times Square area generated about $4.4 billion for the city's economy, including production costs, theatre expenses, and estimated visitor spending. Apparently, the Broadway mega-musical has found a new and expanding niche that even the thrills of direct participation in new media cannot touch.

BMc

Key references

Atkinson, B. (1974) *Broadway*, New York: Macmillan.

Carlson, M. (1989) *Places of Performance: The Semiotics of Theatre Architecture*, Ithaca and London: Cornell University Press.

Roach, J. (1996) *Cities of the Dead: Circum-Atlantic Performance*, New York: Columbia University Press.

Sagalyn, L.B. (2001) *Times Square Roulette: Remaking the City Icon*, Cambridge, M.A.: MIT Press.

Taylor, W.R. (1991) *Inventing Times Square: Commerce and Culture at the Crossroads of the World*, New York: Russell Age Foundation.

Traub, J. (2004) *The Devil's Playground: A Century of Pleasure and Profit in Times Square*, New York: Random House.

CASE STUDY: Media and theatre: Niche marketing

Two major questions hover over any discussion of the history and nature of theatre and performance in the second half of the twentieth century. How did the theatre respond to 1) the increasing cultural diversity of modern societies and 2) to the competition from the increasingly popular film and television productions, with their efficient distribution on tapes and discs for convenient home video use? One answer is that, at the same time, theatres, like the media, were increasingly defining themselves for particular markets, seeking "niche" audiences.

Every reader of this text who has another life as a consumer in capitalist markets will recognize the term "niche marketing." The term is derived from general niche theory that was developed by ecologists and then economists in their studies of the use of resources and the competition for those resources, in nature and in the marketplace. Ecologists, for example, use niche theory to explain competition and coexistence among different species within a natural environment (Dimmick 2003: 23–24). Niche marketing describes the capitalistic, competitive process in which sellers identify and pursue potential consumers in a well-defined segment of the population. The "target" markets are identified through well-researched demographic studies of factors such as age, gender, family size, levels of income and education, ethnic or racial self-identification, uses of leisure time, and geographic location.

Niche programming has proliferated in western media. Radio stations in the United States, for example, target specific audiences with black rap, Latin American music, sports talk, conservative news talk, jazz light, rock hits from the 1950s, classical music, Christian rock, and Christian talk. Their audiences might be described as discrete "interpretive communities," to borrow a phrase from high literary theory (see the Chapter 3 case study on kutiyattam for reception theory). That is, radio stations seek listeners with cultural backgrounds and values in common. Niche marketing has converged in the U.S. radio market with culturally-divisive political talk shows, as stations seek to build listenerships under the labels, "conservative" and "liberal." By the mid-1990s, cable television companies in the U.S. and Western Europe were offering somewhere between 120 and 180 channels ranging from CNN's news channels to the Nickelodeon film channel to specialized sports programming – a video smorgasbord for every possible interest. Migrating Hispanic populations in the U.S. have been followed by Spanish-language radio and cable television channels. Technology has recently refined niche programming down to individual households; cable subscribers receiving music channels can be monitored for their music preferences and then targeted for commercials on products fitting their apparent lifestyles. Satellite radio by subscription in cars (music à la carte) is a recent niche mutation. Newspapers and magazines now reach for different users with websites offering variations on, and extensions of their print content. The marketing staffs of both radio stations and regional theatres commonly bring in "focus groups" to help them identify the tastes of their audiences, and both adjust their programming accordingly.

Even before niche targeting became sophisticated, media and theatre were seeking their niche audiences. To take examples from the American theatre, not long after commercial television had evolved into a medium of easily accessible, commodified entertainment for popular consumption, America's regional, "not-for-profit" theatres began developing an identity apart. (Not-for-profit is a U.S. federal tax category of organizations exempt from taxes.) They defined themselves in artistic, literary, and intellectual terms, somewhat on the European national theatre model, offering a repertory of "classics," ancient and modern. They were constructing themselves as noncommercial alternatives for upscale, educated, and "cultured" audiences in urban areas outside of New York. In the early 1950s, Arena Stage in Washington, D. C., added "theatre in the round" as the architectural signature of its artistic identity. It promised a stage free from encumbering scenery (a signifier for "commercial" trappings) and one conducive to intimate relationships between actors and local audiences (signifying access to psychological and poetic truths). The early regional theatres had another identity marker: their acting companies were in permanent residence. This was to support the artistic ideal of ensemble playing throughout each season, as opposed to the commercial practice of star-centered productions from "out of town." In all these ways, the regional movement was also defining itself as artistically independent of Broadway, although any transfer of one of its productions to Broadway was a source of pride. These theatres were, in effect, configuring themselves in several ways for a new niche audience, although the artistically idealistic directors of these theatres would have been loathe to use the money term.

The United States' regional theatre movement was soon followed by the development of professional theatres in residence in universities, private and public. These targeted the slightly different niche of academic communities where, ostensibly, more artistic risks might be taken. The 1970s and 1980s also brought the construction of many performing arts centers (with theatres and concert halls in the same facility) in developing urban areas in the U.S. and at state universities. These regional arts centers imitated the metropolitan arts centers, such as New York City's Lincoln Center. Their mission was to provide access to the performing arts for a wide spectrum of audiences far from such large urban centers. About the same time, the term "black box theatres" came into common use to describe flexible performance spaces with many possible configurations of playing spaces. (Black curtains, minimal scenery, and area lighting were typical.) Initially, this term signaled experimentation with new forms and sometimes

with unorthodox political material, aimed at small, special audiences. These anticipated the diversification to come. By the 1990s, some regional theatres had both "mainstage" and black box theatres, the latter sometimes as venues for developing new works for culturally diverse audiences.

From the mid-1960s forward, many "alternative" theatres developed to serve audiences defined by their interests in issues of race, ethnicity, or gender. African-American theatres developed in the U.S. following the civil rights movement. Among the most notable were the Free Southern Theatre, the Harlem-based New Lafayette Theatre (1967–1973) and the Negro Ensemble Company, founded by Douglas Turner Ward in 1968. These helped pave the way for the wide critical interest in black playwrights, including Amiri Baraku, Ed Bullins, August Wilson, and Susan-Lori Parks. Wilson's *Fences* (1985) and *The Piano Lesson* (1988) are parts of a ten-play cycle on the African-American experience. Largely in the form of familiar, accessible American realism, they were successful on Broadway and, in recent years, were produced by some U.S. regional theatres, such as Center Stage in Baltimore, Maryland. Notable gay and lesbian theatres have included the Ridiculous Theatre Company, headed by the playwright, Charles Ludlam (1943–1987), and Split Britches in New York. The Lilith Theatre in San Francisco and the Women's Project of the American Place Theatre in New York are just two examples of theatres promoting the work of new women writers and directors. Among the finest plays by an American woman in the era were the emotionally compressed works of Cuban–born María Irena Fornés (1930–), including *Fefu and Her Friends* (1977) and *Conduct of Life* (1985), which focus on the subjugation of women. The performance group, Spiderwoman, begun in New York in 1976, has created pieces derived from the experiences of Native American women, lesbians, sisters, and older women. El Teatro Campesino was founded in 1965 by Luis Valdez (1947–) to dramatize the exploitation of Mexican farm workers and has continued to nourish plays reflecting Mexican-American experiences. Latin American theatre groups representing intersections of U.S. cultures and Cuban, Chicano, and Puerto Rican cultures proliferated in the 1980s. The Intar Theatre in New York, under the direction of Eduardo Machado (1950–), who was strongly influenced by Fornés, is devoted to producing new plays by Latino writers. Plays on the Asian-American experience are the specialty of the East-West Players, founded in Los Angeles in 1965, and three other companies in Seattle, San Francisco, and New York. Regional theatres have had to respond to increasing cultural diversity. By the 1990s, these theatres were building seasons in which individual play choices often reflected, in part, a reach for a different population segment, such as plays that would appeal to African-American audiences (August Wilson's *Piano Lesson*) or 1950s Broadway musicals (*Damn Yankees*) that would have nostalgia appeal for older, middle-class white audiences.

Festivals became a major theatre industry in this era. As we have seen in Chapter 10, international festivals proliferated from the 1990s forward as a phenomenon of globalization, with mobile productions and mobile audiences. Festivals serve many interests and many kinds of audiences. Theatrical niche marketing is nowhere so striking. Artistic idealism sometimes mingles with chamber of commerce development strategies. Festivals have been used to heighten the profile of cities and nations because they often mean both tourism and the promise of resident artistic vitality that attracts new growth and investment, which in turn improve the long-term economic base of a city or nation. As markers of wealth, political stability, and enlightenment, festivals raise a city or nation's profile in the global marketplace in the same way that sponsoring the Olympics or building a signature concert hall designed by Frank Gehry does. In Iran, the Shiraz Festival of the Arts begun in 1967, raised the nation's international cultural profile by bringing in the

work of many international contemporary artists, including Robert Wilson, Jerzy Grotowski, Peter Brook, Terayama Shûji, and Tadeusz Kantor. The Shiraz Festival ended with the Islamic religious and political revolution of 1979.

Festivals define themselves by their niche programming for what are mostly pilgrimage audiences, whether the destination is summer Shakespeare in the park or a gathering of political theatre groups in a Latin American city. Innumerable festivals have been built around Shakespeare, from Ashland, Oregon, through Stratford, Ontario (see Chapter 10), to Stratford-upon-Avon. A Chekhov festival was founded in Moscow in 1992. The Bible is onstage in festivals in more conservative areas of the United States. Christian Bible pageants with spectacular staging have become major attractions, such as the *Great Passion Play* in Eureka Springs, Arkansas, or the Christian musical, *Noah*, in Lancaster County, Pennsylvania. Many festivals, American and international, have been created to nurture new work. Notable annual festivals of international theatre in Edinburgh and Avignon have developed into two-track festivals (see Chapter 10), mainstream and experimental, targeting two different audiences. Edinburgh's Fringe Festival offered 1,700 shows in 250 theatres in August of 2004; one million people attended. (See Chapter 10 for more on international festivals.) The Actors Theatre in Louisville, Kentucky, began its Humana Festival of productions of works by new writers in 1977, sending D. L. Coburn's *Gin Game* to Broadway that season. In 1997, New York City began offering an annual International Fringe Festival, linked with Edinburgh's, and it has since hosted festivals featuring Asian and Hispanic works. San Francisco's Magic Theatre in 2000 was devoted to the international festival-like theme "Playwrights in Danger," and featured works by writers from Nigeria, Argentina, Algeria, Singapore, and elsewhere, whose plays had put their lives at risk. A 1981 festival in Buenos Aires of new plays critical of Argentina's oppressive government, organized by

Osvaldo Dragún, resulted in loyalists burning down the theatre.

In the increasing traffic of globalization, some of the imported fare of international festivals, such as that at Lincoln Center in New York, seems to be carefully shaped (including the use of supertitles) to be accessible for international audiences – an understandable niche development, if a culturally very problematic one – an issue we take up in Chapter 12.

Festivals, then, have defined themselves by niche programming for culturally well identified audiences. Even this brief overview illustrates many of the ways in which theatres, like the media, have been targeting different segments of populations. This seems an inevitable response to the contemporary racial, ethnic, and sexual diversity amid globalization. The development may contribute to community formation in some cases, but the proliferation of niche theatres may also reflect cultural anxieties and fragmentation.

GJW

Key references

See also the listings at the end of the Introduction to Part IV.

Crane, D., Kawashima, N. and Kawasaki, K. (eds) (2002) *Global Culture, Media, Arts, Policy and Globalization*, New York and London: Routledge, 2002.

Dimmick, J.W. (2003) *Media Competition and Coexistence, the Theory of the Niche*, Mahwah, N.J. and London: Lawrence Erlbaum Associates.

Durham, M G. and Kellner, D.M. (eds) (2001) *Media and Cultural Studies, Keyworks*, Oxford: Blackwell Publishing Ltd.

Turow, J. (1997) *Breaking Up America: Advertisers and the New Media World*, Chicago: University of Chicago Press.

CHAPTER 11

Director, text, and performance in the postmodern world

Aristotle to postmodernism: Texts and contexts

Challenges to the western theatre tradition in which the play text was understood to be the source and controlling authority for all meaning in a performance were among the most significant developments in theatre globally between the 1960s and the end of the century. As we have often seen, and will again in this chapter, in indigenous theatres of India, Southeast Asia, and Japan, performances were never viewed as being as text-centered as they were in western-influenced theatre. In the West, and in western-influenced theatres elsewhere, ideas about the role of the director and the place of the text began to change in the 1950s and 1960s. At first in experimental theatres, theatre artists explored new relationships between texts and performances and began to redefine the idea of the nature and purpose of performance and the audience experience. Socially committed directors began to use classical texts to raise political and social issues. Others went beyond rearranging the textual furniture to challenge the conventions of representation and to offer performance itself as theatre's only authentic work.

This chapter and its case studies explain these and other developments and the cultural and theoretical forces underlying them.

Aristotle had set the western pattern of privileging the play text and the author in his *Poetics* (*c*.330 B.C.E.), the first serious philosophic inquiry into the nature of theatre – or, more accurately, drama. Aristotle focused on the formal attributes of tragedy, viewing it as a naturally evolved, self-standing literary form. In this discourse, theatrical production was seen as a kind of messy supplement at best. "Song" was an "embellishment," and "spectacle" was the "least artistic" element, "connected least" with "the art of poetry." "For the power of tragedy, we may be sure, is felt even apart from representation and actors," Aristotle wrote (Aristotle 1971:52). To be sure, Aristotle offered insights about dramatic structure are still valued. On the whole, however, his was a rationalized processing of that complex theatre art that the Greeks had developed from the sixth century B.C.E. forward in their Dionysian festivals, and which encompassed choral song and dance, masked actors, carefully designed performance spaces, and plays that sometimes caused controversy and would have always spoken to more than aesthetic interests (see Part I, Chapter 2). However, Aristotle's textual analysis was ultimately transmitted with the canon of Greek philosophy, and ultimately through western print culture (see Part II Introduction), as were play texts – and western drama criticism for centuries thereafter looked more upon the language and structure of the stand-alone play text rather than upon the vocabularies and dynamics of performance. Many of the West's great professional playwrights, such as Shakespeare and Lope de Vega, did not always adhere to the Aristotelian dictates beloved of the academy. By the early twentieth century, a few theatre artists were challenging the whole Aristotelian scheme, including Alfred Jarry (1873–1907) (see the first case study following this chapter). But the first widely resonant challenges to the western concept of the play text as the controlling center of meaning in performance came after World War II, along with many other challenges to western philosophical traditions. The most visible locus of the challenge in theatre was in the staging of the classics; it was here that the new role of the director first stood out sharply.

In western theatre in the first half of the twentieth century, the role of the director of a classic – whether by the Greeks, Shakespeare, or Molière – was, in effect, to function as a kind of surrogate for the playwright. The Aristotelian privileging of the text converged with the modernist aesthetic goal of a seamless marriage of text and production. A production of a classic was to be the warm animation of a play's (ostensibly) universal meanings, at the center of which was assumed to be a view of human potential in a meaningful world. Some stylistic variations in settings and costumes were acceptable as long as all sign systems led back to the text and to an idealizing and aesthetically-ordered vision.

By the 1960s, these aesthetics and ideals were coming under scrutiny. The experience of World War II, including the industrial-scale slaughter of Jews by the Nazis at Auschwitz and other killing

camps made it hard for some to believe in that "divinity that shapes our ends" of which Hamlet speaks. It was equally hard to credit Hamlet's idealistic, renaissance characterization of humankind: "What a piece of work is a man! How noble in reason . . . in apprehension how like a god" (5.2.10; 2.293–2.296). Many European playwrights, such as Samuel Beckett, took a dark, existential view of the human condition. The Polish critic, Jan Kott, in his influential *Shakespeare Our Contemporary* (1964), found in Shakespeare's histories and tragedies a process of history that was violent, stark, and relentless, with no redemptive end. Directors began to explore classical texts for opportunities to give voice to their despair over what seemed to be an endless cycle of meaningless suffering. By contrast, in East Germany, playwright and director Bertolt Brecht took the Marxist initiative and led his Berliner Ensemble in creating a theatre intended to provoke social critique. The purpose of this politically proactive theatre was to lead audiences to re-examine and challenge inhumane systems and institutions, including western capitalism (see the case study on Brecht's *Mother Courage*, Chapter 9). The East German Shakespeare scholar, Robert Weimann, made the case that in the West, Shakespeare's plays had been reduced to a bland "classical" ideology, when in fact they had offered audiences of their time a complex blend of politics and play. Contemporary performances of his plays could never recover the past; they were bound to generate new meanings. Both the existentialist and the Marxist views challenged the modernist views of art as an aesthetic sphere, dedicated to beauty and universal themes, self-enclosed, set apart from the contemporary world. Both trends had wide influence in Europe and Asia. Both trends meant more active directorial intervention. Directors began to shape "concept" productions of ancient and modern classics. In effect, these often foregrounded the production itself as an encounter between a lapsed world and an anxious contemporary one. By the late 1960s and early

1970s, the idea of the director as the primary artist, or at least a coequal with the playwright, was emerging. It was becoming commonplace to speak not of Shakespeare's but Peter Brook's *A Midsummer Night's Dream* (1970), not of Molière's but Roger Planchon's *Tartuffe* (1962, 1973), not of Euripides's but Suzuki Tadashi's *The Trojan Women* (1974).

To be sure, theatres in the past had always remolded the classics to the sensibilities of their audiences, but from within relatively congenial cultural discourses around a common legacy, and always behind a façade of due diligence in honoring the legacy. Now, more profound gaps had opened. Some directors deconstructed the plays of the Greeks and Shakespeare to critique any grand views of human potential embedded in them and to mine any darker elements (for an explanation of "deconstruction," see the case study following this chapter). When Peter Brook (1925–) directed *King Lear* with the Royal Shakespeare Company (1962), he countered any

possibilities that the text itself offers to show that the human spirit can make meaning out of human suffering. Brook instead emphasized in his staging any possibilities the text offered for an existential vision of a endlessly cruel, godless universe. By 1974, Klaus-Michael Grüber's *The Bacchae* at the Berlin Schaubühne had taken matters much further, going beyond any attempt either to "recover" the ancient Euripides or to reinvent him as a postwar existentialist. Grüber's production instead critiqued those solutions, staging a never-ending process of the stitching and restitching together of ancient fragments, open to varying readings (Fischer-Lichte 1999:16–17). At the opening of the production, the weakened Dionysus, god of the theatre, was rolled out on a hospital gurney, barely able to speak his name (Figure 11:1).

The latter production and such a directorial approach may be described, among other things, as postmodern. Some explanation of this term will help

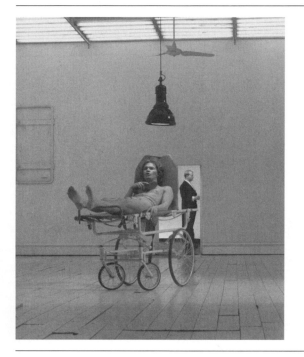

Figure 11.1 Dionysus (Michael König) on the hospital gurney in Euripides's *The Bacchae*, directed by Klaus-Michael Grüber, Schaubühne Theatre Company, Berlin 1974. Photo © Helga Kneidel.

clarify why increasing responsibility was devolving onto the director to be a creator of a world-vision for a production. Postmodernism is a much-debated term that has had many applications and many theorists, including Jean-François Lyotard, Fredric Jameson, and Hans Bertens (see Website Bibliography). But among the chief attributes of postmodern work, in the theatre and other arts, has been an interest in critiquing traditional processes of representation. This is born in part of a deep skepticism of modernism's desire to wrap experience in a single, unified, pleasingly cohesive vision. Grüber's *The Bacchae* foregrounded the performance process to stage a skepticism about what traditional representation can accomplish. For such a radically postmodern approach, Steven Connor's characterization is apt: it asserts "the presence of performance against the inauthenticity of representation" (Connor 1989: 154). In the theatre world, one of the most urgent and influential voices describing what was perceived as a crisis of representation was that of Antonin Artaud, as we shall see.

The new directorial strategies – reinterpreting texts, reading texts resistantly, or "interrogating" texts – sometimes were influenced by developments in twentieth-century literary theory, which grew from the same cultural soil. Structuralist critics had suggested that the structures in literary works, like the structures of language, are simply the means by which humankind tries to make meaning out of chaos. Meaningful structure in literature is a projection of human consciousness, as are the structures of all other cultural phenomena such as myths, social rituals, sports, or forms of entertainment. Then in the mid-1960s, Jacques Derrida critiqued the structuralist assumption that language was a stable system of references to stable meanings. Derrida argued that language was a system of constructed signs disseminating a variety of possible meanings; language was always a dance of relative signifiers around the absence of any foundational center with transcendental meanings. As a human construction then, all

language – and all texts – can be seen as being embedded with ideologies – value systems and social practices. "Text" began to be used as a term for any symbolic system a culture might construct, be it a religious ritual, clothing fashions, or *Hamlet*. The critical movement that Derrida's work inspired, known as deconstruction, began to investigate the array of meanings (often conflicting) available in a text, and the ideological premises implicit in them, with special interest in the self-contradictions in a text. Given the flux of meanings a work generates, it often can be seen to be at cross-purposes with itself. Criticism also began to recognize the roles of different readers/viewers in determining the meaning of a work; the notion of a heroic author as the source of unifying meaning began to look like a comfortable humanist assumption, impossible to grant in the face of the instabilities and constructedness of language. Feminist critics saw the classics reproducing oppressive patriarchy. Materialist critics saw them reinforcing mythologies congenial to capitalism. Brecht offered, in theory and practice, an anti-Aristotelian, non-illusionistic theatre that aimed at critiquing those mythologies. One effect of these critiques was to remove literary works from the exclusive status in which they were viewed as self-enclosed high art and to view them as cultural constructions. The operations of language and of text needed to be deconstructed if we were to understand the rule over us of their unspoken ideologies.* In a landmark work of theatre theory specifically, the French theatre visionary, Antonin Artaud (1896–1948), called for a "theatre of cruelty" that would "break through language" to access the mysterious and darker forces of life left untouched by literary masterpieces and the sterile reverence accorded them (Artaud 1958:7). His book, *The Theatre and Its Double*, challenged the foundations of

---

* For cogent summaries of these critical movements and their relation to theatre, see Marvin Carlson's *Theories of the Theatre*, expanded edition (Ithaca and London: Cornell University Press, 1993), Chapters 21–22.

representation as theatre's reason for being and, from the 1960s to the present, profoundly influenced the work of many directors (his ideas are discussed below and in a case study following this chapter).

The western re-evaluations of theatre practice were also the result of an increasing interest in other cultures. One important development was the turn by directors to the theatre traditions of the East. Prominent directors and visionaries, including Artaud, Brecht, Jean-Louis Barrault, Jerzy Grotowski, Peter Brook, and Ariane Mnouchkine, found inspiration in traditional Asian and Japanese performance arts, including Balinese dance, Beijing Opera, Indian kathakali, and Japanese noh and kabuki theatres. These represented traditions with no binary division between performance and text. The Sanskrit poetics of theatre, Bharata's *Nāṭyaśastra*, the foundational work for traditional Indian theatre (written sometime between 200 B.C.E. and C.E. 200), offered an encyclopedic account of play forms and all elements of performance, including music, dance, and acting (Bharata 1967,1961) (see Chapter 3). Traditional Japanese theatre theory focused on the work of the actor, from works by the playwright Zeami Motokiyo (1363–1443), who articulated the concepts of noh theatre, through the four volumes on kabuki theatre published in the eighteenth century, called the *Actors' Analects*. The scripts of traditional Japanese theatre include much more than dialog, and because of the fluidity in narrative voices, texts are not limited to dialog spoken "in character." Asian martial arts methods, such as *taiquiquan*, *kendo*, and *kạlarippayaṭṭu*, are often incorporated into training performance, serving as holistic approaches to physical control, heightened awareness, and creative expression. For some western artists, eastern theatre traditions seemed creatively liberating, and some found in them alternatives to exhausted western spiritual traditions. Sometimes the cultural road ran two ways; directors in Asia and Japan were discovering Artaud, Brecht, and Grotowski. Artaud's *The Theatre and Its Double* was published in Japan in 1965.

This chapter now turns to selected major works by some of the experimental directors between the 1960s and the 1990s, sometimes characterized as *auteur* directors. This term, borrowed from film criticism, points to the director as the primary artist rather than the writer. The borrowing itself reminds us of the profound impact that film, as a medium of images, circulating internationally, had on the word-based theatre. The powerful imagery in the films of directors such as Sweden's Ingmar Bergman and Japan's Akira Kurosawa challenged stage directors and designers to enlarge their own expressive vocabularies. The examples selected here represent directors' negotiations with classical texts and the creation of new "texts" by directors and theatre collectives between the 1960s and the turn of the century. It will be useful to begin with explanations of the influential theories and practice of Artaud and Grotowski, which allow consideration of the changing concepts of both the director and texts. The chapter concludes with examples of what has been characterized as image theatre.

Director and text in Antonin Artaud's "theatre of cruelty"

In the opening pages of *The Theatre and Its Double* (a collection of writings originally published in 1938), Artaud wrote of a deep "rupture between things and words, between things and the ideas and signs that are their representation" (Artaud 1958:7). He saw a cleavage between spirit and body and between civilized culture and the dangerous forces at the heart of existence. To restore unity, the theatre must give direct access to these forces, without the obstacle of indirect representation, without written language. He called provocatively for a "theatre of cruelty" and sought to liberate audiences from linear storytelling, from keyhole realism with its character psychology, and from all the masterpieces of the past (Artaud 1958:7–13, 33–47, 84–92). The famous title of his Chapter 6 is "No More Masterpieces." Plot (Aristotle's "imitation of an action") and character – the all-absorbing spheres of modernist directors and actors until the Theatre of the Absurd – were vestiges of a diminished form of theatre. Artaud envisioned a primal, non-verbal theatre affecting the whole organism, with performances enveloping the spectator using incantation, ancient musical instruments, rhythmical dance, symbolic gestures, masks, manikins, and ritual-like costumes. He was inspired by the Balinese dance theatre, admiring its color, ceremonial movement, sensuousness, prodigality, and connection to the metaphysical. Artaud writes mystically of the need for the actor to access a realm of passions through the body. The contact between performers and the audience would be intense; performances would take place in a whitewashed hall with galleries above; audiences would follow the actors to different acting areas (ibid.:89–100).

In Artaud's theatre, the director would be the author of such theatre works; there would be no playwright in the conventional sense. As to the material to be performed, "we shall not act a written play," he writes, but "make attempts at direct staging, around themes, facts, or known works" (ibid.:98). He suggests, for example, performing a tale by the Marquis de Sade, staging incidents about the conquest of Mexico, Elizabethan plays "stripped of their texts," and romantic melodramas – any material that would allow "a passionate and convulsive conception of life," and correspond to "the unrest characteristic of our epoch" (ibid.:89–122).

At the fierce heart of his vision, the ultimate goal was an embodied performance that would give access to some metaphysical plenitude, unimpeded by the secondary representations of written language and character impersonation. (This is more fully explained in the case study following this chapter.) This impossible goal – theatre without representation – was one neither Artaud nor his followers ever achieved, of course. But Artaud's mystical jeremiad against a text-based theatre opened a path for experiments toward a more sensuous one.

Experimental directors in many nations took up his charge to become authors of a sensuous *mise en scène*. Many assembled "texts" for productions that privileged theatrical vocabularies over the textual. In Paris in 1968, Jean-Louis Barrault (1910–1994) staged a three-hour adaptation of writings by Rabelais, and Ariane Mnouchkine's Théâtre du Soleil company assembled a collage of sketches on the French revolution for *1789*. *The Serpent* (1969), created by American director Joseph Chaikin (1935–) with his Open Theatre company, was a collage of material from the Bible and scenes from the assassinations of John. F. Kennedy and Martin Luther King. Japanese director, Suzuki Tadashi, created several collages of material from a range of plays in his own hybrid style Called *On the Dramatic Passions* (1969), these included the kabuki classic, *Kanadehon Chûshingura* (*The Treasury of Loyal Retainers*), *Cyrano de Bergerac* (1898) by Edmond Rostand, and *Zô* (*The Elephant*, 1961) by Betsuyaku Minoru. Polish director, Tadeuz Kantor (1915–) created his *The Dead Class* (1975) using an amalgam of his own writings and works by other Polish writers. The "text" of Peter Brook's *Orghast* (1971), was an arrangement of musical phonemes and fragments of ancient languages by poet Ted Hughes, intoned by the actors along with ancient music. Performed in the ruins of Persepolis at the Shiraz Festival in Iran, it opened with the Prometheus myth (Brook's epic *Mahabharata* (1985) is taken up in a case study in Chapter 12).

Artaud himself had tried his concepts without success in his 1935 staging of an adaptation of *The Cenci* (1819), a romantic revenge play by Percy Bysshe Shelley (1792–1822). But his writings were pervasive. By the late 1960s, Artaud was influencing directors in Japan, and "No More Masterpieces" was the title of a directing course in the Yale School of Drama in the United States. By the end of the century, as we shall see, it was clear that Artaud had offered much more than the anti-authoritarianism the 1960s counterculture found in him.

The holy actor as text in Jerzy Grotowski's "poor theatre"

The Polish director Jerzy Grotowski (1934–1999) may be said to have brought Artaud's anti-textual vision into practice, but with a special emphasis on a communal theatre that would be the modern equivalent of the old communities of belief. At its center would be the "holy" actor. Grotowski conceived of a "poor theatre," stripped of elaborate production elements of the commercial theatre. Scripts were to be tapped for their archetypal human dimensions and productions forged in collective collaborations. The "holy actor" would be an ascetic athlete of the soul, physicalizing the sufferings and ecstasies of the human spirit, uniting psychic and bodily powers to achieve "translumination" (Grotowski 1968:15–59). The actor, creating "his own psychoanalytic language of sounds and gestures in the same way that a great poet creates his own language of words," was now, in effect, the chief poet. In this morally astringent theatre, the actor was to sacrifice personal psychology and eliminate in the body any resistance to full expression through a *via negativa*, an eradication of the self to expose primal truths. Grotowski limited his audiences to 100 to assure immediacy. His theoretical language was sometimes obscure and mystical, redolent of both his Catholic background and existentialist despair. But clearly, performance itself was to be the authentic center, the object and subject of performance, and not a representation of another thing. Among the sources on which Grotowski drew were Stanislavski's method of physical actions, Meyerhold's bio-mechanics, Indian kathakali, the Beijing Opera, Japanese noh theatre, and Carl Jung's theory of archetypes that activate the collective unconscious.

His productions in his intimate Laboratory Theatre in Wroclaw included a free adaptation of

Figure 11.2 Ryszard Cieslak as Esau, one of the Jewish prisoners in Auschwitz, dreaming of the freedom of the life of a hunter, in Jerzy Grotowski's production of *Akropolis* at the Polish Laboratory Theatre, Wroclaw, 1962. © The Grotowski Center, Wroclaw.

Akropolis (1962), a play by Polish playwright, Stanislav Wyspiański (1869–1907). In the original, set in the Royal Palace at Krakow (a Polish version of the Athenian acropolis – the height of civilization), figures from its tapestries come alive and are led by the resurrected Christ to redeem Europe. In Grotowski's dark, ironic conception, the acropolis was the extermination camp at Auschwitz (not far from Krakow), the cemetery of western civilization, where Jewish prisoners labored to build cremation ovens and fantasized about love and happiness. In this and *Apocalypse cum figures* (1969), the performances by Grotowski's key actor, Ryszard Cieslak, seemed to realize Grotowski's vision. He reportedly achieved a trance-like state, an interpenetration of actor and role in an externalization of inner suffering – the actor becoming both subject and object. Here, an actor's intense creative process became one with the performance, became the "text" (Figure 11.2).

When Grotowski's company played in New York in 1970, American theatre critic John Simon ridiculed Grotowski's pretensions to a non-verbal and mythic theatre, and described *Akropolis* as "nonsense," "repulsive," "humorless," and "theatre of collective self-analysis" (Simon 1975:143–163). But Grotowski's productions toured the world, and together with his writings and workshops, influenced many directors. In the late 1970s, he renounced this phase of his work, believing his ideas had been misunderstood, especially in America, and that he had not broken through theatre's division between the actor and the passive spectator.

Peter Brook's Shakespeare and contemporary authenticity

The productions of British director Peter Brook (1925–) represent a wide array of experiments across 40 years that have established him as one of the most innovative directors in twentieth-century theatre, and at times a controversial one. He has symbolized the auteur director, on a quest to revitalize western theatre, renegotiating with old texts and creating new ones.

He brought Artaud, Brecht, and Beckett to bear on his 1962 *King Lear* with the then-new Royal Shakespeare Company, and all within an impeccable aesthetic typical of Brook. He saw the play through an existential lens similar to that of Jan Kott. Kott compared the play to Beckett's *Endgame*, reading it as a depiction of the suffering of humanity in a world without hope of meaning and redemption. Brook staged the blinding of old Gloucester with unsparing cruelty, locating it at the downstage edge of the stage, near the audience, cutting the sympathetic lines of the servants in the scene, and, in a gesture toward anti-illusionistic theatre, brought up the houselights as the blinded, bleeding Gloucester staggered upstage. Brook conducted theatre of cruelty experiments in 1964 with members of the Royal Shakespeare Company which culminated in their production of *The Persecution and Assassination of Jean-Paul Marat as Performed by the Inmates of the Asylum of Charenton Under the Director of The Marquis de Sade*, written by Peter Weiss. Weiss's verse text rendered a morally chaotic world in grim corporal imagery. The madness of the inmates was graphically physicalized by the actors in an intimate acting space. Charotte Corday's murder of Marat in his bath was performed ritualistically. When a courtier's epilogue at the end of the inmates' play offered pompous platitudes about the glory of France and the progress of rationalism, its effect was to agitate the inmates into a frenzied march and threats to overtake the asylum. Insofar as the madness within the asylum seemed to have more to recommend it than the sanity without, the ending could be read as a comment on the "civilized" political powers that in 1962 seemed intent on destroying each other with nuclear weapons.

For Brook and others, theatre and society had to be revitalized, and a new relationship established between actors and audiences. In his manifesto, *The Empty Space* (1968), he called for a "holy theatre," marked by sincerity and authenticity, which would replace the packaging processes of the "deadly theatre" of a consumer society. Brook's *A Midsummer*

Night's Dream with the Royal Shakespeare Company (1970) sought to achieve some of these goals with a bright, contemporary theatricality that supplanted the long-defunct romantic stage traditions for this play. With its fairies on trapezes, its non-illusionistic white box setting, its flower-children young lovers, and its playful eroticism, the production seemed to embody the work of liberating imaginations in defiance of a repressive and dishonest past (see Figure 11.3). It also seemed to offer a New World of authentic young love amid the youthful social revolution against an older order. The full text of the play, spoken with rare spontaneity, registered as fresh, but the performance itself became the ground of authenticity and the coequal of the text.

Brook's *Dream* was not the first to do this with Shakespeare (see the following case study on global Shakespeare), but its impact in an era of social upheaval and its mainstream visibility (it toured world capitals for three years) made it a reference point for performance practice for Shakespeare and other classics long after memories of its flower children had faded. It did more than make a case for "contemporizing" Shakespeare (although it spawned many superficial imitations). It altered popular notions of what productions of classics do. Any production of any classical play represents a transaction between past and present, and, as Robert Weimann and others have noted, it is bound to generate new meanings (Williams 1997:213–233; Worthen 2003:28–58). Joseph Roach has usefully characterized performance as an act of surrogation, recalling and performing the past in the form of the present (Roach 1996:221). From the 1970s forward, performance negotiations with the classics – with varying degrees of aggressiveness and by directors and companies representing different points on an increasingly broad cultural spectrum – became commonplace. By the end of century, Julie Taymor's film, *Titus* (1999), based on Shakespeare's *Titus Andronicus*, and Baz Luhrmann's film, *William Shakespeare's Romeo + Juliet* (1996), were offering in the mainstream marketplace a postmodern dialectic between the historical pastness of these plays and a hyperreal contemporary present. In both, performance and text critiqued one another. These films juxtapositioned the plays' Elizabethan verse with contemporary film's hyperspeed language of images, sometimes with dissonance, and sometimes with remarkable synergy.

Among a new generation of Japanese theatre artists who sought to revitalize their theatre,

Figure 11.3 Oberon (Alan Howard) casts a spell on Titania (Sara Kestelman) in her "bower," assisted by Puck, in Shakespeare's *A Midsummer Night's Dream*, directed by Peter Brook with the Royal Shakespeare Company, 1970. Setting by Sally Jacobs. Photo by Thomas F. Holte. © Shakespeare Centre Library, Stratford-upon-Avon.

especially important were the directors Terayama Shûji and Suzuki Tadashi, both considered in this chapter, and Ninagawa Yukio (1935–). discussed in the case study on global Shakespeare that follows. All emerged during the Little Theatre movement (angura – underground) in the 1960s in which many directors and playwrights rebelled – in various ways – against the western-derived drama and theatre practices in Japan (shingeki). Many were also involved in radical anti-Vietnam War and anti-government demonstrations. Overall, their work reflects Japan's complex and sometimes vexed negotiations among its cultural longings – to be a presence on the global stage as a modern nation and a major economic power, to assimilate western culture yet remain connected with its own pre-western past, and to preserve its own traditions.

Terayama Shûji and the disquieting critique of theatrical convention

Terayama Shûji (1935–1983), playwright, poet, director, filmmaker, and essayist, led his experimental company, Tenjo Sajiki, from 1967 until his death at 47 in 1983. He created an arc of fresh, eclectic work that challenged theatrical conventions and left a reputation of legendary proportions. Early works written and directed by Terayama, such as *The Hunchback of Aomori* (*Aomori-ken no semushi otoko*. 1967), *Inugami, The Dog God* (*Inugami*, 1967) or *Heretics* (*Jashûmon*, 1971) featured surreal evocations of Buddhist superstitions and old-time side-shows, coupled with psychedelic music and the discontent of postwar youth. Some works might be characterized as "metatheatre," a term usually used to point to works that trigger audience awareness of the operations of dramatic invention. Plays such as *Opium War* (*Ahen sensô*, 1972) and *Blindman's Letter* (*Môjin shokan*, 1973) forced audiences into terrifying total darkness; black-robed, sword-wielding actors in *Heretics* literally assaulted audience members, resulting in hysteria, claustrophobia, and even

violence. From the early 1970s, Terayama also created outdoor "city dramas" that often involved unsuspecting citizens as audience or even as actors. For example, *Knock* (*Nokku*, 1975) consisted of sites and events spread across 27 locations throughout a district of Tokyo, to which spectators could journey over a 30-hour period. Critic Senda Akihiko wrote of following a map leading him to various sites, including a clock shop with an array of broken clocks lined up in front, a pile of broken toys in the window, and no one inside. Had it been so arranged for this event, or had it always looked that way? When Senda and others followed a married couple arguing their way loudly through the streets, what did bystanders make of the spectacle? Who were the actors? Who were spectators? What was Senda to make of the four people emerging from a manhole, swathed in bandages? The experience led Senda to a reappraisal of his own decoding processes (Senda 1997:56–60). The work seems akin to the "Happenings" in New York in the 1960s. By blurring the boundaries that audiences expect to separate their experience of art from other experiences, such projects hope to provoke reassessments of the processes by which theatres and spectators construct meaning. Other major works written and staged by Terayama included his own unorthodox plays, as the sado-masochistic *Directions to Servants* (*Nuhikun*, 1979), or the similarly subversive *Lemmings* (*Remingu*, various versions 1979–1983), a series of visually striking scenes in which the walls around people imprisoned in private pursuits of individuality dissolved, exposing them to random, sometimes violent experiences.

Suzuki Tadashi's contemporary Japanese Euripides

Suzuki Tadashi (1939–) founded a company in 1966 with playwright Betsuyaku Minoru (b.1937), who was influenced by Beckett and who went on to write plays critical of the Japanese middle class. By 1970, Suzuki had become the sole director and was constructing collages of texts and performances that privileged no one author. He developed a now famous physical training method. Suzuki perceived the upper body as the origin of the conceptual and the conscious, the lower body as the physical and the unconscious, grounded in reality, and the two as always in tension. He devised acting exercises, influenced by noh and kabuki acting and Japanese martial arts, through which the actor is to create a powerful stage presence through highly energized but restrained physical motions. These include slow ritualized movements, rhythmic foot stamping, crouching, and tension-informed stances, sometimes combined with vocalizations (Carruthers and Yasunari 2004:70–97), all of which have become expressive parts of his productions. Suzuki's "grammar of the feet" is his means of forcefully imprinting the presence of the body on the performance; it is an existential affirmation but one also rooted in noh traditions. Japanese critics sometimes have wrongly characterized his work as neo-noh.

Suzuki's radical adaptation of *The Trojan Women* was the first time a Japanese director had not imitated western staging conventions for a Greek classic – which is some indication of just how far Japan had gone in its attempt to assimilate western theatre in its *shingeki* movement. From its opening in Tokyo in 1974 through its final performance in Helsinki in 1989, *The Trojan Women* played in 34 cities around the world and was compared for importance by some with Brecht's *Mother Courage* and Brook's *A Midsummer Night's Dream* (ibid.:124). Suzuki's production combined Euripides's play, in a Japanese translation by Matsudaira Chiaki, with commissioned pieces by the modern Japanese poet, Ôoka Makoto. For the ancient tragedy about the destruction of Troy and the suffering of its women, Suzuki resisted all conventional ideas of an ancient, noble classical world and created images evoking memories of the nuclear annihilation of Hiroshima, still fresh in the minds of the Japanese. A homeless elderly Japanese woman who had lost husband, sons, and daughters in the war, entered carrying a small bundle of the remnants of her life and sat downstage, imagining/remembering the events taking place behind her, at one point delivering a requiem by Ôoka. In the premiere version, well-known actors from noh and *shingeki* (respectively, Kanze Hisao as an old homeless person and Ichihara Etsuko as Cassandra and Andromache), worked in their acting styles alongside the Suzuki-trained Shiraishi Kayoko, playing the role of the homeless person who in the fantasy becomes Hecuba. Major characters were presented in a kabuki-style dumb-show (*danmari*), led on by Jizô, Buddhist guardian deity of children, who watches impassively, unable to intervene in the horrors of war. The chorus women were survivors of both Troy and Hiroshima; the Greek soldiers were kabuki samurai who violently raped Andromache and dismembered her son (a doll) on stage. At one point, the chorus of Trojan women circled in a slow, rhythmic dance, defiantly stamping their feet, lifting their knees to their chests. Suzuki experimented with various endings that disrupted any easy consolations. In the premier, a group of Japanese tourists (including a giant Japanese soldier) appeared on a guided tour of the battlefield at Troy. In the 1979 touring version, the cast exited to leave the old homeless woman sorting through her few belongings and trying to sleep, somewhat reminiscent of a character from Beckett, watched over by Jizô (ibid.:124–153).

Suzuki also staged adaptations of Euripides's *The Bacchae*, Shakespeare's *Macbeth* and *King Lear*, Chekhov's *Ivanov*, and directed a notable revival of *John Silver* (*Jon Shirubâ*, 1965) by Kara Juro (1940–), one of Japan's most important postwar playwrights, known for his non-linear, myth-like works. Suzuki is very clear about his role as an *auteur* director. Speaking of his freedoms with Shakespeare's text in his *Tale of Lear*, he said "But the first responsibility of a director is to define what interests him the most, what resonates with his current concerns" (Mulryne 1998:84). Since 1976, much of Suzuki's work has been done in the rural village of Toga, in the mountains of central Japan, six hours from Tokyo, to which he moved seeking greater artistic freedom. With the help of government subsidies, Toga Art Park there has become a large complex of theatres and rehearsal halls, providing a laboratory for experimental collaborations with international visiting artists and a pilgrimage destination for the tourists who come to its festivals.

Other negotiations with the classics: Roger Planchon's Molière

Molière began to be reworked in France in the midst of the student demonstrations against cultural institutions and the worker's strikes that peaked in 1968 French director Roger Planchon (1931–) led the French revolution in directing in the period, viewing the director as an equal of the author. Influenced by Artaud, Brecht, and Marx, Planchon is known both for his political commitment and his "scenic writing" (his term), that is, his creation of vivid stage images that convey his vision of a play (Bradby and Williams 1988:51–56). In his staging of Molière's *Tartuffe* (1962) at his theatre in a working-class suburb of Lyon, Orgon's home was a kind of mini-Versailles palace. Orgon's devotion to the bogus cleric Tartuffe, had an unconscious homosexual side adding sexual confusion to blind religious devotion The final scene, in which Orgon is saved at the last instant, was staged as a chilling demonstration of the absolute power of Louis XIV. In the 1973 version Orgon's house seemed to be being dismantled room by room, and Orgon and his family were herded into a dungeon beneath the stage floor before being released. There have been many interpretations of the ending of Molière's play (see the Chapter 4 case study); Planchon apparently was suggesting that the bourgeois Orgon was being stripped of far more than his delusions about Tartuffe. (The work of the French director, Ariane Mnouchkine, is taken up in Chapter 12.)

The United States: The performance group, La Mama, and the Wooster Group

Canonical texts from Euripides to Arthur Miller were reworked by radical United States theatre companies. *Dionysus in 69* (1969), was a rendering of Euripides's *The Bacchae* by Richard Schechner (1934) with his Performance Group. Staged in a converted garage on Wooster Street in lower Manhattan, it combined narrative and extra-textual, faux-ritual scenes. Dionysian sexual freedom was set in conflict with repression, with some suggestion of the dangers of unrestrained liberation. Orgiastic nude scenes, which audience members entered into, gave the production considerable notoriety. Schechner's notions of "environmental theatre" were tried: no demarcation between actor and spectator space; multiple events competing with each other around the hall to diffuse any single focus; and actors interacting with audience members in character and personally (Aronson 2000: 97–102). The search for authenticity in the communal experience was typical of American collective theatres in the 1960s. Amid the sentimentality of the American hippie and drug culture, the ostensible communal event, not the text, was the priorty.

The Romanian director, Andrei Serban (1943–), brought rigor to the American experimental scene at Ellen Stewart's La Mama Experimental Theatre Club in the early 1970s. Artaud was the inspiration for his *Fragments of a Greek Trilogy* (1974), composed of portions of Euripides's *Medea*, *Electra*, and *The Trojan Women*, which he developed over a three-year period. Serban had worked with Peter Brook on the non-verbal *Orghast* project in Iran in 1970–1971, and his chief objective here was to create a non-verbal, aural score to communicate the power and passion of the Greek plays. Fragments of Senecan Latin, Greek, and English, were woven together with primitive vocalizations of the actors and Elizabeth Swados's original score. The *Trilogy* was staged in spaces throughout an empty, rectangular, galleried hall, much as Artaud had called for, and the audience moved to follow the action. Critics of a wide-range of sensibilities thought the basic emotions of the plays – fear, love, hate – were communicated powerfully in *Trilogy*, and it achieved nearly legendary status.

The Wooster Group is known for radical reworkings of canonical works. This American company develops its pieces in collective improvisations and experiments, from which director Elizabeth Lecompte (1944–) shapes the final collage product. Departing from the quest for communal authenticity that was characteristic of the 1960s, the Wooster Group performs deconstructive critiques of the processes by which meaning is produced; they are keen to perform a skepticism about meaning-making in a postmodern, mediatized culture. In the 1980s, the group deconstructed both *Our Town* (1938) by Thornton Wilder (1897–1975) and *The Crucible* (1953) by Arthur Miller (1915–2005). *Route 1 & 9* (1981) juxtaposed portions of *Our Town* with a black-face vaudeville routine and a sexually graphic film to explode Wilder's picture of an all-white, small-town America as an embodiment of universal human experience. The routes in the title referred to the film's scenes of sexually explicit behavior during a van ride on highways running not through Wilder's Grover's Corners but New Jersey industrial sites and oil refineries. The Wooster Group frequently uses technology – video-taped segments, microphones, recorded music or voices, calling attention to technologies' processes of constructing, and our processes of interpreting a performance, a self-reflexive move that short-circuits any continuities. In *L.S.D. (. . . Just the High Points . . .)* (1984), the Wooster group critiqued Miller's play, a picture of hysteria over witchcraft in colonial America that Miller intended as a metaphor for the "red scare" of the McCarthy investigations into communists in America at mid-century. A number of devices were in play in a discontinuous collage of scenes. Portions of the dialog were read at a table with microphones, seeming to evoke and query both the

infamous televised McCarthy hearings and Miller's play itself as processes leading to truth. The women were dressed in historical costumes, suggesting their historical, gendered position. The men, by contrast, wore contemporary clothes and, unlike the women, were given microphones, tools of authority. This and other devices pointed to the limits of Miller's play, which as Philip Auslander writes, seems "unable to represent the persecution of witches as the effort of a patriarchal society to suppress independent women" (Auslander 1992:92). The formidable white actress, Kate Valk, played Tituba, the black slave girl (Miller's invention), blacked up in minstrel-style, with a fake "darky" accent (Figure 11.4). By invoking an American theatre tradition of racist representation in minstrel shows and Aunt Jemima figures (Rouse 1992: 148–151), the performance probed the authority of Miller's representation of race in America. Such summations of Wooster's work always risk reducing to rationalized themes its flow of images, in which Wooster's ultimate subject is meaning-making processes. With *L.S.D.*, the group was performing a deconstructive (and sometime confusing) process of interrogating a play that had been written in a mode of realism and grounded in an American version of liberal humanism. (See the discussion of realism and liberal humanism in the Chapter 9 case study on Ibsen's *A Doll House*.)

The postmodern uses by these American directors of copyright-protected texts led to two notable legal confrontations. Postmodern performances that would deconstruct written works still protected by copyrights are, in effect, challenging property rights. Miller's threat of legal action forced the closing of *L.S.D.*, even after the Wooster Group had eliminated Miller's actual words. In 1984, Samuel Beckett and Grove Press threatened legal action against the American Repertory Theatre at Harvard University when director Joanne Akalitis (b.1937) set Beckett's *Endgame* in a subway station that suggested the aftermath of a nuclear holocaust. Beckett's text was spoken almost unaltered, but Akalitis did not follow

Figure 11.4 The *Crucible* sequence from the Wooster Group's *L.S.D. (. . . Just the High Points)*, directed by Elizabeth LeCompte. L–R: Matthew Hensell, Ron Vawter, Nancy Reilly, Peton Smith, Elion Sacker, Kate Valk (in blackface), and Anna Kohler. Photo © Nancy Campbell.

the explicit stage directions of the playwright who is especially adept with stage images in his minimalist poetics. (See the Chapter 8 case study on Beckett.) One sympathetic critic asked, "Is a radical change in setting not *truly* a textual alteration?" (Oppenheim 1994:4). At the eleventh hour, the parties agreed to a program insert in which Beckett, deeply distressed, wrote: "Any production of *Endgame* which ignores my stage directions is completely unacceptable to me. . . . Anybody who cares for the work couldn't fail to be disgusted by it [the American Repertory Theatre production]" (Kalb 1989:79). Arguably, Akalatis's setting reduced Beckett's metaphor for humankind struggling in an endlessly meaningless world by giving the play a local habitation and one particular catastrophic cause. Jonathan Kalb notes that this was not the first time that directors had not

followed Beckett's stage directions scrupulously (see the Beckett case study), but by 1984, instances of such directorial practice were accumulating and becoming more visible. Both of these cases highlight the differences between the modernist faith in the self-sufficient, unified text and the postmodernist insistence on resistant negotiations with the text. They help us see the differences between a theatre practice in which the play text is the source and controlling authority for all meaning in a performance and a practice that foregrounds the process of performance itself as a ground of authenticity – performance as at least the co-equal of the text. These cases also put into high relief the difference between text-authorized practice and a practice like that of the Wooster Group which perform critiques of meaning-making processes.

Theatre of images: Robert Wilson and others

This rubric is useful for performance works that in the 1970s began to move away from texts to a multi-media theatre of visual and aural landscapes and choreographed movement, works in which effects were no longer predetermined by the usual laws of artistic order, continuity, and time. The works of Robert Wilson are considered here from among a field of artists whose techniques vary widely, and among which dancers and choreographers were major contributors. Among other artists who may be described as theatrical imagists are Richard Foreman, Merce Cunningham, Meredith Monk, Martha Clarke, Ping Chong (discussed in Chapter 12), Pina Bausch, Laurie Anderson, Robert LePage, and Ahn Min Soo. The inquiries into the limits and possibilities of language also led German playwright, Peter Handke (1942–) to his "play," *The Hour We Knew Nothing of Each Other* (1992) which consists of stage directions prescribing a wordless sequence of actions and images (Handke 1993:93–105).

The major image theatre productions of Robert Wilson (1944–) have offered surreal landscapes of discontinuous dream-like images, encompassed by music and sound; the few words spoken are part of a trance-inducing aural score. Meticulously choreographed performers move in and out of tableaux in front of giant projection screens on which may float Magritte-like clouds or everyday items in iconic size (a huge shoe). Performers move in measured motions through everyday tasks to communicate Wilson's notion of the "natural rhythms" of life. Spectators are to make whatever associations they please, meditate among the half-remembered archetypes as they wish, or perhaps ponder their own perceptual processes. The refined aesthetic sense that governs the highly formal, modernist images works hand in glove with an earnest postmodern indeterminacy and irony. Wilson seeks to displace rational perceptual processes and reach the spectator at an intuitive, pre-language level. As Arnold Aronson has pointed out, Wilson's spectacles require the spectator to develop "a new kind of watching" (Aronson 2000:125). The subject of his *Einstein on the Beach* (1976), written with composer Philip Glass, was Einstein the dreamer and scientist. Its repeated images of a train, a spaceship, and a trial seemed to raise issues concerning scientific progress, but it was the overall orchestration of images, trance music, and hypnotic movement that audiences found compelling. His monumental *CIVIL warS* (1984) was more thematic though no more linear, dealing generally with human conflict at many levels through evocative images and icons, among them battlefield gunfire and a pageant of historical and fictional figures that included King Lear, Marx, Abraham Lincoln, and an American Indian tribe. Each section premiered in a different

Figure 11.5 Scene from *CIVIL warS*, directed and designed by Robert Wilson, 1984. © George Méran.

city (Figure 11.5). Wilson's *Life and Times of Joseph Stalin* at the Brooklyn Academy of Music in 1973 was a 12-hour "opera" in seven acts, requiring 140 actors, and constituted an anthology of his previous works, including the *Life and Times of Sigmund Freud* (1969). American born, Wilson is now an expatriot living in Germany, where many of his productions have been done, and where state subsidies support his monumental and expensive staging.

The first case study that follows below explains further the reasons for the practices of theatre artists in the postmodern world as it examines Artaud and Jacques Derrida's critique of Artaud and the general crisis of representation. The discussion of directors and texts also figures in the second case study, which surveys Shakespearean texts and postmodern performances globally, focusing especially on *The Tempest* in the light of postcolonial criticism and production.

GJW

Key references

Aristotle (1971) *Poetics*, trans. S.H. Butcher, in H. Adams, *Critical Theory Since Plato*, New York: Harcourt, Brace, and Janovich.

Aronson, A. (2000) *American Avant-garde Theatre: A History*, London and New York: Routledge.

Artaud, A. (1958) *The Theatre and Its Double*, trans. M.C. Richards, New York: Grove Press, Inc. (originally published in French in 1938). [For selections from the large body of commentary on Artaud: see the Website Bibliography.]

Auslander, P. (1992) *Presence and Resistance: Postmodernism and Cultural Poltics in Contemporary American Performance*, Ann Arbor: University of Michigan Press.

Bharata (1967, 1961) *Nātyásatra*, trans. M. Ghosh (ed.) 2nd rev., vol 1: Calcutta: Manisha Granthalaya (1967); vol. 2: Calcutta: Asiatic Soceity (1961).

Bradby, D. and Williams, D. (1988) *Directors' Theatre* London: MacMillan Publishers Ltd.

Brook, P. (1968) *The Empty Space*, New York: Avon Books

Carruthers, I. and Takahashi, Y. (2004) *The Theatre of Suzuki Tadashi*, Cambridge: Cambridge University Press.

Connor, S. (1989) *Postmodernist Culture: An Introduction to Theories of the Contemporary*, Oxford and New York: Basil Blackwell.

Dunn, C.J. and Bunzô, T. (eds, trans.) (1969) *The Actors' Analects*, New York: Columbia University Press.

Fischer-Lichte, E. (1999) "Between text and cultural performance: staging Greek tragedies in Germany," *Theatre Survey* 40(1):1–29.

Grotowski, J. (1968) *Towards a Poor Theatre*, E. Barba (ed.) New York: Simon and Schuster; New York and London: Routledge (2002).

Handke, P. (1993) *The Hour When We Knew Nothing of Each Other*, trans. G. Honegger, *Theater* 1:93–105.

Kalb, J. (1989) *Beckett in Performance*, Cambridge and New York: Cambridge University Press.

Kott, J. (1964) *Shakespeare Our Contemporary*, trans. B. Taborski, Garden City, N.Y.: Doubleday.

Mulryne, J.R. (1998) "The Perils and Profits of Interculturalism and the Theatre Art of Tadashi Suzuki," in T. Sasayama, J.R. Mulryne and M. Shewring (eds) *Shakespeare and the Japanese Stage*, Cambridge: Cambridge University Press.

Oppenheim, L. (ed.) (1994) *Directing Beckett*, Ann Arbor: University of Michigan Press.

Roach, J. (1996) "Kinship, Intelligence, and Memory as Improvisation: Culture and Performance in New Orleans," in E. Diamond (ed.) *Performance and Cultural Politics*, London and New York: Routledge.

Rouse, J. (1992) "Textuality and Authority in Theater and Drama: Some Contemporary Possibilities," in J.G. Reinelt and J.R. Roach (eds) *Critical Theory and Performance*, Ann Arbor: University of Michigan Prress.

Senda A. (1997) *The Voyage of Contemporary Japanese Theatre*, trans. T. Rimer, Honolulu: University of Hawaii Press.

Simon, J. (1975) "Grotowski's Grotesqueries," in J. Simon, *Singularities*, New York: Random House.

Sorgenfrei, C.F. (2005) *Unspeakable Acts: The Avant-Garde Theatre of Terayama Shûji and Postwar Japan*, Honolulu: University of Hawaii Press.

Weimann, R. (1978) *Shakespeare and the Popular Tradition in the Theatre: Studies in the Social Dimension of Dramatic Form and Function*, trans. R. Schwartz (ed.) Baltimore: Johns Hopkins University Press.

Williams, G.J. (1997) *Our Moonlight Revels: A Midsummer Night's Dream in the Theatre*, Iowa City: University of Iowa Press.

Worthen, W.B. (2003) *Shakespeare and the Force of Modern Performance*, Cambridge: Cambridge University Press.

Zeami, M. (1984) *On the Art of Nō Drama. The Major Treatises of Zeami*, trans. J.T. Rimer and Y. Masakazu, Princeton, N.J.: Princeton University Press.

Audio-visual resources

Grotowski, J. (1988) *Akropolis*, video recording, based on scenes from the play by Stanislav Wispianski, staged and directed by J. Grotowski. Film directed by James MacTaggert, New York: Arthur Cantor Films.

CASE STUDY: The crisis of representation and the authenticity of performance: Antonin Artaud and Jacques Derrida

Antonin Artaud's *The Theatre and Its Double* (first published in 1938) challenged the western foundations of theatre, as we have seen in Chapter 11. At first, many dismissed his work as that of a madman (he suffered from mental illness, and his family committed him to an asylum, where he spent nine years). However, Artaud gave a dramatic, even prophetic voice to what may be described as the crisis of representation perceived by many twentieth-century philosophers and language theorists, most especially, Jacques Derrida (1930–2004). This French theorist, who was influenced by Friedrich Nietzsche, Martin Heidegger, Edmund Husserl, Ferdinand Sassure, and Sigmund Freud, among others, profoundly critiqued western concepts of language. From Derrida's theories came the influential critical operation known as "deconstruction," a term often misunderstood and maligned. Deconstruction can be useful for analyzing plays or understanding the effects of a production. Deconstruction is helpful for understanding contemporary directorial practice. This case study explains the concept and the way in which Derrida brought it to bear in a sympathetic and penetrating critique of Artaud's writings.

In order to explain what language is doing and what it does to us, theorists have had to develop some specialized semiotic terms. (For an explanation of semiotics, see the case study on Brecht's *Mother Courage*, Chapter 9.) However, our everyday experiences with language prepare us to deal with terms such as "sign" and "signified" or "transcendental signified." We know that spoken language can be slippery and ambiguous. (Written language is unstable, too, of course, but it will be useful to use examples involving speech first.) The variables of spoken language multiply when the expressive means of voice, gesture, and body come into play. Our daily conversations are filled with phrases that indicate our recognition that oral communication is often problematic: "What does she want from me?" "You know what I'm sayin'?" We even act out puzzling transactions: "And he goes, 'I am so not here' . . . and I'm like, 'What do I do with that?'". A professor who says, "The variables in this play require your scrutiny" is, consciously or not, sending different signals (communicating formality, authority) than the one who says "Are you getting any mixed messages here?" Our words are always colored by the ways in which we use them – whether on the page or in speech. Actors often explore interpretive possibilities (and their own sensibilities) by experimenting with different "readings" of lines, changing meanings by altering the emphasis on words or by using different phrasing, inflection, pacing, or tone. (Try reading the opening phrase of Hamlet's soliloquy "To be or not to be, that is the question" as a meditative, philosophic inquiry. Then read it as if to say, "Big deal — what else is new? Can we move on?")

To move to a deeper level, language is always fluid; it is never anchored in some fixed truth. A rose is not always the same rose. The meaning that gets attached to it (the "signified") can vary, depending on who is sending the rose and for what reason. The "signified" of a rose (the "signifier") might be love, apology, or sympathy. Also, it may help to understand that language is a construct by considering that our computers operate with different "programs" and "languages," from different "platforms," built around certain assumptions for certain tasks. Language always comes with ideologies — inherent beliefs, social practices — built into it. (For more on the term "ideology," see the case study on Ibsen's *A Doll House*, Chapter 9).

Derrida demonstrated that language is but a chain of signifiers, always in play, never stable, always disseminating an infinite number of possible meanings as each signifier operates within a dynamic chain of others. The "meaning" that a word has is produced by its difference from other signifiers. Language is a kind of dance around an absence of fixed meaning, a dance in which meaning is continually being deferred around the chain of signifiers. This led Derrida to recognize that there is no "outside" of language. The assumption that language returns us to some grounding principle outside of itself where eternal, stable truth resides, be that Plato's perfect Forms, God, or rationalism, is a western "logocentric" notion. That is, western ideas of how we deal with reality were based on the assumption that language gave access to truth. Derrida challenged this fundamental notion in a landmark paper in 1965, in which he observed that "the absence of a transcendental signified extends the domain and the play of signification infinitely" (Derrida 1986:84–85). That is, given that language is not anchored in any transcendent source of meaning, it is always, eternally, a work in process.

Artaud, writing some 20 years earlier, was also challenging western assumptions about language. At the root of the confusion of our times, he wrote, there is "a rupture between things and words, between things and the ideas and signs that are their representation" (Artaud 1958:7). Western theatre, Artaud believed, had long since been diminished by being reduced to language, to the words of the playwright. Theatre, by its nature as enfleshed performance, offered the possibility of being much more than an archive of literature. Theatre as only language and Aristotelian imitation could never be more than mere representation for Artaud, a mere second-hand report. Artaud called for a primordial, visceral, nonverbal theatre that would affect the whole organism of the spectator, returning the spectator to some (ostensible) experience of the undivided self before matter and materialization, to the unity of body and spirit prior to dissociation. Artaud's path to this vision included his founding in the 1920s of a theatre named after Alfred Jarry (1873–1907). Jarry's *Ubu Roi* (*Ubu the King*, 1896), blows up the notions of elevated language, nobility, and humankind in general in a dark, grotesque, scatological comedy. King Ubu represents the monstrous stupidity and savagery of humankind that resurfaces throughout human history. Oversized blasphemous performance is essential to its realization. In Artaud's ultimate vision, performance is essence.

INTERPRETIVE APPROACH: Deconstruction

Contrary to the opinion of some, deconstructing a poem, a play, a performance or an essay is not the work of some devilish demon of nihilistic destruction. It is a critical process that engages closely with a text to open up its possibilities rather than closing down a text to some comfortable notion of a single unified meaning. It assumes that texts, like language, are never stable. It is especially useful for analyzing a theatrical performance, in which there are many "texts" in play – the script, the setting, costumes, the actors' performances, the architecture of the theatre, and the occasion of the performance. A theatrical performance is a veritable pyrotechnical pinwheel of sign systems.

A deconstructive analysis seeks 1) to unpack the array of meanings available in a text or a performance, 2) to understand the processes and materials by which it generates those meanings, and 3) to understand the ways in which these are at cross-purposes. A text or a performance, being unstable, is not, then, an object for passive consumption; the deconstructing reader looks beyond any overt ideological project of the work to ask especially about any contradictions, inconsistencies in the work. The deconstructive reading, so far from destroying or distorting a text, actually shows how the complex work is deconstructing itself, revealing its own multiple meaning-making operations. Deconstructive analysis is useful in many types of criticism, including feminist, materialist, and postcolonial studies. It sharpens critical thinking in general.

The case study on Ibsen's *A Doll House* in Chapter 9 is a materialist critique that deconstructs that play to show the contradiction between its idealistic ideological project of freeing Nora and the limits of the play's realistic form for really addressing the material forces that confine her. To take another example, Catherine Belsey's valuable handbook, *Critical Practice*, considers the compelling final scene in Shakespeare's *The Winter's Tale*. In this scene, the statue of Hermione magically comes to life, and this is followed by a reconciliation between her and Leontes, her once abusive, jealous husband, who believed her to be dead and is now repentant. Belsey shows that, on the one hand, the play is asking for our belief in a miracle of art that it presents in its final act to resolve the play. On the other hand, the play is, at the same time, surrounding this miracle with reminders of many kinds of implausible fictions and artistic constructions. Among them are multiple mentions of "old tales" – such as the play's title refers to, the love songs that the ever-opportunistic ballad-seller, Autolycus, hawks to optimistic young lovers, and the reference to the skills of a famous Italian painter (Belsey 1980:98–102). With a little effort, spectators will hear and see the play doing two contradictory things: it asks for our faith in a statue of Hermione "magically" coming to life and the subsequent reunion of husband and wife, and the play calls attention to its construction of its own improbable fiction.

To take an example of deconstruction in a larger sphere, Edward Said has shown how colonizing language constructed the idea of the "Orient" in nineteenth-century western

▷

▷

discourse. He opens the first chapter of his landmark work, *Orientalism*, deconstructing the language of a member of the House of Commons to show that while he seems to speak sympathetically of Egypt ("the problem" of Egypt), his discourse is embedded with colonialist assumptions (Said 1979:31–35). (We develop this example further in the next case study.) Sue-Ellen Case has shown how Europeans tried to frame Sanskrit aesthetics within nineteenth-century western paradigms, referring to Sanskrit, for example, as a "classical" language. One result was that Indian drama was compared to Greek tragedy, resulting in the suppression or misunderstanding of important attributes of a drama of a very different culture (Case 1991:111–127).

As we have seen in Chapter 11, many productions of the classics in the late twentieth century have been, in effect, deconstructing their texts. (Of course, a deconstructive performance is not of the same systematic order as an intellectual critical analysis.) They embody the assumption that texts are not stable, in themselves or in our transactions with them. The director is now no longer seen as the author's proxy, taking protective custody of some (ostensible) single meaning. A variety of meanings being available within any text and within the encounter between a text and a reader, the director's responsibility is for the authenticity of a performance, as a transaction with a text in the present. The productions of Brook, Suzuki, Mnouchine and others have staged their problematic relationships with classical texts, simultaneously occupying and displacing them, each offering this dialectic as all the authenticity there can be. Peter Brook's *King Lear* emphasized any possibilities the text afforced for an existential vision of an endlessly cruel, godless universe. Tadashi Suzuki's *The Trojan Women* imaged contemporary Japanese suffering and confusion, disrupting the conventional elevations of Greek tragedy even as his production evoked comparisons. Elizabeth LeCompte's Wooster Group performed a deconstruction of Miller's *The Crucible* by calling attention to the inadequacy of its signifiers for penetrating American ideologies.

Here are some key questions one might ask in the process of deconstructing a play or performance.

KEY QUESTIONS

1   What possible meanings are available in the work? From what events, sequences, or particular passages of language do you derive each of those meanings?

2   Are there available meanings that contradict each other? (If you wanted to make a case for a single meaning of the play, what evidence would you have to overlook or play down?) How strong, comparatively, is the evidence for one or the other?

3   Although a play is likely to set up a binary, is the difference between the two opposing spheres distinct and absolute by the end?

4   What would be the overt ideological project of the play?

Derrida deconstructs Artaud

Derrida's own characteristic procedure in decon-struction is to work through a sequence of close readings of a work, as he does with Artaud's *The Theatre and Its Double* and other works, interweaving passages from Artaud with his own paraphrasing and elaborations. His two essays on Artaud offer the clearest philosophical critique of Artaud available. Chapter 11 provides a summary of Artaud's vision. With some necessary brevity and risking oversimpli-fication, we now go to the heart of the matter for Derrida: the issue of representation, on which Derrida finds Artaud is sometimes of two minds.

Citing Artaud's renunciation of "the theatrical superstition of the text and the dictatorship of the writer," Derrida sympathetically explains that this is a rejection of the representation of writing and of classical stages, which is to say, ". . . stages of repre-sentation [that] extend and liberate the play of the signifier, thus multiplying the places and moments of elusion" (Derrida 1978:191). The stage is theo-logical – under the rule of the "author-god" – for as long as it is dominated by speech, Derrida explains. It is the domain of a "master" artist who "lets representations represent him through repre-sentatives, directors or actors, enslaved interpreters who represent characters who, primarily through what they say, more or less directly represent the thought of the creator" (ibid.:235). Released from the text and the author-god, the theatre would be returned to its creative and founding freedom, Derrida explains. In Artaud's theatre of cruelty, speech is not altogether abandoned, and the stage is not given over to anarchy. Artaud writes of "speech before words," and, as we have seen in Chapter 11, calls for spectacles of dance, costumes, symbolic gestures. He writes of "spectacle acting not as reflec-tion but force." Derrida explains that Artaud seeks, in effect, a theatre of "pure presence," where there is only meaning itself, with no intervening language symbols, a theatre in which writing has not erased the body, where there are no deferring signifiers,

where there is only the present (Derrida 1978:237, 240, 247). Derrida compares Artaud to the meta-physical theorists who seek a fundamental unity, some "metaphysical plenitude," as Marvin Carlson puts it, behind writing and representation, of which these are but a pale reflection (Carlson 1993:503). Like the old romantic poets, Artaud seeks the freedom of the spirit from the body and social repres-sion, but unlike them has no faith in language to do this. As Susan Sontag pointed out, his anxieties and hungers are like those of Gnosticism, with its passion for the spirit's transcendence of the material world, and the reach for ecstatic speech beyond words (Sontag 1976:xlv–liii). Only a theatre of cruelty could take us to pure presence, to "the unity prior to dissociation." "For what his howls promise us," Derrida writes:

> articulating themselves under the headings of existence, flesh, life, theatre, cruelty, is the meaning of an art prior to madness *and* the work, an art which no longer yields works [of art], an artist's existence which is no longer a route or an experience that gives access to something other than itself; Artaud promises the existence of a speech that is a body, of a body that is a theatre, of a theatre that is a text because it is no longer enslaved to writing.
>
> (Derrida 1978:174)

As Derrida points out, fully understanding the crisis of representation for Artaud, "there is no theatre in the world today which fulfills Artaud's desire." A theatre without representation is not possible; achieving his vision would mean the erasure of theatre. Director and theorist Herbert Blau also pointed to the problem in Artaud. "There is nothing more illusory in performance than the illusion of the unmediated" (Blau 1983:143). Artaud himself recog-nized the paradox inherent in the representation of pure presence. He offered suggestions for spectacles in material, practical terms. He even speaks of

creating a written record of the results of the experimental processes: "all these groupings, researches,
and shocks will culminate nevertheless in a work
written down [his italics], fixed in its least details,
and recorded by new means of notation" (Artaud
1958:111–112). Nevertheless, Derrida writes admir-
ingly, Artaud worked at "the limit of theatrical possibility," knowing "that he simultaneously wanted to
produce and to annihilate the stage" (Derrida
1978:249). Derrida's exploration of the paradox in
Artaud's vision is the result of, and characteristic of
the interest of deconstruction in the contradictions
within a work. He reveals how Artaud's work ultimately deconstructs itself.

As we have seen, however, Artaud's vision of an
impossible theatre helped make possible a profound
re-evaluation of a logocentric western theatre tradition and had a profound influence on directors.
Artaud's intense vision ultimately moved theatre
artists to probe the issue of the source of the authenticity of a performance. The influence that he has
had on that quest of artists around the world cannot
be overestimated. He also anticipated the work
of the performance artists of the 1980s and 1990s,
for whom the body becomes a text. (See the
Introduction to Part IV.)

GJW

Key references

Artaud, A. (1958) *The Theatre and Its Double*, trans. M.C.
Richards, New York: Grove Press, Inc. (originally
published in French in 1938). [For selections from the large
body of commentary on Artaud; see the Website
Bibliography.]

Artaud, A. (1968) *Collected Works*, trans. V. Corti, 4 vols,
London: Calder and Boyars.

Belsey, C. (1980) *Critical Practice*, London and New York:
Routledge.

Blau, H. (1983) "Universals of performance; or, amortizing
play," *Sub-stance* 37–38.

Carlson, M. (1993) *Theories of the Theatre, A Historical and
Critical Survey, from the Greeks to the Present*, Ithaca and
London: Cornell University Press.

Case, S.-E. (1991) "The Eurocolonial Reception of
Sanskrit Poetics," in *The Performance of Power, Theatrical
Discourse and Politics*, eds S.-E. Case and J. Reinelt, Iowa
City: University of Iowa Press.

Derrida, J. (1978) *Writing and Difference*, trans. A. Bass (ed.)
Chicago: University of Chicago Press. [Contains two essays
on Artaud cited here, "The Theater of Cruelty and the
Closure of Representation," and "La Parole Soufflé."]

Derrida, J. (1986) "Structure, Sign and Play in the
Discourse of the Human Sciences" [1966], in H. Adams
and L. Searle (eds) *Critical Theory Since 1965*, Tallahassee:
Florida State University Press.

Said, E. (1979) *Orientalism*, New York: Vintage Books.

Sontag, S. (ed.) (1976) *Antonin Artaud, Selected Writings*,
New York: Farrar, Straus, and Giroux.

CASE STUDY: Global Shakespeare

What country, friends, is this?
Twelfth Night 1.2

By the end of the twentieth century, William
Shakespeare (1564–1616), had reached a global level
of name-recognition matched perhaps only by Elvis
Presley or *Coca-Cola*™. He had become – it should
give one pause to consider – the most performed
playwright on the planet. On the World Wide Web,

there are nearly five million Shakespearean sites. The
plays have been translated into every major language.
The *World Shakespeare Bibliography*, with editors in
44 countries, now shows some 4,000 articles, books,
editions, and productions appearing *every year*.

Consider a few of the Shakespearean enterprises
in the last 25 years. In Tokyo, the Panasonic Globe
Theatre, a rough evocation of Shakespeare's, was
built in 1983 to house the visiting Royal Shakespeare

Company, touring in that decade as no company in the history of the theatre has ever toured. In 1990, 17 different productions of *Hamlet* were done in Tokyo, many of them at the new Globe. In China in 1986, 28 different productions of 18 of Shakespeare's plays were done in China's first Shakespeare Festival. (He had been banned during the Cultural Revolution.) In London in 1997, a scrupulous replica of the Globe was built on the South Bank, validated by recent excavations there of the remains of the original Globe and the nearby Rose Theatre, where some of Shakespeare's plays were also performed. (See the photograph of the Globe replica, Figure 4.10.) The Rose ruins were then encased for public viewing in a dark chamber beneath a new office building, like the crypt of St. Peter. In the United States, a replica of the Blackfriars Theatre, the indoor theatre where Shakespeare's company served the wealthy elite of London, was built not long after in the mountains of Virginia. A replica of the Rose will follow soon in Massachusetts. Over 100 American theatres are devoted primarily to Shakespeare. Several complete plays have been performed on websites. At least 25 major Shakespeare films were made in these years in Brazil, Britain, India, Japan, South Africa, and the United States, all designed for major markets. They include six directed by, and starring British actor-director, Kenneth Branagh, including *Henry V* and *Hamlet*; Richard Loncraine's *Richard III* (1995), in which Ian McKellan rendered Richard as a louche Adolf Hitler; and Julie Taymor's visually rich *Titus* (1999) (Rothwell 1999:Filmography, 308–340). This count does not include the BBC filming of the complete plays for television (1978–1984) or derivatives such as *Shakespeare in Love* (1998).

All of this could be claimed as evidence of Shakespeare's universality, of the ease with which his plays leap all historical, linguistic, and cultural boundaries. Such claims are often accompanied by the citation of the pretty line by Shakespeare's contemporary, Ben Jonson: "He was not for an age,

but for all time!" Jonson might be said to have been thinking rather imperially, for the two lines that precede it are: "Triumph, my Britain, thou has one to show / To whom all scenes of Europe homage owe." Of course, when Jonson wrote those lines for his eulogizing poem in the First Folio of 1623 (the earliest collection of Shakespeare's work), he could not have imagined a world as culturally diverse and as interlocked as it is today, nearly four centuries later. The term "universality" wants some critical reflection.

As with Jonson, the idea of Shakespeare's universality was framed and promoted by English-speakers, with the English language in mind. It also belongs to a western tradition of aesthetics absorbed with art's transcendent values. Shakespeare's presence as an international writer has been the result not only of the power of his poetry but of the power of his sponsors. Even in the West, each age and nation has, to a considerable degree, reinvented the Shakespeare it needed. This is especially evident in the always-public sphere of the theatre, as is clear from any culturally-informed performance history of any of the plays, from *Hamlet* to *A Midsummer Night's Dream*. (See also the Chapter 5 case study on David Garrick.) Gary Taylor, culturally astute editor of Shakespeare, reveals the same thing in his history of the editing and literary criticism of the plays in the West (Taylor 1989:Chapters 1–6). To be sure, the poetry of the plays, their characters, their complex dialectics on the human condition, and their ambiguities have proven to be rich and malleable for reinventing. But a facile notion of universality will not help us understand globalized Shakespeare.

Globalized Shakespeare is, among other things, a wide-screen version of Shakespeare's long-standing presence as cultural capital, a readily recognized legacy with which nations, corporations, and foundations want to be associated. Globalized Shakespeare is the marketable prestige commodity, *Shakespeare*™, ready to be packaged and distributed by global capitalism through all its technological platforms. Global

Shakespeare is western modernity, to which developing nations aspire. Global Shakespeare is sometimes a problematic byproduct of colonialism.

Dependably, original artists in theatre and film in their negotiations with Shakespeare, have drawn attention to these very issues in a shrinking world in which there are crossings of all kinds of boundaries and barriers – racial, national, cultural, and linguistic. As early as 1965, James Ivory and Ismail Merchant's film, *Shakespeare Wallah*, told the story of a British theatre company touring in India with Shakespeare's plays, validating British authority at the very time of the demise of the empire and the rise of the Indian film industry. To take the issue of *Shakespeare™*, images of the commodified Shakespeare are seen everywhere in Baz Luhrmann's film, *William Shakespeare's Romeo + Juliet* (1996). In its hypermodern "Verona Beach," advertisements everywhere borrow Shakespearean lines ("Out Damned Spot Cleaners"). Romeo meets his friends in a poolhall called the Globe; and there is even "product placement," with a copy of the Yale Shakespeare resting on Juliet's nightstand. Luhrmann renders the beginning and ending of the play in a "news at eleven" format, showing the tragedy being thoroughly mediatized for consumption. The double suicide will be off the screen in time for the Late Night Show. Early in the film, Romeo and his friends visit a decaying seaside amusement center. There, at the edge of the sand, are the ruins of an old proscenium theatre, remnant of an older medium whose style of heroic representation is no long viable in this Verona. Romeo's friend, the poetic Mercutio, dies there.

This case study now turns to Shakespearean translations, editions, and electronic conversions. It then examines intercultural productions of the plays and the issues these have raised. (Chapter 12 continues the discussion of interculturalism.) This case study concludes with a section on postcolonial approaches to Shakespeare's *The Tempest*, the colonial resonance of which connects it to the discussion of intercultural theatre.

Shakespeare in other words

At the outset, let it be said that any production of a Shakespearean play might be described as a "translation." Theatrical productions speak many languages besides that of the text, including the visual languages of scenery, costumes, properties, gesture and facial expression, the languages of voices and music, and the language of the movement of the body in space. Productions in the twentieth century up to the 1960s usually sought to give the impression of seamless aesthetic harmony between the text and the scenic vocabulary. Productions thereafter, especially from the 1980s to the present, have been more apt to emphasize dissonances and ruptures. The latter strategy reflects an increasing suspicion of a harmonized Shakespeare, impermeable to troubling contemporary questions. In a production, the language of the text is one of many.

Then again, we cannot really speak of *the* text of a Shakespeare play. The idea of definitive texts of the plays was challenged in the late 1970s by a new generation of Shakespeare scholars, including Steven Urkowitz, Gary Taylor, Michael Warren, and Grace Ioppolo. They stressed the differences between the earliest editions of some of the plays (half of which were published in two or more versions between the 1590s and the 1620s). Previous editors had taken it as an imperative to use one early version of a play as a master text and take "variants" from any other early version(s) to compile a conflated edition for modern readers, one that ostensibly best represented the master's voice. But the earliest texts of *King Lear*, the 1608 "quarto" edition of the play (a small, inexpensive paperback) and the version in the 1623 folio (a large-format, deluxe collection), are different in substantive ways. For example, the 1608 edition has 300 lines (including one whole scene) that are not in the 1623 version, and the 1623 version has 100 lines not in the 1608 edition. Both versions have virtues, and both are Shakespeare's. It was not that Shakespeare could not make up his mind, as Gary Taylor once remarked, but that he made it up twice.

(The existence of multiple versions of a play is not an uncommon result of theatre practice; see the discussion of Tom Stoppard's play, *Jumpers*, in Gaskell 1978:245–262.) A modern edition of the play that conflates the two Lears is a version that no audience in Shakespeare's time ever read or saw performed. To put it another way, what modern theatre audiences usually get is a *King Lear* that Shakespeare never wrote. There are also substantive differences between other early Shakespeare texts. Such a destabilizing idea was very disturbing for those who required one true text of the one true Shakespeare. The new views were disseminated in the 1980s in the prestigious new Oxford Shakespeare editions, under the leadership of eminent Shakespearean Stanley Wells. Shortly after, the Oxford principles were packaged into W.W. Norton's widely used textbook of the complete works. This included three versions of *King Lear* – quarto, first folio, and a modern conflation, a do-it-yourself *King Lear* kit for backpacks.

Destabilized Shakespeare in print is only a part of a larger story. As film directors exploited the visual vocabularies of film more imaginatively, Shakespeare's words were, in effect, decentered; images were, at the very least, as important. Filmed Shakespeare, on video tape and compact discs, became widely available. By the turn of the century, it was possible to access the play texts from multiple online sources. (See our Website Bibliography.) Hypertext versions, on compact discs and online, allowed users to construct their own textual experience, to compare quartos and folios, to read a play while listening to music inspired by it, or to put scenes from past productions alongside the text. (See the websites, *Internet Shakespeare Editions* and *Interactive Shakespeare*). In these environments, Shakespeare's texts have become as electronically fluid as any other text in the cybersphere, at once ever accessible, ever permeable, ever malleable. In these media, Shakespeare became not only disseminated more widely than ever but more democratically – horizontally, rather than from the top down.

Shakespeare's translation into foreign languages always involves cultural adaptation. As Dennis Kennedy points out in his *Foreign Shakespeare*, Shakespeare in translation is always at a cultural remove from the Shakespeare that the Anglophone world claims is "universal" (Kennedy 1993:2). Kennedy also makes the point that the linguistic remove of foreign Shakespeare, together with the absence of literary protectionism that has surrounded Shakespeare in English, may account in part for the interpretive freedoms of foreign directors (ibid.:4–6).

For German-speaking peoples, the voice of Shakespeare from the early nineteenth century to the present, with a few exceptions, has been the voice of their German romantic poets, August W. Schlegel and Ludwig Tieck. Their combined translations (1839–1840) acquired the status of an original, "der deutsche Shakespeare" (Hortmann 1998:86). Few translations of any classic have had so long a shelf-life. (The conventional wisdom is that new translations of the classics are necessary with every new generation.) In communist East Germany in the 1970s, where Marxist readings of Shakespeare prevailed, Maik Hamburger's modern German translations were, Wilhelm Hortmann writes, "direct, dramatic, precise," designed for actors and for "the immediacy of actional impact," in the spirit of Brecht (ibid.:248). In 1990, director and playwright Heiner Müller staged a seven hour *Hamlet/maschine* at Berlin's Deutsches Theater, a hybrid of Shakespeare's play and Müller's own *Hamletmachine* (1977). Müller's production came amid the fall of communism and presented an ineffectual Hamlet who was facing a worn-out Europe, more irrevocably in ruins than it had been at the end of World War II (Hamburger 1998:428–434). The opening lines of Müller's own play, now inserted into Shakespeare's, are: "I was Hamlet. I stood at the shore and talked with the surf BLABLA, the ruins of Europe in the back of me" (Müller 1984: 53).

Directors of Shakespeare in France, Japan, and Russia have sought out new translations congenial to their approaches. In 1946, French director Jean-Louis Barrault was using André Gide's translation of *Hamlet* in search of some rapport between Shakespearean language and classical French taste. By 1974, classical French would have been wholly inappropriate for Peter Brook's approach to *Timon of Athens*. (On Brook and his landmark staging of *A Midsummer Night's Dream* in 1970, see Chapter 11.) Producing *Timon* in Paris for his International Center for Theatre Research, Brook directed Shakespeare's play as a contemporary fable of a modern, young affluent liberal whose world has collapsed. He staged it simply and in the barren shell of an abandoned Victorian theatre, itself a symbol of the decline of the West. Brook commissioned film writer Jean-Claude Carrière to prepare a text in modern French, with the aim of making Shakespeare's play as accessible to a contemporary French audience as a contemporary French play would be. The translation was clear and economical to the point of being prosaic, with a few select passages in verse (Williams 1979:182–184).

Brook's project is a corrective for the Anglo-centric view of universal Shakespeare. Poetry will be lost in translation, but Shakespeare will be more accessible to foreign audiences hearing him in relatively modern translations than he is for many in English-speaking audiences who are hearing him in archaic English. Dennis Kennedy makes this point about the Schlegel-Tieck translations, noting that they are still "infinitely closer to the language spoken on the street in Berlin or Zurich or Vienna than Shakespeare's language is to that of London or Los Angeles or Melbourne" (Kennedy 1993:5). Hearing Boris Pasternak's idiomatic Russian translation of *Hamlet* (1939), another translator said: "We have never been so intimately acquainted with the real persons of great tragedy. We had not ever known that it was possible to be so closely acquainted with them" (Golub 1993:159). (Pasternak's translation was also used by Grigory Kozintsev in his 1964 film of the play.)

When Yury Lyubimov staged *Hamlet* in 1971 at Moscow's Taganka Theatre in the post-Stalin era (it played over a nine year period, 1971–1980), he, too, used Boris Pasternak's translation. Inherent in this translation is Pasternak's concept of a suffering, Christ-like Hamlet, called to a fate beyond his control but enduring it with dignity. In Lyubimov's production, Pasternak's translation took on a localized, contemporary dimension. Hamlet was played by Vladimir Vysotsky, who had been chronicling the difficulties of life in the Soviet Union since the 1960s in his songs and poems. This Hamlet, writes Spencer Golub, "recognized that in this life of struggle, the prisoner is punished for acting independently and for speaking his thoughts aloud" (ibid.:162).

Japan's long interest in Shakespeare is tied in some part to the anxious formation of its national identity *vis à vis* the West. Shakespeare was imported in the Meiji era in the last half of the nineteenth century, when Japan was opening to western influences. The first versions were *shimpa* adaptations meant to glorify Japan's new colonial enterprise. For example, a version of *Othello* dealt with the annexation of Taiwan. These adaptations were based not on Shakespeare's texts, but on Charles Lamb's story summaries. Translations of Shakespeare began to appear early in the twentieth century, concurrent with the growth of the *shingeki* companies who were attempting to establish a modern, western-influenced Japanese theatre, distinct from the traditions of noh and kabuki. Tsubouchi Shôyô's translations, the last volumes of which were published in 1928, were widely used. James R. Brandon points out that Japanese translations were valorized by claims of being faithful to Shakespeare, bringing western text-centered thinking to Japan, where the kabuki tradition, by contrast, allowed the actor considerable freedom (Brandon 2001:43). After World War II, interest in Shakespeare grew, cultivated by the universities. Assimilating Shakespeare was seen as important to Japan's cultural profile as a western, modernized culture. From the 1960s to the

1990s, Japan saw a wave of important Shakespearean productions, mainstream and then experimental.

Translating Shakespeare's language into Japanese is difficult, by any account. In the 1970s, after the youth movements of the 1960s and as Japan's little theatre movement was developing, Yûshi Odashima translated the plays into modern Japanese, treating them as though they were contemporary Japanese dramas (Senda 1998a:18–19). Even opponents of this modernizing, such as translator and scholar Anzai Tetsu, acknowledge the difficulties of translating Shakespeare. To take one example, while Japanese can be powerful for emotionally expressive passages, the delivery of such passages in Japanese requires a deliberate stress on words and many pauses (which kabuki theatre capitalizes on), and this requires more time than their delivery in English. (Anzai 1998:124–126).

It was probably in part to compensate for the translation dilemma that by the 1980s some Japanese directors were turning more to the theatre's visual resources for staging Shakespeare. Kurosawa Akiro's films were the prelude to this, especially his internationally admired *Macbeth, The Throne of Blood* (1957). The most notable stage examples were the visually complex productions of Ninagawa Yukio (b.1935), a major figure in experimental and political theatre of the 1960s and early 1970s, who thereafter had many commercial successes. He set what he called the *Ninagawa Macbeth* (1980) in the Japan of the late sixteenth century, the era of samurai warriors, using scrupulously historical costumes, as had Kurosawa. He also used Odashima's modern translation (Figure 11.6). Ninagawa's setting was a full-stage version of the small Buddhist altar (*butsudan*) used in Japanese homes for prayers for the

Figure 11.6 Kurihara Komaki as Lady Macbeth and Tsukayama Masne as Macbeth in the *Ninagawa Macbeth*, directed by Ninagawa Yukio in Tokyo, 1980 (translation by Yûshi Odashima), seen here in a performance at the Lyttleton Theatre, Royal National Theatre, London, 1987 (International Theatre '87). Photo © John Haynes. Courtesy Royal National theatre.

dead. The play took place inside of the oversize altar. Lady Macbeth was played by a female, but male impersonators in the kabuki tradition (*onnagatas*) played the three witches, lending them sexual ambiguity. The porter was played as a laughable kabuki figure. Cherry petals fell in the scene when Burnam Wood advanced on Dunsinane. Senda Akihiko notes that the altar, the blossoms (symbolizing both beauty and ephemerality for the Japanese), and the characterization of Macbeth as a sullen revolutionary who comes to power in a period of social upheaval signaled a contemporary political motif in Ninagawa's staging. The nation and Ninagawa in particular had been horrified to learn, when the New Left youth movement collapsed in a military confrontation in 1972, that Japan's young, idealistic revolutionaries had lynched eleven of their own. The *Ninagawa Macbeth* was, Senda writes, "a requiem for the dead of his generation, who had failed in their struggle against the system" (Senda 1998a:233; Senda 1998b:23–25). Ninagawa's visual vocabulary was key in his attempt to render the Shakespearean play about a Scottish king in a traditional Japanese world, albeit with contemporary Japanese overtones. There was some disagreement over whether Ninagawa's staging was simply a beautiful "Japanning" of Shakespeare, made for international export. Ninagawa's production was exported to the Edinburgh Festival in 1985 and the Royal National Theatre in London in 1987, where surely some of the appeal to western audiences was seeing Shakespeare in the exotic images of samurai Japan.

Shakespeare in other worlds

Intercultural productions of Shakespeare – the *Ninagawa Macbeth* is one type – have presented wonders and dilemmas amid globalization. Intercultural theatre usually seeks to actively incorporate in its work (to varying degrees) the texts, acting styles, music, costumes, dance, or scenery of a foreign culture. For some, this has offered prospects of artistic exploration and improved understanding across

cultural borders. However, when a western director adapts an eastern text and/or uses eastern performance modes for the staging of western classics, it raises the specter of colonialist exploitation. Such "appropriations" may seriously misrepresent both the theatre and the culture of the source culture, rendering the source culture as the exotic "Other" (explained further below). Peter Brook's staging of an adaptation of the Indian epic, the *Mahabharata* (1985), which toured the world, incurred this type of criticism. (See the case study in Chapter 12.) Intercultural productions of other kinds, like Ninagawa's, have raised other kinds of questions, as we shall see. Among other prominent western directors of intercultural productions in the 1980s and 1990s were Ariane Mnouchkine (1940–) and Eugene Barba (1936–).

In the 1980s, Ariane Mnouchkine borrowed, impressionistically, from the kabuki theatre for her staging of three of Shakespeare's history plays. She set her *Twelfth Night* in India and drew impressionistically from Balinese and kathakali performance traditions. Her productions, then and now, evolve in lengthy collaborative company processes with her resident company, the Théâtre du Soleil, which in the 1980s enjoyed large endowments from France's socialist government. They are done on a vast stage created in an old cartridge factory on the outskirts of Paris.

Mnouchkine believes that Shakespeare's plays have been poorly served by western realist traditions, from Shakespeare's time forward. For her, Asian theatre forms offer vocabularies for doing theatre's work of transforming reality into metaphor and achieving an intensity of effect that she believes impossible in western realism. Her aim is to vivify the Elizabethan history plays with ceremonial size, stylized acting, dance, and music. In her productions of Shakespeare's history plays, the courtiers were dressed in rich costumes that combined features of both Elizabeth and seventeenth-century Japanese court dress. Their faces were whitened or masked in styles influenced by kabuki or noh theatre. In the opening scenes of both *Henry IV* and *Richard II*, these courtiers entered running on to the kabuki-like stage from ramps – somewhat like the kabuki *hanamichi* – and circled the large stage, samurai swords held high. In *Richard II*, when the court received the news of old John of Gaunt's death (2.1.149–151), King Richard, dressed in an elegant white costume reminiscent of the swan in a noh play, did a ritualized high leap of power amid his flanking lords. When the king intervened in the scene of the trial by combat between Mowbray and Bolingbroke (1.3) to banish both lords, they lay prostrate on the ground at his feet. The text, in Mnouchkine's own translation, was, Adrian Kiernander notes, "declaimed rhythmically and at high volume rather than just spoken," and more often than not it was delivered directly to the audience (Kiernander 1993:113). In

these ways, Mnouchkine hoped to avoid the usual absorption in individual psychology. (Mnouchkine has denied being influenced by Artaud [see the previous case study], but much of her work clearly has congenial interests.) Characters were to be defined in clear, precise visual strokes, the better to convey an archetypal world. Rendering Shakespeare as "our contemporary," in any explicit way has not been Mnouchkine's goal.

The *Ninagawa Macbeth* and Suzuki's *The Tale of Lear* (1988 and after) present very different Japanese uses of Shakespeare. Suzuki's best known version cut *King Lear* to about 100 minutes of playing time and, in effect, set the play in two intersecting/conflicting frames. One frame was the fantasy of an old man in a hospital or perhaps a nursing home, perhaps placed there by his daughters. Having the read the play, he now identifies with Lear and acts out the play. As

Figure 11.7 *Richard II*, directed by Ariane Mnouchkine at the Théâtre du Soleil, Paris, 1982. King Richard (Georges Bigot, center) responds to the news of the death of old John of Gaunt with a dance-like leap, flanked by his lords. Photograph © Martine Franck/Magnum Photos.

Takahashi Yasunari recounts the production, a nurse, picking up the playbook from the floor, begins to read it silently. The old man reenacts, she reads, sometimes in tandem, mostly not. She often cackles at what normally would be grim or tragic moments. Music from Handel and Tchaikovsky are sometimes heard. For the famous Dover scene, in which Lear is seen to be mad ("Let me have a surgeon, I am cut to the brains"), the nurse, functioning like Lear's fool, wheels Lear on stage in a hospital trash cart. From there he delivers his lines, "When we are born we cry that we are come / To this great stage of fools" (4.5.172–173). When Lear dies, the nurse finishes her book at the same time, bursting into unstoppable laughter again (Takahashi 2001: 113–118).

This is a landscape reminiscent of Beckett or of Jan Kott's Beckettian reading of *King Lear* (see Chapter 11). In Suzuki's contrasting frames of the old man's enactment and the nurse's laughter, Takahashi found "a dramaturgy that can both move us towards a tragic emotion and at the same time, cast a cold eye on it" (ibid.:116). In the *Ninagawa Macbeth*, the Japanese director would seem to have used the western text to seek a unifying, archetypal tragic resonance. In *The Tale of Lear*, Suzuki sought a western tragic resonance but in order to bring audiences to question its premises. Both productions toured internationally, Ninagawa's with a Japanese cast, performing in Edinburgh and London. One version of Suzuki's adaptation toured North America with an American cast performing in English. The version performed in London was played by a Japanese cast in Japanese.

Let us review the issues that intercultural Shakespearean productions raise. The debate over these has been extensive. (See the bibliographies and especially Phillip B. Zarrilli's discussion of a *Kathakali King Lear* [Zarrilli 1992:16–40].) The controversy over whether borrowings from Asia by western directors amounts to neocolonial exploitation was set off by Peter Brook's *Mahabharata*, with its reworking of an Indian religious text into a western theatre mode (see the case study following Chapter 12). Mnouchkine has drawn less criticism; she has made impressionistic use of Asian performance styles and has not westernized an Asian text. In the debates over western directors' work, aesthetic interests and the argument that intercultural production improves cross-cultural understanding have been countered by an ethical concern for the distortion and dislocation of what is borrowed from the source culture. It also may be asked if the human complexities of Shakespeare's plays are being lost amid the sensuous eclecticism. Intercultural productions of Shakespeare on any side of the world raise questions about cultural reception. Whose Shakespeare is this? To what culture or country do these productions belong? Given the international tours of many intercultural productions, what meanings are available (and not) to audiences of different cultures? For mixed audiences, what is the signified behind all the signifiers borrowed from noh, kabuki, or kathakali? Are these productions dreams of a world of one culture? Doesn't all theatre have to be local? Is the West's mining of the East a symptom of a western exhaustion? Is the eclecticism a postmodern pastiche, a stand-in for the absence of a moral center? Are these productions any more than the global marketing of the exotic?

Given the increasing cross-cultural contact that globalization continues to bring, the debate over intercultural productions is likely to continue. (Interculturalism is further explored in Chapter 12.)

The Tempest and colonialism

In writing *The Tempest* (1610–1611), was Shakespeare bringing echoes of British imperialism to the Globe? It is possible that his imagination was nourished, in some part, by a contemporary account of a hurricane striking a British fleet headed for the Virginia colony at Jamestown in 1609, leaving one ship wrecked on an island in the Bermudas and its survivors struggling to govern themselves. Did

Jacobean audiences see Prospero's slave, Caliban, as a colonized native of America? The answer to the last question is probably not. If Shakespeare read William Strachey's account, the imaginary geography of Prospero's island seems to be somewhere between Milan (from which Prospero was exiled) and Algiers (from which, Prospero says, Caliban's mother, Sycorax, was banished). What can be said is that this play is charged with a consciousness of England's move under James I from nation toward empire in the early 1600s and questions about power. Certainly from the perspective of the last half century, *The Tempest* seems to prefigure the painful issues of colonization.

This resonance came to the forefront for critics, poets, and directors as the hold of European nations over many colonies worldwide was rapidly dissolving in the 1960s as these colonies sought self-governance. Postcolonial criticism has had much interest in Prospero, the aristocrat who rules by coercive magic, and his enforced servants: Ariel, the fabulous "airy spirit" who earns his freedom from Prospero, and Caliban, the disturbing, unruly creature of the cave, in rebellion against Prospero. Whoever Caliban was to Jacobeans, he has long intrigued artists, poets, directors, playwrights, and critics, as Alden T. Vaughan and Virginia Mason Vaughan have shown in their study of him (Vaughan and Vaughan 1991).

INTERPRETIVE APPROACH: Postcolonial criticism

Postcolonial criticism seeks to understand where in literature, art, music, and theatre we see the workings of, the mindsets behind, and the effects of colonial domination. It has been applied broadly to works reflecting colonialist attitudes but with special interest in works in which such domination is critiqued or resisted. Postcolonial theatre of the kind that we examined in African nations in the Introduction to Part IV represents active critiques of, and resistance to imperialism.

Colonialist oppression was, and still is the result of the expansionism of wealthy nations and assumptions about the right of the powerful to control those who are less so. By the end of the nineteenth century, Britain, in pursuit of wealth and power, had extended its empire over one quarter of the earth's surface, including India, Ireland, Australia, and multiple territories in Africa, Southeast Asia, and South America. To the English and other Europeans, one mark of those needing to be "civilized," was a skin color other than white. Colonial exploitation impoverished nations economically. Its patriarchal governments eroded the cultural identity and self-esteem of those they ruled. Britain's colonial empire, like that of other European powers, began to subside, slowly, only after World War II. Postcolonial criticism seeks to expose the effects of empire and of unequal power relationships between cultures, past and present, and with an activist agenda for related contemporary issues.

Colonialist attitudes become deeply embedded in language. Assumptions about the superiority of the West are evident today, for example, in such terms as "First World" (Britain, Europe, and the United States), and "Third World" ("developing" nations such as India and those of Africa, Southeast Asia, and South America). In his book, *Orientalism* (1978), which was influential in establishing the field of postcolonial criticism, Edward Said

▷

▷

(1935–2003) begins with colonialist language. Said deconstructs a speech given by Arthur James Balfour in 1910 to the British House of Commons on Britain's occupation of Egypt. Balfour's speech represents a discourse in which an educated Englishman can assume that what *he* knows about Egypt *is* Egypt, and that his is the superior vantage point for prescribing *for* Egypt. Balfour constructs Egypt chiefly as a British mission that will vindicate western imperialism "We are in Egypt not only for the sake of the Egyptians . . . but for Europe's sake" (Said 1978:31–39). Said's main argument is that the "Orient" is a western construction. The West has imagined the Orient as the Other, projecting onto Arabia, India, or China. as convenient, such characteristics as dishonesty, promiscuity, cruelty, and dirtiness – the opposite of all that the West values. Paul Brown adds the point that in their language, colonial powers must constantly, continually construct the Other to justify their continuing colonia domination (Brown 1985:48–70).

Postcolonial criticism, feminist criticism, and African-American criticism share some common concerns. In a patriarchal culture, women are defined and controlled by men. They are thought of as being intrinsically inferior, irrational, and incapable of self-governance. Seen as sexually threatening, they must be controlled as the property of men. Women without power to alter this ideology have difficulty defining their own independent identities. (See the case study on Ibsen's *A Doll House*, Chapter 9.) In a white racist culture, the same terms apply to blacks. Black women are in double jeopardy.

Postcolonial criticism points out that a double consciousness is common in colonized peoples. They may mimic the culture of their conquerors while at the same time trying to maintain their own. Some indigenous authors write in the language in which they were educated by their colonizers – English or French, for example. Some, like the Kenyan playwright, Ngugi wa Thiong o, write in their own local languages (see the Introduction to Part IV). This double consciousness persists in de-colonized and migrating peoples, caught between cultures. Some critics, like Arjun Appadurai (see the Introduction to Part IV), suggest studying this landscape as a site of an inevitable and creative dynamism, in which there is an evolving hybridity, or syncretism, of indigenous and adopted cultures. Critic Homi Bhabha, in his *The Location of Culture*, suggests another kind of postcolonial strategy: investigating world literature to understand the ways in which cultures have experienced slavery, colonization, revolution, the loss of cultural identity, and other traumas (Bhabha 1994:12).

Postcolonial criticism may also be concerned with the neocolonialist pressures of multinational corporations that move into poor countries, or the "cultural imperialism" of global media (especially the American media), bombarding other cultures with the corrosive fantasies of a consumer culture.

These are some key questions that postcolonial critics might ask when analyzing a play or a performance:

▷

KEY QUESTIONS

1   Where are the instances in the play or performance in which one race, class, or gender has power over another or continually constructs it as the Other in order to maintain power?

2   Where in the play do we see double consciousness?

3   Where, if any, is there any resistance to colonial ideology in the play? What is the result?

Postcolonial critics would agree with Walter Cohen's assessment that "*The Tempest* uncovers, perhaps despite itself, the racist and imperial bases of English nationalism" (Cohen 1985: 401). But the play has had relevance for postcolonialism in general. Ariel and Caliban were used as metaphors for oppressed peoples of the world in Octave Mannoi's 1964 study of colonization and revolt in Madagascar. In Latin America, where Shakespeare has not been much present, "Arielism" has been an important anticolonialist concept, a dream of self-realization referring, of course, to Ariel, the bright native spirit of the island who yearns for his liberty from Prospero and who is the antithesis of the earth-bound Caliban. Aimé Césaire (b.1913), poet, playwright, essayist, and politician born in Martinique in the Caribbean, reworked *The Tempest* in 1969 as "an adaptation for a black theatre." Césaire was a progenitor of Negritude, a diasporic black pride movement, and internationally known for his anticolonialism. His Ariel is a mulatto slave and his Caliban a black slave whose sentiments are much like those of a radical black intelligentsia educated under colonialism: "Prospero, you're a great magician: / you're an old hand at deception. / . . . Underdeveloped, in your words, undercompetent / that's how you made me see myself" (Césaire 2002:61–62). In Césaire's ending, Prospero remains on the island with Caliban.

Shakespeare's Caliban has been played as black, although he probably was not so conceived. Prospero's line "This thing of darkness / I acknowledge mine" (5.1.278–279), goes deeper than pigmentation. To the postcolonial critic, that line might suggest colonialism's production of the Other. African-American actor, Canada Lee, played Caliban in Margaret Webster's 1945 Theatre Guild production in New York, and African-Americans Earle Hyman and James Earl Jones did the role in 1960 and 1962, respectively. If the casting of these productions suggested anything about black-white power relations, it remained subtle, with little else reinforcing it. There have been more explicit stagings, such as Jonathan Miller's in England in 1970, in which Prospero was colonial governor, Ariel his mulatto house slave, and Caliban his darker field slave. In a more general, heavy indictment, Liviu Ciulei's staging at the Guthrie Center in Minneapolis in 1981 surrounded Prospero's island with the decaying detritus of western civilization. The Caliban in Giorgio Strehler's 1978 production was an African noble savage, reduced to slavery. Strehler's production did not aim at single-minded political critique, however; it was known more for its spirited theatricality and optimism.

We close, appropriately, on two important intercultural productions late in the twentieth century – those of Ninagawa Yukio (1987) and Peter Brook (1990) – which took the play into that global Ilyria of amazement, lost and found identities, and missing signifieds. Ninagawa's production was a rehearsal of a noh theatre version of the play, with a small noh theatre on the proscenium stage, and Prospero as director. It was set on the remote Sado island, to which Zeami, founder of noh theatre, had once been banished. The play's masque was done in noh costumes and masks, its comic scenes in something like kyogen style. Caliban wore kabuki-like make-up. But the language was that of Odashima's contemporary, colloquial Japanese translation. The general modality of Brook's production was African, with his customary international cast. Prospero, Ariel, and Antonio were portrayed by Africans and Caliban by a white German actor. All theatrical virtuosity was eschewed for spontaneity and simplicity in the acting. Neither of these intercultural stagings showed any interest in the imperial resonance of the play. Ninagawa's seemed to have been a meditation on the nature of theatre, although it puzzled both Kishi Tetusuo, a Japanese scholar steeped in noh and kabuki, and Robert Hapgood, an American scholar steeped in Shakespeare in western theatre (Sasayama et al. 1998:110–115; 251). French scholar Patrice Pavis, known for intricate and largely aesthetic theoretical adjudications of intercultural theatre, approved of Brook's "intercultural aesthetic" (Pavis 1992:281). Any explicit critique of colonialism was apparently put aside for the universalism and the interest in global harmony that has characterized Brook's work at his International Center for Theatre Research.

Dennis Kennedy has speculated thoughtfully that we may be moving from words and ideologies to images, and in this rapidly changing world Ninagawa, Brook, and Mnouchkine turn to Shakespeare because his status is useful and his work a stable referent (Kennedy 1995:62–63). With all the codes in play in these intercultural productions, especially the visual ones saturated with cultural meanings, we are bound to be as challenged as Viola is in *Twelfth Night*, as she emerges from her shipwreck on the coast of Ilyria to ask, "What country, friends, is this?"

GJW

Key references

Anzai, T. (1998) "Directing *King Lear* in Japanese Translation," in T. Sasayama, J.R. Mulryne, and M.

Shewring (eds) *Shakespeare and the Japanese Stage*, Cambridge Cambridge University Press.

Bhabha, H. (1994) *The Location of Culture*, New York and London: Routledge.

Bhatia, N. (2004) *Acts of Authority/Acts of Resistance, Theatre and Politics in Colonial and Postcolonial India*, Ann Arbor: University of Michigan.

Brandon, J.R. (2001) "Shakespeare in Kabuki," in M. Rutua, I. Carruthers and J. Gillies (eds) *Performing Shakespeare in Japan*, Cambridge: Cambridge University Press.

Brown, P. (1985) "'This thing of darkness I acknowledge mine': *The Tempest* and the Discourse of Colonialism," in J. Dollimore and A. Sinfield (eds) *Political Shakespeare*, Ithaca and London: Cornell University Press.

Césaire, A. (2002) *A Tempest*, trans. R. Miller, New York: TCG Translations. [Based on Shakespeare's *The Tempest*, an adaptation for a black theatre.]

Cohen, W. (1985) *Drama of a Nation: Public Theater in England and Spain*, Ithaca, N.Y.: Cornell University Press.

Dawson, A.B. (1995) *Shakespeare in Performance: Hamlet*, Manchester and New York: Manchester University Press.

Gaskell, P. (1978) *From Writer to Reader: Studies in Editorial Method*, Oxford: Clarendon Press.

Golub, S. (1993) "Between the Curtain and the Grave: The Taganka in the *Hamlet* Gulag," in D. Kennedy (ed.) *Foreign Shakespeare*, Cambridge: Cambridge University Press.

Hamburger, M. (1998) "Shakespeare on the Stages of the German Democratic Republic," in Wilhelm Hortmann, *Shakespeare on the German Stage, the Twentieth Century*, Cambridge: Cambridge University Press.

Hortmann, W. (1998) *Shakespeare on the German Stage, the Twentieth Century*, Cambridge: Cambridge University Press.

Kiernander, A. (1993) *Ariane Mnouchkine and the Théâtre du Soleil*, Cambridge: Cambridge Cambridge University Press.

Kennedy, D. (ed.) (1993) *Foreign Shakespeare*, Cambridge: Cambridge University Press.

Kennedy, D. (1995) "Shakespeare and the global spectator," *Shakspeare Jahrbuch* 131:51–64.

Kleber, P. (1993) "Theatrical Continuities in Giorgio Strehler's *The Tempest*," in D. Kennedy (ed.) *Foreign Shakespeare*, Cambridge: Cambridge University Press.

Müller, H. (1984) *Hamletmachine and Other Texts for the Stage*, trans. C. Weber (ed.) New York: Performing Arts Journal Publications.

Mulryne, J.R. (1998) "The Perils and Profits of Interculturalism and the Theatre Art of Tadashi Suzuki," in T. Sasayama, J.R. Mulryne, and M. Shewring (eds) *Shakespeare and the Japanese Stage*, Cambridge: Cambridge University Press.

Pavis, P. (1992) *Theatre at the Crossroads of Culture*, trans. L. Kruger, London and New York: Routledge.

Rothwell, K.S. (1999) *Shakespeare on Screen*, Cambridge: Cambridge University Press.

Said, E. (1979) *Orientalism*, New York: Vintage Books.

Sasayama, T., Mulryne, J.R. and Shewring, M. (eds) (1998) *Shakespeare and the Japanese Stage*, Cambridge: Cambridge University Press.

Senda, A. (1998a) "The Rebirth of Shakespeare in Japan," in T. Sasayama, J.R. Mulryne, and M. Shewring (eds) *Shakespeare and the Japanese Stage*, Cambridge: Cambridge University Press.

Senda, A. (1998b) Entry on Japan, *The World Encyclopedia of Contemporary Theatre*, Vol 5: *Asia/Pacific*, London and New York: Routledge.

Shakespeare, W. (1999) *The Tempest*, V.M. Vaughn and A.T. Vaughan (eds), The Arden Shakespeare, Walton-Thames, Surrey: Thomas Nelson and Sons Ltd.

Sponsler, C. and Chen, X. (eds) (2000) *East of West, Cross-Cultural Performance and the Staging of Difference*, New York: Palgrave.

Takahashi, Y. (2001) "Suzuki Tadashi's *The Tale of Lear*," in M. Rutua, I. Carruthers and J. Gillies (eds) *Performing Shakespeare in Japan*, Cambridge: Cambridge University Press.

Taylor, G. (1989) *The Reinvention of Shakespeare, A Cultural History from the Restoration to the Present*, New York: Weidenfeld and Nicolson.

Tyson, L. (1999) *Critical Theory Today, A User-Friendly Guide*, New York and London: Garland Publishing, Inc.

Vaughan, V.M. and Vaughan, A.T. (1991) *Shakespeare's Caliban, A Cultural History*, Cambridge: Cambridge University Press.

Williams, G.J. (1979) "*Timon of Athens*: Stage History 1816–1978," in R. Soellner (ed.) *Timon of Athens, Shakespeare's Pessimistic Tragedy*, Columbus: Ohio State University.

Williams, G.J. (1997) *Our Moonlight Revels: A Midsummer Night's Dream in the Theatre*, Iowa City: University of Iowa Press.

Zarrilli, P.B. (1992) "For Whom is the King a King? Issues of Intercultural Production, Perception, and Reception in a Kathkali *King Lear*," in J.G. Reinelt and J.R. Roach (eds) *Critical Theory and Performance*, Ann Arbor: University of Michigan Press.

CHAPTER 12

Interculturalism, hybridity, tourism: The performing world on new terms

Globalization and cross-cultural negotiations in theatre

With globalization has come a variety of cross-cultural negotiations in theatre/performance Scholars have developed a megabyte of terms to describe them including intercultural, intracultural, extracultural, transcultural, multicultural, transnational, and touristic. They all point to the fluidity of performance in a borderless world. As we noted in the Introduction to these final chapters, theatre artists have been working at the junctures and disjunctures between cultures in this era, negotiating the border crossings, giving artistic expression to the dialectic between traditional communities and the forming of next-generation communities. This chapter and the two case studies that follow illustrate some of these terms and relate them to the concepts of syncretism and hybridity. In the process, we take up a wide variety of kinds of performances, from that of the rock group, Queen, to a healing ceremony of a shaman in the Peruvian Andes; from Greek tragedy influenced by kathakali dance-drama to a contemporary Chinese play that draws on traditional Chinese performance modes; and from the puppet theatre of West Java to a production of *Wilhelm Tell* in a small town in Wisconsin celebrating its Swissness. Taken together, these cultural performances shed light on each other and on the particular phenomenon of cross-cultural theatre today. The conversation among them stimulates us to reflect on the dimensions of what we think of as theatrical.

Historical cross-cultural conversations

Cross-cultural conversations are not new in theatre history. The ancient Greek theatre came into being in the sixth century B.C.E. in the festival of Dionysus, the god of fertility who was probably imported from the Near East. Roman drama and theatre architecture were the godchildren of Greek forms. Japan was importing masked dance forms from Korea, China, and India between the sixth and eighth centuries, C.E. When the humanist academies of the sixteenth century attempted to resurrect Greek tragedy, it resulted in the fusion we know as opera. Among the myriad classical borrowings of renaissance playwrights, Spain's Lope de Vega, England's Shakespeare, and France's Molière borrowed from

Rome's Plautus. The kathakali dance-drama, born in Kerala in the seventeenth century, was woven from strands of several indigenous performance traditions, including the Sanskrit temple dance-drama, kutiyattam. Japan's *shingeki* (new theatre) movement in the late nineteenth century brought western drama and acting to Japan. Irish playwright, William Butler Yeats, was influenced by Japanese noh drama. Bertolt Brecht's theory of estrangement in acting drew – somewhat mistakenly – on his observation of the Chinese actor, Mei Lanfang. Such historical perspective may be helpful amid the postcolonial anxiety over intercultural theatre, in which there has been a tendency to think of cultures as unified and static, and to suppose that traditional theatre forms (kabuki for example) exist pure and unchanging in some parallel universe of timeless authenticity, or ought to.

Intercultural theatre

Today, productions that borrow the texts, acting styles, music, costumes, masks, dance, or scenic vocabularies of one culture and adapt them to another have been described as "intercultural theatre." These productions occur within the context of globalization, with its imbalances of power, and against the backdrop of historical colonialism. Such productions have often toured internationally, often to festival venues, their spectacle and music playing a large role in making them accessible to audiences of different cultures and languages. Many have been designed for such venues. Productions in which western artists have borrowed (some have said "kidnapped") Asian performance modes have been of keen interest and hotly debated. They raise ethical concerns over the ostensible western exploitation and misrepresentation of the source cultures. As we have seen in the case study, "Global Shakespeare," the French director, Ariane Mnouchkine, borrowed impressionistically from Japanese kabuki and noh for her experimental staging in Paris of three of Shakespeare's history plays, including *Richard II*. She

set Shakespeare's comedy, *Twelfth Night*, in India and drew from Balinese and kathakali performance traditions. As we will see in a case study following this chapter, Peter Brook staged an adaptation of the Indian epic, the *Mahabharata*, with his experimental company in Paris in 1985, which then toured internationally. All drew criticism for exploiting and distorting the materials of the source cultures, especially Brook's production, which stood accused of insensitively reworking an Indian religious text into a western theatre mode. Because intercultural theatre has, in effect, sought to be transcultural – dealing with universals that are (ostensibly) accessible across cultural boundaries – it has modified the materials of the source cultures in order to appeal to its target cultures. It may be said to manifest some of the conflicts inherent in globalization – seeking cross-cultural connections even while erasing cultural differences.

In one of the more elaborate and aesthetically well-developed intercultural productions to date, Mnouchkine again took inspiration from Asian theatre and dance for her staging of four Greek tragedies, collectively titled *Les Atrides* (*The House of Atreus*, 1990–1993). For Mnouchkine and her Théâtre du Soleil company in Paris, this was an experiment in recovering the tragedies as works to be acted, danced, and sung. She hoped to liberate them from logocentric, literary scholarship and western staging conventions (Williams 1999: 186–194). Her interests went deeper than surface stylistics. She began the cycle with Euripides's *Iphigenia in Aulis*, in which Agamemnon sacrifices his daughter to the gods so they will expedite his army's assault on Troy. This familiarized audiences with the reason for Agamemnon's eventual murder by his wife, Clytemnestra, and in effect put Clytemnestra (played by Juliana Carneiro da Cunha) at the center of the cycle (Salter 1993:59–65). The production then continued into Aeschylus's three-play cycle, *Agamemnon*, *The Libation Bearers*, and *The Eumenides*. In these, Orestes avenges his father by killing his mother and her lover, Aegisthus, in a web of revenge and suffering that is finally broken by the god, Apollo, with a new covenant. The production used new contemporary French translations by Jan Bollack, Mnouchkine, and Hélène Cixous.

For *Les Atrides*, one entered the auditorium of the hangar-like building that houses the Théâtre du Soleil by crossing a bridge over a simulation of the site of a recent archeological dig in China. It uncovered thousands of life-size Chinese soldiers in terra cotta protecting the burial chambers of China's first Emperor, Qin Shi Huangdi (247–210 B.C.E.). The costumes of the principals in the Greek tragedies were influenced by those worn by the Chinese figures. Humanistically-constructed ancient Greece was not the reference point here. The wide playing area was no imitation of a Greek amphitheatre but reminiscent of a bullring, enclosed by shoulder-height walls of earthen-colored wood. Each production began with a long crescendo from a large tier of ancient percussion instruments above stage right. Drums propelled the chorus on stage and drove the

plays forward thereafter. The chorus dances were derived mostly from Indian kathakali dance-drama, as were their costumes of black tunics and white skirts over pantaloons and elaborate headdresses. Their faces were whitened and their eyes dramatically highlighted. The chorus hovered around the action, peering over the walls and around panels in front of the bullring walls, intriguing even sometimes amusing creatures. The most affecting and memorable images of the productions came in their dances and those of the principals. Emerging from gates upcenter, the dancing chorus moved into ranks and files, filling the space, hands above their heads, stamping, kicking, whirling, and leaping high with their white skirts flying and their legs tucked beneath them (Figure 12.1). Their percussion-accompanied dances were marked with an ecstatic energy of a kind never seen in conventional western staging of the Greek tragedies, in which choruses are usually static, draped in stone-like robes, speaking in grey unison, freighted with gravitas. The Théâtre du Soleil chorus delivered their verses in between

Figure 12.1 Dancing chorus members in Euripides's *Iphigenia in Aulus*, in the *Les Atrides* cycle of the Théâtre du Soleil, directed by Ariane Mnouchkine, Cartoucherie, Paris, 1990. Photo © Martine Franck/Magnum Photos.

their dances. They and the principals delivered their lines in combinations of speech and chant. One key dance in *Agamemnon* captured Mnouchkine's sense of the violence and suffering in the play. After Orestes had killed his mother and her lover, he dragged their bodies onstage on a bloody mattress from a vomitorium (an entranceway from beneath the seating area) at house center. The energies of his savage murder of them then bled into an ecstactic but precise dance around their bodies, ending in his collapse as he came to recognize the burden of his terrible guilt (Figure 12.2). His ecstatic dance was horrifying, the more so for seeming so emotionally organic.

Mnouchkine's production was successful with audiences in France and on tour in Vienna, Montreal, and New York. Like some other inter-cultural western productions, it was criticized for its Asian appropriations and ostensible Orientalism, although less so than Brook's *Mahabharata* because Mnouchkine had not reworked an eastern text. For some, the production's exotic, fable-like milieu sometimes seemed a world set apart, socially remote; for others Mnouchkine's vision was large and epic, transcultural, offering a god-like view of the human condition rather than a myopic one. As with other

intercultural productions, its global touring life raises the question of what meanings it made available to what audiences. For many, *Les Atrides* succeeded, as few intercultural productions have, in making clear how word-bound, emotionally constrained, and chained to individual psychology twentieth-century western theatre had become.

Intercultural productions have not been limited to those originating in the West. In New Delhi in 2004, director Amal Allana staged *Eréndira*, an adap-tation of a short story by Gabriel García Márquez, the Colombian Nobel Prize winner. Like Márquez's well-known novel, *Chronicle of a Death Foretold* (1981), his story, "The Incredible and Sad Tale of Innocent Eréndira and Her Heartless Grandmother," is an example of "magical realism." In this genre, fable-like elements are woven into the fabric of a compelling tale. In its imaginary worlds and its blur-ring of the lines between fantasy and reality, magical realism reflects the double consciousness typical of postcolonial peoples, caught between the past and the future. It has become a medium of the cultur-ally dislocated and marginalized in a globalized world, giving Márquez and other Latin American writers a medium that allows an exuberant voice. The New Delhi company clearly found familiar

Figure 12.2 Orestes (Simon Akarian) dances around the dead bodies of Clytemnestra and Aegisthus in Aeschylus's *Agamemnon*, in the *Les Atrides* cycle. Théâtre du Soleil, directed by Ariane Mnouchkine, Cartoucherie, Paris, 1990. Photo © Martine Franck/Magnum Photos.

ground in Marquez's postcolonial sensibility and adapted the story into the Rajasthani dialect of Hindi.

In Márquez's story, a grandmother who was once a prostitute and who has pretensions to grandeur, is served, hand and foot, by her grand-daughter, Eréndira (Figure 12.3). Blaming Eréndira for a fire that destroys their home, the evil grand-mother prostitutes her. She takes her, chained to her bed, on an epic journey lasting years, with men lining up for miles to enjoy the legendary Eréndira. The New Delhi company of six women and one man staged the journey in a sequence of striking visual images intended to function as correlatives of Marquez's verbally rich narrative. They used music, dance, and masks, drawing on Indian and Spanish sources, including Rajasthani folk music and Colombian carnivals. *Eréndira* toured in India and played in Singapore and London, always using super-titles in English.

In the northern Indian state of Manipur, Ratan Thiyam (1948–), artistic director of the internation-ally recognized Chorus Repertory Theatre in Imphal, staged Sophocles's *Antigone* (1985). Thiyam drew on Manipuri performance traditions, including movement techniques from the traditional Manipuri martial art *thang-ta*. Thiyam is well known for his spectacular staging of Indian epics derived from the *Mahabharata* that speak to the volatile political condi-tions in this region.

There has been a wide variety of approaches to intercultural theatre. The work of Chinese-American director, Ping Chong (1946–) might be described stylistically as image theatre (see Chapter 11). Chong's theatre pieces and his films of the 1970s and 1980s were collaboratively developed, plotless,

Figure 12.3 The grandmother in *Eréndira*, an adaptation from Gabriel Marquez's short story, directed by Amal Allana, New Delhi, 2004. In this scene, several actresses play the granddaughter, Eréndira, bathing the grandmother. Photograph © Kaushik Ramaswamy.

carefully choreographed, sometimes meditative works. They often involved themes of cultural and spiritual dislocation, deriving from Chong's own experiences as an outsider in America. In his amusing film, *Noiresque: The Fallen Angel* (1989), an Asian-American girl, a modern Alice-in-Wonderland, boards a train bound for an Orwellian technocracy that is inhabited by dehumanized, mechanized residents. Chong's *A.M./A.M – the Articulated Man* (1982), took up the Frankenstein legend and featured a robot who, unable to become socialized, kills and flees into the city. In what seems to be a clear reference to the sense of spiritual dislocation of many Asian-Americans, Chong said of this production, "When human beings in a society fail to have a rich psychic life, then it's ripe for fascism" (Leiter 1994:62). His *Nosferatu* (1985) alternated portions of F.W. Murnau's early vampire film with scenes from the lives of a soulless yuppie couple in Manhattan who confront a vampire.

In Japan, as we saw in the previous case study, director Ninagawa Yukio transferred Shakespeare's Scottish *Macbeth* to sixteenth-century, samurai Japan, and the production toured to Scotland and England. In Korea, at the Seoul International Theatre Festival in 1988, the Theatre Group Ja-Yu staged *Blood Wedding* by Spanish playwright, Federico García Lorca (1898–1936), using traditional Korean funeral ceremonies in the final act. For the New York Shakespeare Festival in 1988, director A.J. Antoon created an African-Brazilian world for Shakespeare's *A Midsummer Night's Dream*, with bossa nova dances and voodoo spells. For Brazil's Teatro Ornitorrinco in 1991, director Cacá Rosset created an Amazonian world for the same play. In it, the Greek ruler, Theseus, presided over a Spanish colonial court amid the jungle. This production transferred to the New York Shakespeare Festival. Features of intercultural theatre at a popular level can be seen in the Broadway stage production of *The Lion King* (1997),

Figure 12.4 The Lionesses from the original London company of *The Lion King*, directed by Julie Taymor, 1997. Photograph: Catherine Ashmore © Disney.

directed by Julie Taymor (1952–), produced by the Disney corporation. Taymor, who had created an international theatre company in Indonesia in the 1970s, drew on various Asian traditions of puppetry and masked dance theatre for the production's animal puppets, including lions, elephants, and giraffes (Figure 12.4). Its musical score included pieces by South African composer, Lebo M, including African chants and the song "Shadowland," which blends African and European rhythms and orchestration, as well as rock songs by Elton John and Tim Rice. *Lion King*'s accessible story and spectacle have made it globally popular. With ten touring companies, it has played to 25 million people worldwide. Intercultural theatre productions in general have exploited the languages of the theatre – spectacle, music, dance – to be accessible to various international audiences.

Intracultural theatre

"Intracultural theatre" is a term that has been used to describe works combining performance modes from different cultural traditions or communities within nation-state boundaries, rather than across them. In India, a major movement known as "theatre of roots" developed in the 1950s and extended into many cities. It sought to draw on rural Indian folk forms and performance styles for contemporary urban Indian theatre. Director K.N. Panikkar of Kerala (1928–) was a major figure in the movement. In recent years, it has declined, however, criticized for decontextualizing the traditions it has borrowed and reducing them to exotica.

In New York, Mabou Mines, a New York theatre collective led by Lee Breuer (1937–), created *Gospel at Colonus* (1984), one of the group's most popular productions. It crossed Sophocles's *Oedipus at Colonus* (associated with a western high art, white upper-class cultural tradition) with a contemporary African–American gospel choir (popular art, black middle- and lower-class cultural tradition). In another unlikely cross-cultural American pairing

Bernice Johnson Reagon (1942–), African-American composer, civil rights activist, and founder of the women's gospel choir, Sweet Honey in the Rock, collaborated on an original music-dance theatre work with director-designer, Robert Wilson, known for his postmodernist theatre of images and indeterminacy (see Chapter 11). In their *The Temptation of St. Anthony*, based on Gustave Flaubert's novel of the same name (1874), Anthony and a black choir sang gospel-influenced music and, inside Wilson's serene, elegant temple-like setting, they moved to African, rock, and jazz rhythms as Anthony went through his spiritual trials. The work was produced for the Next Wave Festival of the Brooklyn Academy of Music in 2004.

The Chinese composer, Tan Dun (1957–), whose music melds modernist styles and eastern and western classical traditions, is collaborating with Chinese-American novelist, Ha Jin, on an opera, *First Emperor of China*, commissioned by New York's Metropolitan Opera. It will star the Spanish-born tenor, Placido Domingo, as the Qin dynasty emperor, Qin Shi Huangdi, and ultimately will be staged near the Great Wall for a cultural festival connected to China's Olympic Games in 2008.

A case study follows this chapter that deals with an intracultural play in a shifting political landscape within mainland China. *Wild Man* (1985) by the Nobel Prize winner, Gao Xingjian (1940–), gives voice to both China's rural, traditional cultures and its new, urban social realities, and it draws on both traditional and contemporary performance modes. At the time of its premiere, in the era after the Cultural Revolution and before the crackdown in Tiananmen Square in 1989, it corresponded to the new regime's narrative of nationhood.

Syncretism and hybridity

Such intercultural and intracultural performances are among the many manifestations of the syncretism and hybridity that have resulted from globalization. Syncretism refers to the merging of different systems of beliefs, social practices, or aesthetics, from sources inside and/or outside of cultures. The resulting hybrids or fusions may represent a disproportion of influence by the dominant power; they may represent an integration that respects the influences of the less powerful. Historically, syncretism has typically been the result of colonialism, with its military conquests, religious evangelism, settlement, and commerce. Ritual hybrids, such as a Roman Catholic mass with indigenous music, are common.

Let us consider an example of the merging of different cultures in a modern ritual performance that has roots in a centuries-old colonial context. In the Peruvian Andes near Cuzco, not far from the ancient Incan site of Machu Picchu, a middle-aged Andean man regularly performs an ancient Andean healing ritual for groups of foreign tourists. Dressed in the colorful, traditional costume of the rural people of the Andes, this *curandero* prays in the Quechuan language over a carefully prepared packet of herbs and healing plants. His ceremony is an amalgam of many influences, including ancient Incan folk medicine, Hippocrates, and modern beliefs about psychic phenomena. It culminates in the *curandero*'s prayer of blessing over individuals who wish to participate. This modern shaman is also Roman Catholic; he ends each blessing with the Catholic invocation, "In the name of the Father, the Son, and the Holy Ghost." His ritual combines strains from pre-colonial Incan culture, Spanish colonial culture, Roman Catholicism, and the traditional rural Andean culture, and it is performed for audiences of international tourists.

With the development of globalization, hybrids have evolved rapidly, to the extent that hybridity is becoming a global norm. This is in some part the result of the rapidity of globalization and of its horizontal processes, both of which distinguish it from the old colonialism. Globalization is often criticized as capitalistic imperialism that exploits less powerful cultures much as the older colonialism did. However, globalization is more complex; it has not been entirely vertical and hierarchical. Cross-cultural relations occur at an individual level every day in our globalized world, on a large scale. Migrations to urban centers have meant that the populations of the world's cities have become much more culturally and racially complex than they were half a century ago. International travel of the middle class has become a major industry. In developed nations, international concert tours have become commonplace, as have educational exchanges. Above all, the electronic media – television, film, radio, video and audio recordings, and the Internet – have become key in horizontal, cross-cultural relations, and negotiations of cultural change. Neither governments nor the corporate electronic media are wholly in control of these relations. (On these points, see the section, "Globalization, Media, Theatre and Performance," in the Introduction to Part IV.) Of course, many poor and remote peoples, especially in sub-Saharan Africa, are still not so globally linked.

Contemporary popular music, globally distributed through electronic media, presents many examples of the horizontal processes and the new hybridity. In 1977, the British rock group, "Queen," recorded a song, now internationally known, whose beat they derived from the rhythms of a Muslim rite of self-flagellation practiced by Iranian males. "We Will Rock You" has become a thundering victory chant performed by fans at athletic events worldwide (the song title is the title of the Queen musical now touring internationally). In the mid-1980s, American vocalist Paul Simon created a fusion of American popular songwriting with the music of the South African group, Ladysmith Black Mambazo, led by Zulu South African, Joseph Shabalala. The music, which originated with poor black miners in South Africa, is known as *Isicathamiyu*. The group and the influence of this music was heard in Simon's *Graceland* album (1986), including its hit songs such as "Under African Skies" and "Diamonds on Her Shoes." A subsequent album by Shabalala's group alone achieved success, and the group collaborated with Chicago's Steppenwolf Theatre on a Broadway musical in 1993, *The Song of Jacob Zulu*, which was not successful.

Returning to theatrical hybridity, we can see an extraordinary example of the merging of traditional cultures and the forces of globalization in the changing configuration of *wayang golek* – the highly popular puppet theatre of the province of West Java in Indonesia – as it moved into television. In *wayang golek*, three-dimensional, carved and painted wooden puppets tell stories in the Sundanese language. It is related to *wayang kulit*, in which puppets made of thin hide perform in Javanese. It may date from the sixteenth century and was probably associated with the importation of Islam. Its repertoire of plays draws on the *Mahabharata* and the *Ramayana*. Performances are in part improvisatory as the artists adapt to each audience's responses, and the old tales may take on some contemporary resonance. Among *wayang golek*'s characters is an array of gods, warriors, ogres, clown servants, demons, knights, kings, queens, and princesses, all portrayed by puppets 15 to 30 inches high, manipulated by rods by a highly skilled, visible puppeteer (*dalang*). Music for the performances comes from singers and an orchestra of gamelans (tuned kettle gongs), xylophone-like instruments, and drums. Most live performances are held in conjunction with a ritual at which food is served and prayers recited, such as a wedding, circumcision, or a ceremony dedicating a new building. Performances may last eight hours or more, from 8:30 in the evening to 4:30 in the morning.

Wayang golek has long been an entertainment integral to the social life of the West Java (predominantly Sundanese). Because of its popularity – live performances draw large crowds – and its cultural authority, *wayang golek* has been used by national governments to communicate ideologies and instruction, as Andrew N. Weintraub shows in his detailed account, *Power Plays*. From the Japanese occupation in World War II through the regimes of Presidents Sukarno (1945–1966) and Suharto

(1967–1998), *wayang golek* has sometimes been allied with, and has sometimes been a site of resistance to government mandates as it has adapted to cultural sensibilities. It has been a dynamic medium reflecting the national imagining and re-imagining of an Indonesian nation state.

As Indonesia modernized and entered the global economy, *wayang golek* artists created hybrid forms that took advantage of the new communication technologies. In the 1970s, performers of this highly visual and essentially social art began to record and promote performances on audio cassettes. In the mid-1980s, *wayang golek* moved onto the national television channel, where both the government agenda and the reframing for the media resulted in new variations. Broadcasts were limited to about 45 minutes. "Don't play all night! Today's spectators are busy," said one government official (Weintraub 2004:196). This meant that plays intended to last as long as eight hours were drastically edited, compromising the performances of the tales whose elaborated epic form is essential to the metaphysical view of the human condition that the puppets represent. Some artists compensated by serializing their plays. They also learned how to exploit multiple camera angles to heighten scenes of spectacle, such as battles. The hybrid, televised *wayang golek* reached the same audiences as live shows did, and it also suited the autocratic Suharto government well, because the studio performances were done without live audiences. In the customary interactions with *wayang golek* performers, live audiences often registered their reactions to state messages or otherwise made a performance unpredictable.

However, in 1996, one well-known puppeteer, Asep Sundandar Sunarya, developed a new *wayang golek* derivative for television, a hybrid comic form featuring the traditional puppet character, Cepot. Weintraub describes Cepot as "a boisterous, outspoken country bumpkin whose obscene language and carnivalesque humor challenge elitist social conventions and class hierarchies" (ibid.:202).

In daily programs that were part sketch and part sitcom, *The Asep Show* dealt with topical concerns in the final years of Suharto's scandal-ridden regime – bank scandals, money laundering, narcotics, and crooked land-developing schemes. Cepot, the honest, earthy, regional figure with a simple lifestyle, became the foil to the wealth, sophistication, and corruption of Indonesian politics and business. Performances were given in the Indonesian language for a national audience, but with strong regional strains. Quite distinct from the spirit of the Suharto's New Order, which emphasized unity while compartmentalizing regions and ethnicities, the television world of Cepot emphasized diversity, difference, and cross-cultural realities.

The hybrid *Asep Show* continued after the fall of Suharto and the collapse of the national economy in 1998, and through the ethnic and religious strife of the volatile years that followed. Cepot instructed listeners on such matters as the effects of a decline in investor confidence and continued to tell old tales with topical links. Meanwhile, *wayang golek* continued to be performed in traditional style for live audiences in West Java, although affected by the new hybrids. One consequence is an ongoing debate over how explicitly political the art should be.

Tourism and performance

The desire to explore other lands and know other cultures is evident in the travel literature and travel pictures of many cultures over many centuries, which record pilgrimages to capital cities, religious shrines, and scenic natural wonders. Whether travelers are seeking historic/legacy sites and/or different cultures, they seek their own sensuous confirmation of the existence of the world they have imagined and anticipated, and they seek an experience of authenticity. Often, performances of various kinds are part of their experience.

By the end of the seventeenth century in Europe, the "grand tour" to sites of classical monuments and to museums and galleries became a regular

rite in the education and maturing of sons of aristocracy and gentry. With the development of the middle class, and "leisure" time, tourism grew, and tourist destinations responded with improved presentation of sites and added attractions. Today, national and international tourism is a major industry, serving a large middle class in developed nations. Sites once remote have become easily accessible via inexpensive air travel and package tours.

Travel to special performance events has become common. Sports events, such as the Olympics, draw thousands of tourists to their athletic performances and the related rituals and pageantry. Richard Schechner has aptly described the Olympics as "Globalism's signature performance" (Schechner 2002:238). The Olympics are a utopian performance of cultural diversity within an imagined frame of world community, even as the competitive games appeal to nationalistic fervor. Governments know that performing in the games will bring them recognition as respected members of the world community. Developing nations aspire to host the games, knowing that this will testify to a level of prosperity and stability that will assure long-range tourism. Internationally-known architects are selected in competitions to create stadiums that will become skyline signatures of Olympic cities as tourist destinations. Orbiting around the Olympics in recent decades have been intercultural arts events, such as those spawned by the Los Angeles Olympics in the 1980s and those planned for China's Olympics in 2008.

As we have seen, theatre festivals have become destinations for pilgrimage audiences, some seeking the shrines of Shakespeare, some seeking adventurous artistic experiments (see Chapter 10 and the accompanying case study on niche theatre). Suzuki's Toga Art Park in the mountains of central Japan, with its complex of theatres and international festivals, has become a tourist destination. In the summer of 2005, New York City's Lincoln Center offered several weeks of intercultural performance events in a festival environment intended to draw tourists. It included intercultural productions by Robert Wilson, Ninagawa, and Mnouchkine, among others.

Tourist companies and state agencies have helped develop performances or exhibitions for travelers that draw on indigenous cultures. Folkloric performances – usually music and dance – are staged for tourists in major world cities including Mexico City, Warsaw, Prague, Cuzco, and Marrakech. In India, Jaipur's Rex Tours arranges for urbanized Rajasthanis and foreign visitors to observe "authentic" rural Indian life in a specially built village, where they watch craftsmen work and enjoy traditional food, dance, and music. The tour company brochure invites the traveler to "take a peek into the lives of rural folk, their abodes, social setup, religious beliefs, and innovative cuisine" (cited in Schechner 2002:236). In Ireland, one can visit a "real" Irish village near Shannon International Airport. We have seen the Peruvian *curandero*, performing his healing rites for tourists in the Andes. In Kenya, tribal dances of the Maasai tribe have been staged for tourists. As the economic and racial gaps widen between the tourist and the people on display, such performances raise ethical questions. When do they become demeaning exhibitions for the consuming gaze of tourists? Do the historical villages and heritage tours create an appealing "eternal past" that spectators can view with comfortable detachment, even nostalgia, a past unconnected to any problems of the past or the present? Is the tourist seeking escape, or will she/he be proactive in asking questions about such issues?

Some performance artists have devised presentations for tourist settings that are related to the issue of the touristic gaze. Mexican-American performance artist, Guillermo Gómez-Peña, arranged such an event in 1992 in Madrid's Columbus Square on the 500th anniversary of Christopher Columbus's "discovery" of America. It was designed to help spectators recognize the ways in which "exotic peoples" have been exploited and conceptually colonized. Gómez-Peña and his then frequent collaborator, Coco Fusco, set up a 12-ft square golden cage in which they "played" recently discovered "primitive" Amerindians, the fictive "Guatinauis," supposedly from an island in the Gulf of Mexico. The couple was dressed exotically, spoke gibberish, watched TV, and posed for photos (Figure 12.5). Ethnographic handouts described the "specimens" and their typical behavior. Spectators' responses varied. Some believed they were seeing rare natives; some complained that the display was inhumane (ibid.:261).

For the Vienna Festival in the summer of 2000, German director Christoph Schlingensief (1960–) created a performance work that scandalized Austria, the moreso for being set up next to the Vienna State Opera, a prime site for tourists, whom it was designed to reach. Entitled *Please Love Austria*, it employed a "residential container" in which 12 actual refugees (anonymous) from different countries who were seeking asylum in Austria, stayed awaiting their fate. They were guarded and their daily routines filmed and shown on television screens in the plaza. Over the container was a slogan representative of the extreme right-wing politics of the Freedom Party and its leader, Jörg Haider, "*Ausländer raus*" (Foreigners Out). Schlingensief shouted extreme right-wing slogans from a nearby rooftop, and shocked tourists in the plaza below by welcoming them to Austria, "the Nazi factory." As Gitta Honegger explains, "The container installation was the simulation of a culture that had absorbed Haider's extremist rhetoric" (Honegger 2001:5).

In our final case study, we see a community theatrical production which is both a performance of community identity and a performance for tourists. In 1938, a small town in Wisconsin with historical Swiss origins and a long history of celebrating its ethnicity, began what became the annual staging of Friedrich Schiller's play, *Wilhelm Tell*. Schiller's play, often performed in Europe in the nineteenth century, celebrates the legendary Swiss

Figure 12.5 *A tourist photographs Two American Indians Visit.* Guillermo Gómez-Peña and Coco Fusco played fictive "Amerindians" as caged, exotic specimens in this performance work, created in 1992 in Madrid's Columbus Square on the 500th anniversary of Christopher Columbus's "discovery" of America. Photo © Coco Fusco.

figure as a hero embodying the freedom and independence of the human spirit. The residents of New Glarus offer it as both a self-conscious performance of the village's historical Swiss origins and ethnic identity, and as a collective (re)invention intended to attract tourists. Here, tourism, ethnicity, and community identity intersect in a continual reimagining of social relations.

GJW

Key references

Barucha, R. (2000) *The Politics of Cultural Practice, Thinking Through Theatre in an Age of Globalization*, Hanover and London: Wesleyan University Press.

Blumenthal, E. (1999) *Julie Taymor: Playing With Fire: Theatre, Opera, Film*, New York: H.N. Abrams 1999.

Carlson, M. (2000) "The Macaronic Theatre," in C. Sponsler and X. Chen (eds) *East of West, Cross-Cultural Performance and the Staging of Difference*, New York: Palgrave.

Fusco, C. and Gómez-Peña, G. (1992) *Two Amerindians Visit*. [A thirty-minute video tape is available from Data Bank in Chicago: Info@ydb.org, or +1 800 634 8544. A list of Fusco's performance works and publications is at http://www.thing.net/~cocofusco/. For works by Gómez-Peña, see the bibliography for the Introduction to Part IV.]

Honegger, G. (2001) "Austria: school for scandal," *Western European Stages* 13:5–12.

Jaywant, J., Singh, R. and Chaturvedi, R. (1994) Entry for India, in D. Rubin (ed.) *World Encyclopedia of Contemporary Theatre*, vol 5, London, New York: Routledge.

Kiernander, A. (1993) *Ariane Mnouchkine and the Théâtre du Soleil*, Cambridge: Cambridge University Press.

Lee, M. (1989) "The Seoul international theatre festival and forum 1988," *Asian Theatre Journal* 6:202–207.

Leiter, S. (1994) *The Great Stage Directors*, New York: Facts on File.

Lo, J. and Gilbert, H. (2002) "Toward a topography of cross-cultural theatre praxis," *TDR* 46:31–47.

Pavis, P. (1992) *Theatre at the Crossroads of Culture*, trans. L. Krueger, London and New York: Routledge.

Salter, D. (1993) "Hand eye mind soul: Théâtre du Soleil," *Theater* 24:59–65.

Schechner, R. (2002) *Performance Studies, an Introduction*, London and New York: Routledge.

Weintraub, A.N. (2004) *Power Plays, Wayang Golek Puppet Theater of West Java*, Southeast Asia Studies No. 110, Athens, Ohio: Centre for International Studies.

Williams, D. (ed.) (1999) *Collaborative Theatre, the Théâtre du Soleil Sourcebook*, New York and London: Routledge.

CASE STUDY: Whose *Mahabharata* is it, anyway? The ethics and aesthetics of intercultural performance

On 7 July, 1985, the international theatre world witnessed the debut of one of the most theatrically brilliant yet controversial productions of the late twentieth century: director Peter Brook's nine-hour, three-play adaptation of the Hindu epic, *Mahabharata* (Figure 12.6). That first performance (in French) in an abandoned stone quarry as part of the 29th Avignon Festival was followed by an English-language world tour in 1987–1988. A 5½ hour English language film was released (and televised) in 1989. According to director Brook, he and playwright Jean-Claude Carrière were "not presuming to present the symbolism of Hindu philosophy" but trying to "suggest the flavor of India without

Figure 12.6 In Peter Brook's *The Mahabharata*, the archery tournament for the young cousins, in *Part I: The Game of Dice*, from the 1986 production at the Bouffes du Nord, Paris. Photo © Gilles Abegg.

pretending to be what we are not." They were "trying to celebrate a work which only India could have created but which carries echoes for all mankind" (Carrière 1987:xvi).

In addition to adapting a sacred Hindu text said to be 15 times longer than the Bible, the authors borrowed and adapted a wide variety of spectacular performance styles, exotic music, and visual aesthetics derived from India and other non-European cultures. Supported by a huge budget, the international, multi-racial, and multi-lingual cast spent several years in research and rehearsal (including travel to India). The resulting piece provoked both extreme praise and extreme condemnation.

Here, chosen from among many, are examples of the opposing views, offered by respected theatre scholars. First, a criticism from Indian critic, Rustom Bharucha:

> Peter Brook's *Mahabharata* exemplifies one of the most blatant (and accomplished) appropriations of Indian culture in recent years. Very different in tone from the Raj revivals, it nonetheless suggests the bad old days of the British Raj . . . through the very enterprise of the work itself [and] its appropriation and reordering of non-western material within an orientalist framework of thought and action, which has been specifically designed for the international market. . . . [Brook] does not merely take our commodities and textiles and transform them into costumes and props. He has taken one of our most significant texts and

decontextualized it from its history in order to "sell" it to audiences in the West.

(Bharucha 1990 [1993]:68)

In contrast, Maria Shevtsova praises the work:

> [U]niversal theatre [is] represented as never before by Brook's *Mahabharata*, ... Its aesthetic is driven by a vision set on eroding hierarchies between nationals, races, castes or classes, or any other socially determined privileges [*sic*]. In this respect, too, Brook creates in *The Mahabharata* a totally new theatrical genre for which existing names are inadequate. By modeling its own features, this genre both anticipates coeval audiences and presupposes it can help create them. . . . [T]he notion of "world community" underpinning Brook's work is [close] to the spirit of synthesis and, for that matter, to the humanist perspective . . . , not to mention its humanitarian and even utopian impulse.

(Shevtsova 1991:221–222)

Two decades after its premiere, Brook's *Mahabharata* continues to be a touchstone for heated debates regarding the ethics and aesthetics of a genre variously termed "intercultural," "cross-cultural," "transcultural," "multicultural," or "syncretic." For the sake of simplicity, this essay will use the term "intercultural" theatre. For discussions of alternative terms, see Lo and Gilbert (2002) and Pavis (1996).

INTERPRETIVE APPROACH: The historian between two views of intercultural performance

Bharucha and Shevtsova were responding in opposite ways to issues raised by Edward Said in his influential book *Orientalism* (1979), which helped shape postcolonial criticism. We have already seen some of the ways postcolonial criticism works (Chapter 11 case study,

▷

▷

"Global Shakespeare"). Here, we consider both sides of the particular issue that post-colonial critics often describe as the "appropriation" of indigenous cultural properties by artists from an outside culture. Said notes that western artists, like politicians and soldiers, have often seen non-European cultures (such as those of India, Japan, China, Africa, or the Middle East) as objects that are available for their use, rather than as important and equal civilizations. Like colonizers or conquerors, artists have power. By labeling the "Other" as exotic, childlike, primitive, dangerous, or incomprehensible, the artist or colonizer can justify "controlling" or "appropriating" cultural properties. Said does not suggest that the intent is always destructive or even profit-oriented. Artists have often "appropriated" aspects of the art of other cultures to enrich or rejuvenate their own, and benevolent efforts have been made by outsiders to preserve or protect works of ancient cultures that seem in danger of disappearing.

American director Peter Sellars believes that intercultural artistic encounters can have positive results: "Each human operates across cultural lines – between ourselves, between other cultures. . . . The most profound encounters still take the form of the Homeric journey, the quest where you go abroad and come back transformed. That journey doesn't always need to be imperialistic. . . . We are all of us travelers, strangers, visitors, even at home" (quoted in Sorgenfrei 1995:52).

The issue of appropriating or representing another culture in an art work, however, can be problematic, as Said points out in discussing orientalism:

> The things to look at are style, figures of speech, setting, narrative devices, historical and social circumstances, *not* the correctness of the representation nor its fidelity to some great original. The exteriority of the representation is always governed by some version of the truism that if the Orient could represent itself, it would; since it cannot, the representation does the job, for the West, and *faute de mieux*, for the poor Orient.
>
> (Said 1979:21)

To come then to the issue of intercultural theatre, we offer a basic definition by Jacqueline Lo and Helen Gilbert:

> Put simply, intercultural theatre is a hybrid derived from an intentional encounter between cultures and performing traditions. It is primarily a western-based tradition with a lineage of modernist experimentation through the work of Tairov, Meyerhold, Brecht, Artaud, and Grotowski. More recently, intercultural theatre has been associated with the works of Richard Schechner, Peter Brook, Eugenio Barba, Ariane Mnouchkine, Robert Wilson, Tadashi Suzuki, and Ong Keng Sen. Even when intercultural exchanges take place within the "non-West," they are often mediated through western culture and/or economics.
>
> (2002:36–37)

▷

▷

Some of the cultural elements that might be transported between cultures (or fused into new genres) include narratives, rituals, myths, philosophical or religious concepts, music, language, settings, costumes, properties, makeup, staging, and training methods of performers. When done thoughtfully, the results have been aesthetically satisfying for many audiences. For example, *The Lion King*, a hit musical in London, New York, and on tour, directed by Julie Taymor and based on the Disney animated film, featured puppetry, music, scenic design, costumes and masks derived from various African, Indonesian, and Japanese performance genres (Figure 12.7). Japanese director Ninagawa Yukio's acclaimed production of Euripides's *Medea* employed Japanese kabuki acting, ancient Greek and Cretan costuming, and classical European music (Figure 12.8). French director Ariane Mnouchkine and her company, the Théâtre du Soleil, have produced critically acclaimed intercultural productions of Shakespeare and the ancient Greeks (see the Chapter 11 case study, "Global Shakespeare," and Chapter 12), as well as of original plays.

▷

Figure 12.7 Roger Wright as Simba in the original London company of Julie Taymor's production of *The Lion King*. The production showed the influences of various African, Indonesian, and Japanese performance genres. Photo © Catherine Ashmore, Disney.

Figure 12.8 Ninagawa Yukio's *Medea*, at Tokyo International Theatre, 1987. Costume designs fuse Japanese kabuki with Greek/Cretan elements, such as the ram's horns headdress shown here. Photo © Maurizio Buscarino.

Despite the pleasure many find in such works, some scholars feel that intercultural productions raise ethical questions. Does an artist have a right to use whatever she is inspired by, regardless of its source? Are certain subjects or cultural products (such as sacred rituals) off-limits? Does using cultural elements out of context promote stereotypes? Does it aid in understanding and appreciating other cultures? Is it possible to create and/or evaluate a work of art without considering the social or political implications? In other words, is there such a thing as "art for art's sake?"

Evaluating the intercultural performance

Lo and Gilbert acknowledge the wide differences in artists' goals and methods. They suggest imagining intercultural theatre as an elastic dialog between cultures, a kind of

▷ "two-way flow" that sometimes pulls one way, and sometimes the other. To judge a work, they recommend considering 1) the artistic and sociological/anthropological/political elements of the "source" culture or cultures, and 2) those same elements of the proposed "target" culture or cultures (the assumed audience). They note that each case will be distinct, due to the specific circumstances of its creation and performance. The elastic pull might be more towards aesthetics or more towards social/political/cultural context. In judging any intercultural work, then, one must determine, according to one's own priorities, whether there is an acceptable balance.

Before analyzing Brook's *Mahabharata*, it will be useful to consider how this production fits into Brook's work at the International Center of Theatre Research in Paris. (See Chapter 11 for an overview of Brook's major work and his contribution to the changing role of the director.)

Peter Brook and the International Center of Theatre Research

Brook has been one of the most visible practitioners of "intercultural" theatre at least since 1970, when he helped found (with financial backing from the Ford Foundation, UNESCO and other sources) the International Center of Theatre Research in Paris (as of 1974, the International Center for Theatre Creations [CICT]). With actors, dancers, mimes, musicians, acrobats and other artistic collaborators from around the world, the Center attempts theatrical creation and experimentation that transcends national boundaries and commercial considerations. Plays are often rehearsed for over a year; productions occur only when (and if) they are ready. The Paris theatre that is home to the Center is the *Bouffes du Nord*.

The history of CICT suggests the path that led to the *Mahabharata*. Brook sought to create "performance texts" by emphasizing those elements traditionally considered secondary (gesture, movement, vocal tone, spatial relationships, etc.) and de-emphasizing the written text, traditionally elevated

to greatest importance. In its first three years, the company undertook extensive "fieldwork" research in such places as Iran, Africa, and America. The goal was to provide a collective experience that would bind the company together, open them up as artists, and transform them by confronting the unknown. They did not attempt to learn new techniques, but to unlearn old ones, to reveal intuitive or "authentic" responses in the actor's body, and to rediscover a kind of imagined purity or innocence. This idea is similar to the *via negativa* advocated by Jerzy Grotowski (see Chapter 11).

CICT's first production was *Orghast*, performed in 1971 at the Shiraz/Persepolis Festival in Iran. It was an experiment in non-representational, abstract music and poetry inspired by the myth of Prometheus. It was performed in an invented language composed of over 2,000 word-sounds derived from musical phonemes, ancient Greek, Latin and Avestan. Playwright Ted Hughes described his goal: "If you imagine music buried in the earth for a few thousand years, decayed back to its sources, not the perfectly structured thing we know as music, that is what we tried to unearth" (Williams 1991:5). *Orghast* attempted to communicate on a pre-rational level; it presumed and sought to reach some common emotional core in the audience without social, linguistic or cultural barriers.

Orghast was followed by other experiments, such as *The Conference of the Birds* (1972–1973). Based on the twelfth-century Sufi poem by the Persian Farid Uddin 'Attar of Nishapur, the play was developed through improvisation during a three-month trek in jeeps across the Sahara desert and northwest Africa, and later during residencies in California with Luis Valdez's El Teatro Campesino, at a Chippewa reservation in Minnesota, and at the Brooklyn Academy of Music.

Analyzing Brook's *Mahabharata* as intercultural performance

Brook's goals and methods have been both praised and criticized. In regard to *The Conference of the Birds*, David Williams reported that "the lack of any verifiable evidence that the group's foray into African culture involved a real exchange enraged [some people], who immediately wrote off the entire exercise as symptomatic of a radical utopianism, even of a neo-colonial ethos" (1991:7). While Williams acknowledges that such criticism may result from taking the work out of context, he also emphasizes that:

> [T]he Centre's initial work was structured around a series of questions that intrigued Brook. They are avowedly essentialist and humanist – idealist in formulation and concern, signaling Brook's intuitive sympathy with Jung's foregrounding of a mythopoeic sensibility, to the detriment of a rationalist or materialist discourse.
>
> (ibid.:4)

By "essentialist," Williams means that Brook (like psychologist Carl Jung) believes that all people always share a common, unchanging core or essence. "Humanism" is a set of values that has been embedded in western thought since the so-called "renaissance". In general, it placed the emphasis on human potential, putting life more at the center of human concerns than the Christian afterlife (although not excluding the Christian deity). Both concepts have been challenged in recent years as the creations of an elite class of European males. Critics of these terms consider the ways in which such concepts are the constructions of historical conditions flowing from such material factors as class, race, ethnicity, and gender ("rationalist and materialist discourse").

Said suggests that one method of evaluating an artistic work is to examine its narrative structure. In their *Mahabharata*, Brook and Carrière transformed a cyclical, digressive, religious narrative into a linear, secular one. Cyclical narratives tend to distribute their focus across disparate tales and characters and to spread out philosophical considerations rather than zeroing in on a singular topic or issue. They are typically lyrical, dream-like, non-logical and ambiguous. In contrast, linear, forward action emphasizes an orderly or logical progression, for example from ignorance to knowledge. Linear progression is deeply embedded in Judeo-Christian philosophy and forms the rationale for traditional European dramatic structure, beginning with the ancient Greeks. For the *Mahabharata*, Brook and Carrière wanted to shorten and concentrate their work, so they eliminated aspects they thought unrelated to a main action. They divided the rest into three parts, creating a trilogy reminiscent of Greek tragedies or the three-act play structure, and emphasizing the linear concept of Aristotle's definition that a tragedy must have a "beginning, middle, and end." They created a framing device by having the tale told to an Indian child. Did such choices suggest an incoherent or incomprehensible original? Did they imply that the audience was like a child who needed difficult ideas explained in familiar ways? As Said noted, " . . . if the Orient could represent itself, it would; since it cannot, the representation does the job, for the West, and *faute de mieux*, for the poor Orient" (Said 1978:21).

Similarly, if we look at the episodes they chose for inclusion, we notice many that emphasize bizarre or supernatural sex. Examples include 100 brothers born from a giant iron ball that only emerges from their mother's womb after her stomach is beaten, and two wives who summon various gods to impregnate them because their joint husband has been cursed to die if he has intercourse. The adapters selected the stories of five brothers married to a single wife and the sexual encounter of a human with a demon. All of these elements exist in the original but with stories of different kinds. Were these selected primarily for exotic appeal, or did they help audiences discover the original narrative's "interior" meaning?

Such questions require us to examine any particular performance in detail, aesthetically and ethically. We must assess that elastic pull between aesthetic pleasure and social value and between the source and target cultures. There is no simple "score card" with which to assess the extent to whether a work is a troubling, orientalist appropriation. One must assess one's own sensibilities together with an awareness of the possible moral implications of the work. Some may find this comment of Peter Brook's helpful (he was speaking to actors, but his words are relevant to audiences).

> The only thing I can say that may be of some use is that there are two ways of making theatre. One can make theatre . . . to create things that improve on life. . . . The other possibility is to use one's contact with theatre to live in a better way. . . . All one can do is pursue the kind of work that opens one up and makes one available. . . . One can say that theatre is good or bad. And how does one feel that? By tasting it. The proof is in the pudding.
>
> (Williams 1991:278)

Ultimately, it is up to the individual spectator – and the historian – to determine, which careful reading and viewing can help.

CFS

Key references

Bharucha, R. (1993, 1990) *Theatre and the World: Performance and the Politics of Culture*, London and N.Y.: Routledge.

Brook, P. (1968) *The Empty Space*, Harmondsworth: Penguin.

Carrière, J.-C. (1987) *The Mahabharata: A Play Based Upon the Indian Classic Epic*, trans. P. Brook, New York: Harper and Row.

Lo, J. and Gilbert, H. (2002) "Toward a topography of cross-cultural theatre Praxis," *The Drama Review*, 46(3):31–53.

Pavis, P. (1992) *Theatre at the Crossroads of Culture*, trans. L. Kruger, London and New York: Routledge.

Pavis, P. (ed.) (1996) *The Intercultural Performance Reader*, London and New York: Routledge.

Said, E.W. (1978) *Orientalism*, New York: Random House.

Shevtsova, M. (1991) "Interaction-Interpretation: *The Mahabharata* from a Socio-Cultural Perspective," in D. Williams (ed.) *Peter Brook and the Mahabharata: Critical Perspectives*, London and New York: Routledge.

Sorgenfrei, C.F. (1995) "Intercultural Directing: Revitalizing Force or Spiritual Rape?" in M. Maufort (ed.) *Staging Difference: Cultural Pluralism in American Theatre and Drama*, New York: Peter Lang.

Williams, D. (ed.) (1988) *Peter Brook: A Theatrical Casebook*, London: Methuen.

Williams, D. (ed.) (1991) *Peter Brook and the Mahabharata: Critical Perspectives*, London and New York: Routledge.

Audio-visual resources

Brook, P. (director) (1989) *The Mahabharata (Part 1: The Game of Dice; Part II: Exile in the Forest; Part III: The War)*. [Available for purchase from Parabola Video Lab or Insight Media.]

CASE STUDY: Imagining contemporary China: Gao Xingjian's *Wild Man* in post-Cultural Revolution China

In 2000, playwright/novelist Gao Xingjian (b.1940) became the first Chinese author to be awarded the Nobel Prize in Literature. Surprisingly, China did not celebrate this achievement as a national victory. Instead, the announcement was buried in a small article deep inside China's state-run newspapers. To understand the reasons for this dismissive behavior, we must consider both the history of spoken drama (*huaju*) in China and contemporary China's sense of itself as a nation.

INTERPRETIVE APPROACH: Theories of national identity

In *Imagined Communities*, Benedict Anderson argues that it is nationalism or "nation-ness" (the sense of belonging to a unique nation) – not internationalism or globalism – that defines the contemporary world. He suggests that nationalism results from forces set in motion in the eighteenth century, several of which we have considered earlier. Among these are the rise of print-capitalism, the establishment or re-definition of national borders, the inclusion or exclusion of groups based on imagined classifications such as race, religion, social class, or language, and the invention of national mythologies of antiquity and legitimacy.

Anderson maintains that nations are always created by an abrupt rupture with the past that redefines both time and space – for example, by invasions, revolutions, civil wars, declarations of independence, coups, or the dismantling of empires. All members of the nation share a national narrative (or history) that is "remembered" (and sometimes "forgotten" or revised) by everyone, although outsiders may "remember" a different version.

Governments develop and support cultural and natural monuments, education, arts, literature, museums and archeological sites (which are often also valuable economic assets) that help define and "legitimize" the nation and the national narrative. For example, the Grand Canyon, once imagined as a vast, barren chasm that created a barrier to American expansion, is today a national park visited by countless international tourists, and it appears on stamps and postcards as emblematic of the United States' natural beauty and bountiful resources. In Cambodia, the medieval Buddhist monuments of Angkor, lost for centuries in jungle overgrowth, are now important international tourist destinations. Images of the restored temples and palaces appear on the national flag, suggesting an ancient, powerful and eternal realm (despite a recent history of widely-divergent political regimes and the fact that the restoration was instigated and originally funded by colonial France).

In her book *The National Stage* Loren Kruger suggests the ways in which theatre is sometimes used to create national or state legitimacy. She maintains that official notions often

▷

> conflict with how "the people" see themselves. Theatre can become a "battleground" for this often contradictory relationship. Both play texts and the location of performances can help determine legitimacy. For example, in both Elizabethan England and Edo Japan, theatre "for the masses" took place in special districts that were across a river and outside the city limits. In contrast, elegant courtly entertainments were presented within the confines of the ruler's palace. These aristocratic performances suggested the absolute power of the sovereign, and only these were shown to visiting dignitaries.
>
> In order to create a sense of legitimacy, governments have often felt the need to transform, tame or confine public theatrical events. For Kruger, an analysis of theatre's varied artistic, political and economic "spheres" can help us understand the complex, often contradictory relationships between national self-image and the practice of national power.

China's ancient culture extends back thousands of years. A single written language unites over 300 distinct ethnicities and vernacular languages, many of which are mutually incomprehensible when spoken. For centuries, Chinese writing (print culture) and Confucian ideology were the dominant influences in East Asia, especially Vietnam, Korea, and Japan. To be educated or to enter government, non-Chinese speakers throughout Asia needed to learn to read the Confucian classics in Chinese. Often they journeyed to China's capital to gain knowledge and culture. The power of the written Chinese language is one reason why China, which always referred to itself as "the Middle Kingdom," was the center and model for many realms.

Foreign colonization and imperialism eroded Chinese domination and independence. European nations forced a militarily-weakened China to accept unfair trade agreements; the British importation of opium (traded for items such as tea) enfeebled many Chinese who unwittingly became addicts. From the late nineteenth through the middle of the twentieth centuries, various Chinese military and political factions fought each other as well as European and Japanese colonialists.

During the mid-twentieth century, both the nationalists (led by Chiang Kai-shek) and the communists (led by Mao Zedung) supported re-inventing "China" as a "modern nation." Eventually, the communist forces defeated the nationalists, who retreated to the island of Taiwan, where they established the Republic of China, imagined as the legitimate government of all China. In contrast, the mainland People's Republic of China (established in 1949) claims hegemony over Taiwan, which they see as a renegade Chinese province. The issue is further complicated by the desire of some residents of Taiwan to form a separate nation unrelated to the mainland.

Both "Chinas" have created national narratives that are passionately believed in and which are deployed to support legitimacy. For example, when the nationalists fled to Taiwan, they took many priceless works of art. These are displayed in the National Museum in Taipei, the capital of Taiwan. To the Chinese of Taiwan, this act suggests the government's legitimacy and its concern for protecting and saving the ancient Chinese cultural heritage from wanton destruction; to the Chinese on the mainland, however, it represents the act of a bandit regime that plundered the national treasures.

The development of "modern" Chinese theatre

In the early twentieth century, after the humiliations of European imperialism, military defeat in the Sino-Japanese War of 1894–1895, and the shift toward western culture ("The May Fourth Movement") China reversed the ancient practice of cultural pilgrimage. Rather than non-Chinese students journeying to China for advanced education, progressive Chinese students went to university in Japan. There a student group called the Spring Willow Society (*Chunliu she*) produced the first Chinese language spoken drama, *The Black Slave's Cry to Heaven* (*Heinu yutian lu*, 1907), based on Harriet Beecher Stowe's novel *Uncle Tom's Cabin*. For these culturally colonized Chinese students, the theme of freedom (and the spoken style they imagined to be typical of modern western drama) resonated deeply. Thus, the first spoken drama (*huaju*) – and the first play to grapple with the idea of modern national identity – was produced outside of China.

Western models fueled early *huaju* such as Cao Yu's influential *Thunderstorm* (*Leiyu*, 1934), a psychologically-based family drama. However, such realism was deplored during the radical, violent Cultural Revolution (1966–1976), which called for the elimination of everything considered decadent, obscene, or opposed to the public welfare. In theatre, this meant re-writing or "forgetting" the past by eradicating the "feudal" stories and performance styles of "Chinese Opera" (*ixqu* a term referring to all types of traditional theatre, of which the most well known is *jingxi*, or "Beijing Opera"). Optimistic socialist realism was preferred, but most other foreign influences were forbidden. Mao Zedung's wife, Jiang Qing, a former actress who had once played Nora in Ibsen's *A Doll House*, was a central figure in the Cultural Revolution. She advocated a new style of musical drama, permitting only a few "model revolutionary operas" and "model ballets." These featured proletarian heroes and heroines, approved ideology, and contemporary themes, costumes and scenery. The melodramatic, relatively realistic style was, ironically, somewhat akin to both western movie musicals and Russian ballets.

Professional *jingxi* and *huaju* actors, as well as doctors, intellectuals, teachers, and others, were vilified as "dangerous" to the nation's new self-image. They were beaten, imprisoned, or sent to the countryside to be "re-educated." Among these was Gao

Figure 12.9 A performance of *dixi* masked "opera" in Caigun village, Anshun county, Guizhou, China. Photo by Carol Fisher Sorgenfrei, 1990.

Xingjian, who spent six years as a farmer, and later as a teacher, in southwestern China. He escaped the more violent fates of many other intellectuals by "volunteering" to destroy a suitcase filled with his early manuscripts.

Gao's forced sojourn in the provinces exposed him to the culture of China's ethnic minorities. Despite communism's official atheism, many rural peoples practiced the ancient *wu* religion – pre-Confucian shamanism featuring spirit possession, exorcism, and ritualized, theatrical performances (*dixi* or *difangxi*) using carved, brightly painted wooden masks, dance, drama, mime, song and music (for more on shamanistic performance, see Chapter 1). Such influences are evident in Gao's 1985 play *Wild Man* (*Yeren*), written after he returned from the countryside.

Brecht modified for China

With the end of the Cultural Revolution came a period of intellectual openness and artistic experimentation. Many artists sought ways to combine Chinese "tradition" and "modernity." One solution embraced by Gao and other theatre artists, including Sun Huizhu, Sha Yexin, He Zishuang, Wang Peigong and Ma Zhongjun, was the reimportation and reinterpretation of styles and theories attributed to Bertolt Brecht.

Brecht claimed that his theories were partially inspired by seeing performances by *jingxi* star, Mei Lanfang (1894–1961), in Europe and Russia in the 1930s. For Brecht, Chinese Opera seemed so unrealistic that he assumed that both actor and audience were distanced from emotional involvement and (his major interest) freed for critical, rational

Figure 12.10 On Sundays at Green Lake Park in Kunming, Yunnan, China, minority peoples gather to watch and to perform their local dances and plays. Photo by Carol Fisher Sorgenfrei, 1990.

Figure 12.11 A shaman dances with incense sticks as he prepares to go into a trance. Green Lake Park, Kunming, Yunnan, China. Photo by Carol Fisher Sorgenfrei, 1990.

analysis. However, Mei Lanfang felt his art was "realistic"; what seemed strange and unemotional to Brecht was moving and believable to the Chinese. As noted in the Chapter 3 case study on Japanese noh drama, western feminists such as Elin Diamond have suggested adapting Brechtian acting to oppose the power of male-dominated theatre. Similarly, Chinese theatre artists and theorists since the 1980s have espoused reintroducing aspects of "traditional" Chinese performance that correspond to Brecht's misunderstandings in order to emphasize social and political contradictions. They advocate a frontal, presentational acting style, episodic structure, the dialectical juxtaposition of disparate ideas and elements, and a clear awareness of theatre as theatre (stylized gestures, mime, on-stage musicians, direct address to the audience, song, and so on). Brecht's Marxism also coincides with mainland Chinese political philosophy.

In both style and content, *Wild Man* combines Brechtian elements with *dixi*, the ritual, shamanistic performances of rural ethnic minorities. Prior to this play, Gao's most famous work was *Bus Stop* (*Che zhan*, 1983) clearly inspired by Samuel Beckett's *Waiting for Godot*. Unlike Beckett's absurdist play, *Bus Stop* had offered a social message, suggesting that people must actively take charge of their own lives, not passively wait for a savior. Nevertheless, the play was criticized as being "too western" and was condemned for contributing to "spiritual pollution" (*jingshen wuran*). Playwrights wishing to experiment were ordered to turn to Chinese models. Although the excesses of the Cultural Revolution were over, the government dictated (and continues to dictate) approved ways for theatre to represent the nation

Gao's *Wild Man*

Wild Man is about an ecologist assigned to teach forest conservation to peasants in a remote region of the Yangzi river valley. The play demonstrates two conflicts – between ecological conservation and local economic/social realities, and between "factual" science and "superstitious" belief, a conflict exemplified by the urbanized, educated ecologist's refusal to believe in a "mythical" forest creature that the locals revere.

The ecological devastation predicted in the play is real. Deforestation and the resultant severe flooding are consequences of China's rapid industrialization. For example, due to increased education, the academic publishing industry requires more than twice as much paper (made from trees) as it needed in 1985. Gao poses questions about rapid modernization in a society where many rural people still practice ancient rituals and customs, but offers no solutions. For example, both the rural characters forced to marry partners chosen by their parents, and the urban ecologist and his wife who married for love, are equally unhappy.

Wild Man demands a cast of 41, plus singers, musicians, and 12 separate groups of crowds. Each actor portrays many characters. The action takes place in the ancient past as well as the present, in fields, houses, offices, villages, cities, forests and so on, without a break. Scenes flow into and are juxtaposed against each other; time is not chronological. Multiple scenes are performed simultaneously, and locales shift on stage through creative use of sound, lighting and other theatrical or cinematic effects. A traditional singer and his assistant "narrate" the action. Ancient *wu* rituals are performed, including the sacrifice of a live rooster, and local styles of ethnic minority dancing, music, choral recitation, and singing alternate with psychologically-motivated acting.

Both the concern with difficult social issues, presented in a dialectical manner without offering any simple solution, and the use of "epic" performance styles, demonstrate the Chinese appropriation of Brecht. Gao and others who have re-invented Brecht for use in China maintain that they have avoided Brecht's tendency to exoticize the Orient by employing Chinese performance styles. However, it can be argued that turning to ancient Chinese rituals and traditional "Chinese Opera" actually presents these internal genres as "exotic" or "primitive," further marginalizing the rural population and suggesting that ritualistic *dixi* and *jinxgu* are dead (or nearly dead) "museum pieces" in need of preservation (Sorgenfrei 1991). Nevertheless, the Chinese government supports such "intra-cultural" experimentation as honoring both the past and the present by creating theatre that conforms to what mainland China today imagines itself to be.

The question we opened with remains: why didn't official China rejoice when Gao won the Nobel Prize? After the mid-1980s campaign against "spiritual pollution" (a reaction against the liberalization following the end of the Cultural Revolution), a period of political liberalization and artistic experimentation ensued. However, fears that this process was excessive led to another government crackdown. On 4 June 1989, the Chinese government sent military tanks into Beijing's Tiananmen Square in a brutal attack on students and intellectuals who were demanding greater democracy and artistic freedom. Some dissidents fled the country. Although Gao had left China in 1987, many foreign advocates of human rights view him and other Chinese exiles as exemplars of the need to force change on the Chinese government.

Official Chinese versions of the events at Tiananmen Square vary considerably from versions "remembered" outside of China. Inside China, it is not considered a major event, and official Chinese sources estimate far fewer deaths than western histories report. Thus, one reason for the lukewarm reaction to Gao's Nobel Prize may be that China sees the award as a western attempt to influence internal Chinese policies relating to perceived human rights violations. Gao, who now lives in Paris, may be imagined as a person who has abandoned his home-land; indeed, some Chinese intellectuals and artists suggest that he has successfully manipulated western intelligentsia for his own benefit. To them, Gao Xingjian's plays and novels are no longer imagined as part of China's quest for a sense of nation-ness in the contemporary world. If he should return perma-nently to China, it would be intriguing to see if that view would change.

CFS

Key references

Anderson, B. (1983 [rev. edn 1991]) *Imagined Communities: Reflections on the Origin and Spread of Nationalism*, London and New York: Verso.

Fei, F.C. (1999) *Chinese Theories of Theatre and Performance from Confucius to the Present*, Ann Arbor: University of Michigan Press.

Feugi, J., Voris, R., Weber, C. and Silberman, M. (eds) (1989) *Brecht in Asia and Africa: The Brecht Yearbook XIV*, Hong Kong: The International Brecht Society, Depart-ment of Comparative Literature, University of Hong Kong.

Gao, X. (1990) "*Wild Man:* A Contemporary Chinese Spoken Drama," trans. B. Roubicek, *Asian Theatre Journal*, 7:184–249.

Kruger, L. (1992) *The National Stage: Theatre and Cultural Legitimation in England, France and America*, Chicago and London: University of Chicago Press.

McKerras, C. (ed.) (1983 [paper, 1988]) *Chinese Theatre From Its Origins to the Present Day*, Honolulu: University of Hawaii Press.

Sorgenfrei, C.F. (1991) "Orientalizing the Self: Theatre in China after Tiananmen Square," *The Drama Review* (Winter):169–185.

Tian, M. (1997) "'Alienation-Effect' for Whom? Brecht's (Mis)interpretation of the Classical Chinese Theatre," *Asian Theatre Journal*, 14:200–222.

Tung, C. and McKerras, C. (eds) (1987) *Drama in the People's Republic of China*, New York: State University of New York Press.

Yan, H. (ed.) (1998) *Theatre and Society: An Anthology of Contemporary Chinese Drama*, Armonk, N.Y. and London: M.E. Sharpe.

CASE STUDY: Backstage/frontstage: Ethnic tourist performances and identity in "America's Little Switzerland"[1]

Ladies and Gentlemen, with the *Wilhelm Tell Overture* serving as an introduction, we are about to begin the . . . annual presentation of Schiller's classic drama, *Wilhelm Tell*. Welcome again to historic and picturesque New Glarus, named after Glarus, Switzerland. New Glarus is the home of *Wilhelm Tell*, and this drama depicts the story of the famous Swiss struggle for the God-given rights of independence and freedom. It contains a message which is relevant for our times. The Wilhelm Tell Guild would like to request that you do not leave the seating sections with your cameras. All members of the cast will be happy to pose for your pictures at the close of today's perform-ance. Thank you.

(Opening announcement:
New Glarus community performance
of *Wilhelm Tell*, 1981)

Each Labor Day weekend in September, one mile from the small town of New Glarus, Wisconsin (population 1,800) on Green Country Road W, at

1 The original research on which this case study is based was undertaken collaboratively with Deborah Neff between 1981–1984.

the crest of a hill overlooking the village, members of the American Legion, Fire Department, and Lion's Club direct cars and buses toward a grass parking lot. They are arriving for the annual outdoor community performance of Friedrich Schiller's (1759–1805) *Wilhelm Tell* – English performances on Saturday and Monday, and the original German on Sunday.

The walk to the outdoor Tell grounds takes visitors down a long shaded pathway through a thick forest. Toward the bottom of the hill, to the left through the trees, parts of the "backstage" area can be seen: horses are saddled and ready, waiting to take their places. Spectators are greeted by teenage usherettes dressed in "authentic" hand-sewn reproductions of thirteenth-century Swiss costumes. A lush green field opens up at the bottom of the hill. A row of loud speakers separates the main aisle from the huge performance area. The boundaries of the playing space are irregularly formed by the thick

forest – a backstage area with eight entrance pathways.

As the audience is seated – numbering between the hundreds (German performance) and several thousand (English performance) – pre-play entertainment begins with the Swiss Miss Folk Dancers. The welcoming announcement (above) introduces the production. After Rossini's *Overture*, alpenhorn players with their 15-ft-long horns emerge from backstage to call home the herds of brown Swiss cattle and goats from the mountains before winter. In response to the plaintive calls of the alpenhorns, young boys and men appear herding raucous, often unmanageable goats and cows. Peasant women, children, and elders from the "village" gather to welcome the herders home. Traditional Swiss songs and yodeling intermingle with the lowing of the cattle, their clanging bells, and the bleating of goats. As the songs conclude, the cast of over 100 disappears into the forest. The audience applauds the

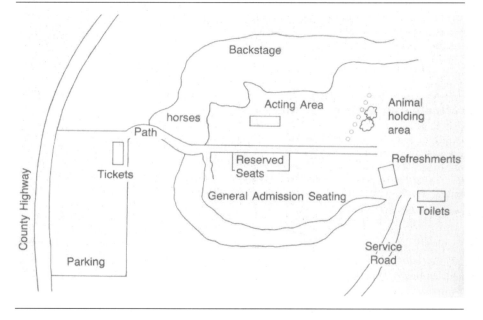

Figure 12.12 Diagram of the grounds for the performance of *Wilhelm Tell*, located just outside the village of New Glarus, Wisconsin. © Phillip B. Zarrilli.

Figure 12.13 Opening scene of the Tell play in New Glarus, with "villagers" herding the Swiss cattle down from the "mountains", Photo © Phillip B. Zarrilli.

Figure 12.14 The Tell production in Interlaken, Switzerland (from 1912). One model for the creation of New Glarus's production. Photo Courtesy Marilyn Christiansen, Tell Guild, New Glarus.

Figure 12.15 In New Glarus, one of the "usherettes" holding the American flag at the conclusion of the performance of *Wilhelm Tell* when the cast poses for photographs. Photo by Phillip B. Zarrilli.

opening spectacle. Thus begins the annual perform-ance of *Wilhelm Tell* as it builds toward the climax when Tell shoots the apple off his son's head. What the audience has witnessed is a literal realization of the pastoral scene described in Schiller's text:

> . . . high rocky shore of Lake Lucerne. . . . Across the lake one sees the green meadows, vil-lages, and farms of Schwyz, lying in the bright sunshine . . . one hears the cowherd's tune and the harmonious ringing of the herd-bells.
>
> (Schiller 1954:7)

Since the play's first performance in German in 1938, this small mid-western community annually garners its collective human resources (over 200 people) to stage *Wilhelm Tell*. Before and after the production, the swell of visitors nearly overwhelms the village. Some will order Swiss specialties such as Kaesecheuchle (baked cheese pie) in local restaurants such as the Glarnerstube, order a Glarnerbier, dance a polka, browse the gift shops stocked with Swiss cuckoo-clocks and cassettes featuring local Swiss music, or visit one or more of its tourist attractions – the Chalet of the Golden Fleece (1937), or the Swiss Historical (pioneer) Village. Overt trappings of "Swissness" dress the town: "Swiss Miss Lace Factory," "Swiss Lanes," Swiss-style architecture, the Wilhelm Tell crest, colorful Swiss family shields on lamp-posts, and the omnipresent red and white Swiss flag on menus, wallpaper, outside buildings, or as a swizzle stick. New Glarus represents itself today as "America's Little Switzerland." This case-study considers how New Glarus provides one site for considering the historical interaction between performance, tourism, ethnicity, and identity.

INTERPRETIVE APPROACH: Sociological theories of tourism and everyday performance

In *The Tourist: A New Theory of the Leisure Class*, Dean MacCannell examines "actual" tourists, that is, the mainly middle-class sightseers scouring the world "in search of experience," and the "tourist" as a meta-sociological model through which to examine the totalizing experience of modernism. The contemporary middle class "systematically scavenges the earth for new experiences to be woven into a collective, touristic version of other peoples and other places," writes MacCannell (1976:13). Sightseeing is an attempt to overcome the discontinuity of modern experience by creating the illusion of a unified experience – an impossibility since "even as it tries to construct totalities, it celebrates differentiation" (ibid.:13). Indeed, the differentiations created by the modern world are structurally similar to tourist attractions in that "elements dislodged from their original natural, historical and cultural contexts" are fitted together with other displaced, modernized things and people. "The differentiations are the attractions" (ibid.:13). Sightseeing allows the tourist to construct totalities from his different experiences. "Thus, his life and his society can appear to him as an orderly series of formal representations, like snapshots in a family album" (ibid.:15). For MacCannell, tourism becomes a primary ground for the production of new cultural forms as it reshapes "culture and nature to its own needs" (1992:1).

Tourism engages the tourist and her/his hosts in a series of face-to-face interactions which are by definition formulaic and time-limited. Sociologist Erving Goffman developed a "dramaturgical model" of the commonplace conventions that govern the performance of face-to-face interactions in contemporary everyday life (Goffman 1959). Whether one is in a doctor's reception room, an airplane, or on tour one is in a context that has a "front" and "backstage." In "front" the "setting," "costumes," and behavior are carefully staged. Conduct and emotions may require training (Hochschild 1983). What is said is often circumscribed or "scripted." In contrast, "backstage", the social roles and conventions governing behavior and interaction can be dropped, knowingly contradicted, or parodied.

Frontstage at Plimoth Plantation and in New Glarus

Some tourist attractions, such as Colonial Williamsburg (1930s) and Plimoth Plantation in Massachusetts (1959) self-consciously constructed their "fronts" as recreated historical villages. Plimoth Plantation became a "living museum" in 1969 when it replicated as seamlessly as possible the "actual" life of the pilgrims of the Plimoth of 1627 by having full-time professional first-person interpreters role-play, "in character," scenes from everyday life "as if" they were the actual pilgrims (Snow 1993). Tourists today encounter a variety of pilgrim characters throughout the village in semi-improvised everyday life and activities – from marriages to a "Court Day," where culprits are brought before the Magistrate.

New Glarus is not a living museum of Swiss or Swiss-American life, but performs its ethnicity while remaining what it is – an economically and increasingly diverse, primarily middle-class, semi-rural small town. Its "Swiss" "front" is not seamless and has been built piece-meal over the years. Residents are aware of the fact that their self-conscious performance of the village's Swiss origins and "identity" are historically factual, but also a collective (re)invention intended to attract tourists. Local historian Millard Tschudy explains without a trace of irony that New Glarus is a "for-real community" in that it developed its early performances for itself rather than for outsiders, but once outsiders started coming to see "the Swiss" in great numbers in the 1960s, the community "naturally" provided them with all the signs of Swissness that outsiders wanted to see.

New Glarus before Tell: Early celebrations for itself and others

New Glarus's self-conscious ethnic identification as "America's Little Switzerland" is an historical fact. The original immigrants – 193 men, women, and children – those most affected by a failed local economy – left their native canton of Glarus, Switzerland, on 16 April 1845, to make the arduous journey to the New World. Organized by the Glarus Emigration Association, they were preceded by advance scouts who procured 1280 acres of land by the Little Sugar River in Wisconsin. On 17 August, 108 of the original group arrived and divided the land by communal lot. After a difficult first winter and within four years, the community thrived by growing wheat. When wheat prices plunged in the 1860s, the community diversified, turning to dairy farming and cheese-making – quintessentially Swiss occupations. After 1910, the single most important non-agricultural employer was a milk-condensing company (originally Helvetia, later Pet Milk), employing 80–140 workers and serving 300 local farms.

Throughout the nineteenth century in Europe, crop failures and unemployment caused by rapid industrialization brought immigrants to the U.S. in unprecedented numbers. Throughout the upper mid-west, new communities formed a patchwork ethnic quilt juxtaposing Germans, Norwegians, Irish, Swiss, and Dutch. Customs and traditions from "home" were maintained through dance, music, language, and key symbols – markers of identity to insiders and a curiosity to outsiders. An Irish woman residing in "Irish Hollow" recorded how she and her family decided to go and "look at the Swiss" on 4 July 1853:

> The two families had decided to spend the Fourth . . . at Belleville. . . . But on the morning of the Fourth, Uncle's horses could not be located. . . . It was noon before we [found them and] had them hitched to the wagon. . . . Then someone remembered it was a long drive – eight miles – to Belleville. "Let's stay home like sensible folk," suggested Mary.
>
> "No, do let us go some place," said Aunt. "It is only five miles to New Glarus; we can look at the Swiss, if we can't understand them."
>
> "I hate to be beat," acknowledged Uncle Alex. "Let us take a look at the Dutch."

Deciding on "the Swiss" rather than "the Dutch," the diarist describes the celebration:

> New Glarus was celebrating the Fourth of July, but it was a Swiss celebration. Gessler was there and William Tell, to shoot the apple from his son's head. There were Swiss wrestlers and Swiss dancers in the dining room of the hotel, where a Swiss music box with weights was wound up [. . .]. Round and round the couples would glide while at certain intervals in the music the men would stamp their feet and emit wild whoops.
>
> (Wallace and Maynard 1925)

The Swiss immigrants readily associated the celebration of American independence with the commemoration of a battle that delivered their ancestors from the tyranny of their Austrian oppressors on 9 April 1388. As early as eight years after the founding of the community, Tell was already a key symbol mediating Swiss and American identities, and providing entertainment for others.

A variety of local accounts confirm how key symbols of Swiss identity remained integral to local celebrations. An 1891 newspaper report on the 600th anniversary celebration of the birth of Switzerland notes that over 6,000 visitors traveled by special train to New Glarus for speeches, eating, dancing, and the parade with living-picture tableaux featuring Wilhelm Tell; Lincoln freeing the slaves, and Helvetia and Columbia – the "Swiss and American goddesses of liberty" (Neff and Zarrilli 1987:6). In 1928, the Men's Choir (Maennerchor) sponsored the first annual celebration of Swiss independence – Volksfest with song, dance, competitions, and food.

For the 90th anniversary celebration in 1935, the grandest community-wide celebration of its history and identity saw a fully-mounted production of an historical drama authored by prominent local citizen, Dr. Schindler (ibid.:6). A dramatic commemoration of the village's settlement, it was translated into the Glarner dialect for performances in English and Glarnerdeutsch. The cast included the first settlers and their families, dancers, yodelers, Civil War veterans, Helvetia, and Uncle Sam. Thematically, the play emphasized the courage, endurance, and cooperation of the early community, admonished the audience to be proud to be Swiss while enduring the hardships of life, and emphasized the virtues of strength, courageousness, unity, freedom, love, and industriousness. The text contrasted the settlers and heroes with the Italian Blackshirts, the German Brownshirts, and the Russian Redshirts, urging caution against "dictatorship, fascism, and Communism in our own land." In contrast, the "truly American shirt was the Buckskin

– standing for steadfastness of purpose, firmness of action, and clarity of union." The play concluded with the entrance of Helvetia and Uncle Sam from separate ends of the stage. The three-day celebration was presided over by Governor P.F. LaFollette.

Tell comes to New Glarus

The festivals and commemorations described above were celebrations of the community's dual Swiss-ethnic and American identities, undertaken in and of themselves. The first steps toward a more self-conscious (re)construction of the community as "Swiss" for outsiders were prompted by an "inside-outsider" – Mr. Edwin Barlow (1885–1957). Although "related" to the community by birth (his mother was Madelena Streiff), Barlow was raised after the death of his parents in nearby Monticello by his aunt and uncle (Mr. and Mrs. Jacob Figi). He attended college in Washington D.C., served in World War I, and lived in New York where he was involved in minor theatrical activities. After being adopted by a New York socialite and distant relative, he traveled Europe and spent nine years in Lausanne, Switzerland.

During the 1930s, Barlow visited New Glarus and Monticello where he experienced Volksfest, and perhaps the 1935 commemorative drama. Inspired by his residence in Switzerland, Barlow decided to build an authentic Swiss chalet for his aunt – an architectural anomaly at the time. When Mrs. Figi died before the "Chalet of the Golden Fleece" was completed in 1937, Barlow made it his home.

Remembered by community members as being "different," "highly dramatic and theatrical" (Neff and Zarrilli 1987:9), Barlow introduced his plan early in 1938 for the community to stage its own outdoor pageant production of Schiller's *Tell*. Barlow was inspired to do so by his experience of the Swiss festival-productions of *Tell* at Altdorf (bi-annually from 1899) and Interlaken (annually outdoors from 1912) – the productions which immortalized Tell "as the Swiss national 'hero'." Barlow was persuasive.

Key community leaders were convinced, and the town was mobilized. On 4/5 September, 1938, with a cast and crew of between 120–140, the first two performances in German played to audiences of approximately 1,500 on the fourth, and "several hundred" on the fifth, who braved cold, drizzly conditions. With a profit of $535.44, the Tell pageant became, as hoped, "one of the traditions of New Glarus" (1938 program). By 1941, the numbers directly involved in the productions (then German and English) had grown from approximately 140 to 290, plus crew. The Tell Festival had quickly become an integral part of the community's social and institutional fabric; the "Tell Guild" was formed to manage the production, invest proceeds in community projects, and interact with other community organizations like the Chamber of Commerce.

Barlow directed the productions between 1938 and 1945/6 when he turned direction over to his assistant, Mrs. Fred Streiff. In 1954 Barlow gifted the Chalet and its contents to the village "with the stipulation that it be maintained as a museum." Barlow died in 1957.

We know from as early as the 1853 Irish diarist that at least some outsiders always attended New Glarus's festivals, but the annual Tell productions attracted a steady stream of tourists. With the closing of the major local non-agricultural employer (Pet Milk) in 1962, village leaders and entrepreneurs saw tourism as a possible year-round economic fillip – and a self-conscious, if gradual village remake began. In 1965, the New Glarus Hotel (built 1853) was renovated into "an authentic Swiss-style restaurant," with "pure basic . . . Bernese-style architecture." Swiss-style store-fronts (Glarnerstube) were erected. Additional "authentic" Swiss architecture (Chalet Landhaus Hotel; Schoco-Laden) followed later. To the traditional Maennerchor were added numerous new folk-dance and music groups – Roger Bright and his Orchestra, the Edelweiss Stars, the Swiss Miss Dancers, and others. New annual festivals – the Heidi Festival (June, 1965) and Little Switzerland Festival (winter, 1985) – were added to Volksfest (August) and Tell (September), attracting tourists year-round.

Backstage

In Goffman's terms, what has a "frontstage" always has a "backstage." Both New Glarus and Plimoth Plantation "stage" their authenticity, but do so in different ways and with a very different relationship between "front" and "back." At Plimoth Plantation, there is a formal division of front and back as the actor/historians clock in and out, and/or take breaks where they step "backstage" into the "goathouse" to have a cigarette. It is transgressive for both when a tourist accidentally wanders backstage and sees a performer out of role. Plimoth Plantation "works" best when there is a constant sense of "playful deceit" between the actor/historians and their visitors (Snow 1993:172).

In New Glarus there is no "seamless" front, no "authentic" historical roles to play, and front and back constantly bleed into one another. There is still a sense of "playful deceit" at work, but the deceit is the tourist's conceit – whether he wishes to see, acknowledge, or document the unhidden "back." It is tourists who stage New Glarus's authentic "Swissness" when their cameras focus selectively on Swiss-style buildings, performances, and costumes and leave out of the frame the ranch-style home next to the Chalet.

Within the community's "backstage," enthusiasm over Tell and Swissness is not universal. Some "don't want to be Swiss." But for many, the annual experience resonates with what Francis Hsu calls the "intimate layer" of social and cultural life – those places, people, things, or activities by means of which a person develops "strong feelings of attachment" (1985:29). Backstage at Tell is a family affair – literally a picnic, and therefore a time when status and interpersonal differences are to a much greater degree than usual suspended while the community plays at making Swiss "history."

It's something people grow up with here. They need you to be there. That's a part of it. Then you get new people into town and they get involved. There is a spirit there.

(Neff and Zarrilli 1987:34)

Once involved, families commit themselves to the production year-end-year-out. Paul Grossenbacher played the original Gessler in 1938 and continued in the role for 24 years before taking over direction of the German production. Gilbert Ott, who with Ed Vollenweider created the first Tell, took the role in the 1941 English version and continued until 1961. He died several weeks after his final performance. Many adults began their involvement as children progressing through such non-speaking roles as choirboys, goatherders, dancers, soldiers, towns-people, and then to speaking roles. Their children, in turn, are playing roles they once played. From this "backstage" perspective, involvement allows residents to experience and (re)fashion their individual, familial, and/or collective identities; explore their relationship to "real" or "imagined" Swiss and middle-American sentiments and values embedded in their performances; stimulate the local economy; and serve their community by raising funds. Tourism, identity, and ethnicity meet and are constantly (re)imagined as New Glarus performs its Swiss/American "cultural heritage."

PZ

Key references

Goffman, E. (1959) *The Presentation of Self in Everyday Life*, Garden City: Doubleday.

Hochschild, A.R. (1983) *The Managed Heart: Commercialization of Human Feeling*, Berkeley: University of California Press.

Hsu, F. (1985) "The Self in Cross-cultural Perspective," in A.J. Marsela, G. De Vos and F.L.K. Hsu (eds) *Culture and Self*, New York: Tavistock.

MacCannell, D. (1976) *The Tourist: A New Theory of the Leisure Class*, New York: Schochen Books.

MacCannell, D. (1992) *Empty Meeting Grounds: The Tourist Papers*, London: Routledge.

Neff, D. and Zarrilli, P.B. (1987) *Wilhelm Tell in America's 'Little Switzerland*,' Onalaska: Crescent Printing Company.

Schelbert, L. (1970) *New Glarus 1845–1970: The Makings of a Swiss American Town*, Glarus: Kommissionsverlag.

Schiller, F. (1954) *William Tell*, Woodbury, N.Y.: Barron's Educational Series Inc.

Smith, V.L. (ed.) (1989) *Hosts and Guests: The Anthropology of Tourism*, 2nd edn, Philadelphia: University of Pennsylvania Press.

Snow, S.E. (1993) *Performing the Pilgrims*, Jackson: University of Mississippi Press.

Urry, J. (1990) *The Tourist Gaze*, London: Sage.

Wallace, E.M. and Maynard, L.W. (1925) "This side the gully" (type manuscript).

Audio-visual resources

"*Backstage Frontstage:*" *Wilhelm Tell in America's "Little Switzerland*," DVD-Video (50 minutes). [Research: Deborah Neff and Phillip Zarrilli. Edited by Sharon Grady. Produced by Folklore Program, University of Wisconsin-Madison. Documentary of the *Wilhelm Tell* play and its production in New Glarus. Narrative edited from interviews with community members reflecting on *Tell*. Available from: University of Wisconsin-Madison, Folklore Program, Ingraham Hall, Madison, Wisconsin 53706.]

Website: Center for the Study of Upper Midwestern Cultures (http://csumc.wisc.edu).

Index

Note: Page references in *italics* indicate illustrations.

152448